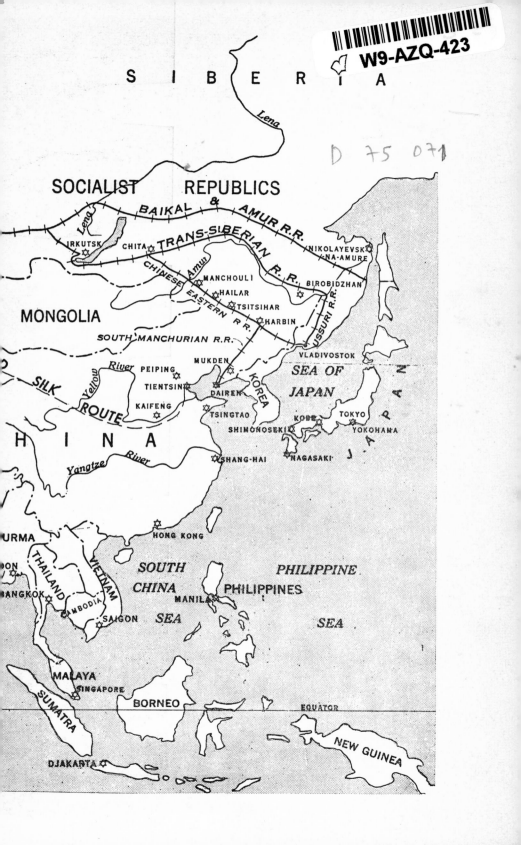

SIBERIA

Lena

SOCIALIST   REPUBLICS

BAIKAL & AMUR R.R.

TRANS-SIBERIAN R.R.

Lena

IRKUTSK   CHITA

CHINESE   Amur   MANCHOULI

EASTERN   HAILAR

R.R.   TSITSIHAR

HARBIN

NIKOLAYEVSK-NA-AMURE

BIROBIDZHAN

USSURI R.R.

MONGOLIA

SOUTH MANCHURIAN R.R.

Yellow   River   PEIPING

SILK   TIENTSIN

ROUTE   KAIFENG

MUKDEN

DAIREN

TSINGTAO

SHIMONOSEKI

KOREA

VLADIVOSTOK

SEA OF
JAPAN

HINA

Yangtze   River

SHANG-HAI

KOBE   TOKYO

YOKOHAMA

NAGASAKI

JAPAN

HONG KONG

URMA

THAILAND

BANGKOK

VIETNAM

CAMBODIA

SAIGON

SOUTH
CHINA
SEA

MANILA

PHILIPPINES

PHILIPPINE

SEA

MALAYA
SINGAPORE

SUMATRA

BORNEO

EQUATOR

NEW GUINEA

DJAKARTA

JAPANESE, NAZIS & JEWS

JAPANESE, NAZI

the Jewish Refug

david kranzler

Foreword by Abraham G. Duk

& JEWS

Community of Shanghai, 1938-1945

Yeshiva University Press

ifria Distributors

New York

976

Library of Congress Cataloging in Publication Data
Kranzler, David H.   1930-
    Japanese, Nazis, and Jews.
    Revised version of the author's thesis, Yeshiva University, 1971.
    Bibliography: p.
    Includes index.
    1. Jews in Shanghai—History. 2. World War II, 1939-1945—Jews.
    3. Shanghai—History. I. Title.
DS 135.C5K7   1976   951.'132'004924   76-20771
ISBN 0-89362-000-9 Lib. Bdg.
ISBN 0-89362-001-7 Pbk.

BALSHON PRINTING & OFFSET CO.
480 SUTTER AVENUE, BROOKLYN, N.Y. 11207
Printed in the United States of America

In loving memory of

Yerachmiel Kranzler ז״ל   Moshe Kranzler ז״ל
(1888-1966)   (1875-1968)

Patriarchs and victims of
oppression, who transplanted
and transmitted their
deep commitment to
their ancient
heritage
"even
unto
the
fourth
generation"

FOREWORD

DR. ABRAHAM G. DUKER

Professor of Judaic Studies and Editor of "Jewish Social Studies"

In reflecting on the periodization of Jewish history, I have often speculated on the validity of the division of its entire span into three periods on the basis of the availability of shelter for Jews in times of extreme adversity. Thus, Jewish history can be divided into three periods. The first, a free and Open Gates Period, ranges from Abraham until 1924, the year of the passage of the Johnson Act, that not only reduced Jewish immigrations to the United States to a trickle, but also served as the example for restrictions by other countries, hitherto fairly open. Thus began the second period, that of Closed Gates, 1925-1948. Of the six million Jews who perished during World War II, directly in consequence of the Nazi-genocide policy or as "normal" military and civilian casualties, too many were victims of the refusal of all the countries of the world to offer even temporary shelter to any sizeable number of Jews. This policy was vividly illustrated before the outbreak of World War II by the United States government's refusal to admit the over 900 passengers of the St. Louis, forcing them to return to Nazi Germany. At the Evian and Bermuda Conferences, Great Britain and the United States showed the entire world, including the Nazi Axis part, their indifference to the

7

fate of European Jews. There was no question of the availability of ammunition and manpower for the bombing of the Roumanian oil fields, but none could be spared for the destruction of Auschwitz or even the railroad tracks that led to that charnel center. The struggle against the establishment of Israel can also be interpreted as the continuation of the war against Jewish immigration. The Jewish state introduced a new reality through initiating the third, Open Gate period, which began with the declaration of the guaranteed entry to every Jew in need of shelter, without any conditions or degrading unofficial quota such as the 1948 U.S. Displaced Persons Admissions Act. One cannot stress strongly enough that in the twentieth century, closed gates constituted a main instrument of genocide, if not invitations to it.

Dr. Kranzler's volume deals with a miniature and short-lasted Open Gate, a small but significant exception in the history of the Closed Gate Period, that of the International Settlement in Shanghai, which required no entry visa. Some 17,000 Jews escaped the Holocaust, practically on their own initiative, and in face of the impotence of the U.S. domestic and of the international Jewish organizations, whose leadership failed to take stock early enough of the inadequacy of their relief and reconstruction formulas of the twenties and whose bureaucrats were not always sufficiently empathetic, as the JDC's Miss Laura Margolis, in Shanghai.

Based upon archival, press, memoirs and oral sources, Dr. Kranzler's study covers most aspects of the life of the Jews in Shanghai during this crucial period and includes earlier historical background. He surveys their community and self-help organizations, clashes and cooperation between the earlier arrivals, the Sephardic (mainly Iraqi) and Russian established communities and the newcomers from Germany and Poland in the late 1930's and early war years. An important contribution is the coverage of the Japanese relations with the Jews, the Jewish refugees and her response to Nazi pressure for the introduction of racist antisemitism in a country almost without Jews.

The book also brings out many other interesting sidelights. For instance, the backing of restrictions on Jewish immigration by the Allies and Jewish organizatons, the functioning of charities, of an important yeshiva and other cultural institutions, the long road to Shanghai via Siberia and Kobe, Japan—all these are brought out in this erudite and important contribution to the history of the period of the Closed Gates.

Research on a complex subject such as this, involving as it does the knowledge of several languages and backgrounds, a variety of scattered sources and the ability to obtain and evaluate oral information, presented many difficulties. Dr. Kranzler faced them indomitably and dauntlessly overcame them, as he was gathering his material for the continually expanding doctoral dissertation on which this work is based. It covers hitherto neglected and fascinating aspects of modern Jewish history. It contains important additions to the knowledge of migrations, World War II, antisemitism, international relations and the Far East. It will be found useful to those interested in refugee adjustment, Jewish self-help, community organizations, relief activities and policies. Dr. Kranzler deserves high commendation for the enrichment of our knowledge of recent Jewish history.

DR. ABRAHAM G. DUKER

CONTENTS

PREFACE

As a fugitive from Nazi Germany who was fortunate enough to find a haven in the United States even prior to Crystal Night, and whose family was active in rescue work, I grew up naturally sensitive to the refugee plight. This work however, was originally inspired by the brilliant lectures on the Far East by Professor Hyman Kublin, and my acquaintance with some recently-arrived refugees from Shanghai. These factors led eventually to the completion, in 1958, of my Master's thesis on *The Jewish Community of Shanghai 1937-1957,* at Brooklyn College. This first essay on the Shanghai Jewish experience was written under the guidance of Dr. Kublin, who has shared unstintingly of his profound knowledge, keen insight and critical scholarship all these years until the very conclusion of this study, for which I am most grateful.

The present work is an outgrowth of a doctoral dissertation written under the supervision of Professor Abraham G. Duker, at the Dov Revel Graduate School of Yeshiva University. He has been my steady guide and mentor who has nurtured my research in numerous ways, supplying stimulus and critical insight long after the completion of the dissertation. I am also indebted to Dr. Duker for his gracious foreword to this book. Any contribution this work might make bears the imprint of these two teachers par excellence.

Research on a work of this kind by its very nature involved the use of thousands of documents, found in dozens of institutions and private collections and in the memories of scores of involved

13

individuals. I take great pleasure in acknowledging my obligations. Although every source is cited in its proper place and all the numerous interviews, unpublished manuscripts and collections of documents are given due credit in the bibliography, I would like to single out those who have gone beyond the call of duty in the sharing of their time, experience and resources. If commonplace, it is no less sincere or proper to state that the contributions by these people does not imply any responsibility for my interpretations, which is mine alone.

LIBRARIES and INSTITUTIONS: YIVO Institute for Jewish Research, Ezekiel Lifschutz for making available to me the extensive Shanghai collection and providing me with a congenial atmosphere for research; Zosa Szajkowski, who opened the HIAS-HICEM and National Refugee Service collections, guided me new vistas in the history of Jewish Immigration and relief, taught me the ABC' of Jewish archival sources and encouraged me in the publication of this work, *Yasher Ko'ach;* The National Archives, Dr. Robert Wolfe, Dr. George O. Kent, two great historians and archivists, Edwin R. Flatequal and Colonel David Conard of the Department of the Army Map Service; Department of State, Dr. Arthur G. Kogan, Director of the Historical Office; The Library of Congress, Andrew Y. Kuroda, Head of the Japanese Division, Philip M. Nagao, reference librarian, for fantastic service; K. T. Wu, Head of the Chinese Division and the staff of the newspaper collection; American Jewish Committee, Blaustein Library, Harry Alderman, librarian; United HIAS Service, Jack Diamond.

Herzl Institute, Sylvia Landress, librarian; Leo Baeck Institute, Fred Grubel and Mr. Galliner; Wiener Library and its efficient staff; Yad Washem Institute (Jerusalem), Dr. J. Kermisz and Mr. Krakowsky, archivists: Institute of Contemporary Jewry, Oral History Division of the Hebrew University (Jerusalem), Dr. Geoffrey Wigoder, Director.

FOUNDATIONS: It was only due to the generous grants from the National Foundation for Jewish Culture and the Memorial Foundation for Jewish Culture that enabled me to reproduce the thousands of relevant documents for the dissertation. My special thanks to Harry I. Barron and Mark Uveeler, respectively. A post-doctoral grant by the Memorial Foundation enabled me to concentrate on the Japanese relations with the Jews, and a SUNY Summer Fellowship permitted additional study of the Russian Jewish Communities in the Far East. I am indebted to both Dr. Jerry Hochbaum of the Memorial Foundation and the SUNY Research Foundation; Dr. Leonard Kranzler and Congregation Warsaw Bikur Cholim, Rabbi Solomon Hecht, for their generous support toward the revision of the manuscript.

INDIVIDUALS: One of the pleasant by-products of this type of research is the opportunity to form acquaintances and friendships with many highly intelligent people acknowledging a common bond. My special thanks to Joseph Hayim Abraham, who so patiently answered my numerous inquiries on tape or the telephone; My colleagues at Queensborough Community College Library, Profs. Al Chmela and Jim Neal, for their valuable criticism and suggestions, Prof. Mary Nutley and her capable assistant May O'Dougherty, for their speedy inter-library loan service, Dr. Shick-Hong, for translations from Japanese; Rabbi Joseph D. Epstein, who provided some interesting documents and who always inspired one to consider the meta-historical significance of mere concrete events; Menachem Flakser, for the use of two volumes of *UNSER LEBEN;* David Rabinovich (Tel Aviv) who read the entire manuscript and permitted the use of the rest of the volumes of that newspaper; Dr. Theodore Friedrichs, who critically reviewed parts of the manuscript and who loaned his memoirs and the medical journal for reproduction; Prof. Nathan Goldberg, for reviewing part of the manuscript; Dr. Samuel Didner, who read the entire book; Rabbi Shraga Moshe Kalmanowitz, for permission to reproduce part of his father's papers; Ernst Keller (Amsterdam), for access to valuable Dutch documents; Dr. Ernst Landau, for documents and careful review of the manuscript; Rabbi Joseph Lookstein, *Yasher Ko'ach*; David L. Bloch for some of his original illustrations; Rabbi Solomon Tarshansky, for valuable suggestions on one chapter; My good friend, Rabbi Marvin Tokayer (Tokyo), for our long and fruitful correspondence on a subject of mutual interest and exchange of documents; Dr. Herman Dicker, who returned the use of my Master's thesis five-fold by permitting the reproduction of the Kogan Papers; The Bender Family, for some valuable docu-

ments; Prof. William Deman and Ms. Joan Deman for important
documents and insights; H. Peter Eisfelder, for permission to reproduce his manuscript and for providing some excellent photos;
Ernest Heppner, for his keen and active interests, his documents,
tape and extremely useful illustrations; Mrs. Kattie Kohn, for permission to reproduce her late husband's (Philip) volumes of
Shanghai newspapers; Frank Newman, for his Kobe diary; Dr.
Rudolph Loewenthal, for making available his excellent collection
of manuscripts, newsclippings, photos, and his steady encouragement and suggestions; Dr. Kurt Redlich, for his warm friendship,
fascinating correspondence, his penetrating insights, and critical
review of the entire manuscript which hopefully helped to avoid
some glaring pitfalls; Dr. Irving Levitas, who gave so magnani-
mously of his time, energy and knowledge, at any hour, and to
whom I turned time and again in moments of difficulty, to be met
only with unfailing patience and encouragement far beyond the
call of friendship; Gerhard Gerechter, President of the Association
of Former Refugees from Shanghai, who willingly shared his experience, reviewed the entire manuscript and maintained great
interest in the publication of this work with patience; Pearl Kardon,
whose indefatigable patience, humor and sound advice, provided
the human touch during my graduate studies and who has remained
a moral support to the present time.

PUBLISHERS: Twayne Publishers and Dr. Dicker for
permission to use some illustrations from his *Wanderers and
Settlers;* A. Watkins, Inc., and George Spunt, for permission to use
a map from his *"A Place in Time"*; Conference on Jewish Social
Studies and Dr. Abraham G. Duker, for permission to include
material originally published in the journal *Jewish Social Studies*
(January 1974); The Union of Orthodox Jewish Congregations
and Rabbi Yaakov Jacobs, for permission, likewise, to use material
that had previously appeared in the September 1975 issue of
Jewish Life;

To Dr. Samuel Belkin, talmid chacham, scholar, and revered
Chancellor of Yeshiva University and Dr. Leon D. Stitskin, editor
of Yeshiva University Press, my sincere appreciation for their
steadfast encouragement.

I also want to express my debt to THE PAST: my dear

parents, Yerachmiel Meir Leib and Chanah Kranzler ל"ז, whose
love of Torah and learning inspired three generations; my sisters
Mali and Rose ל"ז, to whom I owe more than I could express; my
father-in-law, Rav Yaakov Bein ל"ז, whose rescue work amidst
extreme danger should serve as an example of "what might have
been done."

THE PRESENT: to Judy, whose own war experiences and
unerring sense of historical perspective served as an invaluable
sounding board throughout this study, and who managed to retain
her enthusiasm, patience and good humor despite many conflicting
demands.

THE FUTURE: to Moshe, Shani and Yaakov Meir who
hopefully, will someday learn to appreciate their people's heroic—
tragic history . . . thanks for those delightful interludes.

*   *   *

. . . ואחם תשבחס עלי רעה א-לקים חשבה לטובה למען עשות כיום
הזה להחיית עם רב (בראשית נ : כ).

אסתר מן התורה מנין ? "ואנוכי הסתר אסתיר פני", פי' רש"י בימי
אסתר יהיה הסתר פנים, (חולין קלט:).

As the Megillah epitomizes the hidden hand of the Almighty in the warp and woof of history, so too, the incredible
saga to be unfolded in these pages manifests, for those with vision,
the design of the Creator. How little did Jacob Schiff realize, for
example, the far reaching consequences of his actions on his fellow
Jews 35 years later, when in 1904, as a protest against the Czar's
persecution of his coreligionists, he helped to finance Japan's
victory over Russia.

Not even the talmudic scholars, aware of the "miraculous"
nature of their escape from Lithuania to Japan, could have been
aware of the many facets of that miracle that spared them and the
17,000 German refugees from the fate of the Holocaust.

בעזהש"י   Brooklyn, N.Y.
Purim 5736

INTRODUCTION

> *Fun danen treibt men uns arois*
> *Und dorten losst men nit arein*
> *Zog shoin Tatenyu*
> *Vee lang vet dos zein?*
> > From here we are driven out
> > And there we may not enter
> > Tell us, dear Father [in Heaven]
> > How long will this go on?
> > > *(Niggun (Hassidic folk song) Herzman.*
> > > *Toire in Golus)*

Holocaust studies have thus far focused primarily on the catastrophic fate of Jews on the European continent. The present work shifts the focus from *how Jews died, to how they survived* in the Far East where thousands of potential victims built a new life and successfully transplanted their communal institutions. This response to Hitler's murderous scheme has never before been chronicled in a scholarly comprehensive way.

While the Nazis were carrying out their "Final Solution" to the Jewish problem, about 18,000 Jewish refugees found a haven in the only place in the world whose doors were open without a visa: the International Settlement of Shanghai. This study unfolds the dramatic story of how these refugees from

Germany and Austira, as well as a smaller group from Poland, got to Shanghai, and how they adjusted to life in that extra-ordinary Far Eastern community.

The Shanghai experience for the refugees may be divided into five broad categories: the flight from Central Europe—and later Poland—to Shanghai; the relief efforts by Shanghailanders and American Jewry; the creation of a full-fledged Jewish community; the Japanese and the Jews; the War in the Pacific; and the establishment of a Jewish ghetto in Shanghai. In each of these major areas, the events and circumstances are described and documented in detail, many for the very first time. Whenever possible, numerous factors involved are analyzed in light of both local and world-wide conditions.

The year 1938 was a watershed for world Jewry. The doom of the thousand-year-old communities of Central Europe was clearly foreshadowed by the Crystal Night of November 1938. The pogrom created fear and hysteria and almost every Jew now wanted to escape from Hitler's Greater Germany. Those who held American or other visas got out as soon as possible, but the majority became victims of almost universal restrictions. Shanghai was the only place in the world that offered asylum to the desperate, persecuted Jews.

A teeming city of over 4 million Chinese and nearly 100,000 foreigners (including Japanese), the International Settlement in Shanghai was an open city, requiring no papers or visas of any sort for entry. This condition lasted until August 1939 when the first restrictions on immigration were imposed by the Japanese authorities. Even so, Shanghai, so far removed from the European continent, with its strange environment and culture and its reputation as a hotbed of international intrigue and immorality, would hardly have appealed to so many of the fleeing German and Austrian Jews at any other time; and these same factors inhibited many potential emigrants until it was too late. Nevertheless, between 1938 and 1941, some 17,000 to 18,000 refugees, including 1,500 Gentile "non-Aryans" and 1,000 Polish Jews, found their way to Shanghai.

Upon arrival in Shanghai, the German refugees, surprisingly, found not one but two existing Jewish communities: a small group of Sephardim; and a much larger group of Ashkenazim. The Sephardim had come from Baghdad by way of India as early as the latter half of the nineteenth century, while the Ashkenazim came primarily from Russia, getting to Shanghai by way of Harbin, Manchuria, during the first quarter of the twentieth century. These Jews had come to a thriving port whose expanding economic frontiers permitted many of the capable and ambitious Sephardim to rise to the pinnacle of economic and social achievement. Their Ashkenazi coreligionists, if not so preeminent, at least achieved a modest level of prosperity. The refugees, although they by far outnumbered the older Jewish settlers, could not participate in Shanghai's former economic success, since it was still in the throes of the devastating Sino-Japanese hostilities of 1937. With Japan in control of the harbor, and Shanghai cut off from its natural economic base—the huge Yangtze River Basin and hinterlands—this formerly thriving port was unable to absorb the talent and experience of the refugees who were predominantly middle and lower-middle class professionals, merchants and craftsmen.

Much of this study concentrates on the uphill struggle faced by the refugees in the economic as well as other areas. With some help from the local and American Jewish communities—but more so by sheer dint of hard labor, resourcefulness and imagination—the refugees created a number of

viable institutions and formed a new community within a
Jewish environment—for many a first-time experience—that
moulded a sense of kinship out of what had been an amorphous,
heterogeneous mass of individuals. Foremost among these
institutions was the *Juedische Gemeinde,* the European type
all-encompassing religious and social community. It even
included an Arbitration Board, a sort of People's Court, which
adjudicated the vast majority of the refugees' disputes.

Achievements in the educational and cultural arena
were equally impressive. A variety of elementary, trade and
adult education institutions alongside a thriving German-
language press, theatre and musical life was created that would
do proud to a normal community many times its size. This
is all the more astounding considering the all-pervading abject
poverty of most of the refugees. In fact, were it not for the
local and American relief efforts—however inadequate and
amateurishly administered—it is doubtful whether a majority
of the refugees would have survived the prewar years, let alone
the more difficult war years, and especially the period after
1943 in the ghetto.

One of the central themes of this work concerns an
extraordinary and ironic twist of fate, or *Hashgocho Protis*
(Divine Providence), as the believing Jew would have it,
the incredible role of the Axis Powers, especially Japan, in
actually making possible the survival of 18,000 Jews. When,
due to primarily economic reasons, opposition to the refugees
arose among Western inhabitants of Shanghai—including
Jews—this was communicated through their respective governments, including the United States, England and France.
These tried to persuade the German Jews and the German
Government to halt further emigration to the economically
unstable refuge of Shanghai. At the same time, and for their
own reasons, the Axis Powers not only permitted but even

encouraged such emigration. Germany continued her pressure to make thousands of Jews leave even without visas; Italy permitted the use of her ports and ships; and Japan, since 1937, the real power in Shanghai, granted the refugees asylum in Hongkew, part of the Japanese-controlled sector of the International Settlement. The mystery of Japan's most unusual behavior proved to be among the most difficult historical problems to unravel. Its solution opens the door to a broader study of the Japanese attitudes and policies relating to Jews.

These attitudes spawned in the minds of a few middle-echelon officers, so-called "experts on Jewish affairs" with a unique "pragmatic" approach to antisemitism, and promulgated at the highest level of Japanese government, offer the key to an understanding of the entire Shanghai experience. This is true of the entry of the Central-European refugees in 1938-1939; the transit of the smaller Polish group through Siberia to Kobe, Japan and later to Shanghai; the change from a favorable prewar stance toward the Jews, to one more influenced by the Nazis, which led to the establishment of a ghetto in 1943, and the peace feelers to the United States, using Jews living in China as intermediaries.

Since the unique stance of the Japanese was predicated upon the image of the Jews as created and fostered by the "experts," who belonged to the radical military ultranationalist cliques, it was necessary to provide a historical framework for such groups, their ideology and the place of the Jews within their *Weltanschauung*. Moreover, since these ideologes were close to and influential with Tokyo's policy makers, the reader is presented with a cursory sketch of Japan's foreign policy; its architects; their relations to the ultranationalists; and the role they assigned to the Jews in "Japan's Greater East Asian Co-Prosperity Spheres."

In addition to the Japanese attitudes and policies relating to Jews, this study brings to light for the first time a number of other fascinating aspects of life in Shanghai: the refugee participation in the underground; the story of "illegal" and the "two-day Yom Kippur" in Japan; the serious proposals refugees; the life-saving relief work by the Joint Distribution Committee throughout this period; the gripping saga of the Mirrer Yeshiva from its first refuge in Kovno to Shanghai through Siberia and Japan; the "Jewish" international dateline and the "two-day Yom Kippur" in Japan; the sreious proposals to exchange 15,000 Nisei, interned by the United States, for the Jewish refugees; the effect of Pearl Harbor and the establishment of a Nazi-inspired ghetto on the refugee community; a portrait of Ghoya, the self-styled Japanese "King of the Jews"; and the devastation wrought on the refugee center in 1945 by American bombers.

It is the author's hope that this research which illuminates a hardly-known aspect of Jewish and Holocaust History, will also contribute to a broader understanding of the recent history of Japan and the Far East.

1 | "TO SHANGHAI!"

To Shanghai! But you've only three more months to wait before your visa from America comes. Why go to the Orient? . . . I almost took my life last week. Only this news that one can get easily to Shanghai, kept me from doing it.
(Helen Hilsenrad. *Brown was the Danube*).

The tenth of November [1938] had released a panic which thousands had suppressed in order to keep going from day to day. Now there was a wholesale urge for exodus from Vienna. Every office connected with departure of any kind was choked with swarms of terrified Jews. Many people like us, who had affidavits [from the US] but had to wait for quotas, simply could wait no longer and plunged into maniacal routes of escape. When news of their capture came to us it was like hearing of suicides. Dr. Westheimer . . . visited us constantly. He was badly off these days, a man bedevilled with terror. One morning he had interestnig information: "Jim, Helena, I'm going to Shang-hai!"

"To Shanghai! But you've only three more months to wait before your visa from America comes through. Why go to the Orient?"

25

". . . I almost took my life last week. Only this news, that one can get easily to Shanghai, kept me from doing it."

Helen Hilsenrad (*Brown was the Danube*)

Shanghai! By the end of 1938, the name had become a talisman for thousands of German and Austrian Jews, a talisman with which they could transform the nightmare of their lives into a hope of salvation. It was the only place where one could hope to escape the Nazi terror without that magic formula, that open sesame, a visa. The terror had begun in 1933; it culminated in the debris and shattered glass that bestrewed hundreds of Jewish stores, synagogues and homes during the pogrom known as Crystal Night, of November 10 to 11, 1938. Crystal Night shattered more than the windows of German Jewry; it shattered their deeply entrenched illusions of security and rootedness.[1]

Jews had, after all, lived in the region known today as Germany for over sixteen centuries, and had come to feel at home there.[2] It is true that, after the unification of the country in 1871 with its accompanying rise in nationalistic feeling, there had been rumblings of antisemitic propaganda, but the Jews, strong and stable in their self-image as upstanding Germans, did not take it seriously. They felt it would pass away if it were fought with the "truth."[3] More and more they were assimilated, and modern Germany's eminence in science, culture and scholarship owes much to its Jewish citizens.[4]

Looking back, it seems obvious that during the first third of the twentieth century the German Jews were living in a fool's paradise. What burst in their faces in the early 1930's had been building up steadily under their very eyes, long before Hitler assumed power, and certainly long before he unleashed his program of "scientific genocide."

It began on a small scale after Hitler assumed power in

1933 — harsh economic persecution, mass arrests and attacks. The Jews were thrown into panic and there was a rush to escape, although few thought it would last. In this period, 37,000 crossed the borders, mostly to West European countries, although a few got as far as Palestine.[5] A very small group, mostly physicians, traveled, in search of a freer economic and political climate, clear across Europe and Asia to that most unlikely place of refuge, Shanghai.[6] These were to become the nucleus of a large community of refugees, numbering about 17,000, chiefly of German and Austrian origin.[7]

THE NUREMBERG LAWS

At the first mammoth Nazi Party rally, held in Nuremberg in 1935, the so-called Nuremberg Laws were laid down. Citizens were divided into two classes, Aryan and non-Aryan. The high degree of assimilation of Jews in Germany had naturally led to extensive intermarriage, and as a result there was no clear line of demarcation. Nonetheless, those classified as non-Aryan were deprived of both their rights as citizens and government protection, an act, as will be shown later, that had profound implications for the Jewish refugees in Shanghai after Pearl Harbor and the ensuing War in the Pacific.[8]

During Hitler's first five years of power, 150,000 Jews emigrated from Germany.[9] But many, even among those who had obtained visas for the United States and other "desirable" lands, hung on, hoping against hope—in some cases as late as 1939—that things would change in Germany. The hope was so strong, the inability to accept the worst so tenacious, that a large number allowed their visas to expire. It was this attitude that forced so many, so late, to have to choose Shanghai as a place of refuge, because it required no entry visa.[10]

THE EVIAN CONFERENCE

At the end of 1937, as conditions in Germany grew

worse and the plight of the refugees more desperate, President
Roosevelt called an intergovernmental conference to be held in
Evian, France, in the summer of 1938. The complete failure of
this conference to make German Jewry an international responsibility had the darkest consequences. The Nazis gloated over
the fact that the democratic nations liked the Jews as little as
they did, and with a clear conscience could pursue their antisemitic policy.[11]

CRYSTAL NIGHT

The last vestige of wishful thinking on the part of the
German and Austrian Jews, that they might still, somehow, find
a place in the Third Reich, was finally wiped out by the aforementioned events of November 10, 1938.[12] The immediate cause
of the vandalism of Crystal Night was the action of a young
Polish Jew, Herschel Grynszpan, in Paris. Half-crazed by the
news that his family had been forcibly deported from Germany
into the no-man's-land near the Polish border, he bought a
revolver and went to the German Embassy, intending to kill the
German Ambassador. Instead he shot and killed the Third Secretary, Ernst von Rath.

THE PENALTY FOR CRYSTAL NIGHT

Josef Goebbels, the Minister of Propaganda in Germany,
lost no time in announcing the news of "spontaneous" reprisals
against the Jews. But the vandalism that occured that night and
the following day cannot be dismissed as a spontaneous outburst of mob violence. It was too quick, too well planned and
executed, to have been the work of an undisciplined mob. Over
7,500 stores were looted and 191 synagogues destroyed. The
reign of terror and destruction struck hardest among the Jews
of Austria and the Sudetenland who had already been initiated
into the Nazi terror methods following Hitler's *Anschluss* of

Austria on April 10, 1938. Jews were seized and beaten in the streets; many were shot when they attempted to escape. Suicides of individuals and whole families became a common occurrence.

The official penalty to be inflicted on the Jews for their collective guilt in von Rath's murder was announced on November 12. It was to be a threefold punishment. First, a collective fine of one billion Reichsmark was to be assessed on the entire Jewish community, including Austria and the Sudetenland. Before a Jew could have his emigration papers cleared, he was required to submit a certificate that he had paid his share of the indemnity. Second, Jews, although insured, were to pay for the damage inflicted on their own establishments. Third, a series ot acts was promulgated, aimed at the complete elimination of the Jews from Germany's economic life. All Jewish enterprises were to be "aryanized," that is, taken over by the state trustees and sold to "Aryans." Similar decrees were passed applying to real estate, objets d'art, securities and even jewelry.

Meantime, Heinrich Mueller, chief of the Gestapo at the time, ordered the arrest and shipment to concentration camps of about 20,000 wealthy Jews. There, "proper treatment" was applied to induce their families to ransom them at a high price.[13]

PSYCHOLOGICAL EFFECTS OF CRYSTAL NIGHT

At last the Jews of Germany and Austria realized the utter hopelessness of their plight, and everyone was ready to leave. Under conditions infinitely worse than during the early days of Hitler's rule, thousands crossed the borders, where they floundered hopelessly or were interned by "friendly" countries. And the spirit of the German Jews was utterly broken by the knowledge that their beloved Germany was no more.[14]

PLANS FOR SETTLEMENT OF JEWS

As more and more doors were closed to Hitler's victims, a variety of plans were proposed by both Jews and non-Jews, to solve the refugee problem.[15]

Although we have now seen the capacity of Palestine to absorb thousands of refugees, it did not at the time prove the promised haven most Jews dreamed of. Political considerations seemed more important to the British (who had held it as a Mandate since the Treaty of Versailles after World War I) than the rescue of a few thousand Jews. Nonetheless, between 1933 and 1939, over 50,000 German and Austrian Jews did succeed in getting to Palestine.[16]

Other schemes, chimerical or occasionally half-serious, were proposed for the settlement of this enormous population displacement—Madagascar, Southern Rhodesia, Kenya, Tanganyika, the Philippines. However, only the Dominican Republic came up with a serious offer—to relocate 100,000 refugees in agricultural settlements.[17]

Eventually the only place that offered any hope, and where, with a real effort on the part of the relief agencies, thousands more could have been saved, was Shanghai.[18]   ,

THE US QUOTAS AND THE REFUGEE PROBLEM

For close to two centuries the United States had been a haven for immigrants, more so than any other country on earth. But this mass migration, mostly from Europe, came to a halt before 1933, at the very time when an open-door policy was most needed. After World War I, the United States had withdrawn into a position of relative isolationism, and this mood was reflected in profound changes in the immigration laws. The underlying philosophy of the "national origins" system, with its accompanying "quotas," on which the Johnson Immigration Act of 1924-1929 was based, was an expression of racist, ideological prejudice. It gave preference to immigration from "Nordic" countries. Changes in frontiers and national boundaries since the

Treaty of Versailles had affected such origins. A person now living in Germany but born in a territory called Hungary before World War 1 and since occupied by Roumania, would be considered Roumanian by "national origin" and fall into the miniscule Roumanian quota.[19] This aspect of the policy greatly affected the thousands of Polish Jews living in Germany, as well as the Austrian Jews born in some part of the former Austrian Empire that was now considered part of Greater Germany.[20]

But besides the quota system, there were other severe strictures in the enforcement of the United States immigration laws. Section 7(c) required the applicant for entry to supply a police certificate of good character for the past five years. As a great many Jews were escaping illegally from the Nazi terror, or were survivors of concentration camps, they could hardly produce certificates of good character from their home-town Nazi police.[21]

Another provision denied admission to those "likely to become a public charge." The United States consuls meticulously enforced this clause, and many refugees might have been saved by greater leniency. Other democratic countries emulated these restrictive measures and followed the American example.[22]

These are the crucial conditions that forced many refugees to turn to Shanghai as the only available haven. It was over 7,000 miles away; its climate in sharp contrast to that of central Europe; its oriental environment alien and its economic outlook wretched. But the International Settlement in Shanghai required neither visa, nor affidavit, nor police certificate, nor assurance of financial independence. It therefore offered the only asylum, in many cases the only alternative to a return to prison or concentration camp.

NOTES: TO SHANGHAI

1. For an excellent overall picture of the Nazis' early antisemitic measures and the eventual holocaust, see Lucy S. Dawidowicz, *The War Against the Jews*, 1933-1945 [Dawidowicz, *War*] (New York: Holt, Rinehart and Winston, 1975), and its excellent bibliography. Cf. also Nora Levin, *The Holocaust*; *The Destruction of European Jewry* 1933-1945 (New York: Thomas Y. Crowell Co., 1968). Among the more specialized works see Raul Hilberg, *The Destruction of the European Jews* [Hilberg, *Destruction*] (Chicago: Quadrangle Books, 1961), Gerald Reitlinger, *The Final Solution: The Attempt to Exterminate the Jews of Europe* 1939-1945 (New York: Barnes and Noble Co., 1961).

A brief bibliography on the holocaust may be found in Henry Friedlander "The Holocaust: Anti-Semitism and the Jewish Catastrophe," in *The Study of Judaism: Bibliographical Essays* (New York: Ktav, 1972), pp. 207-229.

More detailed bibliographies on this subject may be found in two excellent series titled, *Yad Washem—YIVO Bibliographical Series* and the *Wiener Library Catalogue Series,* respectively. Additional bibliographies can be located through Shlomo Shunami, *Bibliography of Jewish Bibliographies* (Hebrew) (Jerusalem: Hebrew University Press, 1969).

In addition to articles and parts of books on "Crystal Night," found in the above-mentioned literature, see especially Lionel Kochan, *Pogroms* 10 *November* 1938 [Kochan, *Pogrom*] (London: Andre Deutsch, 1957); Reitlinger, *Solution,* pp. 10-18; Rita Thelmann and Emanuel Finerman, *Crystal Night;* 9-10 *November* 1938 (New York: Coward-McCann, 1974); William L. Shirer, *The Rise and Fall of the Third Reich: A History of Nazi Germany* [Shirer, *Rise*] (New York: Simon and Schuster, 1960), pp. 430-435. For reaction to Crystal Night in the United States, see Sander A. Diamond, "The Kristallnacht and the Reaction in America" [Diamond, "Krystallnacht"], *Yivo Annual* of Jewish Social Science, Vol. XIV [YAJSS] (New York: Yivo Institute for Jewish Research, 1969), pp. 196-208; K. J. Ball-Kaduri, "Die Vorplanung der Kristallnacht," [Ball-Kaduri, "Kristallnacht"], *Zeitschrift Fuer Die Geschichte der Juden* (Tel Aviv: Olamenu, 1966), pp. 211-216.

2. For a popular history of the Jews in Germany see Marvin Lowenthal, *The Jews of Germany: A Story of Sixteen Centuries* [Lowenthal, *Germany*] (Philadelphia: Jewish Publication Society, 1939). Cf. also H. G. Adler, *The Jews in Germany: From the Enlightenment to National Socialism* (Notre Dame, Ind.: University of Notre Dame Press, 1969).

3. Two examples of apologetic literature include one by a Protestant theologian and one by a Jew. Hermann L. Strack, *The Jew and Human*

Sacrifice: *Human Blood and Jewish Ritual* (London: Cope and Fenwick, 1909); Joseph Bloch, *Israel and the Nations* (Berlin: Benjamin Harz, 1927).

4. For some statistics on intermarriage see the following: Arthur Ruppin, *The Jewish Fate and Future* [Ruppin, *Jew Fate*] (London: MacMillan, 1940), esp. chap. 6; Eric Rosenthal, "Trends of the Jewish Population in Germany, 1910-1939", *Jewish Social Studies* [*JSS*], Vol. 6 (1944), pp. 233-274; Bruno Blau, "The Jewish Population of Germany, 1939-1945", *JSS*, Vol 12 (1950), pp. 161-172. Blau includes statistics on "non-Aryans" not available to Rosenthal.

For a brief but excellent evaluation of the position of German Jewry during this period, see Robert Weltsch, "Introduction" [Weltsch, "Introd."], *Yearbook of the Leo Baeck Institute* [*YLBI*], Vol. I (London: East and West Library, 1956), pp. XIX-XXI.

For the contributions of German Jewry see for example, Sigmund Kaznelson, *Juden in Deutschen Kulturereich* (Berlin: Juedischer Verlag, 1960); Arnold Zweig, *Bilanz der Deutschen Judenheit* 1933 (Amsterdam: Querido Verlag, 1934); Ernst Hamburger, *Juden in Oeffentlichen Leben Deutschlands: Regierungsmitglieder, Beamte und Parlamentarier in der Monarchischen Zeit* 1848-1918 (Tuebingen: J. C. B. Mohr, 1968); Abraham Myerson and Isaac Goldberg, *The German Jew: His Share in Modern Culture* (London: Hopkinson, 1933).

A good depiction of the Jews in Austria is found in *The Jews of Austria: Essays on Their Life, History and Destruction*, Josef Frankel, editor (London: Vallentine, Mitchell and Co., Ltd. 1967).

5. This was the largest number of emigrants in one year during the Nazi period until Crystal Night. See table in Werner Rosenstock, "Exodus 1933-1939: A Survey of Jewish Emigration from Germany" [Rosenstock, "Exodus"], *YLBI*, Vol. I (London: East and West Library, 1956), p. 373.

For the statistics of those going to Palestine see *ibid.*, p. 379. Rosenstock gives the following breakdown of the percentage of emigrants and their countries of destination in 1933: Europe (including repatriates), 72-74 per cent; Palestine, 19 per cent; Overseas, 7-9 per cent.

6. See for example, Cable of [Bernhard] Kahn to Joint (American Jewish Joint Distribution Committee, better known as the Joint or JDC. See below, Chapter 3), December 14, 1937. (This document is part of the extensive JDC collection relating to Shanghai and China [JDCCA]. All the documents quoted were reproduced by the author, courtesy of the JDC). Kahn gives a figure of about 100 German Jewish families.

This figure of 100 tallies with the one given by Fritz Kaufmann, a German Jewish businessman who came to Shanghai in 1931. At that time, he notes, there were about 10 Jewish families, and during the four years following the rise of Hitler, about 300 German Jewish refugees, mostly professionals, especially doctors, came to Shanghai. Fritz Kaufmann, *The Experiences of the Shanghai Jewish Community Under the Japanese in World War II* [Kaufmann,

Experiences]. (16-page unpublished manuscript of a speech made by the author on February 12, 1963). Reproduced courtesy of the Blaustein Library of the American Jewish Committee.

7. For the statistics of the refugee community, see Appendix.

8. For the Nuremberg Laws, see for example, Hilberg, *Destruction,* pp. 43-53. Cf. also Dawidowicz, *War,* pp. 63-69.

The loss of their status as *Reichsburger* (full citizen of the Reich) in 1935, and even the lesser status of *Staatsangehoerige* (subject of the state) for those Jews who left Germany, was to adversly affect the refugees in Shanghai with the establishment of a ghetto in 1943, inspired by the Nazis.

For a table of anti-Jewish legislation including the 13 decrees comprising Nuremberg Laws, see the *Black Book: The Nazi Crime Against the Jewish People [Black Book]* (n.p.: The Jewish Black Book Committee, 1946), insert, following p. 106.

9. Rosenstock, "Exodus", p. 387. His figure is 140-150,000 for the period up to and including the first six months of 1938. A similar figure, of 140,000, up to the beginning of 1938 is given by Mark Wischnitzer, *To Dwell in Safety: The Story of Jewish Migration Since* 1800 [Wischnitzer, *Migration*] (Philadelphia: Jewish Publication Society, 1948), pp. 192-193.

10. Gerhard Gerechter. Taped Interview April 16, 1968 (and subsequent dates) [Gerechter Interv.]. Mr. Gerechter who worked for the Berlin Police Department prior to Hitler's assumption of power and afterwards worked with the *Hilfsverein der Deutschen Juden* (which helped direct and finance German emigration until 1941) until 1938, when he went to Japan, where he worked with both the Yokohama and Kobe Jewish community relief agencies. He remained in Japan until the spring of 1943, when he relocated to Shanghai. There he was active in the Jewish "Underground". Presently he is in the United States and is the president of the "Association of Former Refugees from Shanghai. Mr. Gerechter granted the writer three taped and countless telephone interviews and reviewed the entire manuscript. He also provided the writer with many leads and valuable documents for reproduction.

Also, Israel Heuman, Interv. August 15, 1968. Mr. Heuman left Germany in the fall of 1939 and related an incident concerning one family that returned to Germany from the United States as late as mid-1939.

See also Wischnitzer, *Migration,* p. 195; *Mrs. Ruth Fischel, Taped Interview.* December 6, 1965 and subsequent dates [Fischel Interv.]. Mrs. Fischel, whose husband was the President of the *Juedische Gemeinde* in Shanghai for several years, left Germany in 1940, and had previously given her Shanghai entrance permit to relatives, in early 1939. Mrs. Fischel granted one taped, and several additional interviews, and provided the writer with important, original copies of documents; "Adjustment of the Professional Refugee", *Annals of the American Academy of Political and Social Science, [Annals]* Vol. 203 (May 1939), p. 155.

11. For the conditions of the refugees at this time, Jewish as well as non-Jewish, see John Hope Simpson, *Refugees*: *Preliminary Report of a Survey* [Simpson, Refugees] (London: The Royal Institute of International Affairs, 1938). This report was drawn up for presentation to the members of the Evian Conference, held on July 6-15, 1938. Also Arieh Tartakower and Kurt Grossman, *The Jewish Refugee* [Tartakower, Refugee] (New York: Institute of Jewish Affairs of the World Jewish Congress, 1944).

For an excellent summary of the refugee problem and the political maneuvers involved in the Evian Conference, see Henry L. Feingold, *The Politics of Rescue*: *The Roosevelt Administration and the Holocaust*, 1938-1945 [Feingold, *Politics*], chapter 2. Cf. also Saul S. Friedman, *No Haven for the Oppressed*: *United States Policy toward Jewish Refugees* 1938-1945 [Friedman, *No Haven*] (Detroit: Wayne State University Press, 1973), chapter 3; Arthur D. Morse, *While Six Million Died*: *A Chronicle of American Apathy* [Morse, *Six Million*] (New York: Random House, 1968), chapter 11; Tartakower, *Refugee,* pp. 412-20; S. Adler-Rudel, "The Evian Conference on the Refugee Question", *YBYB,* Vol. XIII (1968), pp. 235-273; Hans Habe, *The Mission*: *A Novel* [Habe, *Mission*] (New York: Coward-McCann, 1966). In a thinly disguised fictional form, Habe, a former journalist who covered the Conference, gives a detailed analysis of every aspect of this international gathering, including the arguments and rationalizations for each of the partisan views.

Originally the conference was to include only representatives from European countries, except, of course, Germany. Britain, however, insisted that invitations be issued on a broader basis to include non-European countries as well. Limiting the invitations would merely have highlighted the importance of Palestine as the only feasible solution of significance to the refugee problem. Britain, in no mood to antagonize the Arabs who had been making a good deal of trouble in Palestine, demanded that Palestine not be discussed at the Conference at all. In another condition for her participation, Britain insisted that the Conference explore only the problem of "actual" refugees and not those merely "threatened" with persecuteion. See Morton Blum, *From the Morgenthau Diaries*: *Years of War* 1941-1945 [Blum, Morgenthau] (Boston: Houghton-Mifflin Co., 1927), pp. 207-208. Also Morse, *Six Million,* pp. 210-211.

For the Nazis' gloating over the failure of the democratic countries to help alleviate the refugee problem, see Habe, *Mission,* p. 127; Finegold, *Politics,* p. 36; Morse, *Six Million,* pp. 205-206.

12. For the story of "Crystal Night", see above, note 1.

A personal account of this event as it affected the Jews in Vienna is found in Helen Hilsenrad, *Brown Was the Danube*: *A Memoir of Hitler's Vienna* [Hilsenrad, *Brown*] (New York: Thomas Yoseloff, 1966), pp. 321-322.

13. Reitlinger, *Solution,* p. 10. According to Reitlinger, neither the Ambassador nor the Third Secretary were antisemitic. Moreover, von Rath had been under surveillance by the Gestapo for some time because of his reported anti-Nazi activities in Paris.

The event which preceded these deportations was an act by the Polish Government on October 28th of that year, which invalidated the passports of all its nationals residing continuously in foreign countries unless they were periodically renewed. In effect, this made these nationals "stateless."

Actually there were two deportations of Polish Jews. The first took place on the evening of October 28, 1938. When the Polish Government refused to accept their nationals, the Germans permitted this group to return to their homes in Germany. A few days later the second deportation took place when about 10,000 Polish Jews were again sent to the Polish border (Zbaszyn), where they were caught between the armed guards of the two countries, neither of which would permit their crossing the border. Many Jews perished in this no-man's-land from shooting, starvation and freezing weather. *Ibid.,* p. 9.

For the text of the deportation order of October 28, 1938, see *Black Book,* p. 120.

14. Reitlinger, *Soluteion,* p. 17.

Black Book insert cites the decree of November 12 in the (Reichsgesetzblatt, Teil I [Reich Law Gazette Part I]) [*RGBL, I*], p. 1579, concerning the atonement fine for Jews. This fine was popularly referred to as the *Judenabgabe* (Jew's tax), while the fine on objets d'art, etc., was popularly referred to as the *Silberabgabe.* Gerechter Interv.

See *Black Book insert,* re decree of November 12, 1938, to eliminate Jews from German economic life (*RGBL, I,* p. 1580).

For the arrest of the 20,000 "rich" Jews see Reitlinger, *Solution,* p. 14.

The many suicides and the utter hopelessness of the Crystal Night are graphically depicted in Hilsenrad, *Brown,* pp. 316-321.

15. See below, note 17.

16. For the "political considerations, see Ben Halpern, *The Idea of a Jewish State* [Halpern, *Idea*], 2nd ed., rev. (Cambridge: Harvard University Press, 1969), pp. 39, 357. See also Blum, *Morgenthau,* pp. 206-207; Wischnitzer, *Migration,* p. 200.

For a good chapter on how the British policy concerning the entry of Jews into Palestine evolved into the "White Paper" in 1939, see Yehuda Bauer, *From Diplomacy to Resistance: A History of Jewish Palestine, 1939-1945* [Bauer, *Palestine*] (Philadelphia: Jewish Publication Society, 1970), chapter I.

The statistics of the immigration to Palestine are found in Wischnitzer, *Migration,* p. 217. Cf. also Rosenstock, *Exodus,* p. 387. Rosenstock estimates the number to be 44,000.

17. A few of these plans are discussed by Wischnitzer, *Migration*, pp. 217-221 and his sources, esp. note 99. Cf. also Finegold, *Politics*, chap. 5; Tartakower, *Refugee*, chap. 10.

Wischnitzer notes that one plan for settling Jews in Australia was made by a non-Jewish family which offered the refugees a 10,000 square mile tract. *Migration*, p. 238.

For the Madagascar Plan, see Reitlinger, *Solution*, chap. 4. One fascinating plan to settle 100,000 refugees in Yunnan Province in South China was proposed in 1939 by Dr. Jacob Berglas, a former Viennese banker. He even visited the United States in that year in an effort to obtain financial support for his plan. For details, see Jacob Berglas to DALJEWCIB (Far Eastern Jewish Central Information Bureau for Emigrants, affiliated with HIAS-HICEM), Harbin, Manchuria, June 15, 1939 (HIAS-HICEM File at the YIVO [HH] C-4). Made available to the author, courtesy of Zosa Szajkowski, historian and archivist at the YIVO. See also *China Weekly Review*, September 16, 1939, p. 9; *Israel's Messenger*, June 14, 1939.

See also Anna Ginsbourg, *Shanghai: City of Refuge: Jewish Refugees in Shanghai* [Ginsbourg, *Shanghai*] (Shanghai: *China Weekly Review*, 1940), pp. 26-32. This booklet is an edited and revised version of a number of articles which originally appeared in the *China Weekly Review* by Julius Rudolph.

For one of the few settlement projects that worked out, the one proposing to settle the Jewish refugees in the Dominican Republic, see Wischnitzer, *Migration*, p. 203. The financial conditions of this plan included the stipulation that all expenses be paid by the Jews. See also Feingold, *Politics*, pp. 111-113. For the most complete information on the *Sosua Colony* (as the outgrowth of the Dominican plan was called), see Hyman Kisch, *The Sosua Settlement of Jews from Central Europe in the Dominican Republic 1939-1969* (unpublished doctoral dissertation, The Teachers' Seminary and People's University, 1971) (courtesy of the author).

18. See below, chap. 6.

19. See for example, Marcus Lee Hansen, *The Atlantic Migration, 1607-1860: A History of the Continuing Settlement of the U.S.* [Hansen, *Atlantic*] (New York: Harper Torchbooks, 1961), p. 4. During the peak year of 1913, over one million new arrivals landed on the American shores.

For the odd circumstances arising out of the quota system, see, William S. Bernard, "American Immigration Policy: A Reappraisal" [Bernard, "Policy"], *Immigration as a Factor in American History*, Oscar Handlin (New York: Prentice-Hall, Inc., 1959), p. 198.

20. See chart for the quota system in Francis J. Brown and Joseph S. Roucek, *One America: The History, Contributions, and Present Problems of Our National Minorities* [Brown, *One America*], 2nd ed. (New York: Prentice-Hall, Inc., 1945), pp. 634-35.

21. The police certificate was known in German as *Polizeiliche Fuehrungszeugnisse.* Gerechter Interv. In addition to a "certificate of character", the potential refugee had to provide a record of military service, two certified copies of a birth certificate and two copies of all other available public records retained by the authorities of the country of departure. Despite the fact that by law these were required only "if available", many American consuls demanded the complete dossier, particularly the police certificates. Morse, *Six Million,* p. 137. Also, Tartakower, *Refugee,* p. 87.

22. Wischnitzer, *Migration,* p. 173. Actually, it was President Herbert Hoover who, during the Depression, on September 8, 1930, revived the stringent adherence to the "public charge" provision. Morse, *Six Million,* pp. 130-146. Also, Finegold, *Politics,* p. 16; Friedman, *No Haven,* pp. 22-25; Tartakower, *Refugee,* p. 86.

2 | SHANGHAI, A HUMAN KALEIDOSCOPE

. . . [Shanghai was] a place where two civilizations met and neither prevailed. To the foreigners, it was out of bounds, beyond the knowledge or supervision of their own culture, where each man was a law unto himself, or where he easily adjusted to the prevailing mores with no qualms of conscience. Morality was irrelevant or meaningless in Shanghai, an atmosphere which was apparent to even the casual visitor.

(Murphy. *Shanghai*)

What kind of place was Shanghai, which so suddenly beckoned to thousands of refugees from Hitler's persecution? Although hardly a household word in the average Jewish family of Germany or Austria, Shanghai was no primitive village in some distant place. It was, in fact, the world's seventh largest port, and contained a sizeable cosmopolitan population, which resided in two foreign concessions under Western control.

The city that was to become the haven for the Jewish refugees, however, was much more than a busy commercial and financial center. The titles of a few books describing life there make it quite evident that Shanghai was a *Paradise of Adventurers,* a *City for Sale,* the *Key to Modern China* and *Hostage to Politics.* As the very name implies, kidnapping was common-place and crime was rampant, especially since the tangled legal web of "extrality" made justice difficult to implement. At one and the same time, Shanghai's foreign concessions were the centers for Christian missionizing and a "den of iniquity", with the highest ratio of brothels in the world. It was a place where everything could be and was bought or sold. Where fortunes were made quickly and dissipated even faster. Its Western facade belied its essentially Chinese character, which yet was somehow, different from the rest of China.

Shanghai was the battlefield for ideas and ideologies where Confucianism, modern secularism, communism, Chinese nationalism (infected with anti-Western and later anti-Japanese fervor), fought for the minds of the Chinese and eventually the hegemony of all of China.

She was, in he words of one modern historian:

> . . . a place where two civilizations met and neither pre-vailed. To the foreigners, it was out of bounds, beyond the knowledge or supervision of their own culture, where each man was a law unto himself, or where he easily adjusted to the prevailing mores with no qualms of conscience. Morality was irrelevant or meaningless in Shanghai, an atmosphere which was apparent to even the casual visitor . . . For the Chinese, Shanghai was equally off limits. Those who had chosen this new kind of life, like the mer-chants, were by that choice cut off from traditional China and from the sanctions which it imposed.

> . . . on top of this was the continually fluctuating popula-tion. Few people, Chinese or foreign, came to the city with the hope of remaining there long; most of them aimed to make a fortune in a few years and then leave. Many of

them did remain, but so did the frenzied atmosphere. The international, intercultural nature of the city added to its excitement. Foreign hotels found it necessary to advertise their ability to speak with patrons in English, French, German, and Russian as a minimum . . .

[In other words] Shanghai was an exciting and colorful place which travel folders could not exaggerate.[1]

Surprisingly enough, this heterogeneous international city included not one, but two distinct Jewish communities, which were there to welcome their coreligionists. The older one consisted of a small Sephardi (Baghadi) community, which had arrived close to a centry before, and which included some of the most illustrious names of Shanghai's commercial and social roster. The second, a much larger and more recent group, was composed of Ashkenazi Jews who hailed primarily from Russia, and who were never to match the commercial success of the Sephardim.[2]

Superimposed upon this diversity were the Japanese, who, through a significant civilian and military presence, especially since the Sino-Japanese hostilities in 1937, were the real power in Shanghai.[3] Not forgetting the basically Chinese character of the city, this account will provide some idea of the human kaleidoscope that was Shanghai in 1938, that eventful year which saw the arrival of the German-Jewish refugees.[4]

THE FOREIGN CONCESSIONS

The Foreign Concessions of Shanghai had been a haven for Chinese refugees long before 1938, when the last wave of Jews, the victims of Hitler's oppression, began to arrive. Its ambiguous political status had made it an international enclave. There was no passport control: especially after the 1937 Sino-Japanese hostilities. In fact any traveler after clearing customs, could simply debark and be on his way.[5] The foreign merchant was therefore unencumbered by the complications of Chinese mercantile law—regulated at every point by semi-official Chinese merchants—which gave him an enormous economic advantage.[6]

Historically, this came about as a result of the Treaty of Nangking (August 1842) at the conclusion of the Second Opium War, which opened up five ports in China to Western trade. These included the then, very minor port of Shanghai. The conditions of the treaty imposed upon the defeated Chinese included the granting of extraterritorial rights to Britain, rights which were soon to be extended to other Western powers. These "rights" placed the citizens of all the powers which had most-favored-nation agreements with China under the jurisdiction of their own national laws, wherever they went in China, and the law was administered to foreigners by their own consular courts. From this period on there were really two Shanghais, the Chinese and the foreign.[7] The first, or Greater Shanghai, which by the 1930's would encompass the major portion of the population—about two million Chinese—was completely under Chinese jurisdiction. The other half, known as the Foreign Concessions, consisted of two independent sectors, the International Settlement and the French Settlement or Concession.[8] The non-Chinese population of the foreign sectors did not exceed 60,000 during the 1930's, as compared to 1,500,00 Chinese but the administration of each sector lay solely in the hands of the Municipal Council of the International Settlement, and the Consul General of the French Concession.[9]

Thus, according to the 1936 census, the non-Chinese population of Shanghai consisted of 20,000 Japanese, 15,000 Russian, 9,000 British, 5,000 Germans and Austrians (non-Jewish), 4,000 Americans and 2,500 French[10] Though only a small percentage of the total population, the foreigners, especially the British and Americans, represented the upper stratum in wealth and social position. Immediately below them on the socio-economic scale were the Swiss, Scandinavians, Portuguese, and the strong, German-speaking colonies, all of whom had large investments in Shanghai. The French, despite their control of their own concession, were never numerically important either in their own territory or in Greater Shanghai, while the lowest on the scale were the White Russians, who, on the whole, had been unable to establish themselves economically.[11]

The Chinese had used the comparative safety as well as the economic opportunities of the foreign settlements, to escape from upheavals in their homeland from various causes, economic and political, provincial, national, or international. The Taiping Rebellion (1850-65), the Franco-Chinese disturbances (1884-1886), the beginning of the Sino-Japanese hostilities in 1931-1932, and their resumption in 1937, sent hundreds of thousands fleeing into the foreign concessions. The result was the enormous growth of Shanghai's population, which had reached from three to four million by 1937.[12]

Of course, as relatively stable conditions were reestablished at home, many of the refugees returned to their villages or towns, but enough remained to increase the value of land and to supply the cheap labor, which raised Shanghai's manufacturing potential.[13] Their presence created enormous food, health and sanitation problems, and caused serious social disorganization.[14] Except for a few private charitable institutions operated by missionary groups, there was no organized communal effort to care for the sick and homeless, who would often be found lying frozen in the streets during cold winters. The Shanghai Municipal Council reported that in 1937 over 20,000 corpses were collected in the streets of the International Settlement alone.[15]

ECONOMIC CONDITIONS

But Shanghai remained a Chinese city, despite the huge foreign investments and the political and social dominion of foreigners. Labor was of course Chinese, and so were the entrepreneurs in industry, commerce and management. By 1920, a majority of the flourishing businesses were in Chinese hands, even though the ultimate economic and political power belonged to the small non-Chinese minority who owned the capital.[16]

The location of Shanghai was the single greatest factor in its economic growth. Built as it is near the Yangtze Delta, it is the only port in China not cut off from the interior by high mountains. On the contrary, the Delta is the gathering place of an extensive waterway system within a fertile hinterland. Goods from more than half of China could be shipped, easily and cheaply, in the days before industrialization, to the port of Shanghai. At the same time, foreign goods, entering Shanghai, could be as easily and cheaply distributed to this highly populated area. The port of Shanghai, which is also the most westerly port in China, standing where the coast extends farthest into the Pacific (called here the East China Sea), flourished as a two-way trading center. It was destined to become the financial center of China, and its stock exchange and banking system thrived.[17]

During the latter half of the nineteenth century, the commodities that contributed most to the growth of Shanghai were tea, silk and opium. Trade in these items had declined by the turn of the century, but textiles, food and clothing, in that order, were replacing them, as Shanghai developed into a highly industrialized city. Cheap labor and inland water transportation more than compensated for the lack of fuel and raw materials.[18]

A large part of the industrial output was produced in small plants or shops. They were often housed in private homes, or slightly altered dwellings, and operated by members of one family with the aid of a few recruited workers. Electricity was cheap and even these small factories were run by power motors.

These shops had a high rate of turnover and very small capitalization.[19] These conditions enabled some of the newly-arrived Jewish refugees to successfully enter the market.[20]

SINO-JAPANESE HOSTILITIES OF 1937

In July 1937, when fighting broke out between China and Japan, the long period of Shanghai's economic expansion and prosperity ended. It was never to fully recover. The city was cut off from the hinterland, and the cost of food rose steeply. Business was in a precarious state and many of the European firms moved to Hongkong and Singapore. This meant, of course, that, during the period from 1937 to 1940, few investors were willing to risk capital as long as such uncertain conditions lasted.[21]

THE SEPHARDI-JEWISH COMMUNITY

All through the nineteenth century there were mass migrations of Jews from eastern and central Europe to such countries as England, France and the United States. At the same time, a small but very significant group of Jews from Baghdad were moving in a thin but steady stream to the Far East. These Baghdadi Jews are usually called Sephardim, and between 1820 and World War I they migrated to India, China, the Malayan Peninsula and Japan. Both migrations, east and west, were to contribute enormously to the economic development of their host areas.[22]

The Rothschilds have come to represent, to Jew and Gentile alike, the successful western Jew, whose family cohesiveness was the source of his fortune. The family tradition of close loyalty combined with native ingenuity to create a powerful economic dynasty. The Sephardi-Jewish community included other families from Mesopotamia and Arabic-speaking countries, but the Sassoons were the pioneers. They were to remain the single most influential Jewish family in the Far East until the establishment of the Chinese Communist regime in 1949. This event would deprive them of their Chinese sources of wealth and leave them only a limited sphere in India and Southeast Asia, where things had changed at the conclusion of World War II.[23]

David Sassoon, the patriarch of the dynasty, was the scion of a well-known family of Baghdadi merchants and communal leaders. Under the Turkish Pashas, especially during the latter half of the eighteenth-century, conditions changed and even grew unfavorable for the Jews in general and for Sheikh Sason ben Saleh, the Nasi, (the titular head of the Jewish community), in particular. It was then that his son David left Baghdad for the freer atmosphere of India, and by 1832 had settled in Bombay.[24] He became deeply involved in trading and banking operations under the protection of the British Crown. For various reasons, the expansion of the Indian and Chinese markets had coincided with the breaking up of the monopoly previously held by the East India Company. Trade and banking were very lucrative for Sassoon and he branched out during the latter part of the nineteenth century, by placing his sons in other economically developing communities of the ever widening markets of China and India.[25] The advantages of Shanghai as an open city, with all that that implied, did not escape the sharp eye of many an incoming merchant, British and other, including that of David Sassoon. Trade in opium, tea and silk made wealthy tycoons of many petty merchants in the course of the nineteenth century.[26] An enormous trade developed in Shanghai, which by the 1930's had become one of the largest ports in the world.[27]

Elias David Sassoon, the second son of the founder of the family, soon established Hongkong and Shanghai as his business domain. He had arrived in China in 1844. By 1850, Shanghai had become his headquarters, though he traveled constantly between Hongkong, Canton and Bombay. He was probably the first Jew to reach Shanghai, but the first permanent settlers were more likely the three assistants to David Sassoon and Sons, Company, Ltd. Within five years the company was established along the entire China coast, and had branches in Japan when that country opened to western trade in 1858.[28]

The Sassoons were a close-knit clan, and their policy was to admit only the immediate family to the inner council of the business. They did however encourage many of their coreligionists from Baghdad to join their staff, and after training them in Bombay sent them to their various branches in the Far East. This policy provided them with extremely loyal and trustworthy employees. It also meant that they always had a sufficient number of Jews for the daily Minyan (the quorum for prayer). In this the Sassoons can again be compared with the Rothschilds. Especially during the nineteenth century, their business, as well as their personal lives, were influenced by strict adherence to the traditional practices of their faith: observance of the Sabbath and all Jewish Festivals, giving tithes, etc. For instance, it should be noted that every member of the Sassoon family was taught to slaughter chickens ritually, to enable them to eat Kosher even where there was no Jewish community. Even the business checks and notes had the name of the firm in Hebrew. As Shanghai and its business opportunities grew, there was an influx of coreligionists, from Baghdad, as well as from more recently established colonies such as Bombay, Calcutta, Singapore and Hongkong, and from as far away as Egypt and Greece. The Sephardi Community in Shanghai reached a peak of approximately 700 souls.[29]

The Sassoons dominated Shanghai's Jewish scene, but other families such as Kadoorie, Hardoon, Abraham. Edward

Ezra and Solomon, also made significant contributions to the civic, religious, social and economic life of the city. Some started out as clerks or managers in the Sassoon establishment, but soon ventured out on their own. For instance, Silas A. Hardoon became a multimillionaire after leaving the offices of David Sassoon and Company. Others came directly from Baghdad or Bombay and made a fortune in Shanghai's expanding economy.[30]

LEGAL STATUS

David Sassoon had known no English when he arrived in India in 1832. However, along with many of his fellow Sephardim he soon acquired British citizenship and remained unswervingly devoted to the British Crown. India was, of course, at that time, still part of the British Empire.[31] One of the Sephardim is reported to have opted for Spanish citizenship after 1924, when a Spanish law enabled the descendants of the Jewish exiles of 1492 to become subjects of the Spanish Crown. The majority however retained Iraqi nationality or remained stateless.[32]

RELIGIOUS INSTITUTIONS

We have seen that David Sassoon, the founder of the family fortune, was very devout. As he grew in wealth and his business expanded to employ many workers as well as his family, he set up a miniature, self-contained welfare state. The family policy was the same throughout the nineteenth century, whether in India, Shanghai or England, and it is probable that facilities were similarly provided for the religious requirements of his staff in Shanghai, including a room set aside for prayer. The first record of such religious fringe benefits is the donation of the Mohawk Road Cemetery in 1862.[33]

Religious organization of the Community began in all

seriousness when subscribers to the Beth El Synagogue met on August 2, 1887. At first they only rented space, and continued to do so until 1920. A second synagogue rented quarters in 1900 on Seward Road, and called itself Sheerith Israel.[34] However, it was not the sudden growth of the community that warranted a second congregation. Rather it came about as a result of a breaking off the more Orthodox element from Beth El. This occurred at about the turn of the century, when, during the High Holy Days, one of the staunch pillars of the Synagogue witnessed, to his chagrin, another member driving up in his carriage to the sanctuary, a flagrant violation of Jewish law. The ensuing fracas ended in the aggravated officers of Beth El establishing a more traditional congregation.[35] The new quarters included space for a Talmud Torah (afternoon Hebrew School) and a Mikveh (Ritularium). Ten years later, the community in which the Sephardim predominated was large enough and sufficiently varied in its activities to warrant the establishment of an official organization, the Shanghai Jewish Communal Association, or SJCA.[36]

The life of the Sephardi Community of Shanghai reached its zenith during the 1920's, and two beautiful synagogues were built. The first, Ohel Rachel, the successor to Beth El, was built with a legacy from the recently deceased Sir Jacob Sassoon in memory of his wife. It was consecrated in 1920 by the newly appointed minister from England, Rabbi W. Hirsch.[37] The second synagogue, Beth Aharon, an architectural gem, was built with a donation from Silas A. Hardoon, to succeed the rented quarters of the Congregation Sheerith Israel, through the influence of his relative David Ezekiel Joshua (D.E.J.) Abraham. Hardoon himself had little connection with the religious life of his people, and was one of the few Jews who had married a Chinese woman. This last synagogue was never as bustling with activities as it was to become after the arrival of the last wave of Jewish refugees.[38]

Rabbi Hirsch, the first minister to the Ohel Rachel Synagogue, was disappointed in his hopes of developing in this community greater spiritual ardor. He found what he regarded as a flaw in the character of the Sephardi Jews, and in a retrospective article incisively characterized his former flock:

> a desert people to this day, disorganized and loosely connected . . . There is no inner cohesion, no force or attraction to draw the separate individuals into massed units . . . They find cooperation within the community very difficult. Each is a world to himself, splendid in isolation, charming and gentle in his own orbit, but hard and intractable when you try to draw him from his sphere. It goes without saying that it is extremely difficult to organize among them a community in the modern sense, especially as some individuals are strong, with larger or smaller spheres of influence.[39]

Hirsch, in fact, felt that the failure of communal life in the Far East was illustrated by the building of synagogues, which was never a unified effort, but a gift of some wealthy individual. He maintained that benefactors on this scale were a mixed blessing, although amid the noise, the conflict and the differences of opinion attendant on communal effort, they may seem desirable.

> [Where] the individual is not called upon to contribute substantially, and as he is not a giver, neither a getter . . . the synagogue never becomes a center of Jewish life, where interests cross and intersect, and where a communal soul is born. It just remains a house of prayer, where worshippers come to pray in self-detachment and go home, as they came, in a happy self-sufficiency. People do not meet there as children in their home, but as guests in the house of a stranger. There is no common interest no mutual responsibility to draw the hearts and minds together.

Rabbi Hirsch, at the conclusion of his three-year term, left for a pulpit in South Africa.[40]

Events may have substantiated Rabbi Hirsch's characterization. No rabbi officially succeeded him. The Reverend Mendel Brown, who in 1932 became principal of the Shanghai Jewish School, in its newly built structure on the grounds of Ohel Rachel Synagogue, acted as unofficial rabbi of this synagogue. The Sephardi Jews turned to Rabbi Meier Ashkenazi of the Russian-Jewish Community for guidance in matters concerning Jewish law. Particularly during the early years, they occasionally sent religious questions, especially those about custom, to the Chacham, or spiritual leader, in Baghdad.[41]

At first, the Sassoons, by engaging private tutors, saw to it that Jewish as well as secular education was provided for the children of the community. As the numbers increased, however, it became clear that not everyone could afford this, For this reason, when Sheerith Israel was founded in 1900, D.E.J. Abraham made sure that it included a Hebrew School. This later became the Shanghai Jewish School, where the Bible, Hebrew and secular subjects were taught.[42] A more spacious and modern building was erected in 1932, but most of the students belonged to the poorer class, including many of the children of the Russian Jews and, at a later date, some refugee children.[43] The Sephardim preferred to send their children to the Shanghai Public (i.e. private) School in the International Settlement, which was completely under the British influence.[44]

SOCIAL CLIMATE

Not all the Sephardim, of course, belonged to the same economic class as the Sassoons, Hardoons, Kadooris or even lesser financial luminaries. In fact, the great majority of the 600 to 700 that made up the Sephardi community were of the poorer class of the non-Chinese society of Shanghai, both financially and socially. They were chiefly the clerks and other workers in the establishments of their wealthier coreligionists, some of them giants of Asian industry, banking, trade and real estate.[45] For example, in one listing of the members of the Shanghai stock exchange, the Sephardim made up close to 40 per cent of the total membership.[46] A recent book about the Sassoons abounds in accounts of the fabulous events they sponsored whether in India, England or Shanghai, events that glitter with royalty, heads of state, and socially or financially prominent people. It was at the Cathay Hotel built by Sir Victor Sassoon, that Chiang Kai-shek's £10,000 wedding took place. Noel Coward was one of the first to be impressed with the magnificence of this hotel when he visited Shanghai in 1930. He wrote the first draft of *Private Lives* while staying at the Cathay.[47]

Dr. H. H. Kung, Chiang Kai-shek's brother-in-law and China's Finance Minister, became a close friend of Sir Victor. Sassoon would go out of his way, often against his own interests and those of his fellow Jews, to publicly avow his solidarity with the Kuomintang government, and his dislike of the Japanese policies in China. And there were few politicians or industrialists in the International Settlement or the French Concession who would take a stand without consulting Sir Victor's views in advance.[48]

When the problem of the arrival of the Jewish refugees at the end of 1938 arose, the Sephardi community, particularly its wealthy members, were immediately drawn into relief activity[49]

Although commerce was the base and *raison d'etre* of life in Shanghai for the Sephardi Jews, many of its early leaders were scholars, inclined to feel more at home with the Talmud than a ledger sheet. They left it to their subordinates to carry on the business. Among these was S. J. Solomon, who worked for the firm E. D. Sassoon. He was revered as a scholar, student of

the Talmud and ardent communal worker, who befriended young
and old alike, introducing many of the former to Jewish law and
lore He also helped one of his "disciples" Nissim Ezra Benjamin
(better known as N.E.B.) Ezra to establish *Israel's Messenger,*
a respected Anglo-Jewish newspaper which Ezra edited from
1904 until his death in 1936, and to which Solomon periodically
contributed.[50] S.J. Solomon also amassed a large library of Hebrew and classic works and inspired others to do the same.
D.E.J. Abraham should be mentioned as another leading scholar
merchant.[51] Rabbi Hirsch has left us an interesting account of
their homes:

> Their houses, charmingly Jewish, were a refuge for Jewish
> traditions which, made more quaint by the Oriental blend,
> were lovingly cherished and affectionately practiced. It was
> very refreshing to come across such homes. They stood
> out with all the attractiveness of an oasis in the midst of a
> desert. Unhappily, they were few and far between.[52]

During the 1860's, interest was aroused among Shanghai's Sephardim in the fate of their fellow Jews in the ancient
and almost totally assimilated community of Kaifeng in China.
The immediate cause of this interest was the founding, in 1864,
in London, of a society for rescuing Kaifeng's Jews with the help
of David Sassoon and Sons Co., in Shanghai.[53]

Although the plan for the spiritual resuscitation of this
community did not materialize, such ideas must have inspired
S. J. Solomon, D. E. J. Abraham and others to establish the
Shanghai Society for the Rescue of the Chinese Jews, on May
14, 1900.[54] The fascinating story of the exotic community of
Chinese Jews, whose history goes back perhaps a millenium or
more, seems to have come to an end at the turn of the century,
when reports indicated that, at the most, there remained fifty
families comprising 250 souls. They retained the appellation

T'iao-chin Chiao ("the religion which extracts the sinew," i.e.
Judaism) and continued to abstain from pork; but they neither
had rabbi, synagogue, or knowledge of Hebrew, nor followed
any other Jewish practice.[55]

Two months before the official founding of the Society,
on March 13, 1900, the Sephardi community sent a letter, in
Chinese and Hebrew, by messenger, to their fellow Jews in Kaifeng, which read in part as follows:

> We assure you that we are eager to help you accord-
> ing to our ability, so that you may walk again in the foot-
> steps of your forefathers. If you desire to rebuild the House
> of God, which is now become a waste place, we will collect
> money and send it to you; if you want a teacher to instruct
> you, we will send you one; if it should please you to come
> hither and settle here in the city of Shanghai, we will help
> you to do so, and put you in the way to earn a livelihood by
> starting you in trade, and all that you may require we will
> endeavour to supply you with, for there are in this city
> men of our faith, great and wealthy, men of affairs and
> business, who can help to maintain yourselves and your
> sons and daughters.
>
> Wherefore we beg you not to part with scrolls still left
> to you. On this letter reaching you, send two or three men
> to us whom we may question, and from whom we can find
> out what we can do for you. We will pay all the expenses
> of the messengers; we will give them their sustenance, and
> pay them their expenses until they reach again your city.[56]

The Boxer Rebellion, then in progress, prevented reasonable communication with the Jews in Kaifeng, though even
with the return of peaceful conditions these good intentions
were too late to rehabilitate what was no longer a viable community. A final, similar attempt by the reorganized Society in

Shanghai, in 1924, to breathe new life into the already moribund community also failed.[57] The only practical result of the
first of the two attempts was the arrival of several Kaifeng Jews
in Shanghai in 1900 and 1902. Two of these were retained by
the businessmen journalist brothers, Arthur and Theodore
Sopher, who edited the *China Press*. Another remained with
D.E.J. Abraham, that active communal worker whom we shall
meet again in another context, hard at work, together with two
generations of his family, in the rescue of a Jewish community
—the refugees fleeing from Nazi Germany in 1938 and 1939.[58]

SEPHARDI CONTRIBUTIONS TO SHANGHAI

The Sephardim not only cared for Jewish education and
the religious needs of their community, but also supported medical care for impoverished members. They endowed beds for
indigent Jews in the Shanghai General Hospital and the Country
Hospital, both excellent medical institutions. It was soon apparent
that this was insufficient. The establishment in 1934 of B'nai Brith
Polyclinic overcame the insufficiency to some extent.. Eventually, by 1942, the clinic grew into the Shanghai Jewish Hospital,
which was to serve as host to a number of refugee doctors.[59]

The Sephardi magnates were, in fact, both devout and
charitable. They were generous to their own community and no
less so to China in general and Shanghai in particular. They
believed in the future of China, and took great risks in helping
Shanghai grow in the future of China, and took great risks in
helping Shanghai grow into one of the world's great ports. They
also contributed more than their share to civic, communal and
charitable causes.[60]

One director of David Sassoon Co. always served as an
honorary member of the Shanghai Municipal Council.[61] Silas A.
Hardoon had the unique distinction of being elected simultane-

ously to the Municipal Councils of the International Settlement and the French Concession. He had much to do with the development of the International Settlement, and his name, with that of the Kadoories, looms large in all matters concerning Chinese schools, colleges and hospitals.[62]

ZIONISM

Although Zionism never played the same role in the lives of the Sephardim as in that of the later arrivals, the Russian Jews, it did have several achievements to its credit. In 1903, the Sephardim had already sent a delegation to the Sixth Zionist Congress in Basle, Switzerland.[63] And the establishment of *Israel's Messenger* served to strengthen the Zionist element among the Sephardim, since the paper prided itself on being "the fearless exponent of Traditional Judaism and Jewish Nationalism." It also served as the "official organ of the Shanghai Zionist Association and the Jewish National Fund for China."[64]

Sun Yat-sen, the founder of the Kuomintang, recognized early the great Jewish contribution to the development of China, and reciprocated with his support of the Zionist movement. He expressed this in a letter, dated April 24, 1920, to N.E.B. Ezra:

> and I wish to assure you of my sympathy for this movement —which is one of the greatest movements of the present time. All lovers of Democracy cannot help but support whole-heartedly and welcome with enthusiasm the movement to restore your wonderful and historic nation, which has contributed so much to the civilization of the world and which rightly deserves an honorable place in the family of nations.
>
> I am
> Yours very truly,
> (signed) Sun Yat-sen

In 1947, Sun Fo, Sun Yat-sen's son, endorsed these views in a letter to Judith Hasser of the Zionist Revisionist Movement in Shanghai.[65]

THE RUSSIAN-JEWISH COMMUNITY

The Sephardi community was well established in Shanghai when a second, and eventually far larger wave of Jewish emigrés began to arrive. They were mostly Russian Jews, and their Community came to be known as the Shanghai Ashkenazi Jewish Communal Association (or SAJCA) to distinguish it from the Sephardi Community, previously referred to as the Shanghai Jewish Communal Association.[66]

The Ashkenazim, like the Sephardim before them, came to the Far East partly to escape oppression, but even more in search of greater economic opportunity. By World War II, their numbers in Shanghai had increased to about 4,000.[67] The immigration of the Sephardim had taken the form of a consistent, small but steady annual increase. In contrast, the Russian Jews flooded into the Far East in successively greater waves, in response to cataclysmic events in Eurasian history. These waves covered four periods:

> 1895–1904
> 1905–1917
> 1932–1934
> 1937–1939[68]

At first, events carried the exiles only as far as Manchuria, and they settled primarily in Harbin, which, by the 1920's had grown from a provincial little town to a bustling Russian city with a population of 300,000. The Chinese Eastern Railroad, which had been built in 1895, greatly faciliated travel east and provided economic opportunities. The Jews found a more tolerant atmosphere in Manchuria than in Russia; the Russian authorities, in fact, were anxious to encourage the settlement and development of Manchuria.[69] Even during the earliest wave of emigration (before 1905), however, many Jews found their way farther south to Tientsin and Shanghai.[70]

These early Russian-Jewish settlers were not especially welcomed by the well-established, "respectable" Sephardi community. They included many ex-soldiers, escapees from Siberian exile, political exiles, and adventurers. Many of them became involved in such shady enterprises as dope peddling, white slavery, and the opening of bars in disreputable parts of the city.[71] The already wide social and cultural gulf between the two Jewish communities increased and became more impassable. It would take many years and shared vicissitudes before any bridging of this chasm would be possible; and the early developed stereotype of the Ashkenazi Jews as *Schnorrers* would linger on, long after the Russian-Jewish community came to belong to the "respectable" middle and lower-middle class.[72]

The years 1909 to 1917 saw the gathering of the storm of the Russian Revolution, until its great outburst in the October Revolution of 1917. A mighty wave of emigration, in all directions, followed, and included 200,000 White Russians, as well as Russian Jews.[73] Once again, the majority of those who went east remained in Manchuria, but more and more reached Shanghai. By 1924, the Russian-Jewish population of that city had reached between 800 and 1,000.[74]

The rate of increase slowed down until the 1931-32 period, when Japan occupied Manchuria. This occupation resulted in an economic squeeze on all foreign interests, and an unofficial reign of terror, in which kidnapping by White Russian thugs was among the weapons used against rich foreigners, including some Jews. Harbin's Jewish population fell from about 10,000 in 1929, to approximately 2,500 ten years later.[75] Many emigrés went to Shanghai, but others settled in the South Man-

churian cities of Mukden and Dairen. Another large group
ended up in Chinese cities like Tientsin and Tsingtao, where the
economic frontier was still open. As noted, Shanghai's Russian-
Jewish population increased to over 4,000 in the late 1930's.
There it remained relatively constant until after the period of the
War in the Pacific.[76]

Despite the loss of three-quarters of its Jewish population, Harbin retained its position as the leading Russian-Jewish
community in the Far East until 1941. With the arrival of the
Polish and German refugees, a thriving Jewish religious and
cultural life developed in Shanghai, and Harbin lost is pre-
eminence. The reason for Harbin's long dominance arose from
its very dynamic secular and religious leadership under Dr.
Abraham Kaufman and Rabbi Aaron Moshe Kiseleff, respectively.[77] For example, the three annual Conferences of Russian-
Jewish Communities in the Far East held from 1937 through
1939, in which the Japanese authorities actively participated and
gave some kind of national recognition to the stateless Russian
Jews, were organized and led by Dr. Kaufman. And the trap-
pings of a healthy Jewish life, including two synagogues and a
good Hebrew Day School, functioned under the spiritual guidance of Rabbi Kiseleff.[78]

ECONOMIC LIFE

The Russian Jews in Shanghai were never to reach the
pinnacle of economic success achieved by the Sephardi magnates. They were, nonetheless, in the course of less than a
generation, able to fit in to Shanghai's still viable economy.
Many were engaged as subcontractors in the import-export
trade. A few small industries, such as the fur and grain import-
export markets, were almost exclusively in their hands. They
established connections in Russia, Western Europe and the
United States, through which they were able to find markets.

Most, however, owned small shops and specialized stores, or engaged in the export of such things as bristles or wool. A number of the professionals found employment in medicine, engineering, law, music, architecture, etc.[79] But the Sino- Japanese War disrupted economic life and many Russian Jews were destitute when, in 1938, the refugees from Hitler's Germany began to arrive.[80]

RELIGIOUS LIFE

The number of Russian Jews in Shanghai before 1902 did not warrant the establishment of their own congregation. Those who wished to worship went to the Sephardi synagogues. However, as their number increased to approximately twenty-five families, the need for a congregation was felt and they organized one in 1902, which in five years was established as the Oihel Moishe [sic] Synagogue. It was named after Moishe Greenberg, one of the early Russian settlers, and a leader of the small community.[81] Despite the cool relationship with the Sephardi Jews, the nascent Russian-Jewish Community was welcomed and was allotted rooms in the Sheerith Israel Synagogue.[82] When their numbers had grown to approximately 1,000 in the 1920's the Russian-Jewish Community appointed a rabbi, Rabbi Meier Ashkenazi, who was to be recognized as a spiritual leader both by the Orthodox among the Sephardim and Polish refugees.[83]

Rabbi Ashkenazi had previously served eight years in Vladivostok. He was a scholar and a member of the *Lubavitch Hassidic* group.[84] With his Rebbetzin (wife) Taube, he was, throughout their twenty-one year stay in Shanghai, in the forefront of all humanitarian Jewish communal activities, both religious and secular.[85] One of the rabbi's first activities was to organize a building committee for a synagogue, the rented quarters having become inadequate for the growing community. Success crowned his efforts, and in 1927, the Oihel Moishe Congregation moved to its newly converted home at 62 Ward Road in the Hongkew section of the International Settlement.[86] Newcomers from Harbin continued to arrive steadily, and many of the Russian Jews were able to move from the poorer Hongkew district, (especially from those areas devastated by the 1937 Sino-Japanese hostilities) to the French Concession, a residential area of Shanghai. As their economic situation improved, they began to feel the inadequacy of their synagogue and to plan for a new one nearer where they lived. These plans did not materialize until 1941, when the New Synagogue was built with a seating capacity of 1,000, at 102 rue Tenant de la Tours, and was dedicated just before Passover of that year.[87]

OTHER COMMUNAL INSTITUTIONS

We have seen that the Russian Jews did not succeed in a worldly sense to the same extent as the Sephardim. According to one reliable source, only about one to two percent could be considered wealthy, and even these never reached the pinnacle of social and political power achieved by some of the Sephardim. Few had managed to come from Harbin with their assets intact. Around 60 percent were middle or lower-class shopkeepers. Of the remaining portion, a good number were unemployed or partially employed, especially after the disrupting effects of the 1937 Sino-Japanese hostilities.[88] It is, therefore, not surprising to find that one of the first institutions to be established by the Russian-Jewish Community, after their synagogue, was the Shanghai Relief Society and Shelter House in 1916. This benevolent society provided an old-age home, as well as direct and indirect financial and medical aid to the needy and indigent. Its most important feature was a Free Kitchen, which was eventually to serve about 300 meals a day.[89]

Within a few years of the founding of the Shelter House,

the Community was able to establish a Chevra Kadisha (sacred Burial Society) in 1922, and an Educational Aid Society shortly thereafter. The Chevra Kadisha, jointly with its Sephardi counterpart, maintained two cemetries which were used by both groups and provided free burial for the indigent deceased. This amounted to about 40 percent of the burials in the early 1940's. The Educational Aid Society gave financial assistance to pupils unable to afford the tuition at the Sephardi-established Shanghai Jewish School.[90]

Both institutions reflected the steady influx of impoverished newcomers who could not afford two of the basic necessities of a Jewish community: education and ritual burial. Conditions improved, but even during the 1940's, after a full generation, the difficulties had not been completely resolved.[91]

EDUCATION

Unlike their parent community in Harbin, which supported a fine Hebrew Day School, the Russian-Jewish Community of Shanghai followed the example of their Sephardi coreligionists by sending their children to the more secularly oriented Shanghai Jewish School, while those with more means sent their children to the aforementioned Shanghai "Public" School or the Shanghai American school.[92] For the higher education of their children, the choice lay between universities abroad and the two in Shanghai which foreigners attended. St. John's and Aurora, both of which were run by Christian missionary groups for the Chinese.[93]

ZIONISM

The Zionist movement was not new to Shanghai when the Russian Jews began to arrive on the scene. As noted the Sephardi community had been represented at the Sixth Zionist

Congress, in 1903. However, the Sephardi Jews largely channeled their religio-nationalist feelings into synagogue-oriented
activities, which did not jeopardise their standing as good British
citizens during the period when Palestine was a British mandate. His British loyalties, however, did not prevent, for example, Sir Victor Sassoon from expressing his strongest opposition to Great Britain's handling of the 1937 riots in Palestine.
But this indignation expressed the feelings of a British Jew
rather than a Zionist, and the leaders of political Zionism did
not feel kindly disposed toward the Sassoon family.[94]

It was the Russian Jews who brought to Shanghai a
stronger Zionist sentiment. This feeling had already found an
outlet in Harbin, where several Zionist organizations had flourished. In 1916 the Shanghai Zionist Association, "Kodimah"
[sic] was founded, and its primary aim was the rebuilding of
Palestine through the Keren Kayemet (Jewish National Fund).
It enabled the stateless Russian Jews, through multiple organizational activities to identify with a country of their own.[95] A
second Zionist group was the New Zionist Organization (Zionist
Revisionists) with their youth affiliate, Brith Trumpeldor (Betar). Except in their emphasis on youth the Revisionists differed
little from the Kodimah. Betar maintained a very dynamic
ideology with spirited, disciplined, militant units devoted to the
ideals of Jewish culture, the settlement of Palestine, and training
for Hachsharah (for agricultural settlement). Their idol, the
international figure, Zev Jabotinsky, had captured the imagination of the younger generation with his emphasis on physical
training, sports, and the study of the Jewish heritage.[96] The
youth of both Jewish communities, scattered in different schools,
found a common interest and ideal in Betar, just as the children
of the refugees would later. The formation of Betar along strictly paramilitary lines—which included marching in brown shirts
—did not endear it to the older generation. Among the most

illustrious alumni of Shanghai's active Betar group is Joseph
Tekoah (Tukaczynski), Israel's representative at the UN.[97]

SAJCA

By the mid 1930's, the Russian Jews had matured sufficiently as a community to feel the need for an organization to
promote their cultural, as well as their religious interests. In
1935 the aforementioned Shanghai Ashkenazi Jewish Communal
Association (SAJCA) was founded, and, two years later, registered with the Shanghai Municipal Council, and, after the outbreak of the Sino-Japanese hostilities in 1937, with the Chinese
authorities.[98].

SOCIAL AND CULTURAL ACTIVITIES

It was the custom of the various nationalities in the foreign
concessions to have a club as the center of their social activities.
The Russian Jews similarly established such a club (called The
Club) which became the hub of their cultural and social concerns, while prominent Sephardim belonged to the very exclusive Shanghai (British) Club. It came to resemble closely a
well-equipped American Jewish community center.[99]

Among the multifarious cultural activities that were often
going on simultaneously at the Club, were ballet, choral singing,
theatrical productions, and concerts. There were lectures on a
variety of both sacred and secular subjects, Zionist groups used
the Club as their headquarters. There were also numerous charity
drives which increased in number during the later refugee
period.[100] During the 1930's, the artists who provided the entertainment were mostly White Russians; and their level of artistic
performance in ballet, music, opera or theater was as high as
any in Europe. Many of these exiles and impoverished White
Russians depended for a livelihood on these performances, and
they always found sympathetic patrons at the Jewish Club[101]

The Jewish Recreational Club (JRC) was not part of the Club It sponsored many sports activities, including a soccer team, which participated in the Shanghai Football League. The JRC became even more prominent and active during the later refugee period.[102]

MILITARY ACTIVITIES

In 1933, perhaps in response to the news of Hitler's rise to power, and certainly in line with their strong nationalist feelings, the Russian Jews formed a separate Jewish Company of 135 men in the Shanghai Volunteer Corps (SVC). The SVC was a part-time military unit comprising "national" groups drawn from all the diverse elements in international Shanghai, and its backbone was a large contingent of White Russian ex-soldiers. The Sephardi volunteers preferred to join the British units of the SVC, though about thirty-five German refugees joined the Jewish Company upon arrival in Shanghai.[103]

It is interesting that the Jewish Company, led by an Englishman, Captain Noel S. Jacobs, was among the first modern military units to fight under a Jewish flag[104]

THE JAPANESE PRESENCE

The largest single element in Shanghai's multi-national population was the Japanese. From a total of seven in 1873, they reached 20,000 according to the 1936 census, and increased more than threefold just before the outbreak of the War in the Pacific.[105] As members of a coterie who exercised the right of extraterritoriality, Japan maintained in the Settlement a 3,500-man Naval Landing Party (marines), comparable to the contingent of American Marines, or to the British Army units, all of which were ostensibly there to protect their nationals.[106]

BACKGROUND

The presence of the Japanese had made itself felt in modern China not long after Japan's opening to the West by Commodore Perry of the US Navy in 1854. It was the result of a closely related, two-pronged Japanese policy; first, to join as quickly as possible, as an equal partner, with the powerful European imperialist nations who were gradually, but firmly, dividing up the sprawling, weakened Chinese Empire into their respective spheres of influence and control; and second, to build up its own military and industrial might in order to ward off a similar fate—complete dismemberment by the Western nations.[107]

Spurred by Japan's rising sense of nationalism it did not take long for the realization of this policy. Japan was small, densely populated and poor in natural resources and the huge potential market for manufactured goods in China, and the wealth of the raw materials that Japan so needed in spacious, sparsely settled Manchuria were irresistible. Manchuria was also a perfect buffer zone against their feared Russian neighbor.[108] These were among the reasons for Japan's expansion to the Chinese mainland and such ambitions were advanced by the first Sino-Japanese War (1894–1895) and the Russo-Japanese War (1904–1905).

SECOND SINO-JAPANESE WAR

Disorders in Manchuria in 1931 gave them the excuse to strengthen the garrison they kept there to protect Japanese property, and hostilities soon broke out with the Chinese. These hostilities in faraway Manchuria found a battleground also in Shanghai, long a stronghold of rising Chinese nationalism, as well as of Communism. In Shanghai, the Japanese forces met unexpectedly stiff resistance from the Chinese Army.[109]

Five years later, in a continuation of the Sino-Japanese

struggle for domination of the Chinese mainland, Shanghai, including its International Settlement, again became the scene of Chinese resistance. This ended only with the defeat of the Japanese by the Allies in 1945, because, after the bombing of Pearl Harbor, the Sino-Japanese War merged with World War II, and China declared war on the so-called Axis Powers (Germany, Italy, and Japan).[110]

During both the 1932 and the 1937 fighting, Chapei and the northern sector of the Settlement, especially Hongkew, were the scenes of the heaviest fighting, which, combined with the "scorched earth" policy of the retreating Chinese forces, destroyed much of the former heavily Chinese-populated and industrialized sector of Shanghai.[111]

Over one million Chinese refugees crossed the Soochow Creek Bridge into the Settlement fleeing from the battle zones, this almost doubled its population. The Japanese authorities now took full control of Greater Shanghai (the all-Chinese city), and placed the devastated Hongkew sector of the Settlement under the direct command of the Japanese Naval Landing Party. It was no longer considered part of the International Settlement.[112]

These conditions, as will be seen, were to have profound significance for the refugees from Nazi Germany, who fled to Shanghai one year after the Sino-Japanese hostilities of 1937.[113]

NOTES : SHANGHAI

1. The quotation comes from Rhoads Murphy, *Shanghai: Key to Modern China* (Murphy, *Shanghai*) (Cambridge, Mass.: Harvard University Press, 1953) pp. 7, 9. Murphy's book is the best economic history of Shanghai. The other titles mentioned are, G. E. Miller, *Shanghai: Paradise of Adventures.* [Miller, *Paradise*] New York: Orsay Publishing House, Inc., 1937); Ernest O. Hauser, *Shanghai: City for Sale.* [Hauser, *Shanghai*] (New York: Harcourt, Brace and Co., 1940; Robert Barnett, *Economic Shanghai: Hostage to Politics* 1937-1941. [Barnett, *Hostage*] (New York: Institute of Pacific Relations, 1941. Additional titles for the history, economic and political conditions, and especially first-hand accounts of the colorful aspects of Shanghai include, Eleanor Hinder, *Life and Labor in Shanghai.* [Hinder, *Labour*] (New York: Institute for Pacific Relations, 1944); Percy Finch, *Shanghai and Beyond.* [Finch, *Shanghai*] (New York: Scribners, 1953); Arch Carey, *The War Years at Shanghai* 1941-45-46. (Carey, *War Years*) (New York: Vantage Press, 1967); J. V. Davidson-Houston, *Yellow Creek: The Story of Shanghai.* [*Yellow Creek*] (London: Putnam, 1962); F. L. Hawks Pott, *A Short History of Shanghai.* [Pott, *Shanghai*] (Shanghai: Kelly and Walsh Ltd., 1937.

2. For brief, earlier accounts of these two communities, see the author's *The Jewish Community of Shanghai, 1937-1957.* [Kranzler, *SJC*] (Unpublished Masters thesis at Brooklyn College, 1958, chapter 1, and Herman Dicker, *Wanderers and Settlers in the Far East: A Century of Jewish Life in China and Japan.* [Dicker, *Wanderers*] (New York: Twayne Publishers, 1962), pp. 65-73.

3. Albert Jovishoff, "A City of Refugees," [Jovishoff, "City"]. *The Menorah Journal* volume 27. (Spring 1939), pp. 209-216. Cf. also (Michael) Speelman Report, June 21, 1939 (JDCCA); J. Arthur Steiner, "American-Japanese Tensions in Shanghai", [Steiner, *Shanghai*] *Annals* volume 215 (May 1944), pp. 140-146; Ginsbourg, *Shanghai*, p. 8. See also below, chapters 6 and 7.

4. For some notion of the human kaleidescope, see above, note 1.

5. Jovishoff, "City", p. 213. Cf. also Hinder, *Labour*, chapter 1. For the foreign concessions see Murphy, *Shanghai*, chapter 2, Barnett, *Hostage,* pp. 1-10 Hinder, *Labour.* For a longer discourse on the status of the two foreign concessions, see Ching-lin Hsia, *The Status of Shanghai: A Historical Review of the International Settlement.* [Hsia, *Shanghai*] (Shanghai: Kelly and Walsh, 1929), and William Crane Johnstone, Jr., *The Shanghai Problem.* [Johnstone, *Shanghai*] (Stanford, California: Stanford University Press, 1937). See also Miller, *Paradise,* chapter 3 for the easy means of landing in Shanghai without nationality or papers of any sort.

6. *Ibid.* chapter 1. Also Murphy, *Shanghai,* p. 61.

7. *Ibid.* See especially Johnstone, *Shanghai,* chapter 6; Miller, *Paradise,* pp. 35-37, pg. 61; also above note 5. For a personal glimpse of the "real" Chinese by a curious refugee, see H. Peter Eisfelder, *Chinese Exile*: *My Years in Shanghai and Nanking* 1938-1947 [Eisfelder, *Exile*] (A 78 page manuscript. 1972) Xerox copy in author's possession courtesy of Mr. Eisfelder. pp. 26-27, also Miller, *Paradise*, pp. 22-24. For the relative importance of Shanghai as a port even prior to the Western intrusion, see Murphy—Kranzler corres., January 5, 1975.

8. See above, note 5 especially Johnstone, *Shanghai,* chapter 11.

9. Murphy, *Shanghai,* chapter 2. Cf. also Johnstone, *Shanghai,* pp. 45-46, for a lower figure in the 1935 census. By the late 1930's and especially during 1940-41 the Japanese population increased fourfold. See Barnett, *Hostage,* p. 29.

10. Murphy, *Shanghai,* pp. 23-24, quotes the 1936 census, but identifies the 5,000 Germans and Austrians with the Jewish refugees. In 1936 there were not more than 300 of the latter in Shanghai. In a recent correspondence with the author, Prof. Murphy has graciously concurred with the author's view. Murphy-Kranzler corres., Jan. 5, 1975.

For a recent work on the early development of the French Concession, see Michael L. Sinclair, *The French Settlement of Shanghai on the eve of the Revolution of* 1911 (Unpublished dissertation, Stamford University, 1973). The author is grateful to Dr. Frank Shulman of the Center for Japanese Studies at the University of Michigan for bringing this work to his attention.

11. Murphy, *Shanghai, Ibid.* For the White Russians see especially, John Hope Simpson, *The Refugee Problem*: *Report of a Survey* [Simpson, *Survey*] (London: Oxford University Press, 1939), chap. 20 Cf. also Miller, *Paradise,* pp. 28-31; Mark Siegelberg, *The Face of Pearl Harbor*: *A Play* [Siegelberg, *Face*] (Melbourne: View Publishing Co., 1941).

12. Ginsbourg, *Shanghai,* p. III. Also Finch, *Shanghai,* pp. 260-261; Murphy, *Shanghai,* pp. 10, 18-23, Barnett, *Hostage,* pp. 8, 29.

13. Jovishoff, "City", p. 209. Cf. also *The North China Daily News and Herald,* August 6, 8, 10, 1937; Murphy,*Shanghai,* p. 11.

14. See the pages of the *North China Herald and Supreme Court and Consular Gazette,* esp. Dec. 8, 1938, p. 399, March 22, 1939, p. 497; Murphy, *Shanghai,* p. 12.

15. *Ibid,* Cf. also Finch, *Shanghai,* pp. 12-13; Miller, *Paradise,* chap. 1. Barnett, *Hostage,* p. 46; Hinder, *Labour,* p. 128, n. 2.

16. Murphy, *Shanghai,* pp. 17-19, 24.

17. *Ibid.* Chap. 4.

18. *Ibid.* pp. 103-112, 167, and chaps. 7-10.

19. *Ibid.* pp. 170-171. Cf. also Hinder, *Labour.* p. 29.

20. See below, chap. 9.

21. Murphy, *Shanghai,* pp. 114-115; 152-153, Cf. also *Speelman Report,* April 25, 1940 (JDCCA), Michael Speelman, (chairman of the Jewish relief committee (CFA) to be discussed below, chap. 3) notes the rise in prices following the Sino-Japanese hostilities of 1937, due to the latter's taxation of produce brought into Shanghai; *Hilsfond Fuer Deutsche Juden, Shanghai 1934-1938. Report [Hilfsfond Report].*

22. Cecil Roth, "Past, Present and Future of Sephardim [Roth. "Sephardim"] "Le *Judaisme Sephardi* New Series No. 13, January, 1957, p. 570. Cf. also W. Hirsch, "The Sephardi Jewish Community of Shanghai" [Hirsch, "Sephardi"] *South African Jewish Observer,* Sept. 1957, p. 7; Cecil Roth, *The Sassoon Dynasty* [Roth, *Sassoon*] (London: Robert Hale Ltd., 1941) chap. 2; Stanley Jackson, *The Sassoons* [Jackson, *Sassoons*] (New York: E. P. Dutton and Co., Inc. 1968), chap. 1.

23. For the comparison to the Rothschilds see Jackson *Sassoons,* p. 1 et passim. Cf. also Roth, *Sephardim* p. 574; Roth, *Sassoon,* pp. 40, 48. The most complete description of the Sassoon's Far Eastern domain is given by Jackson. See also David Solomon Sassoon, *A History of the Jews In Baghdad* [Sassoon, *Baghdad*] (Letchworth: S. D. Sassoon, 1949), chap. 33; Mendel Brown, "The Jews of Modern China", [Brown, "Jews"] *The Jewish Monthly,* vol. 3 (June 1949), p. 159. Reverend Brown was the principal of the Sephardi Jewish school in Shanghai and served to some extent as a religious leader among the Sephardim in Shanghai. Joseph Zeitin, "The Shanghai Jewish Community", [Zeitin, "Shanghai"] *Jewish Life,* vol. 41, no. 4, Oct. 1973, pp. 54-68. Dr. Zeitin, a German refugee, was rabbi in Shanghai, and a member of the Shanghai *Beth Din.* He maintained close relations with the Russian and Sephardi Jewish communities. He also wrote "The Shanghai Jewish Communal Association" [Zeitin, "SJCA"] in the *Shanghai Almanac* 1946/47 [*Almanac*] edited by Ossi Lewin, pp. 49-52. A slightly revised version of this article by the same auhtor is titled, "The Sephardi Community of Shanghai: a Short Historical Sketch", *The American Sephardi,* Vol. 2, No. 1-2, 1968, pp. 73-76; N. E. B. Ezra "Shanghai", [Ezra, "Shanghai"], *The Jewish Encyclopedia,* (New York: Funk and Wagnalls Co., 1905) XI, pp. 231-232.

Another brief account of the Sephardi community in Shanghai is by Almoni [pseud.], "A Short Account of the Sephardic Jewish Community in Shanghai" [Almoni, "Sephardic"] *Le Judaisme Sephardi* New Series, No. 13 Jan. 1957, pp. 605-606. *Almoni* (Hebrew for "so and so") is obviously a pseudonym, whom the author believes to be Reuben Abraham, scion of a well-known Shanghai Sephardi family whom we shall come across again later.

The author will use the term "Sephardim" for the Jews from Baghdad, although there may be possible "scientific" objections, since the term is usually applied to descendants of Spanish Jewry. Moreover, Rabbi Solomon David Sassoon, formerly of Letchworth, England, the chronicler and archivist of his family, noted to the author that according to his father, David S. Sassoon, author of *A History of the Jews of Baghdad*, Iraqi Jews are the direct descendants of Babylonian Jewry. Sassoon-Kranzler, August 13, 1968.

Still, since the problem has not been solved completely, and since the Iraqi or Baghdadi Jews in Shanghai frequently referred to themselves by the term "Sephardim", the author feels at liberty to follow suit. All the more so, since Cecil Roth in the aforementioned article on the Sephardim notes, that with few exceptions, the Sephardi (Spanish) rite of prayers has superseded those of other Oriental Jewries. Roth, "Sephardim", p. 573. In addition, many Sephardim settled in Baghdad after their expulsion from Spain in 1942. See also below, in this chapter re the Ashkenazi Jews.

24. Jackson, *Sassoons*, pp. 6-17. Cf. also Roth, *Sassoon* chap. 1 and 2.

25. Jackson, *Sassoon*, pp. 22-27. Roth, *Ibid.* chap. 2.

26. *Ibid*, p. 47, Cf. also Jackson *Sassoons*, pp. 23-24.

27. *Ibid.*, p. 1.

28. Jackson, *Sassoons*, p. 23. The three assistants were E[zekiel] Abraham, father of D. E. J. Abraham (whom we shall meet again), M. S. Mooshee (grandfather of Mrs. D. E. J. Abraham), and J. Reuben. Mendel, "Jews", p. 160.

29. Jackson, *Sassoons*, chaps. 1 and 2. Roth, *Sassoon*, esp. pp. 54-67, 70-96. Brown, "Jews", pp. 159-160. For the practice of *shechitah* or kosher slaughter, see Roth, op. cit. p. 60. Joseph Hayim Abraham and his older brother, grandson of the aforementioned D. E. J. Abraham, were taught the method of *shechitah* during the 1930's, as young men, though they never found it necessary to practice it. Interv. Jan. 19, 1975. Mr. Abraham granted one taped interview on January 16, 1969 and answered numerous additional queries by phone or mail.

Brown, Jackson and Roth mention the Hebrew checks and notes, *op. cit.* For the arrival of Sephardim in Shanghai as far away as Greece; Egypt, and England, see Ginsbourg, *Shanghai*, pp. V-VI. Also Brown, "Jews", pp. 159, 161-162.

For the statistics of 700, see Almoni, "Sephardic", p. 605. The number seems to vary between 500 and 700.

30. Jackson, *Sassoons*, pp. 57, 230, 235, re Hardoon and Sir Victor Sassoon. For other names, see esp. Zeitin, "SJCA", pp. 49-51. Also Roth, *Sassoon*, pp. 66-67. A list of 38 names of prominent Sephardim may be found among the 99 members of the Shanghai stock exchange of 1932. See list on

the back of a quotation sheet of the Shanghai Stock Exchange, August 1932, [Sh. Stock Exch.] in the author's possession, courtesy of Ezekiel Abraham, brother of the aforementioned Joseph Abraham.

31. Jackson, *Sassoons*, pp. 19, 35.

32. Joseph Hayim Abraham, Interv. June 17, 1975. He thinks the gentleman refers to N. E. B. Ezra.

33. See Roth, *Sassoon*, pp. 66-67. Also Jackson, *Sassoons*, pp. 30-33, 45. Although the author has no definite documentation for the "Jewish welfare state" in Shanghai, he assumes it on the basis of the Bombay and other East Asian models. For example, Zeitin notes that Sir Jacob Sassoon of Bombay conducted services in his home all year round. "SJCA", p. 50.
For the gift of the cemetery, see Brown, "Jews", p. 160. Almoni ("Sephardic", p. 605) gives the date as 1860, but since Brown did some first-hand research in the cemetery, the author is inclined towards his findings.

34. Zeitin mentions a synagogue committee being founded as far back as 1870, "SJCA", p. 49. For this date Ezra notes the renting of a hall for services. "Shanghai", p. 231. Almoni merely notes that from 1880 to 1922, services were held in houses rented for that purpose.

35. The incident was related to the author by Joseph Abraham without disclosing the name of the irate gentleman. Ezra and Zeitin, however, clearly state that D. E. J. Abraham founded Shearith Israel. He was the staunch defender of Jewish tradition throughout his life, during which time he served as the president of the Sephardi community. We will have the opportunity to come across Mr. Abraham's defense of orthodox practice during the refugee era of 1938-1942.

36. Zeitin, "SJCA", p. 49.

37. Hirsch, "Sephardi". Although Almoni gives the date of the synagogue's consecration as 1922, the author is inclined towards the earlier date, since Hirsch is more likely to remember the date of his arrival and the official ceremony. Still, it is possible that the official inauguration took place in 1920 while the synagogue was not completely ready until two years later.

38. Abraham Interv. See also Joseph David Epstein, "Yeshiva of Mir", *Jewish Institutions of Higher Learning in Europe: Their Development and Destruction* [Eipstein, "Mir"] (Hebrew). Edited by Samuel K. Mirsky (New York: Histadruth Ivrith of America, 1956), pp. 127-128. Mr. Abraham noted that this is contrary to the current apocryphal story about Hardoon's decision to build the synagogue, following a dream in which he was reprimanded for not doing anything for his fellow Jews. This story is found in Chunah Hertzman, *Mirrer Yeshiva in Golus* [Hertzman, *Mir*] (Yiddish) (New York: C. Hertzman, 1950), p. 22.

39. Hirsch, "Sephardi".

40. *Ibid.* Also Rabbi Hersh Millner and Rebbetzin Taube Ashkenazi, Interv. (the son-in-law and wife of Rabbi Meier Ashkenazi, respectively).

41. Zeitin, "SJCA", p. 51. For the inquiries of religious customs, see Abraham, interv.

42. Abraham, Interv. and Ezekiel Abraham to Joseph Hayim Abraham, February 9, 1975. D. E. J. Abraham founded both Shearith Israel and its Hebrew school. He was also the president of the Sephardi community until his internment by the Japanese, in 1942. He died while in an internment camp in May, 1945. Abraham Interv.

Although Ezra ("Shanghai") places the date of the opening of the Hebrew school at 1902, and Almoni ("Sephardic") three years after, the author feels that perhaps two years elapsed from the establishment of Shearith Israel and the opening of the Hebrew school. The 1905 date by Almoni seems less likely, especially since Ezra, the editor of Shanghai's Anglo-Jewish newspaper, *Israel's Messenger*, wrote his article in 1904 or 1905, while Almoni wrote his in 1956.

43. *Ibid.* See also CFA Minutes, April 23, 1939, p. 3 (JDCCA); Bertha Elkan, interv. by H. Dicker, March 20, 1958 [Elkan, Interv.] (DP). For one refugee student's experience at this school, see Eisfelder, *Exile*, pp. 11-12.

The curriculum was geared toward the Cambridge Certificate.

44. Abraham Interv. Cf. also Mrs. David Lew Interv.; Minutes of the Meeting of the Investigating Committee for International Sufferers, January 5, 1938 (JDCCA). This document reveals that of the 240 students in the Shanghai Jewish School, 150 were needy, and provided with one meal per day. A similar fact is borne out by Manfred Rosenfeld, a refugee journalist, in his brief *History of the Shanghai Jewish Communities* [Rosenfeld, *Hist.*], Part II, p. 4. In a description of the Jewish Educational Aid Society which provided scholarship and breakfast for 120 pupils of this school. (The Rosenfeld manuscript [Rosenfeld, *Hist.*], in three parts, is located in the YIVO Shanghai Collection, folder No. 1. This collection consists of 68 numbered folders of documents [YIVO No.   ].

45. David Rabinovich, "Yidn in China", (Yiddish) [Rabinovich, "Yidn"], *Goldene Keyt*, Vol. 7 (1951), p. 218. Cf. also Jackson, *Sassoons*, p. 20; Roth, *Sassoon*, p. 98.

46. See above, note 30. The Shanghai names were checked off by Ezekiel Abraham.

47. *Ibid.*, pp. 229, 235, *et passim.*

48. *Ibid.*, pp. 235, 249-256. Cf. also Spielman to Troper, March 4, 1940; [Naval] Capt. Koreshige Inuzuka to Herzberg, September 17, 1941, p. 2 (JDCCA); articles quoting Sir Victor and rejoinder by Ellis Hayim, under Japanese pressure, in the *North China Daily News, February 25, 27, 28, 1940.*

For the Japanese concern about Sir Victor's anti-Japanese stance and their attempts to influence him towards their side, see also German Foreign Office Documents Inland II A/B Microcopy No. 4667, Roll T-120, "Juedisch-Japanische Beziehungen" (National Archives) [Inland II] Deutsche Botschaft to Foreign Office in Berlin, April 5, 1940, "Judesches Werben um Japan" [Inland II, April 5, '40] wherein it is noted that Dr. Abraham Kaufman of Harbin has to mitigate Sir Victor's anti-Japanese remarks; *ibid.*, February 29, 1940, where the German Consulate reports on similar attempts by Michel Speelman and Ellis Hayim, heads of the CFA, the Shanghai Jewish relief organization, (see below, chap. 3).

For one of the numerous reports by the Japanese about Sassoon, his interests in Shanghai and his attitude toward the Japanese, see the top secret Japanese Foreign Office document, No. S-9460-3-1035, sent by Wagasuki, the Japanese Counsul General in New York, to Foreign Minister Arita, on February 18, 1939, following Sassoon's visit there. This document is part of the "Kogan Papers", [KP] a valuable collection of Japanese position papers concerning Jews and the Jewish Problem, including top secret Foreign Office documents [FO], many of which are found in John Young's *Checklist of Japanese Army and Navy Archives* 1968-1945 (L.C.). This collection was found right after World War II in a Tokyo second-hand bookstore, by a Jewish student at Wasada University named Peter Berstein who gave it to M. Kogan, who in turn, made the collection available to Chaplain Herman Dicker, who had translations made of a large part of this collection utilized in his *Wanderers and Settlers in the Far East* [Dicker, *Wanderers*]. He graciously permitted the author to reproduce these translations in return for the use of the author's master's thesis, *SJC*. The author also possesses a complete Xerox copy of the Kogan Papers, courtesy of Mr. Hideaki Kase and Rabbi Marvin Tokayer. The Kogan Papers and translations are now part of the author's collection called Dicker Papers (DP).

49. See below, chap. 3.

50. Brown, "Jews", p. 163. Cf. also Jackson, *Sassoons*, p. 33.

For some Japanese reports about Ezra, his editorials, etc., see Foreign Office Secret Report No. 402, February 15, 1934; FO S-9460-3-490, December 18, 1934; FO Confidential No. 647, December 27, 1934; FO S-9460-3-541, quoting FO No. 845, November 19, 1935. These deal primarily with Ezra's concern about the treatment of Jews by the Japanese authorities in Manchuria (DP).

Cf. also Dicker, *Wanderers*, pp. 37-39.

51. Brown, *ibid.* For Mr. Abraham's Jewish scholarship, see Joseph D. Epstein Interv. See also Roth, *Sassoon*, pp. 91-92.

52. Hirsch, "Sephardi", p. 7.

53. For Sassoon's interest in the Jews of Kaifeng, see Edward I. Ezra and Arthur Sopher, *Chinese Jews* [Sopher, *Chinese*] (Shanghai: [Arthur

Sopher], 1926), p. 283. Copy in author's possession, courtesy of Arthur and Theodore Sopher. Cf. also Roth, *Sassoon*, pp. 61-62.

For the literature on the ancient Jewish community of Kaifeng, in addition to the aforementioned book by Sopher, see the following three works: Donald David Leslie, *The Survival of the Chinese Jews: the Jewish Community of Kaifeng* [Leslie, *Kaifeng*] (Leiden: E. J. Brill, 1972); Hyman Kublin (ed.), *Jews in Old China: Some Western Views and Studies of the Chinese Jews: Selections from Journals East and West* [Kublin, *Jews*] (New York: Paragon Books Reprint Corp., 1971); William Charles White, *The Chinese Jews: Compilation of Matters Relating to the Jews of Kaifeng Fu,* [White, *Chinese*] 3 vols. (Toronto, 1942), 2nd ed., 3 vols. in 1, with an introduction by Cecil Roth (New York: Paragon Books Reprint Corp., 1966).

54. Sopher, *Chinese*, p. 283. See also the *Minutes of the Founding Meeting of May* 14, 1900 and the subsequent meeting of October 30, 1900. At the former meeting, held in E. M. Ezra's residence in No. 5 Sassoon Building, S. J. Solomon was elected as the secretary. (Hebrew University Library).

55. Cf. Leslie, *Kaifeng*, pp. 67-68. Concerning the title of "sinew extractors" (Bible, Genesis, 32 : 32), see especially Rudolph Loewenthal, "The Nomenclature of Jews in China", in Kublin, *Jews in China*, pp. 72 *et passim*.

56. Sopher, *Chinese*, pp. 63-64.

57. Leslie, *Kaifeng*, pp. 67-68.

58. *Ibid.*, pp. 68-69. Concerning the two that remained with the Sopher family, see Sopher-Kranzler corres., November 13, 1970. Also Sopher-Loewenthal corres., May 18, 1973 and June 8, 1975 (courtesy R. Loewenthal). For the one retained by the Abraham family, see Abraham Interv.

59. Zeitin, "SJCA", p. 51. In reference to the Shanghai Jewish Hospital hosting refugee doctors and patients, see Dr. Max Steinman, Taped Interview, July 1, 1975. Dr. Steinman was the head of this hospital which eventually grew into a 70-bed institution.

60. See especially Zeitin, "SJCA", pp. 50-51. Cf. also Jackson, *Sassoons*, pp. 235; Roth, *Sassoon*, pp. 65.

61. Jackson, *Sassoons*, p. 214.

62. Zeitin, "SJCA", p. 51. Cf. also Zeitin, "Shanghai", pp. 56-57. Concerning the saga of the "Kadoorie School" for German refugees, see below, chapter 14.

63 Ezra, "Shanghai", p. 232.

64. See the masthead of the newspaper.

65. For a copy of this letter to Ezra, see *Tagar* II, 9, May 1, 1947, and

the endorsement of Sun Yat-Sen's views, by his son, Sun-Fo, a member of the Nationalist Government, see *ibid.*, 14, July 17, 1947.

66. The Hebrew name was הקהילה העברית האשכנזת דשנגהאי See Hebrew calendar for 1941 (Yivo No. 26). The similarity of the English title of the Russian Jewish community to that of the Sephardim caused no little annoyance on the latter's part, who considered the Ashkenazi Jews below their station. Abraham Interview.

The term "Ashkenazi" and "Russian-Jewish" will be used interchangeably for this community, although this group included many who hailed from Poland, Lithuania and other Central and East European countries. "Ashkenazi", is thus used in a broad sense, as including Jews from Northern and Central Europe, whose rites are based essentially upon the decisions of Rabbi Moses Isserles. It does not apply to the "Minhag Ashkenazi", or the Ashkenazi rites of prayer maintained by those North European Jews who did not accept the modified form of Sephardi prayer adopted by Rabbi Isaac Luria (ARI) and subsequently by the Hassidim, during the eighteenth century. See Roth, "Sephardim", p. 573. See also H. J. Zimmels, *Ashkenazim and Sephardim* (London: Oxford University Press, 1958), esp. pp. 9-10; "Ashkenazim", *Encyclopaedia Judaica*, Vol. 3, pp. 719-722, and "Sephardim", *ibid.*, Vol. 14, pp. 1164-1177.

One must also be careful not to confuse the name of the rabbi, Rabbi Meier Ashkenazi, with that of his community. The *Shanghai Ashkenazi Jewish Communal Association* [SAJCA].

67. Jovishoff, "Refugees", p. 215. Cf. also Gerechter Interv.; Rebbitzin Ashkenazi, Interv.; Albert Parry, "Jews in East Asia" [Parry, "Jews"], *Asia*, Vol. 24, No. 9 (September 1939), pp. 513-516. He gives the figure of 5,500, which includes the 500 to 700 Sephardim, but is still too high, in the author's opinion. Rosenfeld, *History*, II, p. 2, places the figure at about 1,000 families or 4,000 individuals. W. Citrin, Interview by H. Dicker, (April 14, 1958 [Citrin, Interv.], (DP), confirms this figure. Cf. also A[leksander] Isgour, "Shanghai Jewish Center in Eastern Asia" [Isgour, "Shanghai"], Part II, *Unser Leben*, English Supplement, p. 2, August 28, 1942 (a trilingual Jewish newspaper published by the Russian-Jewish com munity and edited by David Rabinovich). The main section was in Russian with English and Yiddish supplements, edited by Anna Ginsbourg and Menachem Flakser, respectively.

The first two volumes (1941-1942) were loaned to the author by Menachem Flakser, while the rest of the set (1943-1945 was borrowed from David Rabinovich.

While Isagour cites the 5,000 figure, Dicker, *Wanderers*, p. 69, gives Rosenfeld's more accurate count of 4,000.

68. See especially L. D. Epstein, "The New Jewish Settlement in China" (an address before the Jewish Club on October 25, 1931), *Peking and Tientsin Times*, October 27, 1931[Epstein, "China"]. Evidently, this address

was based partly on a survey of the fur industry in Shanghai by the author, and is an excellent introduction to the history of China's Russian-Jewish community. Cf. also Dicker, *Wanderers*, pp. 69-73; Shmuel Rabinowich, "Hayishuv Hayehudi Besin, Shigeshugo Vehurbano" [Rabinowich, "Hayishuv"] (Hebrew) (The Jewish Settlement in China, its Development and Destruction), *Gesher*, Vol. III (July 1957), pp. 108-121.

For the White Russian migration to the Far East following the Bolshevik Revolution in 1917, see Simpson, *Refugees*, pp. 495-513. He also includes some data on Russian Jews as part of this group.

Russian Jews had fled even earlier to Manchuria following pogroms in Crimea during the latter two decades of the nineteenth century, and the turn of the century. See especially Abraham Kaufman, *Testimony Concerning Jewish Life in Manchuria* (an 85 page manuscript of an interview (in Yiddish) of Dr. Kaufman by Yitzchok Elfrowitz, translated into Hebrew, May 1967), (Yad Washem) [Kaufman, *Manchuria*].

This excellent source covers the full range of Dr. Kaufman's life-long activities in Manchuria, especially in Harbin, where he resided from 1912 to 1945. There he served as medical doctor, heading the Jewish hospital; journalist, editing *Yevreskaya Zhizn*, presided over the Jewish community of Harbin; Harbin; organised the Russian-Jewish communities of the Far East, vis-a-vis the Japanese authorities; chaired the three Far Eastern Jewish Conferences during 1937-1939; headed the major Zionist groups and wrote a number of books on different aspects of Jewish life, one which was translated into Japanese. His main work, a monumental one, on the Jews in the Far East until 1937, (in Russian) is still in manuscript form in the possession of his son, Theodore Kaufman. It is an untapped source of history for a little-known facet of modern Jewish history.

Some aspects of this phenomenal man's activities can be gleaned from the above-mentioned interview, as well as from an insert by Menahem ben Iyar in a book by Dr. Kaufman, *Rofeh Hamachaneh* (Hebrew) (Doctor in the [Bolshevick Labor] Camp) (Tel Aviv: Am Oved Publishers, Ltd., 1971). Copy of the book in the possession of the author, courtesy of Theodore Kaufman, who also granted the author an interview, August 15, 1971.

Cf. also Eliahu Lankin, Interview. The Oral History Division of the Institute of Contemporary Jewry at the Hebrew University, No. 850, a 300-page memoir which includes a section on the Jewish communities in Manchuria and China [Lankin, *Far East*]; Epstein, "China".

For the "freer" atmosphere of the Far East for the Russian Jews, see Kaufman, *Manchuria*, pp. 10-12; Epstein, "China"; Lankin, *Far East*, p. 3.

69. See above, note 68. Cf. also Rudolph Loewenthal, "Harbin" ["Harbin"], *Encyclopaedia Judaica*, Vol. 7, p. 1331. Also Epstein, "China".

70. As the formation of a "synagogue committee" in 1902, makes clear. See Zeitin, "The Shanghai Ashkenazi Jewish Communal Association" [Zeitin, "SAJCA"], *Almanac*, p. 53.

71. Epstein, "China". Cf. also Sokolsky, "China", p. 455; H. Drucker, interview by Herman Dicker, February 22, 1958 [Drucker, Interview] (DP).

72. See Almoni, "Sephardic", p. 606, for the chasm between the two communities. Cf. also Rabinowich, "Yidn", p. 217.

For the final, harmonious period, see also *Reports of the Council of the Jewish Community in Shanghai*, 1952-1953, 1954-1955, 1955-1956, 1956-1957. Reproduced courtesy of H. Dicker (DP).

73. See above, note 69, especially Simpson, *Refugees*.

74. Citrin Interview.

75. For Harbin's Jewish population, see Dicker, *Wanderers*, p. 42. The figure of 13,000, also quoted by Loewenthal, "Harbin", is a bit exaggerated, and is based on Parry, "Jews". 10,000 is probably more accurate. The low figure of 2,500 for the late 1930's through 1945 is quoted by Isgour, "Shanghai", and is the more accurate one for this period.

For the occupation of Manchuria by Japan and its effect on the Jews of that country, especially Harbin, see Dicker, *Wanderers*, pp. 35-60; Emmanuel Pratt, "Exodus from China" [Pratt, "Exodus"], *Hadassah Magazine*, Vol. LI (January 1970), p. 26; Loewenthal, "Harbin".

See also the Kogan Papers and Foreign Office documents for the period of 1934-1939.

76. For Shanghai's population, see above, note 67. Dicker's statement (*Wanderers*, p. 42) that 4,000 to 5,000 left Harbin for Shanghai (based on Parry) is unacceptable, and contradicts his more accurate figure of 4,000 on p. 69. Cf. also Citrin, Interview.

77. Isgour, "Shanghai". See also below, chapter 12; Kaufman, *Manchuria*.

78. Dicker, *Wanderers*, especially pp. 24-29. Cf. also Loewenthal, "Harbin".

For Rabbi Kiseleff's own works, which reflect the activities with which he was involved, see especially his volume of sermons and talks upon various occasions titled *Sefer Imre Shefer* (Hebrew) (Tel Aviv: published privately by Rebbetzin Fayge Kiseleff, [1952]), including the biographical sketch in the preface by the author's widow.

Rabbi Kiseleff was born in 1863 and studied in the Yeshiva of Volozhin, then headed by Rabbi Chaim Soloveitchick. He was ordained, among others by Rabbi Chaim Ozer. Upon the urgings of the Lubavitcher Rebbe, Rabbi Kiseleff went to Harbin, Manchuria in 1913 to accept the rabbinical position he was to remain with until 1945.

At the first of the three Far Eastern Conferences in 1937, he was unanimously elected the Chief Rabbi of Russian-Jewish Communities of the Far East. (Preface. Cited also by Dicker, *Wanderers*, pp. 25-26). In 1941 he published *Nationalism and Judaism* in which Rabbi Kiseleff attempted to instill pride in Judaism among the youth. (*Ibid.*, Dicker gives a 1931 date, while the preface gives the later one).

See also Rabbi Kiseleff's earlier volume, titled *Sefer Mishberei Yam* (Hebrew) (Harbin: published privately, 1926), a collection of responsa on a variety of halachic themes, including several that touch upon the life of Jews in the Far East.

Copies of both his Hebrew works were reproduced courtesy of Rabbi M. Tokayer (TP).

For Dr. Kaufman's activities, see above, note 68.

79. See especially Epstein, "China". Epstein noted that Jewish grain dealers fled Crimea prior to 1905, during the pogroms, and settled first in Harbin and then Shanghai. Cf. also Nehemiah Robinson, *The Jewish Community in China in Dissolution* [Robinson, *Dissolution*] (New York: World Jewish Congress, 1954) (a 10-page mimeographed booklet).

For some of the professions, see Dr. Zelik Albans, Interview by H. Dicker, April 9, 1958 [Albans, Interview] (DP). By 1942, the Russian-Jewish community included at least 200 enterprises of varying size, as indicated by the registration of this number in the Jewish Chamber of Commerce organized by the Japanese authorities. (*Unser Leben* [English Supplement], July 17, 1942).

80. Concerning the appeals in 1937 and 1938, for the Jewish (mostly Russian) victims of the 1937 Sino-Japanese hostilities, see the JDCCA files for the period of August 1937 to February 1938.

See also KP S-9460-3-566, May 29, 1936, "Jewish Bodies in Shanghai", Zeitin, SAJCA, p. 54; Rosenfeld, *History*, II, pp. 3-5, for a description of the various communal relief agencies and their activities. See also Elkan Interview; "Shanghai Hebrew Relief Society and The Shanghai Jewish Women's Benevolent Society", financial statements for period of 1933-1943 [SHRSH] (YIVO No. 35). The latter, for example, financed the distribution in 1943, of over 19,000 free meals to the indigent. (*Ibid.*, Statement for 1943).

81. Rosenfeld, II, p. 2. Cited by Kranzler, *JCS*, 3; Dicker, *Wanderers*, p. 69. Cf. also Zeitin, "SAJCA", p. 53.

82. Almoni, "Sephardic", p. 605.

83. *New York Times,* August 27, 1954, p. 21 (obituary). Cf. also Simcha Elberg, "Shanchai und ir Rov" [Elberg, "Rov"] (Yiddish), *Dos Yiddishe Wort*, Vol. 13 (January 1967), pp. 14-16; Abraham, Interview.

See below, especially chapters 12 and 15. Rabbi Ashkenazi left his position in Vladivostok in 1926, after pressure by the Communist regime caused the dissolution of his congregation. See *Israel's Messenger,* June 4, 1926, p. 12. Cf. also Drucker, Interview.

After leaving Siberia, Rabbi Ashkenazi stayed briefly in Harbin where he was married, and from there he went to his new position in Shanghai. Drucker Interview.

84. See the article about Rabbi Ashkenazi's reception dinner tendered in his honor, by the Lubavitch Hassidim, *The Day* (Tog), January 8, 1947.

His father, Shneiur Zalman Ashkenazi, was named after the founder of the Lubavitch Hassidic movement.

86. Zeitin, "SAJCA", p. 53. Rosenfeld, *History*, II, *Ibid.*, gives the date for the establishment of *Oihel Moishe* as 1929. Here, too, the two dates are not necessarily mutually exclusive, since one can refer to the completion of the renovation. and the other to the dedication of the synagogue.

87. Rosenfeld, *History*, II, *Ibid.* Cf. also Zeitin, "SAJCA", p. 54; Drucker Interview. The name "New Synagogue" was now applied to the new building in the French town while the one on Ward Road retained the name "Oihel Moishe". See the titles on the printed Jewish calendar for the year 5702 (1941-1942) which listed both names and addresses. The architect of the New Synagogue was one of its congregants, a Mr. Albans, brother of Dr. Zelik Albans. Albans Interview.

Although the New Synagogue first opened its doors in 1941, those Russian Jews who had already moved from the poorer section of Hongkew to the more residential sections in the Settlement and the elegant Frenchtown, formed *shtibels* (small, more informal, one-room synagogues) in those neighborhoods even earlier. Thus, since 1934, some Ashkenazi Jews utilized a room in the Sephardi Ohel Rachel Synagogue on Seymour Road, while three years later another room was rented in the Concession on Rue Bourget. Zeitin, "SAJCA", p. 53.

The Sephardi *Mikveh* (Ritualarium), however, was still used after 1941, since no new one was built in the New Synagogue. Drucker Interview. The Polish refugees, however, were responsible for the opening of a new *Mikveh* in Hongkew. See the epilogue to *Meor Torah* [*Meor Torah, epilogue*] (Hebrew), Vol. 2 (Shanghai: 1946), p. 62. (This is a journal devoted to Torah Novella, edited by Rabbi Mordechai Ginsburg and published by the students of the Mirrer Yeshiva). Copy reproduced, courtesy of Rabbi Hillel David.

88. Citrin Interview. Also Rebbetzin Ashkenazi Interview. Although during the period of the War in the Pacific many Russian Jews succeeded economically, there were very few really wealthy among them. *Ibid.* This is so in spite of the view by the poverty-struck refugees, who considered all the Russian Jews who had Chinese help as "millionaires". For example, see Elberg, *op. cit.*, pp. 14-15; Rosenfeld, *History*, II, p. 3. He notes that the Chevrah Kadisha (Sacred Burial Society) arranged for free funeral arrangements for approximately 40 per cent of those buried in its cemetery, probably around 1942. Undoubtedly German refugees were among the "free burials". See also *SHRH*, 1943.

89. Rosenfeld, *History*, II, p. 4. See also *SHRH*, 1933-1943. For example, during 1940, prior to the arrival of the Polish refugees, the Society provided over 57,000 meals. *Ibid.*

91. See above, note 88. Also, by 1942, the Educational Aid Society was still subsidizing the education of about 120 children, though not all were from the Ashkenazi community. Rosenfeld, *History*, II, p. 4.

92. See above, note 44. Cf. also Elkan Interview; Irving Levitas Interview, July 28, 1968 and subsequent dates. Dr. Levitas visited Shanghai during 1937-1938, where he was engaged in research; Mrs. D. Lew, Interview; Krasno, Interview.

93. *Ibid.* The former was run by the American Episcopal Church, while Aurora was a French Jesuit institution. See also Pott, *Shanghai*, p. 123.
See also *Israel's Messenger,* December 16, 1921, p. 37, for Rabbi Hirsch's complaint about these "convert" [sic] schools, attended by Shanghai Jews. Cited by Dicker, *Wanderers* (ms.), p. 84, note 17.

94. Levitas Interview. Dr. Levitas had interviewed Sir Victor during this period. Cf. also Jackson, *Sassoons*, pp. 112-113.

95. Rosenfeld, *History*, II, p. 5. Cf. also Dicker, *Wanderers*, pp. 33, 44.

96. Rosenfeld, *History*, II, p. 6. Cf. also Elkan Interview; Mrs. D. Lew Interview. Among those that criticized the "paramilitary" stance of Betar was Gerechter (Interview). Also Theodore Kaufman, Interview. Mr. Gerechter lived in Shanghai from 1943 until 194 . Mr. Kaufman, son of Dr. Abraham Kaufman of Harbin, referred to Betar in his community.
The Shanghai Betar financed the arms shipment to the Irgun in Palestine on the ill-fated "Altalena". Elkan Interview.

97. See, for example, the spirited portrait of Betar's ideals, in an article by the young Tekoah (then Tukaczynski), in *Unser Leben,* January 17, July 8, 1942 (English Supplement).

98. See above, note 66. See also Dicker, *Wanderers*, p. 69; Shannon Interview.

99. See, for example, Carey, *War Years*, p. 163. Cf. also Miller, *Paradise*, pp. 19-20; Pott, *Shanghai*, p. 297. Mr. Levitas noted that the Sephardim rarely visited the Russian-Jewish "Club". Undoubtedly the lack of kosher food was one of the reasons. Interview. also Abraham Interview.

100. For some of the variety of cultural activities during the early periol of the 1920's and early 1930's, see Epstein, "China"; Elkan Interview. For some of the activities during the "refugee" period, see Rose Shoshana-Kahan, *In Faier un Flamen* (Yiddish) [Shoshana, *Faier*] (Buenos Aires: Central Farband fun Poilishe Yidn in Argentina, 1949), pp. 286-287, 291, 296.

82   JAPANESE, NAZIS & JEWS

Cf. also the pages of *Unser Leben* and the numerous tickets to performances of the Club in the YIVO file Nos. 56, 57, 58.

101. Elkan Interview. Cf. also Shannon Interview; Simpson, *Refugees*, pp. 509-510. Carey, *War Years*, p. 59.

102. See Dagobert Levithan, "The Jewish Recreation Club" ["JRC"], *Almanac*, pp. 70-76.

103. Johnstone, *Shanghai*, pp. 258-260 *et passim. Yellow Creek*, pp. 131, 141, 146; Dicker, *Wanderers*, pp. 72-73. Cf. also "Die Jewish Company des Shanghai Volunteer Corps" ["Jewish" SVC], *Shanghai Jewish Chronicle [SJC SE]*, March 1940, p. 20. Hauser, *Shanghai*, pp. 166-167 *et passim*. The latter source gives the more accurate figure of 135 and 35 refugee volunteers.

The Sephardi members of the SVC usually belonged to the British units, another indication of the social and religious chasm between the two older Shanghai Jewish communities. Abraham Interview.

104. "Jewish" SVC. Also Dicker, *Wanderers, ibid*.

105. For the 1873 figure, see "Yellow Creek" p. 94. The 1936 census figures are quoted by Murphy, *Shanghai*, p. 23, and Barnett, *Hostage*, p. 10. The latter also cites the high figures of 70,000 to 80,000. *Ibid.*, p. 29.

106. *Ibid.*, p. 10. See also *Yellow Creek*, p. 150 and especially Murphy, *Shanghai*, p. 16.

107. See, for example, Herbert E. Norman, *Japan's Emergence as a Modern State* [Norman, *Japan's*] (Westport, Conn.: Greenwood Press, 1940), pp. 197-201. Cf. also Nobutaka Ike, "War and Modernization", in *Political Development in Modern Japan*, Robert E. Ward, editor (Princeton, N.J.: Princeton University Press, 1968), pp. 189-211; John Toland, *The Rising Sun* [Toland, *Rising*] (New York: Random House, 1970), p. 7.

108. See, for example, James B. Crowley, *Japan's Quest for Autonomy* [Crowley, *Quest*] (Princeton, N.J.: Princeton University Press, 1966), pp. 159-168. Cf. also Mamoru Shigemitsu, *Japan and Her Destiny: My Struggle for Peace* [Shigemitsu, *Destiny*] (London: Hutchinson of London, 1958), pp. 42-43, 140.

109. See, for example, Crowley, *Quest*, chaps. 3 and 4. Cf. also Richard Storry, *A History of Modern Japan* [Storry, *Japan*] (Baltimore: Penguin Books, 1960), chap. 8; *Yellow Creek*, pp. 139-142.

110. Re Shanghai and the 1937 hostilities, see *ibid.*, pp. 145-156. Cf. also Shigemitsu, *Destiny*, pp. 139-144; Crowley, *Quest*, chap. 6; Toland, *Rising*, chap. 2.

111. *Yellow Creek, ibid.* Cf. also Barnett, *Hostage*, chap. 2; The Shanghai

Ashkenazi Jewish Communal Association to [Jacob] Alkow, August 23, 1937 (JDCCA); see also below, chap. 4.

112. Barnett, *Hostage,* frontispiece, for photo of the mass of refugees crossing bridge into Settlement. Also *ibid.,* pp. 44-47; Ginsbourg, *Shanghai,* pp. 5-8.

For Japan as the real power, see *ibid.,* p. 8. Also Speelman Report, June 21, 1939, p. 1; Barnett, *Hostage,* pp. 16-16, 28; Mark Siegelberg, *The Face of Pearl Harbor: A Play* [Siegelberg, *Pearl Harbor*] (Melbourne: View Publishing Co., n.d.), pp. VII-VIII; KP No. 7, May 26, 1939, p. 21.

113. See below, especially chpas. 4-6.

*Welcome to Shanghai. Now you are no longer
Germans, Austrians Czechs or Roumanians. Now
you are only Jews. The Jews of the whole world have
prepared a home for you.*

*(Delegate of the Relief Committee
greeting the incoming Refugees.
Kamm. Europaeische Emigration)*

The long trek from Hitler's Germany to the Far East
started for some as early as 1933. The story of one man's
odyssey illustrates some of the obstacles encountered by the
initial surge. "A" had fled to Spain after the first wave of arrests
in 1933 inspired by Hitler, but he was forced to leave when
the Spanish Civil War broke out in 1936. For two years he
found asylum in Italy, until Mussolini began aping Hitler's
antisemitic legislation. At the end of 1938, he went to Switzerland, and was granted a four-week permit. He planned to go
to Ecuador, where he had relatives, but first had to travel to
Paris to acquire a visa through an agent. The visa was vali-
dated by the Equadorian consul in Switzerland, but only after

landing, did "A" find out that it was not valid. Since no other Latin American country would accept him, he had to cable his relatives for a return ticket to Europe. Neither France nor Switzerland would grant him entry, and the best he could manage was a two-day permit for Italy. It was in Italy that he was able to purchase a ticket for Shanghai, the only place not requiring a visa. He finally arrived in Shanghai after a sixteen-week circuitous route.[1]

The journey of "A" was of course an extreme case, but the difficulties he encountered were by no means untypical experiences for those attempting to escape. It is no wonder that many desperate men and women fell victim to swindlers peddling phony visas.[2]

Two major routes lay open to the Far East, depending on the period during which the flight took place:

1. By sea — end of 1938 to June 10, 1940
2. By land — June 11, 1940 to December 7, 1941.

The first leg of the sea route was, for most, passage to Italy by either train or boat. From there the refugees, generally using the Italian Lloyd-Tristino Line, traveled through the Suez Canal or around the Cape of Good Hope, to Shanghai or other points of destination in the Far East. This stream of refugees reached its peak during the first half of 1939.[3]

In addition to paying dearly for visas, the harried refugees were at the mercy of the ship companies, who often charged up to ten times their normal rates for tickets. Still, with space at a premium and ships booked up to six months in advance, those who managed to secure tickets considered themselves very fortunate.[4] Ironically, the refugee, whose last *mark* was used to purchase a visa or ship ticket, or whose relatives had furnished him with the required amount, often found himself in a first-class berth on a luxury cruise, because high-priced tickets were the only ones available.[5] This meant that the unfortunate refugee might have to travel with people who could afford the luxury class, who dressed and behaved accordingly, and who frequently displayed very unsympathetic attitudes. The *Hilfsverein*, the German-Jewish relief agency, often paid the difference between second and first-class passage. They also had to guarantee the ship owners a return trip.[6]

The route usually followed was Trieste to Alexandria, via Suez to Bombay, Hongkong, Shanghai. At the first stop (Alexandria or Port Said), representatives of three Egyptian Communities, having been notified by the Shanghai relief agencies, often boarded the ship to greet the refugees.[7] These welcome visitors brought gifts of refreshments, cigarettes, underwear, pocket money, and, most important, some light clothing appropriate for the tropical climate.[8] Besides the Jewish representatives, the refugees were greeted by Arab vendors loudly peddling their wares, which the refugees, because of the general prohibition against taking more than 10 RM in cash out of Germany, were usually unable to purchase. But this ban could be manipulated: anyone taking the route from Bremen was allowed to take along 150 RM as "board money" (required to be spent on board).[9] This was reduced to 75 RM for those who first boarded a ship at Trieste.[10] This money could be utilized for the purchase of resaleable luxury items, such as cameras or tools, etc. Some refugees made spare pocket money on board, giving haircuts to the crew.[11]

After passing through the Suez Canal, the ships usually sailed across the Indian Ocean, making stops at Bombay, Singapore, Hongkong (where those with British visas could go ashore for a few hours), sometimes Manila, and finally reached

Shanghai.[12] Others continued their journey to Kobe and/or
Yokohama which were to serve as transit centers to the United
States, Canada, Australia and Latin America, for about 4,600
refugees.[13] These included 2,000 Polish refugees whom we shall
encounter again later. Occasionally, the captain of the ship
would try to avoid the tolls at the Suez Canal, by sailing around
the Cape. But this added six more weeks to the already four-
week-long journey.[14]

Despite its length, the voyage proved beneficial for
many. Some were to look back on the four to ten weeks at
sea as perhaps the only relaxing and enjoyable period in their
many years spent in the Far East.[15] Those with first or second-
class accommodations found the food very good and the atmosphere often cheerful.[16] It was the first time in months—even
years—that these people were able to relax since escaping the
Nazi terror. They had an opportunity to recoup physically, as
well as psychologically, on a luxury liner, perhaps after a stay
in Dachau or Sachsenhausen. The large contingent of Jewish
refugees aboard the ship—ranging from one hundred to one
thousand—found a sense of solidarity and kinship that often
resulted in marriages or business partnerships.[17]

On the other hand, there were those who found the
voyage but a continuation of the dreary and humiliating
experience that had begun in a concentration camp, and was to
conclude only with the end of the war, or later. For these, the
journey on board ship was the first opportunity to vent the
pent-up emotions of the previous terrifying months in Germany
or Austria. It is not surprising to find that this first taste of
freedom prompted reclusion and often precipitated a nervous
breakdown. Others vented their emotions in quarrels, even
sometimes in physical violence that required the Captain's
interference. Despite their first-class accommodations, some

were snubbed by the regular passengers, and by some of the higher officers, who felt that refugees belonged in the steerage.[18]

THE LAND ROUTE

When the Mediterranean was closed by Italy's entry into the war, in June, 1940, the only way of reaching the Far East, particularly Shanghai, was the land route across Russia and Siberia. This meant that thousands who had booked passage on a boat, lost their chance of fleeing when their visas were invalidated.[19] Since Russia was still on friendly terms with Germany, arrangements could be made with Intourist, the Soviet Government Travel Bureau, for tourists from foreign countries to travel by rail through Siberia, a trek of six thousand miles, at the Intourist price of US $170-240.[20] The NKVD (the Russian secret police) would secure Soviet transit visas for those who possessed end-visas to another country.[21] Fortunate possessors of such visas, to countries like the United State, Canada or Latin America, usually proceeded across the USSR (via Siberia) to Harbin (Manchuria), Pusan (Korea), Shimonoseki, Kobe, or Yokohama, from whence they would sail across the Pacific to their final destination.[22]

The first stop in Manchuria (or Manchukuo, as the Japanese renamed it after their conquest in 1931-1932) was Manchouli, where the refugees were greeted by delegates of the National Council of Jews in East Asia, who helped clear the passport formalities, etc.[23] Those without other visas set their immediate sights on Shanghai, where they were still permitted entry with only a landing permit.[24] Many reached Shanghai, their final destination, via Harbin, by boat from Dairen (a port on the southern tip of Manchuria).[25]

ARRIVAL

The earliest arrivals were destined to receive a warm

welcome, which cooled rapidly as the flood gained momentum. Sebastian Steiner has left us an account of his own family's arrival, a couple from Austria with two children. Neither Steiner nor his welcomer, S. Gruenberg, a fellow Austrian and old-time Shanghailander, was aware that the Steiners were the vanguard of a refugee community which was to reach 17,000. Gruenberg met the Steiners at the boat, the *Conte Biancamano*, arranged customs clearance, and took them to the apartment he had found for them in the French Concession, at the unheard-of rent of (Sh)$150 a month. They were entertained by Rabbi Ashkenazi and his wife, and had time to accustom themselves to their surroundings before facing the economic realities of their new home.[26]

Such a welcome and period of adjustment were not to be the lot of the thousands who followed in a steady stream of ocean liners from Nazi-dominated Europe. Care could no longer be administered on an individual basis, and concern had to give way to sheer subsistence on a mass scale. The devastated sector of Hongkew replaced the elegant residential area of Frenchtown. And even that was beyond the means of many, who had to make do with the hastily set up refugee camps. Even the friendly atmosphere faded as the refugees came to outstrip in numbers both the old-time Sephardi and the Russian communities. Little help was forth-coming from Jews in other parts of the world.

The panic migration of German Jews trying to escape what they called the "ignited powder keg" of Europe continued unabated, and reached its peak during the months of June and August, 1939, when the total number of refugees approached 14,000.[27] If allowed to continue at this rate, between 20 and 25,000 would have arrived by the end of 1939.[28] Two important factors brought about a gradual tapering off. First, a severe shortage of shipping space closed bookings

months in advance on any ships going to Shanghai.[29] Of far
greater significance was the restriction imposed upon refugee
immigration during August of 1939, by both the Japanese
authorities of the Northern District of the International Settlement, and the Municipal Councils of the International Settlement and French Concession.[30] It was the combined impact of
these factors which prevented the Jewish refugee population in
Shanghai from going above approximately 17,000, before the
outbreak of the War in the Pacific, when all immigration into
Shanghai ceased.

LOCAL JEWISH RELIEF COMMITTEES

Despite the severe economic crisis wrought by the
Sino-Japanese hostilities of 1937, the Sephardi and the Russian-
Jewish communities responded instantly and generously to the
appeal for relief of these newcomers to Shanghai. In fact the
Jewish community, Sephardim and Ashkenazim alike, had
appealed unsuccessfully in 1937 to American Jewry for
financial aid for the Russian-Jewish victims whose homes had
been devastated during that fighting.[31] The *Hilfsfond,* the oldest
local refugee relief organization, set up in 1934 by the early
German arrivals for their less fortunate co-religionists, was
able to take care of the first arrivals from Austria, after the
Anschluss. It continued to provide for the relatively few
indigent refugees until the summer of 1938.[32] That summer,
however, the *Hilfsfond* found itself unable to cope with the
hundreds of new refugees.[33] It was then that assistance was
sought outside of the chiefly German-Jewish circle which supported the Hilfsfond.

On August 8, 1938, a new relief committee, called the
International Committee for Granting Relief to European
Refugees (or abbreviated, IC), was organized by prominent

old-time Shanghailanders of various nationalities and creeds. These included Jews and non-Jews, of Hungarian, Czech, Austrian, British and Dutch nationalities.[34] This organization was commonly referred to as the Komor Committee, for its first secretary and administrator, Paul Komor, a Shanghai business-man of Hungarian origin, who was to head its activities until the outbreak of the War in the Pacific.[35] The IC's original plan followed the pattern of the *Hilfsfond* in the collection of monthly contributions from a list of subscribers and friends. For the first few months, they successfully provided the refugees with room and board and some assistance in securing employ-ment, or in establishing a business.[36] Private rooms were rented in boarding houses, and arrangements were made with the Salvation Army and a Chinese YMCA. However, soon the first of many refugee camps better known as the *Heime* had to be leased by the IC in cooperation with the *Hilfsfond*.[37] The author will utilize the German term *Heim* (singular) or *Heime* (plural) for two reasons: first, it was the term used most often by the refugees; second, the German term denoted the irony of what was soon to become the antithesis of a "home," a fact noted by many of the observers. The first camp was housed in a building which had previously been used by the British as an Old Women's Home, and later, remodeled to house sixty bachelors.[38] In addition, subsidies of (Sh) $60 a month per refugee were granted but when funds ran low, this was reduced to (Sh) $55 (US $3.30). An additional source of revenue to support relief activities was a (Sh) 10c. tax on every kosher slaughtered fowl, instituted by N. M. Nissim, the secretary of the Sephardi Community.[39]

Provision had to be made for the immediate housing and feeding of the refugees already in Shanghai, as well as the additional hundreds who began to arrive in the fall of 1938. The cumbersome practice of investigating each refugee for eligibility for relief involved endless paper work. Several people were required for instance, merely to translate all the relevant German documents.[40] At the same time all the newcomers had to be received and provided with room and board. The officials of the Sephardi Beth Aaron Synagogue granted permission for their large and beautiful edifice to be used as a reception center and refugee kitchen. Appeals for funds and supplies were made to both the Jewish and the non-Jewish residents of the foreign settlements. The youth of the Betar (see below) transported bedding and other necessary items in trucks. Mattresses were placed on the floors and benches, even in the sanctuary of the synagogue to provide room for the incoming refugees. A public kitchen, run by both resident and refugee volunteers, was organized by the Abraham and Toeg families to serve food to about 600 refugees a day.[41] This served as the main kitchen until it was replaced by the Ward Road *Heim* Kitchen at the beginning of 1939. As the number of arrivals increased daily, even this proved insufficient. Sir Victor Sassoon then donated an office building, known as the Embankment Building, to serve as a refugee center. It served for about a year as the central receiving station for the incoming refugees, and provided good temporary quarters including a pool, for several hundred people, despite lack of proper sanitation facilities.[42]

The people behind the various relief agencies soon realized that the local financial resources were totally inadequate to cope with the rising influx of refugees. Help would have to come from Jews outside of Shanghai if there was to be any steady commitment to solve the relief problem. In order to avoid costly duplication and wasted effort, greater cooperation and coordination of relief efforts also had to be achieved. The prominent and wealthy Kadoorie family arranged a meeting in the offices of Sir Elly Kadoorie and Sons, on October 19, 1938. Representatives of all the existing Jewish religious organizations and relief institutions were invited—both Sephardi and Russian—in addition to members of the IC and *Hilfsfond*.[43]

This concerted effort was one of the first of the few communal endeavors attempted by the Sephardi and Russian-Jewish communities.[44] On the board of the newly formed committee were representatives of the Sephardim such as Reverend Mendel Brown, D.E.J. Abraham and his son, Reuben D. Abraham. The Russian Jews were represented by the Chairman, H. Gensburger, Rabbi Meier Ashkenazi, Louis B. Greenberg, and H. Kammerling; while the earlier German-Jewish refugees were represented by Dr. Bernard Rosenberg and Dr. Kurt Marx.[45] The new organization was named the Committee for the Assistance of European Jewish Refugees in Shanghai, or abbreviated, CFA.[46] Since the active leadership of this committee would soon pass into the hands of its first treasurer, Michel Speelman, it was commonly known as the Speelman Committee.[47] The members unanimously agreed to amalgamate and coordinate all existing relief agencies into a single representative committee. Its initiative raised about (Sh) $50,000, or about (US) $8,000 by the end of 1398.[48]

The problem of providing shelter and various other forms of relief became too complicated for a single committee, and it was decided to form seven subcommittees to handle specific areas of relief. Eventually, as the need arose, several additional committees were set up.[49] The most important of these subcommittees were:

1. The Executive Committee, soon to be headed by Michel Speelman, was in charge of the entire relief operation. This committee was also responsible for dealing with the authorities of Shanghai's foreign-controlled sectors: the Municipal Councils for the International Settlement, the French

Concession, and the Japanese authorities occupying the Hong-kew areas, where as it happened most of the refugees settled. Ellis Hayim, an influential Sephardi, was the Vice-Chairman of the CFA's Executive Committee.[50]

2. The Finance Committee's function was to handle all finances, including the appeals to the various Jewish organizations abroad, such as the American JDC and the Council for German Jewry in London.[51] Its chairman was Michel Speelman.

3. The Housing and Disbursement Committee took over the functions of the old *Hilfsfond*, whose paid secretary, Dr. Kurt Marx, was retained by the CFA. His primary responsibility was the provision of room and board. In practice, this meant setting up and running the *Heime* and public kitchens.[52]

4. The Medical Committee was originally staffed by German-Jewish physicians, and was eventually headed by a Shanghai Hungarian Jew, Professor Dr. Frederick Reiss.[53] His task was to provide proper medical care for the refugees both in and outside the *Heime*. These activities will be described in detail below.[54]

5. The Educational and Cultural Committee, was led by Horace Kadoorie and Reverend Mendel Brown and provided for the education of the refugee children and adults.[55]

6. The Employment Committee tried to locate jobs for refugees with marketable skills.[58]

7. The Rehabilitation Committee's aim was to make the refugees self-sufficient through loans and advice for new business ventures. After the formation of the CFA, the IC (which had begun its work as an all-round relief agency), concentrated primarily upon the legal and consular aspects of relief.[57] This was made necessary by the complicated problems

of the refugee's status, extraterritoriality, and the Chinese legal system.[58]

As problems were encountered, new departments were formed to handle different relief services. Noted below are a few of the significant additional programs run by the relief committees.[59]

The IC maintained the most complete files on the refugees, largely because application for assistance, even of a temporary nature, required registration with this agency. It also set up a Passport Department which issued identification cards to refugees which were recognized by the Shanghai Municipal Police and the Japanese authorities. It also issued the IC Pass, which enabled many stateless refugees to travel to other parts of Japanese-controlled China, or to those countries that recognized its validity, such as Australia. Though Paul Komor had hoped for international recognition of these IC passes, they lost all validity with the outbreak of the War in the Pacific.[60]

Most refugees were too poor to afford bank accounts, and the IC provided a Banking Service which, among other things accepted deposits and cashed their checks from overseas.[61] The IC Milk Fund provided a supplement to the meagre diet of the younger children and invalids. Funds for this essential program were solicited from the Shanghai public at large through various charity affairs.[62]

Immigrants wishing to sell their belongings were assisted by the Thrift Shop, also set up by the IC. It sold family heirlooms and other objects brought along for resale at bargain prices. Crystal, furs, silver and procelain were among the items that found their way into the homes of the well-to-do natives of Shanghai. This shop also marketed fine handmade articles produced by women in a special workshop set up in the Kinchow *Heim* at the expense and under the direction of Sir Victor Sassoon.[63]

The Rehabilitation Fund, administered primarily by the IC, was considered, even by contemporary critics of the refugee work, to have the most beneficial and durable impact. It orginated in the early attempts of the *Hilfsfond* and IC to promote self-sufficiency and independent livelihood. The small sum of (Sh) $17,000, or about (US) $2,500, collected during the first few months would not have gone very far had it not been for a £5,000 (US $25,000) contribution by Sir Victor Sassoon to the Council for German Jews in London. This organization was one of the principal supporters of Shanghai's relief activities until Britain's entry into the War in Europe.[64]

(Sh) $150,000 was thus earmarked by Sir Victor for a Rehabilitation Fund.[65] This revolving fund, of which a small percentage was eventually paid back, was used to finance promising refugee business ventures, usually upon the condition of restoring a war-damaged shop.[66] By December 1939, over 1,300 people, amounting with their families to 3,300 refugees, achieved some measure of economic self-sufficiency.[67] Perhaps more significant than the purely economic gains was the restoration of dignity which resulted from their newly found economic independence. The failure of many of the budding entrepreneurs, unfamiliar with the complexities of business in Shanghai, does not in any way diminish the value of this Fund.[68] The rebuilding by refugees of many of the war-torn blocks of Hongkew, owned by Sir Victor Sassoon, illustrates the mutual benefits derived from the Rehabilitation Fund.[69]

HICEM*

HICEM was the oldest of the Jewish immigrant aid societies. Even prior to the establishment of the *Hilfsfond,*

---

* The acronym HICEM stands for combination of HIAS (Hebrew Immigrant Aid Society) and JCA (Jewish Colonization Association). The American office is called HIAS, while in Europe and

HICEM, through its constant association with the German-Jewish relief organizations since the first large-scale persecutions in 1933, had played an important role in drawing attention to Shanghai as a haven for refugees.[70] It had been located in Harbin, Manchuria, since 1922, and conducted an elaborate correspondence with potential refugees to China and Manchuria.[71] By providing checks for (US) $50 to $150, HICEM made possible the resettlement of several hundred otherwise penniless former inmates of concentration camps. In this manner over (US) $31,000 reached Shanghai by mid-1939.[72] These HICEM checks often made the difference between economic success or failure, since, in mid-1939, the cost of feeding one person amounted to but (US) 8c. a day.[73] For those already in Shanghai, the vast effort made by HICEM to keep organizations, relatives, and friends overseas in touch with each other gave several thousand refugees an income from abroad, at least until Pearl Harbor.[74]

During the first year of immigration to Shanghai, the task of carrying out the HICEM activities in Shanghai was handled by an old-time Shanghai resident and businessman, B.S. Barbash. His amateurish, though well-intentioned efforts to provide the necessary aid to the thousands of refugees, forced HICEM to move its Harbin office to Shanghai by September of 1939, and put it under the direction of Meyer Birman.[75]

Immigration affairs were also being handled inefficiently, and the CFA set up its own Emigration Department in Shanghai, headed by Eduard Kann.[76] Since the CFA had been dealing with emigration for almost a year before Birman stepped into

---

other countries it was known as HICEM. In the Far East, especially during the period of World War I, and until the outbreak of World War II, it was referred to as DALJEWCIB (acronym for The Far Eastern Jewish Information Bureau).

the picture, overlapping activities and clashes of personalities resulted, a circumstance which did not always serve the refugees' interests.[77]

In the meantime some *modus vivandi*, though not ideal, was worked out. The financial responsibility and authority remained in the hands of the CFA, while most of the traditional work for HICEM was performed by Birman and his staff.[78]

RELIEF ORGANIZATION OUTSIDE SHANGHAI

The Council for German Jewry, a British organization set up in London in 1935, in response to the needs of victims of Nazi terrorism, was a partner of similar organizations in Egypt and New York. It supported some of the needs of the Shanghai refugees until August 1939, a month prior to Britain's entry into World War II. Shortage of funds then stopped its activities as far as Shanghai was concerned.[79]

THE JDC

The relief organization which was to have the greatest impact on the refugees, and without whose assistance it is doubtful that they would have survived their stay in Shanghai, was the American Joint Distribution Committee. The Joint or JDC, as it came to be called, was the largest Jewish relief organization, with help in various forms dispensed to needy Jews the world over. It had started in 1914, under the leadership of Felix M. Warburg, to help the "Jewish war sufferers" in Europe, and was an amalgam of three earlier relief organizations with a similar aim. These three represented the wealthy German Jews, the Orthdox leaders, and a labor group, respectively.[80]

After the United States entered World War I in 1917, it became of course impossible to help victims in enemy territory. The State Department gave the Joint permission to distribute funds from neutral Holland. This situation was to arise again when the United States entered World War II, as we shall see.[81]

At the end of World War I, special and varied relief programs were set up, especially in Poland and Russia. In 1933, when the Jewish persecutions began in Germany, these programs were augmented, and it was not long before financial resources, raised in the United States, came to the aid of the refugees streaming into Shanghai. Its failure to make a steady commitment, and to send trained social workers to oversee the relief situation, will be taken up later.[82]

NOTES : "WELCOME TO SHANGHAI!"

1. Ginsbourg, *Refugees*, p. 3. For the treatment of refugees in Italy, see Tartakower, *Refugee*, pp. 39-40. Cf. also Dawidowicz, *War*, pp. 369-371.

2. Re the sale of valid and invalid visas to Latin American countries see Nathan Eck, "The Rescue of Jews with the aid of Passports and Citizenship Papers of Latin American States", [Eck, "Passports"] *Yad Washem Studies, I: On the European Jewish Catastrophe and Resistance*, edited by Ben Zion Dinur and Saul Esh. (Jesusalem: Yad Washem, 1957), pp. 125-152. Cf. also Morse, *Six Million*, p. 343; Finegold, *Politics*, pp. 101-102, 143; Wischnitzer, *Migration*, pp. 198-199, 231.

3. For four personal accounts of such routes to Shanghai and their experiences there, see three unpublished manuscripts and one published account; Theodore Friedrichs, *Geschichte Unser Auswanderung Aus Deutschland* [Friedrichs, *Geschichte*] (A 321 page manuscript) 1963; Irma Friedlander, *Sieben Jahre Shanghai, 1939-1946* [Friedlander,*Sieben*] (A 56 page manuscript); Eisfelder, *Exile*. Copies of the first two are found at the Leo Baeck Institute. The Friedrichs manuscript was reproduced courtesy of the author. The third manuscript, in author's possession, was reproduced courtesy of Mr. Eisfelder. The fourth account, is a volume by Hugo Burkhard, *Tanz Mal Jude: Von Dachau bis Shanghai* [Burkhard, *Tanz*] (Nurnberg: Richard Reichenbach KG, 1967).

For the predominance of the Lloyd-Tristino Line, see for example, Michel Speelman, "Report", June 21, 1939, p. 1 (JDCCA); Laura Margolies, "Race Against Time", [Margolies, "Race"] *Survey Graphic*, Vol. XXXIII (March, 1944), p. 11.

The Lloyd-Tristino Line was the main carrier by far, and was followed by the German Hamburg-American Lines, as well as ship companies from Japan, France, Holland and other nationalities.

For a more detailed list of most of the steamship lines and the names of the ships, see DALJEWCIB to HICEM (Paris), April 6, 1940. *Report for the Year* 1939, Section A. *Ship Arrivals* 1939 [HICEM, *Report* 1939]. DALJEWCIB represents The Far Eastern Jewish Central Information Bureau for Emigrants which was associated with HICEM. Located since 1922 in Harbin, Manchuria, until September 1939 when it moved to Shanghai. The title was changed to its cable address of HICEM (HH XV C-3); CFA Minutes, April 23, 1939 [CFA Minutes, April 23, '39], p. 2 (JDCCA); Speelman to Council for German Jewry (London), February 10, 1939 [Speelman to Council, February 10, '39], pp. 1, 4, 5 (JDCCA); S. Ishiguro (the Japanese Consul in Shanghai) to Norddentsche [sic] Lloyd, October 28, 1939 [FO Ishiguro to N.D. Lloyd] (DF).

For the Norddeutsche Lloyd see also Alvin Mars, *A Community by Necessity: the Story of the German Jewish Flight to Shanghai*. (Unpublished History Seminar Paper at Temple University, May 1964. (Based to a great extent on Kranzler, *SJC* and Dicker, *Wanderers*). [Mars, *Community*] p. 6.

4. Wischnitzer, *Migration*, p. 231. Also Walter Silberstein Interview by Alvin Mars, April 27, 1964, [Silberstein Interview]. He paid $540 for his ticket.

5. *Ibid*. Cf. also Ginsbourg, *Shanghai*, p. 17; Burkhard, *Tanz*, p. 145.

6. Silberstein Interview. Concerning the awkward situation of the refugees, see Friedrichs, *Geschichte*, pp. 46-48, 55, 61. Cf. also Eisfelder, *Exile*, pp. 5-6.

7. Some refugees began their route in Bremen, and then went to Genoa, Italy, via the North Sea, Suez—Port Said, Singapore, Colombo, Hong Kong, Manila, and finally Shanghai. Gerechter Interview.

Some went to the Philippines, Australia and even Burma. Among the most active ship lines along this route were the German Nord-Deutsche Lloyd and the Italian Lloyd Tristino. Gerechter Interview. Also, Burkhard, *Tanz*, p. 145. *Chronicle* (January 20, 1939), p. 15. Ginsbourg, *Refugees*, p. 17.

The three Jewish communities were Cairo, Alexandria and Port Said. (London) *Jewish Chronicle*, January 20, 1939, p.15. Cf. also Friedlander, *Sieben*, p. 4; E. H. Nahum to Rabbi Stephen Wise, January 13, 1939, (JDCCA).

8. Burkhard, *Tanz*, p. 146. Also *Chronicle, ibid*. The pocket money usually amounted to a few dollars—enough for a few days' food and lodging in Shanghai (*ibid*.). On Passover, the Committee distributed Matzohs. Burkhard, *Tanz*, p. 146.

9. Silberstein Interview.

10. These refugees reached Italy by train via Switzerland. *Ibid*.

11. *Ibid*. Cf. also Friedlander, *Sieben*, p. 4. For the earning of money aboard ship, see Burkhard, *Tanz*, p. 145.

Many of those who managed to take along such valuable items as tools, instruments, sewing machines or even crates of books—all of which were permitted by the Gestapo—used these later in Shanghai as a source for earning a livelihood. Fischel Interview. Also Felix Gruenberger, "The Jewish Refugees Shanghai" [Gruenberger, "Refugees"], *JSS*, Vol. XII (1950), p. 330.

12. Burkhard, *Tanz*, p. 146. Cf. also Friedrichs, *Geschichte*, pp. 49-57. In Hongkong only those refugees with British visas could go ashore for a few hours. *Ibid*. pp. 60-61. Cf. also Friedlander, *Sieben*, p. 4. A similar problem involved the refugees stopping at Bombay. Kurt Redlich—David Kranzler correspondence, November 10, 1973, p. 4. Dr. Redlich contributed much con-

structive criticism and added many valuable insights to the revised manuscript, through his lengthy and detailed correspondence with the author.

13. The Jewish Community of Kobe (Japan) (Ashkenazim), Committee for Assistance to Refugees [JEWCOM], *Report*: *July* 1940—*November* 1941 [*Kobe Report*] (Kobe: JEWCOM, 1942), p. 9 (DP).

14. Ginsbourg, *Refugees,* p. 17. The reason for using the long, circuitous route via the Cape rather than the short way through the Suez Canal was the fact that the tolls at the Canal had to be paid in pounds sterling rather than in Reichsmark, HICEM, *Situation in Shanghai* (Report) [HICEM, *Situation*], n.d. (ca. June 1939). It was probably written by B. S. Barbash, the early, unofficial representative of HICEM in Shanghai, until the arrival of M. Birman in September 1939. (HH XV C-4.).

15. Gruenberger, "Refugees", p. 330.

16. Burkhard, *Tanz,* p. 145. Also Silberstein Interview.

17. Gruenberger, "Refugees", p. 330. Cf. also   Horst Levin, Interview, August 6, 1974. [Levin Interview].

18. Ginsbourg, *Refugees,* p. 17. See also above, note 6.

19. Wischnitzer, *Migration,* p. 235. Also Ginsbourg, *Refugees,* pp. 24-25. Cf. also Friedrichs, *Geschichte,* p. 121.

For the closing of the Mediterranean and its effect on the refugee route to the Far East, see   Wischnitzer, *Migration,* p. 225. Cf. also "Jews in the Far East" [Jews F.E.], *Jewish Affairs,* Vol. 1 (January 1942), p. 4. The last ship to leave Italy was the S.S. Rodi, which sailed on June 4, 1940, with Polish-Jewish refugees. Wischnitzer, *Migration,* p. 239. By then, the North Atlantic route was already not feasible due to the war. For the plan by Mr. Gabriel to switch to the trans-Siberian land route in May 1940, see Hans Gabriel to HIAS (N.Y.), April 5, 1940 (HH XV C-6A).

Among the arguments for this change, Gabriel notes the lower cost of the trans-Siberian route, particularly in view of the practical monopoly enjoyed by the Italian Line on travel to Shanghai. Such   near monopoly was a big factor for some of the outrageously high prices charged for ship tickets. Moreover, Gabriel noted, the land route provided a safer alternative to the already mine-infested Atlantic. He argued that if Japanese shipping lines were used instead of the Italian, one might be able to lower the exorbitant prices charged by the latter. At the same time, this action would make the Japanese authorities more amenable to the refugees.

Not the least of his points was also the fact that during 1940 one was still able to pay for the trip across Russia in German currency. The matter of currency, however, soon changed during the latter part of 1940.

For the trans-Siberian route of the refugees, see the folders from the files of the Japanese Embassy in Berlin containing applications for transit visas

for Japan and Manchuria. (German Records Microfilmed at Alexandria, Va.,
No. 15. Records of Former German and Japanese Embassies and Consulates,
1890-1945 [GRMA], Roll T-176, Serial 67 [T-176, S-67].

A plan advocated still earlier for this "land route" is found in a report
sent by Meyer Birman to HICEM (Brussels), January 25, [1940], [Birman to
HICEM (Brussels, January 25, 1940)], p. 2. (HH XV C-5). This route was
used only on a very small scale until the closing off of the Mediterranean
Sea route in June 1940.

20. The exact amount depended upon the type of accommodations purchased. (Solomon Tarshansky, Taped Interview, June 11, 1968). [Tarshansky
Interview] Rabbi Tarshansky worked with the JDC in Vilna as well as in
Kobe, Japan. Cf. also Shoshana, In Faier, p. 258; Wischnitzer, Migration,
pp. 233-35; Epstein, "Mir", p. 123.

21. For the trans-Siberian route of the German refugees, see the many
microcopy documents in the GRMA, No. 15, T-176, S-67 series. Cf. also
Friedrichs, Geschichte, pp. 121-139.

22. Kobe Report, p. 1. A separate transit visa would be required for
each of the countries traversed, such as Latvia, Lithuania, U.S.S.R., Manchuria, and Japan. (Fischel Interview). Mrs. Fischel's passport is marked by
the stamp of each of the five "transit" countries. (Passport in author's
possession, courtesy of Mrs. Fischel).

23. Kobe Report, p. 1.

24. For the "landing permits", see below, chapter 8.

25. Kobe Report, p. 1.

26. Sebastian Steiner, "Als Erste Emigrantenfamilie in Hongkew", [Steiner,
"Erste"]Shanghai Jewish Chronicle, (Special Issue) [Chronicle S.I.] March,
1940, p. 27.

27. Julius Weinberger, Annual Report of the Central Management of the
I.C.R. Homes, 1939 [Weinberger, Report], p. 7. I.C.R. probably refers to the
International Committee for Granting Relief to European Refugees, or I.C.
at the Inaugural Meeting, August 8, 1938. YIVO No. 3. Cf. also Lawrence
Kadoorie to S. Frieder, August 2, 1939 (JDDCA).

28. Speelman, Report, June 21, 1939 (JDCCA), p. 2. See Mars, "Community by Necessity", p. 10, citing Cf. North China Herald, May 24, 1939,
p. 327, cited by Mars, "Note", p. 288.

29. See above, note 4.

30. See below, chapter 8.

31. See Jovishoff, "City", pp. 211-212. For the appeal to the American
Jewish Joint Distribution Committee (JDC), see SAJCA to Alkow, August

23, 1937 and the response by the JDC, Hyman to Alkow, September 29, 1937. (JDCCA).
See *Hilfsfond Fuer Deutsche Juden Shanghai: Report* 1934-1938 *[Hilsfond, Report]*, p. 1   YIVO No. 38).

32. *Ibid.*

33. *Ibid.*

34. Speelman to Troper, January 12, 1940 (JDCCA). See also *By laws of the International Committee for Granting Relief to European Refugees [IC Bylaws]*, August 8, 1938, (YIVO No. 38). This document gives the date for the inaugural meeting and a list of the 27 original trustees present at the meeting. Cf. Mars, *Community,* pp. 19-20. Additional, later sponsors included Elly Kadoorie and Sir Victor Sassoon.

After the Speelman-Sassoon split and the reorganization of the IC, its full name was changed to the International Committee for the Organization of European Immigrants in China. See especially Sassoon Memo to CFA, December 20, 1939 (JDCCA) in which Sir Victor Sassoon gives his analysis of the reorganization of the old IC and the guidelines for the functions to be carried out by the new IC as distinct from the work involving the CFA.

See also M. C. Troper to JDC (N.Y.), February 15, 1940 (JDCCA) [Troper, JDC (N.Y.), February 15, 1940], p. 1.

35. A receipt for a donation to the IC on May 22, 1940, shows Komor retaining his official title of "Honorary Secretary". YIVO No. 60.

A note from the IC dated August 7, 1942, bears the signature of Robert Peritz for the IC. Paul Komor was arrested in February 1942 by the Japanese, who soon released him, but forced him out of the IC. He was replaced by Robert Peritz. Margolies, *Report,* 1941-43, p. 12. Paul Komor had lived in Shanghai since 1898, and took part in the relief work for Central Europeans in Shanghai in 1907. See Paul Komor. *"Meine Arbeit fuer die Immigration"* [Komor, "Immigration"], *Chronicle (S.I.),* p. 15. Komor was technically the Honorary Secretary and Treasurer of the IC while Eduard Kann, another Hungarian, converted Jew, was its first chairman for a brief period. YIVO No. 60, November 10, 1938. Cf. also Kann, "The Problem of the European Refugees in Shanghai" (a talk before the members of the Shanghai Rotary Club held on August 24, 1939, at the Cathay Hotel) [Kann, "Refugees"], p. 5. On the basis of this clipped article, the author was unable to ascertain the title of the periodical from which it is derived. (JDCCA).

For Kann's religious persuasion, see Birman, Cable Confirmation, September 16, 1939. (HH XV C-4). For Komor's Jewish background, see Birman, HICEM, *Report,* January 16, 1940, p. 5. (HH XV C-6).

36. Ernst Pollak, "Menschen die uns Helfen", *SJ Chronicle (SI)* [Pollak, "Menschen"] p. 6. Cf. also Komor, "Immigration".

37. Abraham Interview. He worketd his father, R. D. Abraham, and his grandfather, D. E. J. Abraham, on the various committees of the CFA,

which helped house the refugees. This committee at first provided room and board at the rate of about (Sh) $45 per person per month. Also Tibor Kunfi, *"Der Existenzkampf der Refugee Aerzte"* [Kunfi, "Aerzte"], *Chronicle (S.I.)*, p. 26.

38. Speelman to Council, February 10, 1939, p.2. (JDCCA).

39. Ginsbourg, *Refugees*, p. 19. At that time the ratio of the Shanghai dollar to the American was approximately 6½ to 1. As prices rose, the ratio jumped at various intervals at a reasonably steady rate, e.g. to 10 to 1, 15 to 1, 18½ to 1 (by mid-1940) until the period near the end of the war in the Pacific when the inflation sky-rocketed to unmanageable proportions. See also below, chapter 9.

During 1938, a low-salaried office clerk (many White Russians were in this category) earned (Sh) $70 a month. George Leonof, "Jewish Refugees Here Facing Lean Future" *China Press*, April 14, 1939, [Leonof, "Lean"] pp. 1, 3. For the tax on the kosher fowl, see letter by Nissim, 1939, (YIVO No. 9).

40. Jovishoff, "City", p. 211.

41. Among these trustees were R. D. Abraham and I. E. Toeg. From the end of 1941 until mid-1944 it served as the Mirrer Yeshiva's study hall (*Beit Midrash*). For its use as an early refugee center, see Speelman to Council, February 10, 1939, p. 1; Ing M. Rosenberg, "Die Embankment-Kueche" [Rosenberg, "Embankment"]; Weinberger, *Report*, p. 4.

For the Betar activities see Pana Samsanovich, "Up to 1945 History of Shanghai Betar", *Betar in China 1929-1949*. [Shanghai, *Betar*], p. 87. Also Louis Greenberg, Interview, September 16, 1968.

42. Kann, "Refugees", p. 15. Cf. also Speelman, *Report*, June 21, 1939, p. 2; also Weinberger, *Report*, 1939, p. 4. Ginsbourg, *Refugees*, p. 19. Cf. also Rosenberg, "Embankment"; Abraham Interview; Kann, "Refugees", p. 15; Ginsbourg, *Refugees*, p. 19; Speelman to Council, February 10, 1939, p. 1; Speelman to Troper, December 14, 1939, p. 1; "Die Zentralheimleitung erstatetet ihren Taetikeitsbericht" ["Zentralheimleitung"], *S.J. Chronicle* (S.I.), p. 9.

For a personal experience, see Friedlander, *Sieben*, p. 7. Cf. also Eisfelder, *Exile*, pp. 16-17, re Embankment Building pool.

43. *CFA* to *JDC*, October 28, 1938, especially pp. 2, 5. In addition to the IC and *Hilfsfond*, the meeting was attended by representatives of the following organizations and institutions: The Shanghai Jewish Communal Association (Sephardi); The Shanghai Ashkenazi Jewish Communal Association; The Shanghai Home for Aged Jews and The Shanghai Jewish Women's Benevolent Society, (Ashkenazi); The Shanghai Jewish School; The Shanghai Lodge for Bnei Brith, Sephardi and Ashkenazi); The Ohel Rachel Synagogue (Sephardi); The Oihel Moishe Synagogue (Ashkenazi); The International Committee for Granting Relief to European Refugees; The Hilfsfond.

44. For example of the lack of cooperation between the two Jewish groups, see Jacob Alkow to Hyman, August 19, 1937 (JDCCA). Also Abraham Interview. Cf. also Fritz Faufmann, "The Experiences of the Shanghai Jewish Community Under the Japanese in World War II" [Kaufmann, "Experiences"], from a manuscript of a speech by Fritz Kaufmann on February 12, 1963, before the Shanghai Tiffin Club, New York, pp. 1, 4.

45. CFA to JDC, October 28, 1938. This is the first correspondence I was able to discover of the newly-founded CFA.

46. CFA is the abbreviation I will utilize throughout this paper. For an example of its use, see Margolies to Pilpel, August 11, 1941, p. 3 (JDCCA). Though it was also, at times, referred to in another abbreviated form as the COMAR Committee, it is too readily confused with the Komor Committee or IC to warrant its use.

The author has been unable to ascertain for certain the real reason for the establishment of the CFA in competition with the already existing IC. A telephone talk with Paul Komor (November 20, 1969) failed to solve this problem. Mr. Komor was of the opinion that the CFA was closer to the more Orthodox Jews, such as D. E. J. Abraham. This is somewhat satisfactory in view of the fact that the IC from the outset included and even encouraged membership from Shanghai's non-Jewish population as well as Jews. Moreover as will be noted later, the IC maintained a separate Arbitration Board, for the non-Jewish refugees, as late as 1942. However, there were very few Orthodox individuals on the CFA other than Abraham.

Heinz Ganther thinks that the IC concerned itself more with the Austrian refugees, especially at the beginning—Komor himself was Austrian—while the CFA continued the work of the Hilfsfond, which took care of German refugees since 1934. *Drei Jahre Immigration* (Shanghai: Modern Times Publishing House, 1942) [Ganther, *Drei Jahre*].

47. See H. Gensburger to J. C. Hyman, October 28, 1938. For example of the term "Speelman Committee", see Shoshana, *In Faier*, p. 289. It was also sometimes referred to simply as the "Committee". See Speelman to Troper, January 12, 1940, p. 1.

As Speelman readily admits, in practice the IC under P. Komor retained its identity as a distinct organization, which was taken over completely by Sir Victor Sassoon sometime at the end of 1939. *Ibid.*, p. 2. Cf. also Sassoon, *Memo*, December 20, 1939, (JDCCA).

48. *Ibid.*, p. 3.

49. Speelman to Troper, December 14, 1939, pp. 2-3.

50. The original members of the CFA included Joseph Hollzer, Michel Speelman, Ellis Hayim, David E. J. Abraham. After some shifting and resignations, the following remained on the Executive Board: Ellis Hayim, Chairman; Michel Speelman and Reuben D. Abraham.

The chairmanship alternated between Hayim and Speelman. In practice, however, Speelman was the more active administrator while Hayim remained the more dominant voice. See Margolies to Pilpel, August 11, 1941 (JDCCA).

51. Speelman to Troper, December 14, 1939, pp. 2-3.

52. *Ibid.* Cf. also Margolies to Pilpel, August 11, 1941, p. 3.

53. *Ibid.* Laura Margolies in this letter gives her usually frank, incisive and biased sketches of the leading personalities, including Professor Reiss. For some of the backgrounl, Cf. also Frederick Reiss, "Die Aerztliche Fuersorge Der Emigration", *S.J. Chronicle (S.I.)*, pp. 11-13.
For the resignations of the committees including the German-Jewish doctors, see Margolies to Pilpel, August 11, 1941, p. 1. Also Speelman, *Report,* June 21, 1939, Annex I, p. 1 (JDCCA).

54. See below, chapter 10.

55. See below, chapter 14. Sir Elly Kadoorie and his two sons, Lawrence and Horace, who were among the wealthiest Sephardi Jews in Shanghai, made education their specialty. They established schools and special educational institutions in all parts of the Far and Near East, including Israel. See Margolies to Pilpel, August 11, 1941, p. 4.
Reverend Mendel Brown was the principal of the Shanghai Jewish School and the unofficial Rabbi of the Sephardi community. He was very active in all the Jewish communal affairs. Laura Margolies, whose critical characterizations spare very few personalities active in the relief activities, has only the kindest words for Reverend Brown. Margolies to Pilpel, July 17, 1941, p. 2 (JDCCA).

56. Speelman claims that by December of 1939, this employment agency located jobs for about 935 individuals, excluding families. Speelman to Troper, December 14, 1939, p. 5. Both the IC and the CFA had employment agencies which were of some help. "Ein Jahr Internationales Komitee" ["1 Year IC"], *Chronicle (S.I.)*, pp. 15-16.

57. This was particularly so after Sir Victor broke with the CFA and took over the IC, with Paul Komor remaining in charge.
For the Speelman-Sassoon controversy and split of the IC from the CFA, see the (JDCCA) for December 1939—January 1940. See especially the following documents: Sassoon, *Memo,* December 20, 1939; Speelman to Troper, January 12, 1940; Sassoon to Speelman, January 15, 1940; Speelman to Troper, January 17, 1940; Joint (Paris) to Joint (N.Y.), February 15, 1940; Troper to Speelman, February 15, 1940; Margolies to Pilpel, August 11, 1942, p. 2; Margolies to Pilpel, November 5, 1941, p. 1; Kann, "Refugees", p. 39.

58. For the problems of extraterritoriality and the Chinese legal system, see Johnstone, *Shanghai,* pp. 159-168. See also above, chapter 2; Eisfelder, *Exile,* pp. 3-4.

59. See especially Speelman to Troper, December 14, 1939, p. 2.

60. When thousands of refugees, whose German passports were not renewed, remained stateless even prior to the German removal of citizenship in 1941, the IC provided them with IC Passes. These were recognized by the Australian government for immigration purposes and the Japanese authorities for those few who received permission to travel further into Japanese occupied China. See "1 Year IC", p. 16; Friedrichs, *Geschichte*, p. 64.

See Speelman, *Report*, June 21, 1939, Annex I, June 22, 1939, p. 1, re registration for the German Consulate, and the conflict this produced among refugees. See also Ginsbourg, *Refugees*, p. 22.

61. "One Year IC", p. 16.

62. *Ibid.* Also Kann, "Refugees", p. 32; Ginsbourg, *Refugees*, p. 22.

63. Ginsbourg, *Refugees*, p. 22 Cf. Kann, "Refugees", p. 32.

64. Troper to JDC, July 12, 1939, p. 1. See also below, note 79.

65. Troper to Joint (N.Y.), July 12, 1939, p. 1. Also Speelman, *Report*, December 14, 1939, p. 6; Speelman to Council for German Jewry, February 10, 1939, p. 5. *American Jewish Yearbook*, Vol. 41 (5700-1939), p. 417. Cf. Sassoon's personal contribution to the "British War Fund" in Shanghai of £25,000. *Ibid.*

The Rehabilitation Fund was started by E. Hayim, M. Speelman and E. Kadoorie. *Ibid.* Speelman to Troper, December 14, 1939, p. 6; Kann, Problem of European Refugees, pp. 38-39.

66. For the repayment by the refugees, see CFA Minutes, February 6, 1940, p. 1. For the "condition", see Eisfelder, *Exile*, p. 18.

67. See Speelman, *Report*, December 14, 1939, p. 6; also Heinz Ganther, "Sieben Jahre Immigration" [Ganther, "Seven Years"], *The Shanghai Herald* (German Language Supplement), (Special Edition, April 1946) [*Herald* (*S.E.*)], p. 2.

The 1,300 probably includes those enterprises that never lasted very long, since other reliable statistics point to lower figures, e.g., Friendlander on p. 26 quotes 400 households.

68. For the number of failures, see Ginsbourg, *Shanghai: City of Refuge*, p. 17. Also Ganther, "Seven Years", p. 2.

69. Ganther, "Seven Years", p. 2. Cf. also Eisfelder, *Exile*, p. 18.

70. "Twenty-nine Jahre HIAS (HICEM) in Fernen Osten" ["Twenty-nine Years HIAS"], p.

71. For the activities of HIAS-HICEM in Shanghai, see the valuable HIAS-HICEM Files at the YIVO, Section XV [HH XV]. These documents were given to YIVO by Meyer Birman who managed the HICEM office in the

Far East for about 30 years. This collection was put at the author's disposal courtesy of its cataloger, Mr. Zosa Szajkowski.

See also the (JDCCA) in whose collection one occasionally finds duplicates of those in the HH XX files. In addition, the JDCCA files often shed much light on HICEM personalities and activities in Shanghai. See, for example, Margolies to Pilpel, August 11, 1941, p. 2; and July 29, 1941, pp. 2-3.

A few summary articles about HICEM activities may be found in the following: "Der Wirkungskreis der HICEM in Shanghai" ["HICEM"], *S.J. Chronicle (S.I.)*, p. 23; "Twenty-nine Years HIAS", *Shanghai Herald* (German Language Supplement, April 1946, Special Edition) [*Herald (S.E.)*], "Thirty Years in the Far East" ["Thirty Years F.E."], *Almanac.*

72. Herbert Katzki, *Memo,* June 6, 1939 (JDCCA). Cf. also Birman, *Report,* January 16, 1940, p. 1. Speelman, *Rreport,* June 21, 1939, p. 3. The HICEM checks of (U.S.) $50-150 sent along with those refugees leaving the concentration camps for Shanghai are not to be confused with the (U.S.) $400 sent by HICEM for the refugees to the shipping companies as "Guarantee Money" after the August 1939 restrictions.

73. Sir Victor Sassoon to Paul Berwald [sic], April 5, 1939 (JDCCA).

The purchasing power of (U.S.) $50 at that time in Shanghai can be gauged from the fact that when a representative of the Nanking Chinese government seriously discussed possible Jewish mass migration to the South-western section of China, he accepted the (U.S.) $50 as sufficient guarantee for a small family for several months. See James Bernstein to HIAS (U.S.) re Jewish Immigration to China, April 27, 1939 (HH XV C-4).

74. "Twenty-nine Years HIAS".

75. See copy of article in the *S.J. Chronicle,* October 29, 1939 (n.p.) (HH XV C-4). Also Birman to HIAS (U.S.), September 21, 1939; Birman to HICEM (Belgium), January 15, 1940 (HH XV C-4).

76. Ibid. Cf. also Eduard Kann, "Europaeische Emigration nach China", *S.J. Chronicle (S.I.),* April, 1940, [Kann, "EE"], p. 7; Kann, "The problem of the European Refugees in Shanghai", (unidentified article from a Shanghai newspaper) August 24, 1939, [Kann, "Refugees"], pp. 15-16, (JDCCA).

77. See, for example, Birman to HICEM (Belgium), January 25, 1940, where Birman complains that the CFA employees of the Emigration Department hinder his work despite a disclaimer by the Chairman, Ellis Hayim. Moreover, he complained that despite his transfer to Shanghai for the past three months, the various HICEM organizations in Europe still sent their correspondence to Barbash, who referred them to him, or worse, to the CFA.

See also Margolies to Pilpel, September 10, 1941, p. 2; August 11, 1941, p. 2; CFA Minutes, February 6, 1940, p. 6 (JDCCA).

78. Margolies to Pilpel, August 11, 1941, p. 2; and July 2, 1941, p. 1.

79. For the background of this organization, see Norman Bentwich, *They Found Refuge: An Account of British Jewry's Work for Victims of Nazi Oppression* (London: Cresset Press, 1956), chapter III. Cf. also CFA Minutes April 23, 1939; Troper to *JDC*, July 12, 1939, p. 1; Speelman *Report*, June 21, 1939. See especially, James Bernstein [of HICEM, Paris] to HIAS of America, August 18, 1939, (JDCCA).

80. For a general history of the JDC, see the first of a projected two volume work by Yehuda Bauer, *My Brother's Keeper: A History of the American Jewish Joint Distribution Committee* 1929-1939 [Bauer, *JDC*] (Philadelphia Jewish Publication Society, 1974). Cf. for example pp. 290-292. For some critical analyses, see Zosa Szajkowski, "Private and Organized American Jewish Overseas Relief and Immigration", *American Jewish Historical Quarterly* Vol. 57, No. 1 (September, 1967), pp. 52-106 and *ibid*, No. 2 (December, 1967), pp. 191-253.

81. Bauer, *JDC*, p. 8. For the Shanghai parallel, see below, chapter 16.

82. Bauer, *JDC*, chapter 2. For the Shanghai situation, see below, chapters 3-5.

THE TRANSFORMATION OF HONGKEW

They started delicatessen stores and opened sidewalk
cafes. Chusan Road, once a typical Chinese lane, in
1941 looked like a little street in Vienna.

(Laura Margolies. *"Race Against Time"*)

What high hopes and keen anticipation the skyline of
Shanghai must have aroused in each successive shipload of
refugees! The impressive outline of tall buildings alongside the
Bund (the harbor highway) could be seen from shipboard as
they docked after the pleasant but uneventful four-week
voyage.[1] Now they were to meet the challenge of a new life.
And the words of the delegation from the relief committee,
which greeted them on board, augmented this sense of challenge and innovation: "Now you are no longer Germans,
Austrians, Czechs or Rumanians, now you are only Jews. The
Jews of the whole world have prepared a home for you."[2] Many
of the arrivals were soon to discover that the refugee camps or
Heime, to which many of them were guided, and in which they
were destined to spend up to ten years, meant something quite
different in Shanghai than it had in better times in their
Fatherland.[3]

113

The customs and medical formalities were taken care of after an interminable wait to collect baggage from among the 6,000 pieces aboard a typical ship's load. The refugees, unsuitably dressed, as they were unprepared for the humid weather, walked off the ship bathed in sweat. They were at once besieged by crowds of coolies eager to earn a few pennies by transporting their baggage.[4] Those lucky immigrants whose friends or relatives had prepared a room for them in advance went there directly, while the less fortunate were taken to the refugee reception center at the Embankment Building, or its later replacement, the Ward Road *Heim*.[5]

HONGKEW

Until the restrictions on immigration to Shanghai were imposed in August of 1939, there was no legal barrier to the settling of refugees in any of the foreign sectors of Shanghai, such as the French Concession, the International Settlement, and Hongkew, the Japanese-controlled former part of the Settlement, north of the Soochow Creek.[6] These sections were called the "foreign" concessions, because as we know, the vast majority of the over four million residents of Shanghai were Chinese rather than foreigners.[7] During the period 1937 to 1941 the foreign population (apart of course, from the refugees) had not increased to more than about 100,000, including the Japanese.[8] The Western facade belied the Chinese character of most of even the foreign sectors.[9]

Of the three above-mentioned sections, the French Concession (or Frenchtown, as it was called) was the residential and most beautiful sector. Its planned, broad, tree-lined avenues resembled the Crown Heights section of Brooklyn.[10] Although there were some commercial areas downtown, the French Concession contained few of the large industrial complexes or factories that were situated in Hongkew or even in the International Settlement.[11]

Most of the better class among the Russians, both Jews and non-Jews, as well as the Sephardim, resided in Frenchtown, especially after the 1937 hostilities. The commercial areas had a Russian flavor, since all the shops, even the Chinese-owned bore signs in that language. Among the most prominent thoroughfares was the Avenue Joffre, which traversed the Concession and was lined with the finest shops.[12]

Those refugees able to afford the higher rents moved to this Concession, where they enjoyed both the greater comfort and the proximity to the commercial advantageous, "proper" connections.[13] Until they were forced out by the edict establishing the ghetto in May 1943, about 4,000 out of the approximately 17,000 refugees managed to live in the Concession.[14] They were, however, rarely able to afford anything beyond a single room. Only the wealthy, even among the older settlers, rented apartments of five to six rooms.[15]

The International Settlement, or at least that part controlled by the Shanghai Municipal Council, consisted of both large industrial and commercial sections and residential areas.[10] Approximately 1,500 refugees were able to find homes in this quarter of Shanghai.[17]

It was, however, in Hongkew, the third of the foreign sectors, that the majority of refugees made their homes during the seven to fifteen years of their stay. Hongkew, strictly speaking, was only one of the three parts of the Japanese-occupied sector of the International Settlement, the others being Wayside and Yangtzepoo, but it was the term applied by the refugees and even Shanghailanders to the whole sector north of Soochow Creek.[18]

A formerly heavily industrialized area, Hongkew or little Tokyo as it was also called, had suffered from some of

the heaviest fighting, raids, and after effects of the Chinese
scorched-earth policy, which left stretches in complete or
partial ruins.[19] It was primarily inhabited by the lower-class
Chinese laborers, the poorest elements among the Russians,
Jews and non-Jews, and Japanese. Many of the latter had come
in the wake of the military occupation that followed the 1937
hostilities.[20]

At best, Hongkew, even after much of it had been
rebuilt, could only be described as ugly and depressing; only
one street, Broadway, was lit up at night.[21] Yet its very limita-
tions were a boon to the majority of the refugees, who could
not afford housing in the other foreign sections.[22] Rents in
Hongkew were lower by as much as 75 per cent.[23] Hongkew's
market prices, too, were cheaper than in the Settlement or the
Concession, in part due to the Japanese policy of encouraging
settlement in Hongkew, according to one contemporary
journalist. The Japanese viewed the International Settlement as
an alien enclave. This meant that employees living in Hongkew
but working in the Settlement in late-evening-hour establishments, such as night clubs or restaurants, had to meet the 2 a.m.
curfew established by the Japanese authorities at all the bridges
linking Hongkew with the Settlement. For example, at the
Garden Bridge, which was used most frequently to enter Hongkew, the Japanese sentries required all entering Chinese to bow
low and to refrain from smoking in their presence. Rifle blows
and kicks awaited those who responded too slowly; but the
Chinese usually won out by smiling back at their tormentors.

But whatever the disadvantages, Hongkew satisfied the
two major needs of the refugees, low rents and cheap food. To
give an illustration: One could enjoy an excellent six-course
"tiffin" (lunch) at a fashionable restaurant in the Settlement
for one Chinese dollar, or (US) 16c. In Hongkew one could

eat "Russian style" for considerably less, while at home it was still cheaper.[24]

The remarkable transformation, within two and a half years, of whole streets in Hongkew into European-style avenues, which reflected the refugee optimism, has been noted by several observers.[25] Such streets as Tongshan, Kungpin, Seward and Wayside Roads, actually most of the Wayside district of Hongkew, was completely rebuilt, while a revitalized Chusan Road became the commercial hub of "Little Vienna."[26] In fact, a minor economic boom was created through the initiative of some enterprising refugees, who helped rebuild Hongkew's ruins out of its own rubble.[27] From the ruins there emerged new but simple houses, in European style, with indoor plumbing and bathrooms. One shop after another opened up, especially restaurants, open-air cafés, provision stores, snack bars and bars, which proliferated and stood side by side where there was previously but a single coffeehouse. Due to the Chinese disdain for milk or cheese, such products were not readily available to the Westerners except at high prices. The refugees opened up milk bars where one could purchase this luxury, though a milk shake was beyond the means of most of the refugee patrons, as were such delicacies as chocolate and ice cream.

There were also numerous, excellent nightclubs. The night life in which these clubs and bars played a role, catered to nationals of all varieties, some, such as the White Horse Inn and the Roof Garden, boasting top musical and comedy entertainment. The latter even featured a Miss Shanghai contest. The refugee girls who serviced the nightclubs were the best-dressed women in Shanghai. They were also known to be generous to worthy causes.[28]

Many non-Jews, including Chinese, Japanese and Europeans, frequented the refugee stores and establishments for items and atmosphere previously unobtainable in Shanghai.[29]

On the other hand, the refugees often patronized Chinese and Japanese stores. Within a year or two, many of its former Chinese inhabitants returned, the electric trolley resumed full service to the rest of Shanghai, and sections of Hongkew acquired a more respectable appearance despite areas still desolate and grim.[30]

HOUSING, LANE SYSTEM

The most common kind of housing utilized by the refugees in Hongkew outside the *Heime* was the lane system, which predominated in most of Shanghai. It is most fully described by Manfred Rosenfeld, one of the most astute contemporary chroniclers of refugee life in Shanghai.[31] The term "lane system" applies to the peculiar street and housing arrangement prevalent in Hongkew and in much of other sectors of Shanghai. It consisted of a long, wide, main street with many dark, narrow lanes or alleys extending from both sides and lined with fairly solidly-built, single, or at the most double-storied houses next to each other. They were low because they were built on land which was formerly swampy rice paddies, unable to take the weight of taller buildings.[32] At night, these lanes were closed by gates and sometimes guarded by one or two Sikhs, those excellent tall East Indian guards, members of the Shanghai Municipal police force. These Sikhs were found primarily in the Settlement rather than Hongkew, and were known to intimidate the Chinese.[33] The entire scene had a distinctly medieval flavor.[34]

The ground floor of these lane houses, which ranged from ten to forty feet long and eleven to twelve feet wide, usually contained several rooms. One side, facing an alley or lane, might have a glass-covered entrance or foyer, and a kitchen with one side facing a tiny courtyard, where much of the cooking was done. On the other side of the kitchen was the toilet, the only one for the building, which contained the "tub," for the "night soil," or when newly rebuilt, and more expensive, a modern water closet and sink.

Further back would usually be the stairway up, which on the in-between level usually had a tiny meter room, which frequently served as "home" for a single refugee occupant. Behind the stairway towards the back was usually a large room. The outside of this room facing the other lane usually consisted of a larger courtyard with a gate to the lane, whose "fences" to the neighboring house were stone walls. This courtyard often contained a large bamboo stick upon which hung the family laundry.[35]

Though originally meant to house a single family, the frugal, enterprising Chinese found themselves able to earn extra money by renting out each of these rooms to an entire family.[36] These "extra" rooms were often nothing more than partitioned-off backs of former larger rooms by Japanese-style lattice work, sliding panels. Such rooms would often be without windows. It was difficult to fit the large, heavy European furniture into the small, narrow lane houses. Occasionally a piece had to be lowered through a skylight, or a room enlarged to accommodate it.[37]

The main tenant usually rented from a landlord who after some alteration, produced what looked like a cubbyhole for each of the families.[38] The refugees soon caught on to this means of renting and imitated it.[39] In this manner, refugees with a little money were able to become independent entrepreneurs, by purchasing and rebuilding the lane housing.[40] One such refugee, for example, was able to leave the *Heime* and refurnish two lane houses with the (US) $200 sent to him by relatives in the United States.[41]

Most lane houses were owned by English and American companies, though Chinese and Japanese too numbered among the proprietors.[42] These usually constituted the principal landlords, who in turn leased them to the above-mentioned individual entrepreneurs. The larger companies were most happy to welcome the refugees, who rebuilt much of the war-torn property and profits were suddenly derived from previously inactive real estate.[43]

During 1939 and 1940, rooms in such lane houses rented anywhere from (Sh) $10 to (Sh) $150 per month, depending upon whether they had indoor plumbing, or a bath and a toilet. Two or three-room apartments cost several hundred Shanghai dollars per month.[44] The more affluent refugees, and the professionals who usually rented the larger apartments ran into lots of difficulties and red tape when they tried to have phones installed.[45] The majority of these apartments had running water but very few had toilets. Their place was taken by the above-mentioned tubs, which were emptied every morning by a "tub man," who earned his livelihood by selling this "night soil," a product highly valued by the Chinese as fertilizer.[46]

With the increasing inflation during the next few years, prices for rooms rose, though not at the same rate as other items.[47] Since these houses were built along narrow side lanes, the rooms were generally dark, airless and humid. Their flimsy partitions were hardly more effective than curtains in preserving the privacy for the families residing there. Anything above a whisper could be heard which often caused psychological strain, as well as marital strife. It is not surprising that such conditions often brought out the worst in people. Petty thievery and loose moral behavior were not uncommon among the lane dwellers. Most problems involving theft, however, were traceable to the numerous poor Chinese in the sector, who were very skillful in sneaking out objects right under an unsuspecting European nose. A story is told by one refugee who had his hat

"swiped" from his head on an open streetcar, and found himself buying it back from the thief a few blocks away. This
incident was not an isolated case, as several reports testify.[48]

Another, more insidious racket practiced on the
unsuspecting lane residents was known as the "rice swindle."
This episode, as recalled by one refugee, went as follows:

> . . . One day, a young Chinese man knocked at our
> door in Kungping Road, and told aunt Bertha in broken
> English that he had a bag of rice for her. She made it
> clear, that she had not ordered any nor wanted any, but
> this was countered by him, that 'the other man' in the
> house had ordered it and paid for it and all he wanted to
> do was to give it to her. So she took the bag, assuming that
> either my father or one of the other people we were
> sharing the house with, had bought it. A few minutes later,
> the man came back, saying: 'So sorry, mistake, was for
> man next door' and took the bag of rice away again. Half
> and hour or so later, there is a great commotion outside,
> a screaming Chinese child in the centre of a milling
> multitude and finally the arrival of a policeman. There is
> some difficulty in getting each others message across but
> aunt Bertha is taken to the police station, where she is told,
> that the young boy had arrived from the country with a
> bag of rice to be sold and had been approached by her
> (aunt Bertha's) servant, who had told the boy that his
> mistress wanted to buy the rice and after the young boy
> had seen the 'servant' hand over the bag to aunt Bertha,
> the 'servant' had told him to wait a few minutes, his
> mistress would soon hand over the money. Her assurance,
> that she had no servants, nor the bag of rice, fell on deaf
> ears. There were several 'witnesses' who would swear that
> they had seen her taking the bag from the young man.

Any protestation, that the gentleman had been back shortly afterwards to retrieve the rice, were countered with: 'Well, the young boy has lost his bag of rice and you had better pay for it, or we'll have to lock you up until the matter can be resolved by a court.' And what that meant, everyone knew only too well. So we, on behalf of aunt Bertha had to pay up, but this did not stop the team from repeating the same performance, with the same cast and the same bag—which heaven knows, might only have contained sand—day after day. Many warnings were published, but they always managed to find new and ignorant suckers.[49]

Although Hongkew was drab, one could still enjoy a few of the simple amenities of life. During the hot summer months, for example, one could enjoy the shade of several lovely "Public Parks" for a small entrance fee. A walk across the race-course, in the middle of the Settlement, or the lovely Jessfield Park, with its small zoo, were popular places. Less so, was the largest, but not as beautiful, Hongkew Gardens, located in the northwest corner of Hongkew, some distance from the Wayside area. Other than distance, the fact that the imposing headquarters of the Imperial Japanese armed forces were located alongside the park's entrance, must have kept down the number of visitors.

A much more popular spot was the Public Garden below the Garden Bridge at the junction of the Soochow Creek and Whangpoo River. There one could enjoy the cool breeze while being entertained by the passing busy river traffic.[50]

NOTES : LITTLE VIENNA

1. See above, Chapter 3. Cf. also, Malkah Raymist, "The Shanghai Myth" [Raymist, "Shanghai Myth"], *American Hebrew* (September 29, 1939), p. 5. Cf. also Eisfelder, *Exile*, pp. 6-7.

2. For the delegations greeting the incoming vessels, see Kann, "EE". Also, *Chronicle* (March 17, 1939), pp. 36, 41 (cited by Mars, *Necessity*, p. 23); Erich Peckel Correspondence from Shanghai, June 1, 1939 [Peckel Correspondence] (JDCCA).

Sometimes no delegation was available to greet the disappointed incoming refugees, who then felt totally neglected. This problem, however, was due primarily to the fact that not all vessels and/or ship lines notified the Committee in advance of their arrival. The Lloyd-Tristine Line was the only company that was always prompt in this manner. Cf. Herbert Katzki, *Memo*, June 6, 1939 (JDCCA).

The quotation is taken from an article in the *Berliner Illustrierte Zeitung*, No. 10 (June 15, 1940), pp. 9-12 (JDCCA). Though someone at the JDC assumed this article to be a typical piece of Nazi propaganda, as the scrawling across the page indicates, the author found it to be quite an accurate, though only partial, picture of the refugee conditions in Shanghai. The picture painted is perhaps too bleak for the taste of the JDC. However, all the written reports sent to its offices by the CFA in Shanghai, and the oral reports submitted by Sir Victor Sassoon and Michel Speelman to the JDC, concur in the portrait drawn by the *Berliner Illustrierte*.

3. Ganther, "Seven Years", p. 3. See also below, chapter 5.

4. When the refugees lacked even the little money required for customs, they had to leave their baggage until they could redeem it later on. See Peckel correspondence. The customs inspection, which took hours for clearance but cost very little, was the only formality undergone by the arrivals until the restrictions of August 1939. After that date, a member of the Shanghai Municipal Police would always board with the Committee's delegation to make certain that the new regulations were fully complied with and that the refugees were properly registered. See also A Hertzberg, "Suggested Mode of Procedure for Landing Permits and Landing of Immigrants in Shanghai" [Hertzberg, "Procedure"], February 12, 1940, p. 2 (JDCCA); Kann, "EE"; Raymist, "Shanghai Myth", p. 5.

It was not even necessary to have one's passport visaed by the Chinese consulates abroad, because no inspection of the immigrants of any nation took place since the outbreak of the 1937 hostilities. See Kann, "Refugees", p. 1. Cf. also Speelman, *Report*, June 21, 1939, p. 1; Jovishoff, "City", p. 213; Eleanor Hinder, "Labour", p. 11.

124   JAPANESE, NAZIS & JEWS

For the "coolie longshoremen", see Shoshana, *In Faier*, p. 282. Also Silberstein Ineterview; Fischel Interview; Friedrichs, *Geschichte*, p. 61.

Cheaper Chinese labor replaced the refugees who previously earned a livelihood working for some 40 small Jewish firms by mid-1939. Dr. Kurt Marx, the paid director of the CFA at the time, was responsible for this change.

For one individual's experience on arriving in Hongkew, see Eisfelder, *Exile*, pp. 6-8.

5. Shoshana, *In Faier*, p. 282. Also Raymist, "Shanghai Myth", p. 5; Friedrichs, *Geschichte*, p. 62. The Embankment Building was used as a reception and CFA office building as well as a dormitory for up to 200-300 people. See the "Shanghai Municipal Council Report", March 18, 1939, p. 4 [SMC, *Report*] (JDCCA).

6. See below, Chapter 8 for the restrictions.

7. See above, Chapter 3. Cf. also Eisfelder, *Exile*, pp. 25-26.

8. See above, Chapter 3, especially, Murphy, *Shanghai*, p. 18.

For the rapid increase of Japanese "civilians" in Hongkew during 1940-1941, see also Hans H. Hinzelmann, *O China: Land Auf Alten Wegen* [Hinzelmann, "O China"] (Braunschweig: I. M. Schlesser Verlag, 1948), p. 73. Copy of this volume reproduced courtesy of Dr. R. Loewenthal.

9. Murphy, *Shanghai*, pp. 18-19. See also Raymist, "Shanghai Myth", p. 5; Jovishoff, "City", p. 215; Burkhard, *Tanz*, p. 147; Eisfelder, *Exile*, pp. 25-26.

10. Abraham, Interview.

11. Burkhard, *Tanz*, p. 147; also Abraham Interview.

12. Simpson, *Refugee*, p. 153; also Burkhard, *Tanz*, p. 147; Miller, *Paradise*, pp. 27-36.

13. Ganther, "Seven Years", p. 3. He voices the refugees' complaint about having to live in Hongkew, an ugly, poor section, which also isolated them from the rest of the Jews, and potential connections for business. Ganther and others felt that this isolation was a deliberate attempt by the Shanghai Jewish residents to keep the refugees "at a distance".

See also Manfred Rosenfeld's, incomplete three-part typewritten manuscript about the Jewish community in Shanghai. [Rosenfeld, *History, III*], p. 57; Gruenberger, "Refugees", p. 333.

14. F.O. S-9460-3-1688, January 19, 1940, lists the following breakdown for the refugee population and its places of residence: 11,000 in the Japanese-occupied area (Hongkew); 1,500 in the British Concession (International Settlement); 4,000 in the French Concession. Cited by Dicker, *Wanderers*, p. 101.

15. Rosenfeld, *History, III*, p. 4. Many of the later, East European arrivals lived in the French Concession, partly because of their greater affinity to the Russian Jews. Margulies Interview. Many refugees tried to live in the Con-

cession as long as their money lasted and moved to Hongkew only as a last resort. Shoshana, *In Faier*, pp. 288-289.

16. Abraham Interview. Also Shoshana, *In Faier*, p. 288.

17. F.O. S-9460-3-1688, January 19, 1940. Cf. also Rosenfeld, *History, III*, p. 4; Eisfelder, *Exile*, p. 13.

18. Jovishoff, "City", p. 213. Also Abraham Interview.
Even some Shanghailanders applied the term "Hongkew" in this loose manner. For example, Ginsbourg, *Refugees*, p. 8; Kann, "Refugees", p. 40. This sector was occupied by the Japanese Naval Landing Party during the 1937 fighting. See Francis C. Jones, *Japan's New Order in East Asia: Its Rise and Fall* [Jones, *New Order*] (London: Oxford University Press, 1954), pp. 46-48. See also Finch, *Shanghai*, pp. 258-61. Hinder, *Labour*, pp. 12-13.

19. See Margolies, "Race", p. 11. Cf. also Kann, "EE", p. 7; Shoshana, *In Faier*, p. 283; Gruenberger, "Refugees", p. 332; Rosenfeld, *History, III*, pp. 67; Friedrichs, *Geschichte*, p. 62; Eisfelder, *Exile*, pp. 7-8.
The appellation of "Little Toyko" was due to its large Japanese population. Ginsbourg, *Refugees*, p. 8. Though some of the refugees lived within the Japanese enclave in Hongkew, most lived among the Chinese, who were located primarily in the Wayside and Yangtzepoo areas. Gerechter Interview.
20. Hinzelmann, *O China*, pp. 55-60. Also Rosenfeld, *History, III*, p. 4; Eisfelder, *Exile*, pp. 718.

21. Shoshana, *In Faier*, p. 283. Cf. also Ginsbourg, *Refugees*, p. 8; Rosenfeld, *History, I*, p. 7; Ganther, *Drei Jahre*, p. 15; Friedlander, *Sieben*, p. 12.

22. Rosenfeld, *History, I*, p. 7.

23. *Ibid.*

24. Ginsbourg, *Refugees*, pp. 7-8. For the Garden Bridge incident, see Friedrichs, *Geschichte*, p. 65. Cf also Siegelberg, *Face*, pp. vii-viii; Eisfelder *Exile*, p. 7. For the cheap price of food, see *idid.*, p. 10.

25. *Ibid.* Cf. also Margolies, "Race", p. 11; Gruenberger, "Refugees", p. 333; Burkhard, *Tanz*, p. 146; Ganther, *Drei Jahre*, p 15; Friedrichs, *Geschichte*, pp. 115-116; Friedlander, *Sieben*, p. 14.

26. Gruenberger, "Refugees", p. 333. Also Rosenfeld, *History, III*, p. 8; Eisfelder, *Exile*, pp. 8, 18.

27. Margolies, "Race", p. 14. Cf. also Ganther, *Drei Jahre*, p. 15.

28. *Ibid.* Cf. also Gruenberger, "Refugees", p. 333; Burkhard, *Tanz*, p. 146; Rosenfeld, *History, III*, p. 8; Carey, *War Years*, p. 146; Ganther *Drei Jahre*, p. 15.
For Hongkew's night life, see Friedlander, *Sieben*, p. 14. Cf. also Horst Levin, Interview, August 6, 1974 [Levin, Interview]. Mr. Levin attended such a beauty contest as a judge. He was also active in promoting entertainment and variety acts in night clubs. See the documents and photos provided the author by Mr. Levin (Levin Papers); Eisfelder, *Exile*, pp. 14-15. See the latter source also for the price of dairy products, *ibid.*, p. 21.

29. Carey, *War Years,* p. 108. Also Burkhard, *Tanz,* p. 146.

30. *Ibid.,* pp. 146-17, for the refugees patronizing Chinese shops. For the purchase of Japanese goods and the patronizing of Japanese stores, see Ginsbourg, *Refugees,* p. 9. For the resumption of the trolley service and restoration of Hongkew, see Eisfelder, *Exile,* p. 18. See also above, note 25.

31. Rosenfeld, *History, I,* pp. 9-14. Cf. also Rosenfeld, *History, III,* pp. 4-5; Hinder, *Labour,* pp. 83-84; Fritz Friedlander, "Jewish Mass Immigration and Settlement in Shanghai, 1939-1941" [Friedlander, "Migration"], *Ort Economic Review,* Vol. II (November-December 1941), p. 27 (copy given to author courtesy of Mr. Roder of ORT); Kranzler, *JCS,* pp. 18-19; Dicker, *Wanderers,* p. 101; Mars, Necessity, pp. 28-29. Rosenfeld is the basis of the latter three sources.

32. Rosenfeld, *History, I,* pp. 9-10. The main streets were at the most about 32 feet wide. *Ibid.* See also Fuchs Interview.

33. Friedlander, "Migration", p. 27. These Sikhs were so effective that they were retained even by the Japanese after Pearl Harbor, especially since they frequently hated the British. See Fuchs Interview; Eisfelder, *Exile,* p. 7.

34. Friedlander, "Migration", p. 9.

35. Rosenfeld, *History I,* pp. 9-10. Also Hinder, *Labour,* p. 83; Redlich, Interview; Eisfelder, *Exile,* pp. 42-43 and floor plan, at the end of his manuscript, of his lane house.

36. Rosenfeld, *History, I,* p. 10.

37. *Ibid.* Also Hinder, *Labour,* p. 83. For the furniture problem, see Friedrichs, *Geschichte,* pp. 73-74; Fuchs Interview.

38. Hinder, *Labour,* p. 83. The Chinese name for such cubby-holes was *pai ke hsiaung. Ibid.*

39. Rosenfeld, *History, I,* pp. 11-12.

40. *Ibid.* Also Friedlander, *Sieben,* p. 12.

41. Tobias Interview. Cf. also Rosenfeld, *History, I,* p. 12.

42. *Ibid.,* p. 11.

43. *Ibid.*

44. Rosenfeld, *History, I,* p. 12.

45. Rosenfeld, *History, I,* p. 12. Friedlander, "Migration", p. 27. For the phone problems, see Friedrichs, *Geschichte,* p. 75.

46. Friedlander, "Migration", p. 27. Cf. also Eisfelder, *Exile,* pp. 9, 42-43.

47. Rosenfeld, *History, I,* p. 12.

48. Rosenfeld, *History, I,* p. 13. Though it was still not as bad as in the *Heime.* For the numerous cases of petty thievery, see Friedlander, *Sieben,* p. 13; Burkhard, *Tanz,* p. 149; Friedrichs, *Geschichte,* p. 140.

49. Eisfelder, *Exile,* pp. 49-50.

50. *Ibid.,* p. 20.

5 | A HOME IN THE *HEIME*

> *What day of the week is today—red beans or white beans?*
>
> (Fred (Fritz) Melchior. *The Hongkew Ghetto.*)

The old, the sick, the needy and all the unfortunate refugees who, for financial, physical or psychological reasons were unable to adjust, and were therefore, completely dependent on the relief committees, found refuge in the *Heime*. After processing at the reception center, that epitome of bureaucracy with its endless forms to be filled out, they were assigned to one of the five *Heime*.[1] The trip there, through dark, rubble-strewn, half bombed-out Hongkew, quickly dispelled any vestige of optimism left over from the four-week sea voyage.[2]

They stepped from what was merely the façade of a Western metropolis into a city teeming with four million Chinese, where the world's prime examples of utter squalor existed side by side with unheard-of luxury. In the beautiful French Concession, to which the more affluent refugees would go, there were daily scenes that depressed even those recently released from Dachau. During this one ride to their future home (often in a coolie-drawn rickshaw), the refugees were likely to

127

encounter such spectacles as screaming, deformed beggars; stiff corpses of children and adults left in the streets by their unfortunate families; people dying from various diseases or starvation who dragged themselves to certain spots in the city to die in a common resting place, which might be merely one alley turn away from the spacious luxurious mansions of the rich.[3] These repulsive sights were only a prelude to what the helpless refugees were to encounter in one of the *Heime*.[4]

TEMPORARY SOLUTIONS

The *Heime* which were to become such a bone of contention among the refugees, and the objects of almost universal criticism, were an ad hoc solution of the local relief committees to the immediate problem of providing room and board for a growing clientele with diminishing funds.

Long-range planning was made difficult by several factors. For one thing, the majority of the refugees, and their Shanghai mentors, regarded Shanghai as a transient center, with the real goal one of the countries in the Western Hemisphere, especially the United States or Canada. And, in fact, prior to the outbreak of the War in the Pacific, several hundred did manage to leave Shanghai for other countries, and only the tightening of entry requirements to the United States, in June 1941, prevented many others from doing so.

Moreover, among the heads of the relief organizations in Shanghai and their local staffs, there was not a single professional social worker, whose skill and experience in relief work could have set up a smoothly running operation. For example, the single hour a day spent on refugee affairs by Ellis Hayim, the vice-chairman of the CFA, about which the JDC's professional, Laura Margolies, was later to complain, happened to be the daily lunch hour of a busy executive, wealthy stockbroker and financier.[5]

Finally, as previously discussed, is the fact that the JDC did not make a steady commitment to the financial support of the refugees until September 1939, when most of the relief work was already set up.

WARD ROAD HEIM

The earlier policy of the three relief committees of a cash subsidy of (Sh) $60 per month for room and board for each refugee had undergone a radical change by the end of 1938, as the influx of refugees grew swiftly.[6] A method had been sought to cut down the mounting expenses by mass feeding and housing. The well-meaning, but inexperienced members of the relief committees proposed the building or refurnishing of a large refugee center to solve what seemed to them an overwhelming problem. Such a unit would not only replace the unsuitable, temporary, Embankment Building as a reception center, but also serve as a central feeding and housing unit for indigent refugees. The first of these "permanent" refugee camps located at Hongkew was the Ward Road *Heim*. Located at 138 Ward Road, this had been originally a White Russian barracks, and was remodeled and designated as the Refugee Center No. 1.[7] Like the later-to-be-established *Heime,* the buildings on Ward Road had been damaged extensively during the Sino-Japanese hostilities of 1937. After some hasty repairs, which transformed the barracks into dormitories, the Ward Road *Heim* was officially opened in January 1939, ushering in a new phase of mass refugee relief.[8] Though not the largest in capacity, this *Heim* became the prototype for the later ones.[9] In addition to housing, the Relief Center No. 1 had a kitchen that provided food for the refugees living in the *Heime* and for those outside. According to its director's report, by the end of 1939 the kitchen was able to serve 6,000 to 7,000 meal three times a day.[10] There were three types of recipients of food from the

Heime. First, there were those fully supported by and resident in the Heime. There were also a few special cases who were granted rent subsidies outside but received their food free there. Finally there were those who had sufficient means for private rooms outside the *Heime,* but who paid for their food at reduced rates of up to (Sh) $10 per month.[11] It is significant that in the period prior to Pearl Harbor (at which time outside food subsidies were cut off), the last category numbered about 4,000 refugees.[12]

Before the establishment of the Ward Road *Heim* and its facilities, the refugees were served by two kitchens, one at the Museum Road Synagogue, the other at the Embankment Building. The latter was operated by a Chinese caterer.[13]

With the establishment of the Ward Road *Heim,* a Central Management, headed by an Austrian Jewish refugee, Julius Weinberger, operated all the kitchens.[14] The Central Management maintained other *Heime* in addition to the one on Ward Road.[15]

At least during the first few years, at the insistence of the Committee, all the kitchens observed the Dietary Laws, although only a minority of the refugees were observant.[16] The establishment of the Ward Road *Heim* reduced the cost of feeding the refugees from a previous (Sh) 50c. to (Sh) 30c., or (U.S.) 5c. per day. Sir Victor Sassoon pointed out that at this price, Shanghai was the cheapest place in the world to feed refugees.[17]

OTHER HEIME

It did not take long for the Ward Road *Heim* to fill up, as immigration increased by 1,500 to 2,000 a month during the first half of 1939.[18] Additional camps had to be established in order to provide for the many new refugees unable to afford private rooms. The Shanghai Municipal Council, probably through the influence of Ellis Hayim, as Vice-Chairman of the

CFA, placed three sites at the disposal of the refugees at a nominal rent of (Sh) $100 each per year. These were turned into the Wayside, Alcock and Kinchow Road *Heime*.[19]

The London Mission Society did its share in providing scarce real estate for the refugees, by donating its large former Mission Compound on Chaoufoong Road, while Sir Victor Sassoon provided his property on Pingliang Road. The latter was a larger and more suitable substitute for the Embankment. Building, which was henceforth used only as a food distribution center for the refugees.[20]

All of these valuable pieces of real estate had been extensively damaged during the 1937 Sino-Japanese hostilities. For example, four out of five buildings in the Chaoufoong Road Compound were damaged so severely that it did not pay to have them repaired.[21]

The method of dispensing relief by the CFA was changed with the opening of the Chaoufoong Road *Heim* on April 30, 1939. The rent subsidy of (Sh) $15 was eliminated for most of the refugees, who were now required to move into the *Heime* if they could not afford to pay for even the cheapest private room. Exceptions were made for those over seventy, the seriously ill, and for families with children under three years of age.[22]

The subsidies provided by the Committee were technically not grants, but loans, meant to be repaid as soon as the refugees became financially independent, and each refugee had to sign notes for the amount received. The Committee did not actually expect the loans to be repaid, but they went through the formalities for the purpose of retaining a legal recourse if and when a refugee did prosper. Thus, while the amount of the subsidies to refugees reached over (Sh) $400,000 between the last month of 1938 and February 1940, only about (Sh)

$10,000 to $12,000 was repaid by the refugees during that period.[23]

DESCRIPTION

What were these *Heime* or refugee camps like, and what did they offer to those unable or unwilling to rent a private room even in the low-cost Hongkew section?[24] Though their primary task was to provide room and board, they were not alike in size, physical setup, facilities offered, or in the type of refugees housed therein. The housing capacity of the *Heime* ranged from approximately 300 to 600 people and only one provided even that minimum privacy necessary to families or couples.[25] In the others, the men were separated from the women in different dormitories, which led to much criticism.[26] This situation lowered both the morale and the moral standard of many of the inhabitants of the *Heime*.[27]

The capacity of the rooms, or dormitory facilities, also varied from one Heim to the other, from a low of 6 to 14 and a high of 150 people in a room.[28]

In addition to the above-mentioned large facilities of the Ward Road *Heim,* the Pingliang Road *Heim* had a small kitchen which served only its residents.[29] Those needy refugees who worked in the Settlement were served in the Embankment Building, which merely distributed the food sent from the Ward Road kitchen.[30]

By 1940, the CFA provided full medical treatment for its inhabitants by establishing an outpatient clinic in each of the *Heime* for immediate medical needs. Three hospitals were also established there. A Refugee Hospital and a Maternity Ward were located at the Refugee Centre No. 1 on Ward Road, while the third medical center, an Isolation Ward, was maintained at the Chaoufoong Road *Heim*.[31]

The officers of the Housing and Disbursement Department were removed from the Embankment Building to their new quarters at the Alcock Road *Heim*. An excellent workshop for producing women's wear was set up by Eduard Kann's wife in the Pingliang Road *Heim*.[32] The latter also maintained a vocational training center in such fields as the building trades and electricity, for one to two hundred youngsters, though it was primitively equipped and poorly financed.[33]

Thus, within one year's time, the relief committees, despite their mistakes, inefficiency, and strictly amateur handling, had established a complete setup which attended to most of the enormous, immediate and varied needs of major portions of the 16,000 refugees in Shanghai, by the end of 1939.[34]

ACTIVITIES AND SERVICES

A closer look at some of the activities and services provided by the relief committees, especially in the *Heime,* will reveal many of the positive as well as negative aspects of this huge undertaking.

The most pressing need for many of those entering Shanghai almost penniless was of course room and board.[35] The arrival at the *Heime* was anything but cheerful. With hundreds coming in weekly, every additional refugee was looked upon as a "new burden and a new responsibility."[36] As one of them, relating his experience in one of the more gloomy reports on the *Heime,* wrote:

At last after a long drive through all this human misery and sorrow, we arrived at the Immigrants Home . . . We climbed a steep staircase and came into a long corridor, sad and gray, like something out of a bad dream, It looked as if the corridor would never end. Then we came into a bare room, and were taken into the bedrooms. Women

and children went one way and men the other. There were
no beds, or at least not what we usually call a bed. Only
a sort of wooden frame with a piece of linen of doubtful
cleanliness stretched over it. We had to sleep on those.
These so-called beds stand so close together that there
is no space between them and you have to climb into this
cot through the only free place, at the foot. Unnecessary
to mention is the doubtful pleasures of such close proximity to one's roommates, who are not what you would
like to be . . . There is no chair or stool in the whole
dormitory. No table, not even a nail in the wall to hang
your clothes on, not even a little shelf at the head of your
cot where it touches the wall is there; just a row of cots
on one side, close to each othe rand another row just like
it, on the other side of the bare, long room; . . . no sheets,
no pillows, just a grey flannel blankete, which looks as
if it had served several generations. It is impossible to
unpack even the barest of everyday necessities.[37]

The method of food distribution did nothing to improve
the pervading cheerless atmosphere. Since the main kitchen for
cooking and distributing food was located at the Ward Road
Heim, each meal required three shifts. The incongruity of
hundreds of fairly well-dressed refugees, who only recently came
from obviously better circumstances, tin plate in hand, demonstrated perhaps more than anything else the state to which they
were reduced.[38]

The food itself, particularly during the first year, was
filling, edible, but singularly monotonous. By mid-1939 a typical
menu might consist of : Breakfast—coffee, bread, margarine;
Lunch—noodle soup, meat, bread, dessert; Dinner—potato
soup, bread and apple.[39] After the first year, when funds were
insufficient, quality and quantity were cut down. By the end of

1940, dinner was dropped from the menu, and after Pearl
Harbor, only one meal a day was served. This meal usually
consisted of a hot stew of vegetables with a little meat.[40] The
only item always available and in quantity was hot tea, since
unboiled water was unsaniteary.[41]

The kitchen itself was a rather inefficient, makeshift
affair that used up five-sixths of the cost per meal for coal, while
a long line of refugees had to wait up to two hours for their
meal..[42] Only after Pearl Habor, through the initiative and
perseverance of Laura Margolies, one of the two JDC representatives in Shanghai, was a modern, efficient kitchen finally con-
structed.[43]

The meager diet was obviously insufficient for most of
the inmates of the Heime, who tried by various means to supplement it. Those lucky enough to receive money from their friends
or relatives overseas were able to buy the extras needed to keep
body and soul together. Others sold whatever possessions they
brought along, to earn a few pennies for food.[44] During the War
in the Pacific, as conditions deteriorated, some of the inmates
went as far as selling the shirts off their backs for a little addi-
teional food and wandered around Shanghai in rags or sack-
cloth, to the shame of all the refugees.[45]

"Extras" were to be had at the concessions set up for the
neediest refugees by the CFA in each of the *Heime*, where they
sold all sorts of sweets, fruit, cigarettes, etc. The *Heime* also
maintained coffee shops which sold sandwiches and cake. Some
of the refugees even attempted to keep goats and chickens in the
Heime, feeding them on leftovers. It was not successful.[46] One
of the *Heime* also served as a detention quarter for those youths
caught involved in petty theft. In view of the deep psychological
problems of many of the *Heime* residents, there was surprisingly
very few cases of alcoholism, despite the low price of alcohol and
its availability, during the first few years. [47]

In retrospect, despite the steady, and fairly valid criticism of the Committee and its handling of the food distribution, the number of meals served both in and out of the Heime seems incredible. For example, over four million were served to about 8,000 refugees during 1939, when food was still relatively ample and three meals were given a day.[48]

SANITARY CONDITIONS

The sanitary conditions in the *Heime* were deplorable even by Hongkew's low standards. For example, one of them had no other washing facilities than a few basins, while the latrines were simply ordinary, white-enamelled buckets.[49] Anothei Heim, in better condition, had over one hundred taps installed in long rows. Each *Heim* had shower or bath facilities, the use of which entailed a price of (Sh) 1c. per bath.[50] One can imagine that it was often the refugee most in need of a bath that was least able to afford even this low price, particularly in the view of the omnipresent dust in the streets.[51]

At the behest of the Municipal Council and the Japanese authorities, every refugee was innoculated several times against the many diseases common to the Far East and practically unknown to the refugee physicians from Central Europe, However, the generally low resistance caused by an insufficient diet prevented the innoculations from being very effective. The refugees lived in constant dread of catching any one of the innumerable communicable diseases so prevalent in Shanghai.[52]

ADMINISTRATION

The emergency conditions under which the *Heime* came into existence did not favor the development of democratic rule for their residents. The CFA, which was primarily interested in housing and feeding the tremendous daily influx of arrivals, formed a Central Management Department which, in effect, proved to be the practical authority within the *Heime,* while discipline was maintained by a "Home Police Service" consisting of about 36 men.[53]

The first paid secretary of the Housing and Disbursement Committee, which ran the first *Heim,* was Dr. Kurt Marx, who had previously worked for the *Hilfsfond.*[54] By mid-1939, he left for the Philippines, and Julius Weinberger was appointed to succeed him. He remained at this post throughout 1939, but was replaced some time early in 1940, following charges of mismanagement.[55] Despite criticism of his administration from various sources, one contemporary Shanghailander, deeply involved in the relief work and who had closely observed Weinberger's work, testified to the great amount of physical labor he exerted in setting up the Ward Road and other *Heime.*[56]

As head of the Central Management, Weinberger supervised a staff of over 500 refugees, to run the kitchens, hospitals, administrative offices, etc.[57] In effect, this meant that one out of every five residents of the *Heime* served as an employee.[58] The mere existence of such a large paid staff, most of whom had started out as volunteers, practically assured the existence of a lethargic bureaucracy, whose chief pleasure, according to one contemporary critic, was the production of paperwork. If anything, it was Parkinson's Law run wild.[59] Many were friends of the administration, and were as dictatorial towards the refugees as their chief.[60] Such conditions fostered a lack of initiative and interest, so that those with originality and fresh ideas did not stand a chance.[61] The refugees had no voice in the management, though most of the money supporting them was not contributed by the local Jews who made the major decisions, but came from the JDC overseas.[62]

What critics of the system failed to realize, however, was the fact that many refugees found that real work, and a daily routine added purpose, dignity and self-respect to many who had never known or had forgotten it during long-enforced layoffs. As one observer put it,

> . . . they [the Jewish leaders] organised an enormously com-
> plex administration in which very many were given employ-
> ment carrying trays full of forms from one desk to another.
> While in practice, little real work was accomplished . . .
> a Camp Police was created . . . [that] could pride them-
> selves with the uniforms they wore, even if the equipment
> was limited to a steel helmet, a baton, a whistle and some
> rope. After all, there was always the chance of promotion
> and raising through the ranks.[63]

After Weinberger was dismissed, the CFA selected a local executive director of German origin, Captain A. Herzberg, who turned out to be a hard-working, honest and efficient administrator.[64] Margolies, whose confidential reports are the chief source of information concerning Herzberg, felt that, in some respects, the refugees in the *Heime* fared a lot worse under his rule than under the allegedly lax and corrupt Weinberger. The key factor was Herzberg's personality and his manner of treating the refugees. He had worked at the docks all his life in charge of coolie labor. He was a strict disciplinarian and organizer, who brooked no back talk or criticism, and he "had absolutely no understanding of handling people". He treated the refugees worse than he had the coolies, and regarded them all as "a bunch of crooks and thieves".[65] Those who tried to protest in any way were threatened with being cut off from relief.[66]

Some of his assistants were described by Margolies as "Prussians", who followed his lead in the "heel clicking" and "obedience to and fear of authority". She adds, "One has the constant feeling of being in the German army".[67] There was no recourse to a higher authority, especially since the CFA Chairman, Michel Speelman, was only too happy to leave most of the decision-making to Herzberg. One can imagine one of the poor refugees trying to see Herzberg with a complaint. It was easier, Margolies noted, to get to see President Roosevelt than to get near even one of Herzberg's assistants.[68]

Under such conditions, it is no wonder that friction and tension often pervaded the Heime, and "terrific hatred" was felt towards the Committee and its leadership.[69]

Only after Pearl Harbor was the aforementioned more democratic form of self-government instituted in the *Heime*.[70] Experimenting with the largest *Heim*, at Seward Road, Laura Margolies, and Manuel Siegel, the JDC representatives in Shanghai, and some members of the Society of Friends (Quakers), helped the refugees elect their own governing board (*Heimausschuss*), which later became the basis for the postwar *Zentral-Ausschuss*, which controlled all the *Heime*.[71] The Friends also organized classes in English and discussion groups in the *Heime*.[72] Margolies was amazed at the infusion of real spirit and life into the refugees "at a time when they were probably hungrier than ever before".[73]

Undoubtedly, Margolies was unaware that it was more the depressed psychological state of the *Heime* residents than their lack of a tradition of democratic practice, as she contends, that caused the previous lethargic state of affairs. An astute insider, with far better insight of the refugee mentality, interpreted the new zeal for elections as a means whereby "These people, who had lost any status, any dignity, any purpose, all of a sudden became important as voters or even as candidates for the camp committee". From her "superior" stance, as an American, she noted that these refugees "were very clumsy in using the technique of democratic organizations, which do not come naturally to those of German background".

> . . . Miss Margolies' remarks reveal, that she did not know that the Jews in Germany and Austria were in the forefront [sic] in the fight for democracy since the middle of the 19th century, that Jews valued highly democratic institutions . . . Jewish participation in elections was always nearly 100 per cent and that the Jews themselves in their *Juedische Gemeinden* and *Kultusgemeinden* enjoyed self-government with democratic rule for many decades. So democratic rule was a very natural way for Jews in Central-Europe.[74]

RECREATION

Some attempt was made by the Committee to provide recreation for the residents of the *Heime,* particularly the youngsters. With the acquisition of the Kinchow Road *Heim,* which was soon to be transformed into a school, there were sufficient grounds, including a large sports field.[75] Soccer was the most popular sport among the refugees and Sunday tournaments were often attended by as many as 2,000 spectators. Other well-attended tournaments including boxing, ping-pong and handball.[76] For evening entertainment, the Central Management organized free or low-priced-entrance variety shows, played by refugee performers, in all the *Heime,* which allowed the audiences to forget the miseries of their lives for a few hours. The proceeds went to the most indigent of the refugees.[77]

EDUCATION

Though the domain of academic education remained out of the hands of the Central Management of the *Heime,* they did attempt to provide for the vocational training of several hundred youths.[78] Classes were held at the Kinchow Road *Heim,* where workshops were set up, and English classes taught by Professor Wilhelm Deman, who also set up a cultural department.[79] Some of the students were able to utilize their new skills in helping to convert the recently acquired Pingliang Road property into a reasonably liveable *Heim.*[80]

Religious services were held in the synagogues set up in each of the *Heime.* An *Oneg Shabbat* (service for children) was prepared for several hundred children. At these services, fruit and cake were handed out.[81]

Thus, while where there was much to justifiably criticize in the management, facilities and lack of long-range planning provided by the relief committees for the *Heime,* given the circumstances, the inexperience and the attitude of various concerned parties, these refugee camps did an admirable job. Under the worst circumstances, while they kept together the body and soul of the poorest of the lot, the *Heime* always left the door open for those with more initiative and drive, to explore the possibilities of success or failure of life on the outside. Secure in the knowledge that should their dreams not materialize, these refugees could always return to their *Heim.*

NOTES : A HOME IN THE HEIME

1. At one point there were as many as seven *Heime*, and if one counts the various locations used at one time or another, there were actually 10. By 1940, however, there remained but five permanent *Heime* throughout the war. During the postwar period, additional *Heime* were added. Cf. Mars, *Necessity*, p. 31, n. 107; Dicker, *Wanderers*, p. 101.

For the bureaucratic aspect, see Friedrichs, *Geschichte*, p. 63.

2. Gruenberger, "Refugees", p. 330. Cf. also Raymist, "Shanghai Myth", p. 5; Shoshana, *In Faier*, p. 283; Friedrichs, *Geschichte*, p. 62; Redlich-Tischler, Correspondence, January 28, 1974, pp. 1-3 (RP).

3. For the effects of such scenes on the arriving refugees, see Raymist, "Shanghai Myth", pp. 5, 17. Cf. also Shoshana, *In Faier*, p. 283; Friedrichs, *Geschichte*, p. 66.

For the general conditions in Shanghai with its extremes of poverty, see Finch, *Shanghai*, pp. 11-13. Cf. also Miller, *Paradise*, especially Chapter I; Georges Spunt, *A Place in Time: Shanghai Between the Two World Wars* (New York: Putnams, 1968) [Spunte, *Place in Time*], whose autobiographical novel presents a picture of wealth during the 1920's and '30's in Shanghai, oblivious of the surrounding filth, poverty and disease.

See Barnett, *Hostage*, p. 46, concerning the frozen bodies in the streets. Cf. also Hinder, *Labour*, p. 128, n. 2.

4. Raymist, "Shanghai Myth", p. 17. Cf. also Margolies to Pilpel, May 28, 1941, p. 1; Tobias Farb Correspondence (JDCCA). The latter was sent to relatives in the United States and was not intended for publication, making it all the more valuable as a source.

For an excellent analysis of the refugees' shock upon arrival in Shanghai from the luxurious, first-class accommodations to the rubble-strewn Hongkew, the *Heime*, and the feeling of utter helplessness, on the part of different groups of refugees, see Redlich-Tischler, Correspondence, January 28, 1974, pp. 2-5.

5. For the transient nature of Shanghai, see Rosenfeld, *History, I*, p. 2; Rosenfeld, *History II*, pp. 53, 57. Cf. also Redlich-Tischler, Correspondence, April 9, 1974, pp. 1-3. For Margolies' complaint about Ellis Hayim's "devoting only one hour to the refugees" see Margolies to Pilpel, August 11, 1941, p. 5. Joseph Abraham, who worked for the refugees together with his grandfather D.E.J., and his father Reuben, explained to the author the nature of this hour. This, in addition to at least one hour of poring over, CFA papers every morning, and frequent meetings in the afternoons. Ernst Lustig, taped interview, September 25, 1975. Mr. Lustig, an accountant

for the CFA used to bring the work to Hayim every morning at 8 a.m. Interview.

6. Joint *Memo* re Shanghai, March 14, 1939, p. 2. Cf. also CFA Minutes, April 23, 1939, p. 3 (JDCCA); Ginsbourg, *Refugees*, p. 19; Rosenfeld, *History, III*, p. 9. The original (Sh) $60 (equivalent to (U.S.) $3.30), was a low but reasonable amount. At that time, a poorly paid White Russian clerk earned about (Sh) $70 per month. Professor Nathaniel Peffer, Memo to J. P. Chamberlain, Member of the League of Nations High Commission for Refugees, April 6, 1939 [Peffer, "Memo"] (JDCCA). Article from the *China Press*, April 14, 1939 (n.p.) (JDCCA). The (Sh) $60 was at first cut to (Sh) $55 per month as the rate of immigration increased rapidly. Ginsbourg, *Refugees*, p. 19.

7. CFA *Report*, March 2, 1939, p. 1 (JDCCA). Also Weinberger, *Report*, 1939, pp. 3, 8; "Unsere Heime", *S.J. Chronicle*, p. 9. This article was undoubtedly written by Julius Weinberger, since it is very similar to his *Report;* Kann, "Refugees", p. 20.

Technically, the Washing Road *Heim* was the very first building rented as a dormitory. It housed about 60 young men, but it was far too small to serve the larger number of arrivals. It was changed into the Washing Road [Refugee] Hospital by January 1939, until June 1940, when it had to be evacuated. *"Unsere Heime"*, p. 9. Also Weinberger, *Report*, 1939, p. 4. The Embankment Building, too, was one of the transitory *Heime*, which served as a dormitory and reception center for several months. It was then replaced by the larger, more suitable Pingliang Road *Heim*. The kitchen at the Embankment Building, however, was retained to serve about 500 refugees who worked in the Settlement. Its food was delivered daily from the Ward Road *Heim* in Hongkew. CFA, *Report*, 1940, p. 8.

The Ward Road *Heim*, however, was the first to be reconstructed specifically for the housing and feeding of a large number of refugees. Other "temporary *Heime*" included the Hongkew branch of the Hongkong and Shanghai Banking Corp. Kann, "Refugees", p. 20. For the use of the Museum Road Synagogue, see "Embankment-*Kueche*", *S.J. Chronicle (S.I.)*; also Weinberger, *Report*, p. 4.

During the Pacific War, the Ward Road *Heim* unwittingly became the model for the internment camps built by the Japanese for enemy nationals, according to Joseph Abraham, who was interned in 1942 by the Japanese authorities. This is evidenced from the fact that shortly after Pearl Harbor, the Japanese authorities frequently "visited" the Ward Road *Heim*, asking many questions about its construction, but saying little. Only after his internment did Mr. Abraham realize the purpose of the visits by the Japanese. Interview. For additional information on this and other internment camps, see Carey, *War Years;* also Davidson, *Yellow Creek;* Langdon Gilkey, *Shantung Compound* [Gilkey, *Shantung*] (New York: Harper and Row, 1966).

8. Weinberger, *Report*, p. 6. Also see *"Unsere Heime"*, p. 9. It was leased from the China Realty Company for the relatively low sum of (Sh) $8,400 per year. Speelman to Troper, December 14, 1939, p. 4.

9. *"Unsere Heime"*, p. 9.

10. Weinberger, *Report*, 1939, p. 7. The kitchen was constantly enlarged to accommodate the increasing number of refugees. Cf. Kann, "Refugees", p. 32; Peckel Correspondence, June 1, 1939.
Since we have found Weinberger's statistics generally exaggerated, we feel that 6,000-7,000 might also be too high; 5,000 would be more accurate. Cf. Laura Margolies, "Race Against Time", [Margolies, "Race"], *Survey Graphic*, Vol. 33 (March 1944), p. 14.

11. CFA Minutes, February 6, 1940 (JDCCA), p. 3. Also Kann, "Refugees", p. 32; Ginsbourg, *Refugees*, p. 19.
Laura Margolies claimed that many refugees outside the *Heime* who received their food gratis, or at a very low price did not justifiably deserve it. She felt that a poor system of checking plus "cronyism" were the cause for this uneven distribution. Margolies to Pilpel, May 28, 1941, p. 1 (JDCCA).

12. Cf. Margolies, "Race", p. 12. Cf. CFA Minutes, February 6, 1940.

13. Weinberger, Report, p. 4. Cf. also "Embankment-*Kueche*"; Redlich-Tischler Correspondence, January 28, 1974, p. 4.

14. Weinberger, *Report*, pp. 4-6.

15. *Ibid.*

16. Weinberger, *Report*, p. 8. Weinberger claimed that the majority of the refugees came from traditional homes, but according to all my interviews and sources, at best 10 per cent to 20 per cent observed Kashruth.
According to Margolies, it was at the insistence of R. D. Abraham that only kosher food be served. Her anti-religious *Weltanschauung* becomes evident from her appraisal of R. D. Abraham, one of the few she singled out for praise, but about whom she added, "They are absolutely blind on the subject of their orthodoxy". See also Margolies to Pilpel, October 26, 1941, p. 4. According to Horst Levin, during the later period, most likely after Pearl Harbor, the kitchens no longer observed Kashruth. Interview.

17. Sassoon to Landau, August 5, 1939 (JDCCA). Also Lawrence Kadoorie to S. Frieder, August 2, 1939 [Kadoorie to Frieder, August 2, 1939], p. 2 (JDCCA). Cf., however, Sassoon to Berwald [sic], April 5, 1939.

18. Speelman to Troper, December 14, 1939, p. 4.

19. *Ibid.* Cf. also Kann, "Refugees", p. 32; Speelman, *Report*, June 21, 1939, p. 2.

20. *Ibid.* Cf. also Speelman to Troper, December 14, 1939, pp. 2-3; Kann,

"Refugees", p. 32. Kann lists the addresses, donor or source for the *Heime* and the rental paid for the then six *Heime* (August 1939).

Address	Rental from [sic]	Rental
1. 138 Ward Road	China Realty Co. (Speelman was on its Board of Directors)	(Sh) $8,400
2. 150 Wayside Road	S.M.C.	(Sh) $ 100
3. 680 Choufoong Rd.	London Mission Society	(Sh) $ 12

Address	Rental from [sic]	Rental
4. 100 Kinchow Road	S.M.C.	(Sh) $ 100
5. Pingliang Road	Sir Victor Sassoon	free
6. 66 Alcock Road	S.M.C.	(Sh) $ 100

The Kinchow Road *Heim* was used only temporarily as a dormitory; it was turned into a school by late 1939. The Embankment Building, the Museum Road Synagogue and the Washing Road *Heim* were also used only temporarily. The Seward Road *Heim,* the one with the largest number of residents, was first acquired after August 1939. Cf. Kadoorie to Frieder, August 2, 1939, p. 1.

21. Speelman to Troper, December 14, 1939, pp. 3-4.

22. Kadoorie to Frieder, August 2, 1939, p. 2. Cf. also Kann, "Refugees", p. 32; DALJEWCIB (HIAS), Report, May 19, 1939 [HIAS, *Report,* May 19, 1939], p. 3 (HH XV C-4). Kadoorie notes that during this period of August 1939, about 1,800 refugees were granted the rent subsidies. By 1940 the number had been reduced to 549. CFA Report, 1940, p. 5 (JDCCA).

23. CFA Minutes, February 6, 1940, p. 1.

24. That there were those in the *Heime* that had the means to rent private quarters is attested to by various contemporary observers, as well as former inhabitants of these *Heime.* See for example, Margolies to Pilpel, May 28, 1941, p. 1; Rosenfeld, *History, I,* p. 15; Fischel Interview.

25. Despite the various reports and newspaper articles, quoted by Dicker and Mars (Cf. Dicker, *Wanderers,* p. 102, and Mars, *Necessity,* p. 30), which gave the capacities of the various *Heime* to 1,500 for the Pingliang Road *Heim.* Cf. also Weinberger, *Report,* p. 5; or the Speelman *Report,* June 21, 1939, p. 2), these figures are gross exaggerations. They were due either to the tendency to blow up the figures for their public relations value, and/or they involved the anticipation of a far greater number of refugees than actually came.

My estimates are based on two premises: first, every report or correspondence dealing with the total number of refugees in the *Heime* invariably arrive at the figure of about 2,600 or less. The sources for the exaggerated figures would bring the total far above this number. See for example Kann, "Refugees", p. 32; Margolies to Pilpel, May 29, 1941, p. 1; August 11, 1941, p. 1; CFA, August 2, 1939, p. 2.

Moreover, the CFA *Report*, 1940, p. 4 (DP) gives the total number of beds at 2,388 (including those unoccupied). Undoubtedly the potential was greater, but no evidence of greater utilization is found.

26. The Wayside Road *Heim*, which was occupied by approximately 300 refugees, provided for "private" quarters. CFA *Report*, 1940, p. 4. Also Weinberger, *Report*, p. 7. For the criticism, see George Leonof, "Jewish Refugees Here Facing Lean Future" [Leonof, "Lean Future"], *China Press* (April 14, 1939), p. 3.

27. See Rosenfeld, *History, III*, p. 6.

28. For the lowest figure of 6-14, see Leonof, "Lean Future", p. 3. Rosenfeld reports up to 150. *History, III*, p. 6.

29. CFA *Report*, 1940, pp. 4, 8. Cf. also CFA Minutes, February 6, 1940, p. 2 (JDCCA).

30. CFA *Report*, 1940, p. 8.

31. *Ibid.* The original Washing Road Refugee Hospital had to be vacated by the summer of 1940 and was moved to the Ward Road *Heim*, which also maintained the Maternity Ward and a central Pharmacy. Kunfi, "Medizinische", p. 9.

32. Weinberger, *Report*, 1939, pp. 10-11. It was backed by Sir Victor and set up by Mrs. Kann. This shop was set up not as a training center, but as a small plant which utilized indigenous labour for the production of ladies' garments, suits, knitted goods and other items. Cf. also Rosenfeld, *History, III*, p. 12. Rosenfeld remarks that though it was one of the few worthwhile projects set up in the *Heime*, it never lived up to its potential.

33. Weinberger, *Report*, 1939, p. 10. Weinberger's typically exaggerated figures place the number of students at about 300. A more accurate figure of 100 is found in Speelman to Troper, December 14, 1939, p. 4. Cf. also Rosenfeld, *History, III*, p. 11. Here, too, the superficial picture belies the actual conditions, since very little was actually accomplieshed in this vocational center due ot the lack of tools and materials. Leonof, "Lean Future".

34. Even Laura Margolies, the most severe critic of the CFA, agreed that "the local Committee had done a magnificent job in meeting the emergency here when it arose". Margolies to Speelman, August 4, 1941, p. 1 (JDCCA). Cf. Friedrichs, *Geschichte*, p. 64.

The maximum of 17,000 refugees was not reached until the 1,000 East

European refugees arrived from Japan during the latter half of 1941. Most of those refugees that did not require direct subsidies for room or board received help in one way or another from one of the many relief agencies such as CFA or HICEM, etc.

35. Kann, "Refugees", p. 32.

36. Peckel Correspondence, June 1, 1939, p. 5. Also Leonof, "Lean Future"; Farb Correspondence, April 28, 1939; Raymist, "Shanghai Myth", p. 5; Margolies to Pilpel, May 28, 1941, p. 1.

37. Raymist, "Shanghai Myth", p. 5. See also Rosenfeld, *History, III*, p. 10; Mars, *Necessity*, p. 36.

38. Leonof, "Lean Future", Also Peckel Correspondence.

39. Kann, "Refugees", p. 32. See also Leonof, "Lean Future", p. 1; Rosenfeld, *History, III* p. 10; Mars. *Necessity*, p. 36. Eggs were always plentiful. Lustig Interview.

40. A report from the Peiping Chronicle stated "that due to the decrease in funds from the Joint, there would be a reduction from three to one meal a day". This must either have been a release intended to display a financial crisis, or it was modified in reality. News item in the *Peiping Chronicle*, November 12, 1940, (n.p.) [*P. Chronicle, November* 12, 1940]. From the collection of news clippings gathered by Dr. Rudolph Loewenthal from the *Peiping Chronicle* and other Anglo-Chinese newspapers re the Jews in Shanggare. Courtesy of Dr. Loewenthal [LP].
Margolies stated that two meals a day were served in mid-1941, though she called their quality "less than edible". Margolies to Pilpel, June 18, 1941, p. 1. Only after Pearl Harbor and the complete cutoff of funds from the United States was the food reduced to one meal per day. Laura Margolies, *Report of Activities in China, from December* 8, 1941 *to September* 1943 (JDCCA) [Margolies, *Report*, 1941-43], p. 2. In her article, however, she noted that by the spring of 1941, the refugees were receiving only one meal per day. "Race", p. 11. Perhaps the one meal was granted only to those outside the *Heime* whereas the residents still received the two meals. Cf. also Rosenfeld, *History, III*, p. 10.

41. Margolies, "Race", p. 11. Cf. also Redlich-Tischler Correspondence, January 28, 1947, p. 3.

42. Margolies, "Race", *ibid*. For the long lines and wait, see Rosenfeld, *History, III*, p. 29.

43. Margolies, *Report*, 1941-44, pp. 8-9. Also Margolies, "Race", p. 11.

44. Rosenfeld, *History, III*, p. 10. Also Leonof, "Lean Future", p. 1. For information concerning money sent from abroad, see Rosenfeld, *History, III*,

p. 10, and especially Peckel Correspondence, June 1, 1939; Friedlander, "Mass Migration", p. 25.

45. Rosenfeld, *History, III*, pp. 6, 10. Also Fuchs Interview; Rosenfeld, *History, I*, pp. 17-18.

46. Leonof, "Lean Future", p. 1. Also Rosenfeld, *History, III*, pp. 6, 10, 45; Friedlander, *Sieben*, p. 14.

47. Fuchs Interview. Cf. also Gerhard Gottschalk Interview, November 24, 1973.

48. Weinberger, *Report*, 1939, pp. 16-17. Cited by Dicker, *Wanderers*, p. 103.

49. Leonof, "Lean Future", p. 3.

50. Weinberger, *Report*, 1939, p. 6.

51. Cf. Peckel Correspondence, June 1, 1939.

52. *Ibid.* Cf. also Raymist, "Shanghai Myth", p. 17; Speelman to Troper, April 25, 1940, p. 3. For the outbreak of scarlet fever and other diseases, see below, chapter 10.

53. This department, in turn, was "ruled" by Ellis Hayim of the CFA. See especially Margolies to Pilpel, June 18, 1941, pp. 1-2; July 17, 1941, p. 1; August 11, 1941, p. 5.

54. See Arthur and Theodore Sopher, *The Profitable Path of Shanghai Realty* [Sopher, Shanghai] (Shanghai: *Shanghai Times*, 1939), pp. 385-86. A copy of this work sent to the author, courtesy of the authors.

55. Margolies to Pilpel, August 11, 1941, p. 3. C. E. Gauss, American Consul General to the U. S. Secretary of State, Concerning Jewish Refugees in Shanghai, January 24, 1939 [Gauss to State Department, January 24, 1939], National Archives, State Deprtment Decimal File (NA/SDDF No. 893.55 J/6).
The author has seen no direct source establishing the date of the inception of the Central Management Department. Weinberger, in his 1939 Report, mentions its functions, during that year. It is not clear whether this department was already organized under Dr. Marx's direction or only after Weinberger was appointed, although Weinberger already headed the Ward Road *Heim* while Marx was still working for the CFA. See, for example, CFA *Minutes,* April 12, 1939, p. 3 (JDCCA). At any rate, his title was probably that of executive director (or its equivalent), in German *Zentralheimleiter.* Courtesy Gerechter. On a document signed by Capt. A. Herzberg (CFA Financial Report, September 30, 1941, p. 1), his title is listed as Executive.
For the various accusations concerning Weinberger's administration, see the correspondence between the CFA and the JDC (N.Y.), and the CFA with Sir Victor Sassoon for the period of November 1939-January 1940 (JDCCA).

56. Though unable to deny any allegation of misconduct on Weinberger's

part, Mr. Abraham is very definite, however, about granting him the credit for being the first to really work hard at the huge task of erecting a complex institution that would grant at least a minimum of food and shelter to thousands of helpless refugees. Interview. Cf. Margolies to Pilpel, July 29, 1941, p. 3.

57. The CFA *Report*, 1940, p. 3, lists 516 employees, including 437 administration, 29 doctors and 50 nurses. Also, Margolies, *Report 1941-45*, p. 7.

58. On the basis of an average population in the *Heime* of about 2,500.

59. Rosenfeld, *History, III*, p. 9. Also Friedrichs, Geschichte, p. 63.

60. Margolies to Pilpel, July 17, 1941, p. 1. Cf. also Margolies to Pilpel, August 11, 1941, p. 3; June 18, 941, p. 1.

61. Rosenfeld, *History, III*, p. 9.

62. Although prior to September 1939 the JDC shared the cost of relief in Shanghai with the London Council for German Jewry and the Cairo Jewish Communities, among others, it assumed the full responsibility by the time of the outbreak of the war in Europe.
For the assistance by the Council and the Jews from Egypt, see, for example, Speeiman to Gauss, April 27, 1939 (NA/SDDF No. 893.55 J/13). Also CFA Minutes, April 23, 1939, pp. 1-2 (JCCA).

63. Eisfelder, *Exile*, p. 50. Also Redlich-Tischler Correspondence, April 9, 1974, p. 4.

64. Margolies to Pilpel, May 28, 1941, p. 1. Cf. also Margolies to Pilpel, August 11, 1941, p. 3; July 29, 1941, p. 3.

65. Marpolies to Pilpel, May 28, 1941, p. 1. It must be noted that Margolies did not even get her information from the numerous refugees who tried to give their version of conditions. For example, she refused to listen to anyone who would not recite his criticism in front of Herzberg. Rather, her sources were the many disinterested outsiders, as well as personal experience in dealing with him. *Ibid.*

66. *Ibid.*, August 11, 1941, p. 2.

67. *Ibid.*, May 28, 1941, p. 1.

68. *Ibid.*, August 11, 1941, p. 3. Margolies felt that Speelman was really a decent person who had been in this from the very beginning, and was simply too tired to fight. He felt Herzberg to be his lifesaver, since he did so well, and had removed some of the causes of the criticism revolving around the previous director. *Ibid.* Although, as one refugee noted, it was not very easy to get to see Margolies either. Zacharia Silberpfenig, "Shagrire

Yisrael Bemizrach Harachok" [Zilberpfenig, "Shagrire"] (Heb.), *Hadoar*, Vol. 12 (May 1, 1942), pp. 371-2.

69. Margolies to Pilpel, August 11, 1941, p. 3. She wondered why, under such circumstances, no one had attempted any physical violence on Herzberg. *Ibid.*, p. 1.

70. Margolies, *Report*, 1941-44, p. 12. Also Margolies, "Race", p. 14.

71. "Sieben Jahre Ward Road Heim", 1946. An unidentified news clipping (possibly from the *Shanghai Journal*, ca. February 1946) (JDCCA).

72. See Margolies, *Report*, 1941-43, p. 12; Margolies, "Race", p. 14; "Sieben Jahre Ward Road Heim" [Ward Road Heim] (JDCCA). Unidentified news clipping ca. January 1946, probably from the *Shanghai Journal*).

Manuel Siegel arrived on the Shanghai scene in November 1941, six months after Laura Margolies. (Margolies, "Race", p. 12).

73. *Ibid.*

74. Margolies, "Race", p. 12. For the "insider's" view, see Redlich-Tischler Correspondence, April 9, 1974, p. 4. See also below, Chapter 15.

75 "Unsere Heime", p. 10. Also Weinberger, *Report*, 1939, pp. 14-15. For general sports and recreation, see Jewish Recreation Club" [Levithan "JRC"], *Almanac*, p. 70-76. For the sports field, see *ibid.*, p. 73.

76. *Ibid.;* see also Ludwig Guggenheim, "Sport" [Guggenheim, "Sport"], *Herald* (S.E.), pp. 22-23.

77. Weinberger, *Report*, pp. 14-15. The entertainers were paid a very small sum for their talent. See also Friedlander, *Sieben* p. 14. For the library see Rosenfeld, *History, III*, pp. 11, 42-43.

78. The CFA was also in charge of education, though this aspect was not administered by Central Management.

79. See Weinberger, *Report*, pp. 10-11. Also Deman-Kranzler Correspondence, October 22, 1974, p. 2.

80. Weinberger, *Report*, pp. 10-11.

81. *Ibid.*, pp. 13-14.

6 | NO MORE REFUGEES!

NEGATIVE REACTION TO THE REFUGEE INFLUX

> *. . . It is a physical impossibility for us to cope with the situation, unless world Jewry comes to our aid so that we may continue the relief work, and later be able to direct emigrants to other cities where they may earn a living.*
> *(Report—Shanghai Committee for the Assistance of European Refugees in Shanghai. February 14. 1939 (JDC)*

We have seen the goodwill and sympathy that the well-established Jewish residents of Shanghai extended to the refugees. However inept the relief administration, however awkward and bureaucratic the local agencies, the underlying warmth and concern which had greeted the exiles at each stage of their journey was equally present when they arrived in Shanghai.

But such feelings were neither universal nor lasting. By December 1938, as the number of refugees approached 1,500 and the tempo of their arrival increased almost daily with no end in sight, all the residents of Shanghai's International Settlement, including the Jews themselves, began to fear that this influx could not be absorbed.

FEAR OF INFLUX

This fear, emanating as it did from various elements of the city, spread through the Municipal Council to the various governments involved in the Settlement. The efforts of these

151

combined forces, as will be demonstrated below, took on the character of a universal conspiracy to prevent further emigration from Germany of those thousands of potential refugees whose only haven was Shanghai. Thus arose the ironic situation whereby, during the first six months of the refugee influx, the governments of the United States, Britain and France, and their major Jewish organizations, such as the American Joint and HICEM-HIAS, attempted to curtail the flight of Jews from Germany to Shanghai. They worked to convince the German government not to permit the use of its ships, and to persuade the Jewish *Hilfsverein* in Germany to discourage Jewish emigration. All this at a time when the Axis powers, for their own diabolical reasons, and in their own way, were not only permitting, but even encouraging such emigration. Germany maintained its pressure to make thousands leave even without visas: Italy allowed the use of its ports and shipping lines; and Japan the real power in Shanghai, maintained a public silence amid the clamor for restrictions, while thousands of Jews were pouring into Shanghai.[1]

ECONOMIC COMPETITION

Objections to the refugees were manifested in different ways, reflecting Shanghai's complex and varied population. But whether overt or covert, most of the negative reactions arose from the overriding fear of economic competition, and from Shanghai's severe housing shortage.[2] Such fears, it is important to note, did not involve the majority of the Chinese, whose coolie standard of living was far below the possible competitive level of any European. The Chinese were hardly affected by the arrival of 17,000 refugees. It is irrelevant to speak of the impact of 10,000 or even 25,000 refugees on the economy of the overwhelming majority of the four million Chinese; the problem related to the foreign population and to a much smaller group of Western-trained, lower-middle-class Chinese. Even the consumptive capacity of these refugees made little impact on the larger Chinese community. Most affected were the 20 to 30,000 White Russian emigres, and some Russian Jews who had not yet found their niche within Shanghai's economy, and had not fully recovered from the results of the hostilities of 1937. Many of these were out of work or employed at unskilled, low-paying jobs that offered salaries of no more than about (Sh) $70 a month.[3]

In early 1939, a rumor circulated that the China General Bus Company was considering firing its White Russian employees and hiring Jewish refugees instead. This had to be quickly and publicly denied by the bus company. An editorial in the *North China Herald* read in part:

> It is unfortunate that the rumor was ever allowed to gain currency, for it is quite clear that the best interests of Shanghai lie in doing everything to prevent any outbreak of anti-Jewish sentiment in this city . . . Of late there has been much speculation concerning the possibility of the replacement of Gentile labour by some of the Jewish refugees. It should be made quite plain from the outset that this proceeding is wholly undesirable, and that any employer doing such a thing is rendering a definite disservice to the community as a whole.[4]

There was more than fancy to this rumor as is borne out by at least two documented cases involving the use of refugees as strike breakers.[5] There is also no doubt that some employers maintained a policy of hiring refugees as a means of exploiting available skill.[6] In some cases, the refugees would work for nothing for a period of time in the hopes of eventually ousting the lower class Russian or Chinese employees.[7] On the other hand, Paul Komor of the International Committee prevented

154

well-qualified refugees from accepting jobs which would replace Shanghailanders despite his realization that some would criticize the refugees as lazy and unwilling to work.[8] Such practices were vehemently denounced in a lead article in the *Shanghai Evening Post and Mercury,* entitled "Economic Threat Caused by Jewish Refugees," and subtitled "Emigres from Europe soon to Form Fourth of Foreign Population."[9] The author, John Ahlers, seemed to speak for most, though by no means all, of the foreign nationals, when he clearly voiced his apprehension at the so-called "German invasion."[10]

ANTISEMITISM

Fear of economic competition exacerbated the already existing antisemitic feeling among the White Russians.[11] Remarks by Sir Victor Sassoon, lauding the refugees while slighting the White Russians, only strengthened such feelings.[12] The small Western-trained Chinese middle class had to meet competition from some of the refugees, but only a limited number— including a few of the Chinese intelligentsia, surprisingly—were infected by the prevailing antisemitic atmosphere. The long history of China's tolerance toward all religions and the generally excellent economic relations which the refugees maintained with their neighbors kept trouble at a minimum.[13] One source explains the exceptions by pointing to the American training received by many such Chinese, who may have picked up their antisemitism during their college days in the United States, and returned with it to China. Other Chinese intellectuals became receptive to the Nazi propaganda through their sympathy for Germany. Illustrative of the effectiveness of antisemitic propaganda on some Chinese is an incident, reported by Owen Lattimore, concerning the reaction of some important Chinese officials to the appointment of two American Jewish traffic experts to posts in China. They asked whether the fact that the

U.S. sends over people *"who had an inferior status in the U.S.* did not indicate that the U.S. also regarded China as an inferior country?" [italics mine].[14]

Local antisemitic material was also disseminated by Nazi followers among the old German Gentile colony in Shanghai to all sectors of its international element. Such propaganda, in the form of vicious, scurrilous attacks on the incoming Jewish refugees, played on the fears of Orientals and Occidentals alike.[15]

LOSS OF FACE

Shanghai's wealthy international community, which was not affected economically by the new arrivals, had its own reasons for what soon became a generally unsympathetic attitude. "Loss of face" was suffered in general by the white community with the arrival of the refugees: in a society where the white man was respected only for his power and wealth, manual labor on his part was unthinkable. The impoverished refugees, therefore, lowered the already weakened status of the Occidentals in China.[16] They came, too, in the wake of the White Russians, who had never made a good economic adjustment, and this aggravated the situation.[17] A report from the Shanghai Municipal Council echoed the fears of the international element when it expressed alarm that failure to absorb the Jews might lead to a new crime wave, such as had followed the White Russian influx — this at a time when only 4,000 refugees had arrived.[18]

It also must be remembered that the political situation in the Settlement was delicate vis-a-vis the Japanese, especially following the outbreak of the European war, and the SMC expressed the additional fear that this balance might be upset by the newcomers' political activities.[19] A critical Council election was held on April 10 and 11, 1940, in which the

Japanese hoped to more fully represent their much larger share
of the foreign population, by gaining a majority at the expense
of the dominant British and American representatives.[20] The
Japanese, therefore, tried to sway a large part of the non-
Chinese population residing in the sector of Shanghai under
their control. As noted in the *Shanghai Evening Post and
Mercury,* these residents—including White Russians, the old
German Gentile colony, and ironically, the Jewish refugees—
held the key to the balance of power in the forthcoming elec-
tion.[21] This led to the paradoxical situation in which the
Japanese simultaneously wooed the German Nazis and the
German-Jewish refugees.[22]

The big inducement to the Jews was a promise of 1,000
permits to enable them to bring their relatives out of Europe,
at a time when, following the August 1939 restrictions, the
Japanese were issuing almost no such permits.[23] A political
fiasco was suffered by the Japanese at the election, as a result
of a clever scheme utilized by the British and American residents, whereby the number of voters, i.e., those paying property tax, was suddenly increased, and a great deal of ill will
was generated toward the refugees, several of whom had openly
campaigned for the Japanese.[24]

ANTI-REFUGEE RUMORS

Anti-refugee sentiment was also fanned by a canard that
many of them had come with their own capital but were nevertheless soliciting financial aid. The aforementioned Council
report, in which this allegation was aired, categorically denied
the charge after a full investigation.[25] Still, the rumor had its
effect on receptive minds, particularly when it was seemingly
verified by an unfortunate incident concerning the HICEM
"Guarantee" money. A group of 37 refugees arrived after the
1939 restrictions, with the (US) $400 guarantee provided by

HICEM in Europe, to meet one of the conditions imposed on refugees desiring to enter the International Settlement. Of this money, $300 was to be paid back to HICEM in Shanghai, to enable additional refugees to enter. This particular group refused to do so on the grounds that it had not realized how difficult economic conditions in Shanghai were. Eduard Kann, chairman of the Immigration Department of the CFA, was not alone in his opinion that "most of the people concerned here are not only ungrateful, but unworthy of support.[26]

Further, the rise in rents and the additional crowding of certain sectors by thousands seeking living quarters increased the resentment of many Shanghailanders toward the newcomers. Their ill will, however, did not prevent some of them from taking advantage by overcharging the refugees for their rented quarters.[27]

Some of the resentment appeared in advertisements for tenants, where it was specifically stated, "not to let to refugees." One journalist investigated the source of 10 such advertisements and found five of them to be Russian, two British, one Italian and two German.[28] Others, especially among the White Russians, went so far as to provoke street brawls with the refugees.[29]

One incident following the outbreak of the War in Europe caused not only resentment among the local population, but even greater consternation among the vast majority of refugees. This involved a news report that a number of young refugees had volunteered for the service at the German Consulate. As a result, some refugees lost their jobs at British owned firms. Such a climate of opinion was exacerbated by the natural tendency of the refugees to speak German, their mother-tongue, on the street, a fact which was resented by many "patriotic" English subjects.[30]

JEWS AGAINST JEWS

By the middle of 1939, the Jews themselves, in Shanghai as well as in other parts of the world, were contributing to this negative, resistant attitude toward the refugees. As we consider how this arose, and how it gained momentum, we must not forget for a moment the enormity of the undertaking: that of absorbing over 15,000 destitute persons already in Shanghai, plus the anticipated additional thousands yet to come into a city whose economy was contracting and whose settled Jewish population consisted of less than 5,000, with little consistent help from outside. Of the 5,000 Jewish residents, few were wealthy; most belonged to the lower middle class.[31] Nor could anyone imagine, or allow himself to imagine, at this early date what the alternative was, total annihilation, for any Jews left in Europe.

Economic and social self-interest alike led many of Shanghai's Jewish residents to share the fear and resentment of their gentile neighbors. The Municipal Council expressed this concern, as did the relief organizations, when they questioned the ability of Shanghai to absorb so many refugees. The Sephardim had always had a strong influence with the Council, and this was to be felt when, in August 1939, in conjunction with the authorities of the two Concessions and the Japanese military establishment, restrictions on immigration were finally imposed.[32]

Voluminous reports sent by Laura Margolies demonstrate that most of the CFA had been at best indifferent, at worst clearly hostile to the refugees. She quotes Kann as saying that his greatest fear was "that there would be too many refugees in Shanghai."[33] We have seen what a threat the refugees were to the Russian Jews, and how cool relations existed between the Central-European Jews and their Russian counterparts. This was reinforced by the age-old historic antagonism between these two Jewish groups, with their varying religious and cultural backgrounds. The large number of "converted", as well as completely assimilated refugees among the former, tended to draw an additional curtain of mistrust between them and the more nationalistic Russian Jews.[34] These feelings help to explain the poor, or relatively poor, participation of the Russian Jews in refugee relief work. Their attitude tended to be, "Leave it to the rich Sephardim," while they concentrated their communal efforts on the New Synagogue and the Club.[35]

THE ROLE OF THE JDC

And what was the role of the Jewish relief organizations throughout the world? We know that both the JDC and the London Council for German Jewry had refused to commit themselves to help on a steady basis, and had left the local committees to struggle with the job of absorbing the refugees on an uncertain financial footing.[36] We have only to read the response of the JDC director, Joseph C. Hyman, to an appeal for assistance: amid the usual mouthings about the Joint's wide commitments and limited resources, he promises a grant of $2,500, and adds, significantly, a firm assurance that they would *exert their influence to prevent other refugees from coming to Shanghai* [emph. mine]. Among other Jewish relief organizations that adopted this "policy of limitation" were the London Council for German Jewry, HIAS-HICEM and the B'nai B'rith.[37] Far from offering more money and social workers, the JDC could only promise less refugees! Most of the valid criticism of the relief effort could have been avoided, had the personnel been sent in 1938 or at least 1939 instead of May 1941.[38] Long before that, both the SMC and the relief committees on the spot, had been forced to adopt the policy of stemming the flood of refugees by any and all means. A telegram

on December 27, 1938, sent by the Council "earnestly requests
your assistance in preventing any further refugees coming to
Shanghai [or] the Council may be compelled to take steps to
prevent them landing in the International Settlement."[39]

A concerted effort was made to convince the overseas
organizations to discourage emigration by painting a picture of
the terrible refugee situation in the city, or to frighten potential
refugees in Germany and Italy by posters and press publicity
concerning the adverse economic conditions awaiting them.[40]
Under consideration was even a plea to the German and Italian
Consulates in Shanghai to use their influence with their home
governments to stop people from leaving for Shanghai, and to
forbid the use of Italian ports as points of departure.[41] Irony
is heaped on irony when one reads Michel Speelman's reports
to the CFA, where his account of such petitions stands side by
side with his complaints that the Gestapo and the Italian Lloyd-
Triestino Lines are openly encouraging emigration.[42]

UNIVERSAL CONSPIRACY

Even the governments of Britain, France and the
United States were to be drawn into the conspiracy, apparently
not without some tentative success. In a confidential dispatch of
February 18, 1939, U.S. Secretary of State Cordell Hull suggested to the American Embassy in Berlin that:

> . . . in your discretion and after you have learned the
> German reaction to the British demarche, you mention
> informally to the German authorities the desirability of dis-
> couraging the travel of Jews to Shanghai on German
> vessels.[43]

Above this barrage of official voices can hardly be heard
the faint cry of one refugee, speaking for all his fellow victims
of Nazi persecution:

We are going to Shanghai. We know that war is raging in China, that Shanghai is being ravaged, that perhaps there is no place for us, but we are going anyway. Since in face of all other doors closed to us, it was the only one remaining open and our only desire was to flee Germany no matter what happened. [sic][44]

The Japanese alone, the real authorities in matters of emigration into Shanghai at this time, refrained from public utterances concerning the refugee influx, from December 1938 until May 1939. When they did eventually change their minds, their reaction was to be the most significant for the restrictions of August 1939.[45]

Not only were the Japanese silent, but they did not even seem to object to the refugees residing in their territory, "Little Tokyo," the northern sector of Hongkew—this despite the fact that the Chinese who had fled the city in 1937 were not permitted to return to Hongkew until 1939.[46] An American writer on the Far East, at the time, found it "rather difficult to believe the rumor that the Japanese authorities in the Chinese part of Shanghai were collaborating in the settlement of these Jews."[47]

Nevertheless, the ever-increasing number of refugees arriving in Shanghai during the first half of 1939 illustrates the impotence of the Shanghai Municipal Council, the foreign offices of some of the major powers, and the Jewish organizations to prevent immigration to that place of refuge in the face of the wishes of the Japanese, the "real" power in Shanghai. Through their control of the harbor, the Japanese continued to permit and even encourage (via their German and Italian allies), for their own reasons, the immigration of Jews to Shanghai.

Such conduct on the part of the Japanese calls for an explanation and that can only be found in the extraordinary nature of Japanese policy toward Jews as a whole.

NOTES : NO MORE REFUGEES!

1. This chapter in a slightly revised form, was first published in *Jewish Social Studies*, Vol. 36, No. 1 (January 1974), pp. 40-60. The author extends his appreciation to the editor, Dr. Abraham G. Duker, and the Publishers, The Conference on Jewish Social Studies, for permission to reprint the article.

2. See especially John Ahlers, "Economic Threat Caused by Jewish Refugees," *Shanghai Evening Post and Mercury* [Ahlers, "Threat"], April 15, 1939, p. 8.

3. *Ibid.* Cf. also Peffer, Memo; Ginsbourg, *Shanghai*, p. 6; Jovishoff, "City," pp. 209-16; "Another Tragedy of a Tragic Era" (unidentified document, dated December 31, 1938) (JDCCA). From its tone it would appear to be a copy of a news article; Kann, "EE," p. 7; Ganther, "Seven Years," p. 2; Gruenberger, "Refugees," p. 332; Robert W. Barnett, "Shanghai's German Refugees Face Uncertainties" [Barnett, "Uncertainties"], *Far Eastern Survey*, Vol. 8 (October 25, 1939), p. 252; FO, "A Joint Report of Investigation on Jewish Problems in Shanghai." Carried out by Col. Senko Yasue (Army), Capt. Koreshige Inuzuka (Navy), and Shiro Ishiguro (Consul), July 7, 1939, p. 4 [FO No. 10, July 7 1939].

Cf. also F.O., "An Investigation Report Concerning the Problems of the Entry of Japanese, Manchuria [sic] and Chinese Nationals Especially Jewish Refugees," presented by Mr. Kumabe at a meeting of the "Moslem and Jewish Problems Committee," January 18, 1939, p. 3. [FO January 18, 1939] (DP). This committee was established in Tokyo to "debate and discuss various issues connected with Moslem and Jewish elements under Japanese Control." See Dicker, *Wanderers*, pp. 80, 82, 88, 90; cf. also B. Barbash to the editor of the *North China Daily News* (February 15, 1939) [Barbash Corres. February 15, 1939] (YIVO No. 60); H. Kadoorie to Barbash, July 21, 1938 (bid.); *North China Herald* (August 16, 1939), p. 267 (cited by Alvin Mars in "A Community by Necessity: The Story of the German Jewish Flight to Shanghai" (Temple University, 1964) [Mars, "Necessity"], p. 11. This unpublished senior paper leans heavily on Kranzler, *S.J.C.* and Dicker, *Wanderers*; *North China Daily News* (February 3, 1939); Editorials from the *Peiping Chronicle* (November 26, 1938; May 12, 1939) (n.p.). The latter two are part of the Loewenthal Papers (LP).

4. *North China Herald*, January 4, 1939, p. 45. This editorial is quoted in Peffer to Chamberlain, April 6, 1939 (JDCCA). The *North China Daily Herald* editorial is cited by Mars, *Community*, p. 12.

5. Hinder, *Labour*, p. 77. Cf. also Rosenfeld, *History III*, pp. 36, 40, 60.

6. Meyer Birman, "Report of the Jewish Refugee Activities in Shanghai," January 16, 1940, p. 2 [Birman, "Report," January 16, 1940]. (HH XV C-6) (YIVO).

7. Ahlers, "Threat." Many local Jews gave their coreligionists preference when making purchases, buying from refugee peddlers whenever possible. Abraham Interview. Cf. also P. Komor to B. S. Barbash, April 15, 1941 (YIVO No. 60).

8. SMC *Report*, p. 6.

9. April 15, 1939, p. 8.

10. *Ibid.* For sympathetic views toward the refugees, see Ginsbourg, *Refugees*, p. 9; and Arthur and Theodore Sopher, *The Profitable Path of Shanghai Realty* (Shanghai, 1939) [Sopher, *Shanghai*], pp. 380-88, in which the authors defend the refugees against unnamed but obvious critics.

11. "Another Tragedy," December 31, 1938, (an unidentified document in the JDCCA). The author notes that "scurrilous" antisemitic propaganda has already started in Shanghai. The fears of the poor Russians who are doorkeepers and bus drivers are played upon when they are told that they will be dispossessed by these refugees. Cf. also Peffer to Chamberlain; Summer Welles to American Embassy in London, January 5, 1939 [Welles to American Embassy, January 5, 1939], NA/SDDF No. 893.55 J/2.

For such negative attitudes on the part of Shanghailanders even prior to the arrival of the refugees, see J. Hyman to Judge Holzer, February 1, 1938 (JDCCA). Cf. also David Benz, "Refugees in Shanghai" [Benz, "Refugees"], *Congress Weekly*, Vol. 8 (May 9, 1941), pp. 11-12.

For street fighting between refugees and White Russians, see Capt. Inuzuka to Herzberg, September 17, 1941, p. 1 (JDCCA).

12. Articles in the *North China Daily News*, February 25, 27, 28, 1940. These include rejoinders to Sir Victor's remarks, by Michel Speelman and Ellis Hayim, under obvious Japanese pressure. Cf. also Speelman to Troper, March 4, 1940; Inuzuka to Herzberg, *ibid.*

13. Ahlers, "Threat." Cf. also Layle Silbert, "Report from Overseas: Shanghai" [Silbert, "Shanghai], *Congress Weekly*, Vol. XV (January 16, 1948), p. 14; Speelman to Troper, March 4, 1940, p. 2 (JDCCA).

That antisemitism on the part of the Chinese was the rare exception has been attested to by all interviewed. In fact, Menachem Flakser, editor of *Unser Leben*, a tri-lingual Jewish newspaper in Shanghai, maintained that the Chinese peddlers and small merchants who often suffered from Jewish competition were quite tolerant, and even sympathetic, about this condition. Isaac Margulies attested to the rapidity with which the Chinese merchant would grant goods on credit to the refugees, though he hardly knew them. Still, there was rarely any social contact between the two. Interview. Cf. also Hans Hinzelmann, *O China: Land Auf Alten Wegen* (Braunschweig, 1948), concerning his personal experiences and contacts with the Chinese.

14. For Chinese antisemitism, see "Memorandum of talk between Mr. Landau and Owen Lattimore," May 5, 1942 (JDCCA). Owen Lattimore, who was FDR's political advisor to Chiang Kai-shek, noted the existence of antisemitism among some of the Chinese intellectuals, which he felt to be due to German influence. This, he explained, was caused by the fact that the

Chinese were more sympathetic to the Germans, who, after World War I, had lost their rights of extraterritoriality, and with it their independent jurisdiction, which in principle was so abhorrent to the Chinese. Moreover, Germany extended military and diplomatic assistance to China ever since the First World War. This relationship would make them more receptive to Nazi propaganda. Cf. also Speelman to Troper, March 4, 1940 (JDCCA); Murphy, *Shanghai*, pp. 82-83; C. P. Fitzgerald, *Birth of Communist China* [Fitzgerald, *Communist*] (Baltimore: Penguin Books, 1964), pp. 54-55; Meskill, *Hitler*, p. 102.

15. See the letter by Carl O. Hawthorne (American Vice Consul in Tsinan, China) to Cordell Hull, the U.S. Secretary of State, January 9, 1939 [Hawthorne to Hull] (NA/SDDF No. 893.55 J/5). Attached to this letter was an example of such typical Nazi propaganda entitled "A Warning to all Chinese, Japanese, and Gentiles Alike," and subtitled "The 'Chosen People' Have Invaded Shanghai." The copy in the State Department Papers is only a typed version. Dr. Loewenthal was kind enough to provide a xerox of a complete, original copy with the illustrations (LP).

16. For the importance of the "loss of face," in Shanghai re the newcomers, are Gruenberger, "Refugees," pp. 331-32. Cf. also Margolies to Pilpel, August 11, 1941, p. 5; October 26, 1941, p. 2; *Ginsbourg, Shanghai*, p. 6.

17. SMC *Report*. Cf. also above note 3; Simpson, *Refugees*, pp. 155-61.

18. SMC *Report*, pp. 3-4. Though the report states that at that time (March 1939) only two cases of crime (fraud) had been reported, they were afraid that with the expected increase in the number of refugees, a larger crime wave would follow. Cf. also the "apologetics" on this matter by Kann of the CFA in his address to the Shanghai Rotary Club. Kann, "Refugees," pp. 39-40.

As early as December 27, 1938, at a time when the number of refugees in Shanghai numbered fewer than 1,500, Cornell S. Franklin, Chairman of the Shanghai Municipal Council, in a letter to Dr. A. J. Alves, the Consul-General for Portugal and Senior Consul of the International Settlement, similarly voiced his "grave concern" at the turn of events that had brought hundreds of refugees into Shanghai. In this letter were summarized most of the basic arguments maintained by the Shanghailanders against the influx of Jewish refugees. He noted:

> "There is already in Shanghai an acute refugee problem which is taxing to a grave degree the resources of both the municipality and of private philanthropy. There is to be considered not only the provision of accommodation and subsistence, *but the degree to which any further number of refugees could be absorbed without still further impairing the standard of living of the present community.* [italics mine]
>
> "I have the honor to request that the *interested consuls may take any steps within their power to prevent any further arrival* of Jewish refugees in Shanghai . . . [italics mine] . . . should this problem increase in magnitude it would be the Council's duty to protect the community of

the International Settlement *by taking steps to prohibit the landing in the International Settlement of any further Jewish refugees* without adequate means of subsistence or promise of employment [italics mine]. It is hoped that the interested Consuls may be able to bring this view to the notice of interested organizations and shipping companies concerned. It is further hoped that the Council's view has the approval of the Consular Body."

See FO S-9460-3-879 (circular 399-G-vii). Annexed Paper [sic], December 27, 1938, for the full text. [FO S-9460-3-879, December 27, 1938] (DP). Cited by Dicker, *Wanderers*, p. 82. Mars cites the *North China Herald* (February 15, 1939), p. 284, for part of this letter. *Community*, p. 13.

19. SMC *Report*, p. 7. Cf. also the text of the telegrams sent by the CFA to New York, London and Paris, on April 14, 1939. CFA Minutes, April 23, 1939, p. 5. For the delicate political situation, see Barnett, *Hostage*, pp. 29-30, 32; *Yellow Creek*, Chap. X, esp. pp. 162-66.

20. It must be remembered that the composition of the Council, which included five Chinese, five British, two American and two Japanese members, did not reflect, for example, the ratio of over 60,000 Japanese to less than 10,000 English subjects.

21. *Shanghai Evening Post and Mercury [Mercury]*, April 5, 1940, p. 1. Cf. also Barnett, Hostage, pp. 29-30, 32; Barnett, "Uncertainties," p. 253. In the latter article, written in October 1939, the author already recognized the importance of the refugees in the clash between Western and Japanese interests for the control of Shanghai.

Since the majority of the Jewish refugees resided in Japanese-controlled Hongkew, the Japanese authorities attempted to make use of the many potential voters.

22. Speelman to Troper, April 25, 1939. Those able to buy the Japanese permits had to pay anywhere from $150-300. Friedrichs, *Geschichte*, pp. 107-108.

24. Speelman to Troper, April 25, 1940, p. 2. Also Barnett, *Hostage*, p. 30.

Suffrage was limited to rate payers, i.e., those paying a certain amount of taxes on rented properties, including stores or lofts, etc. A recent change in the rate of exchange enabled any individual, including many refugees, to become rate payers by paying a mere (Sh) $70 on taxes a year. This, plus the scheme of subdividing one's property into many shares, and each share placed under a different name, created a sudden increase in the number of rate payers and voters. Abraham Interview.

25. SMC *Report*, p. 2.

26. Birman, *Report*, 1939, p. 2. Cf. also Kann to Association Belge pour l'Emigration de Refugies, January 10, 1940 [Kann to Belge], p. 2 (JDCCA).

27. Mars, *Community*, pp. 10-11. In addition to rent, the refugees had to pay a stiff price for "key" money, a sort of bonus for the landlord, a require-

ment for leasing an apartment or business. *Ibid.* Cf. also Ginsbourg, *Shanghai,* p. 7. Gerechter Interview.

28. Ginsbourg, *Shanghai,* p. 8.

29. Inuzuka to Herzberg, September 17, 1941, p. 7.

30. For the news report, see Friedrichs, *Geschichte,* pp. 81-82. The antagonism vs. the use of the German language is recorded in Ginsbourg, *Shanghai,* pp. 14-15. The author noted that the relief organizations advised the refugees to avoid the use of German on the outside. Cf. also Friedlander, *Sieben,* p. 6 and below, Chap. 14, where the antagonism to the teaching of the German language in the refugee school is discussed.

31. See above, Chap. 2.

32. For the Japanese part in the restrictions, see below, Chap. 8. The influence of the Sephardim in the SMC can be seen from the following sources: Margolies to Pilpel, September 10, 1941, p. 2; August 11, 1941, p. 3; Jackson, *Sassoons,* p. 214; Arthur Sopher to David Kranzler, April 22, 1969.

33. Margolies to Pilpel, August 11, 1941, p. 4. Cf. also Kann to Belge.

34. For additional sources on the friction between the Russian Jews and the German refugees, see FO KP No. 10, July 7, 1939, p. 4; taped interview with Dr. Georges Ginsbourg, June 7, 1969, and below, Chaps. 12 and 15.

The historic feud between Eastern and Western Jewry has been only sparsely documented. Among the works that touch upon this problem are the following: H. G. Adler, *Ostjuden in Deutschland* 1880-1940 (Lubigen:

, 1959); Abraham G. Duker, ed., *Europe Between the Two World Wars:* 1919-1939 (Jewish Postwar Problems; a Study Course, Unit IV) (New York: American Jewish Committee, 1942), p. 25; Robert Weltsch, "Introduction," *YLBI,* Vol. I, pp. xx-xxi; Herman Schwab, *A World in Ruins: Life and Work of German Jewry* (London: Edward Goldston, 1946), pp. 78-79.

35. Dr. Josef Zeitin, taped interview, August 5, 1968. Also Menachem Flakser, Interview, June 16, 1968.

36. See Elisha Friedman, *Inquiry of the United Jewish Appeal: Report for Refugees and Overseas Needs* 1940 [Friedman, *UJA Report* 1940] (N.C.: United Jewish Appeal, 1941), p. 57. Copy presented to the author, courtesy of Mr. Jack Diamond.

For the cessation of funds from Cairo and London, even prior to the outbreak of the War in Europe, see CFA to Council for German Jewry, August 18, 1939, p. 1 (JDCCA); Troper to JDC (N.Y.), July 12, 1939; Katzki, *Memo,* September 11, 1939, p. 1. At that date the JDC had not yet granted definite assurance of financial aid. *Ibid.*

For more detail on this entire problem of the role of the Jewish organizations and the restrictions to immigration to Shanghai in 1939, see Kranzler, *JRC,* Chaps. 5 and 6, or David Kranzler, "Restrictions against German-Jewish Refugee Immigration to Shanghai in 1939," *Jewish Social Studies,* Vol. 36, No. 1 (January 1974), pp. 40-60.

37. Hyman wrote that "We are asking our European office to advise us on the degree to which the emigration to China can be controlled." Hyman to CFA, December 12, 1938. Cf. also Troper to Joint (N.Y.), February 25, 1939,

p. 2; CFA, *Report*, March 2, 1939, pp. 2-3; Katzki, Memo, May 4, 1939, p. 2; Katzki, Memo, September 11, 1939, p. 1.

For concurring views, see the opinion of a "Jewish" expert on the Far East, Professor Nathaniel Peffer to Joseph Chamberlain (Chairman of the National Coordinating Committee), April 6, 1939 (JDCCA).

For HICEM's views, see the following previously mentioned documents: Hyman to CFA, December 12, 1938, p. 2; Hyman to Troper, February 10, 1939; Katzki, Memo, May 4, 1939, p. 2; Katzki, Memo, September 11, 1939, pp. 1-2; Birman to HIAS, September 16, 1939 (HH XV C-4). In the latter document, Birman, head of the Far East branch of HICEM (Shanghai), noted that "we advised not to have too many persons emigrate to the Far East, but there have been too many persons during the last few months." Cf. also Dr. James Bernstein (Head of Paris Bureau of HICEM) to HIAS of America, August 15, 1939, p. 1 (HH XV C-4). Bernstein inadvertently points out the fact that HIAS was more concerned for "enhancing its prestige" than in sending "only moderate" sums to Shanghai which would not solve the relief problem anyhow. *Ibid.*

The B'nai B'rith was also notified of refugee conditions in Shanghai by the JDC, which openly admitted its intention of cutting down the influx despite full knowledge of conditions in Germany. Hyman to Bisgyer, December 27, 1938. Similarly, in a letter to Roswell Barnes of the Federal Council of Churches of Christ in America, Herbert Katzki of the JDC clearly delineated his organization's policy, and noted that

> ". . . on the advice of local authorities in Shanghai we have advised the European agencies so far as is in their power to try to discourage further emigration to Shanghai. To stop it altogether, as you undoubtedly know, is most difficult, for large numbers sail for Shanghai without consulting the agencies; and, then again, even though warned, these people, harassed as they are, take the earliest boat for any country in which they might be permitted to land."

Katzki to Barnes, February 17, 1939 (JDCCA). Cf. also Troper to Joint (N.Y.), February 25, 1939, p. 2.

The Council for German Jewry (London) which was among the first organization to send financial assistance to Shanghai, and which maintained its one-time grants throughout the first seven months of 1939, joined the chorus for preventing further immigration into Shanghai, by advising all Jewish organizations in Germany to do likewise. Speelman, *Report*, June 21, 1939, p. 1.

Thus, the lack of a critical response to the Joint's communications regarding their policy of limiting immigration at the time implicates those Jewish organizations that accepted this policy.

38. Some of the "appeals" for trained relief personnel are found in the following JDC documents: Hyman to CFA, December 12, 1939, p. 1; Speelman to Council for German Jewry, February 10, 1939, p. 6; Speelman to Hyman, April 26, 1939; JDC (N.Y.) to JDC (Paris), July 2, 1939; JDC

(N.Y.) to JDC (Paris), February 15, 1940, pp. 2-3. Only in the later correspondence is the definite need for the JDC to send a representative to Shanghai noted. The shortage of such trained social workers at the time was noted by Dr. Joseph Schwartz, former head of the European JDC, in a taped interview with the author, July 28, 1969.

39. J. C. Hyman to M. Bisgyer (Executive Secretary of the B'nai B'rith), December 27, 1938 (JDCCA). This document indicates that the JDC made efforts to control emigration to Shanghai even prior to this notification by the Shanghai Municipal Council. Such efforts to "stem the flow" by the JDC came in response to a request for financial aid by the CFA on October 28, 1938. CFA to Hyman, October 28, 1938. The SMC's telegrams merely spurred its efforts in this direction.

40. Hull to Amembassy (Berlin), February 18, 1939 (NA/SDDF No. 893-55 M/RR); Summer Wells to American Embassy (London), January 5, 1939, ibid, J/3.

Cf. also Hyman to Bisgyer, December 27, 1938.

41. See letter by the Consul-General for Italy in Shanghai, Commander L. Neyrone to Cornell S. Franklin, Chairman of the Shanghai Municipal Council, *North China Herald,* February 15, 1939, p. 284. A copy of this article is also found in the files of the JDCCA. Also cited by Mars, *Community,* p. 13; FO KP No. 7, May 26, 1939, p. 7. Such requests were made in December 1938. This document records the failure of such an attempt; Gauss to U.S. Secretary of State, January 3, 1939. NA/SDDF No. 893.55 J/2.

See also above, note 40.

42. Speelman, *Report,* June 21, 1939, p. 1. On the encouragement of the Gestapo and the Italian Lines (in obvious cooperation with their respective governments) in abetting Jewish emigration to Shanghai, see *ibid.* Cf. also Troper to JDC (N.Y.), February 25, 1939, p. 1; *Black Book,* p. 120; Arthur Prinz, "The Role of the Gestapo in Obstructing and Promoting Jewish Immigration," *Yad Washem Studies II on the European Jewish Catastrophe and Resistance,* edited by Shaul Esh (Jerusalem, 1958), pp. 205-18.

43. See above, note 40.

44. "German Jews en Route for China," p. 5 (JDCCA). Cf. also the retort by the *Hilfsverein* to American Joint, February 10, 1939 (JDCCA); Malkah Raymist, "The Shanghai Myth" [Raymist, "Myth"], *The American Hebrew,* Vol. 145 (September 29, 1939), p. 17 (JDCCA).

45. For the Japanese as the "real" power in Shanghai, see above, Chap. 2. For their share in the August Restrictions, see below, Chap. 8.

46. Y. Miura (Japanese Consul-General in Shanghai) to E. Bracklo (German Acting Consul-General in Shanghai), August 10, 1939. (DP).

47. Parry, "Jews," p. 4.

INTRODUCTION

> [*The Jews are*] *just like a swellfish dish. It is very*
> *delicious but unless one knows well how to cook it,*
> *it may prove fatal to his life.*
> (Captain Koreshige Inuzuka. *Report to Naval General*
> *Staff. January 18, 1939, cited by Kase, "Jews in*
> *Japan")*

The singular behavior of the Japanese authorities in dealing with the Jewish refugees in Shanghai and later in Kobe (Japan) can only be grasped if the influence exerted on Tokyo by a number of Japanese "experts" on Jewish affairs and by their form of antisemitism is understood. How these middle-echelon officers came to influence Japan's national policy, seemingly in opposition to their Axis partner, Nazi Germany, and how the cause these experts advocated fits into the intricate pattern of Japanese internal and external affairs is part of the story to be unfolded below. Clarification of this will require brief, but frequent leaps in time, excursions into complex Japanese economic, social, military and, above all, political spheres, and some general probing into the Japanese mentality and its approach to the Jewish problem.[1]

Men like Colonel Senko Yasue of the Army, and

169

his naval colleague Captain Koreshige Inuzuka were the experts responsible for formulating and carrying out the Japanese policy. Few Japanese in those days had any knowledge of Jews or Judaism, as there had never been a Jewish community of any size in Japan—and to this day the average Japanese has difficulty in distinguishing between a Christian and a Jew. It was the occupation of Manchuria in 1931 and 1932, and of North China in 1937, which brought a sizeable Jewish population within the Japanese orbit for the first time. This sprawling area of the Far East contained at least eight communities, with a combined Jewish population of about 27,000, including as we know, Sephardim, Ashkenazi Jews from Russia, refugees from the Bolshevik Revolution, and— after 1938—victims of Nazi Germany.[2]

This confrontation between Japanese and Jew, particularly during the period of 1938 to 1945, gave rise to policies and attitudes which seem to present paradoxes. The free immigration of refugees into Shanghai, permitted by the Japanese in the face of the opposition from the various nationalities governing the International Settlement, as well as the Jews of Shanghai themselves, is but one phase of this drama.

Colonel Yasue was at the time Chief of Dairen (Manchuria's) Military Mission, and the liaison with the Jewish Far East Council for the period of 1938 to 1940, yet under the pseudonym of Hokoshi, he translated *Protocols of the Elders of Zion,* authored such antisemitic tracts as *The Revelation of a Revolutionary Movement* and the *Jewish Control of the World,* and disseminated propaganda worthy of Goebbels or Streicher. Here is a composite statement from his works:

> The Bolshevik Revolution is part of the Jewish plot; Zionism seems to be the goal of the Jews, but they actually want to control the world's economy, politics and diplo-

macy. Unless the Japanese realize this danger Japan will
be left behind in the struggle for world supremacy; The
League [of Nations], Freemasons, May Day Celebrations
are under Jewish Control.

The Jews are revolutionaries and they are encroaching
on the Manchuria economy (1933), and the Japanese
should guard their interests in both Japan and Manchuria
against the Jews [read: Western Powers].

I dwell on the Jewish problem . . . besides such powers
as Great Britain, the U.S., France . . . there is a nation
with no statehood and settled in those countries and *have
an influence there surpassing* that of the native people so
as to have a good control of the states. Furthermore, they
are maintaining close contact among themselves and are
boldly fighting to get the world at their mercy and achieve
their ultimate ideal . . . almost every state is a double
state, a compound of two opposing nations . . . The U.S.
Government on the surface, and internally a Jewish U.S.
Government. Therefore, we must handle international
problems of diplomacy, politics and economy from such
a twofold viewpoint . . . [italics mine].[3]

At the third Convention of the Jewish People of the
Far East, held in Harbin in 1939, Yasue is, however, singled
out for particular praise for his help to the Jews by Dr.
Abraham Kaufman, the Convention Chairman, and the spokesman for close to 30,000 Jews living in Manchuria and North
China under Japan's hegemony. Sitting to the left of Dr. Kaufman, on a platform decorated with the Japanese, Manchurian
and Zionist flags, and flanked by uniformed members of Betar,
the militant Zionist youth group, Colonel Yasue responded in
kind to Dr. Kaufman's praise; spoke of the common fortunes
of the Japanese and the Jews, and stressed the need for their

friendship in the future. He concluded with the hope that the Jews of the Far East, belonging to one of the world's "oldest races," would be the ones "to esteem the nationalities of both Japan and Manchuria." Dr. Kaufman notes in his memoirs, written eight years ago, that Yasue was a true friend of the Jews, whom they could always count on to intercede with Tokyo on their behalf. Furthermore, this same Yasue was, two years later (1941), to be inscribed in the Golden Book of the Jewish National Fund for his services to the Jewish People. He was instrumental in setting up the Three Conferences of Jewish Communities in the Far East between 1937 and 1939. He was also responsible for closing down the antisemitic newspaper *Nash Put,* an organ of the large White Russian population of Harbin; and he interceded on behalf of Peking's tiny Jewish community to prevent the obnoxious *J* from appearing on their passports.[4]

Yasue's colleague, Naval Captain Inuzuka, under the pseudonym Kiyo Utsunomiya, also wrote antisemitic tracts and articles and translated the *Protocols* and other antisemitic material.[5] Most of the latter were published in the antisemitic yearbook *Kokusai Himitsu-Ryoku No Kenkyu* and its successor journal titled *Yudaya Kenkyu,* (1936-1943).[6] There is some evidence that he was one of the founders of these outlets for Japanese antisemitism, men like General Ennosuke Higuchi, Lt.-Gen.Nobutaka Shioden, Toshio Shiratori, Masao Masuda, etc.[7] Among the special oriental twist given by Inuzuka to the *Protocols* are the following:

> The League of Nations is a tool of Jewish financiers . . . They intend to drive the Japanese out of China . . . The British, French and German Jews have given a loan of $200,000,000 to China for the development of Southwest China in order to forstall a further advance of Japan

southwards . . . The Sassoon is in control of the Chekiang
financiers through his close relations with the Chinese
National Government which in turn controls the Central
Bank of China . . . The Jews are in control responsible
for the American and European "control" of the Chinese
Nationalist Government . . . the kindnapping of General-
issimo Chiang Kai-shek in Sian (December 1936) [can
be explained as being due to] the rivalry of two Jewish
groups . . . the Jewish plot must be destroyed by force . . .
The anti-Japanese activities in England are all instigated
by Jewish freemasons . . . They are responsible for the
immorality of the Japanese youth by showing of their
[Jewish] films . . . the Jews control the American press
and thereby public opinion, turning it against Japan . . .[8]

Moreover, in a lecture at A Naval Paymaster School, which
became an oft-revised text, Inuzuka labelled the Jews (as
quoted by Kase)

The source of evil thoughts, "saying that" I warn you
that there is a by far greater national peril" than the
danger of an armed conflict and that a "gang of 'Masonic'
Jews have incessantly been master-minding international
intrigues against Japan behind the scene in Britain, the
United States, China and Russia ever since the Manchurian Incident. Japan is not fully prepared for these
intrigues.[9]

Yet it was these very men who were formulating the
Japanese policy which permitted the entry of German-Jewish
refugees into Shanghai at a time when there was an otherwise
almost universal conspiracy against them to restrict such entry.
Two years after the August 1939 restrictions were put into
effect, Inuzuka was again responsible for the formulation of

the Japanese policy which permitted over 1,000 Polish refugees stranded in Japan, to enter Japanese-controlled Hongkew. One of Inuzuka's treasured mementos, and one which was to save him from being tried in the Philippines in 1946 as a war criminal, is a silver cigarette case inscribed with the following message:

To Captain Inuzuka I.J.N.
In Gratitude and Appreciation for
Your Service For The Jewish People
[from the]
Union of Orthodox Rabbis of the U.S.

Frank Newman
Purim 5701 [March 1941]

UNIQUE CHARACTERISTICS

The key to such a policy and to the men behind it lies in the special interpretation these experts gave to modern anti-semitism, and the manner in which their theory became the practical policy of the Japanese Government. The Japanese antisemites, such as Yasue or Inuzuka were *sui generis,* in that they were not interested in eliminating the allegedly powerful and wealthy Jews, but rather in utilizing their great wealth and influence for Japan's "Greater East Asia Co-Prosperity Policy."[11]

Inuzuka, Yasue and others of their type really believed that Jews controlled the financial and political forces, as well as the mass media of the United States and Great Britain.[12] During the crucial weeks prior to Pearl Harbor, when last-minute negotiations to avert war were conducted by the Japanese Foreign Office with Washington, Inuzuka, with the full knowledge of the higher authorities, contributed his own little campaign on behalf of peace. He pressured the Jews of Shanghai to send a cable to the major Jewish organizations in the United States imploring them to stop the impending war.[13]

JEWISH IMPACT ON JAPAN

One must review the historical impact Jews have made on Japan during the past century in order to understand how such notions about Jews could become part of Japan's Western legacy. Though small groups of Baghdadi and Russian Jewish merchants are known to have resided in Japan ever since Perry's arrival in 1853, and one, Alexander Marks, even served as its Honorary Consul in Australia before the turn of the century, knowledge of Jews and Judaism in Japan was restricted primarily to individuals, especially Japanese Christians, who maintained a purely theological and historical interest. Among the latter, one must include Bishop Juji Nakada, the members of whose church were to welcome the refugees in Kobe with baskets of food and fruit.[14]

The most lasting impact upon the Japanese and their attitude towards the Jews was made by Jacob H. Schiff, the German-born president of the New York banking firm Kuhn, Loeb and Company. He arranged the floating of several crucial loans to Japan during the Russo-Japanese War of 1904-1905. These loans, among other things, financed about half of the Japanese Navy which later decisively defeated Russia's Baltic Fleet. Perhaps of greater significance than the cash value of these loans, as admitted by Baron Korekiyo Takahashi, who negotiated them, was the confidence in, and support of Japan by European governments and financial circles skeptical of Japan's viability as a modern nation. Schiff's first loan, for example, was completed even before Japan's first victory, at the Yalu River.[15]

The timing and circumstances of these loans must have made a deep impression on the Japanese who came to view Schiff as the epitome of *the* Jewish financier. Takahashi, who was later to become Finance Minister and then Premier of Japan, discovered upon inquiry that Schiff, unlike the rest of

the financial community, immediately responded in the affirma-
tive to the request for the crucial first loan because he had a
personal grudge against Russia. Moreover, Takahashi, and
other Japanese, were undoubtedly aware of Schiff's Jewish connections in Germany (such as M. M. Warburg and Company
of Hamburg and Sir Ernest Cassel in England) which enabled
him to float Japan's desired multi-national second and third
loans. The fact that Schiff was one of the key targets of the
antisemites who accused him of financing the Bolshevik Revolution must have added to his "prestige" and mystique in the
eyes of the Japanese antisemites—and those who read the
German and especially the Nazi versions that later appeared
in Japan.[16]

    To the present day, Schiff, who was the first foreigner
to be awarded the Order of the Rising Sun by the Emperor
himself for these loans, is still considered a true friend of
Japan and is spoken of with reverence. His continuing influence will be demonstrated in the following pages.[17]

    Another steady, though less significant factor in
developing an image of the Jew in the eyes of many Japanese
as having influential international connections is the fact that
from the very opening of Japan to the West through to the
present, there has been an unusually large number of Jewish
import-export firms and agents in Japan, which helped spread
Japan's products throughout the Western Hemisphere. This
view was reinforced during the boycott of Nazi Germany by
Jewish importers during the 1930's, a boycott which benefited
the Japanese, and seemed ironically to confirm the Nazi view
of an all-powerful Jewry.[18]

GENESIS OF JAPANESE ANTISEMITISM

    A little known episode in modern history had a pro-
found effect on the Japanese attitude toward the West in general

and the Jews in particular. This was a military expedition of Japanese armed forces into Siberia during 1918 and 1922, ostensibly on a cooperative mission with units of the Allied Armies to help the remnants of the White Russian forces under Admiral Alexander Kolchak to prevent the advancing Bolshevik army from reaching the Far East. This venture was totally unsuccessful and resulted in thousands of White Russians fleeing south to Harbin, Tientsin and Shanghai. Their presence as refugees undermined the respect for the Europeans of the Japanese officers and made these Westerners lose face, as we have seen, in the eyes of the Chinese population.

The Siberian expedition, however, provided a training ground for many of the younger Japanese officers in the political machinations and intrigue they were to put to good use in Manchuria, a decade later. A lesser-known unfortunate result of the contact between the White Russian and the Japanese officers was the latter's inculcation with the crudest form of antisemitism. The peculiar form it would take could, however, not have been comprehended, let alone pleasing, to the Russian "Teachers."[19]

Among such apt pupils of this antisemitic propaganda in Siberia were General Kiichiro Higuchi, Colonel Senko Yasue, Captain Koreshige Inuzuka and General Nobutaka Shioden, all Russian-language experts.[20] The White Russian generals infected the Japanese officers with their hatred of Bolsheviks and Jews, and made them synonymous to some Japanese. The Japanese were also introduced by their Russian mentors to such antisemitic translations from the Russian as *The Essence of Radicalism* (1919) and of course the *Protocols of the Elders of Zion*, which had already been disseminated, but achieved international infamy as the Bible for the world's antisemitism during this period.[21] In essence, the *Protocols* consists of a number of lectures in which a member of the supposed Secret

Jewish Government—the Elders of Zion—outline a plot to achieve world domination. The *Protocols* were soon proven, by an astute reporter of the London *Times,* to be a complete fabrication based upon a Frenchman's satire on Napoleon III. Maurice Joly, in a brilliant work sought to criticize Napoleon III's despotic methods while making a good case for liberalism. Ironically, in this parody, the author foretold much of the contemporary trend toward totalitarianism. This exposure as a forgery, however, was no bar to its widespread appeal to antisemites, and was certainly no problem for the Japanese experts, who implicitly believed in the authenticity of its very contradictory notions and "facts," especially that of the Jews as the prime secret proponents of world revolution under the guise of Bolshevism, a movement of an all-pervading concern to the Japanese of every political and social persuasion. This belief however did not lead most of them to the same fatal conclusions as it did other antisemites.[22]

For the Japanese, the 1920's and early 1930's were periods of theoretical study of Jews and Judaism by the soon-to-be experts, who indiscriminately digested material both in the original language and in Japanese translations ranging from the *Protocols* and the many works it inspired such as *The International Jew,* to more objective and philosemitic works, such as Ruppin's *Soziologie der Juden* or Dubnow's *Neueste-Geschichte des Judischen Volkes.*[23] This type of audience proved to be extremely limited in Japan, until later when the distribution of Nazi propaganda broadened it by the end of the 1930's. And the Jews and Judaism did not lack champions. In two recent articles, for example, Prof. Masayuki Kobayashi, Japan's foremost contemporary scholar of Jewish history, in "Mitsukawa's War against antisemitism," has described the campaign carried on by Kametaro Mitsukawa, one such pioneer, against the antisemitic trash circulating in the 1920's.[24]

JAPANESE FOREIGN POLICY AND RISE OF ULTRANATIONALISM

To comprehend the policies and personalities of the Japanese antisemites, it is necessary to highlight some of the major political trends and the climate of opinion that existed in the crucial two decades following World War I,

It will be remembered that ever since Japan's entry into the Western world, its designs on the Asian mainland had taken the form of a two-pronged policy "the enhancement of national security, and the enhancement of the economic well being of the state." These served as the consistent standard for Japan's domestic and foreign policy throughout the nineteenth and twentieth centuries. During the earlier period it was reflected in the slogan of "a rich country and a strong arm"; in the late thirties, in the formulation of the "Co-Prosperity Sphere." These two goals also became increasingly identified in the minds of the imperial government with the hegemonial position in East Asia and they were not to be argued until the conclusion of the War in the Pacific.[25]

In other words, if Japan was to avoid the fate that had befallen China, her formerly powerful neighbor, she had to build up her military might. Similarly, in order to become a full-fledged member of the Western imperialist nations, Japan had to "establish a new, European-style empire on the edge of Asia."[26]

Small in size, poor in natural resources, and burdened with an ever-increasing population, Japan early looked toward the "edge of Asia," i.e., Manchuria and Korea and China, to solve her problems. Sparsely settled and immensely rich in undeveloped natural resources, Manchuria was a natural choice. There one could settle Japan's overflowing population and Manchuria's unlimited source of the raw material would make her ideally suited to feed vast industrial and manufacturing potential. Moreover, Manchuria would provide a buffer zone between Japan and ever-encroaching Russia, its much feared enemy. China and Korea, from which two countries in previous centuries Japan had drawn much of its cultural heritage, were now fair game in the great power hunt for political and economic concessions, and a vast market for her manufactured goods. In addition to the purely economic and political motives, Japan adopted a fraternal attitude toward China as "the energetic younger brother scolding and goading into life the lazy, corrupt, and backward elder brother." We find that China's first revolutionary movement, at the turn of the century, headed by Sun Yat-sen, received unofficial support from and sanctuary in Japan.[27]

These expansionist views were at first spurred by its early ally, Great Britain, whose desire to check Russia's imperialist aims in the Far East coincided with that of Japan. In more ways than one, Britain, another island empire, became a model for Japan in her emulation of the best in Western tradition. Successful military ventures in 1895, 1904 to 1905, 1910 and World War I, and the concomitant creation of a host of almost legendary military heroes, encouraged the development of the patriotic, national impulses that were to play such a crucial role during the 1930's.[28]

Still, after the conclusion of World War I, Japan appeared for a while to be heading in a different direction. The Washington Naval Conference of 1921, in which Japan accepted a 5:5:3 ratio of capital ships with Britain and the United States and maintained the status quo for naval bases in the Pacific, seemed to leave Japan in a relatively secure position. A liberal age in Japanese politics seemed to be opening up such democratic tendencies as the passage of universal manhood suffrage. Parliamentarianism and the political primacy over the military, coupled with the desire on the part of big business to reduce armaments, the twenties experienced a change of climate and even the Minister of War concurred in such an unmilitary stance. In the words of one modern scholar, "the carefully controlled revolution of the Meiji period [1867-1912] was developing into a runaway liberal movement of the urban middle classes."[29]

The twenties found Japan in the process of even greater changes in its social fabric than the earlier decades. The process of modernization which in previous decades achieved its greatest success in the army and the technological sphere now began to take place in the rest of the nation, particularly its urban population.[30] Modernism, frequently meaning little more than adoption of the latest fads, took hold, as American-style taxis, dancing, jazz and movies became the rage. This era, which is characterized in Japan by the expression "ero Guro, Nansensu" (namely, eroticism, grotesquerie, and nonsense), or, as others put it, the three *S*'s (Sex, Sports, Socialism), gave birth to *mobo* ("modern boy") and the *mogo* ("modern girl") dressed in the latest Western fashions, who daringly walked down the Ginza (in Tokyo) holding hands. This seemed symptomatic of the subversive ideas that caused the deterioration of traditional Japanese family life. Even the imperial throne was no longer immune from these inroads of modernization. The Crown Prince, with his liberal and democratic leanings, and his fervent interest in his hobby, marine biology, alarmed the conservatives.

The process of modernism which gripped Japan during this period aroused interest in various radical ideologies from the left to the right, among the burgeoning student body at the universities and some of the younger officers of the armed forces. Modernism, however, also had its manifestation, at least in the critics' eyes, in the post World War I labor strikes, rice riots, inflations, and the bankruptcy of many small business establishments. All these fed the ultranationalist revulsion against what they considered subversive foreign ideologies which had to be eliminated before the "Showa Restoration" could take place.[31]

The Great Depression of 1930, that cataclysmic event that had such universal economic and political repercussions, made the strongest contribution to the decline of Japan's liberal era, and to the rise of the militaristic one that was to end in the attack on Pearl Harbor on December 7, 1941. The shrinking economy and the systematic shutting out of Japan's exports to many countries, particularly raw silk to the United States, and the ensuing mass unemployment, fomented unrest and criticism that had lain dormant during the relatively good years of the 1920's. Charges of bribery and corruption involved big business and politicians, with such episodes as the "Railway Scandal" and the "Matsushima Red-Light District Scandal." A revulsion against parliamentary democracy and unbridled capitalism was triggered among many of the idealists from the left and the right.[32] The Western powers were still unwilling to accord Japan full recognition as a major power and this rankled.[33] Moreover, the rising tide of nationalism in China and Manchuria under the leadership of Chiang Kai-shek, supported morally and financially by the British and Americans, threatened Japan's special economic privileges and rights in China. The London Naval Disarmament Conference in 1930 reduced Japan's naval power far below the standard acceptable to the General Staff in Tokyo, and there was an outcry from the young Japanese military officers. These ultra-nationalist radicals felt that the Western powers, especially the United States and Britain, were denying Japan's rights as a great power, and strangling her economically. This view saw Japan's primary sources of raw materials from the United States, Britain, China and the Dutch East Indies (called the ABCD powers) systematically cut off, while the two Western powers were strengthening their Pacific naval bases. This became known in the nationalist literature as the *ABCD Encirclement* whose real and imagined implementation was eventually to lead to war.[34]

Following the political assassinations and the aborted military coup of February 1936 and the beginning of the Sino-Japanese hostilities in 1937, even greater efforts were made to achieve a "patriotic unification movement." Almost overnight, membership in ultranationalist parties doubled from 300,000 to 600,000, and efforts were made to create fundamental changes in both formal and informal education. Kingoro Hashimoto, the founder of the radical Cherry Blossom Society, "wanted to create a huge youth society working toward the goal of spiritual renovation," which one recent historian, Delmer M. Brown, states, "had an appeal to the conservative militarists who were in power."[35]

At the same time the government formulated a program of "thought control." Toward this end it set up a central bureau of information with the responsibility "for the collection, evaluation, and dissemination of all information, both at home and abroad."

> This central bureau would also supervise . . . intelligence bureaus in each ministry . . . control all organizations that could be of assistance in directing the thoughts and attitudes of the people, all the political, social, cultural, religious, labor, youth and business organizations were to be encouraged . . . to unite into a single body.

This body would also supervise the entire field of "communication and entertainment, including press, radio, moving pictures, publication," etc.[36]

To insure the development of a proper *Weltanschauung,*

the Department of Education, under the newly appointed
General Araki, published a book called *Kokutai no Hongi*
(*Principles of Kokutai*) to serve as an "official interpretation
for the guidance of teachers throughout the Japanese public
school system."[37]

It did not take long for the regulations of the media to
become so restrictive that all editorials, radio broadcasts and
appointments of personnel were subject to official censorship.
For example, after 1938, all radio programs were geared
strictly toward the goal of the National Spiritual Mobilization
movement. The government even supplied radios to the rural
areas so that the widest possible audience could be reached by
such patriotic messages. By 1940 this reached the point of
establishing the New National Structure, an overall instrument
of ideological control and stimulant to further nationalist
sympathies.[38]

As a direct result of this campaign, the Department of
Education prepared another ideological text, this one to be
studied by all students, called *Shimmin no Michi* (*The Way of
the Subject*). It sums up all of Japan's aims and embodies all
the justifications for her course of action and her antipathy
toward Western civilization. For our purpose it is important
to keep their arguments in mind, since they will reappear in
the antisemitic literature in a slightly different form. Again, we
rely on Brown's selections and translations. This book, in
Brown's words:

> . . . was designated . . . toward the destruction of the
> self-centered and utilitarian ideas that had seeped into
> Japan from the West, and toward clarifying the Way of
> the Subject—a way which was based . . . upon service
> to the state.

The first part of the book outlines the development

and expansion of the Western powers. Their march into all parts of the world paved for their subsequent world domination politically, economically, and culturally and led them to act freely as they pleased, fashioning them to believe that they alone were justified in their outrageous behavior" . . . *The Way of the Subject* states that the wars of the last century were caused by Western aggression and emphasizes the inevitability of the disintegration of the old order . . . the foundation of the Western civilization . . . are individualism, liberalism, materialism . . . promote epicurian desires, seek a highly expanded material life . . . "This virulent expansionism and these selfish, materialistic concepts are leading to world collapse . . . the only way to prevent this collapse is for Japan to undertake the "construction of a new world order based on moral principles." Japan . . . had already stirred hopes in the hearts of all Asiatic peoples that they would be free, from the "shackles and bondage of Europe and America."

These Western powers

> . . . obstruct Japan's continental development. "Because of this opposition, Japan was forced to withdraw from the League of Nations, and then to engage in fighting with the Chinese . . . Japan's aims were pure, and that what she wanted most of all was "to enlighten China, to strengthen Sino-Japanese unity, and to realize coexistence and coprosperity, thereby building up a new order in East Asia and contributing to the consummation of world peace." . . . [Japan's] ultimate goal was "elimination of the evils of European and American influences in East Asia."[39]

Inspired by the words of ultranationalists such as Ikki Kita and others, these idealist critics of Japanese society found a solution to all of Japan's deeply felt ills. Kita's book, called *A General Outline of Measures for the Reconstruction of Japan,* was published already in 1919, and in it he advocated a combination of Emperor worship and anticapitalist, antidemocratic notions at home with equally radical expansionist policies abroad. Among other things, he wrote:

> The Japanese are following the destructive examples of the Western nations. The possessors of financial, political and military power are striving to maintain their unjust interests under cover of the imperial power . . . No one be allowed to accumulate more than 5 million yen. Important industries should be nationalized, a dictatorship established . . .[40]

An important element in Kita's and other radical ideologies of this period was the influence of Japanese agrarianism (*Nohonshugi*). Analogous in many ways to the American Populist cause at the turn of the century, the Japanese spread the agrarian myth which idealized the rural life where hard work, devotion, thrift, forebearance and obedience to the throne were the ideals. These radicals "advocated a return to a harmonious agrarian society or unity under the "imperial will." This was somewhat similar to the American version of the myth, which was a "kind of homage the [Americans] have paid to the fancied innocence of their origins." In the words of a recent historian of Japanese agrarianism, this influence was pervasive among the young radicals because:

> In short, it was its vision of a united Japanese nation, forming an ideal society without greed, individualism, or other evils associated with capitalism, that gave *Nohon-*

shugi its greatest appeal to the young enthusiasts in the army and navy officer corps.[41]

Numerous secret societies with programs of the type advocated by Kita and others during the early 1920's were dominated by civilians. But the membership changed rapidly by the late twenties in favor of the military, especially among the young officers. Many of these had come from rural areas and were familiar with the economic plight of these areas and the ideology of Japanese agrarianism. During the 1930's, this change was to have a major impact on Japan's foreign as well as domestic policies.[42]

During the late 1920's and early 1930's, two factions emerged among the ultranationalists in the army, with civilian sympathizers on both sides. The younger and more radical group was known as the "Imperial Way" clique, while the more mature army officers belonged to the "Control Group," though both had the same critical attitude toward Japan's domestic and foreign policies and both desired the replacement of liberalism and individualism with the principles of Nipponism.[43] They differed primarily in their solutions. While the Imperial Way was ready to establish state socialism in Japan by means of a *coup d'etat,* the Control Group was neither against big business nor willing to tolerate such radical change. It agreed that a greater role be assigned to the military. In foreign affairs they differed even more. The younger faction stressed the "Manchurian" panacea for Japan's ills of overpopulation and lack of natural resources. It was they who felt that Manchuria would serve as a natural buffer between the Japanese mainland and the Soviet Union. In their rosy view of the development of Manchuria they saw her as "an autonomous state, a haven for all of its ethnic groups, Japanese, Manchurians, Chinese, Koreans and White Russians." These young radicals of the Imperial Way clique were also

dead set against any action that would bring Japan into conflict with the United States and Britain, as was a likely result
of any move southward into China proper. The Control
Group, on the other hand, was of the conviction that Japan's
only road to self-sufficiency and achievement of her destined
greatness lay in her move south into China beyond Manchuria, with the aim of securing the rich British and Dutch
colonies of the Malay Peninsula and the East Indies, etc., in
Southeast Asia. Realizing fully well the implications of such a
move, they aimed at preparing Japan politically, economically
and, above all, militarily for the eventual battle with the United
States.[44]

A few more details concerning these two ultranationalist factions, with emphasis on the more radical of the
two, the Imperial Way clique, will provide the proper framework for the Japanese relations toward the Jews. It was this
same idealist radical army group, still under the influence of
the fanatical Kita, that was to dominate the changing Japanese
domestic and foreign policies during the period of 1931 to
1936.

Two of the most influential leaders of the Imperial Way
clique were Colonel Ishiwara (or Ishihara) and his close friend,
Colonel Itagaki. John Toland describes the first as a "brilliant,
inspired, flamboyant . . . fountain of ideas," and the second as a
"cool, thoughtful master organizer . . . They made a perfect
team. What Ishiwara envisioned, Itagaki could bring to pass."
Both were staff officers of the Kwantung Army who strongly advocated the Manchurian solution to Japan's problems.[45] Though
only middle-echelon officers, they had greater influence on the
course of the Kwantung Army than their commanding officer.
In this they were merely following tradition in the Japanese
Army whereby the General usually takes the advice, signs the
directives and assumes the responsibility for the plans con-

ceived by his junior officers. Ishiwara and Itagaki were responsible for the eventual takeover of Manchuria in 1931-1932
in the face of ineffectual opposition by the civilian government
in Tokyo.[46]

At this point it is worth looking a bit more closely at the
career of Ishiwara, one of these radical officers who sought the
"Showa Restoration," since his ideology and influence were to
bring him into direct involvement with later Japanese policy
vis-a-vis the Jews. Ishiwara enlarged the narrow nationalistic
concerns of the other ultranationalists to encompass a sense of
universal mission. This doctrine he derived from a combination of
Japan's essential spirit as manifest in *Kokutai,* and a particular
interpretation of Nichiren Buddhism. Peattie, in his study of
Ishiwara, summarizes the three main ingredients of Nicheren's
messianic doctrine: patriotism, an apocalyptic nature, and a
world mission. Patriotism identified religion with national life,
and thereby instilled national pride into the Japanese religion.
Its apocalyptic nature, which divided the world's history into
several periods, would conclude in a golden age, but only
after a period of dreadful conflict. In this golden age, Japan
would unite to create a "Holy See" which "would preside over
world regeneration, peace and harmony." A sense of world
mission meant a zeal to propagate this faith, which made it a
unique feature among Japanese religions. In other words, the
Nichiren faith was "purported to be a religion for all mankind,
and the center of propagation was to be Japan," or as Chigako
Tanaka, a modern interpreter of Nichiren, put it, "Japan is the
Truth of the World, Foundation of Human Salvation and
Finally of the World."[47]

Through Ishiwara this became an ideology which
greatly influenced Japanese military thinking, though he was
most successful with his friends and contemporaries who came
to be known as the Manchurian faction. Under the influence

of Tanaka's interpretation of Nichiren, Ishiwara, in essence, sought to make the *Kokutai* more universal by applying its moral principles at first to East Asia and eventually to the world at large.

In adapting his faith to Japanese geopolitical thought, Ishiwara fashioned an ideology whereby the assault on Japanese ideals by Western concepts, such as democracy, would result in a military confrontation on a global scale. Once the West was defeated by Asia, "its principles of harmony and coopera- tion—the righteous way, could be extended to the world at large, and through the principle of *hakko ichiu* [the eight cor- ners of the world under one roof] or universal brotherhood, could at last become a reality." Since the United States was the prime source of democracy, it became *ipso facto* the principal enemy, whose destruction by Japan would herald the eventual messianic era. In the course of further study and his experience as the Army Chief of Staff during 1935 to 1937, the United States remained the enemy in the apocalyptic future, but was replaced by Russia as the more immediate threat. Thus, Ishi- wara felt that the chief objective, along with other members of the Imperial Way clique, was the isolation of the Soviet Union in cooperation with Germany, and that "every effort was to be made to keep China, Britain, and the U.S. from interceding on the side of the U.S.S.R."[48]

On the positive side, Ishiwara's goals made him press "to establish Japan as the leader of East Asia," and to silence the opposition of the white races. Such a goal could only be reached with the help of his other concepts of "total war" and "national defense state," which would entail the complete subjugation of the economy of Japan, Manchuria and North China, to provide the military tools for a protracted war. Man- churia, particularly, would play a crucial role in this scheme, since a fully planned economy, out of reach of Tokyo's bungling hands, would be developed there by the Kwantung Army. Paradoxically, Ishiwara envisioned Manchuria as an independent, multi-racial nation living in complete harmony, and "possessing complete autonomy in internal matters, but whose defense [and] foreign relations" were to be entrusted to Japan. Slogans such as "racial harmony," "racial equality," and the "righteous way," served admirably as vehicles of propaganda for the Kwantung Army, since Ishiwara felt that

> In order to build a Manchukuo of one people we must work with the other races to establish an ideal state. That is the real meaning of racial harmony.

This attitude of Ishiwara is demonstrated by his denunciation of the blatantly racist conduct by many of his countrymen toward the Chinese, that he witnessed in China.[49]

Although Ishiwara's doctrines found many adherents in the army, his influence, naturally, was greatest among members of the Kwantung Army, many of whom were his peers and classmates. Among the latter one must include General Itagaki, General Higuchi, Colonel Iwakuro and Colonel Yasue, who became closely involved with the Jewish problem. Moreover, through his leadership of the East Asian League (*Toa Remnei*), dedicated to spreading his principles of Pan-Asianism, he influenced many other individuals, even an occasional navy man, such as Captain Inuzuka.[50]

From 1936 until the end of the War in the Pacific, the role of the Imperial Way clique in Japanese affairs diminished greatly when some of their leaders were purged after the mutiny of February 1936. The 1936 affair created antagonism toward this radical faction but the army, or rather the Control Group faction, greatly strengthened its grip on the government. Ironically, the radical reformist views now came to be regarded as the orthodox ideology of the state. This paradoxical situa-

tion arose out of the attention focused by the "mutineers" on
the complaints against the civilian government and big business which were taken to heart by the government. Though
diminished, the Imperial Way clique still retained a great deal
of influence in Japanese affairs both at home and abroad,
especially in Manchuria, where they controlled the powerful
Kwantung Army.[51]

The occupation of Manchuria in 1931-1932, the ensuing condemnation of Japan by the United States and the
League of Nations, and Japan's subsequent exit from that
world body, strengthened the ultranationalist philosophy. The
reaction to the West triggered a backlash against what they
considered to be a hypocritical, unjust and condescending
attitude toward Japan. More and more, Japan reverted from
its former secure, outer-directed pride vis-a-vis the West in its
achievements to its earlier insecure, more inner-directed, fear
of foreign inroads and ideologies. The effects of this trend will
be made apparent shortly.[52]

Japan's triumphant walk out of the League, led by its
delegate Yosuke Matsuoka, and the slowly deteriorating relations with England and the United States, especially during
the latter half of the 1930's, due primarily to Japan's expansionist policies in East Asia, isolated her even more inter-
nationally. She soon sought new allies among the European
powers, primarily Russia and Germany, Although Japan feared
Russia, especially after a good shellacking by the Soviet Army
on the Siberian-Manchurian border in 1936, she attempted at
various times to come to an agreement with her. This would
enable Japan to move south, resulting in a likely conflict with
the United States and Britain, while undisturbed on the northern border. Or, a friendly, or at least a neutral, Russia would
permit Japan to prepare herself more fully for a "total war"
during the next few years, so that the inevitable war with the

Soviet Union would be conducted from a position of strength,
The latter view reflected the thinking of Ishiwara and the
Imperial Way clique, while the former represented the concepts of the Control Group. This successful view eventually
maneuvered Japan into a position of her worst fears, when
during the last days of the War in the Pacific, she had to fight
the United States and the Soviet Union simultaneously.[53]

Nazi Germany and Japan sought each other out for a
number of years, since 1933, for an uneasy alliance in which
each tried to make use of the other. Japan desired Germany's
neutralization of Russia, while Germany's interest in Japan
was based upon her similar idea for the Soviet Union and later
help in the conflict with Britain, while keeping the United
States from intervening. Despite the Anti-Comintern Pact of
1936, the Cultural Pact in 1938, and the Tripartite Pact of
1940, which, with Italy, was to create what was later to be
known as the Axis Powers, there was never the type of cooperation between them that existed between Britain and its ally,
the United States, during World War II.[54]

JAPANESE ANTISEMITES—INTRODUCTION

Why did the Protocols and other antisemitic writing
published in Japan after World War I have so much appeal?
Most of the Japanese as we know had never seen a Jew or
known what a Jew was. The answer must be sought in the prevailing Japanese social and economic conditions during the
1920's and 1930's and the response to these by a small group
of ultranationalists. These saw in the Jew the solution to all
of the economic and social ills, real and imagined, that disturbed Japan's radicals of the right. Such conditions were of
course not unique to Japan. The economic ills plaguing
Europe and the United States that spawned another version of
modern antisemitism are well described in the words of John
Higham:

. . . economic distress functioned as one element in a complex of social and economic dislocations within the western nations. The years from 1873 to 1896 unleashed severe class conflicts and a general unrest that revived during the postwar disorganization after 1918 and reached a culmination in the 1930's. There was good cause to believe that the whole social system was somehow being undermined. The tensions relaxed in the early twentieth century as the achievements of imperialism and social democracy made themselves felt. Again, in the mid-1920's a growing stability revived confidence in the existing social order.

But social and economic frustrations did not stir up ethnic frictions automatically. The recurrent pattern of social and economic strain was accompanied by a persistent ideological disturbance. Each of the crisis periods produced a powerful display of nationalism, and it was the blindly cohesive energy of nationalism that channeled internal discontents into agitation against foreign influences. Consequently anti-Semitism in the modern world has reached maximum intensity as an integral component of movements aimed at defeating the nation from various perils originating beyond its frontiers.

and he continues,

It was a time of mass strikes, widening social chasms, unstable prices, and a degree of economic hardship unfamiliar in earlier American history. On the same scene a strong upsurge of nationalism expressed itself in jingoist outbursts against England and other countries, proliferation of patriotic societies . . . In broad outline, both the social situation and nationalist response paralleled the contemporary experience of western Europe.[55]

In a Japan with conditions that were not too dissimilar such ultranationalists such as Inuzuka, Yasue or Shioden found, that the answer was spelled out in the *Protocols,* with its apparent plot by a unique people, the Jews, to overthrow all governments and create a Jewish world empire. These people, according to the *Protocols,* without a country of their own, were so wealthy and powerful that they controlled and manipulated governments at will. The cunning developed throughout their long diaspora enabled this Jewish nation to use various weapons, such as the debilitating effects of liberalism and class strife, to weaken gentile states. Other weapons included a monopoly of gold, entirely owned by Jews, control of the press, immorality and economic crises. Their allies in this plot included Free Masons, political parties, atheists, speculators and corrupt politicians, all ready to do the bidding of the Jews. After terrorizing the world, the *Protocols* concluded, the leaders of Zion would set up their world empire, under the House of David.[56]

It came as a revelation to these young Japanese officers in Siberia, as they listened to their White Russian teachers, or read the *Protocols,* to discover that a single factor lay behind all the world-shaking events of recent times. The fall of such mighty empires as the Hapsburg, the Hohenzollern and the Romanov, within such a short time, must have substantiated this theory in their eyes. Their own knowledge of the Schiff loans, which had saved Japan at a critical time, verified their stereotype of the influential Jewish financiers able to manipulate world events. Was it not their duty to study more about this unusual people without a country or armies, but whose ideas were as dangerous to Japan as any geographically based enemy?

The eagerness with which such a theory was embraced, even in so sophisticated a region as Europe, demonstrates the

longing for simple solutions for complicated conditions. And
it becomes easier to understand the mentality of those more
parochial Japanese, whose Western education was restricted primarily to technology and military science rather
than the liberal arts to seek a similar, easy solution to their
problems. Add to this the fact that many of these officers who
"studied" Jews and Judaism were of rural and/or landed
gentry background with the "agrarian myth" as part of their
Weltanschauung. Let us take a look at how these budding
Japanese antisemites utilized the arguments of the *Protocols*
or *The International Jew,* and especially what adaptations they
made to suit their specific Japanese situation.[57]

It will be useful to divide the arguments into two
major areas: those affecting Japan's domestic issues, and those
connected with her foreign relations. One must bear in mind
that it was the domestic conditions in Japan during the 1920's
that made the theories propounded in the antisemitic literature
so persuasive; it was not until the 1930's that they were found
to be equally convincing in foreign relations. Japan's expansionist policy in East Asia, starting with the occupation of
Manchuria in 1931 and 1932, brought about a violent negative
reaction in the Western nations, especially the United States
and Britain, and the theories were used to explain this also.

The wrath of many of these young ultranationalists
focused on the United States and Britain, as most representative of the West, so that the term "West" referred usually to
those two.[58] According to the *Protocols* and similar works, the
Jews obviously controlled the political and financial destinies
of these two powerful nations, and the Japanese antisemites
could readily blame them for all subversive ideas which ema-
nated from there. There are numerous books and articles in
periodicals which attest to this theory. For example, in a
Japanese version of the German book *Juda entdeckt Amerika*

(*The Jews Discovered* [*or Developed*] *America*), the Jews were accused of wanting to make Hebrew the American national language.[59] According to another source, Jacob Schiff, Otto Kahn, and Paul Warburg, all Jews, controlled the United States economy and the Congress, while Bernard Baruch and Henry Morgenthau, Jr. controlled President Roosevelt, as they had *President Wilson earlier.*[60] Inuzuka called it their "immeasurably golden power over the financial, political and industrial worlds."[61] The Jews were believed to also dominate and manipulate all the media, including the newspapers, radio, film industry and advertising agencies. Similarly, Britain had become a Jewish dependency.[62] The Jewish influence was of course not limited to these countries: the U.S.S.R. was as fully under their power as the Western nations. Jewish ability to export revolutions, especially in the form of Bolshevism, was used with great skill, employing Russia as a base for such operations.[63] Their ideology of Zionism was merely a coverup for the plot to control the whole world.[64] In the eyes of these extremists, everything American was Jewish, and they also blamed the racist immigration policies directed against Asians on the Jews, forgetting that the Jews themselves were among the worst victims.[65]

As the major exporters of subversive ideas into Japan, the Jews' nefarious influence seemed to be manifest in every walk of Japanese life and undermined its foundations. Such "cunning Jewish ideas" as liberalism, democracy and socialism are concepts that have entered the mainstream of Japanese thought through missionaries and foreign teachers, in the guise of Christianity, a veiled form of Judaism.[66] The British information agencies in Tokyo, for example, were spreading all the Jewish concepts so alien to the Japanese spirit. Jewish mammonism and materialism, the very negation of Japanese spiritual ideas, pervaded the atmosphere of the Japanese universities and struggled for the minds of the students while capitalism and individualism eroded the warp and woof of Japan's social and intellectual life. One of the by-products of such seditious ideas in academia was the Jewish-Communist inspired attack on Emperor Worship, according to Professor Minobe's writings, and the appearance of the "Karl Marx boys," as the students with liberal or Western leanings were called.[67]

Moreover, the youth are contaminated early, through foreign "Jewish infiltration," by Japanese proponents of modern education, under the inspiration of the writings of Pestallozzi and Dewey. Both of these are called Free Masons; both are part of the Jewish plot to undermine Japanese morality and convert all the Japanese to Jewish views.

> . . . The Jews have reinterpreted all philosophies. Thus the motto of modern students in Japan is liberty, equality, and philanthropy. The Jews have used this slogan to destroy other nations . . .
>
> Even the prevalence of "tasty" Western-style food in the colleges is seen as "part of the Jewish plot in order to keep our students weak."

Instead, Japanese educators are urged to return to a system that would teach the young "in the spirit of, that the Tenno (Mikado) is the center of everything."[68]

The Japanese people must also be made aware of the dangers of the alien ideas that pollute the minds of the young, corrupt their morals, and undermine the traditional family and community system, by their contact with the familiar Jewish vices of the three S's (Screen, Sex, Sports). In short, Japanese society, its divine tradition and spiritual culture, are pitted against all the Jewish and Jewish-inspired ideas and intrigues.[69]

At times, the identification of the Jew with the Americans and British is so tenuous, even in the eyes of the Japanese antisemite, that he merely equates them on the basis of their having the same characteristics. Some "experts" in fact write entire books about Jews that hardly mention the word Jew in the text. An example of this is *The Jewish Plot and the anti-Japanese Problem,* which concentrates almost exclusively on the problems posed to Japan by the West.[70]

These antisemites projected all the fears of their fellow ultranationalists concerning the future of Japan, which seemed to be losing its true Japanese character as a result of Jewish (i.e., Western) ideologies. These fears, however, were not confined to the domestic scene, especially after the relatively quiet 1920's. New and even more urgent problems were soon to occupy the mind and pens of these guardians of the *Kokutai* against Jewish encroachments.

FOREIGN RELATIONS ISSUES

Japan's course of expansion on the Asian mainland after 1931, the rising tide of Chinese nationalism, and the ensuing criticism of Japan by the West, especially Britain and the United States, created a number of problems which are illustrated in the literature of the radical ultranationalists. The antisemitic elements or "experts" on the Jews, among these radicals, found in the Jew the perfect scapegoat for these evils as well. High on the list of such evils was the restraint imposed by the Jews (read West) on Japan's "righteous mission" in East Asia. As Iyataka Nakaoka put it:

The American and British Jews . . . are trying to stop the Japanese development and to keep Japan out of China.[71]

The Jewish intrigue carried out this plan in a number of ways. Through its domination of the world-wide press and other mass media, it influenced world opinion against Japan, and no

one ever saw her side of the conflict. Since the Jews controlled
the network of world communications, "all the news about
Japan consists of lies." This was particularly true of the United
States where the Jews were accused of manipulating the press
as an anti-Japanese tool.[72]

Other means of restricting Japan's territorial ambitions,
which the Jews used, were political and military. Through
their control of the American, British, Chinese and Dutch
governments, the Jews, then, were really responsible for the
ABCD Encirclement.[73]

Japan's conflict with the West was similarly seen as an
ideological struggle between Judaism's secular ideas of human-
ism and democracy, and Japan's New Order in Asia. This
order had been introduced by "divine inspiration."[74]

According to Utsunomiya, in his book, *The Jewish
Problem and Japan,* "The League of Nations was planned and
is controlled by the Jews," so it was they, obviously, who were
behind the League's criticism, and the Lytton Commission's
condemnation of Japan's action in Manchuria. Moreover, as
a result of their disapproval, the "British and American Jews
protested the Japanese occupation of Manchuria . . . [and]
took retaliatory economic measures against Japan through the
League of Nations." Once Japan walked out of the League,
the Jews also "began to boycott Japanese goods in China."[75]
Yasue in his book *Jewish Control of the World* advises the
Japanese that "since the Jews . . . are encroaching on the
Manchurian economy . . . [they must] guard their interests in
both, Japan and Manchuria against the Jews."[76]

While some Japanese antisemites only blamed the Jews
for instigating the hostility with China, others went still further.
They blamed the Jews for the Opium War of 1840, the Russo-
Japanese conflict of 1904 to 1905, World War I, and later,
World War II.[77] Even Schiff's munificent loans to Japan in

1904 were misinterpreted by these radicals on the right, and
became a ploy to prevent peace between Japan and Russia.[78]
Similarly, the Jews were held responsible for weakening Japan's
moral fibre and will to fight, by planning the destruction of her
military power, propagating defeatism, creating internal conflicts, forming secret societies, and winning over populations.
Again, the Jew as a symbol for the White Man was condemned
as the exploiter of Asia.[79]

It goes without saying that the Jews were considered
the true rulers of China, both its economy and its leaders.
Chiang Kai-shek's stubborn resistance to the Japanese, aided
by foreign loans especially from Britain and the United States,
is attributed to Jewish control of these two powers, as part of
an anti-Japanese plot. Chiang is considered a mere puppet of
his masters, the Jewish plutocrats, especially Sir Victor Sassoon.
The latter's close relations to T. V. Sung, brother-in-law of
Chiang, was proof of this contention. One article on this theme
is entitled "The Soviet Union and the Chiang Kai-shek regime
have joined the American and British Allies." Another, later
one, asserts that "at the present [1942] the British and American, as well as Soviet Jews are utilizing Chiang Kai-shek in
order to destroy the potential power of Japan."

Already in 1937, Utsunomiya wrote that:
. . . the Jewish financiers . . . intend to drive the Japanese
out of China . . . [Moreover] the British, French and
German Jews have given a loan of $200,000,000 to
China for the development of Southwest China, in order
to forestall a further advance of Japan Southwards . . .
[as part of] an anti-Japanese plot by the Jews . . .

Here is the very man who, under his real name of Inuzuka,
attempted to borrow 200 million yen from American Jews
for a Jewish settlement in Shanghai, writing:

Shanghai is now a Jewish kingdom in the Far East . . .
[and] Chiang Kai-shek is collaborating with the Jews of
Shanghai. He is a stockholder of the Sassoon Building . . .
The Jews made a 50-year plan and wanted to send some
500,000 European Jews to Manchuria, but the Japanese
prevented that. They went to China proper instead, invested there, helped the Chinese government, and agitated
against Japanese influence in China . . . The Jews ex-
ploited the British press to protest against Japanese influence in China; thus encouraging China in her struggle
against Japan.

Or again, the same man who was to be largely responsible
for saving thousands of the victims of Hitler by permitting
their entry to Shanghai, could under his own name term
Hitler's persecutions against Jews as an "unavoidable, imperative move."[80]

One must revert to the circumstances in Japan after
1938, with the emphasis on the mass indoctrination for "spiritual renovation" and "thought control," to understand the shift
in the direction taken by the writings of the Japanese antisemites. This was a time when anti-Bolshevik and anti-British
rallies and exhibits drew hundreds of thousands of visitors.[81]
Prior to this period, individuals, chiefly officers in armed forces,
wrote their tracts in book or pamphlet form independently, or
occasionally lectured to small groups of civilians or servicemen
on the evils and danger of the international Jewish conspiracy,
on a purely theoretical basis. Such tracts or lectures appeared
during the 1920's and early 1930's.[82] By 1936 the critical
changes described above have allowed the antisemites to find
additional, common sponsors and outlets for their research on
the Jewish problem in government-supported channels. It is
during this time that the *Kokusai Seikei Gakkai* (Society for

International Political and Economic Studies, *KSG* for short) was established. This organization was probably one of numerous agencies set up at the behest of the Bureau of Information and under the influence of Inuzuka.[83] It was placed in the Second Section, Research and Analysis Department under the Foreign Ministry, with the mission of gathering pertinent information concerning the Jews.[84] Its financial support came from the secret service funds of the army—most likely because of the military figures involved. Some important politicians and business leaders may also have contributed.[85] Since this people, or race as they are frequently designated, was so closely related to many of Japan's "fears," such as Russia, Bolshevism, and the West, it was imperative that information be available to the government and its different agencies. Moreover, since Japan was now directly involved with a sizeable group of Jews in Manchuria, and indirectly with their influential coreligionists, the pro-British Sephardim in Shanghai, one had to know more of their weaknesses and strengths in order to deal intelligently with them.[86]

The *KGS* also provided an outlet for the antisemitic research of such authors as Inuzuka, Yasue, and Shioden in the pages of its publication. This annual, called *Kokusai himitsuryoku no Kenkyu* (Studies in the International Conspiracy), ran from 1936 through 1940 when it was continued, the following year, by a monthly entitled *Yudaya Kenkyu* (Studies on the Jews). The latter lasted about two years,[87] until mid 1943. The organization sponsored lectures and forums on a regular basis to let the message reach a wide audience. In one such lecture, Inuzuka spoke on the "peril of Semitism," but requested his audience to "keep it only here." Possibly Inuzuka and many other such authors, convinced by their own arguments, feared that some Jews in Japan or elsewhere would discover their identity and do them harm; or that such revelations would hamper their negotiations with Jews.[88] Incidentally, the *KSG* had branches outside Japan; at least, there is mention of one in Shanghai in an article by Inuzuka's wife and former secretary. Inuzuka was certainly in Shanghai, doing research on his favorite topic, long before his official stationing there in January 1940 to set up his Bureau for Jewish Affairs. Occasionally, an objective piece about Jews also found its way into the *Yudaya Kenkyu*.[89]

The Foreign Office also gathered information in hundreds of reports on every aspect of Jews and Jewish affairs in the Far East, the United States and even Europe. Much of the present author's material is based upon the translations of such Foreign Office secret reports by Jewish experts, consuls, and other on-the-spot authorities. For example, we find Foreign Office documents on the Jewish influence in the United States that list the percentage of Jews who voted for Roosevelt in the 1936 election; the plan for a boycott of Japanese goods in 1933 by Polish Jewry; not to mention a detailed account of the movements and statements of Sir Victor Sassoon on his brief visit to Japan in 1939.[90]

Earlier, around 1934, a "Moslem and Jewish Committee," was established by some military officers to get more information on the Jews, as will be discussed below. Again Inuzuka seems to have been either the founder or one of the key members of this committee, together with his colleague, Yasue.[91]

The Foreign Office, however, was not the only government agency to set up research centers on Jewish affairs. The army and navy gathered similar material, beyond that supplied by these two assiduous experts, Yasue and Inuzuka. Kase mentions the following Navy publications, *The Yudaya Joho* (*The Jewish Information*), which in 1938 had already published Volume II and five months later Volume LXX, as well as *The*

Yudaya Gokuhi Joho (The Top Secret Jewish Information) which was published periodically.

In addition, the South Manchurian Railroad, under the later Foreign Minister Matsuoka, published a 50-page periodical once or twice a month, called *The Yudaya Mondai Jipo (The Current Report on the Jewish Problem)*. As Kase has pointed out, not all of these reports and investigations are antisemitic or even negatively inclined toward the Jews. Some are purely objective, and others even sympathetic.[92] In one 1939 report for the South Manchurian Railroad, for example, Kotsuji gave a sympathetic historical study of the Jewish Refugee's Arbitration Board, which we will discuss later.[93]

FOREIGN INFLUENCE

We have noted earlier the influence on the budding Japanese antisemites of the White Russian officers in Siberia, who peddled their hatred for the Jew and especially the identification of Jews with Bolshevism by word of mouth and by distributing copies of the *Protocols*. These emigres did not limit their campaign to the Japanese officers, for they spread the gospels of the *Protocols* throughout the world, in any country that offered them a haven. They were probably the most influential source of modern antisemitism, prior to Hitler. In fact Hitler's basic views of antisemitism were shaped by one such emigre.[94] In sophisticated United States, France and Britain lay fertile soil for such ideas for individuals who, in turn, under the tutelage of their Russian teachers, produced antisemitic literature which they exported elsewhere. *The International Jew,* the most popular antisemitic work after the *Protocols,* on which it was based, appeared originally as a series of articles in Henry Ford's newspaper the *Dearborn Independent. The International Jew* which preached the "truth" of the *Protocols* had a deep effect on Hitler and his Nazi propa-

ganda machine, long before he came to power. It was translated
into 16 languages, including Japanese. Since many of its ideas
were based on Ford's version of the "agrarian myth," they
found a sympathetic hearing among the like-minded, ultranationalist critics of modern industrialized Japan.[96]

Britain, too, provided fertile ground for antisemitic
material, particularly through the activities of Henry H.
Beamish, a fascist, from a well-known English family, who was
pro-Japanese and a personal friend of Hitler. He served as the
intermediary for the English-language antisemitic literature and
his Japanese sympathizers, and was also responsible for the
translation of one of the more popular versions of the *Protocols*
into Japanese.[97]

But it was Germany which provided the greatest stimulus to the budding Japanese antisemites, though the results
were not always to the satisfaction of their Nazi mentors. One
important reason for this strong German influence was that the
model for the Japanese military had been the victorious
Prussian Army, following the Franco-Prussian War of 1870.
This trend, of looking to Germany for technology and ideas,
continued even after Germany's defeat in World War I.
German had become the required language for any aspiring
Japanese officer, which made the Nazi antisemitic literature
immediately accessible to him. It is ironic that the spread of
German culture among the Japanese came largely through
translations of German-Jewish writers, such as Wasserman,
Feuchtwanger and Schnitzler.[98]

If this was true during the quiet 1920's, when no conscious effort was made by Germany to export such ideas, it was
much more so following the rise of the Hitler regime, when
much effort was spent on Japanese translations of Nazi works.
The Japanese officer was able to absorb the current antisemitic
ideas from Germany in its original language in Japan as well

as by direct contact with the Nazi propagandists themselves. Most prominent among the latter, for example, was General Shioden, whose first direct acquaintance with Nazi ideology stemmed from a 1927 visit to Nuremberg, and who renewed and strengthened these ties during an extended tour in 1938. In fact, he made quite an impact on Streicher and his comrades, as was prominently reported in the *Stuermer* and the *Voelkischer Beobachter*, particularly through his participation in the Conference on the Jewish Problem. He was the exception to the rule among the Japanese experts who wanted to make use of the Jews; he followed more closely the true Nazi line of "advocating" the radical elimination of Jewry from the Far East."[99] More true to our previous generalization was the above-mentioned General Higuchi of Manchuria. He too served in Nazi Germany as a military attache, succeeding General Hiroshi Oshima, who then became Japan's ambassador to Germany. Similarly, Colonel Yasue and Captain Inuzuka had been to Germany in 1927 and 1928, respectively, as part of their military tour of Western countries. Yasue even included Palestine in his tour, where he became acquainted with Zionist leaders such as Menachem Ussishkin and Ben Gurion.[100]

The key to the distinction between the Japanese and the European form of antisemitism seems to lie in the long Christian tradition of identifying the Jew with the Devil, the Antichrist or someone otherwise beyond redemption. In Norman Cohn's recent psychological formulation of the nature of modern antisemitism, the Jew in Christian society retained his symbolic value as simultaneously the "bad" son and the "bad" father, and it was in the latter guise that the myth of the Jewish world conspiracy lay. It was this myth that served as a warrant for many massacres, culminating in attempted genocide in the middle of the precent century.[101]

The Japanese lacked this Christian image of the Jew

and brought to their reading of the *Protocols* a totally different perspective. The Christian tried to solve the problem of the Jews by eliminating him; the Japanese tried to harness his alleged immense wealth and power to Japan's advantage. It is this pragmatic approach which we will now examine in some detail and see how it saved thousands of Jewish lives.

AYUKAWA AND THE IMPORTATION OF U.S.
CAPITAL INTO MANCHURIA

As early as 1932 we find a concerted effort on the part of Ishiwara and Itagaki to achieve their dream of an industrialized Manchuria as the key to Japan's national defense by importing American capital. Since the *Zaibatsu,* or the big business conglomerates were anathema to the radical army officers, they joined with Gisuke Ayukawa, a relative upstart in the business world, but who shared their views concerning Manchuria. An integral part of Itagaki's plan, as enunciated in a memorandum of April 1932, was his desire to foster closer relations with the United States, for which he was quite willing to

> . . . acknowledge the spirit of the Open Door and equality of opportunity, import American capital, and force a close relationship with the U.S. based on common interests . . .

Even earlier, in late autumn 1931, we find a similar view expressed in an army document (undoubtedly by the same authors or others who shared his opinions) which stated that:

> Since it is generally unprofitable for us to show marked hostility toward the United States and to make it our enemy, we should *adopt a pragmatic policy* that will lead to actual gains for the empire. As long as there is no fundamental interference with our policies in China, Manchuria, and Mongolia, we should go along

with the principle of the Open Door and equality of opportunity. Even in the establishment and consideration of a new regime in Manchuria, *we should avoid antagonizing the United States* by refraining, insofar as possible, from unnecessary provocation. [italics mine][102]

These proposals, especially the italicized phrases, are the concepts which underlay the Japanese policy, not only in regard to the importation of capital for the development of Manchuria, but also in reference to the later developed policy toward Jews.

This "pragmatic" policy of fostering good relations with the United States was not only a basic element in the often contradictory and fluctuating policy toward the United States, during the crucial decade of 1931 to 1941, but it was the very rock on which the Japanese policy vis-a-vis the Jews under their jurisdiction rested. In fact, the attempt to use the Jews for the above-stated purpose is probably one of the few continuous threads in the variegated pattern of Japanese governmental policy beginning in 1936.[103]

BASIC PREMISE

Thus, we find that the Japanese policy toward the Jews developed during the period of 1936 through 1938 and manifested itself in a number of ways: the three conferences of the Far East Jewish Communities, in 1937 through 1939; the plans for a Jewish home in East Asia, during this same period; the entry of the German refugees into Shanghai in 1939; the transit of German and Polish refugees through Manchuria and Japan in 1940 and 1941, and finally, the peace feelers with Jewish intermediaries in 1945, In each of these instances the Japanese antisemites or ideologes, provided the rationale and information that was used by Tokyo to act favorably toward the Jews. Moreover, the evidence points quite clearly at a small group of about a dozen key individuals in the government, both civilians and military men, that were directly responsible for the decisions that shaped this policy. These ranged in rank from middle-echelon colonels, civil service officials to generals, ministers and even premiers. Most of them were to a greater or lesser degree inbued with the ultranationalist *Weltanschauung* of the Imperial Way clique and belonged to a fairly close-knit group known as the Manchurian faction and under the influence of Ishiwara's ideology. This in no way implies a unanimity on all political and even ideological issues.

The common bond, in addition to their Manchurian experience, was the firm belief in the Jewish power, especially in the United States and Britain. This faith derived from several sources. The primary one was the crucial Schiff loans to Japan, which set the tone for their stereotype of the influential, international Jewish financier as set forth in the *Protocols* and other similar literature. For some, this image was undoubtedly reinforced through the close association with Finance Minister Takahashi, who had arranged these loans with Schiff. For others of this clique, the details of the Jewish stereotype and the identification with the hated communists, were supplied and "proven" to their satisfaction through friendship on a working relationship with Yasue, Inuzuka or Kotsuji.

As far as the first three instances are concerned, there is solid documentary evidence for the Japanese use of the Jews for the dual purpose of encouraging American Jewish capital to invest in the Far East and to create a more favorable atmosphere in the United States toward Japan. For the last two instances, there is sufficient proof to conclude that the motivation for the Japanese policy changed with differing circumstances. This time the Japanese desired to utilize the Jews under their jurisdiction for the purpose of softening America's increasingly hostile attitude toward Japan and perhaps averting the impending conflict. Near the end of the War in the Pacific, we are aware of several unofficial attempts to have the Jews mediate a peace with the United States.

Also quite clear is the fact that the research and anti-semitic writings about the Jews during the 1920's and early 1930's by Japanese so-called experts was conducted and supported primarily by the military, on a purely theoretical basis. In the author's view, this was simply one of the numerous areas of research of potential implication for Japan, such as Communism, and Bolsheviks. Since these experts assumed the identification of Jews and Judaism with these two, they became a natural subject for study. Only by the mid-1930's, when the Manchurian faction sought American capital for investment in Manchuria did the theoretical study of Jews achieve a pragmatic end.

FOUR PHASES

What were these plans, and how did the Japanese policy toward the Jews change from one of indifference to one of marked friendliness? From the occupation of Manchuria in 1931 and 1932, until the conclusion of the War in the Pacific, one can discern four distinct periods. The first, from 1931 through 1935, was, as a whole, one of indifference; the second from 1936 until December 6, 1938, witnessed the development of a distinctly pro-Jewish policy, which received governmental sanction on that last date. From December 9, 1938 until Pearl Harbor, the third phase in this relationship, can be described as the era of goodwill, as manifested in the previously mentioned episodes. The last phase, which covered the war years, brought about a sharp shift from a pro-Jewish posture to one which ranged between neutrality and definite antisemitism—

but which never, even at its worst, touched the extremism of Japan's Nazi allies.

The Japanese had taken a very positive stand on the Balfour Declaration and the Zionist programs at the Paris Peace Conference in 1919. Japan had also proved helpful, at that time, to the Russian-Jewish refugees in transit in Yokohama, in their flight from the Bolshevik armies, again with the help of Schiff's magic name. But no major policy had been promulgated, as the small number of Jews under Japanese jurisdiction, before 1931, made it unnecessary.[104]

The Golden Era of Manchuria's Jewish communities began after World War I but came to an abrupt halt with the Japanese occupation in 1931 to 1932. The deterioration that followed would begin to reverse itself only in 1936, through circumstances that will be discussed below. This period we have already characterized as one of indifference, and Manchuria's Jewish communities, especially that of Harbin, with a Jewish population of close to 10,000, were adversely affected by the various political, social and economic factors attending the occupation. These included the sale of the Chinese Eastern Railroad to Japan which resulted in loss of jobs to Jewish retailers servicing the personnel. The economic squeeze on most businesses by the Japanese forces with its anticapitalist policy whereby Japanese "assistants" were placed in all key enterprises, stifled much of Harbin's formerly vibrant economic life, including that of the numerous Jewish import-export firms and their agents. These now went south to seek the freer economic atmosphere of Tientsin and Shanghai.[105]

In addition, the Jews of Harbin became victims of some vicious antisemitism from the large White Russian population, which found its strongest expression in the pages of the scurrilous newspaper called *Nash Put*, The Russian Jews, like their White Russian compatriots, were stateless citizens (since

Russia had lost her "extrality" rights in 1922). As such, they were represented in Manchuria (as later in Shanghai) by a White Russian society. Many of the Czar's ex-soldiers served both the Japanese and the Soviets, as policemen and officers; as well as spies and con men for some of the bandit gangs still roving around Manchuria. Kidnapping and terrorist tactics, especially against wealthy individuals, including Jews, were frequent enough to add to the exodus from Harbin. This situation in the Jewish community of Harbin came to a crisis with the kidnapping and subsequent murder of Simon Kaspe, the talented pianist son of a rich father. The Chinese judges who condemned the guilty party were themselves arrested, an action condoned by the Japanese authorities. Protests and meetings of Jews in Harbin were led by Dr. Kaufman and in Shanghai by N. E. B. Ezra, in the pages of his *Israel's Messenger* where Ezra gave his full support to this protest against Japanese tolerance of, if not complicity in, this situation. His editorial was read by fellow Jews in Britain and the United States as well as by the Japanese representatives in those countries, but was apparently of little avail. Even a direct appeal by Dr. Kaufman to the Japanese Office of Foreign Affairs and a promise by the vice-minister, Mamoru Shigemitsu, to correct the situation had no effect. The home of Rabbi Levin of Dairen was searched on Yom Kippur, the holiest day of the Jewish calendar, for subversive material. A part of the problem was the lack of any effective voice or representation for the Jews, and they were forced to deal with Eguchi, an extremely biased chief of police, and the author of a slanderous report. There was apparently no sympathetic ear among the Japanese officials, and the Jews were unable to improve the situation.[106]

But even at the height of their despair, motions to change the situation in their favor were afoot. We have already noted the writings and theories of Itagaki and Ayukawa concerning the desirability of developing Manchuria through American capital and Jewish as well as Japanese settlers. These theories were formalized in a series of plans beginning in 1937, when Ayukawa's Nihon Industrial Company (Nissan) was transferred to Manchuria and became the Heavy Industries Development Corporation. Four years earlier, in 1934, a plan by Yotara Sugimura of the Foreign Ministry was publicized for the first time, undoubtedly at Ayukawa's request, for Japan's acceptance of 50,000 German Jews for settlement in Manchuria. According to Mr. S., a Jewish executive who worked under and enjoyed a long and close relationship with Ayukawa, he had long sought such Jewish pioneers with their technical and intellectual endowments for his Manchurian plans. As Chō, in his article, makes clear, the Manchurian settlement plan was eagerly supported by Ishiwara, Itagaki and, somewhat less enthusiastically, by Matsuoka, then president of the South Manchurian Railroad (the quasi-governmental agency that virtually ruled the country).[107]

Two additional important members of the Manchurian faction ideologically and personally, Naoki Hoshino and Nobusuke Kishi, were friends and enthusiastic supporters of Ayukawa and his plan for the importation of American capital. Both were later to reappear as influential members of the central government, after their recall from Manchuria in 1939. Both also seemed to have had their share in supporting the Board and Finance Ministry, respectively. If they did not get their stereotype of the Jews directly from Takahashi, as did Ayukawa, they must have assimilated it during their close association with the latter. These individuals sought to import as much as one billion American dollars for this purpose.

Finally, we find a kindred soul to the Manchurian faction in Hachiro Arita, the foreign minister in the Konoe Cabinet which promulgated the Japanese policy toward the Jews. He was a long-time member of an ultranationalist organization called Genyosha (Dark Ocean Society) and a central figure in the foreign office from 1932 until Pearl Harbor. Arita had worked closely with Toshio Shiratori, later ambassador to Italy and a virulent antisemite. He authored the articles, "The Japanese and the Jews," in the *Yudaya Kenkyu* (August 1942), in which he accused the Jews of plotting to control the world. Mamoru Shigemitsu, later ambassador to China, was another close colleague of Arita's in the foreign office. Shigamitsu, too, believed in the notion of "Jewish influence over world opinion," which undoubtedly helped to shape Arita's views of the Jews as well.[108]

What Chō and others were not aware of was the part played by the Jewish policy in all this. Ayukawa's concept of the Jews as rich, influential and willing to work with Japan was a complex one. The story of Schiff's loans to Japan seems to have impressed Ayukawa as it did many other Japanese, only with one difference. Ayukawa undoubtedly got his information first hand from his long-time colleague and friend Takahashi, Japan's Minister of Finance and one-time Premier, who was assassinated in the 1936 army plot. Takahashi had also at one time thrown his full support to Ayukawa's plans for Manchuria. He will be remembered as the one who met Schiff accidentally in London in 1904 when Japan, still untested as a military power, sought desperately needed loans to keep her war machine going. Schiff's generosity, so apparently unusual for a hardheaded financier, aroused Takahashi's curiosity and made him try to understand Schiff's reasoning. He became well acquainted with Schiff, and in fact sent his daughter to live in Schiff's house when she went to the United States for three years of study. This enabled Takahashi to discuss many details of the loan with Schiff. As he has explained in his memoir, the loans were part of Schiff's urgent protest against Czarist

Russia's mistreatment of its Jews. This loan was especially
timely, coming on the heels of the protests against the Kishinef
Pogroms of 1903. There is little doubt that the concept of universal Jewish wealth and power, especially in the United States
and Britain, and the desire to use this power on behalf of world
Jewry, were very much part of Takahashi's "indoctrination" of
Ayukawa during their numerous discussions. Moreover, Ayukawa's notion of all-powerful Jewry must have been reenforced
by the worldwide boycott of German goods by Jewish importers
during the early 1930's.[109] Nor is it unlikely that Ishiwara and
Itagaki absorbed these views from Ayukawa, their industrialist
protege, as well as from Colonel Yasue, Ishiwara's classmate
and good friend. Armed with such knowledge, these advocates
of Manchurian development, part of a clique known as the
Manchurian faction, were going to make full use of these Jews
for their own plans. The only problem was that until 1936,
when a Five Year Plan for the Industrialization of Manchuria
was officially promulgated by a cabinet decision, all the talk
about importing American capital was nothing but talk. Only
during that crucial year did a number of different factors con-
verge and a major overhaul of the earlier policy toward the
Jews was called for.[110]

It would not be surprising if the aforementioned *Kokusai Sakai Gakhai* were subsidized, at least partially, by Ayukawa and some of his friends in the Imperial Way Clique, such
as Ishiwara and the Minister of Education, General Sadao
Araki, who desired more information about these influential
Jews from such experts on the Jewish question as Yasue,
Inuzuka and Shioden. These "founders" used the antisemitic
journal to spread their Japanese versions of the *Protocols* in
print and in lectures. Yet, when Ayukawa and his Kwantung
Army friends, especially Ishiwara, Hoshino and Kishi, with
the government's blessing, decided to push their plans for

developing Manchuria forward with American, especially
Jewish, capital and Jewish settlers, they called on these same
experts to put their theoretical knowledge of making use of the
Jew for Japan's good into practice by becoming the on-the-
spot advisors in Manchuria and later in Shanghai. This is probably why their antisemitic colleague, Shioden, who had close
ties with Nazi Germany and whose interest lay in the elimination of the Jews, was not chosen to work with the pragmatic
idealists on the Manchurian scheme.[111]

By 1936 we enter the second period of the Japanese
relationship with the Jews, the development of a distinctly pro-
Jewish stance, which reached its height during the three years
prior to Pearl Harbor. This second period includes the three
Far East Jewish Conferences held annually in Harbin during
December of 1937 through 1939.

In the fateful year of 1936 there was a greater output
of antisemitic literature in Japan, and a related event, in
November of that year, the signing of the Anti-Comintern Pact
with Germany, took place. It was designed to counteract the
threat of Soviet Communism and Russian Far East expansion.
In the wake of this agreement with Nazi Germany, there were
some sporadic attempts to appease their racist partner by firing
a number of Jewish academicians, such as the economist Kurt
Singer, though the few cases had little impact on the overall
Japanese policy.[112]

Already in 1935 we have seen voices in the Foreign
Office which expressed anxiety over the effects on public relations in the Western countries of the Jewish protests against
their mistreatment in Manchuria.[113] It was undoubtedly the
same Manchurian faction that was responsible for establishing
the Far Eastern Jewish Council, headed by Dr. Abraham Kaufman, which was the first indication of a changed Japanese
policy toward the Jews. The Council provided autonomous

status recognition for the Russian Jews in Manchuria, and protection from the troublesome, antisemitic White Russian organization. Yasue, a friend of Ishiwara and Ayukawa, was made the liaison officer for the Council with the Army Mission in Dairen. In other words, the Jews of Harbin could henceforth appeal through the Council and Yasue directly to the Japanese authorities for redress of any injustice.[114]

The second move by the Japanese authorities to allay the fears of Manchuria's Jewish community was to close down the antisemitic *Nash Put*. This caused consternation among the large White Russian population. However, the third step followed: preparation for the first annual conference of the Jewish Communities in the Far East, which actually took place in December 1937.[115]

Earlier that year the Sino-Japanese hostilities had erupted in Shanghai, and the United States ship *Panay* was sunk and Nanking occupied. Unable to extricate herself from China by quick military action, Japan became more deeply involved. By November of 1938 she renounced further dealings with Chiang Kai-shek and, at the same time, Prime Minister Konoe declared the establishment of a New Order in East Asia. That same month, impressed by Hitler's success at Munich, Konoe entered into a cultural agreement with Germany. All these events stiffened opposition by the West to Japan's China policy and made them compare Japan with her Nazi partner. The moral embargo by the United States on aircraft and aviation gasoline to Japan was a direct result.[116] Though it may seem illogical that these steps in Japan's foreign policy should lead directly to their pro-Jewish policy, it did receive official sanction in a declaration of a Five Ministers' Meeting on December 6, 1938.

In the fulfillment of the Manchurian dreams of Ayukawa, Ishiwara and Itagaki, one other step in Japan's domestic policy should be mentioned. Ayukawa had become president of the Manchurian Heavy Industries Development Corporation, reorganized from the original Nihon Industrial Company. Despite worsening relations with the United States, Ayukawa's Five Year Plan, which involved the importation of American capital, was finally incorporated into the Four Year Plan for the Expansion of Industrial Capacity of Japan which was officially announced in January 1939. This plan was strongly advocated by their comrade Ishiwara, then on the General Staff, who saw Manchuria as the key to Japan's national defense hopes. It is also quite certain that Ayukawa was supported in these plans by Finance Minister Seihin Ikeda.[117] Despite his affiliations with big business, which was anathema to radical ideology (he was the head of the *Mitsui Zaibatsu*), Ikeda had been offered by Ishiwara in 1937 both the presidency of the Banks of Japan and the job of finance minister, which he refused at the time. Nevertheless, Ikeda accepted the office a year later, in 1938.

As a member of the *zaibatsu*, Ikeda had always opposed those factions in the army that would antagonize America. In fact, he was convinced that deteriorations in relations with Great Britain and America would be disastrous, and he hoped "that somehow or other these two countries could be used to settle the China question."

Moreover, in the fall of 1938, the critical days for the Jewish policy, Ikeda noted that:

> There are those in the army who suggest borrowing money from England; there are others who argue for the overthrow of England. It is really very troublesome that there is no unity of opinion . . . Even when American feeling toward Japan is not good as a result of the German-Japanese tie, the [American] Jews still sell goods to Japan. However, *if Japan imitates Germany's*

*severe control of the Jews, discrimination will develop
in connection with our foreign trade.* [The brackets
above, probably Tiedemann's, italics mine].[118]

It would not be surprising if Ikeda, who had close connections with his predecessor Takahashi, did not get the full
details of the Schiff loan from him.

Just prior to the reorganization of Ayukawa's Nihon
Corporation in 1937, he and Itagaki, then Army Chief of
Staff, and Matsuoka, made a month-long tour of Manchuria,
after which Ayukawa remarked:

To build up the Manchuria Heavy Industries Development Corporation in five years . . . will require 3 billion
yen. We should depend for at least one-third and pre-
ferably one-half of this sum upon foreign capital (principally American dollars) . . . The probable result of
pooling our interests with those of other countries will
be to reduce the danger of a further war.[119]

We may now return to the three Far East Jewish Conferences of 1937, 1938 and 1939, and try to view them in
relation to the overall Japanese policy vis-a-vis the Jews.
Originally, this policy had of course little if any relation to
the German-Jewish refugees entering Shanghai during the last
few months of 1938 and the first seven months of 1939. The
first Conference was held in December 1937, and, described
more fully in Dicker's work, was attended by over 1,000 Jews,
including delegates from five Far Eastern communities. The
entire scene made a profound impression on the attending
Jews, and as one observer noted of the third Conference, "there
was joy all over the town."[120] What were the goals of this and
the subsequent conferences from the viewpoint of the Jews on
the one hand, and on the other, what did the Japanese expect

to gain? We have already seen that the Jews hoped to attain a larger measure of independence from the White Russians, and better and more direct relations with the Japanese authorities. A by-product of the sort of independent status achieved by the Jews was the official recognition of Zionism as the legitimate Jewish goals. As a tiny minority, scattered over the vast regions of Manchuria and China, the Jews also desired to gain a greater sense of unity through stronger national and religious ties. Above all, these Jews wanted to know, and to let it be known, that they were not alone, that others cared about them in their precarious situation. This is why they so eagerly responded to the Japanese suggestions in 1936 and 1937 to establish their Council and Conference. Perhaps this is also the reason why the Jews in the Far East frequently responded in a similar fashion to other overtures, though aware of their being used by the Japanese for their own purpose.[121]

On the other hand, some of the Japanese aims for the Conferences in relation to the Jews of China (especially of Shanghai), Manchuria, and the United States can be gleaned from the reports and lectures by Inuzuka and Yasue. Inuzuka's report was made on October 12, 1938 before the Moslem and Jewish Problem Committee and members of the Foreign Office, and refers primarily to the Jews of Shanghai. In it he noted that since the Sino-Japanese conflict, the Jews of Shanghai, that is, the wealthy Sephardim, had been concerned about the policy of the Japanese authorities. Therefore, he suggested, "now it can be said to be the best chance for us to conduct a Jewish operation" [sic] [i.e. campaign]. As an example, of their attempt to "sound out Japan," Inuzuka pointed to the Sephardim advancing $700,000 credit for a Japanese project. "In making use of the Jewish people," Inuzuka urged a dual approach, combining friendly overtures with firmness, without going to either extreme. Referring to

222   JAPANESE, NAZIS & JEWS

the wealth of the Jews, he continued, "it will be advisable to
make use of their economic power in China to our interests."
This, however, would require the establishment of a basic
Japanese policy toward the Jews.

Inuzuka then went on to present a few practical steps
to achieve a viable policy. First, he advised that a civilian
agency like the Japan Economic Federation (*Nihon Keizai
Renmeikai*) rather than military agency deal with the Jews.
The following year this body established the External Rela-
tions Committee (*Taigai Iinkai*) to attract American investment. The next task was to set up a committee to study the
Jewish problem and "keep in touch with the Government."
In Shanghai, Inuzuka called for greater coordination and exchange of information between the various intelligence-gather-
ing services, including those of the Army, the Navy the Consul
General, the Shanghai branches of the South Manchurian
Railroad and the "International Association of Politics and
Economics" (i.e., the *Kokusai Sekei Gekkai*). He summarized
these notions in the following statement:

> . . . since . . . the Jewish people in Shanghai, especially
> Sassoon . . . have their capital and property in Shanghai;
> . . . [and] our country may be in need of an enormous
> amount of funds for the development of China, it will
> be important to study in detail and find to what extent
> we can make use of the Jewish people, to what degree
> they are incompatible with our purposes, and so forth.
> It is emphatically advised, therefore, that our intelli-
> gence agencies should be strengthened and investiga-
> tions on the spot intensified.[122]

The Japanese, however, had additional things in mind,
which would be greatly enhanced by successful manipulation
of the Conferences. From Yasue's lecture, delivered after that

of his colleague Inuzuka, and distributed to all the Japanese diplomatic channels of the Far East by Prime Minister Konoe, we get an idea of the aims of the Japanese concerning the Jews of Manchuria and those of the United States. As we have seen from the signing of the 1936 anti-Comintern Pact, Japan sought to counteract Russia and Communism. She also desired to promote greater cooperation with the United States in order to help achieve her Manchurian development plans, and at the same time maintain, if not improve her trade relations, since she still depended on the United States and Britain for her raw material. Yasue expressed these two points in his lecture:

1. The Jewish people in the Far East will solemnly denounce Communism and proclaim their gratitude for Japan's efforts in fighting against the USSR, the enemy of mankind.

2. The Jewish people, while both Japan and Manchoukuo [sic] render protection to them, will contribute to the interests of the two countries.

Idealistically we will first solidify [i.e., unite] the Jewish people in Manchuria, then proceed to the indoctrination of those in North, Middle and South China and finally of those all over the world.[123]

In other words, the Jews of Manchuria would serve to influence all the Jews of the Far East in Japan's cause, and they in turn would impress the rest of world Jewry, especially in the United States. What the Japanese also had in mind was that since Russian Jews were less ideologically opposed to the Japanese than the British Jews, such as Sassoon, one should use a Russian such as Topaz (then president of the Russian Jewish community in Shanghai) to "influence his relative"

[sic] Sassoon to modify his open dislike of the Japanese, and take a more neutral posture.[124] Similarly as we shall see, individuals with close ties to American Jewry would attempt to sway this powerful group, which controlled 80 per cent of America's capital, the press, the media, and of course President Roosevelt. The resulting favorable climate of opinion in America would help to offset the recently established Moral Embargo. At the same time the American Jews would be encouraged to repeat the financial assistance rendered to Japan 34 years earlier by Schiff. Such a successful enterprise would fulfill Ayukawa's dream of inducing a large number of technically proficient Jews to settle in Manchuria. And, perhaps most of all, a strong, united Jewish community in Manchuria, as a separate national entity, would serve to counteract *Birobidjan*, the so-called "Jewish" Soviet state bordering on Manchuria.[125]

What were some of the practical steps taken to put into effffect these grandiose ideas of Ayukawa, and his Manchurian faction? And how did such steps lead to a pro-Jewish policy in Tokyo at the Five Ministers' Conference on December 8, 1938, less than two weeks before the second Conference and three weeks prior to the announcement of Ayukawa's Five Year Plan? Formalizing the Far East Council and arranging for the Jewish Conferences was already realized. The initiative for these came from the Japanese, despite disclaimers, such as one in a government report about the first conference which stated, "This conference was *initiated only by Jewish people* who approached special section, Japanese army and received their agreement concerning said conference" [italics mine]. A more realistic view is given by Mr. Z. one of Harbin's major businessmen and a confidant of the Japanese officials, when he said quite explicitly, "the Jewish Council, which *was created by the Japanese Government* . . ." [italics mine].[126]

A speech given by General Higuchi, chief of the Japanese Military Mission, can be paraphrased as follows: Extolling the new spirit of cooperation between the Jewish people and the people of Manchuria and Japan, and expressing satisfaction at the recognition by the Jewish communities of "the present position of Japan and Manchuria" (i.e., Japan's legitimate hegemony) it was the intention of this gathering to spread this notion to the rest of the Jews in the Far East." He continued:

> There is no doubt that in case of regeneration of their motherland the firm nationalism [Zionism] of the Jewish people will be satisfied. *If the Jewish people are given the opportunity to direct their talented activity in the line of economics and science,* this will absolutely destroy the modern acuteness [i.e., difficulties] of the Jewish question.

> The Nipponese having no racial prejudice look friendly towards the Jewish and are ready to cooperate with the Jewish people . . . and *maintaining close business relations* [italics mine].

> For your, Jewish people, Nippon gives a full possibility of an extensive business cooperation of which you have already been convinced.

> . . . Manchu-Ti-Kuo has for the basic for her existence the great idea of "the coordination of all the people" [sic] [better "the whole world under one roof" or "universal brotherhood"].

He added that the representatives at the conference should give the proclamation active support, and not regard it as "a dead statement." As Dicker pointed out, he must have realized that before real cooperation could exist, the suspicion of the Jews had to be stilled. The official resolution went as follows:

> We Jews, attending this racial conference, hereby proclaim that we enjoy racial equality and racial justice under the national laws, and will cooperate with Japan and Manchuria in building a new order in Asia. We appeal to our coreligionists.[127]

Such proclamations and resolutions of the first as well as subsequent conferences were to be sent to all major Jewish organizations and publicized in Harbin's Jewish newspaper *Yevreskaya Zhizn*. In one such issue, for example, six months after the first conference, and duly reported in a foreign office document, there appeared an article entitled "Japan and the Jewish People." As the document expressed it:

> . . . an article in defense of Japan [which] appeared in the *"Jewish Life"* [*Yevreskaya Zhizn*], organ of the Far East Jewish Convention in Harbin.

Which it summarized as follows:

> In some papers in Europe, a false rumor had it that the Japanese Government set an anti-Jewish movement afoot. However, such information is either a mistake or an intrigue. *In defense of Japan, we will explain the fact that on the contrary, the Japanese Government is helping Jews.* [italics mine][128]

Yasue, in some of his concluding remarks in his October 1938 Report, emphasized the public relations aim of the previous conference. Among other things he noted:

> Through the Far East Jews can we advertize our hospitality toward them [the American Jews]. This means, I believe, will be effective also in dealing with the boycott

of Japanese goods problem . . . By means of this magazine we should give to the world an impression that
Far East is the best place for Jews to settle down, make
known the economic situation of Japan and the actuali-
ties of our operation, encourage the Jews for further
investment report in detail the military situations and
the operations for the maintenance of peace and thus
solidify their sympathy with Japan. we will make the
utmost of this means at the all-American Convention
[American Jewish Congress] of November [1939].[129]

In addition to the Jewish newspaper articles and cables
to Jewish organizations, word of the good treatment of Jews
by the Japanese was, as intended, conveyed personally by Mr.
Z. to the key Jewish leaders in the United States. Cyrus Adler,
then president of the American Jewish Committee, and Rabbi
Stephen S. Wise, then president of the American Jewish Congress, were approached. As a so-called confidant of Roosevelt,
Wise was assumed by the Japanese, as well as by many of his
coreligionists, to be the most influential Jew in the United
States. It was expected that he would be able to sway the
President and of course his powerful coreligionists. The
Japanese concept, however, was not as farfetched as it might
seem, since Wise, in the words of one recent historian, "more
than any other figure represented American Jewry and as such
was patronized by Roosevelt, Hull, and other top-ranking
government officials." Nor was Wise's image of himself any
less, as this historian continued, "Wise naturally considered
himself a person of importance and responsibility." Mr. Z. on
a business trip to the United States, was asked by Dr. Kaufman to represent the Jews of the Far East at the American
Jewish Congress convention scheduled for May 1938, and to
submit a report entitled "The Situation of the Jews in Japan

and Manchu-Ti-Kuo," which included statements by Dr. Kaufman and part of Higuchi's address at the 1937 Conference.[130]

We know from the correspondence of Rabbi Wise to Mr. Z. on November 22, 1938 that the former, almost five months after the unsuccessful Evian Conference and only 11 days after Crystal Night, was totally opposed to any concurrence with the request from the Jews of the Far East. He wrote:

> I write to you again in order to say, I am in complete disagreement with your position. I think it is wholly vicious for Jews to give support to Japan, as truly Fascist a nation as Germany or Italy. I do not wish to discuss the matter any further and I deeply deplore whatever your reasons may be that you are trying to secure support for Japan from Jews, I promise you that everything I can do to thwart your plans. I will do. You are doing a great disservice to the Jewish people.
>
> I do not wish to discuss this with you further. I have no desire to speak with anyone who like you is prepared to give support to Japan for reasons which are invalid and without regard for the fact that *Japan is like Germany, Italy, a nation that is bound to take an anti-Semitic attitude, and indeed has already done so.* [italics mine]
>
> > Faithfully,
> > Stephen S. Wise
> > President

In desperation, Mr. Z, replied the next day with the following message:

> In the name of the 15,000 Jews in the Far East I implore you to think of us; not to throw us upon the waves of

disaster and not to take upon yourself the responsibili-
ties of any consequences where there might be at least
the minimum hopes for betterment of our situation.[131]

This unanswered appeal is really the basis for the cooperation
of the Jews with the Japanese in their attempt to survive under
extremely difficult conditions. All they really wanted, in Z's
view, was a letter stating that

> . . . the Committee was glad that the attitude of the ad-
> ministration to the Jews in Manchuria [sic] is improving
> and the Committee believes that the good relationship will
> continue for mutual benefit . . .[132]

For obvious reasons Wise's letter was never communicated to
the Japanese whose pro-Jewish policy was promulgated only
two weeks later.

An invitation to Dr. Kaufman (then in Harbin) to
visit Japan for a month in May 1939, was a further step taken
by the Japanese to create better relations with Manchurian
Jews, in order to impress American Jewry.[133] In Tokyo, Dr.
Kaufman was feted as he made the rounds between one government office and another, in order to gather first hand views
from the highest echelons on the Jewish question. At one meeting, he met a group of bankers and Finance Minister Ikeda,
who discussed financial problems with him, and undoubtedly
touched upon the investment of American Jewish capital in
Manchuria. Ikeda reassured Kaufman that Japan had no
reason to persecute Jews and that racism and other forms
of discrimination were foreign to Japan. In his talk with the
other Japanese bankers, Ikeda voiced fear of German influence on Japan. This was the same person who, as we have
seen, in 1938 disagreed with the Tokyo policy that would
undermine Japanese-American relations. He was therefore the

right man to reassure Kaufman concerning Japanese treatment
Jews. At the office of the Army Chief of Staff, Kaufman met
an old acquaintance from Manchuria (Itagaki?) whom he
considered a friend of the Jews. Dr. Kaufman noted that as
part of the Far Eastern Jewish Council he had established the
Far East News Information Service which would provide free
information about the true situation of the Jews in the Far
East. Before he returned to Harbin, Dr. Kaufman was presented with a gift, a picture of the palace in Tokyo in a special
frame denoting it as an imperial gift—a great honor in the
eyes of the Japanese. This award would one day, near the end
of the war, save Dr. Kaufman's life at the hands of the
Japanese police.[134]

This invitation to Japan of the Jewish representative
in the Far East was preceded, six weeks earlier, by a similar
invitation to a supposedly influential American journalist,
William O. Inglis, "to dispel misunderstandings in the U.S.
about Japan and to bring Japanese-American amity," by the
Japan Economic Federation (*Nihon Keizai Renmeikai*). This
organization, which also probably made the overtures to Dr.
Kaufman, aimed to improve American relations and to attract
American capital for investment in Manchuria.[135] The prevailing social and political climate according to Chō, meant that
the scheme to import capital from the United States especially
from the Jewish angle, had to be carried out with extreme
care. It is not surprising, therefore, to find that there exists
only one public document concerning the aims of the External
Relations Committee. It states:

The External Relations Committee, established within
the [Japan Economic] federation in April 1939, has as
its objective the dissemination of information abroad and
the carrying out of research in order to promote under-

JAPANESE AND JEWS

231

standing and cooperation with various foreign countries concerning the long-term industrial and economic construction of Japan, Manchuria, and China . . .[136]

In June 1940 there was still another invitation by this Federation to prominent Americans for the same purpose. This time, the visitor was a lawyer, General O'Ryan, who spent several weeks in Japan. Nothing, though, seems to be known about the follow-up of either Inglis' or O'Ryan's missions. The expense for these activities was borne by the General Affairs Bureau of the Manchukuo Ministry of State Affairs headed by Hoshino and his vice chief Kishi. Chief among the Japanese attending the meeting was Ayukawa, president of the Manchurian Heavy Industries Development, as well as a number of other key people among Japan's financial circles. As Chō again makes clear, these two attempts to raise American capital and ease Japanese-American tensions failed, since one month after the second attempt, the signing of the Tripartite Pact doomed its success. What Chō was unaware of, besides the Jewish involvement, was the fact that such attempts relating to Jews, as we have already seen, took place prior to, in between and even *after* the visit of the two Americans. Much more concern, activities and proposals involved the Jewish aspect of the attraction of American capital, and it would not be at all surprising to find out one day that the Inglis and O'Ryan venture itself was a by-product of the overall scheme to utilize the Jews on behalf of Japan.[137]

In tying together these various developments, we will notice that by the end of December 1938, there had evolved a definitely pro-Jewish policy, advocated, or at least agreed to, by the highest authorities. This policy came into being, in spite of, or perhaps because of a firmer stand by Britain and the United States against Japan's declared New Order in Asia, and her cultural pact with Germany—in the form of a Moral Embargo by the United States of strategic material to Japan. We believe that this came about as a result of the influence wielded by members of the Imperial Way clique, or more specifically the Manchurian faction under the leadership of Ishiwara and Ayukawa, to use the Jews of the Far East as a means of easing tension between the United States and Japan and encouraging the importation of American Jewish capital to develop Manchuria. In their arguments, such persons as Ishiwara and Itagaki etc., were supported by the "experts," Yasue and Inuzuka. As financial authorities, Ikeda, Kishi and Hoshino must have been particularly effective spokesmen on behalf of this policy. It received its formal recognition at a Five Ministers' Conference on December 6, 1938 suggested by Army Minister General Itagaki, and including the Prime Minister (Konoe), Army (Itagaki), Navy, Foreign Affairs (Arita) and Finance Ministries (Ikeda) in the following declaration:

> Our diplomatic ties with Germany and Italy require that we avoid embracing the Jewish people, in light of their rejection by our allies. But we should not reject them as they do because of our declared policy of racial equality, and their rejection would therefore be contrary to our spirit. This is *particularly true in light of our need for foreign capital and our desire not to alienate America.* [italics mine]

These provisions followed the declaration.
1. At present we will not reject the Jews presently living in Japan, Manchuria and China and we will treat them equally with other foreigners.
2. Jews to enter Japan, etc. in the future will be treated under the same entry as other foreigners.

3. We will not extend a special invitation to Jews to come to our territories, but *capitalists and engineers will be mentioned.* [italics mine][138]

This crucial meeting, mentioned and quoted in a number of sources, set the tone for the Japanese relations to the Jews for the next three years, and was to have a great effect on the flow of refugees from Austria and Germany. The policy owes its creation not to the refugee influx, which by December of 1938 had hardly reached the 1,000 mark, but to the earlier Jewish residents of the Far East. We know this because plans for it were developed and formulated when the number of refugees entering was hardly more than a trickle. As it turned out, however, it was the large contingent of refugees streaming into Shanghai during the first half of 1939, and the smaller group that came through Japan in 1941, that were the beneficiaries of this benign policy.

Once the pro-Jewish policy had been formulated, a special effort followed, relating to the Jews of the Far East and the United States, to effect the hoped-for Japanese plan for the importation of foreign capital, particularly on the part of those dealing with the Third Conference of the Jewish Communities in the Far East, scheduled for December 1939. It was only weeks after the Jewish policy was adopted, on January 1, 1939, that the official incorporation of the former Five Year Plan into a new "Four Year Plan for the Expansion of the Industrial Capacity of Japan" took place. Exactly two months later came the only official public announcement of the Japanese policy toward the Jews, in a reply by Foreign Minister Arita to a question in the upper house of the Japanese parliament. He had expressed anxiety about the large number of Jewish refugees entering Shanghai, which was of some concern to the Japanese public, and "requested a clear-cut enunciation of the Government's policy toward the Jews." Arita's reply as quoted in the *Japan Times* reiterated part of the resolutions passed at the Five Ministers Conference, in stating:

Japan has never made any discrimination against alien people either through legislation or as a matter of fact. In view of public attention attracted by an increasing number of Jews in the Far East since last autumn, the Government has decided on a definite policy toward Jews, according to Foreign Minister Arita who said this policy aims at no discriminations against Jews. Jewish residents in Japan shall be treated just as any other foreign residents who are free.

This reply by Arita was evidently elicited from the former Ambassador to the United States Kotsuji Debuchi who, one imagines, was in on Arita's plans for attracting American capital.

Arita repeated his stand concerning Jews two months later, at the annual conference of Prefectural Governors, at which he said:

Germany has created friction with other countries by her treatment of Jews; Japan wishes to avoid it.

The implications of the first part of this statement are his and the government's desire to avoid friction. Or better, by treating the Jews well, Arita hoped to promote more favorable relations with the United States.[139]

Dr. Kaufman, in his talk with Japanese officials in Tokyo, noted that Arita's favorable comments concerning the Jews in the Far East were well received in *Congress Weekly,* the organ of the American Jewish Congress.[140]

While these efforts to attract American capital were going on in one area, there were activities elsewhere in the Far

East relating to Jews, with the same aim in mind. For example in order, as Inuzuka noted in the report that helped to create the Japanese policy, "to make use of their economic power . . to our interests . . . it is necessary first to find out their [Jewish] desires in detail and then clarify demands on our part. It will be a prerequisite therefore to establish as soon as posible practical measures to make use of the Jewish people."[141]

Dr. Setsuzo Kotsuji was called to serve as advisor to the Research Department of the South Manchurian Railroad (*Mantetsu Chosa-bu*) on the Jewish question. His earlier works on Hebrew grammar and the Semitic alphabet, written in 1936 and 1937, respectively, had established him as the only Japanese scholar of Hebraica. There followed a short stint as a researcher at the *Kokusai Gakkai Sakai* in 1938. It was probably while he was in the latter organization that his expertise on Jewish affairs came to Matsuoka's attention. Matsuoka requested his services in January 1939, but Kotsuji did not go to Manchuria until October of that year. Still he was there in time to provide, as we know, a spectacular appearance for the benefit of the Jews at the Third Conference, when they would hear, for the first time, a Japanese official address them in Hebrew.[142]

We have now seen how the Japanese policy toward the Jews was officially formulated, and the feverish activity which followed to attract American capital for the furtherance of their New Order in Asia. In light of this, Japan's public silence and her permission for thousands of Jewish refugees to enter Shanghai during the first half of 1939 becomes clear. Even the eventual restrictions put into effect in August of that year, after the refugee population reached 14,000, were no indication of a change in Japan's pro-Jewish policy. In spite of pleas by Shanghai's Japanese colony for relief from the overcrowding of Hongkew and the rising economic competition,

Japan still did not act to close the doors. She did so only after
assurances were received by Sir Victor Sassoon that the Jews
all over the world would not protest.[143]

The Japanese policy vis-a-vis the Jews was not altered
by the arrival of so many refugees in Shanghai. In fact, these
circumstances actually increased the efforts to use the Jews
to obtain American Jewish capital.[144] It also came at a critical
period of Japan's relations with the United States whose retort
to Japan's New Order was a hardening of its attitude. One sign
of this was the announcement in July 1939 (at a time the
deliberations concerning the "settlement" and "restrictions")
of America's intention to abrogate its commercial treaty with
Japan. This left the export of vitally needed strategic materials
at the mercy of a critical Washington. The Shanghai/Man-
churian Settlement plans, involving the large body of newly
arrived refugees, illustrates this. We have seen that Ayukawa
long dreamed of settling 50,000, or even 100,000 technically
proficient German Jews as part of his Manchurian Development idea, but it remained pure speculation until the arrival
of the refugees at Shanghai.[145] During the period of pro-Jewish
policy that followed the Five Ministers Conference, there were
several plans proposed and developed by Inuzuka, Yasue and
others, for creating permanent Jewish settlements in either
Manchuria or Shanghai. They fitted in well with the underlying scheme of attracting capital. The immediate presence of
thousands of refugees in Shanghai must have increased interest
in Inuzuka's plan, and we are certain that whatever negotiations were carried on, concentrated primarily on the Shanghai
plan. These projects were also doomed to fail, but much time
and effort were expended on their development. The only
practical result of these proposals was the positive effect they
had on the Japanese approach to the refugee problem.

The first of these plans, probably initiated by Mr. Z.,

centered on a small settlement to be located near Harbin. This involved the setting up of facilities for a leather factory, for about 200 workers and their families, altogether about 600 persons. Z. had offered to cover the expenses involved, including a donation of the land. He did insist, however, on the financial participation by American Jewish organizations of $200,000. This sharing of the responsibilities for settling Jewish refugees was not forthcoming according to Z, and the plan never materialized.[146] One may guess that it was less a matter of money that made the Jewish organizations hestitate, than the fear of appearing to cooperate with the Japanese, as we saw in the case of Dr. Wise.[147]

This project was proposed some time in early 1939, probably in March, and certainly no later than mid-April, during the height of the refugee influx into Shanghai. It was very likely part of a large plan, to be discussed below, for which Inuzuka desired a 200 million yen credit, of which 25 million was to be used to finance the leather factory.[148]

The second, much larger plan involved the creation of a Jewish settlement, in either Manchuria or China proper, for at least 30,000 Jewish refugees, though Inuzuka originally projected a figure as high as 300,000. This project was studied and debated at this very time and in the same reports, which covered the restrictions on the refugee immigration, and these two proposals did not seem mutually exclusive.[149]

A joint report of this plan, which included the views on the forthcoming restrictions, was submitted on July 7, 1939 by Yasue, Inuzuka and Ishiguro, representing the Ministries of the Army, Navy and Foreign Affairs, respectively. The initial plan was researched early in May 1939, which included a "successful" encounter with the leading Jewish representatives in Shanghai. By July 6, Yasue had a combined version in Tokyo for approval by the authorities. The specific data on the proposed settlement was the result of much planning, since the aim included not only the existing refugee colony, but those additional refugees that were expected to be added to it, whether through natural increase or further emigration. Thus, the statistics provide projections for a three-unit population, ranging from 30,000 to 50,000 to 70,000 for a 10 to 20 year period.

The location of this project was a matter of dispute among the members of the Task Force, with suggestions ranging from locations in or near Shanghai, such as Pootoong, or completely newly built sectors of Shanghai, or an island off Manchuria called Tsungming, among the geographic contenders, which included even locations in Korea. The geographic differences reflected the various interests represented. For example, Yasue preferrd a location near Manchuria, his base of operations, though he was by no means dead set against Shanghai. Yasue, in line with his general views, preferred the Manchurian site, where the settlement "shall be in the form of a Jewish autonomous territory like Birobidzhan and shall be placed under the protection of Japan through the new Chinese Regime."[150] No doubt Yasue's thinking was influenced by his visit to Palestine in the 1920's and his desire to create a sort of Zionist state in Manchuria. Yasue may have been familiar with Herzel's early desire to set up a Jewish state in Uganda, a fact which permitted Yasue to think of his Manchurian "Israel" as not too far fetched. However, just as Manchuria itself was never really autonomous in spite of Ishiwara's influence and slogans of "racial harmony," "racial equality," and "the righteous way," so too this Jewish enclave, in the words of the report:

> . . . is to be made to *appear* autonomous, steps will be taken to place our authorities in a position to supervise and guide it behind the scenes. [italics mine]

The Shanghai location was the natural choice of Inuzuka, who was to become permanently assigned there. Some individuals in the army voiced their objections to the selection of the Pootong area, since it was still technically part of the International Settlement, and they would brook no "interference of a third nation."[151]

In line with the forthcoming restrictions, there was to be a much more stringent process of selection, so that only those with the desired "professions and technical *skills required on our part*" would be permitted entry [italics mine].

Yasue and Inuzuka's reports of June and July 1939 make it clear to what an extent this project was only a part of the overall Japanese plan:

> . . . when we say we want to have the Jewish people cooperate in the reconstruction of New-Shanghai, what we have in mind are not only the Jewish plutocracy [i.e,, the Sassoons] but also those from all over the world, *especially their central power in New York.* [italics mine]

And thus, it continues,

> . . . when we give a land of peaceful living to the Jewish people we should make the most of this opportunity to the following effect.[152]

First, a successful approach to the Jews in the Far East would result in a "total cooperation with our country by the Jewish people in the Far East." This important first step would be taken by making use of some of the influential pro-Japanese Jews among the Russian Jews, such as Mr. Z. or Bloch, to work on the Sephardim who were openly pro-British. If they could be convinced, as the Jewish experts were sure that they could be, and invest in a joint venture with the Ashkenazi Jews and the Japanese, it would indicate a great advance in the conversion of the Sephardi tycoons to the Japanese. At the very least, it would subdue their vocal anti-Japanese posture and stop their financial support of Chiang Kai-shek. As a successful example of a joint venture, Yasue pointed to the Pacific Trading Company which had on its board of directors Chinese, Japanese, Sephardi and Ashkenazi Jews. He singled out a Mr. Ezekiel, who was supposed to have been Sir Victor Sassoon's chief accountant and former secretary.[153]

Simultaneously, the already allegedly pro-Japanese Russian Jews in Manchuria and Shanghai, together with their newly won converts, could approach their American coreligionists and create a "favorable turn of the attitude toward Japan of the Jewish people in Europe and America." Such a move would be a most decisive step toward "easing the loan and investment" needs of Japan for her New Order in East Asia. This goal, as we have seen, involved a great deal of investment, primarily of American money and strategic material, which would enable Japan to become self-sufficient in the military and economic sphere of Japan, North China and Manchuria. Yasue's added provision of a Jewish counterpart to Russia's Birobidzhan strengthened his case.[154]

The American Jews could also be won over to the Japanese view, this report notes, by "invitation to Shanghai of leading pro-Japanese Jews in the U.S." The Far East Conferences would work into the hands of the policy by providing "propaganda by means of writings, especially communication of the resolutions of the Supreme Jewish Council." Part of this drive on American Jews would also involve the solicitation of personal loans to Japan by Jewish financiers in the manner of Schiff's. Ayukawa and the Jewish experts could hardly have missed the fact that it was Schiff's Jewish connections in Euro-

pean financial circles that made possible the even more successful second and third multinational loans to Japan in 1904
and 1905. With Schiff's example constantly in mind, it was
assumed that the success of such personal loans would spur
Jewish financiers of Europe, in, say, Holland or Belgium, to
do likewise.[155]

Once the powerful Jewish groups had been won over,
the report continues, it should not prove too difficult to utilize
the "Jewish-controlled" press, advertising agencies and financiers, to sway the minds of the American public toward the
Japanese. Such success would enable Japan to achieve her
ultimate goal of military and economic self-sufficiency, and
rapprochment with the United States, and to concentrate on
defeating her enemy in the north, the Soviet Union. In other
words, Inuzuka and Yasue's plans reflected Ishiwara's dreams,
as advocated in his East Asia Federation and by his Manchurian faction.

In fact, it would not be surprising to find that the endeavors of the Japan Economic Federation, through its
Japanese-American Trade Council, to attract American capital into Manchuria was a by-product of the "operations against
the Jews."[156]

This plan, along with others proposed by Yasue and
Inuzuka,did not lack opposition in the military as well as
among the civilian authorities. In the case of Yasue's plan, we
find that some members of the Middle-China Expeditionary
Army voiced their objections to an "autonomous state," a pure
Ishiwaran concept, even if it were under Japanese supervision.
Others based their opposition to the use of such Jews to pro-
mote economic self-sufficiency for Japan, on patriotic grounds.
Such intent, this party contended,

. . . not only means a disregard of the true significance
of our Sacred War, but also will lead into the same rut

of destruction which the European Countries have been treading.

If we revealed even a little bit of such an intention, they would certainly make light of our Empire Strength and throw doubt on our capability waging a prolonged war. Therefore, Japanese Army will be determined to disregard the immediate interests. And also lead the Japanese people and Government to do likewise.

If we should take a false step in the basic thought, tens of thousands of the souls of the war-deceased and billions of yen would be wasted . . . for the construction of new East-Asia.[157]

In addition to the backstage maneuvering of Inuzuka and Yasue, who were the individuals involved in the negotiations concerning the settlement plans, similar negotiations were carried on at the highest levels of Japanese government. The local authorities, whether military or civilian, were not aware of such dealings. We find that the Japanese ministers were kept informed of the constant stream of Foreign Office and other official communications and research reports. We also know of the participation of the Japanese higher echelons from the Kogan Papers and Foreign Office dispatches, which included direct instructions, for example by Foreign Minister Nomura to the Japanese ambassador to the United States in January 1940. We have seen Foreign Minister Arita's public reply to a query in the Diet, by Japan's former minister to the United States. Similarly, in Kaufman's and Mr. Z. dealings with the Japanese authorities in Tokyo, discussions and meetings only with the highest officials of the government were involved.[158]

Who were the protagonists on the Jewish side? We know from several statements in the Foreign Office reports which mention meetings with "the leading characters [sic] among the Jewish people in Shanghai," and other similar statements, that Sir Victor Sassoon, Ellis Haym, Michael Speelman and possibly D. E. J. Abraham were referred to. We have also seen that, in Manchuria, Dr. Kaufman and Mr. Z. were directly involved. In spite of the paucity of documentation, as far as the American Jews are concerned, the key figure was Dr. Stephen S. Wise. Z's dealings with him are not the only ones we know about. We have a brief correspondence between a Dr. Karl Kindermann, a German Jew in Japan, with Mr. Niwa, a Japanese, and Dr. Wise, wherein Dr. Kindermann, probably at the suggestion of Inuzuka, wrote to Dr. Wise in June 1940 about the settlement plan. Dr. Wise, who had previously displayed a clear anti-Japanese stance in his correspondence with Mr. Z. now seemed open to suggestion. In his reply to Kindermann, Wise wrote that

> . . . any offer to settle Jewsh refugee [sic] in Japan which would come from authoritative sources in Japan would certainly receive the fullest consideration of Jewish organizations . . . any negotiation to be undertaken by any American Jewish organization with regard to Jewish immigration to and settlement in Japan would first have to be submitted to the State Department in Washington for its approval or rejection.[159]

The only follow-up of this letter on the part of the Japanese available is the note sent by the Shanghai Consul General Yoshiaki Miura, to Foreign Minister Yosuke Matsuoka on August 2, 1940, requesting him to review the case, with Inuzuka's added favorable comments.[160] All this took place at the time Matsuoka was preparing the details of his forthcoming diplomatic triumph, the Tripartite Pact of September 1940. Although Inuzuka claims that it was this pact that killed the plan, the present author has his doubts, since he believes that the Jewish organizations were simply suspicious of any plans to transplant Jewish refugees in the Far East under Japanese jurisdiction. Dr. Wise obviously did not publicize his correspondence, and the American Jewish community remained unaware of these plans.[161] In an earlier response to Ernst Baerwald and H. Steinfeld (the unofficial Jewish consulate in Tokyo) by Paul Baerwald, the then Chairman of the JDC and brother of Ernest, we can judge the hesitation of that organization to participate in this plan. Wise was unwilling to participate in any scheme that might smack of a ransom, as we have seen in similar proposals involving deals with the Nazis. The JDC Chairman wrote:

> . . . From your letters I have the impression that the actual settlement plans are still to be worked out in detail before they can be submitted to us. You will understand that, in view of the grave situation in Europe, it is not possible for us to provide extensive funds and keep them in reserve for plans that are not yet definite.[162]

The Japanese authorities, too, seemed to have had second thoughts, as Foreign Minister Nomura indicated in the dispatch to the Japanese Ambassador in the United States as early as in January 1940. The Japanese negotiator, Kozoh Tamura, seems to have been overoptimistic and gone beyond his jurisdiction in his dealing with his American counterpart, Mr. Garson. Mr. Garson has not yet been identified, but he seems to have been a high official of an American Jewish organization, probably the JDC. Perhaps, Garson is a pseudonym that he used to keep such delicate negotiations under cover. What is interesting is Tamura's reply to Garson suggested by Nomura, in which he writes:

. . . in consideration of the necessity for Tamura to reply
to *G* this office has the intention of having Tamura cable,
as if wholly from his own initiative, to the effect that
while the Government was not necessarily in need of the
Jews, it would be prepared to discuss the matter with the
local authorities concerning their accommodation under
certain conditions. *Due, however, to lack* of cooperation
on the part of the Jews *in Shanghai, the prospected*
locality of accommodation, solution to the problem is
having a rough sailing . . . in the event of continued
negotiations with the authorities concerned, if you are
prepared to provide a reasonable amount of funds for
each of the refugees for the constructive purposes of
accommodating the refugees and having them settled,
we should appreciate your reply by cable. [italics
mine][163]

Yet, somehow negotiations did not break down completely, as
the document from the JDC and Kindermann indicate, until
the Tripartite Pact in September 1940. This event is also mentioned by Chō as the death knell of the O'Ryan mission to
import American capital into Manchuria.[164]

By mid-1939, the Jewish refugees and the settlement
plan became the major focus of attention for the Japanese
experts in their overall "operations against the Jews," and the
Third Far East Conference dropped to second place. The
Conference and its by-product of Japanese propaganda could
not hope to compete with the attraction and hostage value of
a complete refugee settlement. All the previous factors for
utilizing the conferences to influence American Jewry, and to
convince the Shanghai Sephardi to change their pro-British
stance, were still valid. Especially the proclamation on the
first day and the resolutions on the last were made to order
for Japan's propaganda aims concerning the Jews, as the

report of June 1939 made clear. Among the points raised in the proclamation at the outset of the convention was the declaration that:

There exists no discrimination or limitation in Japan, Manchoukuo [sic], North or Central China or the religious, educational and cultural developments of the Jewish and other peoples.

This Convention holds *itself responsible for informing the Jewish people in Western Europe* and other parts of the world of the fact that the Jewish people in the Far East are treated with justice and goodwill by the governments concerned,

This Convention hereby thanks Japan and Manchoukuo for their *recognition of the Jewish people as one of the Manchurian nationalities,* and also for enabling the Jewish communities in the Far East to carry out their respective autonomous public affairs with the laws of the countries.

This Convention hereby congratulates the Japanese Empire for her great enterprise of establishing a place in East Asia, and is convinced that when the fighting has ceased, the peoples in East Asia will set on their national construction under the leadership of Japan . . . [italics mine][165]

The theme of the conference was the Jewish refugees and the problem of dealing with them. What was important from the point of view of the Japanese was the help the National Council offered in screening further immigrants, and above all, the follow-up of the above proclamation and similar pro-Japanese resolutions. These were duly adopted and cabled to Jewish organizations in New York, London and Geneva. Besides the speech in Hebrew by Dr. Setsuzo Kotsuji, there was a silent prayer offered on behalf of one of the true Christian friends of the Jews, Reverend Nakada, who had died a few months earlier.[166]

We thus find that the Third Conference and the settlement plan have become part of the larger program by the Jewish experts, in conjunction with their superiors in the Manchurian faction, and with the full knowledge and assistance of Tokyo, to make use of the alleged Jewish wealth and influence on behalf of Japan's New Order.

Thus within the context of the Japanese policy toward the Jews, influenced by the experts on Jewish affairs, and backed by sympathetic officials in various key departments, one can understand not only the permission granted to the Jewish refugee to enter Shanghai until August 1939, but also the kind of restrictions that were finally placed on this refugee influx in that month.

NOTES : JAPANESE AND JEWS

1. The following are among the major sources utilized (in translation) by the author for this chapter. The most important are the Kogan and Foreign Office Papers, part of the Dicker Papers. (DP). Courtesy of Dr. Dicker. In addition, the following were quite useful. An article by Inuzuka's wife, Kiyoko Inuzuka, "The Imperial Navy Protected the Jews: Historical Testimony Now Clearified [sic] by the Secretary of the Department of Intelligence during the Period of Jewish Refugee Influx in Shanghai" ["Imperial Navy"], *Jiyu Magazine* (February 1, 1973), pp. 236-45; Koreshige Inuzuka, "The Secret History of Japanese Jewish Policy: The Japanese Auschwitz was a Paradise, My Great Effort against Pressure Exerted Upon Jews to Set Up a Unique Japanese Policy Concerning Jewish People" [Inuzuka, "Secret"], *Jiyu Magazine* (February 1, 1973), pp. 228-35; Koreshige Inuzuka, "My Faith," a 19-page English version (probably translated by Inuzuka himself) from Inuzuka's personal papers; Hideaki Kase, "Jews in Japan," [Kase, "Jews"], *Chuo-Koron,* Vol. 86, No. 6 (May 1971), pp. 234-47. Kase used the Kogan and Foreign Office Papers, including some not available to the author in translation. Translation of Prof. Masayuki Kobayashi's two articles on the early Japanese antisemites. These are "Kametaro Mitsukawa's War against Antisemitism in Japan: Sidelight on the early years of antisemitic propaganda (1919-1932) [Kobayashi, "Mitsukawa" I], *Kaigai Jijo,* Vol. 21, No. 11 (November 1973), pp. 1-9, and "Kametaro Mitsukawa's War Against Antisemitism: Side Light on the Early Years of antisemitic Propaganda in Japan" [Kobayashi, "Mitsukawa" II], *Kaigai Jijo,* Vol. 22, No. 2 (February 1974), pp. 61-72. The author is grateful to Rabbi Marvin Tokayer for making copies of these and other related documents (a large correspondence and a number of taped interviews with involved subjects) available to the author in our long period of fruitful correspondence and exchange of sources. This chapter could not have been written without his material.

2. The history of the Jews in Japan is still to be written. A good start has been made by Dicker in his *Wanderers.* Tokayer has done much additional research and located many new sources, but at this moment the general reader must rely on the few printed journalistic ventures, all of which must be used with great caution. Among these are the following: "Jews in the Far East ["Jews FE"], *Jewish Affairs,* Vol. 1 (January 1942), pp. 2-7; Albert Parry, "The Jews in East Asia"," [Parry, "Jews"], *Asia,* Vol. 39 (September 1939), pp. 513-16; Mary I. Swartz, "Jews in Japan" [Swartz, "Japan"], *Hadassah Magazine,* Vol. 57, No. 2 (October 1975), pp. 10-11, 50-53; Joachim O. Ronall, "Jews in Japan" [Ronall, "J. Japan"], *Jewish Spectator* (February 1958), pp. 19-21; Lucie Nissim, "My War

Years in Japan" [Nissim, "Japan"], *India and Israel* (April 1952), pp. 18-19 (Wiener Library); Kase, "Jews"; Robert M. Lury, "Jews in Japan," *Review Jewish Community Center 1956-1957 [RJCC]* n.p.: np., n.d. (Tokyo, Japan); Abraham Black, "Jews in Japan," *RJCC 1957-1958* n.p.: n.p., n.d. (Tokyo, Japan), pp. 27-37. The author's estimation of the Jewish population for the late 1930's is broken down as follows:

North China-Shanghai	.. ..	21,000 - 22,000	
Sephardim	.. ..	500 - 700	
Russian	.. ..	4,000	
German Refugees	.. .. ..	17,000	
Tientsin	.. ..	1,500	
Peking			
Hankow	.. ..	500	
Hangchow			
Manchuria			
Harbin	.. ..	2,500	
Dairen			
Mukden			
	.. ..	1,000	
Tsitsihar			
Hailar			
Japan	.. ..	900	
Tokyo			
Yokohama			
Kobe, Nagasaki, Shimonoseki			

For the Shanghai statistics, see Appendix. Also Chapter II. For Harbin, *ibid.* Japan's population can be found in Arthur Ruppin, *Jews in the Modern World* (London: Macmillan and Co. Ltd., 1934), p. 27.

3. For brief biographical sketches of Yasue, see Dicker, Wanderers, pp. 77-80, 91-93 *et passim*. Among the sources used by Dicker and passed on to the author, are: a four-page biographical sketch by Yasue's eldest son Hiroo, written for Dicker in 1958 [Hiroo, "Yasue"]. (Hiroo is presently at work on a longer-biography of his father); a brief, one-page sketch of "The History and Recent Activities of the Japan Israel Association" (DP). Kase in his article mentions Yasue, as of course the Kogan and FO Papers.

A pioneer work on Japanese antisemitism is the article by Hyman Kublin, "Star of David and Rising Sun" [Kublin, "Rising"], *Jewish Frontier*, Vol. 25, No. 4 (April 1958), pp. 15-22.

Kobayashi's aforementioned two articles in *Kaigai Jijo* are important first studies of the rise of the Japanese antisemites as well as philosemites. Hiroo Yasue, already in 1958, wrote a nine-page manuscript for Dicker, titled *Jewish Problem and Japan* [Hiroo, *Jewish*] in which he gave a historical view of Japanese interest in Jews and Judaism, including the role of his father. (DP)

For Yasue's pseudonym of "Hokoshi," see Kobayashi, "Mitsukawa I,"
p. 2. There Kobayashi lists the five pioneers of Japanese antisemitism, and
their pseudonyms. They are Ennosuke Higuchi(not to be confused with
General Hiichiro Higuchi) (pseud. Baiseki Kitagami), Shogun Sakai,
Nobutaka Shioden (pseud. Nobutaka Fujiwara), Yasunori Yasue (pseud.
Hokoshi), Koreshige Inuzuka (pseud. Kiyo Utsunomiya).

Yasue's first name is usually given elsewhere as Senko (see, for example,
JCM, p. 265, or Hiroo, *Jewish*, p. 3). His pseudonym is also given by
Abraham (Setsuzo) Kotsuji, *From Tokyo to Jerusalem: the Autobiography
of a Japanese Convert to Judaism* [Kotsuji, Jerusalem] (New York: Bernard
Geis Associates, 1964), p. 151. Kotsuji gives Yasue's first name as "Nasuke,"
ibid., p. 170.

A very important source on the Japanese antisemites is Rudolph Loewen-
thal, *Japanese and Chinese Materials Pertaining to the Jewish Catastrophe*
[Loewenthal, *JCM*] (a 293-page manuscript). Prepared for the YIVO 1955.
This unpublished volume, including an index added in 1970, contains one or
two-page summaries of a large portion of the Japanese antisemitic literature.
Included are articles from the *Yudaya Kenkyu* and antisemitic books written
by most of the Japanese figures involved with the Jews, including Yasue and
Inuzuka. The author is grateful to Dr. Loewenthal, one of the authorities
on the Jews of ancient China (Kaifeng), for permitting the author to
reproduce this and numerous other documents and news clippings, that
make up the author's Loewenthal Papers (LP).

The titles of Yasue's antisemitic works are taken from Loewenthal, *JCM*,
pp. 265, 268. For his translation of the *Protocols*, see Kotsuji, *Jerusalem*,
pp. 150-51 (such as *Inside the World Revolution* or as the *JCM* translates
it, *Revelation* [*sic*] *of a Revolutionary Movement*, p. 265). A four-page
summary of this book, and an explanation of the cover symbol, is found
in the Dicker Papers [Yasue, "Revolution"].

For the composite statements see, Loewenthal, *JCM*, pp. 265-69.

4. For the three conventions, see above, Chapter II, notes 77-78. See also
FO Public Secret [*sic*] Issue No. 58 Sotaro Tanaka to Kooki [*sic*] Hirota,
February 23, 1938, [FO February 28, 1938], and FO S-9460-3-728, July 7,
1938, Jewish Report No. 14 [FO July 7, 1938], and the KP "Proclamation
of the First Convention of the Far Eastern Jewish Communities" ["First
Convention"] (DP), for information concerning the first of the three conventions.

Several versions of the third convention exist in the KP and FO series.
The Kaufman and Yasue speeches are found in the FO Secret No. 15
[Manichiro] Kubota, Consul-General in Harbin to Yoshijiro Umezo,
Ambassador to Manchuko [*sic*] (DP). This detailed report is a supplement
to FO S-9460-3-1640-1654, Kubota to Umezu, on the "Third Convention
of the Jewish People in Far East," January 11, 1940 [FO January 11 1940].
An additional, detailed report of the Third Convention, lacking a title page,
in the author's collection (DP). ["Third Convention"].

The speech of the Jewish representative from Shanghai is found in FO S-9460-3-1791, Consul-General in Shanghai Yoshiaki Miura to Foreign Minister Hachiro Arita, January 19, 1940 [FO January 19, 1940] (DP). Some aspects of these conventions are discussed by Dr. Kaufman, *Manchuria*, pp. 19, 41, and for Kaufman's high regard for Yasue as a friend of the Jews, see pp. 19, 32, 33, 36 *et passim*. For the annulment of the *J*, see p. 33. See also Kaufman, *Itonot*, p. 83. Kotsuji similarly notes the high regard Jews had of Yasue in *Jerusalem*, p. 151.

See also English summary of an unpublished article on Yasue by R. Sugita and the letter to Tokayer concerning this article, by Hiroo Yasue. (H. Yasue to Tokayer, December 23, 1974) [H. Yasue-Tokayer] (TP).

The problems for the Jews of Manchuria caused by *Nash Put* and the request for its closing are found in an undated cable [probably 1936] sent to Tokyo by the Consul-General in Harbin (S-9460-3-536). Cf. also FO EC (Secret) No. 2221, December 5, 1935, p. 4. The closing of *Nash Put* is reported in October 1938 Report of the 1937 Conference by Dr. A. Kaufman, p. 1 (Z-Dicker correspondence) (DP).

Yasue's being inscribed in the "Golden Book" on July 14, 1941 signed by Menachem Ussishkin, is noted in Morinaka Yokoo, "The History and Recent Activities of the Japan Israel Association," an undated extract of an article [co. 1958] [Yokoo, "Japan-Israel"] (DP). Kaufman, *Manchuria*, p. 19; Kase, "Jews," p. 8; Sugita, "Yasue."

5. For the use by Inuzuka of the pseudonym Utsunomiya, see Kobayashi, *Mitsukawa I*, p. 9. Professor Kobayashi confirmed this statement in correspondence with the author, April 26, 1975, and subsequently, on August 30, 1975. He came to this conclusion after years of studying all the writings of "Inuzuka" and "Utsunomiya." Kobayashi further noted that Shioden, a very close associate of Inuzuka for many years, confirmed this fact in a talk with Kobayashi, *ibid*. Kobayashi once confronted Inuzuka with this fact, to which the latter sheepishly replied, "That book was written by my wife, not by me." *Ibid.*, August 30, 1975, pp. 1-2 [Kobayashi-Kranzler correspondence].

This point was further reiterated in a taped interview by Tokayer, who asked Kobayashi the questions submitted by the author. [Kobayashi Interview] December 25, 1975. Cf. also Loewenthal, *JCM*, p. 230.

6. For the titles, dates and general description, see esp. Loewenthal, *JCM*, pp. 273-75. As noted, many articles from these two journals are summarized in this volume. According to Loewenthal, Utsunomiya was the editor of the *Kokusai Himitsu-Ryoku No Kenkyu*, *JCM*, p. 196. Cf. also Kublin, "Rising," p. 19; Kase, "Jews," pp. 9-11.

7. Kobayashi Interview. See also the pages of Loewenthal, *JCM*, for these authors; "Imperial Navy," p. 9, for Inuzuka's and Shioden's founding of the *Kokusai Seikei Gakkai* (KSG). See also below, note 83.

8. For Inuzuka's composite citations, see, Loewenthal, *JCM*, pp. 234-49.

9. Kase, "Jews," p. 12.

10. For the formulation of this policy see below in this chapter. See Chapter XIII for the 1939 restrictions. Inuzuka's part in helping the Polish refugees settle in Shanghai is found among the following: Inuzuka to Herzberg, September 17, 1941; "Imperial Navy," pp. 8-9; Inuzuka, "Faith," p. 5. The latter two sources also include the text of the cigarette case, as well as the episode of how it saved him from being tried as a war criminal. Photo of this case in author's possession courtesy of Tokayer, who received it from Mrs. Inuzuka (TP).

Cf. also the brief diary of Frank Newman and his mission in 1941, from the *Vaad Hatzalah; Agudas Harabonim* (Union of Orthodox Rabbis) and Agudath Israel [Newman Diary] (an unpublished manuscript, loaned for reproduction to the author courtesy of Mr. Newman). See also Newman taped interview by Dr. Kranzler.

11. See for example, Loewenthal, *JCM*, p. 196. The author is grateful to Professor Kublin and Dr. Avraham Altman for some elucidation of the general theory of Japanese antisemitism. Dr. Kublin also provided much of the bibliographic guidance for this chapter.

12. See below, note 80.

13. Copy of cable in author's collection, courtesy Tokayer (World Jewish Congress Archives).

14. For the background on the Jews in Japan see Dicker, *Wanderers,* Chapter 6. Cf. also above, note 2. Some of the sources for the earlier history of Jews in Japan researched by Tokayer are the following: etchings on the tombstones of the Jewish cemetery in Nagasaki, many of which indicate death and burial before the turn of the century; a series of articles from the (London) *Jewish Chronicle* beginning with 1860 through 1889, attesting to organized Jewish life shortly after the opening up of Japan to the West. Especially interesting is the long letter by Alex [ander] Marks, dated January 7, 1866 (TP).

An article concerning exploits of the Hon. Alexander Marks and his role as Japan's representative to Australia from 1879 through 1896, was written by D. C. S. Sissons, "Early Australian Contacts with Japan," *Hemisphere* (April 1972), pp. 13-15. (TP).

15. See Cyrus Adler, *"Jacob H. Schiff:* His Life and Letters, 2 vols., (New York: Doubleday, 1928), esp. Chapter VII, *et passim.* For the story of his loans to Japan see the memorandum by Korekiyo Takahashi [Takahashi, *Memo*], taken from his autobiography, and quoted in full by Adler, Vol. I, pp. 213-30. This section from the original Japanese is cited by Kase, "Jews," pp. 17-20.

As Adler noted, these loans were so large and far-reaching that they were his most important international undertaking (Vol. I, p. 213). For the financing of the navy, see Kase, "Jews," p. 18. Schiff's loan prior to Japan's first victory is noted by Takahashi, *Memo,* pp. 215-17.

16. See *ibid.,* pp. 213-25 for his connections with Warburg and Sir Ernest Cassel. Even the first half of the first loan offered by the Hongkong and Shanghai Banking Corporations, with its Jewish shareholders, i.e., the Sassoons and Kadoories. See T. Salvotti, "China, Japan und die Juden" [Salvotti, "Juden"], *Mitteilungen Uber die Judenfrage,* October 17, 1939, p. 5 (Wiener Library). Although the author is antisemitic, the statements seem factual. Kadoorie's share in the bank is verified in a nine-page statement, dated 1972, about the concern, "Sir Elly Kadoorie and Sons," on which is listed the H. & S. Banking Corporation as one of the two banks in which the Kadoorie Company has large holdings (TP). For Sassoon's share, see Kann, "Refugees," p. 20.

For Schiff as a target for antisemites, see Cohn, *Warrant,* p. 126. He quotes a Russian document to the effect that Schiff's millions supported the Bolsheviks. As Cohn already pointed out, this was based on the real attempt by Schiff, which Takahashi must have been aware of, to rally his fellow Jewish bankers against floating loans to antisemitic Czarist Russia. *Ibid.* Cf. also Takahashi, *Memo,* pp. 215-16; C. C. Aronsfeld, "Jewish Bankers and the Tsar" [Aronsfeld, "Tsars"], *Jewish Social Studies,* Vol. 35, No. 2. (April 1973), pp. 87-104, esp. pp. 100-104; Loewenthal, *JCM,* pp. 54, 196. Zosa Szajkowski, "Paul Nathan, Lucien Wolf, Jacob H. Schiff and the Jewish Revolutionary Movement in Eastern Europe 1903-1917," *Jewish Social Studies,* Vol. 29, No. 3 (Fall 1967), pp. 75-91, esp. pp. 77-80, 91.

17. Takahashi, *Memo,* p. 235. Cf. also Kase, "Jews," p. 18; S., *Jewish Consulate* [Consulate], p. 99. This manuscript, written by a German-Jewish businessman, was a long-time resident of Japan and maintained close connections with important Japanese officers and industrialists. Among the latter is Gisuke Ayukawa, whom we shall come across again in this chapter. Mr. S., who corresponded with Tokayer and the author, requested anonymity. Parts of the *Jewish Consulate* and the correspondence are part of the author's Tokayer Papers.

18. *Consulate,* pp. 104-105. Also Tokayer—S. correspondence, August 9, 1974; September 19, 1974; Kase, "Jews," p. 22.

19. Richard Storry, *A History of Modern Japan* [Storry, *Japan*] (Baltimore: Penguin Books, 1960), pp. 158-59. A general picture of Japanese military venture in Siberia is given in James William Morley, *The Japanese Thrust Into Siberia, 1918* [Morley, *Siberia*].

20. For the Japanese antisemites' early contact with their White Russian teachers in Siberia, see Kobayashi, "Mitsukawa" I, p. 2. Cf. also Hiroo, *Jewish,* p. 4; Kublin, "Rising," p. 17; Dicker, *Wanderers,* pp. 75-76; Hiroo, "Yasue"; KP Election Bulletin, April 30, 1942, by Nobutaka Shioden. [Shioden, "Election"]. This campaign literature by Shioden includes an autobiographical sketch. (DP). For Yasue, see Hiroo, "Yasue," p. 1.

21. See a chronological list of titles, starting with Ennosuke Higuchi's *Essence of Radicalism,* published in 1919, in Kobayashi, "Mitsukawa" I, p. 3. For the spread of the *Protocols* by the White Russians throughout the world, see Cohn, *Warrant,* Chaps. 5-7. Cohn noted that Admiral Kolchek, chief of the White Russian Forces in Siberia, was so obsessed by the *Protocols* that he published an edition there.

22. A good summary of the plot by the Elders of Zion is found in Cohn, *Warrant,* pp. 60-65. Similarly, for the spread of the *Protocols* throughout the world, Chapters 5-7. For the forgery, see pp. 72-76. The *(London) Times* story is found on pp. 149-53.

Much of Cohn's work concerning the origin and spread of the Protocols is based on Henri Rollin, *L'Apocalypse de Notre Temps: Les dessous de la propaganda allemande d'apres des documents inedits* (Paris: Gallimard, 1939).

23. Much of this material, books and titles are described in Loewenthal, *JCM.* Cf. also the list in Kobayashi, "Mitsukawa" I, p. 3; H. Yasue "Jewish," pp. 3-4.

One good example of this type of literature is Yasue's *Inside Story of the World Revolution,* published in 1925, under his pseudonym Hokoshi. Kobayashi remarked, in a note relating to summary of this book, that "the Protocols of Zion constitutes a major part of the book." (DP).

24. See above, note 1. Kublin also mentions such defenders of the Jews against the *Protocols,* as Professor Sakuzo Yoshino, Professor Sentaro Kemuyama and the churchmen, Donjo Ebina and Kanzo Uchimura." "Rising," p. 18.

25. James B. Crowley, *Japan's Quest for Autonomy: National Security and Foreign Policy 1930-1938* [Crowley, *Quest*] (Princeton, N.J.: Princeton University Press, 1966), pp. XIV-XVI. See also the same author's essay, "Japan's Military Foreign Policies," *Japan's Foreign Policy, 1868-1941* [Morley, *Foreign Policy*], James W. Morley, ed. (New York: Columbia University Press, 1974), pp. 3-30; Storry, *Japan,* pp. 104-107; Edwin O. Reischauer, *Japan: The Story of a Nation* [Reischauer, *Japan*] (revised edition; New York: Knopf, 1974), pp. 147-51.

26. Marius B. Jansen, "Modernization and Foreign Policy in Meiji Japan" [Jansen, "Modernization"], *Political Development in Modern Japan* [Ward, *Modernization*], Robert E. Ward, editor (Princeton, N.J.: Princeton University Press, 1968), p. 175; Norman, *Japan's,* pp. 197-201.

27. Storry, Japan, p. 145. For the earlier, cultural dependency on Japan and the changing attitudes of Japanese scholars toward China, see Marius B. Jansen, "Changing Japanese Attitudes Toward Modernization," [Jansen, "Changing"], *Changing Japanese Attitudes Toward Modernization,* Marius B. Jansen, ed. (Princeton, N.J.: Princeton University Press, 1965), pp. 54-61.

28. Edwin O. Reischauer, John K. Fairbank and Alebrt M. Craig, *East Asia: The Modern Transformation* [Reischauer, *E. Asia*] (Vol. II of *A History of East Asian Civilization;* 2 vols.; Boston: Houghton Mifflin Company, 1965), p. 483. See also Nobutaka Ike, "War and Modernization" [Ike, "War"], *Political Development in Modern Japan*, Robert E. Ward, ed. (Princeton, N.J.: Princeton University Press, 1968), pp. 194-95.

29. Storry, *Japan*, esp. pp. 168-70. The quote is from Edwin O. Reischauer, *Japan, Past and Present* (London: Duckwirth, 1957), p. 155, cited by Storry, *op. cit.*, p. 170. For the political change of the 1920's, see Robert A. Scapalino, "Elections and Political Modernization in Prewar Japan" [Scapalino, "Elections"]; Ward, *Political*, pp 283-91.

30. Ike, "War," pp. 195-98.

31. Storry, *Japan*, pp. 165-67. An excellent overview of the general effects of modernization on Japan in the twenties is found in Reischauer, *Japan*, pp. 168-78. Cf. also Scapalino, "Elections," pp. 285-91; Delmer Brown, *Nationalism in Japan* [Brown, *Nationalism*] (Berkely; University of California press, 1955), p. 169.

32. Toland, *Rising*, pp. 4-5. Cf. also Storry, *Japan*, pp. 169-75; Reischauer, *Japan*, Chapter 10; Reischauer, *E. Asia*, pp. 498-502; Ben-Ami Shillony, *Revolt in Japan: The Young Officers and the February 26, 1936 Incident* [Shillony, *1936*], Princeton, N.J.: Princeton University Press, 1973, esp. p. 15. For one of the main sources of inspiration for the young idealists and their discontent with conditions in Japan, see George M. Wilson, *Radical Nationalist in Japan: Kita Ikki, 1883-1937* [Wilson, *Kita*] (Cambridge, Mass.: Harvard University Press, 1969), see specially Chapter 5; Mark R. Peattie, *Ishiwara Kanji and Japan's Confrontation with the West* [Peattie, *Ishiwara*] (Princeton, N.J.: Princeton University Press, 1975); Yoshikashi Takehiko, *Conspiracy at Mukden: The Rise of the Japanese Military* [Takehiko, *Mukden*] (New Haven: Yale University Press, 1963), esp. pp. 107-18.

33. Ike, "War," p. 210.

34. See Asada Sadao, "The Japanese Navy and the United States" [Sadao, "Navy"],*Pearl Harbor as History: Japanese-American Relations 1931-1941* [*P. Harbor*], Dorothy Borg and Shumpei Okamoto, eds. (New York: Columbia University Press, 1973), esp. pp. 243-44. Cf. also Robert J. C. Butow, *Tojo and the Coming of the War* [Butow, *Tojo*] (Princeton, N.J.: Princeton University Press, 1961), Chapter 8.

35. For the increase in membership and the general patriotic fervor after 1936, see Takashi Ito, "The Role of Right-Wing Organizations in Japan" [Ito, "Right-Wing"]; *P. Harbor*, pp. 493, 501-502; Cf. also Brown, *Nationalism*, esp. chap. 10. The quote is on p. 206; Storry, *Patriots*, Chapters 1-3. Wilson, *Kita*; Peattie, *Ishiwara*; Shillony, *1936*; Reischauer, *Japan*, pp.

194-97. The two good studies of ultranationalists ideologies to help perceive the prevailing patriotic climate of opinion are Wilson, *Kita* and Peattie, *Ishiwara*.

36. Brown, *Nationalism*, pp. 209-15. For the later role of the Bureau of Information, see, for example, *JCM*, p. 59. In the translation of the complete article, which deals with the sponsorship of an antisemitic fair by the "Bureau," among others, Kotsuji translates the name as "Intelligence Bureau." There is little doubt that this was part of its functions. For the translation, see Kotsuji to Kranzler correspondence, August 27, 1973.

37. Brown, *Nationalism*, p. 208. A copy of rather difficult text, and a good introduction is Robert King Hall (ed.), *Kokutai No Hongi: Cardinal Principles of the National Entity of Japan* [*Kokutai*] (Cambridge, Mass.: Harvard University Press, 1949). Hall gives a detailed analysis of this book in his introduction. A brief selection of the Kokutai and other material on Japanese ultranationalism, with brief introductions, are found in Ivan Morris (ed.), *Japan 1931-1945: Militarism, Fascism, Japanism?* [Morris, *Militarism*] (Boston: D. C. Heath & Co., 1963); Reischauer, *Japan*, pp. 198-200.

38. Brown, *Nationalism*, pp. 211-15. Cf. also Peattie, *Ishiwara*, pp.

39. *Ibid.*, pp. 222-23.

40. Quoted by Toland, *Rising*, pp. 5-6. See Wilson, *Kita*.

41. Thomas R. H. Havens, *Farm and Nation in Modern Japan: Agrarian Nationalism 1870-1940* [Havens, *Agrarian*] (Princeton, N.J.: Princeton University Press, 1974), p. 313. See esp. Chap. 13. For a comparison between Japanese and American agrarianism, see *ibid.*, pp. 313-16. The quotation re agrarianism is by Richard Hofstadter, *The Age of Reform* (New York: Random House, 1955), p. 24. Cited by Havens, *Agrarian*, p. 316. Cf. also Maruyama Masao, *Thought and Behavior in Modern Japanese Politics* [Masao, *Thought*] (expanded edition, edited by Ivan Morris; London: Oxford University Press, 1969), esp. pp. 36-41.

42. See, for example, Peattie, *Ishiwara*, pp. 223-29. Cf. also Shillony, *1936*, p. 164; Reischauer, *Japan*, pp. 184-86; Takehiko, *Mukken*, pp. 107-18.

43. Though scholars of Japanese nationalism may differ as to the simplification of this definition, for our purpose of clarifying the relationship of ultranationalism to the "Jewish Problem," it is sufficient. For such a detailed analysis, for example, see James B. Crowley, "Japanese Army Factionalism in the Early 1937's" [Crowley, "Factionalism"], *Journal of Asian Studies*, Vol. 21, No. 3 (May 1962), pp. 309-26. Some simpler versions are found in Toland, *Rising*, pp. 3-10; Reischauer, *Japan*, pp. 191-96; Storry, *Japan*, pp. 192-200, *et passim;* in *Patriots*, Storry gives a detailed account of these two factions and their ideologies, especially in

Chapters 6-7. Cf. also Shillony, *1936;* Wilson, *Kita;* Crowley, *Quest;* Masao, *Thought.* Ivan Morris, *Nationalism and the Right Wing in Japan: A Study of Post-War Trends* [Morris, *Nationalism*] (London: Oxford University Press, 1960). Morris shows how these factions reappeared in the postwar era.

44. See Toland, *Rising,* pp. 6-9; Reischauer, *Japan,* p. 188; Storry, *Japan,* pp. 192-94. Cf. also works in note 43. Among the most detailed discussions of Manchuria as a panacea is found in Peattie, *Ishiwara, et passim.* It was Ishiwara who most clearly defined the concept of Manchuria as a haven for multi-ethnic groups; see Chapter 5, esp. pp. 145-50, 164-65. For the dreams about and the conquest of Manchuria, see Chap. 4, esp. pp. 96-101.

45. Toland, *Rising,* p. 6. Cf. also Brown, *Nationalism,* p. 195.

46. For the influence of middle-echelon officers, see Akira Fujiwara, "The Role of the Japanese Army" [Fujiwara, "Army"], *P. Harbor,* pp. 189-95, esp. p. 191. Cf. also Masao, *Thought,* p. 107; Reischauer, *Japan,* pp. 190-91; Storry, *Japan,* p. 192; idemd, *Double,* Chaps. 4-5. Mamoru Shigemitsu, *Japan and her Destiny: My Struggle for Peace* [Shigemitsu, *Destiny*] (London: Hutchinson, 1958), p. 64.

47. Peattie, *Ishiwara,* esp. pp. 37-48.

48. *Ibid.,* p. 44. On the principle of *hakko ichiu,* see esp. pp. 320-21. Also Brown, *Nationalism,* pp. 208-209; Reischauer, *Japan,* p. 200. For his strategical concerns, esp. re Russia, see Chap. 6, esp. pp. 200-206.

49. *Ibid.,* p. 150.

50. For Itagaki, see, for example, Toland, *Rising,* p. 6 and Peattie, *Ishiwara,* pp. 95-96, *et passim.* For Iwakura, see *ibid.,* pp. 67-68, where his role in Manchuria re the Jews is discussed. He, Itagaki, Iwakuro and Higuchi were all staff officers in the Kwantung Army in Manchuria. Iwakura later worked in the Army Ministry, no doubt brought there by his Manchurian colleague, Itagaki, when the latter became Chief of Staff. See Chichiro Hosoya, "The Role of Japan's Foreign Ministry and its Embassy in Washington, 1940-1941" [Hosoya, "Foreign"], *P. Harbor,* p. 150. For Itagaki's role as army minister, see Katsumi Usui, "The Role of the Foreign Ministry" [Usui, "Foreign"], *P. Harbor,* p. 140; Peattie, *Ishiwara,* pp. 95.

Yasue's very close friendship with Ishiwara dating from their student days is attested to by Yasue's son Hiroo, in his brief biographical sketch of his father. Hiroo characterizes this friendship with the phrase, "General Ishiwara intimate friend of Col. Yasue, classmate." (DP). For Ishiwara's leadership of the East Asian League, see Peattie, *Ishiwara,* pp. 176-77, *et passim.* Yasue's close working relationship with Inuzuka can be gleaned from the numerous joint reports in the KP and FO Papers, and their work at the *KGS.* This has also been verified by Kobayashi Interview. For

Inuzuka's membership in the East Asian League (*Toa Renmei*), see the interview of Inuzuka by Dicker, January 28, 1958 [Inuzuka Interview]. (DP).

51. See Shillony, *1936*, Chap. 9. Cf. also Storry, *Japan*, p. 199; *Reischauer, Japan,p.* 195. Toland, *Rising*, p. 36.

52. See Ito, "Right Wing," p. 493. Cf. also Brown, *Nationalism*, pp. 198-99.

Iriye Akira, "Japan's Policies Toward the United States" [Iriye, "Policies"], *Japan's Foreign Policy 1868-1941: A Research Guide* [*Foreign Policy*], James William Morley, ed. (New York: Columbia Univeristy Press, 1974), pp. 443-44.

53. For Ishiwara's concern about Russia, see Peattie, *Ishiwara*, pp. 200-206. His concept of "total war" is clarified in *op. cit.*, Chap. 6. Cf. also Chihiro Hosoya, "Japan's Policy Toward Russia" [Hosoya, "Russia"], *Foreign Policy*, esp. pp. 397-401; Fujiwara, "Army," pp. 189-91, 194.

54. For the German-Japanese relations, see, for example, Ernst L. Presseisen, *Germany and Japan, A Study in Totalitarian Diplomacy 1933-1941* [Presseisen, *Japan*] (New York: Howard Fertig, 1969); Johanna Menzel Meskill, *Hitler and Japan: The Hollow Alliance* [Meskill, *Hitler*] (New York: Atherton Press, 1966); Frank W. Ikle, "Japan's Policies Toward Germany" [Ikle, "Germany"], *Foreign Policy*, esp. pp. 306-32.

55. John Higham, *Send These To Me: Jews and Other Immigrants in Urban America* [Higham, *Send*] (New York: Atheneum, 1975), p. 129. Cf. also Seymour Martin Lipset and Earl Raab, *The Politics of Unreason: Right-Wing Extremism in America, 1790-1970* [Lipset, *Unreason*] (New York: Harper, 1970), pp. 92-95, *et passim*.

56. See note 50 for Inuzuka's and Yasue's friendship with the ultranationalist Ishiwara. See below for examples from their writings. For Shioden's credentials as an ultranationaliist (aside from his writings), see Shillony, *1936*, p. 162, where he is depicted as a friend of the rebels.

For a summary of the *Protocols'* "plot," see Cohn, *Warrant*, pp. 60-65.

57. For the influence of the agrarian myth on the Japanese, see above, note 41. An American example of a technologically sophisticated individual under the spell of the agrarian myth is Henry Ford. See Cohn, *Warrant*, pp. 156-163, esp. p. 163.

58. For the reaction to the West, see above, note 39. See Peattie, *Ishiwara*, p. 44, for the identification of the United States as the primary source of the evils from the West. Shioden, for example, does likewise. Cf. also *JCM*, p. 73.

59. *JCM*, pp. 106, 75, 77, 108. This last, for example, is found in an article by Michiatu Kubota, titled "The Japanese Spirit and the Jewish Problem," the author notes that the Jews "encroach on the Japanese under

the guise of British and American liberalism." Cf. also p. 116, where it states, "England has become a Jewish dependency."

60. *JCM*, pp. 110-11.

61. FO S-9460-3-1722, January 1940, p. 2 (DP). Cf. also FO S-9460-3-746, October 12, 1938, p. 6.

62. *Ibid.*, pp. 1-3. See *JCM*, p. 116, for England's dependency. Cf. also *JCM*, pp. 75-77, 88, 89, 95, 98, 101, 120, *et passim;* Shigamitsu also subscribed to this theory, as he noted in *Destiny*, p. 95, "to take advantage of Jewish influence over world opinion."

63. See both articles by Kobayashi, "Mitsukawa" I, II. Cf. also some of the titles of the antisemitic works, such as *Jewish World Conquest Movement, The Cabal (Against the World) by the Jewish People* by Ennosuke Higuchi, *The Unstable World* and *Behind the World Revolution* by Shioden, *Jewish Aggression in the World* by Katsugun Sakai. In the latter, for example (*JCM*, p. 202), the author attributes various European revolutions to the Jews, who use such techniques as means of achieving economic control over these countries.

64. Yasue in an article titled "The Struggle Between Two Jewish Trends of Thought" (1936), contends that Zionism seems to be the goal of the Jews, but that is merely a ploy to control the world. As noted, Yasue had studied Zionism at first-hand in Palestine. *JCM*, p. 269.

65. *JCM*, p. 73.

66. *JCM*, pp. 67, 259. Cf. also *JCM*, pp. 72, 75, 108, 115-16, 191, *et passim.*

67. See *JCM* for the following: British Information Office, mammonism and materialism, pp 51, 61, 108, *et passim;* Jewish "individualism," pp. 226, 169; "Karl Marx" boys, pp. 115-16, 121; the distinction of the Japanese education, pp. 115-16, 181, 167; deprivation of the emperor's divine attributes are mouthed by Shiratori. See also Kase, "Jews," p. 10.

68. *JCM*, pp. 115-16. For Dewey and Pestallozzi, see p. 118.

69. *JCM*, pp. 77, 88, 101, 181. Cf. also "Imperial Navy," p. 2.

70. *JCM*, p. 73.

71. *Ibid.*, p. 184. Shioden repeated this line in a similar fashion, p. 214.

72. For the Jewish control of the press, see above, note 62. Cf. also Muto-Teiiti, *Angriff der Juden gegen Japan* (The Jewish Attack on Japan) [Teiiti, *Juden*] (Tokyo: Naigai-Syobo, 1938), pp. 1-2 (a three-page summary is found in Inland II). Inuzuka, FO S-9460-3-1722, January 1940, pp. 2-3; *JCM*, pp. 54, 107, 245, *et passim.*

73. *JCM*, pp. 74, 109. The second item is an article in the *Judaya Kenkyu* 1:5 (September 1941), pp. 61-67, whose author, M. Kubota, explains the use of the snake as a symbol for the Jewish plot to conquer the world. He repeats the canard that when the tail meets the head in the Far East this goal will have been attained. Loewenthal summarizes the essence of this article, that "The Jews are strangling the Japanese economy from Singapore, along the ABCD [American, British, Chinese, Dutch] line . . . They now intend to destroy the rule of the Mikado." Cf. also Butow, *Tojo*, chapter 8.

74. *JCM*, p. 176.

75. *JCM*, pp. 245, 184, 261, 173.

76. *JCM*, pp. 268, 271.

77. Teiiti, *Juden,* p. 1; *JCM*, pp. 189, 74, 115-16, 121, *et passim*.

78. Kase, "Jews," p. 20.

79. *JCM*, pp. 171, 102, 78, *et passim*.

80. For the Jewish support of Chiang's regimé, and their control of China's economy, see Teiiti, *Juden*, p. 1. Cf. also T. Salvotti, *Juden in Ostasien* [Salvotti, *Juden*] (Berlin: Nordland-Verlag, 1941), pp. 25-40, 58-60, *et passim; JCM*, pp. 2, 3, 11, 69, 70, 64, 36, 47, 185.

Utsunomiya's quotes are cited in *JCM*, pp. 242-43; Kase, "Jews," p. 12. For Japanese view of loans to China, see Katsumi, Usui, "The Role of the Foreign Ministry" [Katsumi, "Ministry"], *P. Harbor*, p. 135.

81. Ito, "Right Wing," esp. p. 507.

82. See Kublin, "Rising," p. 17. Cf. also Kobayashi, "Mitsukawa" I, II; Kase, "Jews," p. 12.

83. The date of the *KSG* can be gauged from the inception of its first journal, *Kokusai Himitsu-Ryoku No Kenkyu* (The Study of the International Secret Power [i.e., the Jews]), according to Loewenthal, which began with volume 1 on November 3, 1936, and concluded on April 1, 1940, with volume 6. Its successor, *Yudaya Kenkyu,* appeared from May 1941 to June 1943. *JCM*, p. 83.

Loewenthal (quoting Vol. 1, p. 410) cites a list of five key contributors to the journal, four military and one civilian. These are Minoru Akaike, (member of the Upper House of the Japanese Diet); Yasuzo Hasegawa (Staff Member of the S. Manchurian Railway); Masao Masuda (expert on Russia, China and Jewish affairs); Kiyo Utsunomiya (government official, leading member of the Society, and *editor of the journal*). Loewenthal was already aware of the identity of Inuzuka and Utsunomiya (see index); Unosuke Wakamiya (the one civilian); Jaichi Yanagizawa (expert on Jews, was in France for a long period, and probably derived much of his antisemitic notions there). Senko Yasue (army officer, who published a book *The Jewish People* under the auspices of the Japanese Army Club). *JCM*, p. 84. The author is uncertain why Shioden was left out of this list by Loewenthal, since he too was one of the founders and key contributors. See JCM, pp. 198, 213, 214, 228, 230. Cf. also Kobayashi-Kranzler correspondence, August 30, 1975, and Kobayashi Interview.

For additional information of Inuzuka as the founder (or *a* founder) of the *KSG*, see "Imperial Navy," p. 9, written by his wife and former secretary.

84. Kase, "Jews," p. 10.

85. Cf. Morris, *Nationalism*, p. XXI. The author would not be surprised if an industrialist such as Ayukawa, who was so interested in the Jews, was one of the financial supporters.

86. See, for example, FO S-9460-3-746, October 12, 1938, p. 2.

87. See above, note 83. Cf. the index of the *JCM*, for the numerous articles by the three main contributors.

88. See, for example, *JCM*, pp. 86,93, for such lectures. The quote is from Kase, "Jews," p. 12.

89. FO S-9460-3-746, October 12, 1938, p. 2.

90. For Poland, see FO Dispatch from Shuichi Sakawa to Foreign Minister Koki Hirota, February 17, 1938. For the "visit" of Sassoon, see FO S-9460-3-1300-1304,, July 18, 1939, "Movements of Sassoon . . . During his stay in Japan."

91. Inuzuka, Interview.

92. Kase, "Jews," pp. 9-11. Cf. also *JCM*.

93. KP No. 14, "Essay Concerning the Court of Arbitration of the Jewish People of Shanghai" (DP).

94. Cohn, *Warrant*, Chapters 6-7. Cf. also Dawidowicz, *War*, p. 16.

95. Cohn, *Warrant*, Chapter 7.

96. For Ford's "agrarian myth," see *ibid.*, pp. 156-63. The Japanese concepts are found above, note 41.

97. *JCM*, pp. 30, 31, 85, 101.

98. For some German influence on Japan, see index of Reischauer, *E. Asia*, and Robert E. Ward and Dankwait A. Rustow (eds.), *Political Modernization in Japan and Turkey* [Ward, Modernization] Princeton, N.J.: Princeton University Press, 1964; de la Trobe, "Die Juden in Japan" [Trobe, "Juden"]. Inland II, March 6, 1939, p. 2. For the study of the Japanese by one German (Jewish) professor, who taught for eight years

262

JAPANESE, NAZIS & JEWS

in Japan, see Kurt Singer, *Mirror, Sword and Jewel: A Study of Japanese Characteristics* [Singer, *Mirror*] (New York: George Braziller, 1973); "Jewish Consulate," p. 105.

99. For Shioden and his career, see the following: Kobayashi Interview; *JCM*, pp. 198, 213, 214, 228, 230; biographical details. (TP). KP "Election Bulletin," April 30, 1942 (four-page biographical sketch) (DP); Bondy, *Racketeers*, pp. 245-47; "Jews in E. Asia," p. 6; Salvotti, *Juden*, p. 59; Cohn, *Warrant*, pp. 242-43.

100. For Higuchi, see Dicker, *Wanderers*, p. 46 f. Kase, "Jews," pp. 6-7. Although the author would dispute the number of Jews Higuchi claimed to have saved, Higuchi's role re the Far East Conferences will be discussed below, this chapter. For Yasue's visit to Palestine, see Hiroo, "Yasue," p. 2.

101. See Cohn, *Warrant*, Conclusion.

102. Yukio Cho, "An Inquiry Into the Problem of Importing American Capital into Manchuria: A Note on Japanese-American Relations, 1931-1941, [Chō, "Manchuria"], *P. Harbor*, pp. 386-87. Cf. also Peattie, *Ishiwara*, pp. 208-10, 215. Cf. also S. Tokayer correspondence, September 7, 1974; "Jewish Consulate," p. 100.

103. See especially Katsumi, "Ministry," for the variation in Japan's foreign policy for this period.

104. Dicker, *Wanderers*, pp. 165-67. For Japan's endorsement of the Balfour Declaration, see FO Sakichi Takahashi to Yutaka Ueda, January 6, 1940, p. 2. It was signed by Ambassador to England Uchida and Viscount Ishii. (Uchida was entered into the Zionist "Golden Book").

105. For conditions in Manchuria, see above, Chapter 2.

106. See the KP and FO Papers for 1934-1936, esp. FO S-9460-3-489, December 18, 1934.

107. Dicker, *Wanderers*, p. 38 (citing a Jewish Telegraphic Agency Report from Tokyo, August 5, 1934). See also Shigemitsu, *Destiny*, pp. 94-95; Chō, "Manchuria."

108. Chō, "Manchuria," pp. 389-90. For Kishi's and Hoshino's relationship to Ayukawa and others in the Manchurian faction, see Bantow, *Tojo*, esp. pp. 72-75. There are recounted the friendships of the five individuals, i.e., "Tojo, Hoshino, Matsuoka, Kishi, and Aikawa," known as *ni-ki sansuke:* "the two *ki* and three *suke*," referring to the fact that the first names of Tojo and Hoshino ended in the syllable *"ki,"* and those of the three ended with *"suke." Tojo*, p. 75. Cf. also Dan Kurzman, *Kishi and Japan: The Search for the Sun* [Kurzman, *Kishi*] (New York: Ivan Obolensky, Inc., 1960), pp. 122-40, *et passim*. See pp. 108-109, for Kishi's

adherence to the views of Kita and Okawa; Katsuro Yamamura, "The Role of the Finance Ministry" [Yamamura, "Finance"], *P. Harbor*, pp. 292-94.

108. For Arita's relationships, see Katsumi, "Ministry"; *JCM*, p. 215; Shigemitsu, "Destiny," p. 95.

109. See above, notes 16-18. For the benefit to Japan of the Jewish boycott of Nazi goods, see S. Tokayer correspondence, September 19, 1974. Cf. also Arthur E. Tiedemann, "Big Business and Politics in Prewar Japan," [Tiedemann, "Business"], *Dilemmas of Growth in Prewar Japan*, James William Morley, ed. [Morley, *Dilemmas*] (Princeton, N.J.: Princeton University Press, 1971), pp. 312-13, note 75.

110. Chō, "Manchuria," p. 391.

111. Whether "in practice," Shioden would have acted any differently than Yasue and Inuzuka, can only be speculation. Kobayashi is inclined to see little difference. Interview.

112. See Singer, *Mirror*, p. 11, for his being fired. Others, however, were retained in face of Nazi pressure such as the conductor Rosenstock. Joseph Rosenstock-Tokayer correspondence, April 15, 1974, pp. 2-3. (TP). Cf. also Ambassador [Eugen] Ott to the German Foreign Office in Berlin, March 19, 1940. Inland II.

113. FO S-9460-3-541, October 14, 1935. Cf. also FO September 19, 1936, Shotaro Sato, Consular Officer in Harbin, to Shigeru Yoshida, Japanese Ambassador to Britain.

114. The Council was probably set up in 1937 during the First Conference. Kaufman, *Itonot*, p. 83. The decision for setting it up, though, was most likely made sometime in late 1936, the year of decision for setting up the "Construction of Manchukuo." For Yasue's appointment as the liaison between the Council and the Japanese Military Mission in Dairen, see Dicker, *Wanderers*, pp. 46-50. Cf. also Kaufman, *Manchuria*, pp. 19, 32. Hiroo, "Yasue," p. 2.

115. For the closing of *Nash Put*, see Z-Dicker correspondence, October 1938, p. 2. Cf. also FO Tanaka to Hirota, February 23, 1938.

116. See Irye, "Policies," pp. 443-54.

117. See Yamamura, "Finance," p. 293.

118. *Ibid.*, p. 298. Cf. also Tiedemann, "Business," pp. 312-13. Cf. also Kaufman, *Manchuria*, p. 20, for Ikeda's relation to Jews.

119. Chō, "Manchuria," p. 388.

120. For the Conferences, see Dicker, *Wanderers*, pp. 45-59. The quote is from Z.-Dicker, correspondence, May 20, 1959, p. 3. Cf. also the KP

"Proclamation of the First Convention of the Far Eastern Jewish Communities."

121. Dicker, *Wanderers*, pp. 44-47. This status as a separate entity, fit well into Ishiwara's concept of Manchuria as multi-racial, autonomous state. Z-Dicker correspondence, May 20, 1959, pp. 2-3.

122. FO S-9460-3-746, October 12, 1938, and FO S-9460-3-750, October 13, 1938. For the establishment of the External Relations Committee by the Japan Economic Federation, see Chō, "Manchuria," pp. 377-78.

123. FO October 13, 1938, p. 2.

124. *Ibid.*, pp. 4.

125. KP No. 10, July 7, 1939, pp. 3-11. For the counterpart of Birobidjan, see KP No. 6, June 5, 1939, p. 12 (addition, June 7, 1939); Kase, "Jews," p. 13; S.-Toyaker correspondence, March 1, July 9, September 19, 1974, "Jewish Consulate," p. 100. Cf. also Shigemitsu, *Destiny*, pp. 94-95.

126. For the Japanese view, see FO S-9460-3-1640-1654, January 11, 1940, p. 3. Mr. Z's appraisal is found in his correspondence to Dicker, October 11, 1959, p. 3.

127. FO S-9460-3-1640-1654, January 11, 1940, p. 12 (should be page 7, pagination not clear on Ms.). Cf also Dr. Kaufman's report and version of this speech given to Mr. Z., titled "The Situation of the Jews in Japan and Manchu-Ti-Kuo" [sic], pp. 3-5. Z.-Dicker correspondence; Dicker, *Wanderers*, p. 46.

128. FO S-9460-3-728. Information concerning Jews, No. 14, July 7, 1938.

129. FO S-9460-3-750, October 13, 1938, pp. 8-9.

130. For the Japanese view of Wise, see FO S-9460-3-1369 A, B. Cf. also Karl Kindermann to Mr. Niwa, June 7, 1940, and the response of a letter to Kindermann by Stephen S. Wise, June 10, 1940. For the historian's evaluation of Wise, see Friedman, *No Haven*, pp. 151-52. Mr. Z's assignment is found in Z.-Dicker correspondence, September 30, esp. pp. 2-3; October 5, 11, 1959. For Kaufman's Report, see Z.-Dicker correspondence, 1938. See also Dicker, *Wanderers*, p. 56-58; KP (Bei-3-Confidential-291), Ueda to Arita, May 16, 1939.

131. Letters in Archives of World Jewish Congress, Cf. also Z.-Dicker correspondence.

132. Z.-Dicker correspondence, May 20, 1959, p. 4.

133. See speech by Dr. Kaufman KP Bei-3-Confidential-291. Ambassador Ueda to Foreign Minister Arita, May 16, 1939.

134. *Ibid.* For Ikeda, see Kaufman, Manchuria, p. 20. For the life-saving power of this picture, see Kotsuji, *Jerusalem*, p. 188.

135. Chō, "Manchuria," pp. 377-78. See FO S-9460-3-746, October 12, 1938, p. 2, for the Japanese Economic Federation.

136. *Ibid.,* p. 378.

137. *Ibid.,* p. 379.

138. Even Arita belonged to the ultranationalist camp, and his notions concerning the Jews were no doubt shaped to some extent, by his close association with the antisemite Shiratori and other ultranationalists. See Katsumi, "Ministry," esp. 148.

For the text of the declaration, see Inuzuka, "Secret," p. 3. References to this policy are found in the FO S-9460-3-2516, Code 2149, 2152, January 17, 1942. From the Foreign Minister [Shigenori] Togo to [Mamoru] Shigemitsu, Ambassador to China and others, on the subject of "Emergency Measure for Jewish People." This major document reveals the change in the Japanese policy toward the Jews as a result of the War in the Pacific. See below, Chapter 17.

For the renewal of the Five Ministers Conference only several months before, as means of decision-making instrument, see Seiichi Imai, "Cabinet Emperor, and Senior Statesman," *P. Harbor,* p. 70. The general, political situation related to Japan's foreign policy, especially toward the United States and the New Order in East Asia; see Iriye, "Policies," pp. 443-53.

139. For the "Five Year Plans," see Chō "Manchuria," p. 386. Arita's announcement was carried in the *Japan Times* of March 1, 1939 (TP), and in a small article in the *New York Times* of December 28, 1939. For Arita's second declaration, see Parry, "Jews," p. 514. Cf. also Dr. Kaufman's speech, KP Bei-3-Confidential-291, May 16, 1939; Trobe, "Juden," pp. 3-4. Trobe refers to the inquiry of [Atsushi] Akaike, an antisemite. *JCM,* p. 2.

140. KP Bei-3-Confidential-291, May 16, 1939, p. 2.

141. KP, October 12, 1938, p. 2.

142. Kotskji, *Jerusalem,* pp. 143-44.

143. See below, Chapter 8.

144. See below, this chapter, re various plans by Inuzuka to attract Jewish capital.

145. For the worsening Japanese-U.S. relations, see Iriye, "Policies," pp. 450-53. For the 1934 announcement by Japan of settling Jews, see Dicker, *Wanderers,* p. 38.

146. FO S-9460-3-1155, April 4, 1939. Cf. also KP 11, July 1939, p. 33; Z.-Dicker correspondence, August 30, 1958, p. 2.

147. Symptomatic of this attitude were the memos sent by Miss Schulz to Dr. Tartakower of the World Jewish Congress during May-June 1941. These reveal the suspicions such leaders as Wise, Dr. Goldman and Mr. Lipsky had of dealing with Dr. Kaufman and the Far Eastern Council, whom they suspected as being "too closely allied with the Japanese." In the last memo, dated June 10, 1941, there is the final decision by the aforementioned leaders "that there should be no further communication with Mr. Kaufman." World Jewish Congress Archives (TP).

148. Inuzuka, "Secret," p. 6 and "Imperial Navy," p. 7.

149. For the higher figure, see "Imperial Navy," p. 6. The lower number is found in the KP No. 12 Report titled "Estimate of Space Required for Concentration of the Jewish Refugees" by the Special Investigation Section, Department of Investigation. Yasue was the Chief of the Special Task Force. July 1939. This was part of the July 7, 1939 Report (KP No. 11) which included the opinions of Colonel Yasue, Captain Inuzuka and Consul Shiro Ishiguro.

The restrictions are in the first part of this overall report (KP No. 10, July 7, 1939). Since the Japanese received the assurance of the Jewish leaders that no negative reactions will follow the proposed restrictions, they could feel assured in their plans for both the restrictions and the settlements. See below, Chapter 8.

150. KP No. 13, July 18, 1939, pp. 23-24, 30. For the Korean location, see Herbert Katzki to M. Tokayer, February 7, 1975 (TP). For Yasue's desire to counteract Birobidjan, see KP No. 6, June 7, 1939, p. 12.

151. For Ishiwara's concepts, see Peattie, *Ishiwara*, p. 150. The army's "objections"are found in KP No. 6, June 7, 1939, p. 11. The statement goes far to explain "who was behind the Three Conferences."

152. KP No. 6, June 7, 1939, p. 12.

153. KP No. 10, July 7, 1939, pp. 9-10.

154. *Ibid.*, p. 9. The Japanese were very concerned about Sir Victor's openly anti-Japanese remarks and hoped at least to tone them down.

155. *Ibid.*, pp. 6, 9.

156. See above, n. 122.

157. KP No. 6, June 5, 1939, p. 10.

158. See, for example, KP No. 10, July 7, 1939, p. 13. For Nomura, see FO S-9460-3-1635, January 10, 1940. Almost all the KP and FO Papers involve corespondence among the higher echelons of the Foreign Office. See also Inuzuka, "Secret," p. 6.

159. FO S-9460-3-1369, June 7, 1940 for Kindermann's letter, and June 10, 1940 for Wise's reply.

160. KP (Top Secret) Confidential No. 2116, August 2, 1940, p. 1.

161. The author was unable to locate reference to this correspondence in the press.

162. Herbert Katzki to Tokayer, Feburary 7, 1975. For Wise's hesitation in "deals," see Friedman, *No. Haven*, pp. 58, 75.

163. FO S-9460-3-1635, January 10, 1940.

164. Chō, "Manchuria," p. 379.

165. KP No. 10, July 7, 1939, p. 6. For the resolutions, see FO S-9460-3-1640-1654, January 11, 1940, pp. 6-8. Cf. also other versions; see FO Secret No. 15, January 17, 1940, p. 4; "Imperial Navy," pp. 3-4.

166. FO Secret No. 15, January 17, 1940, pp. 3-7.

8 | THE GATES CLOSE: RESTRICTIONS GO INTO EFFECT

> *. . . there is no authority at present in Shanghai who could interfere with the landing of refugees, except the Japanese Military Authorities, who could only do it at the unanimous request of the whole Consular body. Such a request is entirely out of the question.*
>
> (Speelman. *Report—June 22, 1939*)

As a result of Japan's pro-Jewish policy, the German-Jewish refugee influx into Shanghai continued unabated in the face of numerous pressures. Yet, in spite of hearsay concerning the reasons for Shanghai's open-door toward the Jewish influx, most contemporaries, in the words of one scholar on Asian affairs, found "it hard to believe the rumor that the Japanese authorities in the Chinese part of Shanghai were collaborating in the settlement of these Jews."[1] This refugee policy, as we have seen, was not disturbed, even when Japan finally closed the doors by imposing restrictions to refugee immigration in August 1939.

CAUSE OF RESTRICTIONS

These restrictions were not the result of outside influence. Rather it came about as a result of the reaction by the

267

Japanese civilian colony in Shanghai against the dearth of rooms, the ever-rising rents, and the tougher business competition caused by the refugees streaming into Hongkew.[2] The clamor for action by Tokyo became louder and more insistent as the number of refugees reached close to 14,000 by the end of May 1939 and threatened to double by the end of the year. It was then, and only then, that the Japanese authorities attempted to deal with this problem rather than publicly ignoring it.[3]

This change of attitude is evident in the appearance of anti-refugee articles in the Japanese press during that period.[4] A sign of the modification of official reaction is mirrored in the Foreign Office document of May 26, which noted that "it is necessary to protect Japan from the prosperity of the Jewish immigrants."[5] And even at the last moment the Japanese hesitated to take the final step until reassured by Sir Victor Sassoon that the Jewish organizations in the United States and Britain would not object.[6]

INUZUKA AND SASSOON

On May 25, 1939, the aforementioned interview took place between the Japanese Investigating Committee, consisting of Yasue, Inuzuka and Ishigura, and Sir Victor and Ellis Hayim. These two leading personalities of the Sephardi community and the Shanghai relief committees repeated their oft-told tale of lack of funds, and fear in general of the steadily increasing influx. They complained of the failure of their earlier petitions to foreign consuls in Shanghai, and explained that they were now turning to the Japanese as the only ones who could effectively prevent further immigration.

Sassoon and Hayim maintained that *such restrictions would not meet widespread opposition on the part of Jews in general* [italics mine] since it would be for the good of those already in Shanghai, whose situation the Jewish organizations all over the world were well aware of.[7] "The Committee," the two spokesmen for Shanghai's Jewry assured the Japanese, "will be satisfied if the influx of refugees be restrained somehow or other."[8]

PROPOSALS FOR RESTRICTIONS

The day after this interview, the "On the Spot Subcommittee" of the Moslem and Jewish Problem Committee proposed the first of a series of plans for restricting Jewish immigration. This plan was submitted on May 26 by Inuzuka.[9] A second plan was proposed several days later with a somewhat similar solution though there were distinctions based on the personalities of the authors.[10] By June 10, the Japanese Consul General in Shanghai had already sent a telegram to Tokyo. This included basic concepts found in both plans, namely, immediate restrictions against new immigrants, except for those already on the sea, and direct negotiations with the representatives of Germany and Italy in Shanghai, requesting their help to control Jewish emigration.[11]

The correlation between the Sassoon interview and the Restriction Plan can be further seen from the first paragraph of the *Joint Report of Investigations* [sic] *on Jewish Problems* in Shanghai dated July 7, an amalgam of the Army's and Navy's original plans.[12] At the beginning of the preface to this 14-page analysis of the "Jewish Problem," the author's note:

On May 9, the investigators from the Ministries of the Army, Navy, and Foreign Affairs met in Shanghai and set on investigating Jewish affairs in close mutual contact. First they successfully approached the leading characters [sic] among the Jewish people in Shanghai. Subsequently, when they grasped a general picture of the Jewish situation in Shanghai, they mapped out a plan on the disposition of Jewish refugees.[13]

The author of the analysis goes on with chronology of events leading to the restrictions, stating:

> On June 3, this plan was introduced at a meeting aboard the man-of-war "Izumo" to be explained and discussed by the officers concerned from the Army, Navy, Foreign Ministry and Board of Asian Rehabilitation [Asia Development Board or *Koain*]. Then Col. Yasue went to Nanking where he briefed the Army Commander, the Chief of Staff and the Staff members concerned about the immediate Jewish problems, introducing the above plan . . .

Additional reviews were submitted by various other branches, and with each criticism there were additions and deletions. Finally,

> Investigators Inuzuka and Ishiguro then put together the above-mentioned plans into a new plan. This plan being approved by the Fleet Command and the local station of the Foreign Ministry. Captain Inuzuka brought it to Tokyo on July 6, whose modified version was also submitted by a Naval officer serving in Shanghai.[14]

In order to get a more accurate count of the number of refugees in Hongkew, the Japanese decided to compile a Directory of Jewish Refugees, The Directory would also enable the authorities to keep a tighter control over the refugee movement in and out of Hongkew.[15] Any refugee still residing in Hongkew after August 21 without a permit would be punished by the Japanese authorities.[16]

In a letter to the CFA and in a report to the *Paris*

Temps of August 11, 1939, the Shanghai Japanese authorities stressed the point "that this measure has been taken *at the request of the Jewish Refugee Committee itself* which fears a new influx of refugees"[17] [italics mine]. A Foreign Office Memo, in a slightly altered fashion, similarly noted "that the Jewish leaders among the Refugee Committee wished to see for the benefit of the refugees already in Shanghai that further influx be discouraged in some way or other."[18] Thus, in their correspondence with the CFA, the Japanese reiterated the Committee's own rationale. The Japanese also stressed the fact that even Japanese civilians, let alone Chinese, were not permitted unrestricted return or access to Hongkew.[19]

From the tone of this and other previously mentioned documents, it becomes quite evident that the Japanese were reluctant to carry out this action without the prior approval of the influential Jews of Shanghai, since they feared unfavorable propaganda via the Jews of the United States and England.[20]

RESTRICTIONS GO INTO EFFECT

On August 9, 1939, catastrophe struck the German Jews as Japan issued a policy statement to restrict further immigration into Shanghai. This statement was in a letter to the Shanghai Jewish relief organizations, in which the Naval Landing Party Headquarters listed among the temporary steps to be taken the refusal of admittance to any new arrivals in Hongkew after August 21, 1939.[21] In addition, those residing in Hongkew on August 22 would have to register with the Japanese authorities in order to remain there legally.[22]

In the meantime, on August 10, Y. Miura, the Japanese Consul General, notified E. Bracklo, the Acting Consul General for Germany in Shanghai, and F. Farinacci, his Italian counterpart, of the impending Japanese restrictions.[23]

On August 14, the Municipal Council notified all the consulates and the steamship companies involved, that European refugees would no longer be permitted to enter the International Settlement.[24] On the basis of the Japanese notification on August 9, and that of the Council on August 14, Ellis Hayim cabled the London Council for German Jewry, which in turn informed the JDC that all emigration from Europe must cease. In addition, Hayim noted that the French Concession was expected to follow the lead of the Municipal Council.[25]

It is easy to imagine the agitation among Shanghai's refugees when the news appeared in the local press on August 16.[26] Those whose relatives were about to embark, or were already on the high seas, were hardest hit.[27] There were immediate problems for the ship companies and some lines returned the deposit to those booked after August 14. Then word was received by HICEM that four boats carrying 631 passengers scheduled to leave between August 14 and 21 would be permitted to land.[28] Thus, for the moment, Shanghai was closed to any incoming refugees debarking after August 21, 1939.

As a result of closed discussions during August and September by members of the various ruling authorities in Shanghai, including a representative of the refugees, a tentative agreement concerning the restrictions was brought to the public on October 11, 1939. This agreement was made final, and published in the Municipal Council's *Gazette* and elsewhere on October 22.[29]

NEW REGULATIONS

According to these new regulations, further immigration to Shanghai was limited to: persons able to show a deposit of (US) $400 as "Guarantee Money"; a resident's immediate family; someone with a contract for a job in Shanghai; or the intended spouse of a Shanghai resident.[30]

These rules applied only to the Settlement controlled by the Municipal Council, not to the Japanese-controlled Hongkew, or to the French Concession. From a private report by Eduard Kann, we learn that both the Japanese and the French refused to be bound by them. The Japanese eliminated the "(US) $400 Guarantee Money" clause and said that they would take each application for an entry permit on its own merits.[31] Unofficially, however, it was made quite clear to the CFA that very few refugees would be permitted to enter the Japanese and French sectors. That this "policy of exclusion" was strictly maintained can be seen from the correspondence of January 1940 between Ishiguro and Nash, wherein the Japanese Consul General complained to the Municipal Council of its leniency in granting entry permits to refugees while they, the Japanese, had given out merely 25 up to date.[32]

To obtain an entry permit to the Settlement required filling out an application at the CFA's Immigration Department with a fee of (US) $10.[33] After verification, the CFA either rejected the claim or recommended its approval to the Shanghai Municipal Council Police Department, which in turn did its own checking of all claims, determining, for instance, whether the applicant was assured of a job with a certain minimum income per year.[34]

Once the Municipal Council approved a permit, it was deposited with the shipping company involved, which informed its home office, thereby enabling the refugee to embark at the European port.[35] Those applying under the first clause, requiring the (US) $400 Guarantee Money, had to deposit the funds in special accounts in one of the Shanghai banks before being granted a permit.[36]

Since most of the refugees were unable to produce

such a large sum of money, it was usually sent by relatives or friends in the United States, or by HICEM, which subsidized many penniless German Jews.[37]

Those receiving the $400 HICEM checks were supposed to return (US) $300 for re-use in getting more refugees out of Germany, but some did not do so.[38] At the same time, Kann of the CFA refused to wire to HICEM in Europe the $300 he received from some of the refugees, because he rejected the theory of re-using the money for additional refugees. He argued that

> . . . in close co-operation with the authorities, we have been instrumental in carefully framing the regulations pertaining to immigration. It is our duty not merely to adhere to the spirit of the rules, but also to watch over their execution. Therefore, our Committee is quite unable to carry out your well-meant proposal to employ all the funds returned by the first lot of refugees sent by you as guarantee-money for the next batch. We cannot possibly do that.[39]

It should be noted that after the applications were approved, the refugees were told they could reside only in the Settlement south of the Soochow Creek, and were warned to avoid illegal entry into the Japanese-controlled Hongkew. This policy was reinforced by the Shanghai Municipal Police and the CFA Boarding Committee that greeted each boat as it arrived in Shanghai.[40]

The Japanese Consul pointed out to the Municipal Council that despite such elaborate precautions, many refugees were using the Settlement entry permit as a means of eventually settling in Hongkew, with its cheaper room and board. Though no accurate statistics are available on these illegal entrants to Hongkew, they seem to have numbered in the hundreds.[41]

BLACK MARKET PERMITS

Moreover, a black-market traffic in entry permits, run by some White Russians as well as some refugees, soon began to flourish. It circumvented the interminable red tape and possible refusals in the CFA's handling of applications. In fact, Margolies complained that not only were most of the refugees unable to get their applications processed via the CFA, but they were not even able to get their $10 fee returned.[42]

Since too many refugees were still arriving through entry permits, the Japanese applied pressure on the Municipal Council to revise the regulations. This revision was made, effective July 1, 1940. The major change involved the first clause, requiring the (US) $400 Guarantee Money, which now included the necessity for an entry permit in addition to the money. This was undoubtedly added to maintain a check on the applicant's whereabouts.[43]

The permits were generally valid for only a four-month period. This meant that many refugees who possessed permits lost their chance of leaving Germany, because they were either unable to find shipping space within the allocated time, or could not raise the $400 required.[44]

MEDITERRANEAN CLOSED

Italy's entry into the war on June 10, 1940, further changed the picture. It closed the Mediterranean and cut off the refugees' major avenue. This spelled doom to the 2,000 potential immigrants with entry permits to the Foreign Settlements. For this reason the revision of the Japanese restrictions had no visible effect on the already diminishing influx. New routes were to be worked out, via Siberia, Manchuria, and Japan, but the people waiting in Germany had to start all over again, applying for permits from the Japanese authorities and transit visas from each of the countries to be traversed.[45]

To the credit of a great number of Shanghailanders it

must be added that many refugees received their permits through the application of part B of the second regulation, which allowed entry to those owning a contract for employment by a resident of Shanghai, with projected earnings of (Sh) $250-300 a month. Frequent checks on the veracity of such contracts were made, but a number of firms, both Jewish and non-Jewish, offered them to refugees, even though no such jobs were available.[46]

Thus, with the exception of the 1,000 Polish refugees, who were to arrive in Shanghai in 1941, and the few hundred fortunate Jews able to enter under the new requirements, the gates of the sole unrestricted haven for Jewish victims of Nazism were effectively closed, with the refugee community limited to a maximum of 17,000.

NOTES : THE GATES CLOSE

1. Parry, "Jews," p. 514.

2. Ginsbourg, *Refugees,* p. 8. Fear was also expressed by the Japanese authorities of the possible setting up of a Jewish "Concession" (KP No. 6, June 5, 1939, p. 9).

3. For the statistics, see above, Chapter III. The Japanese by no means ignored the arrival of the refugees in their secret reports. For example, one of the key studies of the refugee influx came as a result of October 12, 1938 investigation by Inuzuka for Jewish and Moslem Problem Committee (see FO S-9460-3-747). By January 18, 1938, the detailed report by Kumabe discussed all the details and problems encountered, in monitoring the arrivals in Shanghai under the existing conditions, where many landing piers were privately owned. See FO KP No. 3 Investigation Report Concerning the Problem of the Entry of Japanese, Manchuria [sic] Chinese Nationals, Especially Jewish Refugees," January 18, 1939 [FO January 18, 1939]. See also Kranzler, *JRC,* pp. 143-45.

4. Ginsbourg, *Refugees,* p. 8.

5. FO KP No. 5, May 26, 1939, p. 6.

6. See below, for the connection between the two dates. Cf. also FO January 18, 1939, p. 3, where Kumabe pointed out the proposals of the Office of Engineers of the Municipal Council to limit the influx was *not in any way to be connected with the Japanese* since "it will be *greatly embarrassing* if the act of the Office of Engineers *is propagandized as influenced by Japan"* [italics mine].
Similarly, even when the measures for the restrictions were formulated, and notice was to be given to Germany and Italy to stop sending the refugees, the leaders of the Moslem and Jewish Problem Committee suggested that it be done "with the greatest possible secrecy" (FO KP No. 13, July 18, 1939, p. 25).

7. FO KP No. 5, May 1939, p. 1. Cf. also Birman to HICEM (Lisbon), October 9, 1940, p. 3 (HH XV C-6).

8. FO KP No. 5, *ibid.* At the same time Sassoon asked the Japanese for help in locating additional badly-needed housing for the refugees, and he invited them to visit the existing *Heime.*

9. FO KP No. 7, June 11, 1939. Although this plan was submitted by the Navy to Tokyo on June 11, it was first submitted in Shanghai on May 26, 1939. See p. 6.

10. The second plan was submitted on June 5, 1939 by the Army, represented by Col. Yasue. KP No. 6, Measures on Jewish Refugees from the Standpoint of Security [FO KP No. 6, June 5, 1939]. For the differences between the two plans, see Dicker, *Wanderers*, pp. 85-86.

11. FO KP No. 6, June 10, 1939 (DF). The "On the Spot Subcommittee" Report of July 1 merely added some details to the June 10 telegram, such as the preparation for registering all the refugees presently residing in Hongkew, and secret negotiations with the German and Italian representatives in Tokyo as well as Shanghai. FO KP No. 9, July 1, 1949, pp. 18-19 (DP).

12. FO KP No. 10, July 7, 1939.

13. *Ibid.*, p. 1. The first plan, Inuzuka's, envisioned registration of all refugees residing in the Japanese sector and the relocation of *all unemployed refugees* [italics mine] and a temporary camp managed by the Refugee Committee. Dicker, *Wanderers*, p. 86, erroneously maintains that "those who had already been settled now [in Hongkew] had to be resettled in a camp," implying *all refugees* in Hongkew, rather than merely the unemployed. Cf. FO KP No. 7, June 11, 1939, p. 7. For additional material see *JRC*, pp. 148-51.

14. FO KP No. 10, July 7, 1939, p. 1.

15. FO S-9460-3-A, August 9, 1939, p. 2.

16. *North-China Herald* (August 16, 1939), p. 280. Also cited by Mars, *Necessity*, p. 14.

17. Joint (Paris), Memo, August 18, 1939, p. 1.

18. FO S-9460-3-A, August 9, 1939, p. 1 (DP).

19. *Ibid.* See also Inuzuka, "Secret," p. 5; "Imperial Navy," p. 5.

20. FO "Jewish Measures" [January 17, 1942]. Cf. also FO S-9460-3-2516, January 17, 1942, p. 1.

21. *North-China Herald* (May 31, 1939), p. 2. Also cited by Mars, "A Note on the Jewish Refugees in Shanghai," *Jewish Social Studies*, Vol. XXXI (October 1969), No. 4, pp. 286-91, esp. p. 389. For further sources see *JRC*, p. 149, n. 38.

22. FO S-9460-3-A, August 9, 1939, p. 1. Cf. also *North-China Herald*, p. 372.

23. FO No. 40-B, Miura to Bracklo, August 10, 1939, and FO No. 17-C, Miura to Farinacci, August 10, 1939 (DF).

24. See the copy of the message received by the *Paris-Midi* on August 14, 1939, Joint (Paris) Memorandum, August 18, 1939, p. 1. Three days later

additional instructions were sent to the ship companies, "not to accept any booking for Shanghai." FO S-9460-3-1474, August 17, 1939 (DF). Cited by Mars, "Notes," p. 290. The author is uncertain whether the August 14 letters were sent to all the ship companies, while those of August 17 merely reiterated these demands, or perhaps the message of August 14 merely gave notice of the Council's intent, but was only implemented by the 17th. According to the Joint (Paris) Memorandum of August 18, p. 3, it seems that the Japanese Office of the Nippon Yusen Kaisya (N.Y.K.) Lines had been notified as early as the 14th.

25. Joint (Paris) Memorandum, August 18, 1939, p. 2.

26. North-China Herald (August 16, 1939), p. 280. Also cited by Mars, "Note," Jewish Social Studies, Vol. XXXI, p. 289.

27. Ibid.

28. Joint (Paris) Memorandum, August 18, 1939, pp. 2-3. Although Eduard Kann, who was directly involved in these negotiations, claims that August 19 was the cut-off date, there probably was no strictly uniform policy carried out by all parties involved. See Kann, "Report on the Problem of Immigration into China on Part of the European Refugees," November 11, 1939, p. 2 [Kann, "Report on Immigration"] (JDCCA).

29. For details concerning these meetings and related matter, see JRC, pp. 151-55.

30. A copy of these regulations in the Gazette is found in the Appendix of the JRC, p. 463.

31. Kann, "Report on Immigration," p. 3. Cf. also FO S-9460-3-1534, October 10, 1939. The French, at a later date, accepted a (US) $300 figure for the first clause of the regulations. Kann to Speelman, June 1, 1940; Kann, Memorandum, March 20, 1940 (JDCCA).

32. See the following FO documents: FO S-9460-3-920, January 19, 1940, No. 1; FO S-9460-3-921, January 19, 1940, No. 2; FO S-9460-3-818, February 1940 (DP). For additional sources see JRC, p. 156, n. 60.

33. Margolis to Pilpel, August 11, 1941, p. 4.

34. See Herzberg, "Suggested Mode of Procedure for Landing Permits and Landing of Immigrants in Shanghai," February 12, 1940 [Herzberg, "Procedure"], pp. 1-2 (JDCCA) Cf. also Birman to HICEM (Paris), April 5, 1940, p. 3 (HH XV C-3). At that time the minimum "salary" required was about (Sh) $250 per month, at the rate of (Sh) $17 to (US) $1. Ibid., FO S-9460-3-920, Nash to Ishiguro, February 2, 1940 (DP).

35. Kann, "Report on Immigration," p. 3.

36. Dicker, Wanderes, p. 100. These sums were usually deposited at the

Shanghai branch of the Chase Bank. As a result of the start of the war in the Pacific, all immigration was cut off and thousands of unclaimed dollars were left in such accounts *Ibid.*

37. See HH XV C-5 for many documents concerning the HICEM checks (US) $400.

38. Birman, *Report,* 1939 p. 2.

39. Kann to *Association Belge pour l'Emancipation des Refugies,* January 10, 1940, p. 2 (JDCCA). Copies of this letter were sent to Messrs. Hayim, Speelman, Ladoorie, and Birman of HICEM (Shanghai). As Margolies already noted, Kann's greatest fear was that more refugees would come to Shanghai. Margolies to Pilpel, August 11, 1941, p. 4. A See also Birman, HICEM, Report, 1939, p. 2. The writer was unable to ascertain whether the money returned by some of the refugees was sent back to HICEM in Europe.

40. Herzberg, "Procedure," p. 2. See also *JRC,* p. 72.

41. FO S-9460-3-921, B. Ishiguro to E. T. Nash, February 2, 1940 (DF).

42. *Ibid.* Cf. also FO 9460-3-1687 Secret No. 195, January 19, 1940. Yoshiaki Miura (Consul General) to Hachiro Arita (Minister of Foreign Affairs), p. 3 (DF).

43. For Japanese pressure, see FO S-9460-3-921, January 19, 1940. The new regulation is found in Kann to Speelman, June 1, 1940, and for the purpose of the new requirements see Birman to HICEM (Paris), June 5, 1940, pp. 1-2 (HH XV C-6A).

44. Margolies to Pilpel, August 11, 1941, p. 4. Cf. also Kann, "Emigration Restrictions," February 13, 1940, pp. 2-3 (JDCCA); Kann, "Report on Immigration," p. 3.

45. Ginsbourg, *Refugees,* pp. 23-24. For the effect on the influx, see Kann to Speelman, June 1, 1940.

46. See Birman to *Reichsvereinigung der Juden in Deutschland,* September 23, 1940, p. 2 (HH XV C-6). Cf. also Birman to HICEM (Paris), June 5, 1940, p. 1 (HH XV C-62).

9 | BREAD AND BUTTER IN SHANGHAI

ECONOMIC CONDITIONS UNTIL PEARL HARBOR

> ... *By the time they [the refugees] arrived, Shanghai's economy had reached a stage of chronic crisis, fluctuating between depressions and booms, of varying degrees of intensity.*
>
> (Barnett. *Shanghai; Hostage to Politics*)

Few among the flood of refugees arriving in Shanghai had any real illusions about what was to greet them there. Most had come more from despair than hope. Nonetheless, there were probably few who did not hope against hope that somehow, somewhere, they might be able to be integrated into the economy of their new home. We shall examine the reasons why relatively few of these hopes could be fulfilled, or at most fulfilled on a very low level.

CONDITIONS ON ARRIVAL

A proper perspective of the economic conditions prior to Pearl Harbor can only be achieved by taking into consideration the numerous negative, as well as the relatively few positive factors that influenced and shaped the integration of the newcomers into Shanghai's economy. Only then is it possible to

281

realize the tremendous odds faced and overcome by a large segment of the over 17,000 Jewish refugees, in quest of a livelihood.

The most serious obstacle confronting the new arrivals in this search was the fact that by 1938 Shanghai's economic frontier was closed. This city, which, as we know, had been able to absorb consecutive waves of refugees in the past, had no longer any potential for economic expansion, or a flourishing trade or industry to make use of their skill and initiative to any appreciable degree. In fact, by the time they arrived, Shanghai's economy had reached a stage of chronic crisis, fluctuating between depressions and booms, of varying degrees of intensity.[3]

QUALIFICATIONS OF THE REFUGEES

Moreover, both their previous socio-economic middle-class, mercantile background, and their age level (the average being over forty) made integration into Shanghai's economy a difficult task. The majority consisted of white-collar workers, skilled artisans, professionals, businessmen, as well as artists, all of whom found no market at all for their skills. Though we have no statistics for the economic or vocational background of the entire refugee body, we do possess several reports from the CFA, the HIAS and the JDC that cover accurately more than half the number of refugees. From these reports a fair picture can be projected for the entire refugee body, since the only major change came with the arrival in 1941 of the approximately 1,000 East European refugees with their very different economic background.[4] Moreover, since neither the children, nor a large number of the women who had no vocational background, are included in these reports, the 6 to 7,000 listed represent a good three-fourths of the refugees.

A "List of Professions," compiled by the Disbursement and Housing Committee of the CFA on December 31, 1939, based on a registration of 7,052 refugees, reveals the following pattern.[5] It divides the vocations of the refugees into eleven categories, with a total of 6,309 listed. These include the following:

    1. *Artisans* (45 categories, total 905). Including bakers, butchers, furriers, plumbers, stonecutters, quiltmakers, distillers, etc.

    2. *Professionals* (11 categories, total 367). Including architects, lawyers, physicians, chemists, journalists, and teachers.[6] The latter are divided into eight subspecialists such as teachers of gym [sic], language, dance, etc.

    3. *Medical and Dental Assistants* (8 categories, total 118). Including baby nurses, dental and lab assistants, etc.

    4. *Sundry (Misc.)* [sic] (13 categories, total 889). Including chauffeurs, farmers, several types of hotel employees, photographers, undertakers, window dressers, etc.

    5. *Artists* (6 major categories, total 267). Including actors, actresses, artists, draftsmen, fashion designers, musicians (including 15 conductors), painters [sic] and piano tuners.

    6. *Dressing, tailor, dry cleaning and ironing* (15 categories, total 924). Including cleaners (dry), cutters, dressmakers (321 women), tailors (105 men).

    7. *Barber, beauty parlor and cosmetics* [sic] (3 categories, total 93). Including barbers, cosmetics and hairdressers.

    8. *Manufacturers* (17 categories, total 89). Including the manufacturers of buttons, cigars, chemical articles (13), perfume, and underwear (19).

    9. *Engineers and mechanicians* [sic] (4 categories,

total 195). Including engineers with diplomas (35), electricians, mechanics, etc.

10. *Clerks and executives* (12 major categories, total 1,328). The largest category with the least number of potential jobs in Shanghai, including accountants, bookkeepers, secretaries, clerks (over 600), bank employees (115), executives, interpreters, etc.

11. *Agents, dealers, and experts* [sic] (44 categories, total 1,124). Including advertising, bookdealers (12), coal, coffee, grain (61), eggs, fruit and foodstuff (100), furniture, hardware, leather (56), radio, tobacco, etc.

This list, though incomplete, indicates the variety of skills and experience possessed by the refugees, who could easily have found a niche for themselves in an open economy. The trouble was, as Fritz Friedlander already pointed out, that the refugees came out of political necessity rather than economic usefulness.[7] A good example of this is the large proportion of white-collar workers (over 1,300 clerks and executives) that came into a market already flooded with competent Western-trained Chinese, and crowded every office or place of business in search of a job.[8] Similarly, the over 200 physicians that came to Shanghai following the German Crystal Night created a "medical proletariat", and caused hardship among that usually affluent element in society.[9]

The age of most of the refugees also hampered their new business ventures. A 1946 report by the JDC substantiates this notion as it indicates that at the time of their emigration from Germany and Austria, more than 55 percent of the refugees were over forty.[10] This meant that the majority had been settled in their vocations at home for perhaps ten to fifteen years, making it difficult for them to change suddenly to a new field.[11]

IGNORANCE OF LOCAL CONDITIONS

Ignorance of local conditions also meant that the immigrants came unprepared for the climatic, sanitary, economic, social and linguistic conditions. For example, the refugees arrived without proper clothing to face the hot humid summers, the freezing winters, and the rainy season in between. The doctors were unfamiliar with the indigenous diseases, and the merchants did not realize that their wares would rot in the humid, hot summers. Everybody thought in terms of francs, marks or gold dollars, and so everything seemed cheap; the fallacy was that everybody's earnings were in Shanghai dollars.[12]

Very few came to Shanghai with a working knowledge of English, the language of its business world. This proved a tremendous handicap for those refugees who might otherwise have possessed the desired skills.[13] There were many and varied attemps by the Committees, as well as by the refugees themselves, to conduct classes and seminars for those interested in learning English.

The fact that no license was required to operate a business or practice a profession, proved advantageous to many refugees, especially doctors; but it was a double-edged sword. More than a few refugees lost their last penny by investing their meager funds with "phonies or sharpies" who made short shrift of the naive or unwary. The tangled web of extraterritorial rights and Chinese jurisdiction made it very difficult to assure protection against such frauds.[14]

SUCCESS AND FAILURE

Ignorance of local conditions was a basic reason also for the failure of over 900 small enterprises started by refugees.[15] Among these one may include the numerous attempts by inmates of the *Heime* to start an independent method of livelihood with a loan from the Rehabilitation Fund, or some money sent from abroad by a friend or relative. Those who failed would usually end up back in the *Heime,* perhaps to try their luck again at a later date.[16]

On the other hand, those refugees who did possess the proper experience, and even the knowledge of local conditions, had to overcome other obstacles. For example, in addition to the money required to establish a business, there was the added burden of having to pay the key money, i.e., the money demanded for the lease of a shop or business as well as for an apartment.[17]

Since a majority of the refugees had to live in Hongkew, because of the cheaper food and lodging, their mobility and means of establishing the "proper" business connections in the Concession or Settlement was severely limited.[18]

Competition with the Western-educated Chinese and the White Russians for many of the white-collar jobs was not only very keen, but also generated friction between the newcomers and many local residents.[19] Some of the refugees attempted to secure jobs by working temporarily without pay in the hope of filling a possible opening, or worse, someone else's job. This merely exacerbated matters, and was loudly condemned in the local English press as we have seen.[20]

Those who were aware of positions available in other parts of occupied China, especially Manchuria or North China, were unable to get permission from the Japanese authorities, who in most cases declined to admit refugees with a "J" stamped on their passport. Those possessing Polish, Hungarian or Czech passports, however, stood a much better chance, though refugees bearing German passports for foreigners (i.e., those born in Poland), called the *Deutsche Fremdenpasse,* fell into the same category as those with passports stamped with a "J".[21]

Not the least of the many hurdles to be overcome by the

refugees in starting out a new life in Shanghai, and particularly for those that had experienced imprisonment in concentration camps, was the psychological block that affected their normal initiative and drive.[22]

Nevertheless, despite all of the above-mentioned obstacles, the majority of the refugees, through a combination of hope, optimism and initiative, did manage to find some means of employment, or to establish a business, however small, and to maintain a minimum standard of living. This enabled all but about 2,500 of the poorest to live outside the *Heime* and to effect a major change in the physical environment of Hongkew. There were even a few, with a combination of skill, experience and some money (which some had been able to send out from Germany prior to 1938), who were able to create quite extensive commercial or manufacturing establishments that were taken note of in the larger Shanghai business world.[23]

STATISTICAL PORTRAIT

A good but rough statistical picture of the refugees' economic condition is given by a contemporary journalist in the *ORT Economic Review* in 1941. The estimate and the proportions he gives, with our qualifications based on statistics, are fairly accurate, though at no time did the picture remain static. Refugees constantly switched from one category into another, as changes in personal fortune or outside circumstances affected them. Pearl Harbor, and the later establishment of the ghetto in 1943 were major factors to change the picture and will be taken into consideration.[24]

It will be remembered that approximately 2,500 refugees resided in the *Heime,* totally dependent on the committees for their room, board and medical care. Another 5 to 6,000 managed an independent but precarious existence outside the *Heime,* though getting their food free or at low cost from the *Heime.* The rest of the refugees, approximately 9 to 10,000, were divided into the following three categories. The first, probably the largest of the three, lived on the money sent by friends or relatives from abroad, particularly the United States. The second, consisting of about 2,500 refugees, formed a middle class that managed an income of (Sh) $200-$500 per month, and received no aid from the committees. The last was the prosperous group, which corresponds closely in number with those that were either successful in business or were high-salaried professionals.[25]

SUCCESSFUL VENTURES

What was the nature of some of the successful business ventures carried on by the refugees during the period 1939-41? It must be noted at the outset that despite extensive economic activities resulting from the refugees' initiative, their impact was insignificant in comparison with Shanghai's overall economy.[26] Still, a few did manage to achieve influence outside the immediate sphere of refugee circles. For example, one of Shanghai's most successful sheet-and-quilt factories was started by a refugee who had arrived in 1934.[27] Others did almost as well in such areas as leather, textiles, clothing, food, real estate, chemical and pharmaceutical industries.[28] One refugee knitting firm, opened in 1940, employed over 350 Chinese and a few fellow refugee workers.[29]

We have already noted above how the necessity for cheap food and housing forced most of the refugees to settle in the Hongkew sector of Shanghai. A direct result of the feverish activity to repair and rebuild hundreds of demolished houses was a minor boom in the construction industries in which both refugees and Shanghailanders participated. The former included architects, builders, and landlords.[30] Whole streets were rebuilt in Hongkew along European models, their buildings having such modern fixtures as indoor plumbing and toilets.

One such refugee builder amassed a sizable fortune in this line and sponsored one of the few large, social events promoted by the refugees, just prior to the outbreak of the War in the Pacific. He hired a full complement of actresses, singers, etc., to celebrate the founding of his firm and to praise its success. This event was attended by many refugees able to pay the entrance fee, while others, less fortunate but more resourceful, managed to sneak in and to participate in this gala affair where the food was both plentiful and delicious.[31]

The newcomers also introduced a variety of products, such as leather goods and certain food items, including European specialties, like Viennese pastry and sausages; services, such as the sale of used stamps to numismatists; and skills, such as industrial arts, previously unknown to Shanghai.[33] These not only provided familiar items for the refugees, but also found new customers among all nationalities in Shanghai, including the Japanese.[34]

Several refugee window dressers introduced their craft to Shanghai, where they modernized and "dressed up" the windows of the fancy shops on Nanking Road and Avenue Joffre. Another enterprising refugee established a snake farm in order to produce the much-desired serum for Chinese drugstores.[35] On the whole a handful of the refugees were able to establish enterprises that required a great deal of capital investment, such as the technological industries. These few, despite difficulties and often great losses, had been able to bring some capital with them to Shanghai.[36] Among the more successful products of these manufacturers were radios and radio parts.[37] In fact, one such firm, utilizing chiefly Japanese material, placed a radio on the market that was 75 percent cheaper than the lowest-priced imported ones.[38]

Some enterprising refugees capitalized on the financial needs of others and their willingness to part with their household goods, or the luxury items they had brought from Europe. They opened up jewelry shops, selling such things as crystal, cameras, antiques, books, works of art, china and porcelain, to Shanghai's wealthier classes. These Shanghailanders were able to drive a hard bargain because there were frequently more sellers than buyers.[39] The above-mentioned Emigrants' Thrift Shop similarly served as an outlet for such goods, particularly for the residents of the *Heime*.[40]

The majority of the shops opened by the refugees were one- or two-man operations, such as those run by skilled craftsmen, shoemakers, furniture repairmen, tailors, smiths, or hatmakers.[41] Despite the stiff competition from Chinese labor, the European craftsmen achieved some measure of success in Shanghai, where their superior skill was sought, notwithstanding its higher cost.[42]

Expert European tailoring, whether designing original clothes or repairing used ones, was appreciated by the Japanese customers. They patronized such refugee shops or individual seamstresses, even to the point of coming into the ghetto, after 1943, to obtain superior workmanship.

Efforts on the part of such craftsmen to unite, in order to overcome competition, resulted in the foundation of the Guild of Craftsmen, organized primarily to secure jobs for its members. It strove to successfully promote the idea that the European craftsmen were worth the higher price that they demanded.[43] The founders of a branch of the ORT Vocational School in Shanghai also recognized the potential for skilled craftsmen, even in competitive Shanghai.[44] Occasionally Chinese businessmen took some of these European refugees into their businesses.[45]

Among the most common stores, albeit not always too successful, were the many food-provision shops started by the newcomers. These consisted chiefly of coffeehouses, cafés, restaurants, bars, or hors d'oeuvres" stores.[46] A popular refugee enterprise was the coffeeshop, the first of these having opened in December 1938, in the French Concession.[47] Some of these coffeeshops or cafés were frequented not only by refugees, but became popular meeting places for individuals of many nationalities, including some from the old German gentile colony.[48]

Almost every avenue of business was explored by the refugees in their quest for a livelihood, whether they possessed the requisite skills or not. Quite a few tried their hand at door-to-door peddling of all sorts of articles, particularly to the local Jewish population, who naturally favored their coreligionists.[49] This often brought them into direct competition with the Chinese or Japanese small businessmen, who resented what they considered unfair competition.[50]

Others tried their hand at what can best be described as "miniature export," since it was possible to produce profitably, even on a very small scale, items in demand overseas, especially in the United States.[51] The very high rate of exchange of Shanghai dollars against US dollars was conducive to such overseas trade.[52] One contemporary noted the busy traffic of refugees to the Post Office to send their parcels overseas.[53] As noted, the War in Europe, in this respect, proved beneficial to the refugees, since it created a demand for items overseas, formerly procured from Europe. In addition, it provided a larger market in Shanghai itself for items formerly produced in Europe.[54]

Two partners in a successful soap factory got their lucky break from Sir Victor Sassoon, who was impressed by their ingenuity and drive. They had attempted to start their business in one of the ruins of Hongkew, with about the most rudimentary equipment possible, bought from a junk dealer. Sir Victor, in admiration of their spirit bought their whole output and they were soon on the way to a prosperous business.[55]

Some resourceful refugees found various unusual means of earning a livelihood. One elderly gentleman, for example, earned his few dollars by establishing a "waking up" service. He made certain that his clientele was awakened at specified hours and gave them the day's weather forecast, which enabled them to dress suitably.[56] Another immigrant, residing in the *Heime,* utilized a package of old clothes sent him, to open a secondhand clothing store. He also bought up similar packages sent to other refugees, and was soon able to leave the *Heime* permanently.[57] A unique occupation for a refugee was serving as a lifeguard at various pools and waterfronts in Shanghai. And as many as thirty refugees were applying for each of the few job openings teaching English or other subjects.[58]

The drive and ingenuity displayed by the refugees in their attempt to fit into Shanghai's economic picture evoked both amazement and hostility among local Shanghailanders.[59] To them, such drive was illustrative of the refugees' quest for the "almighty dollar", a rather odd complaint on the part of Shanghailanders, who were renowned for their preoccupation with material things.[60]

NOTES : BREAD AND BUTTER IN SHANGHAI

1. For the best history of the economic development of Shanghai, see Murphy, *Shanghai*. Cf. also Barnett, *Hostage*.

2. See especially Ginsbourg, *Refugees*, pp. III-VI.

3. Cf. Barnett, *Hostage*, pp. 86-87. Also Hinder, *Labour*, pp. 12-13; Ahler, "Threat," April 15, 1939; Jovishoff, "City," p. 214; Friedlander, "Migration," p. 25.

4. See above, pp.

5. CFA "List of Professions," December 31, 1939 [CFA "Professions"] (HH XV C-4). The titles used for the categories and subcategories are those found in the report. The 7,052 listed as "registered" at the CFA (see title page) could not refer to all the refugees that had registered with the CFA for one reason or another, since the detailed CFA Minutes of February 2, 1940, p. 2, list the total registered with the Committee as 13,500. The latter number probably refers to the combined total of those living outside, but receiving their food from the *Heime*.

Cf. also F.O. Masaki Yano (Consul General) to Kazuo Aoki (Minister of Greater East Asia), July 21, 1943 [Yano to Aoki, July 21, '43], p. 5 (DF).

6. Only a small number of physicians are noted since the list, which includes dentists, adds up to only 57 (CFA "Professions," p. 3). According to a number of sources, there were over 200 refugee physicians in addition to dentists in Hongkew.

Probably the number of physicians here refers only to those who worked for the *Heime*. Cf. CFA *Report*, 1940, p. 3.

7. "Migration," p. 25.

8. HIAS, *Report*, May 19, 1939, p. 3.

9. Friedlander, "Migration," p. 25.

10. This report is cited by Gruenberger, "Refugees," p. 329. Cf. also Nathan Reich to Joseph Hyman, January 21, 1946 (JDCCA). The statistics of the refugees in the document are most likely not based on a 1946 survey, but rather on a Japanese survey of February 1943, when the refugees were ordered into a ghetto. See introduction to this document. Following is the age level of 15,000 refugees: under 30—32 percent; 31-50—45 percent; over 50—23 percent. For a similar age level of 2,200 German refugees who made their way overseas in 1940-41 via Siberia and Japan, see *Kobe Report*, p. 12A.

11. Jovishoff, "City," p. 215. Cf. also Friedlander, "Migration," p. 26.

12. Wolfgang Fischer, "Two Years Shanghai," *Shanghai Jew Chronicle* (March 1, 1941), p. 3. Cf. also Rosenfeld, *History*, III, pp. 51-52.

13. Jovishoff, "City," p. 215. Cf. also HIAS, *Report*, May 19, 1939, p. 3; Rosenfeld, *History*, III, pp. 61-62.

14. Jovishoff, "City," p. 216. Also Hinzelmann, *O China*, p. 67; Kann, *EE*, p. 7. For the legal problems of Extraterritoriality and Chinese Law, see Johnstone, *Shanghai*. Cf. also Miller, *Paradise*, Chapter 1, especially pp. 19-20. According to Dr. Friedrichs, the doctors had to register in the *Shanghai Municipal* medical directory in order to practice. This was not difficult if one had all the papers and certificates from home. *Geschichte*, p. 64.

15. Rosenfeld, *History*, III, p. 52. Cf. also Friedrichs, *Geschichte*, p. 65.

16. Silberstein, Interview; also Birman, *Report*, January 16, 1940, pp. 1-2; Kann, "Refugees," p. 39; Gruenberger, "Refugees," p. 333.

17. *Israel's Messenger*, July 14, 1939 (typed reprint of article), p. 3 (HH XV C-4). Also Barnett, "Uncertainties," p. 252.

18. Ganther, "7 Years," p. 2. The author feels that the "local" Jews intentionally kept the refugees at a distance, i.e., in Hongkew, to have as little contact with them as possible. He fails to see what alternative there was, short of paying the rent for the refugees, in view of the radically cheaper rates in Hongkew.
Cf. also Gruenberger, "Refugees," p. 332; Redlich-Kranzler corres. Aug. 10, 1973, pp. 3-4.

19. The refugee worker usually required a salary four times that of his Chinese counterpart to live even within his circumscribed standard of living. Left out altogther was the possibility of competition with coolie labor, which was impossible for the Europeans. See Hinder, *Labor*, p. 77. Cf. also the Joint "Confidential Summary Report No. 9," August 26, 1940 (JDCCA); Ahlers, "Threat."

20. *Ibid.*

21. Birman, *Report*, January 16, 1940, p. 3 (HH XV C-6).

22. Rosenfeld, *History*, III, p. 3.

23. See below, p. 000. See Redlich-Kranzler, corres. Feb. 27, 1974, p. 3, for examples of a few such successful businessmen who brought money along.

24. Friedlander, "Migration," pp. 26-27. His estimates are based on a total of 20,000 refugees, which the author considers too high. The latter's estimate runs to about 17,000-18,000. Friedlander agrees that "accurate statistics are lacking," and bases his calculations on "well informed sources" (probably estimates given him by the HICEM, CFA or the IC). He gives another figure of 25,000 without discussing it. It is a figure often thrown about, but with no basis in fact.

25. *Ibid.* Cf. also Rosenfeld, *History,* III, p. 3; Birman, *Report,* 1939, pp. 5-6; Gruenberger, "Refugees," p. 334.

26. Barnett, *Hostage,* pp. 73-74.

27. Ganther, "3 Years," p. 30.

28. *Ibid.* Cf. also "Aus Dem Wirtschaftsleben," *Herald* (S.E.), p. 1.

29. Ganther, "3 Years," p. 20.

30. *Ibid.,* pp. 22-23. Also Friedrichs, *Geschichte,* pp. 115-116; *Friedlander, Sieben,* p. 21.

31. *Ibid.,* p. 26. Also *Gruenberger,* "Refugees," p. 333.

32. Gruenberger, "Refugees," p. 333. For the sale of stamps, see Birman, *Report,* 1939, p. 5. For new products, see Barnett, *Hostage,* p. 86; HIAS *Report,* 1939, pp. 2-3; Sopher, *Shanghai,* pp. 387-88.

33. Ganther, "3 Years," p. 20.

34. Gruenberger, "Refugees," p. 333. Also Georg Cohn, Interv. p. 3 and Testimony of Hugo Hoenigsberg, "Experiences in Shanghai," 1932-47, pp. 4-5 (Transcripts of Intrv. of G. Cohn by Peter Zadek, and Testimony by Hoeingsberg, courtesy of Wiener Library, London.)

35. Levin, Interv. Aug. 6, 1974.

36. Ganther, "3 Years," p. 20.

37. *Ibid.*

38. Ginsbourg, *Refugees,* p. 7.

39. "Wirtschaftsleben." See also Friedlander, *Sieben,* p. 15.

40. Kann, "Refugees," p. 32.

41. Gruenberger, "Refugees," p. 333. Also Kann, *EE,* p. 39.

42. Ganther, "3 Years," p. 23 cf. also Georg Cohn, Interv. p. 3; Hoeingsberg, "Experiences," pp. 4-5.

43. *Guild of Craftsmen,* 1943-1947 [Guild], p. 6 (JDCCA). For what the author believes to be its precedecessor, see Margolies to Pilpel, August 11 1941, p. 6.

44. See below, pp. 000.

45. Barnett, "Uncertainties," p. 253.

46. Ganther, "3 Years," p. 24. He notes over 200 such enterprises were started by the refugees.

47. *Ibid.*   48. Gerechter, Interv.

49. Abraham, Interv. Also Greenberg, Interv.

50. Abraham, Interv. Cf. also Barnett, "Uncertainties," p. 262; Ahlers, "Threat."

51. Birman, *Report,* 1939, p. 5.

52. *Ibid.*   53. *Ibid.*

54. *Ibid.* Cf. also Ahlers, Economic "Threat."

55. Redlich-Kranzler corres. Dec. 11, 1973, p. 4. Redlich was not certain if it was Sir Victor or Elly Kadoorie.

56. Gruenberger, "Refugees," p. 334.

57. Mrs. Gerechter, Interv. Her father opened such a store. He later added other secondhand items such as China.

58. Friedlander, *Sieben,* p. 18 for the English language instruction. Cf. the *Almanac,* p. 99, re the position of life-guard.

59. Abraham Interv. Also Greenberg Interv.; Ginsbourg Interv.

60. Lothar Brieger, "Emigration und Kuenstlerische Produktivitaet" [Brieger, "Kuenst"], *Shanghai Jewish Herald (S.E.),* p. 18. For emphasis on the dollar, see Miller, *Paradise.* Also Abraham, Interv.

10 | "PLEASE DON'T DRINK THE WATER"

SANITARY AND HEALTH CONDITIONS

1. Don't remove your hat in the sun.
2. Never drink unboiled water.
3. Don't eat raw fruits and vegetables.

(*from IC "Twelve Golden Rules of Health"*)

Forewarning about the economic conditions in Shanghai had prepared the refugees to some extent for what lay ahead. But no admonition could fully prepare a people accustomed to the temperate climate of Europe for the extremities of the weather in Shanghai. The combination of the semitropical climate and the highly insanitary and crowded living conditions, particularly in the *Heime,* was not conducive to a healthful life for the new arrivals. Temperatures soaring to over 100 degrees Fahrenheit, combined with very high humidity, made them swelter in their dingy rooms or in the overcrowded dormitories of the *Heime,* The often torrential rains and the extreme cold hovering around the freezing point, during the winter months added to the discomfort. When the periodic typhoon came down over Shanghai, the Wangpoo overflowed, and Chaoufoong Road was no longer a thoroughfare, but a flowing river over two feet deep. It found its way into the living rooms of the low, lane-

297

type houses, made linen rot, books mildew and furniture warp. Such ominous climatic circumstances, combined with the poor physical condition of many of the refugees, especially after the food-ration cuts of 1940, precipitated constant fear of contracting one of the many communicable diseases prevalent in the city.[2] The most common were dysentery, typhus, beri beri, cholera, and a host of parasitic-worm diseases. It was certainly miraculous that relatively few epidemics did break out among the refugees, even in the *Heime,* and that these were arrested with minimum fatalities.[3]

A large measure of credit for averting any major medical disaster must go to the Medical Board of the CFA and its devoted staff of doctors and nurses.[4] Its medical services, despite the lack of adequate facilities and food, and the deteriorating conditions that followed Pearl Harbor, were, in the opinion of one of its foremost contemporary critics, among the more praiseworthy activities of the CFA.[5]

Much of the physical discomfort and sickness can be attributed, as in the case of the economic conditions, to ignorance on the part of both the refugees and the doctors of the hygienic conditions prevailing in Shanghai. This ignorance can be ascribed in part to inadequate information about conditions in Shanghai in the news media which circulated among potential refugees in Berlin during 1938-40. Fritz Friedlander, a journalist, described his own experience in January 1939, when he tried to locate data at the *Hilfsverein* in Berlin, for a realistic picture of conditions in Shanghai. He found it to be wholly inadequate.[6] The result of such ignorance manifested itself, for example, in the inappropriate clothing and furniture brought by the refugees to Shanghai.[7]

DIFFICULT ADJUSTMENT

The first year of immigration proved particularly difficult in terms of adjusting to this unfamiliar environment.[8] The problems arising from insanitary water and food, and the generally unhealthful conditions by European standards, wrought havoc among the refugees.[9] The European refugee doctors themselves were unfamiliar with either the new environment or its concomitant diseases, which were rarely found in Europe. Little help in this respect came from native Shanghailanders.[10]

It was some time before there was any adjustment to the climate and environment which would make them immune to the milder forms of the diseases. The IC issued a list of "Twelve Golden Rules of Health," in order to help the refugees avoid, at least, the most common hazards. These included:

1. Don't remove your hat in the sun.
2. Never drink unboiled water.
3. Don't eat any raw fruits and vegetables.[11]

Bread was usually sliced very thin, so that the omnipresent and appetite-killing worms could be easily spotted.[12]

During the first few months of the immigration, most of the refugee patients were sent to Shanghai's various municipal and private hospitals. The expense, however, was too great for the CFA's limited budget, nor was there room for the many refugee patients in the Shanghai General Hospital. The directors of the CFA, therefore, decided to establish their own hospital, especially since a large number of refugee doctors were available.[13]

THE REFUGEE HOSPITAL

The first health establishment, a polyclinic, was set up at the newly established Ward Road *Heim* in January 1939. This was followed shortly by outpatient clinics at the Chaoufoong, Kinchow, Alcock, and Pingliang Road *Heime*. These outpatient clinics treated over 66,000 cases, including 12,000 vaccinations in that year. The crowded, insanitary conditions in the *Heime,* however, pointed to the need for a separate hospital building. Therefore, by March 1939, the Emigrant or Refugee Hospital was opened in the former Washing Road *Heim* under the supervision of Dr. Samuel Didner with a capacity of 60 beds. By the end of 1939, it had treated close to 1,000 patients.[14] Valuable X-ray and iron-lung equipment was donated by Messrs. Kadoorie and Sons and by Sir Victor Sassoon.[15]

The first epidemic of dangerous proportions struck the Hongkew refugees during May of 1939. Eighteen refugees had contracted scarlet fever, and required isolation. One of the buildings, in the newly acquired Chaoufoong Road *Heim,* was quickly transformed into a temporary isolation ward. Meanwhile, there was a daily rise in the number of infected cases, until it reached its peak at 128. The epidemic was finally brought under control by the end of June. As a result of this experience, the CFA established a permanent Isolation Ward, in the Chaoufoong Road *Heim,* by September 1939. Sixty isolation beds were also placed in the Kinchow and Wayside Road *Heim.*[16]

The Emigrants Hospital was removed from the Washing Road *Heim* to larger quarters in the Ward Road *Heim* (House No. 2) which now included 100 beds. Until December 1939, all major operations were performed at the Shanghai General Hospital, while the services of other medical and mental institutions were utilized by the refugees. For example, the American Foundling-House cared for those babies whose mothers were unable to look after their newborn.[17] Through the initiative of Mrs. Reuben D. Abraham, a Maternity Ward was also erected at the Ward Road *Heim.*[18]

Thus, within approximately one year, a complete system of medical care, including outpatient clinics, a central pharmacy, a laboratôry, a dental clinic, and three hospitals with a combined capacity of 200 beds, were made available by the Com mittee to the refugees in the *Heime*.[19] Until the war broke out in Europe, all the medicines, and even the raw materials, i.e., chemicals, came from Germany. A shortage and a corresponding rise in the price of medicine followed. Thus a salve previously costing the druggist about £1 (British money) now went for 18 times that amount. When Dr. Friedrichs attempted to establish a herb industry, to enable the refugee doctors to utilize and experiment with cheap, home-grown Chinese herbs, he was thwarted by the refusal of the Chinese practitioners to teach the Western doctors, for fear of creating competition. Still, some medicines continued to come from Germany in small supply, till Pearl Harbor, when they stopped completely. Moreover, some knowledge concerning the herbs was slowly acquired and adapted by a few refugee doctors.

One such successful attempt involved the discovery of a Chinese "miracle drug," a substitute for the very expensive (after Pearl Harbor) medicine, *emitin*, used for amoebic dysentery, a common ailment among the refugees. Dr. Friedrichs, after much experimentation and with the help of his pharmacist wife, was able to isolate the medicinal part of a special nut. The new drug, called *KuSanTze*, worked so well and was so cheap that it quickly replaced *emitin* as the cure.[20]

CONDITIONS OF THE REFUGEE PHYSICIANS

Still, the picture was far from encouraging. The doctors themselves were often as undernourished as the patients, and many had to take on additional jobs to supplement their incomes. Supplies and medicine were never in overabundance, which increased the difficulties for both the physicians and patients.[21]

About 20 per cent of the approximately 200 refugee doctors were able to establish some sort of medical practice, or gain entrance to a hospital. As noted above, a number of refugee physicians found full-time and others, part-time employment at the Sephardi—run B'nai B'rith Polyclinic and Shanghai Jewish

Hospital, in the French Concession. This institution was headed by Dr. Max Steinmann, an earlier-settled internist, who was to render invaluable help to the East European group during the war years. This small number was in contrast to the experience of many German doctors who had arrived between 1933 and 1934 and who had easily become established.[22] China, unlike other countries, did not then require a special examination for a doctor to open a practice. In fact, anyone, whether genuine or a quack, was able to hang up a shingle or any other sign, and start in business, as long as he reported it to the proper authorities and was registered in the SMC Medical Directory.[23]

As we have noted, those in the *Heime* received their medical service free with their room and board. However, those refugees residing in private rooms, sometimes at the cost of their every penny, found it difficult to pay for the frequent medical services required. The pay scale had to be adjusted to the low but realistic figure of (Sh) $1-$3 per visit.[24]

The above-mentioned lack of contact among the foreign circles made the more lucrative clientele largely unreachable for the majority of the refugee doctors, though, of course, many exceptions existed.[25] Since medical insurance was unknown in Shanghai, it was difficult to establish a practice amongst a poorer economic group. In order to provide such a Medical Insurance Plan, as well as to pool their knowledge and experience concerning so many new diseases, the refugee doctors formed an Association of Central-European Physicians, in 1939.[26] The Medical Insurance Plan cost the subscribers (Sh) $1 per person, per month, which paid for 50 per cent of medical bills, and 25 per cent toward the dental bills. The Association also met twice a month for professional discussion and issued scientific papers.[27] They published a German-language medical journal titled *Journal of the Association of Central European Doctors,* under the editorship of Dr. Theodore Friedrichs. Some of the medical journals which were used to keep up with the most recent advances in medicine came from the United States until the outbreak of the War in the Pacific. Money was raised to publish the journal by presenting a variety show (*Bunter Abend*). That this journal held the interest of a wider circle than only refugee physicians can be seen from the many articles written in English and Chinese.[28]

A brief perusal of one of the more reliable sets of fatality statistics among Shanghai's refugees for the period of 1939-1945 should provide an insight into their overall health situation. For the seven years under review, and with a maximum population of about 17,000, there are recorded 1,581 fatalities, including 36 suicides, an average of about 226 deaths per year or about 13 per 1,000. Compared to the 1974 ratio of 11.8 for West Germany, or 12.6 for Austria, the refugee statistic is not unusually high, particularly when one must take into consideration the very difficult few years after Pearl Harbor with the increase in malnutrition and its concomitant diseases.[29]

Thus, a large share of the credit for preventing, what could easily have become a catastrophe must be given to the medical and health care set up by the refugees with the financial aid of local and American Jews.

NOTES : "PLEASE DON'T DRINK THE WATER"

1. Rosenfeld, *History, III*, p. 5. Cf. also Eisfelder, *Exile*, pp. 8, 20-21. Despite the cold winters, snow fell but once in several years. Abraham Interview.

2. For the condition of avitaminosis and beri beri, and the problem of importing fresh fruit as a cure, see Speelman to Troper, February 15, 1940, p. 2. Speelman hints that the Japanese were the cause of an "artificial" rise of exorbitant prices.

The constant fear of catching the prevalent diseases was a definite factor in the psychological makeup of the refugees, particularly in the *Heime*. See Farb Correspondence, April 28, 1939. Also Dr. Frederick Reiss, *Report of the Medical Board (CFA)* 1939-1940 [Reiss, *Medical Report* 1939-1940], p .12 (YIVO No. 34). For the typhoon rains see Friedrichs, *Geschichte*, pp. 79-80; Eisfelder, *Exile*, pp. 20-22.

3. For health conditions, see Friedrichs, *Geschichte*. Cf. also Dr. F. Reiss, "Die Aerzliche Fuersorge der Emigration" [Reiss, "Aerztliche"], *S.J. Chronicle (S.I.), pp.* 11-13; Dr. F. Reiss, *Report of the Medical Board (CFA)* 1940-1941 [Reiss, *Medical Report* 1940-1941] (YIVO No. 34); Dr. T. Kunfi, "Die Medizinische Betreuung der Immigranten" [Kunfi, "Medizinische"], *Herald (S.E.)*, pp. 9-10. Also Weinberger, *Report,* 1939, pp. 11-13; Rosenfeld, *History, III*, pp. 10-11, 34-39; CFA *Report,* 1940, pp. 6-8; Kann, *EE*, p. 16; Speelman to Troper, December 14, 1939, pp. 5-6; CFA Minutes, February 6, 1940, p. 11; Dr. S. Friedmann, "Ein Jahr Ambulanzdienst", *S.J. Chronicle (S.I.),* p. 13; Speelman to Council, February 10, 1939, p. 2; Birman, *Report,* January, 16, 1940, p. 2 (HH XV C-6); *Der Hongkewer Aerzte-Verein* (Association of Central-European Physicians) *Report* [Physicians' Report], pp. 1-5 (YIVO No. 34); also Birman, HIAS *Report,* 1939, p. 5; *Journal of the Association of Central European Doctors* [JACED], Vols. I, II, III (July 1941-December 1942); *Mitteilungen der Vereinigung der Emigranten-Aerzte* [*MVEA*], Vols. I, II (January-October, 1940). The last two are complete sets, and give technical as well as more popular style information. This set loaned for reproduction courtesy of its editor, Dr. Theodore Friedrichs.

For the small number of fatalities, see especially Theodore Friedrichs, "The Refugees as a '"Folks Unit"', Their Acclimatization and Their Causes of Death' [Friedrichs, "Causes of Death"], *JACED,* pp. 123-24.

4. See n. 3, especially Kunfi, "Medizinische". The author feels this to be true despite Laura Margolies' criticism of Dr. Reiss and his Medical Board. See Margolies to Pilpel, August 11, 1941, p. 13. He places greater weight on the more objective judgment of the usually critical Rosenfeld. See Rosenfeld,

History, III, p. 10. Thus, for example, in Margolies' judgment, the maintenance of their own medical facilities was considered a waste of money which did little for the refugees. She felt that the Shanghai municipal hospitals could have taken care of the refugees' needs more cheaply. According to Dr. Reiss, there were never more than about 20 free beds available in those hospitals. Interview. The CFA originally sent the refugees to the municipal hospitals, and they resorted to the building of their own hospitals as a matter of economy. Speelman to Council, Joint, February 10, 1939, p. 3. They paid $3 per day for 20 cases. Perhaps the refugee hospitals could have been run more efficiently with more experienced help, and less red tape.

Two additional factors must be remembered: first, the proximity of the medical care to the *Heime* meant faster care, an important factor for the weak and undernourished patients. Second, the care given to patients within familiar surroundings, with empathetic doctors who spoke their language, would seem to favor a hospital of their own. Margolies also noted that the many refugee doctors supported by the hospital gave them the opportunity to practice their skill, instead of intellectually rotting away in the *Heime* as did a number of other intellectuals. See SMC, *Report,* p. 3.

Nevertheless, under the dire circumstances, following Pearl Harbor, the JDC had little choice but to close the hospital. Dr. Theodore Friedrichs, Interview. Dr. Friedrichs was present at the meeting when the decision was made to close the hospital.

5. Rosenfeld, *History, III,* p. 11. Cf. also Birman, *Report,* January 16, 1940, p. 2. Birman reports that, for example, the hospital's first misroscope was acquired in 1940. For operations, the refugees were sent to several general and municipal hospitals, especially the Shanghai General Hospital. Reiss, *Medical Report,* 1939-40, p. 11.

6. Friedlander, "Migration", p. 24.

7. *Ibid.* For example, very few were prepared for the hot, humid summer, or owned the proper rain gear for the torrential rains. See also Friedrichs, *Geschichte,* p. 61; Eisfelder, *Exile,* p. 1.

8. Reiss, "Aerztliche". Cf. also Speelman to Troper, December 14, 1939, pp. 4-5. Dr. Friedrichs noted, however, that during the first year or two the refugees were careful and more on their guard in some respects, though later they became more careless. Interview, February 2, 1971.

9. Even when refugees refrained from drinking unboiled water, they were liable to catch dysentery from melons bought from Chinese dealers who injected water into them to boost the weight. Friedrichs, Interview. Cf. also Eisfelder, *Exile,* pp. 20-21.

10. Kunfi, "Medizinische", p. 9. Cf. also *Physicians' Report,* 9. 1; Gruenberger, "Refugees", p. 332. Dr. Friedrichs noted that there were few that were helpful. One of those noteworthy exceptions was Dr. Bernard Rosen-

berg, who had come to Shanghai in 1933, and on invitation of the Hongkew Physicians' Association shared freely his knowledge and experience with his more recently arrived fellow physicians. Interview.

11. Paul Komor, "12 Golden Health Rules" [Komor, "Rules"], *S.J. Chronicle*, August 3, 1941 (n.p.) (YIVO) No. 67).

12. Ruth Fischel, Interview.

13. CFA *Report*, March 2, 1939, p. 2. See also Dr. Samuel Didner, Interview, September 22, 1973.
By 1940 the Heime employed 29 doctors and 50 nurses for their three hospitals, and clinics. CFA *Report*, 1940, p. 3. See also Friedlander, "Mass Migration, 1939-41", p. 24.

14. Kunfi, "Medizinische", p. 9. Cf. also Reiss, *Medical Report*, 1939-1940, pp. 5-12; CFA *Report*, 1940, pp. 6-8. For the number of cases in the clinics, see Weinberger, *Report*, pp. 11-12.

15. Speelman to Troper, December 14, 1939, p. 4. Cf. also L. Kadoorie to S. Frieder, August 2, 1939, p. 3; Jackson, *Sassoons*, p. 253; Reiss, *Medical Report* 1939-1940, p. 12.

16. Kunfit, "Medizinische", p. 9. See also CFA *Report*, 1940, pp. 6-7; Kann, "EE", p. 16; Speelman to Troper, December 14, 1939, pp. 5-6; Weinberger, *Report*, 1939, pp. 11-13; Reiss, *Medical Report* 1939-40, pp. 12-13.

17. Kunfi, "Medizinische", p. 9. For some of the services rendered by Shanghai institutions, see Reiss, *Medical Report*, pp. 11-12.

18. CFA *Minutes*, February 6, 1940, p. 11. Cf. also Weinberger, *Report*, 1939, pp. 12-13; CFA *Report*, 1940, pp. 6-7. It was called the "Mount Moriah" Maternity Ward (*ibid.*, p. 7). Laura Margolies, who pulls no punches in her candid and critical evaluation of relief projects and personnel, has nothing but praise for the manner in which the Maternity Ward was run. She gives Mrs. R. D. Abraham the credit for making it a bright and cheerful place, in contrast to the typical, dreary atmosphere of the *Heime*. Margolies to Pilpel, August 11, 1941, pp. 4-5.

19. CFA *Report*, 1940. Also Reiss, *Medical Report* 1939-1940, pp. 11-13. *Ibid.*, p. 9.

20. Friedrichs, *Geschichte*, pp. 86-89, 157-159.

21. Kunfi, "Medizinische", p. 10.

22. Dr. Tibor Kunfi, *"Der Existenzkampf der Refugee-Aertze"*, *S.J. Chronicle (S.I.)* [Kunfi, "Aertze"], p. 2. About 30 of these got jobs in mission hospitals. Friedlander, "Migration", 1939-41, p. 27. For the number of physicians, see the *Report* of the Association of Central-European Physicians, [ACEP, *Report*], p. 5.

For the information re the B'nai B'rith instituteion, see *Almanac*, pp. 51, 54. Cf. also Dr. Max Steinmann, Interview, July 5, 1975; Menachem Flakser, "Toizend Poilishe Yidn in Shanchai" (Yid.) [Flakser, "Poilishe"], *Jewish Daily Forward*, December 31, 1962, p. 5. (Cony reproduced courtesy of Mr. Flakser.)

23. Kunfi, *"Aertze"*, p. 27. Cf. also Kann, "EE", p. 7; HIAS *Report*, 1939, p. 5; Friedrichs, *Geschichte*, p. 64.

24. Kunfi, "Aerzte", p. 27.

25. *Ibid*.

26. ACEP, *Report*, p. 2. Its original German name was *Hongkewer Aerzte Verein*.

Dr. Friedrichs explained the two different titles for the Physicians Association as follows: Originally there was organized a general association of all the refugees physicians in Shanghai which was named the Association of Central-European Doctors (*Vereinigung der Emigranten-Aerzte*). It was under this title that both the *Mitteilungen* and the Journal were published. Within a year or so, probably sometime during 1940, a new organization was formed, composed only of those refugee doctors in Hongkew i.e., *Hongkewer Aerzte Verein*. (Both had their origin in the meeting of European physicians called by the *Shanghai Jewish Chronicle* on July 6, 1939. Friedrichs, *Geschichte*, p. 67). This was done because the older, more inclusive organization was too poor to rent a central locale, and after only a few meetings it petered out. The newer organization remained active throughout the Shanghai period, although their journal ceased publication (under the original Association's name) by the end of 1942 due to financial difficulties. Interview. See also Friedrichs, *Geschichte*, pp. 89-90.

There were probably around 200 refugee physicians in Shanghai. The Report states that 25 or 14 per cent of its membership died during its eight years (1939-47), which would make it closer to 175. Perhaps with a few doctors who did not join a total of 200 might be reached. Kunfi in his *"Aerzte"*, gives the figure of about 200-250.

27. ACEP, *Report*, p. 2.

28. See, for example, all the Chinese articles in *JACED*, Vol. III. For the American medical journals, and their financing see Friedrichs, *Geschichte*, p. 154.

29. For the statistics of refugee fatalities, see appendix. Cf. also Friedrichs, "Causes of Death". The 1974 figures can be found in the *Reader's Digest* 1975 *Almanac and Yearbook* (Pleasantville: The Reader's Digest Association, Inc., 1975), p. 472.

INTRODUCTION

ומסילת הברזל . . . אשר נסלל לפני שנים רבות לולדיסטוק במזרח
הרחוק, הרי בטוח הוא שתחילתו הוא, במה שבני תורה שנסעו
במלחמה זו לשאנחי, יראו להם דרך נוחה לנסוע, . . . ואם אנו
אין מבינים איך זה אבל הקב"ה עושה מרחוק, ואשר במשך הזמן
בא הדבר אל תכליתו . . .

(חידושי רבינו הגר"ז סאלאווייציק מפי השמועה על התורה,
ס׳ קנ.   בהכרת טוב למוהר"ר הלל דוד שליט"א)

* On February 11, 1941, amidst an outpouring of patriotism and enthusiasm for the national "spiritual mobilization" unequalled since the days of the Russo-Japanese War, the 2,601st anniversary of the divine founding of the Japanese Empire by the Emperor Jimmu was celebrated. Millions of Japanese crowded their shrines throughout Japan to express their reverence to the gods and the Japanese way of life (*Kokutai*). In Tokyo, over 200,000 youths and other groups, many in uniform and shouldering rifles, paraded to the Imperial palace to bow *en masse* before the Emperor, and "thunderously compress the 'sentiments of the nation into a single word, thrice repeated: 'Banzai!' "[1]

On this same day, there could be seen, huddled near the various foreign embassies in Tokyo and Yokohama, or along the streets of Kobe, hundreds of Polish refugees, including bearded rabbis and Yeshiva students, recently-arrived from Kovno, in Russian-occupied Lithuania. They were in transit in Japan hoping to find a permanent sanctuary in the U.S. or other country,after their long flight from Hitler's armies. These circumstances bring us to what was probably the strangest of the various situations that manifested the unique Japanese policy toward the Jews.[2]

KOVNO

Kovno, Lithuania is roughly 6,000 miles from Kobe, Japan, but in terms of culture and milieu, the distance could hardly be measured in light-years. And it was almost by a series of miracles that another group of refugees, very different from their German and Austrian coreligionists, a group of 2,000 Polish Jews, made its way out of Russian-occupied Kovno, across the wastes of Siberia, to Kobe, between 1940 and 1941. Half of these were to end up in Shanghai just before Pearl Harbor.[3]

These 2,000 Polish Jews were among the 4,600 to 4,700 refugees who managed to escape to the Far East by this route. And these 2,000 were also part of the approximately 10,000 Jews who had fled from both German- and Russian-occupied Poland into neutral Lithuania during the period of October 1939 to May 1940.[4] There they congregated chiefly in Vilna, where the JDC—through an ad hoc local relief committee—provided for all refugees.[5] Most of those with end-visas or certificates to Palestine (and sufficient money—usually provided by the Joint in Lithuania and/or by relatives abroad) took the opportunity to emigrate during the early part of 1940.[6]

CURACAO VISAS

It was, however, an extraordinary circumstance that

enabled 2,000 of the 10,000 Polish-Jewish refugees who had no end-visas to cross Siberia and reach Japan. The sudden appearance of a Japanese consul by the name of Senpo Sugihara in Kovno was the source of this fortunate situation.[7] Prior to his arrival there had never been a Japanese consul in Kovno, and Sugihara's stay lasted less than a year, until August 1940. Yet during that short period he became—as a spokesman for the Mirrer Yeshiva put it—an "angel of salvation" for thousands of Jews.[8] According to his recent memoirs of the period, Sugihara was sent to Kovno by Lieutenant-General Hiroshi Oshima, the Japanese Ambassador to Berlin, in order to ascertain more fully German moves on the Eastern Front. He did not quite trust Hitler's promise to invade Russia, a basic premise of Japanese foreign policy.[9] Sugihara issued over 3,500 Japanese transit visas, evidently from humanitarian motives alone. He was not ordered to act in this manner (and in fact ignored orders from Tokyo and requests from the captain of the ship that transported the refugees from Vladivostok to Japan to refrain from issuing any more transit visas) and, unlike consuls from many Latin American countries, derived no monetary gain. On the contrary, his achievement resulted in his early dismissal.[10] Only about 2,000 refugees eventually were able to use these visas, as their legality soon became suspect.[11] What gave these so-called Curacao visas dubious status was the fact that they were all granted to this same final destination (Curacao), on the basis of a legal fiction, invented for the occasion.

Nathan Gutwirth, a student of the Talmudical College of Telshe (Poland), and a Dutch national, requested, and received permission from Dekker, the Dutch Ambassador to the three Baltic States, who resided in Riga, to go to Curacao, part of the Dutch West Indies. With such an end-visa, Gutwirth secured a transit visa from the Japanese consul, and finally was permitted by Russian officials to leave Lithuania. When his friends at the

Mirrer Yeshiva expressed their desire also to utilize this exit route, Gutwirth appealed again to Ambassador Dekker to stamp his friends' passport with a visa to Curacao. Dekker replied that "no visa to Curacao was required but a landing permit could only be granted by the Governor of Curacao." Gutwirth then asked the Ambassador to stamp his friends' passports with only the first half of the phrase, i.e., "no visa to Curacao was required." The Ambassador, fully aware of this life-saving device, authorized the Dutch Consul in Kovno, J. Zwartendijk, to do this for Gutwirth's friends, and soon the entire faculty and student body of the Mirrer Yeshiva obtained these Curacao end-visas, especially after much prodding by Zorach Wahrhaftig, one of the Zionist activists, later to become Minister of Religion in the State of Israel. They, in turn, received their Japanese transit-visas from Sugihara. Word spread quickly to other Polish refugees, and eventually about 2,000 made use of these dubious papers. On the strength of the Curacao visas, the Russians gave permission to all the Polish refugees to leave Lithuania, an otherwise treasonable crime, and the refugees were able to travel across Siberia via Intourist. The price, $170-$240, was a very steep sum to raise—particularly at a time when it was supposedly illegal even to possess foreign exchange.[13] With the assistance of the American Jewish Joint Distribution Committee, Vaad Hatzalah, and relatives in the United States, the money was collected and the tickets bought.[14]

ACROSS SIBERIA

Most of the Polish refugees left Lithuania during the months of January and February of 1941.[15] The journey itself, through European Russia and Siberia, proved to be uneventful and unstrained for most.[16] A stopover was made in Moscow, where the Intourist provided a tour, including a visit for some to the Yiddish State Theater.[17] After travelling 10 to 11 days, they reached Vladivostok, where they boarded an unseaworthy tramp steamer, overcrowded with 550 refugees. What was normally a 36-hour trip was stretched to 60 on account of storms.[18] Although most of the German and Austrian refugees had utilized the trans-Siberian route, chiefly during the latter half of 1940, a sizeable minority also came with the Polish group, during the first half of 1941. Their journey into common exile did not diminish their mutual distrust. Episodes revealing antagonism and friction began on their first encounter on the boat to Japan, and persisted throughout the period of their stay in Shanghai.[19]

KOBE—TRANSIT CENTER

The earlier transients using the overland route (July 1940 to January 1941) followed the Siberia-Manchuria-Japan route to Vladivostok, and from there boarded a ship to Tsuruga, Japan.[20] From Tsuruga they went by rail to Kobe, or from Shimonoseki to Kobe.[21] However, regardless whether refugees reached Japan via Manchuria or Vladivostok, they were greeted at all transit points by delegates of the Jewish communities, the National Council of Jews in East Asia, which was recognized by the Japanese authorities. The Council helped to clear passport formalities and assisted the refugees to embark for the next stop.[21]*

The Jewish Committee from Kobe (better known by its cable address JEWCOM), in conjunction with the Japanese authorities, made all the arrangements for speedy rail service to Kobe, a distance of approximately 100 miles.[22] This was particularly helpful to the hundreds of rabbinical students and rabbis who arrived on a Friday, and were anxious to reach Kobe before sundown, so as not to desecrate the Sabbath.[23] When one such group of about 80-90 students arrived at Tsuruga on Friday after sundown, they refused to violate the Sabbath by signing the required landing papers. The bewildered head of the

Kobe delegation, Mr. Gerechter, had a difficult time trying on the one hand to convince the refugees of the urgency to sign, and on the other to explain to the Japanese authorities why these rabbinical students refused such a simple request. The episode concluded amicably when Gerechter signed the word *Shabbos* (Sabbath) on each refugee's papers in place of their name, and he was dubbed the *Shabbos Goy* (Sabbath Violator).[24]

PORTRAIT OF THE REFUGEES

The cooperation of the Japanese authorities, and the serene beauty of the country, made a deeply favorable impression upon the tired survivors of the 6,000 miles trip across Asia.[25] Kobe, often compared in beauty to Rio de Janeiro, was Japan's second-largest port.[26] Its Jewish community consisted of approximately 50 families, divided about evenly between Sephardim and Russian Ashkenazim.[27] For a while it included about 100 German refugees, of whom only a handful remained in Kobe throughout the war.[28] It was a prosperous community, which maintained very good relations with the Japanese authorities.[29] The migration of over 4,600 souls through Kobe, and especially the Polish refugees, wrought a complete change in the lives of this small tranquil Jewish community.[30] The transit visas granted by the Japanese authorities were normally valid from seven to 15 days, but most of the Polish refugees stayed longer.[31] Over one-third of them had to remain for at least eight months.[32] About 1,000 were able to reach their final destination in the Western Hemisphere, or Australia, before the Pacific War broke out, while the remaining approximately 1,000 primarily Polish refugees, unable to obtain visas to other countries, were eventually transferred during the latter part of 1941 to Shanghai, where they remained until the end of the war.[33]

During this early period, the activities of the Kobe JEWCOM had centered on "tourist aid," namely securing room and board for those unable to pay for hotels, and passage for their next step overseas.[34] The age level of this first group had differed markedly from those that arrived during the second period.[35] According to the tables found in the *Kobe Report*, the Polish group consisted chiefly of young to middle-aged refugees, with males in a three-to-one majority. The German-Austrian group had been divided almost equally between male and female, but with a much larger percentage in the over-fifty category. What can readily be ascertained from even a cursory look at these figures is that the German refugees who arrived in the Far East via the land route during the first period (July 1940-October 1940), although victims of Nazism, were able to leave in family units with many of their belongings intact, and their visas and other papers in order. Compared to the later arrivals by this route (November 1940-September 1941), these were almost like tourists, since their stay in Kobe or Yokohama did not usually exceed the time allowed for holders of transit visas. The Polish Jews by contrast, were victims of war forced to flee for their lives with hardly a shirt on their backs. The majority of the these were younger males who had taken advantage of any opportunity to escape. These were refugees in every sense of the word.[36]

WELCOME TO KOBE

A delightful and surprising complement to the assistance of the JEWCOM and the beauty of the surroundings was the warm welcome extended by the Japanese people which deeply impressed these recent victims of Hitler's oppression. There were anonymous gifts of flowers and money, baskets of fruit were sent by a Japanese Christian organization to the synagogue for the Jewish holidays, contributions arrived from school groups, and free medical attention was made available to hundreds of refugees by a well-known Japanese doctor.[37]

Incidents of almost gratuitous consideration were also
common. One woman went to buy bread, unaware that it was
rationed. Japanese customers, noticing her bewilderment at the
demand of the bakery for ration cards, offered her their own
coupons and, in fact, almost forced them on her.[38]

On the other side there were incidents where the refugees
were at fault and where antirefugee feeling might have been
aroused, had it not been for the goodwill of the populace. A few
cases of shoplifting are known to have occurred, some dealings
in the black market, and an occasional attempt to avoid paying
streetcar fare. Even some of the habits of the European refugees,
their carelessness about littering for instance, might have angered
the extremely civic-minded Japanese.[39] This is all the more
significant in view of the aforementioned tenor of the times,
during which the fear of communist spies was very real,
and when most Europeans were eyed with suspicion.
Even the children used to refer to any Westerner by the
English word "spy."[40] Yet such natural irritation somehow did
not arise, and each incident was handled quietly. The police
inspector took up the matter with the leaders of the JEWCOM.[41]
Perhaps the total experience of the Jewish experience with the
Japanese, during their sojourn in Japan, with both the authorities and the "man in the street," is best summed up in a retrospective account given by Leo Hanin, a member of JEWCOM,
to Rabbi Marvin Tokayer:

> . . . Kobe had very few foreigners living there at the time.
> I would say maximum 300 families, among them 30 Jewish
> families, therefore the appearance in the narrow streets of
> Kobe of a large number of foreigners, specially some of
> them "very strange looking" people to Japanese eyes:
> Rabbis, Yeshiva students in *kapotes*, [kaftans] *yarmolkas*,
> [skull caps] with beards and *peyes* [long, curly sideburns]
> was immediately obvious, and they started asking ques-

tions about these strange people. Articles appeared in the Japanese newspapers with some photographs which described these people as refugees, Jews from the war in Europe on their way to other countries, passing through Japan as a transit point only. Personally with my conversations with my Japanese friends, also in checking with some other Jewish residents and the refugees themselves, I can summarize the attitude of almost all Japanese in one Japanese word: *Kawaisoy* (We were sorry for them).

Here again I can say definitely there was no antisemitism to the refugees in Kobe, only compassion and kindness. At that time in Japan there was a shortage of food, all the Japanese and ourselves (foreign residents), were rationed, some of the foods were not available such as butter, oil, chickens, eggs, etc., but whenever the refugees came to the stores, somehow the shopkeepers would always manage to offer them those rare commodities.

How can I ever forget one day we received a letter [at the Committee] from a farmer telling us that he heard of the plight of the Jews, and that we had 60 children as refugees, and that the farmers would be honored if we allow them to distribute fruits they had grown to these little children. They came the next week with boxes and boxes of fresh, beautiful apples and oranges, and personally presented each child with some of the fruits. They were humble, decent, good people.

As I said above everyone in Japan was then rationed, but the Authorities asked our committee to report on a weekly basis how many refugees were staying, and every evening a truck would drive up to the Community Center with warm loaves of bread, one pound per person, man, woman and child. The refugees did not have to stand in line for this bread, even though all the Japanese and foreign residents had to do so at appointed stores, to get their daily rations of bread and rice.

On one occasion I remember when one of the children became very sick and the Japanese doctor was called to treat him and took him to his private hospital, the doctor refused to accept money for his services and the hospital, when he found out this child was a refugee.[42]

INVESTIGATING THE REFUGEES

Despite the warm welcome the refugees received in Kobe, the Japanese thought-control police (*Kempeitai*) kept a careful watch over their every movement. This treatment, though, was no different from that accorded all other Westerners and even Japanese amidst a pervasive fear of communism.[43] Still, it was the Yeshiva group, with their unusual garb and even more unusual habits, which made them suspect to the authorities. For example, they "set up shop," i.e. established a *Beit Midrash* (Study Hall) to continue their schedule of 18 hours-a-day of Talmudic study, in the ancient, quiet part of Kobe. It took a while for the neighborhood, to get used to the noise of the loud, melodious manner of study, especially during the evening hours. Japanese investigators frequented the yeshiva and often spoke with the students—as with other refugees—during pleasant walks or over tea, One such agent, who investigated these students of the Talmud, was a Mr. Osakabe, a former interpreter for Ambassador Oshima in Berlin. Unlike his former, Hitler-admiring boss in Berlin, Osakabe turned in a very favorable report, dubbing these students "holy idealists."[44]

ROOM AND BOARD

Among the most serious problems that faced the people who were pouring into Kobe was that of securing food, clothing, housing and medical care. Despite the small size of the

Ashkenazi community, the JEWCOM, which was responsible
for such aid, managed fairly well. It had the full financial support
or the JDC and *HICEM* in the United States.[45] These two organizations shared much of the financial burden involved in the care
and arrangements for further travel until funds from the United
States were no longer permitted entry into Japan, by July 1941.
Some money for relief work was raised among Kobe's Jews in
the early stages, as well as during the last months of the refugees'
stay in Japan.[46]

Aid in the form of money and/or goods came to the
refugees from both private sources and organizations, mainly
from the United States to supplement the JDC and HICEM
funds. Two organizzations, Agudath Israel and Vaad Hatzalah,
directed their relief activities to the over 440 rabbis and students
who comprised one-quarter of the Polish-Jewish refugees.[47]
Agudath Israel had spearheaded the drive to rescue Jews from
Europe, pioneering with the "Corporative Affidavit" method.[48]
The Polish Embassy in Tokyo, headed by Count T. de Romer
until October 10, 1941, was helpful in supplying some of the
Polish Jewish refugees with a share of its Canadian and other
visas, as well as providing some financial aid to its countrymen.[49]

PROVIDING FOR THE REFUGEES

Regular houses and hotels were changed by JEWCOM
into dormitories for the use of the refugees under the supervision
of self-governing managers.[50] Although they were much more
comfortable than those in the *Heime* in Shanghai, the houses
were always crowded.

Instead of being fed at a public kitchen, each person
was given 1½ yen (US 25c.) per day, which was reduced to
1.20 yen (US 21c.) in July of 1941, because of the aforementioned restrictions on United States currency importation.[51] This

amount provided a minimal but adequate diet consisting chiefly
of fruits, vegetables, fish and bread, meals being prepared by the
refugees themselves.[52] As noted, the Japanese authorities permitted a rather high allotment of flour for the refugees, despite
a shortage, as Jews were not accustomed to the Japanese diet of
fish and rice.[53] On Passover, Matzot were imported from the
United States and provided for all.[54]

In addition to the drastic change in climate, food, and
living conditions, the long period of travel took its toll on the
health of the refugees, particularly of the yeshiva students.[55]
Close to 800 individuals were treated for various illnesses by a
nurse and doctor provided for by the JEWCOM.[56] The Japanese
doctor who donated his services, administered hundreds of
vaccinations.[57] The fact that only two deaths occurred among
the 4,600 refugees during their stay in Japan is evidence of the
good care provided for them.[58]

TWO-DAY SABBATH AND TWO-DAY YOM KIPPUR

Amidst the many problems of visas, affidavits and the
search for a new home, which faced the refugees in Kobe, one
group, primarily the rabbinic and yeshiva element, was concerned with a rather interesting Halachic problem: on which
day is the Sabbath or Yom Kippur once you have crossed the
Date Line? A difference of opinion existed among Jewish
scholars as to the location of the "Jewish" Date Line. According
to some authorities it lies 180° east of Jerusalem (approximately 125° East Longitude), rather than Greenwich, England.
This difference of opinion resulted in the observance of a two-
day Sabbath and a two-day Fast of Yom Kippur.[59]

The Russian-Jewish communities of Japan and Manchuria already followed the ruling of their Chief Rabbi, Rabbi
Aaron M. Kiseleff, of Harbin, to maintain all Jewish holidays
according to the local calendar. His views, however, were not

considered authoritative by the scholarly students of the yeshivoth, who were unfamiliar with Kiseleff's writings.[60]

While on route to Kobe, Rabbi Aaron Kotler, one of the leading rabbinic scholars, anticipated the problem. He cabled to Jerusalem's scholars for a ruling.[61] Rabbi Isaac Halevi Herzog, Chief Rabbi of the Holy Land, immediately called an assembly of scholars in September 1941, to clarify the law on this matter.[62]

The conclusion reached by this assembly concurred in effect with the ruling of Rabbi Kiseleff, to follow the local calendar for both the Sabbath and the forthcoming Yom Kippur.[63] The only dissenting voice was that of Rabbi Avraham Yeshayahu Karelitz, better known as the "Hazon Ish." This lone, but authoritative scholar ruled that the refugees observe the "Sunday" in Kobe as their "Sabbath," eat on the Yom Kippur as celebrated in Kobe (Wednesday), and fast rather on the following day.[64]

In deference to the great authority of Rabbi Karelitz, yet not desiring to go contrary to the assembly's ruling, the yeshiva students observed the Sabbath for two days. In order to avoid a two-day fast on Yom Kippur, most of the rabbinic groups and yeshiva students left Kobe for Shanghai a few weeks before their deadline.[65] However, a small contingent, which remained throughout Yom Kippur observed it for two days, though only the stronger ones fasted two complete days.[66]

Those who observed the "second day" Sabbath did so also in a minimal fashion, i.e., they refrained from work (*Melacha*), but put on the phylacteries without a blessing and recited the week-day prayers.[67]

VISA PROBLEMS

The primary concern however, of the Polish group while in Japan, was to find a country that would receive them, at a time when more and more countries were tightening rather

322   JAPANESE, NAZIS & JEWS

than relaxing their restrictions. This search presented them with a twofold problem: They had to obtain an extension of their transit-visas, which had been granted on the strength of the so-called Curacao visas (which were of course useless for any further step) in order to find time to badger Western Consulates in Tokyo and Yokohama for real end-visas to their respective countries.

A constant fear of denial of extension added to the already existing sense of insecurity. However, in spite of cases where transit-visas were invalidated by the authorities, and further measures adopted during February to curb the flow of refugees, all those who started out from Lithuania during February through March of that year, were able to make it to Japan.[68] And although the Japanese kept announcing further restrictions, the refugees kept coming. Within several months, the Japanese government not only accepted all these refugees with the "Curacao visas," but even those dozens of refugees stopped at the Siberian port of Vladivostok by the Japanese authorities for using forged passports and other illegal papers. In fact, it was finally Hitler's invasion of Russia on June 22, 1941, that stopped the flood by closing the escape route through Siberia.[69]

How were these extensions of the transit visas secured, extensions which for over one-third of the Polish refugees meant a lengthened stay of from three to eight months? Much of the credit for the successful surmounting of the problem must go to the aforementioned Dr. Kotsuji, the Japanese Biblical scholar, who had amazed his Russian Jewish audience with his welcoming speech in Hebrew at the Third Far Eastern Conference in Harbin, in 1939. It will also be remembered that Kotsuji made this speech in his capacity as an advisor on Jewish affairs to Matsuoka, then President of the South Manchurian Railroad.[70] It was with the memory of the Harbin event in mind that the small, Russian-Jewish community in Kobe, headed by Anatole

A. Ponevejsky, turned to Kotsuji for help when faced with the overwhelming difficulties of ministering to the hundreds of fellow Jews pouring into Japan with no immediate prospects for securing an end visa in the U.S. or elsewhere. It was Kotsuji's mission to persuade his former superior in Manchuria, Matsuoka, now Japan's Foreign Minister, to extend the transit visas. Matsuoka, according to Kotsuji's memoirs, confided in Kotsuji that he was under pressure from the pro-Nazi factions and he could not defy them openly. Nonetheless, after listening to Kotsuji's plans, he gave it tacit approval whereby Kotsuji was able to work with the local police prefecture, while the central government maintained a discreet silence. Bribery, to the tune of 3,000 yen was made use of in an indirect manner, and it became possible to get the visas extended from the usual seven to 15 days, to over eight months for many of the Polish refugees.[71]

Only two months before Pearl Harbor, with Japan already on a war footing, the 1,000 remaining refugees who had been unable during their months-long stay in Japan to find a country willing to open its doors to them, were finally shipped to the Japanese sector of Shanghai.[72]

CENSORSHIP AND A TALIS

One anecdote may be added to the story of the struggle for visas. On one occasion, the Japanese censors sent for Leo Hanin of the JEWCOM, to have him translate and explain a cable which was being sent to Kovno, Lithuania, with the message: *"Shisho miskadshim b'talis ehad."* Hanin explained that it was going from Rabbi Kalish, the Amshenower rebbe, to a colleague in Lithuania on a matter of Jewish ritual, and meant, "Six persons may pray under one prayer shawl." The explanation was accepted and the cable sent.

But Hanin went away puzzled and later approached the venerable rabbi, who looked at him with his deep, sad eyes, as if to say, "how can a Jew be ignorant of such well-known Talmudic dictum?"

"*Wos farshtaist Du nit?* Six persons can travel on one." Then the truth. The rabbi, just out of Europe, was deeply concerned about his coreligionists in Soviet-occuped Lithuania, with the Nazis advancing through Poland. He knew that Japanese visas in Kovno were issued to families and he was suggesting that six strangers should get together as a family.

"*Yetzt farsteh ich.*" (Now I understand).[73]

NAZI PRESSURE ON JAPANESE POLICY

The most unusual behavior by the Dutch and Japanese consuls, and Kobe's general populace, can be ascribed to truly humanitarian impulses and the usually hospitable and polite behavior by Japanese toward guests in their homeland.[74] However, the same cannot be said of the decisions arrived at by the practical, hard-headed government of Premier Konoe and his Foreign Minister Matsuoka, the architect of the Tripartite Pact with Hitler, only months earlier. Matsuoka had to contend with strong pressures exerted both by the German embassy against displaying any overt philo-semitic acts, and by many admirers of Hitler among the militarists, in and out of the government, who were usually unfamiliar with Jews and the Jewish problem. They could see no reason to antagonize Germany over what seemed to be such an insignificant issue.

Earlier we had touched upon some aspects of the Nazi influence on the Japanese antisemites as well on the Japanese policy. Additional instances include the promotion of Nazi antisemitic literature among the Japanese people by subsidizing the publication and distribution of such material through exhibits and lectures. By this means, the Germans could turn the heavily-attended anti-Bolshevik or anti-Freemason demonstrations into popular vehicles of antisemitism. Although this technique was more successful following the outbreak of the

War in the Pacific, we do find such attempts even prior to Pearl Harbor. For example, Nazi literature was subsidized for distribution in all the hotel rooms in Harbin, while a proposed antisemitic exhibit in Fukuoka in 1940, was just nipped in the bud by the vigilant Jewish community in Harbin with the help of Colonel Yasue and other Japanese "friends of the Jews." Still, even Yasue could not prevent an antisemitic rally in Tokyo by the Anti-Espionage League, in September 1941, which adopted a resolution saying that "The Jewish aspiration to dominate the world is not absolutely compatible with the spirit of the Empire."[75]

On the other hand, the German Embassy attempted to apply direct pressure on the Japanese to follow the Nazi line toward Jews. As early as 1936, following the German-Japanese Anti-Comintern Pact, there was Nazi pressure to eliminate Jewish artists from a catalogue published by the Japanese subsidiary of Columbia Records. This attempt was quashed when a Jewish employee showed his Japanese manager the revised catalogue with the names of the Jewish musicians crossed out. Beginning with the violinists, the eliminated included, Elman, Goldberg, Heifetz, Huberman, Kreisler, Menuhin, Szigeti, Zimbalist. The manager, reviewing this distinguished roster, remarked, with deep understanding: "oh, I see, so-called Aryans—I think that is the right word the Germans are now using—are not allowed to play the violin." In January, 1940, the German ambassador, Eugene Ott, noted in a dispatch to Berlin his unsuccessful attempt to have a Jew, Rosenstock, removed from his post as conductor of the Tokyo Orchestra. He was more successful, however, in preventing the opening of the fourth annual convention of the Far Eastern Jewish Communities in late 1940, two weeks before its scheduled opening. This was no doubt a consequence of the recently-signed Tripartite Pact. This enabled the Germans to protest the strong anti-Nazi line adopted at each of the earlier three conventions. Closely related in time and approach was the forced semi-retirement of Colonel Yasue, the "friend of the Jews" undoubtedly under German pressure. Diplomatic channels were also used wherever feasible, to bolster all efforts to spread the Nazi gospel among the Japanese masses.[76]

Then, in the midst of these events occurred a most paradoxical episode. In the fall of 1940, Inuzuka made a pro-Jewish radio broadcast, which advertised Japan's favorable treatment of the Jews as contrasted with their mistreatment by the Nazis. In this speech, Inuzuka recalled the wonderful treatment accorded the Jewish refugees in Shanghai by the Japanese. He drew a picture of how the refugees' early longing to return to Europe changed into an acceptance of the Far East as their home. This came about as a result of their realization of Japan's cardinal principles and policy of true racial equality and religious freedom. Inuzuka also pointed out the great financial talent exhibited by the [Sephardi] Jews of Shanghai, who helped to build up Shanghai and who still led the financial and cultural field,

In comparing Japan's benevolent treatment of the Jewish refugees with that of the Nazis, he noted that the Jews' strong desire to return to the East ("der Drang 'Zureck nach Osten',") manifest in Zionism, is a result of the fact that they are an Asian nation. As such they were unable to adjust to the West's notion of "Individualism." It was natural for Japan, the protector, concerned about the welfare of all Asian nations, to encourage the Jews to participate in the peace and New Order in East Asia.

Inuzuka concluded his incredible remarks, so criticized by the German Embassy in Tokyo, with the statement:

"In our relations with the Jews, we will always deal with them on the principle of equality, so long as the Jews remain loyal to the Japanese authorities."[77]

This broadcast caused uneasiness in the German Embassy in Tokyo, duly reported to Berlin, bringing, in turn, inquiries as to how much influence this "friend of the Jews" had in Japanese official circles. At this very time, the Nazi Embassy, in a report by Ambassador Ott to the Foreign Office in Berlin, gloated over the popularity of two important antisemitic books, one of which was a 500 page tome titled the *Jewish Problem and Japan* by Kiyo Utsonomiya. This book was a rehash of the *Protocols*, with a few original Japanese nuances: blaming the Jews for all the Western anti-Japanese propaganda, and declaring that Jewish capitalists (plutocrats) and communists were the main support of Chiang Kai-shek, etc. What the Nazis were unaware of, was that Utsunomiya, a prolific writer of antisemitic literature, was none other than our very own Inuzuka. Nor were the Nazis, such as Ott, who gloated over the publication of the two antisemitic books, praised their publisher who had also put out Shioden's works, aware, that Inuzuka was his close co-worker at the antisemitic *KGS*.

Neither is it likely that the Nazis would have been able to fathom the mentality of Inuzuka's or Yasue's antisemitism had anyone bothered to explain it to them. They would have been even more confused were they to see this same Inuzuka in the post-war years, promoting Japanese friendship for the State of Israel through his own organization called the Japan-Israel Society. However, to view him as a chameleon-like opportunist, completely misses the mark. Inuzuka and others like him were simply pragmatic Japanese super patriots whose single-minded purpose was to utilize the "influential" Jews, whether in the United States, Shanghai, or Israel, for the best interests of Japan.[78]

While the Tripartite Pact invited greater Nazi influence in Japan, and no doubt put to rest the idea of the "Jewish settlement," for the Japanese they had no desire to completely cancel their pro-Jewish policy promulgated in December 1938. Despite obviously poor relations between Germany and Japan even after their pact it would have been highly unlikely for Japan to have maintained its unique behavior toward the Jewish refugees streaming into the Far East unless there were compelling reasons. Such reasons are not too difficult to discern, given Japan's ambivalent foreign relations during the critical year prior to Pearl Harbor. A brief glimpse at this situation will help to set the stage for the Jewish question involved.

Out of the welter of numerous differing opinions concerning Japan's future course during the final months of 1940 and the first part of 1941, there emerged two opposing schools of thought in the Japanese government. One school, consisting chiefly of the military, including the General Staff and the Navy Ministry, emphasized that the point of no return had been reached. Japan's concern at this point was only *how* to wage future conflict with the U.S. Since the U.S. would not accept Japan's move south further into China and the British and Dutch Colonies, rich with strategic raw materials, it was rightly presumed, that a total American embargo on such vital material would ensue, which in turn would precipitate open conflict between Japan and the U.S.

The second school of thought maintained that, since the purpose of a war with the U.S. would be to assure Japan a steady supply of strategic supplies, an agreement with the U.S. on this point would make such a move south unnecessary. It would, in fact, give Japan a chance to prepare for the eventual battle with Russia, the "collosus of the north." This view predominated among the diplomats, and was advocated at first, even by the arch militarists, General Hidecki Tojo, after his appointment in October 1941, to the post of Prime Minister. At any rate, the more bellicose school was reflected in Japan's preparations for war, her neutrality pact with the U.S.S.R., Japan's move into Indochina, and the steady stiffening of its attitude towards the U.S.

The United States, led by Secretary of State Hull's moralistic and very inflexible attitude toward Japan, (a continuation of Stimson's earlier, similar view), left little room for maneuvering or negotiations. Following Japan's entry into Indochina, in July 1941, the U.S. in conjunction with the British and Dutch, froze Japan's assets and enforced an oil embargo on Japan. This act was seen by Japan as the final step in the completion of its encirclement by the ABCD powers, which ultimately was to spell war.[79]

Yet the other faction was not without influence, as the last-minute attempts at peace negotiations indicate, The Jewish aspect of such peace negotiations played an important part in the maintenance of Japan's pro-Jewish policy during this critical year before Pearl Harbor. One of these, the unofficial peace negotiations initiated by two American priests, involved Premier Konoe, who used this channel to "sound out the U.S. government on the subject of negotiations and to report to Tokyo." The two priests, Bishop E. Walsh and Father James M. Drought, went to Japan on this private mission for peace, armed only with their optimism and letter of recommendation from Lewis Strauss of Kuhn, Loeb & Company. This letter was to Strauss' friend Tadao Ikawa, then Director of the Central Agricultural and Forestry Bank in Japan. Ikawa, an important figure in Japanese financial circles, had become acquainted with Strauss quite well during his stint in the U.S. as a secretary to a member of the Japanese Finance Ministry. He was also, incidentally, the author of an antisemitic work titled, *The Origin of Radicalism*. There is no doubt that Ikawa was on quite familiar terms with Ikeda, the Minister of Finance, whom we came across as one of the supporters of the "Jewish Policy" in December 1938. Ikawa must also have been on good terms with Kishi and Hoshino, from the Finance Ministry and Cabinet Planning Board, respectively, both of whom had been closely involved earlier in Manchuria, with Ayukawa's scheme to import U.S. [Jewish] capital. Moreover, Matsuoka had suggested to Konoe, his superior, that Colonel Hideo Iwakuro of the War Ministry sound out the Army on this plan. Iwakuro was to work very closely with Ikawa on this peace mission, even in the face of Matsuoka's later opposition, since a great deal of negotiations were carried out over the Foreign Ministry's head. This is the same Iwakuro, who, according to Toland, claimed credit (along with Higuchi) for having persuaded his Manchuria superiors to permit the Jewish refugees to go through Manchuria and Japan during 1940-1941:

> on the grounds no true Japanese could deny: a debt was owed the Jews; the Jewish firm of Kuhn, Loeb & Company had helped finance the Russo-Japanese War.

Although this author is sceptical of many of Iwakuro's claims, there is little question of his involvement in the decisions concerning the Jews, in Manchuria and Tokyo. The Schiff Loan and stereotype of the influential American Jewish financiers surely played once again, a key role in this matter.

The Walsh initiative in these peace moves was taken soon after the signing of the Tripartite Pact, and resulted in a ten-months series of negotiations. An interview was even arranged for Bishop Walsh with F.D.R. by Postmaster General Frank C. Walker. The President seemed more amenable to this novel approach to peace than his sceptical and rigid Secretary of State. Anticipating success, Walsh had cabled

Ikawa in late January 1941: "As a result of meeting with the president, hopeful of progress awaiting developments." In response, both Ikawa and Iwakuro went to the United States.[80]

On February 11, 1941, Admiral Nomura, a known friend of America, was sent to the United States by the Konoe government on behalf of Matsuoka and the Foreign Ministry, in an attempt to find a way out of the growing impasse with the United States. We met Nomura earlier, when, in his capacity as Foreign Minister, he was directly involved with the Jewish settlement plan and the Tamura-Garson negotiations. It should be remembered that on this same day the anniversary of the Empire's divine founding was being celebrated and the Polish refugees were seeking extensions of their brief transit visas. Ironically, only about a month after he approved the visa extensions and Nomura's peace mission, Matsuoka went to Germany seeking to further cement relations between the two countries.

Now it becomes easier to understand Inuzuka's pro-Jewish radio broadcast in Tokyo, in November 1940, and why he was sent all the way from Shanghai on this mission. It must be remembered that all radio broadcasting was strictly under government direction and in fact served as one of Japan's key vehicles for its ultranationalist propaganda. In the author's opinion, Inuzuka's mission was to "reassure the Jews" that, in effect, the favorable Japanese policy toward the Jews would not be rescinded or even diminished, despite the recent pact with Hitler. Inuzuka made it clear, that as long as the Jews cooperated with Japan, they had no need to be concerned. The reprinting of this broadcast with very favorable comments by the editor and the Kobe Jewish Community seem to point to at least some degree of success for Inuzuka's mission.[81]

In light of these developments it also becomes easier to see why Matsuoka invited Mr. Z. to a private tea, in December of that year, at which, in Z's words, Matsuoka:

wanted to asure [sic] me and declare that antisemitism
will never be adopted by Japan. True, he said, "I concluded a treaty with Hitler but I never promissed [sic] him
to be an antisemit." [sic]

I lived 15 years in the U.S. and abroad and I know
how unjust people are to the Jews. [sic]

And it is not only my personal opinion but the principle of the entire Empire since the days of her foundation . . . I asked him whether he wants me to tell his
gracious words to my coreligionists in Manchuria or
abroad, and he said; Yes, you can, of course you can.

*His permission to tell it abroad was very important
for me because I wanted that abroad will be known his
assurance;* it was kind of an obligation from his side.
[italics mine]

This assurance to Mr. Z. was deemed doubly urgent
by the authorities in view of their concern of his desire to liquidate his Manchurian assets and stay in Tokyo. Even prior to
Matsuoka's invitation. Yasue was dispatched to Mr. Z's house
to convince him to return to Manchuria.[82]

Similarly, these circumstances go far to render com-
prehensible the favorable response by Tokyo to Higuchi's,
Iwakuro's and Yasue's request for the German Jewish refugee
transit through Manchuria and Japan. One might even
speculate, that given these circumstances, the Japanese Foreign
Office was not really too interested in preventing the wholesale
distribution of transit visas by Sugihara, during this period.
Certainly if Tokyo had made any real efforts in this direction,
it could easily have stopped Sugihara's venture, since there
was no need for Japan to accept all these Polish refugees.
Were it not for the "Jewish image," Japan need never have
concerned herself about foreign negative reaction to her refusal

to permit the entrance of several thousand refugees. In view
of their being "enemies of Japan's friends," and travelling with
papers of dubious value, any democratic country would have
done likewise.[83]

Even more extraordinary was Japan's willingness to
repeatedly extend the refugee's brief transit visas. The fantastic
scheme proposed by Matsuoka some time in January, or
February 1941, seems to be the only rationale.

In Kotsuji's words:

> His idea was truly like something like wisdom revealed
> in Hell. Five thousand refugees were saved because of his
> scheme. I kept that only to myself. No one knew about
> this. After this he entrusted me with a plan to be carried
> out sometime in the future. Nobody will believe me
> today, even if I told about this secret agreement between
> him and me. *His great scheme in dealing with* Jewish
> power has born out of the idea of protecting Japan . . .
> I am not going to reveal the contents of this scheme, for
> I am afraid that it will be laughed at by people of malice.
> [italics mine]

In his autobiography Kotsuji, hints a bit further at Matsuoka's
reasoning:

> Matsuoka was not dissembling. He was eager to win the
> Jewish people over to the Japanese viewpoint. My task
> was to advise him, to tell him what the Jews wanted, and
> *how best to obtain their good opinion.* [Italics mine][84]

This then, helps to explain the circumstances whereby the
Japanese attempted to use the alleged, vast Jewish influence
in the U.S. by helping the Kobe refugees. With the "Jewish
capital" scheme no longer viable, the author believes, Matsuoka

now sought to use the Jews who "controlled FDR., the financial and news media," to help create a more favorable attitude toward Japan in its negotiations with the U.S.

This view was not confined to the Foreign Minister, as is evidenced by an incident recalled by Leo Hanin of that period in Kobe. At a dinner tendered by Anatole Ponve, head of JEWCOM, in honor of the Governor of the Hyogo Prefecture [in which Kobe was situated], Ponve thanked the Governor and his assistants for all the help extended to the Jewish refugees. In his reply, the Governor said:

> We want you to *let your brethren* [sic] *Jews of America know* what is happening here and how kind we are to your Jews . . .[85]

Even the last minute peace negotiations carried on by the much more militant Tojo, during the last weeks prior to Pearl Harbor, can be better understood in light of the Jewish angle. For Tojo, as we have seen, along with Ayukawa, Kishi, Hoshino and Matsuoka, formed a close clique within the Manchurian faction—he was either responsible for, or at least acquiesced in Inuzuka's pressuring the Jews of Shanghai to send the aforementioned following cable to the major Jewish organizations in the U.S., as well as to Henry Morgenthau Jr., F.D.R's Secretary of the Treasury, a Jew:

November 23, 1941

This day when the fate of Pacific is in balance we voicing opinion of a large community deem it necessary to emphasize that *irrespective of the fact that Japan is allied to the Axis* its people are against national hatred and oppression stop War in Pacific would bring untold hardships to many millions and in the interest of humanity we hope a peaceful mutual understanding will be reached

stop convey this sincere unsolicited opinion all influential
organizations [italics mine]

> Shanghai Ashkenazi
> Communal Association
> Topaz President.[86]

Thus we find that Japan's unique policy toward the
Jews not only saved thousands of German and Polish refugees
from the Holocaust, but it also influenced the formation of
Japan's pragmatic approach to relations with the United States
prior to Pearl Harbor, a policy which was far more flexible
than that of the United States during the same period.[87]

Returning to the refugee scene, we find that even prior
to leaving Japan these Polish refugees were fully aware, through
correspondence with friends in Shanghai, of the poor conditions
and prospects that awaited them there. It was with a feeling
of anxiety and sadness that they left behind them the memories
of a lovely landscape and a hospitable people.

NOTES: KOVNO TO KOBE

1. Dan Kurzman, *Kishi and Japan: the Search for the Sun* [Kishi] (New York: Ivan Obolensky, Inc., 1960), pp. 156-157.

2. See below in this chapter. For two earlier developments, see above, chapter 7. Another will be discussed below, chapter 19.

3. For the story of the German refugee flight to Shanghai, see above, chapter 3.

4. The Jewish Community of Kobe (Japan) (Ashkenazim), Committee for Assistance to Refugees [JEWCOM] *Report*: July 1940—November 1941 [*Kobe Report*] (Kobe: JEWCOM, 1942), p. 13. (DP). According to this *Report*, 4,680 refugees reached Kobe, Japan. The rest went directly to the Philippines, Singapore, or even remained in Manchuria. (See HH XV D-1 for the Philippines, and for the Far East in general see M. Birman to HICEM (Paris) (January 16, 1940) [Birman, Report (January 16, 1940)] (HH XV C-6).

As far as the number of Polish-Jewish refugees is concerned, see the *Kobe Report*, p. 22a, which lists the "Polish" group with a total of 2,111 people. According to Tarshansky, the category of "Other" in the table of the Kobe Report, which encompasses 313 individuals, rightfully belongs to the "Polish" group, since most of these came with them from Poland. These include many students of the Mirrer and other yeshivot, who originally hailed from such countries as Germany, Hungary, etc. (Interv.).

For the number of Jews fleeing Nazi-occupied Poland into Lithuania, see *Contemporary Jewish Record* [*CJR*] Vol. 4 (1941), p. 189. Also Tartakower, *Refugee*, pp. 44-45. Lithuania was occupied by Russia on June 16, 1940, and formally annexed into the Soviet Union on July 14-15 (*Ibid.* Vol. 3 [1940], p. 541. Cf. Shoshana, *In Faier*, p. 253; Tartakower, *Refugee*, pp. 44-45.

5. Tarshansky Interv. (Rabbi Tarshansky was employed by the JDC in Poland and in Kobe, Japan. *Ibid.*).

6. Tartakower, *Refugee*, p. 45. Cf. also *Kobe Report*, p. 7; Wischnitzer, *Migration*, p. 234.

On July 15, 1940, Russia gave all those stateless refugees who resided in Vilna since September 1, 1939, a chance to opt for Soviet citizenship. This offer of enfranchisement was accepted by about one-third of the Jewish refugees in Vilna. (*CJR*, Vol. 3 [1940], p. 541. Cf. also Tartakower, *Refugee*, p. 45; Wischnitzer, *HIAS*, p. 165. On the other hand, this offer merely accentuated the drive towards emigration on the part of anyone with the slightest opportunity (Wischnitzer, *HIAS*, p. 165; also Tarshansky Interv.).

Sometime in the fall of 1941, greater pressure was applied for the remaining Jewish refugees in Vilna to accept Soviet citizenship under the threat of exile to Siberia (Joseph D. Epstein Interv., October 15, 1968 and subsequent dates [Epstein Interv.]. Rabbi Epstein, the Secretary of the Mirrer Yeshiva, was one of the last of the Polish refugees to make it out of Russian-occupied Lithuania).

One of the primary goals for many refugees was Palestine. Such a goal became feasible due to the release of thousands of unused "Palestine Certificates" by the British Government, which were distributed by Jewish Agency offices (Palestina Amt) opened up for this occasion in Lithuania. Some of these refugees had to travel to the Far East and a long, two-year trip before reaching Palestine, their destination. Cf. Chart of countries of destination from Japan for the period July 1940—November 1941, in the *Kobe Report*, pp. 22a, 24. See also Laura Margolies (JDC representative in Shanghai) to Robert Pilpel (JDC, N.Y.), November 11, 1941 [Margolies to Pilpel, November 11, 1941], pp. 1-2 (JDCCA); Wischnitzer, *Migration*, p. 234.

See Jacob Goldman, "Rabbi Herzog's First Rescue Journey," *Niv Hamidrashia* (Hebrew) (Tel Aviv, Winter 1964), pp. 5-11, for the story of Rabbi Herzog's successful attempt to convince the Soviet Ambassador in London, Mr. Maisky, to grant exit permits to the many yeshiva students and rabbis so that they could go to Palestine. The author included a telegram sent by Mr. Maisky to Rabbi Herzog attesting to Moscow's agreement in this matter, but advising the students to have Palestine Certificates (entry visas) and Turkish transit visas ready so that they could go to Palestine via Odessa. I assume that once permission for exit visas was granted for this purpose, it was also extended to those owning the Japanese transit visas as well.

Why Russia granted the exit visas, an extremely unusual action on her part, is still not clear. Some speculate that the prime motive behind the permission granted for exit was the desire for U.S. dollars, since all the fares for Intourist had to be paid in this form. Others feel that Russia desired to create a good impression upon the world with its humanitarian gesture or use this route to send spies into Western countries. None of these explanations are fully satisfactory.

7. Abraham Kotsuji, *From Tokyo to Jerusalem* [Kotsuji, *Jerusalem*] (New York: Bernard Geis Associates, 1964), p. 160. See also Senpo Sugihara, *Memoirs* (Hebrew) [Sugihara, *Memoirs*] July 21, 1967, (a four page typewritten manuscript at Yad Washem). Courtesy of Rabbi M. Tokayer.

8. Joseph D. Epstein, "Yeshiva of Mir" [Epstein, "Mir"], *Jewish Institutions of Higher Learning in Europe: Their Development and Destruction* (Heb.), Samuel K. Mirsky, ed. (New York: Histadruth Ivrith of America, 1956), p. 122.

The alternate usage for the Yeshiva of Mir (a small town in Poland) to be used is the Mirrer Yeshiva, a form preferred by the present institution in the United States. (See the Yeshiva's letterhead).

9. Sugihara, *Memoirs,* p. 2. For the Japanese aims re the Tri-Partite Pact with Germany and Italy and their designs covering Russia, see for example Ernst Presseisen, *Germany and Japan; a Study in Totalitarian Diplomacy* 1933-1941 [Presseisen, *Germany*] (New York: Howard Fertig, 1969), p. 82; Meskill, *Hitler,* pp. 4-20.

10. Sugiharo, *Memoirs,* p. 3. Cf. also Kase; "Jews," p. 6.

11. Tarshansky Interv. Fishoff Interview. Copy of transcription in author's possession, courtesy Dr. Dicker. Rabbi Fishoff noted that Rabbi Kalisch, the Rebbe of Amshenov, insisted, against opposition, on the utilization of such visas. He even collected money to buy passports unbeknown to many of those whose lives were saved by their use. Some opposition to even the application for such visas stemmed from the fear that the desire to leave the Soviet Union could prove to be too dangerous a risk. (Epstein, Interv. Cf. also Epstein, "Mir," p. 121.).

12. For the story of the "Dutch" yeshiva student, Nathan Gutwirth, see Nathan Gutwirth to Marvin Tokayer 9/24/74 [Gutwirth] (Tokayer Papers) Cf. also, for slightly different version, Epstein, "Mir," p. 122. Also Moshe Zupnik, Interview, June 23, 1968. He was the student who eventually went to the Japanese consul for the transit visas.

The Japanese, surprisingly enough, still recognized the Dutch Government-in-Exile, until Pearl Harbor. Meskill, *Hitler,* p. 121.

Most of the refugees did not even own a Polish passport, and since there was no Polish consul in Riga, they only received a "stateless visa," authorized by the Lithuanian Government. A number of the yeshiva students got papers from the British Consul in Kovno testifying to their Polish citizenship. Both types of "papers" were later exchanged in Tokyo by the Polish Ambassador, Count de Romer, for full Polish passports. Dr. Ernest Landau, taped interview, June 20, 1968 [Landau Interv.]. Dr. Landau was on the Executive Board of the Polish Refugee Association set up in Shanghai.

13. Tarshansky Interv. Also, Epstein, "Mir," p. 123.

14. Tarshansky Interv. Also Epstein, "Mir," p. 123. He states that Rabbi Kalmanowitz raised the required $50,000 (U.S.) to pay for the transit of the entire Mirrer Yeshiva. According to Rabbi Alex Weisfogel, the then assistant to Rabbi Kalmanowitz, much of this money was raised by soliciting from the American relatives of the yeshiva students (Weisfogel Interv., June 23, 1968).

15. *Kobe Report,* p. 9.

16. See above, Chapter 3.

17. Shoshana, *In Faier,* p. 259. They stayed at Hotel Muscovy. Rose Shoshana, the well-known Polish actress whose diary provides many of the details of this trip, writes appreciatively of the services provided by Intourist, including medical attention. *Ibid.,* p. 261. The Orthodox group, unable to

partake of the regular meals served in the train's restaurant, either ate food taken along prior to the trip (Tarshansky Interv.), or got along on the vegetables, bread or fish, the latter bought at the train stops. (Shkop Interv.). The train restaurant actually provided this group with utensils so they could fry their own fish. *Ibid.*

18. At Vladivostok, the Soviet authorities removed their last valuables such as pens, jewelry, etc. (Shoshana, *In Faier*, pp. 265-66; also Tarshansky Interv.).

19. Shoshana, *In Faier*, p. 266.

20. *Kobe Report*, p. 6.

21. For the alternate route of Shimonoseki to Kobe, see *Kobe Report*, p. 4. Cf. also Birman to HICEM (Lisbon) (Oct. 15, 1940), p. 1 (HH XV C-6).
Those refugees whose end-visas were completely intact would usually travel to Yokohama, and continue from there by boat to their final destination. This usually meant North or South America (*Kobe Report*, p. 5).

21* Among other stops in Manchuria on route were Manchouli, Mukden, Harbin and Dairen (*Kobe Report*, p. 1). See the same Report for the activities of the National Council of Jews in East Asia (Cf. also Moiseff, "Japan," p. 2).
Occasionally the welcoming committee at the stops en route had to provide temporary room and board, when delays in Harbin or Dairen prevented the refugees from the immediate purchase of ship cards to Japan or Shanghai. At times such delays stretched to weeks and even months, with the committee caring for all indigent refugees. *Ibid.*, pp. 2-3.

22. Not to be confused with the EASTJEWCOM of Shanghai. See below, chapter 12.

23. *Kobe Report*, p. 6. Cf. also Tarshansky Interv.

24. Gerechter Interv.

25. *Kobe Report*, p. 6. Cf. also Epstein Interv.; Dobekirer Interv.; Ber I. Rosen, *Geklibene Shriften* [Rosen, *Shriften*] (Yiddish) (Melbourne: Ber Rosen Committee, 1957), chapter 2; Rottenberg, *Shanchai*, pp. 308-12.

26. Kotsuji, *Jerusalem*, p. 159.

27. *Ibid.* Each of the two small communities had their own synagogue and rabbi. Both synagogues were destroyed by an air raid during World War II (Gerechter Interv.).

28. Gerechter Interv. Mr. Gerechter was in Japan from 1938 through the spring of 1943.

29. Kotsuji, *Jerusalem*, p. 160.

30. *Ibid.*

31. Kotsuji notes seven to ten days, whereas the *Kobe Report* claims a stay of seven to 15 days. Perhaps there were different time periods for different groups.

32. *Kobe Report*, p. 9.

33. Over 3,500, since 4,608 made it to Kobe and the remainder, 1,098, were shipped to Shanghai. See *Kobe Report*, p. 32.

34. *Ibid.*, p. 7.

35. *Ibid.*, p. 12a.

36. *Ibid.*, pp. 7-8. Cf. also "Jews in the Far East," p. 5; Epstein to HICEM (Lisbon), August 18, 1941, pp. 6-7. The table in *Kobe Report*, p. 9, shows that of the 1,119 transients arriving between July and September 1940, none remained by the end of the month.

In terms of statistics for the Polish and German refugees, both groups were equal in number. *Kobe Report*, p. 8. The breakdown according to origin is as follows:

Germany	2,116
Poland	2,178
Other countries	315
Total	4,609

The statistics found in the "Jews in the Far East," p. 5, differs slightly from this *Kobe Report*. I am not sure of the sources utilized by the former. The following are the differing statistics as found in "Jews in the Far East": for the period of July 1940 and May 1941, 4,664 refugees arrived in Japan.

Germany	2,498
Poland and Lithuania	1,962
Sub-Total	4,460
Other countries	204
Total	4,664

Thus, there are some differences in the two reports. Perhaps the author of the latter report includes some of the German Jews that settled in Japan. Cf. also Wischnitzer, who uses the latter statistics in both of his books. (*Migration*, p. 234; *HIAS*, p. 164).

37. For the incident of the basket of fruit, the anonymous donations, see *Kobe Report*, p. 6. Also Tarshansky Interv. For the free medical attention see Gerechter Interview.

Due to the fact that the Japanese lacked the concept of embarrassment involved in the "direct giving of charity," to the contrary, to them it was a sign of greater friendship — these baskets were accepted gracefully. However, this was so, due chiefly to the clarification of the honorable intentions of the Japanese, by Sam Evans, an old-time resident. Tarshansky Interv.

See also Lazar-Kahan, *Togbukh*, (Kobe, 1941) [*Togbukh*] pp. 4-5. (The manuscript of a diary, in Yiddish, kept by the writer and husband of Rose Shoshana. Reproduced from manuscript in Yivo (Rose Shoshana) Archiv.

38. Mrs. Joseph Levenson, Interview (September 21, 1970).

39. For incidents involving black market activities and streetcar fares, see Margulies Interv. For cases of shoplifting, see Shkop Interv. Also Togbukh, p. 10.

40. Reischauer, *Japan*, p. 200. Cf. also Story, *Japan*, pp. 194-195.

41. Leo Hanin to Marvin Tokayer [Hamin - Tokayer corres.] March 2, 1973. (TP).

42. *Ibid.* Cf. also Gerechter Interv.; Margolies Interv.

43. Gerechter, Interv. Mr. Gerechter, who left Japan in mid 1943, was similarly investigated by the *Kempeitei*, as were other foreigners. Cf. also *JRC*, p. 49, note 156. For the general climate of opinion for this time, see Brown, *Nationalism*, pp. 209-225; *Kokutai No Hongi*, p. 54; Takashi, "Right," pp. 487-509.

44. Gerechter Interview.

45. *Kobe Report*, pp. 14, 16a. The JDC supplied the lion's share of the funds and the expenses incurred by the refugees, beginning with the money required for the Intourist tickets, the "landing fee," as well as room and board in Japan. Tarshansky Interv.; Hanin-Tokayer, March 2, 1973.

46. Gerechter Interv. Mr. Gerechter said that loans were extended for later payments by the JDC. Also Mr. Evans, the honorary president of the Committee, donated money and also raised funds from the Sephardic community of Kobe. *Ibid.*

The cutting off of funds from the United States, probably coincided with the freezing of the Japanese funds in the United States in July 1941. Feis, *Pearl Harbor*, chapter 30. Also Gerechter Interv.; Young, *Inflation*, pp. 247-248, 259-260.

47. See the chart in the *Kobe Report*, p. 13a, for the number of rabbis and rabbinic students. See also Birman to HICEM (Lisbon) (August 18,

342 JAPANESE, NAZIS & JEWS

1941), p. 8; Margolies to Pilpel (October 26, 1941) (JDCCA), p. 4. She gives a figure of 409, but admits that these figures were only tentative.

For some of the rescue work, particularly concerning visas and affidavits to the United States, see over 200 telegrams communicated between Agudath Israel in New York and various yeshiva groups in Kobe. YIVO No. 49. Cf. also [Moshe Prager] *Disaster and Salvation: The History of "Vaad Hatzalah"* [sic] *in America* (Yiddish) (New York: "Vaad Hatzalah Book Committee, 1957), especially pp. 227-45 [*Vaad Hatzalah*].

For some of the work by Vaad Hatzalah and Rabbi Abraham Kalmanowitz in the support of the Mirrer Yeshiva in Kobe, see the various documents in the Kalmanowitz Files (KF), which were put at the writer's disposal by Rabbi Kalmanowitz's wife, and son, Rabbi Shraga Moshe Kalmanowitz. Among the items one may see the leaflet (Yiddish) which proclaims the dire need of the hundreds of yeshiva students in Kobe, and asks the populace to respond warmly to an appeal by Rabbi Abraham Kalmanowitz to be held in a synagogue on the first day of Rosh Hashanah, September 19, 1941.

Cf. also for similar appeals the *Hapardes* (Hebrew Rabbinic Journal), Vol. 15 (September 1941), pp. 2-5; 45-27; Weisfogel Interv.; Memo by Rabbi A. Kalmanowitz to the State Department in Matters of the Issuance of Visas to the Students of the Rabbinical Colleges now in Japan, June 6, 1941 (KF). Margolies to Pilpel (October 26, 1941), p. 6; Epstein, "Mir," p. 129.

For the amazed reaction of Laura Margolies to the success of the rabbinical group in securing visas, at a time when she experienced the greatest difficulties, see Margolies to Pilpel, October 26, 1941, p. 6. One Agudath Israel bulletin of this period notes 15 affidavits from the United States procured for refugees from Shanghai (out of 1,403) during this difficult period. "Report of the Refugee and Immigration Division, Agudath Israel Youth," June 1941, p. 15. Author's collection.

48. George Kranzler, Interview (June 3, 1968). Dr. Kranzler worked for the Immigration Division of Agudath Israel during this period. For the use of the "Corporate Affidavits" after the war, see Gerechter Interv.

49. *Kobe Report,* p. 28. Cf. also Schwartzbart-Dicker correspondence (September 5, 1958) (DF). Dr. Ignaz Schwartzbart who was a member of the Polish Government-in-Exile Parliament in London and maintained contact with Jan Stanczyk, the Polish Minister in Tokyo, as well as the Jewish community of Kobe.

Shoshana, in her diary, is less enthusiastic concerning Romer's help to the refugees. She claims that the first choice for visas or any other help was extended first to converts and assimilationists. *In Faier,* p. 278. Dr. Ernest Landau, who was later to be appointed by Romer as one of the three representatives of the Polish Refugees in Shanghai, maintains that even the money distributed by the Polish Government-in-Exile came from the JDC. Taped interview with Dr. Ernst Landau (June 20, 1968). See also copy of a telegram sent by the Polish Aid Society to Geneva, No. 352, on August 10, 1943, pp. 1-2 (YIVO No. 40).

Despite Poland's "disappearance" by conquest, it was still recognized by the Japanese Government until October 10, 1941. Meskill, *Hitler*, p. 121. Also Shoshana, *In Faier*, p. 279.

50. *Kobe Report*, p. 16.

51. See above, note 46, for the currency restrictions. For the reduction in relief, see the *Kobe Report*, p. 16a. Cf. also Shoshana, *In Faier*, p. 272.

52. *Kobe Report*, p. 16. Cf. also Epstein, "Mir," p. 126; Shkop Interv.

53. Shkop Interv. Also Gerechter Interv. Jechiel Dobekirer related that when the refugees asked for special allotments of flour for baking challas for the Sabbath, the police granted their request, but suggested that they carry their challas under wraps so as not to cause envy among their Japanese neighbors who had been living under an austerity diet months prior to the outbreak of the Pacific war. Interview (June 23, 1968) [Dobekirer Interv.]. Also Hanin-Tokayer corres., March 2, 1973.

54. *Shoshana, In Faier*, p. 272.

55. *Kobe Report*, p. 16a.

56. *Ibid.*, p. 17.

57. Gerechter Interv. He could not recall the doctor's name. Close to fourteen thousand vaccinations were required. *Kobe Report*, p. 17.

58. Two deaths occurred among the refugees during their stay in Kobe. These were buried in Kobe and Yokohama. *Kobe Report*, p. 17. The latter city at that time had the only Jewish cemetery in Japan (i.e., Jewish section of a cemetery). *London Jewish Chronicle* (October 4, 1957), p. 16.

59. The literature on this subject is quite extensive and I shall merely mention a few important works.

The most recent survey of this field can be found in Samuel Hubner, "Anashim Hanosim Lejapan Keytsad Yinhagu" (Hebrew), *Ha Darom*, Vol. 15 (April 1962), pp. 78-91. An English summary of Hubner's article is located in Immanuel Jacobovitz, *Jewish Law Faces Modern Problems* [Jacobovitz, *Jew Law*], Studies in Torah Judaism Series No. 8, edited by Leon D. Stitskin (New York: Yeshiva University, 1965), pp. 25-30. For an older summary of most legal opinions from Judah Halevi to Rabbi Karelitz, see Menacham M. Kasher, "The Sabbatt [sic] and The East of the World" (Hebrew) [Kasher, "Sabbatt"], *Ha Pardes*, Vol. XXVIII (January 1954), pp. 1-31.

The story of the refugees in Kobe and the problem caused by the Date Line is told briefly by David Kranzler, "The Two-Day Yom Kippur in Japan," *Yom Kippur Anthology*, edited by Philip Goodman (Philadelphia: Jewish Publication Society, 1971), pp. 201-203.

Among the basic sources concerning the legal aspects of this problem, see Avraham Yeshayahu Karelyitz, "Kuntrus Yud-Het Shaot" (Shabbat, Sect. 64), *Hazon Ish* (Bnei Brak: Shmuel Greineman, 1957), pp. 185-92.

Jechiel M. Tikozinsky, *Sefer Hayoman Bekadur Haarets* (Hebrew) (Jerusalem: , 1943); Aaron Chaim Zimmerman, *Agan Hasaar* (Hebrew) (New York: Balshon Press, 1955); also by the same author, *Kviat Kav Hataarikh* (Hebrew) (New York: Hakerem, 1954).

A few articles include Menachem M. Kasher, "The Sabbath of Genesis and the Sabbath of Sinai" (Hebrew), *Talpioth*, Vol. I (April-September 1944), pp. 604-50; Joseph E. Henkin, "On the International Date Line" (Hebrew), *Talpioth*, Vol. II (June 1945), pp. 179-83; Menachem M. Kasher, "Rejoinder" (Hebrew) [to Henkin's article], *Talpioth*, Vol. II (June 1945), pp. 184-89; Simcha Selig Brisk, "A Letter on Sabbath in Japan" (Hebrew), *Talpioth*, Vol. II (June 1945), pp. 177-78. Shlomo Goren, "The Sabbath in the Northern Countries and in the Far Sast," *Mahanayim* [Goren, "Far East"] (Hebrew) Vol. 114 (March 1967), pp. 2-11. (Courtesy Rabbi Tokayer) (TP).

60. Rabbi Joseph Levinson, Interview (September 4, 1970). Also Rabbi Israel Perutinsky, Interview (September 7, 1970). Both rabbis were in Kobe at this time.

61. Gerechter Interview. Mr. Gerechter helped Rabbi Kotler dispatch the cables.

62. For the Assembly, see two articles in the *Hatzofeh* (Hebrew) newspaper published in the Holy Land. The first, "Hadiyun Besheelat Yom Hakipurim Bejapan" (September 30, 1941), p. 1. The second by Meir Berlin, "Mitziyon Tetsey Torah" (Hebrew) (October 2, 1942), p. 2.

63. See especially the letter by Chief Rabbi Herzog and Rabbi Isser Zalman Meltzer in Kasher, "Sabbatt," p. 29.

64. Rabbi Karelitz had already cabled Rabbi Kotler early concerning the observance of the Sabbath. This answer, which is also found in brief in Kasher, "Sabbatt," pp. 24-25, refers primarily to Yom Kippur. His retort to the refugees' query was "eat on Wednesday and fast on Thursday." *Ibid.*, p. 24.

65. Levinson Interview. Also Perutinsky Interview. For the early departure, see Zackheim Interview.

66. Perutinsky Interview. Those who were not as hardy ate on Thursday in piecemeal quantities of less than the minimum measure (slightly less than an average-sizzed egg) for which one was culpable on Yom Kippur. The usual Yom Kippur prayers, however, were omitted on the "second day" as well as the *Yaale Veyovo* in the *Birchat Hamazon*, which was recited by those unable to fast.

67. *Ibid.*

68. For Japan's announcement of restrictions on further Transit visas, see *CJR*, Vol. 4 (1941), p. 263. Cf. also Shoshana, *In Faier*, p. 269. Dr. Landau was refused a Japanese transit visa in Moscow in April 1941, though he possessed a Nicaraguan passport. The explanation given Dr. Landau by the Japanese was that already too many refugees were stranded in Japan. Only

the intercession and personal guarantee on his behalf by the Belgian Ambassador persuaded the Japanese to grant him the transit visa. Interview. The copies of the letter by the Belgian Ambassador and other related documents in the writer's possession, courtesy of Dr. Landau. For the statistics, see the *Kobe Report*, p. 8. The table indicates that from March through August, 1,312 refugees came to Japan, with the bulk coming in May. Only 108 arrived during June-August of 1941.

69. The 46 who managed to make it to Japan during July and August had probably already crossed Siberia earlier.

70. See above, chapter 7.

71. *Kobe Report*, p. 10. The Russian-Jewish community of Kobe had heard of Kotsuji because of the stir he had created at the Third Far Eastern Jewish Conference held on December 23, 1939, in Harbin, Manchuria. "Report on the Third Conference of Jew Race [sic] in Far East," a secret memo sent by the Japanese consul Sueo Shimomura to Yoshijiro Umezu, the Japanese Ambassador in Manchuko [sic] on January 17, 1940, p. 3 [F. O. Shimomura to Umezu, January 17, 1940] For the sum spent by Kotsuyi, Tokayer-Kranzler corres., September 1974. Tokayer was given this information by Kotsuji's family. See above, chap. 7.

72. *Kobe Report*, p. 9. The exact figure is 1,098, *Ibid*, p. 22a.

73. Hanin-Tokayer corres. March 2, 1973.

74. See for example, the letter by Yoshizane Iwasa to the *New York Times*, on May 13, 1973. Iwasa is president of the Japan-U.S. Economic Council.

75. For the distribution of the antisemitic literature and the prevention of the Fukuoka exhibit, see Kaufman, *Manchuria*, pp. 30-35. The successful 1941 exhibit is found in the *Tokyo Record*, p. 173. For the most successful anti-semitic rallies, which were held after Pearl Harbor, see *JNJ*, Chap. 17, note 18a. Cf. also Trobe, *Juden*, p. 3.

76. For the general pressure, see Trobe, *Juden*, pp. 3-4. See also the *Peking Chronicle*, December 3, 1938 (LP). The violinist incident is reported in *Jewish Consulate*, p. 75. Conductor Rosenstock wrote up his own story in his correspondence with Tokayer, April 15, 1974. (TP). Ambassador Eugene Ott's complaint of the failure to remove Rosenstock is noted in Inland II, March 19, 1940. The prevention of the fourth Convention is found in Kaufman, *Manchuria*, p. 23.

77. The speech is summarized in the *Shanghai Jewish Chronicle*, November 24, 1940, p. 7.

78. The following documents from the German Embassy in Tokyo, in Inland II; February 1941, April 23, 1941; May 30, 1941; February 2, 1941, p. 9. For Inuzuka's postwar Japan-Israel Society activities, see *Nippon Times*, December 2, 1952. Cf. also Kobayashi Interv. The author possesses one of Inuzuka's calling cards which lists him as the president of the Nippon-Israel Society.

79. For the two opposing parties, see Irye, "Policies," pp. 454-56. Cf. also Reischauer, *Japan,* pp. 209-10. For a good broad view see the various articles in *P. Harbor,* especially James C. Thomson, Jr., "The Role of the Department of State" [Thomson, "State"], *P. Harbor,* pp. 81-106. For a very critical view of the American position, see Charles Callan Tansill, *Back Door to War: Roosevelt Foreign Policy 1933-1941* [Tansill, *Back Door*] (Chicago: Henry Regnery Co., 1952).

80. For the "Walsh" and official peace initiatives, as well as Ikawa's role, see Toland, *Rising,* Chap. 3. Cf. also Hosoya, "Foreign"; Yamamura, "Finance"; Mira Wilkins, "The Role of U.S. Business" [Wilkins, "Business"], *P. Harbor,* pp. 357-58; Tansill, *Back Door,* pp. 628-33. Ikawa's book is summarized in *JCM,* pp. 62-63. Actually he merely wrote the first of four parts in the book, called "The Plot for a World Revolution," in which he discussed the Freemasons and revolutionaries, calling them all "Jews." The quote from Toland is found in *Rising,* p. 68. Iwakuro's claims of saving 5,000 Jews in Manchuria, might possibly refer to the transit of close to that number (4,600) *through Manchuria,* since only 100 or so refugees settled there. For the transit of the large group, see *JNJ,* Chap. 11.

81. See above, n. 170. The comments by the Kobe Jews was printed alongside the Inuzuka.

82. Z-Dicker correspondence, May 20, 1959, pp. 4-5.

83. There were a number of cases where individuals and groups were originally refused entry into Japan from Vladivostok due to either a lack of even the Curacao visas or having completely forged or illegal papers, who were nevertheless permitted entry, with the obvious permission of the Foreign Office. For such examples, see *JNJ,* Chap. 11. Cf. also the *Peking Chronicle,* March 17, 1941 (LP) re one instance of 200 refugees without the proper visas.

No country, democratic or otherwise, can be shown to have done likewise.

84. See the translation of a section of a biography of *Matsuoka* called *Matsuoka Yoseki, the Man and his Life,* edited by Committee for Publishing Biography of Matsuoka Yoseki, published by Kodansha, 1975.

This section or article was written by Kotsuji for this book. The author is grateful to M. Tokayer for securing this translated portion. (TP). Cf. also Kotsuji, *Jerusalem,* p. 149.

85. Hanin to Tokayer, February 8, 1973.

86. Copy of this and other cables in author's collection, courtesy M. Tokayer (World Jewish Congress Archives).

87. The author feels this to be true despite Masao's opposing view. See Masao, *Politics,* pp. 106-109.

12 | POLISH REFUGEES IN SHANGHAI

A FOURTH COMMUNITY

The Polish and Lithuanian are brought up entirely differently from the other refugees in way of their religious habits, character and language. I do not wish to state that they are better or worse than others, but they are different and must be organized into a separate group.
(Letter, A. Oppenheim of EJC to M. Spechman of
CFA, October 2, 1941)

After their prolonged sojourn in Japan, approximately 900 Polish refugees finally arrived in Shanghai in the fall of 1941.[1] They added a fourth to the three separate Jewish communities already there and, although they were to share the fate of their German and Austrian coreligionists during the next decade (1941-1951), they held themselves apart from their fellow refugees. They were generally younger and differed in socio-economic, religious, political and cultural background. These differences had formed their *Weltanschauung,* and was to dictate their behavior, which was often at wide variance with that of the non-Polish refugees.[2] They were to maintain these differences throughout their stay in Shanghai, in time, their

347

influence was to leave a deep imprint on all segments of Shanghai's Jewry though most pronouncedly on the Russian-Jewish community.

Despite their distinctive character, the Polish refugees were far from homogeneous. In fact, their views covered the full range of prewar Polish Jewry's political, social and religious spectrum. For example, this group included a Hassidic Rebbe, Agudath Israel followers, Bundists, Zionists (ranging from the Poalei Zion through Mizrachi to Revisionists), Yiddish journalists, writers, actors and actresses, teachers, lawyers and other professionals, as well as farmers and artisans.[3]

Most numerous, however, and in many ways most influential in the long run, was an Orthodox group consisting of over 400 Talmudic students, faculty members, and two groups of rabbis. Among these was the only complete yeshiva (Talmudic college) saved from the Nazi destruction, the Mirrer Yeshiva, with its 250 students and faculty. One of the oldest of Europe's yeshivot, it had made its way from the little town of Mir in Poland, as we have seen, across Lithuania, through Russia to Siberia, and then to Kobe, and ended its odyssey in Shanghai. These refugees from Poland's cultural centers truly comprised an elite of East European Jewry, in all its partisan divisions.[4]

Strong nationalist and cultural bonds forged this otherwise far from homogeneous group into the single, most cohesive element among all of Shanghai's Jews, and gave rise among them to a feeling of pride and *esprit de corps* that, prior to Pearl Harbor, was to make them pit their strength against that of the various Jewish relief committees.[5]

They considered themselves superior to the Central European refugees, whose ranks included a large number of both converted and totally assimilated Jews, who felt little if any attachment to their Jewish heritage.[6] Even a common plight amid the vicissitudes of Shanghai was insufficient to abate this deeprooted historic feud between the Central and the East European Jews.[7] Moreover, this spirit of independence manifested itself also in costly opposition to the Japanese military authorities during the Shanghai ghetto period of 1943-1945.

The attitude of superiority on the part of the Polish refugees was felt even prior to their arrival in Shanghai. While they were still in Kobe, they corresponded with Rabbi Ashkenazi, requesting the formation of a separate relief organization.[8] Despite their impoverished condition, they declined to accept the standards of relief established for the German refugees by the CFA, and they absolutely refused to have anything to do with the *Heime*, which they considered far too degrading.[9] It was the good fortune of the Polish refugees that help from several sources enabled them to maintain their proud stance and high standards, as well as their cultural and religious activities throughout their stay in Shanghai.[10] The Polish refugees were especially favored by the fact that the Russian Jews in Shanghai felt more kindly disposed towards East European Jews, with whom they shared a greater cultural, religious and national affinity, than with the Central Europeans. Moreover, a few dedicated and idealistic individuals, such as Rabbi Ashkenazi and Alfred Oppenheim, led the way in marshalling the resources of the Russian Jews to help the Polish refugees, to a degree that had not been possible in response to the needs of the German Refugees.[11] Even this did not come easily, and Rabbi Ashkenazi, for example, had to expend great effort and at times endure much personal abuse, in his efforts to secure help for the newcomers.[12]

EASTJEWCOM

The first relief project for the Polish Jews was the establishment of the separate relief organization called the Committee for Assistance of Jewish Refugees from Eastern Europe, more commonly known as *EASTJEWCOM* or *EJC*, in March 1941.[13] The purpose of this committee was not to replace the aid provided by the Joint via the CFA, but to supplement it by giving them the means for such aid, in a manner that would enable the Polish refugees to avoid recourse to the *Heime* and to afford independent room and board.[14]

After long and arduous negotiations with the CFA in Shanghai, and correspondence with the JDC in the United States, arrangements were made for the Joint to contribute a cash subsidy of (US) $5 per person per month for room and board. This was to be supplemented by extra allowances from the EASTJEWCOM, which would handle all the monies for the Polish refugees. This sum was ostensibly larger than the (US) $3 per capita spent by the *Heime* for its residents, but the Joint's representative, Laura Margolies, admitted that one had to consider the higher costs of food for the very Orthodox Polish refugees, and also of the additional medical cost which was provided gratis for the inmates of the *Heime*. And further, the supplementary aid provided by the IC exclusively for the German refugees made the treatment for both groups relatively equal, despite the discrepancy in cash allowances.[15]

This insistence upon separate private quarters was to bring a group of rabbinical students into open conflict with their former patrons, the Russian Jews, during the relocation to the ghetto.[16] And indeed the spirit of independence of the Polish refugees did not make them easy to deal with.[17] The CFA was furious at having to contend with the "obstreperous" East European refugees, who refused to be treated as *shnorrers,* while the German refugees, on their part, were angry, at the *Ostjuden* for arguing with the Committee. Undoubtedly, some of the German refugees envied the defiant and rebellious nature of these Polish Jews, who were expressing openly the thoughts that they themselves had long suppressed. Moreover, the fact that the Polish refugees received cash from the relief agencies, instead of being required to live in the *Heime,* or at least to secure meals from the free kitchen in the Seward Read *Heim,* that they lived in the Concession, and, wonder of wonders, had chicken for the weekends, caused no little envy among the German refugees.[18]

KOSHER RESTAURANT

Among the most noteworthy forms of aid provided by the Russian Jews to the Polish refugees, in addition to the EASTJEWCOM, was the setting up of a kosher restaurant, which provided good meals at about half the standard price. This enabled the poor refugees, who were ashamed to take the free meals provided at the Shelter House, to buy a decent meal at a price they could afford, and thereby maintain their dignity.[19]

At first this restaurant was subsidized by the EAST-JEWCOM, and at one point there were branches in Hongkew and on the fashionable avenue Joffre in the French Concession.[20]

Other means of helping their Polish coreligionists included the securing of jobs, or helping individuals make their way through the maze of Shanghai's economic world.[21] Many refugees, both Polish and German, earned their livelihood by peddling wares to the older-established Jews.[22]

Help was also extended by the Russian Jews in the cultural realm. They founded and supported such refugee-inspired institutions as a Talmud Torah, an intermediary yeshiva high school for boys, and the Beth Jacob school for girls.[23] They supported the reestablished centers of Torah learning such as the Mirrer Yeshiva and the remnants of the other East European Talmudic academies. They were involved in the reprinting of many Hebrew texts for the use of the Yeshiva, in addition to the printing of original Hebrew and Yiddish works.[24] They not only helped with financial backing for numerous Yiddish shows, but had to provide the audience as well, since the over 400 rabbinic students had little interest in this kind of entertainment.[25]

POLISH "PHILANTHROPISTS"

While it may, be that the Polish refugees were but recipients in the financial sense, in the spiritual sense *they* were the philanthropists.[26] When all is said and done, the cultural impact, and the contribution of the Polish refugees to the Russian-Jewish community more than repaid the financial aid they received. This evaluation requires a fuller treatment than space permits, but a few examples should suffice.

The Russian-Jewish community of Shanghai was the largest Jewish community in the Far East, yet as we have seen, it remained under the shadow of its parent community, Harbin, until well after Pearl Harbor. Harbin's dominant status was due to its flourishing social and cultural institutions, and its able religious and secular leadership.[27] While, at first, the German refugees had little influence upon the Russian Jews, and thus did nothing to change the status of Shanghai vis-a-vis Harbin, the impact of the East European refugees was to leave a deep cultural imprint. The latter helped to strengthen almost all Russian-Jewish institutions and also to create new ones, thus revitalizing what had previously been, at best, a stagnant Jewish cultural life.[28]

UNSER LEBEN

Most significant was the establishment of the trilingual newspaper, *Unser Leben* (*Our Life*), which gave a cohesiveness and provided an avenue of expression, for the emerging Russian-Jewish community.[29] The arrival of some of the leading Polish spokesmen of various Zionist groups did much to strengthen Shanghai's Zionist movement.[30] The relatively small Orthodox element among the Russian Jews was greatly enhanced in both stature and numbers, when several hundred rabbinic students and rabbis arrived, who composed half of the Polish refugee body. Certainly, the prestige of Rabbi Ashkenazi within his entire community rose as a result of the respect accorded him by so many of the new Jewish refugee scholars. This was in marked contrast to the relative neglect and indifference with which he had previously been treated.[31]

While the above-mentioned Yeshiva and Talmud Torahs were supported by the Russian Jews, they more than reciprocated in their spiritual influence, since the students of these institutions came from all elements of Shanghai's Jewry, including the Russian, German and even Sephardi.[32]

YIDDISH CULTURE

The Russian Jews, to whom culture and entertainment had previously meant the Russian language and productions performed by White Russian artists, now became accustomed to hearing Yiddish as a vehicle of both secular and religious learning. Lectures and forums, on topics concerning Jewish history and literature were now introduced by the Polish refugees, in the Jewish Club, or even on the radio. Among the themes presented at such lectures were: "The Struggle for Our National Existence During the Middle Ages," "The Women in Light of the Talmud" and "World Literature," "The Commemoration in Memory of Herzl and Bialik."[33]

Programs of Yiddish song, drama, or dramatic presentations at the Club not only brought a few dollars to the Polish actors and actresses, but added a Jewish dimension to the previously one-sided type of entertainment, and this attracted even some of the Russian-speaking youth.[34]

When *Gittin*, the first of many Talmudic tractates, was reprinted in Shanghai, it became the cause for celebration for the entire community.[35]

JEWISH WASTELAND

Perhaps the best testimony to the impact made by the Polish refugees is the letter sent by a teenage Jewish girl to the editors of *Unser Leben* in 1942. The girl, who grew up in the semi-assimilated Russian-Jewish milieu of Shanghai in the 1930's writes of her surprise at discovering among the newcomers complete and committed Jews, at home with their literature, values, and language. Despairing at the thought that "I am thoroughly conscious of my Jewishness only when our race or one of its members is praised or despised," she goes on to ask, "Must I not be always, permanently impregnated with my Jewishness? But how can I be so? I know nothing of the Jewish religion and of its moral ideals. I know nothing of Jewish traditions, of our ancient and relatively modern history."

She accuses her parents' generation, who in their own youth had contact with a full Jewish life, of failing to pass on this heritage to the young. She demands that her generation at least be given the opportunity to get to know authentic Judaism.[36] The next few issues of this newspaper featured discussion on the answers to the girls' quest, by proponents of varying schools of thought.[37]

POLISH GOVERNMENT

The sympathetic, supporting role of the Polish Government (and later the Government-in-Exile) to its refugees in Kobe and Shanghai, was an additional factor favoring the Polish group above their German and Austrian counterparts. In Kobe and Shanghai the Polish Government representative provided a reasonable share of his country's allotment of British visas to Canada and Australia, to his Jewish compatriots.[38] In Kobe, the Polish Ambassador, Count de Romer, also helped set up a Committee of Relief for Polish Citizens, whose counterpart, the Polish Aid Society in Shanghai, continued the relief work begun in Japan.[39]

In Shanghai, he also helped set up an elected council representing the 19 groups among the Polish refugees. This Organization of Polish War Refugees in China elected an executive committee of five, who, after de Romer's departure, would act as unofficial agents of the Polish Government-in-Exile in London.[40]

The above-mentioned Polish Aid Society, or Pole Aid, as its cable form became, was set up in Shanghai as the agency through which the Polish Government-in-Exile in London channeled the money for the refugees via the International Red Cross in Switzerland.[41] Most of this money reached the refugees through the EASTJEWCOM.[42] For example, at a time, after Pearl Harbor, when the funds borrowed on the JDC Guarantee loan ran low, two large grants of 20,000 Swiss francs each (total equivalent of (Sh) $450,000) arrived from the Polish Government-in-Exile by this route.[43]

Furthermore, the Polish Government arranged for 43 of its Shanghai refugees to be repatriated with the British and other "enemy nationals" on August 17, 1942, to Laurenco Marques, Mozambique.[44]

Besides receiving the assistance rendered to all the Polish refugees, individual groups among this body were the fortunate beneficiaries of aid by other organizations, both in the United States and in neutral European countries. Such groups as the Yiddish writers or Bundists received various grants from their sympathizers in the United States or elsewhere.[45]

AID TO YESHIVOT

Most favored by such sympathizers, especially in the United States, were the yeshiva and rabbinical groups. Through the personal efforts of a few individuals in the United States and Europe, such as Rabbis Abraham Kalmanowitz and Eliezer Silver of Vaad Hatzalah, and laymen like Michael Tress of Agudath Israel, these religious groups were the fortunate beneficiaries in terms of visas, as well as financial help. Through the aforementioned organizations, these three individuals left no stone unturned, whether in Washington, and various embassies and key locations all over the world, such as the Vatican, Stockholm, etc., in their efforts to feed, rescue, transport and repatriate what they considered the Jewish People's most important resource, the students of the Torah.

With the help of the JDC, they were able to rescue the entire student body and faculty of the Mirrer Yeshiva, and the remnants of other schools, and to maintain the students' 18-hour-a-day study period throughout their exile, in Siberia, Japan, and Shanghai, before and even during the ghetto period. Money was sent during 1943 and 1944 via neutral countries, even when the Joint's "super patriotism," constrained them from cabling the assurance of loan guarantees. In fact, the very success of the sponsors of the rabbinical groups roused the envy of other, less fortunate refugees.[46]

Typical of the zeal with which such individuals espoused the cause of saving the remnants of Europe's Torah scholars, is the following incident involving Rabbi Kalmanowitz.

During a taxi ride one late Friday in the winter of 1940, on a mission to collect part of the (US) $50,000 necessary to pay Intourist for the trip out of Kovno to Japan, his secretary, Rabbi Alex Weisfogel went to gently remind the pensive Talmudic scholar that it was already "Shabbos," (i.e., past sundown, when it is no longer permitted to travel on the Sabbath). The venerable rabbi retorted angrily, that these people's lives are in danger and you're telling me about *Shabbos!* (i.e., this is a case of *Pikuach nefesh,* danger to life, which takes precedence over the Sabbath in Jewish Law).[46]

This relief and rescue work provides one of the more heroic but neglected chapters of the Shanghai story, and its nature and import deserve greater recognition.

NOTES : POLISH REFUGEES

1. See *Kobe Report*, p. 22a; HH XV B-21 — B-26; Epstein, "Mir," p. 127.

2. The *Kobe Report*, on p. 22a, lists 1,098 refugees who went to Shanghai from Kobe, including 860 Polish and 37 "others" (than German). Rabbi Solomon Tarshansky, who worked for the JDC in Kobe, told the author that the category "other" definitely referred to refugees of East European origin. He was certain that more than 900 East European refugees traveled through Kobe to Shanghai. Interview. His view is substantiated by the figures from a report by Epstein, a HICEM representative in Kobe, who cites the exact number of 972 for the Polish refugees in Shanghai. Epstein to HICEM (Lisbon), September 1, 1942, p. 1 [Epstein to HICEM, September 1, 1942]. HH XV B-26. A later source, which excludes the 43 Polish refugees that were repatriated in 1942, notes that approximately 940 Polish refugees were in Shanghai. Copy telegram No. 416 sent by the Polish Aid Society via the International Red Cross, October 25, 1943. YIVO No. 40.

3. Dobekirer Interview.; Margolies Interview. For the variety of elements among the Polish refugees see the names of the groups that signed the Statutes of the organization of Polish War Refugees in China [Zosa-Szajkowski] *YIVO Catalog of the Exhibition: Jewish Life in Shanghai* [YIVO, *Catalog*] (New York: YIVO, 1948), p. 13; Menachem Flakser, "Yapan und China: Zeier Baziung zu Yidn in der Tzveiter Velt Milchome" [Flakser, "Yapan"] (original 13-page manuscript of a briefer Yiddish article that later appeared in the *Jewish Daily Forward*. Copy made courtesy of the writer. Menachem Flakser, "Toizend Poilishe Yidn in Shanchai" [Flakser, "Poilishe Yidn"], *Jewish Daily Forward* (December 31, 1962), p. 5 (courtesy author; "Polish War Refugees in Shanghai" [Polish Refugees"], *Shanghai Almanac*, 1946-1947 [Almanac], Ossi Lewin, ed. (Shanghai: *Shanghai Echo*, n.d.), p. 80.
See also below, note 40.

4. The author's statistics for the number of students in the Mirrer Yeshiva in Shanghai are based on those cited by Margolies to Pilpel, October 26, 1941, p. 4. Though Margolies admits that her figures may not be too accurate, they seem to be the most complete, and are at least very close. For example, the Talmudic tractates for the use of the Mirrer Yeshiva were reprinted in runs of 250 copies (Epstein, "Mir"). The following are Margolies' statistics for all the yeshivot in Shanghai: Mir, 238 students; Kletsk, 22; Telse, 12; Lublin, 35; Lubavitch, 29; Misc. (mostly rabbis), 73; total 409. If we include the families of some rabbis, the figures for the rabbinical groups number somewhere close to 500, thus comprising over half the Polish refugees. The *YIVO Catalog*, p. 13, cites 80 as the number of rabbis among the two rabbinical associations, the *Ihud Rabanim* and the *Kolel Kovno-Vilna*.

. 5. Jechiel Dobekirer Interview. Also Moshe Elbaum taped interview, June 6, 1966.

6. The *esprit de corps* of the Polish refugees is described by Shoshana, *In Faier*, pp. 283-85, 310. Cf. also Flakser Interview; Margulies Interview; Elbaum Interview; Epstein to HICEM, September 1, 1940, p. 2.

7. See above, chap. 6, note 34.

8. Dobekirer Interview. Cf. also Birman to HICEM (Lisbon), March 21, 1941, p. 1 [Birman to HICEM, March 21, 1941] (HH XV C-10); Rottenberg, *Shanghai,* pp. 324-27.

9. For the first reaction of some Polish refugees to the Heime, see Shoshana, *In Faier,* pp. 284-85. Cf. also Birman to HICEM (Lisbon), April 9, 1941 [Birman to HICEM, April 9, 1941] (HH XV C-10); Margolies to Pilpel, October 26, 1941, pp. 1, 4; Bitker to CFA, September 26, 1941 [Bitker-CFA, September 26, 1941] (JDCCA); Epstein to HICEM (Lisbon), August 18, 1941, p. 7; "Polish Refugees"; Rottenberg, *Shanchai,* pp. 324-27.

10. Flakser, "Poilishe Yiden." Cf. also Margolies, *Report,* 1941-45, p. 10.

11. Flakser, "Poilishe Yidn." Cf. also *Unser Leben,* September 18, 1942; September 25, 1942, p. 1 (English Suppl.); Margolies, *Report,* pp. 10-11; SACRA Minutes of the Shanghai Ashkenazi Collaborating Relief Association, a Russian-Jewish organization responsible for helping the Japanese authorities to relocate the refugees into the ghetto in 1943). See below, Chapter 18. CCB represented the Central Control Board, the highest governing body over various subcommittees of SACRA (YIVO No. 13). See also below, Chapter 19. SACRA Minutes, CCB, May 23, 1945, pp. 1-2; Speelman to Oppenheim, October 7, 1941 (JDCCA).

12. Report on Arrival of about 300 Refugees from Japan, August 22, 1941 ["Arrival"] (JDCCA); Margolies to Pilpel, October 26, 1941, especially pp. 2-3. See also Simcha Elberg, "Shanchai Und Ir Rov" (Yiddish) [Elberg, "Rov"], *Dos Yiddishe Vort,* Vol. XIII (January 1967), pp. 14-16; Simcha Elberg, "Golus Shanchai" [Elberg, "Golus"], *Dos Yiddishe Vort,* Vol. XIII (December 1966), pp. 14-16, especially p. 14; Zacharia Zilberpfenig, "Shagrire Yisrael Bamizrakh Harochok" (Hebrew) [Zilberpfenig, "Shagrire"], *Hadoar,* Vol. XII (May 1, 1942), pp. 371-73. For Rabbi Ashkenazi's part in the formation of the CENTRAJEWCOM, see *Unser Leben* (September 18, 1942, p.1 (English Suppl.).

13. For the date, see Birman to HICEM, March 21, 1941 (HH XV C-10). Birman gives the title as Committee for the Assistance to East Europeans. Actually, the complete title, as found on the masthead of the organization's letterheads of various dates 1941-1942 (YIVO No. 37) is Committee for Assistance of Jewish Refugees from Eastern Europe. For use of the brief title of EASTJEWCOM or EJC, see for example Margolies to Pilpel, Octobei 26, 1941. The latter two brief forms will be used interchangeably. The EASTJEWCOM is not to be confused with JEWCOM, the cable name for the Jewish Community of Kobe Committee for Assistance to Refugees (see above, Chap. 2). J. Epstein to HICEM (Lisbon), August 20, 1941 (HH XV B-25).

For Oppenheim's chairmanship of the EASTJEWCOM, see Margolies, *Report,* p. 10. Cf. also Oppenheim to Speelman, October 2, 1941 (JDCCA); Margolies to Pilpel, November 9, 1941, p. 2 (JDCCA). For contrast of the CFA to EJC, see *ibid.* Also Rosenfeld, *History,* III, p. 15.

14. See especially Oppenheim to Speelman, October 2, 1941. Also Mar-

golies to Pilpel, October 26, 1941, pp. 2-5. The Polish refugees also desired the freedom to seek business or employment, which was easier when unencumbered by their required presence at the *Heime* during mealtime. Margulies Interview.

15. Margolies to Pilpel, October 26, 1941, especially p. 5. Cf. also Margolies, "Memorandum re Budget," November 5, 1941 [Margolies, Memo, November 5, 1941] (JDCCA); Margolies to Pilpel, September 10, 1941, p. 3; Margolies to Pilpel, November 9, 1941, p. 2.

This arrangement for separate relief allocations continued after Pearl Harbor, despite Margolies' reluctance to make distinctions between East and Central European refugees. This was the time when Margolies raised (US) $180,000 locally, upon the Joint's guarantee. The basic reason, of course, was that she had to rely on the good will of the Russian Jews to raise the money, since after Pearl Harbor the wealthy Sephardim were no longer in a position to extend aid. Margolies, *Report*, pp. 10-11.

16. See below, Chap. 17. The married rabbinic students were immediately provided with individual rooms. Rabbi Moshe Walden Interview, October 10, 1969.

17. Margulies Interview. See also Margolies to Pilpel, September 10, 1941, p. 3; "Arrival". The writer (probably Laura Margolies) notes the "difficulty" involved in the "Pass Control" of a rabbinical group that arrived in Shanghai on a Friday and which would not remain for the luggage control that took place on the Sabbath.

18. Shoshana, *In Faier*, p. 286. Also Friedlander, *Sieben*, p. 32; *Unser Leben*, September 5, 1941, p. 1 (Yiddish Sect.); SACRA Minutes, June 30, 1943, p. 2.

For the general treatment and view of the refugees as *shnorrers*, see Ganther, "Seven Years." Cf. also Rosenfeld, *History*, III, p. 51. Even those refugees outside the *Heime* considered the residents in the *Heime* as shnorrers. Fischel Interview; Flakser, "Poilishe Yidn"; "Polish Refugees." Deman-Kranzler, Corres., July 12, 1974. For a favorable German view of EASTJEWCOM as a model of relief organization, see Rosenfeld, *History*, III, p. 15.

19. The full name of this restaurant was the Polish Refugee Kitchen No. 1 which was first located at the old Jewish Club, 35 Mulmein Road, but transferred in 1943 to the location of the former Altman's (nonkosher) Restaurant on avenue Joffre. It was thus often referred to as Altman's Restaurant. It was also known as the General Jewish Kitchen for Polish and East European Refugees. It was located at the time (March 1942) on Tongshan Road (Margulies to Barbash, March 4, 1942) (YIVO No. 60).

For the full title, see Receipt of the Polish Refugee Kitchen No. 1, August 22, 1944 (YIVO No. 42). For the background of this unique restaurant, see Margulies Interview. Isaac Margulies was its first manager. Cf. also Elkan Interview. (DF).

20. Margulies Interview.

21. Shoshana, *In Faier*, p. 322.

22. *Ibid.* p. 327. For another view of the help rendered by the Russian Jews, see Elberg, "Golus," p. 14.

23. For details concerning these institutions, see below, Chapter 15. See for example the many receipts for donations in Barbash Files (YIVO No. 60); also YIVO No. 50); Flakser, "Poilishe Yidn."

For information on the Beth Jacob schools for girls in Poland, see Miriam Eisenstein, *Jewish Schools in Poland,* 1919-1939 [Eisenstein, *Schools*] (New York: Columbia University, 1950), Ch. 6.

24. See below, Chap. 15.

25. Shoshana, *In Faier,* p. 327.

26. Dr. Simchoni [Elberg], "Yiddish in Shanchai" [Simchoni, "Yiddish"], *Unser Leben,* May 8, 1942, p. 2 (Yiddish Sect.).

27. Rabbi Kissileff and Dr. Abraham Kaufman, respectively. See above, Chap. 2, especially notes 77-78.

28. See *Unser Leben,* February 13, 1942; March 6, 1942; April 24, 1942, p. 1 (Yiddish Sect.). See especially September 4, 1942, p.   (English Suppl.).

29. This newspaper [*Unser Leben*] which was published between 1941 and 1945 contains much information about the Russian-Jewish and the refugee communities. We have made good use of the two volumes covering 1941-1942, courtesy of the editor of its Yiddish section, Menachem Flakser, and the subsequent volumes through 1945, loaned to the author by David Rabinovich, the overall editor. For the effect of this newspaper on the Russian-Jewish community, see Samuel Ivri, "Drei Kehillos-Drei Zeitungen," *Unser Leben* (May 5, 1942) (Yiddish sect.), p. 2.

30. Dobekirer Interview. Also Margulies Interview.

31. Drucker Interview (DP). Also Joseph D. Epstein Interview.

32. See below, Chapter 15.

33. For the White Russian cultural predominance, see *Unser Leben,* November 14, 1941; December 5, 1941; January 6, 1942; January 23, 1942; January 30, 1942; February 13, 1942.

For these lectures, see the pages of *Unser Leben,* e.g., June 19, 1942; July 19, 1942; May 29, 1942 (Yiddish Sect.), p. 1. See also Simchoni, "Yiddish." For the Yiddish Radio, see *Dos Wort—The Word,* November 21, 1941, p. 1, which noted the first of a series of lectures on the Yiddish program on station XMHA. Also see YIVO File No. 54 for the text of these programs (a 28-page ms.).

34. See the pages of *Unser Leben* for the announcements and news items concerning Yiddish dramatic or other forms of entertainment. An assortment of the tickets to such entertainment in YIVO No. 44, 56-58 gives an indication of the range and frequency of such presentations. Cf. also Shoshana, *In Faier,* pp. 287, 290-94, 296, 298, 323. For the number and titles of Yiddish books printed or reprinted in Shanghai, see *JRC,* Appendix.

35. *Unser Leben,* May 1, 15, 1942 (Yiddish Sect.), p. 1. See also Epstein, "Mir," p. 130.

36. *Unser Leben,* August 28, 1942, p. 1 (English Suppl.).

37. See, for example, O. Rapoport, "A Voice in the Wilderness," *Unser Leben* (September 25, 1942) (English Sect.), p. 2.

38. See Epstein to HICEM (Lisbon), August 18, 1941, p. 5 (HH XV B-24).

39. For activities of this Committee in Kobe, see *Kobe Report*, p. 28. The Polish Ambassador himself donated over 1,000 yen to this Committee for the Relief for Polish Citizens. *Ibid.* See also Epstein to HICEM, August 18, 1941. *Ibid.*

40. Ernest Landau Interview. The Polish name of this organization was Organizacja Polskich Uchodzcow Wojennych w Szanghaju (see the Statutes of this organization promulgated May 12, 1942) [Polish Refugees, "Statutes"] (YIVO No. 40). Also briefly noted in the YIVO *Catalog*, p. 13. The Executive consisted of Aleksander Fajgenbaum, Ernest Landau, Szimon Bergman, Rabbi Joseph D. Epstein, and S. Grosfater. Landau Interview. Polish Refugees, "Statutes," p. 7. Also YIVO, *Catalog*, p. 13.

The 19 groups represented were lawyers, Jewish journalists and writers, engineers, merchants, physicians, free professions, rabbis, artisans, manufacturers, farmers, lumber workers, Agudas Yisroel, Betar, Bund, Coordinating Committee of Zionist groups, Combatants, Yeshiva of Lublin, Yeshiva of Mir, Yeshiva of Lubavitch. Polish Refugees, "Statutes," p. 2. Also YIVO, *Catalog*, p. 13.

41. Epstein to HICEM (Lisbon), September 1, 1942, p. 3 (HH XV B-26). The money itself came mostly from Jewish sources. Landau, Interview. Cf. also copies of telegrams sent by the Polish Aid Society to Geneva, especially No. 352 (YIVO No. 40), pp. 1-2; SACRA Minutes, September 14, 1943, p. 2. Also cited by Dicker, *Wanderers*, p. 127. Lewin, *Churban*, pp. 243-44.

42. Polish Aid Society to EASTJEWCOM, August 19, 1942 (YIVO No. 37). Also Zackheim Interview.

43. Birman to HICEM, October 15, 1942, p. 2. In 1944, 100,000 Swiss francs were sent. Birman, *Report*, Extract February 10, 1944, p. 1 (HH XV C-9). See also Isaac Lewin, *Churban Eiropa* (Yiddish) [Lewin, *Churban*] (New York: Research Institute for Post-War Problems of Religious Jewry, 1948), pp. 229-32.

44. Epstein to HICEM (Lisbon), September 1, 1942, p. 3. Also Birman to HICEM (Lisbon), May 14, 1942 (HH XV C-7); Birman to HICEM (Lisbon), October 15, 1942, p. 1. Actually 43 Polish and 18 Czech refugees left with this group of repatriates, consisting of British, Belgian, Dutch, Norwegian citizens. *Ibid.* See also Shoshana, *In Faier*, p. 297.

For a critical view of the means used for the selection for repatriation, see *ibid.*, pp. 294-95; Yaakov H. Fishman, "Shiffn," in *Farvogelte Yidn* (Yiddish) [Fishman, "Shiffn"] (Shanghai: Communal Committee, 1948), pp. 7-16. An answer to this opinion was given by Margulies Interview and Landau Interview. A second proposed repatriation of 300 Polish refugees, never materialized. Epstein to HICEM, September 1, 1942, p. 3.

45. Shoshana, *In Faier*, pp. 320, 322.

46. For the rescue of the Yeshivot from Europe to Japan, see above, chapter 11. For Kalmanowitz's Sabbath ride, see Weisfogel Interview.

The composition of the refugee community resulted in a far above average cultural life of a community of this size. 12-14,000 people represent the population of a small city and you will hardly find a community of this size showing similar cultural achievements.

(Kurt Redlich *to author. December 23, 1975*)

Despite its heterogeneous and factional character, the refugee community recognized its common need for a rich cultural life. Many of the refugees had been part of the intellectual and artistic elite in their own countries and sought to recreate in Shanghai a familiar cultivated life. Surrounded by an alien, often hostile environment, beset by the unending difficulties of mere survival, they unswervingly insisted on, and provided, cultural activities throughout their stay in Shanghai.

A superficial glance at the abundance of newspapers, organizations, schools, libraries, concerts, artistic exhibitions, and other cultural endeavors might readily suggest the cultural life of a normal and peaceful community. But this fertile display of culture barely concealed a harassed community, where the majority were ill-fed, ill-housed, and dependent to a greater or lesser degree on charity. And, especially after Pearl Harbor,

363

initial optimism and hopes of leaving Shanghai were supplanted by increasing bleakness and undiminished adversity.

In light of the cultural life that was created, the criticism of mercenaries leveled at the refugees seems spurious.[1] While no lasting masterpiece of creative work was produced by the refugee community during its stay in Shanghai, no one can deny the unusually high calibre of its intellectual pursuits and sheer variety of cultural endeavors worthy of an active community perhaps ten times its size.[2]

THE PRESS

Perhaps no medium is more illustrative of the heterogeneity of the refugee community's background and political and social opinions than its relatively large and flourishing press.

The only Jewish newspaper in Shanghai at the time of the arrival of the Central European refugees was the Sephardi, Zionist-oriented, English-language weekly, *Israel's Messenger*, edited, as we saw earlier, since its inception in 1904, by N. E. B. Ezra.[3] The Russian Jews, whose parent community of Harbin had supported a Jewish, Russian-language weekly since 1918, were unable to sustain, despite several attempts, a similar publication, until the arrival of the East European refugees in 1941.[4]

The large, non-Jewish German population in Shanghai was served by the only German-language newspaper, the *Ostasiatische Lloyd*, which became a vehicle for Nazi propaganda.[5] The arrival of the German-Austrian refugees saw the establishment of a flourinshing Jewish-German-language press. In fact, during Jewish journalism's heyday, from the end of 1939 until Pearl Harbor, the Shanghai refugee community produced three dailies—two morning and one evening paper. Among the refugees were many able and experienced journalists, who expressed a broad range of viewpoints in a variety of publications, including dailies, weeklies, and monthlies.[6]

The first paper to succeed, after a number of abortive attempts, was the *Shanghai Woche,* a weekly edited by Wolfgang Fischer, which began publication on March 30, 1939. It covered worldwide political as well as local and immigration news. The German-language *Shanghai Jewish Chronicle* appeared shortly afterwards. Initially a weekly, by May 1939, it was transformed into a daily morning paper. Edited by Ossie Lewin, it was to survive until the Chinese Communist takeover in 1949, making it the longest running German-language Jewish newspaper. Its name was changed to *The Shanghai Echo,* following the conclusion of the War in the Pacific. The *Chronicle* was the only daily to receive sanction from the Japanese authorities to continue publication after Pearl Harbor, a fact that later evoked critical sneers from its competitors. They claimed that Lewin was too friendly with the Japanese, this despite his brief incarceration at their hands in the infamous Bridge House jail.[7]

Die Gelbe Post, a monthly under the very able journalist A. J. Storfer, who was also a psychologist and a student of Freud, was considered one of the best-edited papers in Asia. Most of its contents were devoted to articles of a cultural nature, as well as political and local news. In October 1939, Storfer changed his monthly, first into a weekly, and by March of 1940 into a daily, giving the Shanghai Jewish Chronicle tough competition. *Die Gelbe Post,* however, was never able to maintain its former high standard after becoming a daily because, according to one source, Storfer was not geared to the deadlines required of a "daily" writer. He suffered a heart attack in September 1940 as a result of problems due to daily pressure and bad weather. Moreover, according to one close observer, there was really no room among the relatively small number of refugees for two dailies, and certainly Storfer felt unable to compete with the *Chronicle,* which was supposedly financed by the JDC.[8]

In addition, there appeared an evening paper called the

8-Uhr Abendblatt, published by Wolfgang Fischer, thus making three German-language dailies. Of all the havens of refuge for the hundreds of thousands of Jews migrating from Central Europe, including the United States, only Shanghai's German-Jewish community was able to support more than one German-language daily. During this same period several good weeklies also were initiated. These included the excellent *Tribune,* edited by Dr. Dreifuss and Kurt Lewin, and the *Laterne* under the guidance of Heinz Ganther. The outbreak of World War II in Europe aroused a greater interest on the part of the refugees in general world affairs, and was an important factor in the creation of many newspapers during the period 1939-41.[9]

The *Juedische Gemeinde** published its own weekly, the *Juedisches Nachrichtenblatt,* ably edited by Philip Kohn, which also continued publication during the Japanese occupation. After the war it reappeared under the new title of *The Jewish Voice.* Since many refugees could not afford to buy a copy of the newspaper, especially during the ghetto period, the publishers usually provided a free reading room.[10]

Editors and many writers changed positions fairly frequently before Pearl Harbor, some to start their own newspapers. For example, Dr. Frank left the *Chronicle* to publish the *Shanghai Morgenpost,* in conjunction with the English-language *China Press.* Among its contributors were Dr. Fritz Friedlander, Lothar Brieger, and many other fine journalists. The *Morgenpost* has been described as "the high point of refugee journalism in Shanghai." Some competitors were critical of its lack of concern for the plight of the Jews, and its continuation as more of a "German" than "Jewish" newspaper, despite the Nazi terror. The *Morgenpost* was shut down on December 8, 1941. This left the *Jewish Chronicle* without competition. The refugee community could even boast its own scandal sheet, a weekly publication, called *Der Querschnitt,* which was edited by a budding journalist, Egon Varo, sometimes, during 1939. Another young writer published the short-lived *SPORT* magazine in 1939.[11]

An attempt by the Polish-Jewish writers to publish the *Wiadomosci dla Uchodzcow Wojennych w Szanghaju* (*News for War Refugees in Shanghai*) as a supplement in Yiddish and Polish, to the Polish paper *Echo Szanghajskje* (*Shanghai Echo*) was cut short by its own staff when they burned it, for fear of the Japanese authorities.[12] Some of the Polish refugee journalists did have a forum for their views in the Yiddish supplement to the tri-lingual, *Unser Leben,* published by the Russian-Jewish community.[13]

Heinz Ganther and Dr. Alphons [Kramer] published a bi-weekly, *Die Neue Zeit,* which was taken over in December 1945 by Dr. Frank, and renamed the *Shanghai Journal.* Published as a daily, it competed for a while with Heinz Ganther's German supplement to the *Shanghai Herald.*[14]

The medical profession added to the available publications by putting out the short-lived *Medizinischen Monatshefts,* edited by Dr. Kurt Raffael. Dr. Theodore Friedrichs edited a monthly, *Journal of the Association of Central European Doctors,* which appeared from mid-1940 through 1942.[15] This technical journal published many articles in English and Chinese as well as in German, and thus reached a wider audience than the approximately 200 refugee physicians. Right after the war, the Association of Jewish Writers and Journalists, Refugees from Poland, was finally able to raise its independent voice by putting out a physically crude, but journalistically good Yiddish weekly, *Unser Welt* [sic] (Our World). It was edited for the first few months by the president of the abovementioned association, Lazar Cahan, with Moshe Elbaum, until Cahan's death in 1946.[16]

As we have noted, under the Japanese occupation no unrestricted press was permitted. This resulted in unemploy-

ment for a majority of the journalists. Many ended up in the
Heime, where they led a hand-to-mouth existence, particularly
during the ghetto period. The ghetto period found some of these
intellectuals wandering about Shanghai in tattered clothes and
with shattered morale. A few failed to survive this period at
all.[17]

There existed also a religiously oriented press, albeit a
small one. The Agudah (worldwide orthodox organization) of
Shanghai published a shortlived monthly, *Die Yiddishe Shtime
Fun Vayten Mizrekh,* which first appeared in September 1941.
One month later, a weekly, Yiddish-English paper entitled *Dos
Wort* (The Word) appeared, under the editorial tutelage of
Simchoni (Elberg).[18] However, the small group of orthodox
writers was obviously unable to remain united in a journalistic
venture. Another magazine devoted to articles of religious inter-
est and thought was *Der Yiddisher Almanach,* published in
Yiddish, English, Russian and German.[19]

THEATER, RADIO, ART

The theater played a great role in the cultural life of the
Shanghai refugees. Its achievements at times rivaled some of its
European counterparts, which is astounding in the face of all the
obstacles it had to overcome.[20]

One of the main problems, of course, was that of financing decent productions. Raising subsidies, difficult even in richer
societies, was compounded in a community that was struggling
for bare subsistence, and whose artists were often on relief.
Literally every nail purchased to build the most primitive stage
meant a genuine sacrifice for those who were struggling along in
the *Heime.* The results were all the more astonishing. Rehearsals
would take place in freezing, unheated rooms, and usually after
a hard day's labor as a waiter, grocery delivery boy, or car-
toonist.[21]

Refugee audiences were often most difficult to satisfy by a cast itself badly in need of encouragement. The snobbishness of those refugees who came from Berlin or Vienna was evidenced by such remarks as, "This I've seen with Basserman, or with Massary." Such an attitude had to be overcome before objective criticism could be expected.[22]

Nevertheless, a beginning was made. After struggling through the scorching summer of 1939, the first presentation of "Ein Bunter Abend" ("A Colorful Evening"), a sort of variety show, was given in one of the *Heime*. It was directed by Walter Friedmann, the most active of the refugee stage producers.[23] The first major play, a big hit, Frank Wolfmar's "Delila," was played at the Lyceum Theater that year. Fritz Melchior, the noted cartoonist-actor, directed and co-starred with Eve Schwartz in this show.[24]

Many of the plays were performed in the various *Heime,* including some as "benefits" for the residents.[25]

Over 60 German-language plays were produced by the refugees, a formidable statistic in view of the circumstances. The repertoire included well-known European plays by Shaw, Strindberg, Molnar and Hofmannsthal, as well as original scripts written by local talent.

Resident refugee authors, such as Max Brand-Bukofzer, Max Siegelberg and the joint authors E. Engel and D. Gruen, wrote many plays which were performed in Shanghai.[26]

The outbreak of the War in the Pacific brought with it the ubiquitous Japanese censor, who checked every production prior to its performance. For example, Noel Coward's "Private Lives" was removed when the Japanese realized that his play *In Which We Serve* was based on an anti-Axis theme.[27]

The Boris Sapiro Buehne was a small but ongoing Jewish theater which supported quite a few refugee stage artists, both prior to and even after the establishment of the ghetto. His productions included original local, as well as an array of international plays. His operation continued throughout the ghetto period, though no one is sure of his financial source. The fact that he was among the first to receive a postwar visa to the United States, and his steady financial solvency, in a normally insecure field, indicate that he probably had a source of money from the Allies. They may have paid him to maintain some sort of underground activity.

Also popular among the refugees was an excellent Puppet Theater.[28]

YIDDISH THEATER

Yiddish actors and actresses set out to establish a Yiddish theater almost immediately upon arrival.[29] Yiddish plays were performed from late 1941, when the Polish refugees arrived in Shanghai, to mid-1943, when the ghetto was established.[30] Rose Shoshana (the wife of Lazar Cahan) and a small group of fellow entertainers produced such Yiddish classics as Gordon's *"Mirele Efros," "Dos Glick fun Morgen,"* and *"Tevye der Milchiger"* adapted from Sholom Aleichem.[31]

The potential audience for the Yiddish theater was much smaller than that of its German counterpart, since only the older elements of the relatively small Russian-Jewish community understood Yiddish. Also, almost half the Polish refugees were yeshiva students and rabbis, who had no interest in the theater at all. This limited audience created difficulties for the actors, since they could never perform a play more than once.[32] The Yiddish Theater had to close with the establishment of the ghetto in 1943, since the only sizeable potential audience, the Russian Jews, were now outside the ghetto.[33] Even if passes could be secured to leave the ghetto in order to produce plays, the passes were never valid for a period long enough to make all the necessary preparations. The indefatigable Rose Shoshana, how-

ever, did manage to prepare an evening of entertainment, though
not a play, after securing a limited pass.[34]

Yiddish Theater group felt the lack of books containing plays even more so than did its German counterpart, as
the latter received at least one such shipment sometime in
1940.[35] Scripts of entire plays such as *"Tevya"* had to be written
from memory.[36]

Nor did the Yiddish stage escape the ever watchful eye
of the Japanese censor after Pearl Harbor. An example of a
play cancelled by the Japanese was D. Marcus' "A Tour Around
the World," considered unfavorable to Japanese interests.[37]

RADIO

About six months after the start of mass immigration, a
successful attempt was made by Horst Levin and Heinz Ganther
to utilize the radio for programs of interest.[38] Opening on May 2,
1939, Station XMHA provided a series of programs for one
hour every afternoon, that included serious as well as light
cultural entertainment. Newscasting became important after the
outbreak of World War II, in September 1939, with the resultant
greater interest in current events. After the arrival of the East
European refugees in late 1941, a Yiddish program was included,
with lectures, music and news broadcasting in Yiddish, for the
first time in Shanghai's history.[39]

Music on radio ranged from classics to jazz and was
very popular both among the refugees and the old Shanghai
"foreigners." This was made possible by the primarily classical
collection of 10,000 records maintained by the station XMHA
which received copies of all the best records produced by RCA
(NBC), the parent station. One hour a week was devoted to live
performances by all the leading refugee musicians. Since the
radio program was broadcast on shortwave, it reached fellow
refugees who worked deep in China's interior as Mission
doctors, and who were delighted to hear the familiar classical
music, and news, both Jewish and general.

Among the more noteworthy special programs were talks by old-time German physicians, who gave badly needed advice about sanitation and medical problems.[40]

Several refugees found jobs as announcers on other radio stations. For example, A. Storfer and Peter Adams worked for an English station, while Rudolph Schlesinger was active with a Chinese station. Dr. Dreifuss and Hans Koenig, both Communists, worked for TASS in Shanghai.[41]

ART

The designation of the refugee enclave in Hongkew as "Little Vienna," with its European-style architecture and storefronts, can be safely attributed to work of the refugee artists.[42] Still, despite its size and commercial nature, Shanghai had little use for European artistic talent, whether in the fine or commercial arts. Thus, along with many other refugees who were well trained for the society they were forced to leave behind, the artists had great difficulty earning even a meager livelihood.[43]

A few commercial artists found jobs in advertising agencies, while others free-lanced. One architect obtained a position with the Shanghai Municipal Council.[44]

Artists arranged for group, as well as one-man shows, in their attempt to attract friends and customers.[45] In order to gain a larger audience and to interest potential patrons, the refugee artists formed an organization called ARTA (Association of Jewish Artists and Lovers of Fine Art) which included sixty-four artists and their friends. Membership in ARTA enabled a patron to receive one free work of graphic art as well as a reduction on any purchase.[46] Their first combined exhibit, featuring the works of 14 artists, was held in May 1943. The subjects centered around Jewish life in Shanghai and in general, life in this Chinese metropolis, though some Japanese motifs were also included.[47]

MUSIC

Before the Central European refugee influx, Shanghai's musical life did not measure up to the city's stature as one of the world's largest commercial centers.[48] However, when one considers the rather small number of Westerners, about 40 to 50,000, in this Chinese city, the level of its musical talent is seen in a different light.

Aside from one English-language, European theater and one fairly good symphony orchestra, most of Shanghai's musical talent was to be found in the numerous bars, dancehalls, and coffee-houses. Italians, Filipinos, and White Russians predominated among the musicians.[49]

The arrival of over 17,000 refugees, which included a disproportionate number of musically talented people, enhanced both their own cultural life and advanced that of Shanghai's.[50]

The refugee group included two types of musicians, the professional and the amateur. The latter were quite numerous and able. In fact, some of them were the equal of many professionals.[51] For example, two outstanding amateurs were doctors of medicine, Erich Marcuse, whose forte was conducting, and Arthur Wolff, whose original compositions were already well known in Germany.[52]

The great majority of the amateurs joined those who supplied Shanghai with popular music in dancehalls, cabarets and bars. These musicians were usually refugees whose primary career had found no outlet within Shanghai's restricted economy.[53]

The professional artists rarely played in the cafes and bars. They attempted to enter Shanghai's serious world of music and in some measure succeeded, creating professional orchestras or arranging and performing at concerts for the refugee clientele.[54]

As early as the first months of 1939, refugee musicians

were giving recitals in both the Jewish club and the club at the Race Course. Several attempts were made, during 1939 to 1940, to create trio and quartet chamber music ensembles. Only one managed to gain a solid economic foothold.[55]

Many musicians performed as piano, violin, and vocal soloists. Among the more outstanding, for example, were Hans Baer, a pianist, and Ferdinand Adler, a violinist who had already won the coveted Ibach Prize in Germany.[56] Operettas were quite popular. Their light touch after a hard day's grind was found soothing. Such masterpieces as "The Merry Widow," "The Bat," or "The Count of Luxemburg" were among the numerous productions performed by such vocal artists as Rose Albach-Gerstl, Margit Langer-Klemann, and Erwin Frieser, among others. Margit Klemann also founded a popular woman's choir, which provided entertainment, as well as release from tension, for both participants and audience. There were some attempts to produce operas, such as "Cavalleria Rusticana" and "Carmen," but these were not too successful.[57]

Vocal music was not limited to the general field. Jewish music, both synagogal and folk, particularly folk music from the Holy Land, was a popular form of entertainment for the refugee community as well as for the Jewish Shanghailanders. Among the few East European artists to create a popular following among German refugees was Raya Zamina, whose frequent appearances with the comedian Herbert Zernik achieved great popularity. Her Yiddish and other folk songs bridged the almost impassable chasm between these two groups of refugees.[58]

The cantors, both with chorus and in solo, performed in the synagogue and in concert halls. A German refugee, Max Warschauer, Shanghai's chief cantor, was very popular both for his sacred music and his secular concerts.[59] Every sort of concert was performed, in rented halls, the synagogues, the clubs on the radio, and in the *Heime,* to which the many dozens of tickets and programs at the YIVO archives testify.[60] Many of these concerts were prompted by an organization of refugee artists and friends of Jewish culture, called EJAS (European Jewish Artists Society). Its aim was to further the welfare of the otherwise forlorn refugee artists. Its membership included musicians, actors, singers, etc.[61]

Another organization, with similar aims, but limited to musicians, was the Shanghai Musicians Association or SMA, which added "of Stateless Refugees" to its title during the ghetto period.[62]

About ten professional musicians found positions in Shanghai's Municipal Orchestra, while others taught in local schools, such as the Chinese National Conservatory, Shanghai University, or St. John's University. On both levels, the new arrivals raised the professional standard of their respective institutions. The Asia Seminar, a Jewish People's University, led by Y. Tonn, also engagaed a number of refugee musicians in leading positions.[63] Tonn, despite his oriental-sounding name, was really an accomplished German-Jewish Sinologist, who once sent a beautiful poem in Chinese to Chiang Kai-shek, during the post-war period.[64]

The period 1939-41 was thus one of adjustment in most areas of refugee cultural life, including the musical. Pearl Harbor, whose impact adversely affected all other areas of refugee life, had a less severe effect on the cultural sphere than did the establishment of the ghetto in 1943. The latter posed the greatest threat to the Jewish refugee community in general, and the musicians' livelihood in particular. Much of the already precarious refugee economy came close to a standstill in the crowded "restricted area," and the degrading system of ghetto exit passes limited outside employment. As a result, many musicians found themselves without jobs.[65] On only two occasions was permission granted by the Japanese authorities to conduct concerts outside the ghetto. It meant that the entire audience was permitted to leave the ghetto for these two performances, with special passes stamped by the Stateless Refugee Bureau, the administrative office in charge of the ghetto. A request for a third concert was turned down by Ghoya, one of the two key Japanese officials who was in charge of the distribution of such passes.[66] As economic conditions deteriorated during 1944 and 1945, the number of musicians forced to resort to street performances rose sharply though the serious professional never joined these ranks.[67] Some musicians maintained their contacts outside by obtaining their precious passes, while others tried in vain to eke out a bare livelihood within the ghetto.[68]

Attempts to produce concerts were hampered by both difficult economic conditions and the overzealous Japanese censors.[69] Even some of those concerts that had passed the censor were often disrupted by the ever-increasing interference of the police or *gendarme* patrols.[70] Still, the soothing effects of a yet pulsating musical life helped maintain the refugees' sanity in the ghetto under the most adverse conditions.

ZIONISM

As we have seen earlier, Zionism was no newcomer to the Shanghai Jewish scene with the arrival of the refugees, since both the Sephardim and the Russian Jews maintained their long-established "Ezra" and "Kadimah" organizations respectively.[71]

German refugee Zionists did not establish an independent branch until the fall of 1939. Then, as in many other areas, they formed a separate German-speaking unit of the Russian Kadimah branch, under the leadership of Dr. Bernard Rosenberg and Ossie Lewin.[72] In spite of economic pressures and a general ban against political activity, which prohibited recruiting members in the *Heime,* as part of the general ban against political activity, a vibrant organization was soon built up.[73]

Among the pioneers of the refugee Zionist organization were such men as Drs. Jacob Wachtel, Otto Koritschoner, Bezalel Roth, and Salo Guttman, who together founded the first independent Central European Zionist organization in Shanghai, under the name AZO "Theodor Herzl" (Allgemaine Zionistische Organisation) on September 9, 1939.[74] About one month later this organization was given official sanction by the Shanghai Municipal Council.[75]

During its early formative stage, the Theodor Herzl group succeeded in building up its membership and influence to such an extent that it seemed destined to play a major role in the life of the refugee commuity. During this brief period of about a year, it could boast of its own local in Hongkew, with branches in the Concession and Settlement; a membership of over 2,000 and a Zionist-oriented majority of representatives of the *Juedische Gemeinde.* Its headquarters housed a library and spacious rooms that were used for classes in Hebrew and Jewish history, by youth groups and a women's auxiliary.[76]

Its potential, however, was never realized. Factional disputes and personality clashes, among other factors, caused a decline, from which the organization never recovered despite several attempts at resuscitation during 1941. The conflicts gave rise to two additional splinter groups, which were named Zion Zioni and Zionist Association, respectively.[77]

A ladies' auxiliary of the Theodor Herzl branch was organized, but it was unable to maintain a regular program. It certainly could not match the very successful activities of its feminine counterpart in the *Juedische Gemeinde,* which will be discussed later. Only the youth groups called Brith Noar Zioni, under dynamic leadership maintained a strong and active organization.[78] Even during the ghetto period, it managed to publish its mimeographed English-language newspaper, the *Davar.*[79]

The outbreak of the War in the Pacific placed the Zionists in the untenable position of striving for political rights within the enemy's (Britain's) sphere. This limited their wartime activities to the purely social and cultural.[80] Some individuals sought unsuccessfully to win Japanese approval for the Zionist political ideology, by expressing it in terms of "Jews as Asians returning to their homeland." This view was not entirely foreign to some Japanese students of Judaism, especially the influential Capt. Inuzuka, behind whose desk there loomed a large picture of Theodore Herzl.[81]

All the warring Zionist factions continued their internal strife in spite of worsening wartime conditions and police survelliance of every activity. Only the necessity of all refugees to relocate to the ghetto in 1943 forced the three independent Zionist organizations to merge into a single unit, under the name of ZOS (Zionistische Organization Shanghai). A new election voted in Dr. Paul Parnes as president and Markus Halpern as vice-president.[82]

Even such purely mass cultural activities as the weekly Oneg Shabbat, the Purim or Hannukah gatherings, were cause for suspicion on the part of the Japanese authorities during the ghetto period, and were conducted at considerable risk. The headquarters of the ZOS in the ghetto at the "Hungaria" was demolished during the July 17, 1945 air raid, which left the organization homeless and weakened.[83]

REVISIONISTS

In addition to the previously mentioned Zionist organization, there existed in Shanghai a Revisionist (right-wing) militant Zionist party and its youth group the "Betar" (Brith Trumpeldor). These also began life in Shanghai as the German-speaking chapter to the indigenous Russian group in the French Concession as early as the end of 1938[84]

An independent Betar branch soon opened in Hongkew, which used the Ward Road Synagogue as its headquarters. Due to the para-military type of training emphasized by Betar, strict discipline and sports played a large role in their program.[85] Their fellow Betar members among the Russian elements frequently helped the refugees secure the proper certificates and documents of employment to enable them to get passes from Ghoya and Okura to leave the ghetto. For the same reason, many of the youth over 18 joined the Shanghai Volunteer Corps alongside their Russian coreligionists.[86]

With Pearl Harbor came a general slackening of membership, including resignation of refugees from the Shanghai Volunteer Corps.[87] Due largely to the inspiration of their Polish counterparts, the Betar saw a revitalized program and activities during the ghetto period. They made their home in quarters placed at their disposal by the authorities, in the SACRA *Heim* on Muirhead Road, which they shared with the "older" Revisionist groups.[88]

POLISH ZIONISTS

The Polish refugees included approximately 50 to 100 Zionists, representing almost every political shade and ranging from the Aleph and Bet groups of General Zionists to the Mizrachi, Poalei Zion and Revisionists.[89] Despite sharing these widely divergent opinions, the Polish Zionists remained fairly unified and active, a fact greatly admired by their fragmented German refugee counterparts.[90] This cohesiveness helped the Polish Zionists to gain greater influence with the Jewish Agency and the World Jewish Congress. In turn, this influence enabled the small group to secure a disproportionately large share of the Palestine Certificates while still in Kobe, Japan, and later in Shanghai.[91]

Their leaders, such as Ilutovich, Bergman, and Dobe-

kirer, were old-time Zionists from Poland and spoke excellent
Yiddish. They did much to help forge that high morale that was
the envy of the German Zionists.[92] One must remember that
the very same factors which contributed in general to the good
spirits of the Polish group worked also in favor of the Polish
Zionists.[93]

A presidium, representing the various factions, met when
circumstances warranted unified action on common problems.[94]

CONCLUSION

Perhaps the sheer volume and intensity of the numerous
cultural activities are indicative of something more than the
great reservoir of creative energies among the refugees. For the
harried refugee to read a German-Jwish newspaper, to hear his
mother tongue on the radio and to listen to familiar works in
music or on the stage, brought back a bit of home. At the same
time, it provided an escape from the harsh realities of life in
Shanghai, and served as a psychological release for a tense
community.

NOTES : CULTURE AMIDST WANT

1. See Brieger, "Kuenst". Cf. also "Cultural Life and Emigration", in *Almanac*, p. 64 [Almanac, "Culture"].

2. Brieger, "Kuenst".

Perhaps one day the achievement of one refugee, Charles Bliss, presently a resident of Australia, will be sufficiently recognized to refute the author's categorical statement. While in Shanghai, Mr. Bliss, a chemical engineer, invented an international symbol language, appropriately named, "Blissymbolics". This system combines symbols derived from Chinese ideographs, mathematics and chemistry, etc., which can be readily used to communicate with individuals of different nationalities and languages.

Presently the system has been successfully tried out in Canada as a technique for teaching cerebral-palsied children. See the *Melbourne Press,* June 30, 1970; *Melbourne Age,* March 29, 1975; *Time,* June 26, 1972. The author is indebted to H. Eisfelder for this information and copies of the aforementioned newsclippings. Cf. also Eisfelder-Kranzler, August 17, 1975.

3. Though Ezra died in 1937, his wife continued its publication until her death in 1941. Sopher, Interview. Cf. also Dicker, *Wanderers*, p. 67. The first edition after Ezra's death was edited by Rev. Mendel Brown, (as indicated on the masthead).

4. Harbin's Jewish, Russian-language weekly *Yevreskaya Zhizn* (Jewish Life) was edited by Dr. Abraham Kaufman, Harbin's foremost communal leader. See above, Chapter 2.

For various previous attempts by the Russian Jews to publish a newspaper in Shanghai, see the two basic bibliographies on the Jewish Press in China. The first by Dr. Rudolph Loewenthal, is titled *The Jewish Press of China,* which lists six titles of papers published at various times in Shanghai during the period of 1904-1939. Copy reproduced courtesy of the author. The second, more complete bibliography (in Yiddish), titled *Die Yiddische Presse in China,* by Oskar Rozenbes (YIVO No. 52), lists the same six newspapers. Excluding *Israel's Messenger,* published by the Sephardi community, leaves us with the five abortive publication attempts by Russian Jews.

A combined bibliography is found in the excellent, above mentioned, YIVO *Catalog*, pp. 19-23. See Appendix.

5. A set of 17 volumes of this newspaper for the period 1938-1941 is found in the *Institut fuer Auslandsbeziehungen*, 7000 Stuttgart 1, Charlottenplatz 17, Germany. Kranzler Correspondence, April 9, 1968.

6. La France, "Die Presse der Emigration", *Herald S.E.*, [La France,

"Presse"]. p. 11 (pseudonym of Alfred Alphonse Kramer, courtesy Gerechter). His excellent article is the basic source for this subchapter. See also *Drei Jor Jewish Chronicle in Shanghai, Unser Leben* (May 1, 1941), p. 1 (Yiddish Section, p. 2). Cf. also Birman to HICEM, January 16, 1940, p. 3 (HH XV C-5).

7. La France, "Presse". Ossie Lewin also edited the *Almanac 1946-47*, which contains many articles on all aspects of Jewish life in Shanghai, including his experience in the Bridge House. Also Friedlander, *Sieben*, p. 31.

The YIVO *Catalog*, p. 22, erroneously states that the *Jewish Chronicle* was a weekly from May 5, 1939 through 1945. See La France. The date for the *Shanghai Woche* is taken from the first issue of that paper (Levin Papers).

La France notes, probably with tongue in cheek, that no one knows who publishes the *Shanghai Echo* since no masthead is printed. *Ibid.* Obviously La France knew that Ossie Lewin was still the editor of the Echo, as well as of the above mentioned *Shanghai Almanac*. See Stanley Wood, "The International Press of China" [Wood, "Press"], *Almanac*, pp. 17-19.

A volume of the *Shanghai Woche* was reproduced by the author, courtesy of Mrs. Kattie Cohn, whose late husband Philip, edited the *Juedischen Nachrichtenblatt*.

8. La France, "Presse". See also Horst, Interview for information *re* Storfer's background and the Shanghai Jewish press in general. For observations of the competition from the *Chronicle*, see Friedlander, *Sieben*, p. 17.

9. La France, "Presse". *Ibid.*

10. *Ibid.* A complete set reproduced by the author, courtesy Kattie Kohn. For the "reading room" see Kattie Kohn, Interview [Kohn, Interview], June 18, 1975.

11. La France, "Presse". For the critical views of the *Morgenpost's* lack of Jewish identity, see *Unser Leben* (December 5, 1941), p. 1 (Yiddish Section). Also Kohn Interview. For the *Querschnitt* and *Sport* see Eisfelder, *Exile*, p. 18.

12. YIVO *Catalog*, p. 22. This newspaper is not to be confused with the above-mentioned postwar *Shanghai Echo*, the continuation of the *Shanghai Jewish Chronicle*.

13. See below, Chapter 15.

14. La France, "Presse". The April 1946 Special Edition of the *Shanghai Herald* has excellent articles on all aspects of refugee life in Shanghai. YIVO No. 68. It is incomplete, however, only pp. 1-26 extant, with at least five pages missing.

15. *Ibid.* Dr. Friedrichs was the Chairman of the *Hongkewer Aerzte Verein*. The five volumes were loaned for reproduction to the author, courtesy Dr. Friedrichs.

16. *Ibid.* Copy of this newspaper of February 1, 1946 in author's possession, courtesy of Dr. Loewenthal. See also copy of July 26, 1946 issue (YIVO No. 68). The masthead of the February 1, 1946 issue lists L. Cahan, M. Elbaum, and Fishman as "Editorial Committee"; Shoshana, *In Faier*, pp. 371, 383.

17. La France, "Presse". See program for "Autoren Abend" (YIVO No. 36).

18. Lewin, *Churban*, pp. 219-21, 226. Cf. also YIVO *Catalog*, p. 20.

19. YIVO *Catalog*, p. 20.

20. A. [dolf] Dreifuss, "Unser Theater" [Dreifuss, "Theater"], *Herald* (*S.E.*), pp. 13-14. Dreifuss, a director and critic, is our primary source of information concerning the German-language theater in Shanghai. See also *Alamanac*, "Culture"; YIVO folders No. 55, 56, 57, which contain many tickets and programs of both the German and the Yiddish Theater. Cf. also YIVO *Catalog*, pp. 18-19; Friedrichs, *Geschichte*, p. 96.

21. Dreifuss, "Theater", p. 13. Also *Almanac*, "Culture".

22. Dreifuss, "Theater", p. 13.

23. *Ibid.* No name of the particular *Heim* is given. According to the complete listing of plays by Dreifuss of the German language theater in Shanghai, 22 out of the 65 productions were directed by Friedmann. *Ibid.*, p. 14.

24. *Ibid.*, p. 13.

25. Ibid. Cf. also some of the tickets and programs to the performances to such shows as *Dreimal Hochzeit, Bunter Abend,* both at the Alcock Road *Heim,* or the *Bunte Buehne* (YIVO No. 55, 56); *Zentralheimleitung,* p. 10.

26. Dreifuss, "Theater" p. 14. Mark Siegelberg's play *Die Maskenfallen* was translated and printed in Australia, with an excellent introduction. See Siegelberg, *Pearl Harbor.* It presents a vivid picture of White Russian society in Shanghai on the eve of Pearl Harbor and the ensuing conflicts of loyalty within their ranks. It is also quite critical of the Japanese. This fact was responsible for its performance as a propaganda play in the British Press Office, under the latter's protection. See Dreifuss, "Theater", p. 14. A copy of the English version of this play in the author's possession, courtesy of Rabbi Walkin.

27. *Ibid.* Cf. also Shoshana, *In Faier*, pp. 291, 298, concerning the censorship of plays by the Japanese.

28. *Ibid.*, p. 15. For the "Boris Sapiro" venture, see Levin Interview.

29. The author's basic source for the Yiddish Theater in Shanghai is Rose Shoshana's oft-quoted diary, *In Faier*. Shoshana was the producer as well as

384 JAPANESE, NAZIS & JEWS

performer of many Yiddish plays. See also the programs for the Yiddish Theater alongside those of the German-language theater. YIVO No. 55, 56, 57.

30. The last Yiddish production until the end of the War in the Pacific, *Dem Umbekanten*, was played on May 2, 1943, just 16 days before the removal of the refugees to the ghetto. Shoshana, *In Faier*, p. 301.

31. Shoshana, *In Faier*, pp. 296, 293 and 292, respectively. The very successful American musical, "Fiddler on the Roof", was based on *Tevye der Milchiger*.

32. *Ibid.*, p. 327.

33. *Ibid.*

34. *Ibid.*, p. 323.

35. Dreifuss, "Theater", p. 14.

36. Shoshana, *In Faier*, pp. 292-93.

37. *Ibid.*, p. 291.

38. Horst Levin, *Rundfunk fuer die Refugees* [Levin, *Rundfunk*], *S.J. Chronicle*, p. 26. Levin is a very basic source for information concerning the German refugee radio programs. Subsequently the author received the MSS of many of the ghetto programs and other papers relating to this and other cultural activities of Levin, together with two detailed interviews. Among the programs was the MS of the inaugural program with the dates May 2 and 3, 1939. Levin noted that the program was presented on both days. See also Dreifuss, "Theater", p. 15; Hausdorff, *Das Musikleben der Immigranten* [Hausdorff, *Musikleben*], *Herald (S.E.)*, pp. 16-17; Friedrichs, *Geschichte*, p. 151.

39. Levin, "Rundfunk". For the Yiddish radio program, which lasted from November 1941 until Pearl Harbor, see *Dos Wort* (November 21, 1941), p. 1. This was an Agudist newspaper which appeared but sporadically. See copy YIVO No. 54. Cf also script for the Yiddish progress. Station XMHA, Div. of NBC (YIVO No. 54).

40. Levin, *Rundfunk* For the note *re* the large record collection, and for the contact with the Jewish doctors in the Chinese interior, see Levin, Interview. For example, Drs. Mosse and Hecht were among the "cooperating" physicians who had arrived in 1933-34. *Ibid.*

41. Gerechter Interview. Gerechter stated that the two were among the few communists among the refugees. The latter, after the war, became the ambassador for East Germany to Communist China. For other refugees working at various radio stations, see Dreifuss, "Theater", p. 15. See also Hausdorff, *Musikelben*, p. 17.

42. The author's main source for the artistic aspects is D. L. Bloch, *Aus Dem Schaffen Unserer Graphiker* [Bloch, Graphiker], *Herald* (*S.E.*), pp. 30-31. Bloch himself was one of the five artists.

43. *Ibid.*, p. 31.

44. Fritz Kaufmann, taped interview, July 15, 1969 [Kaufmann Interview].

45. We have records for a "Six Artist Painters" [sic] exhibit, which opened in December 1940, consisting of watercolors and paintings. It is possible, however, that group shows had been exhibited earlier. YIVO No. 55.

46. For the date and membership in ARTA, see YIVO *Catalog*, p. 18, which errs, however, in the last part of the organization's title, which it lists as "Association of Jewish Artists and Friends of Jewish Art" (italics author's). For the correct title of this organization, and rules for membership, see the flyer published by ARTA (YIVO No. 55). See also the ticket to the evening by entertainment sponsored by both the SMA (Shanghai Musicians Association) and ARTA. YIVO No. 44.

47. Bloch, *Graphiker*, p. 31. For an interesting composite of signs related to the ghetto, see *ibid.*, p. 30.

48. For the impact of the refugees on Shanghai's musical life, see the following: Hausdorff, *Musikleben*, pp. 16-17; Martin Hausdorff, *Von Gefuehlsgehalt der Musik* [Hausdorff, *Musik*], *Herald* (*S.E.*), p. 21. Alfred Kahn, "*Das Musikleben* in Shanghai" [Kahn, *Musikleben*], *S.J. Chronicle* (*S.I.*), p. 24; *Entwicklung des Musiklebens in der Emigration 1939 bis zur Beendigung des Pazifikkrieges* (The Development of the Musical Life [in Shanghai] from 1939 until the conclusion of the War in the Pacific) (a three-page typewritten, unidentified, manuscript in YIVO No. 32) [*Entwicklung*]; "Cultural Life and Emigration" ["Cultural Life], *Almanac*, p. 64; [Erwin Felber] "Prominent Artists and Musical Teachers at Local Conservatory" [Felber, "Musical Teachers"], *Almanac*, pp. 65-67; Henry Margolinski, "Musical Characters in Shanghai Commissions", *Almanac*, p. 68.

49. Entwicklung, p. 1. Also Friedrichs, *Geschichte*, pp. 68-70.

50. *Ibid.* Cf. also Hausdorff, *Musikleben*, p. 17.

51. *Ibid.*

52. *Ibid.*, pp. 16-17. Cf. also Felber, "Musical Teachers"; Friedrichs, *Geschichte*, esp. pp. 68-70.

53. *Entwicklung*, p. 2.

54. *Ibid.* Cf. also Hausdorff, *Musiklebens*, p. 17; Felber, "Musical Teachers"; Margolinski, "Musical Characters".

55. Hausdorff, *Musikleben*, p. 16.

56. *Ibid.*, pp. 16-17. Cf. also Kahn, *Musikleben;* Margolinski, "Musical Characters", "Musical Teachers", p. 66.

57. Hausdorff, *Musikleben*, p. 16. According to Dr. Friedrichs, an amateur musician himself, Margit Klemann was an outstanding opera singer and an important cultural asset of the refugee community. Interview. Also his *Geschichte*, p. 117.

58. *Ibid.* Cf. also Felber, "Musical Teachers", p. 66. For specific concerts by Raya Zamina, see, e.g., *Unser Leben* (May 15, 1942) (Yiddish sect.), p. 1. Cf. also Program of "Concert of Jewish Soup" (Yiddish) at the Shanghai Jewish Club featuring Raya Zamina and Mark [sic] Warschauer (YIVO No. 56); Levin Interview, August 6, 1974.

59. Hausdorff, *Musikleben*, p. 16. Cf. also Kahn, *Musikleben*; Felber, "Musical Teachers", p. 66. For the concerts given by cantors in general, see YIVO folder No. 32. It also includes information *re* the Association of Precentors.

60. See YIVO folders, Nos. 55, 56, 57, 58. For radio, see Hausdorff, *Musikleben*, p. 17; *Rundfunk fuer die Refugees, Shanghai Jewish Chronicle (S.E.)* (March 1940), p. 26.

61. *Almanac*, "Cultural Life". Cf. also Felber, "Musical Teachers", p. 66; Hausdorff, *Musikleben*, p. 17. *Unser Theater, Herald (S.E.)*, p. 13. Originally, the organization was called Artists Club, and consisted primarily of the Jewish artists. It was later broadened into the EJAS to include friends of Jewish culture. (Dreifuss, "Theater".) Cf. also FO S-9460-3-1519; October 29, 1939, correspondence between Dr. Dreifuss and the Japanese Consul, Y. Miura (DP).

62. Cf. the program for an evening of comedy (YIVO No. 44).

63. Cf. Felber, "Musical Teachers", Cf. also Hausdorff, *Musikleben*, p. 17. For the Asia Seminar, see *ibid.* Cf. also "Modern Adult Education at the Asia Seminar" ["Asia Seminar"], *Almanac*, p. 63; program of concert played by the students of Professor Chao Mei-Pa and Professor Lazareff in May 1942 (YIVO No. 12).

64. Friedrichs, Interview.

65. The specific effect on the musicians is found in *Musikleben*, pp. 2-3.

66. Ibid. For the "pass system" too leave the ghetto, see below, Chapter 17.
For the two concetrs, see the programs of these concerts for July 15, 1944 and August 2, 1944, the first a "shubert" night, the second a "Strauss and Lehar" (YIVO No. 58). See note on back of Shubert program.

67. *Musikleben*, p. 3.

68. See above, note 66.

69. For the censor, see Shoshana, *In Faier*, p. 291.

70. *Musikleben*, p. 3.

71. See above, Chapter 2. For the "Kadimah" organization, see Rosenfeld, *History*, II, pp. 5-6. For the "Ezra" organization and Zionism in general, see Alphons [Kraemer], *Der Zionismus in der Immigration* [Kraemer, *Zionismus*], *Herald* (*S.E.*), p. 5. Dr. Alphons Kraemer, who was later to be elected on the ZOS Presidium, wrote this and many other articles in his career as journalist, under the pen name Alphons. Gerechter, Interview. Cf. also "The General Zionist Organization of Shanghai" *Shanghai Almanac*, [GZOS, *Almanac*], p. 59; Otto Koritschoner, *Allgemeine Zionistische Organisation Theodor Herzl* [Koritschoner, "Herzl"], *S.J. Chronicle* (*S.I.*), p. 19.

72. Kraemer, *Zionismus*.

73. *Ibid*. Also Paul Komor, telephone interview, September 19, 1969.

74. Kraemer, *Zionismus*.

75. Koritschoner, "Herzl". The exact date was October 20, 1939.

76. Kraemer, *Zionismus*.

77. *Ibid*.

78. *Ibid*.

79. YIVO No. 52. An earlier publication, *Chaverim News*, published in 1941, was independent of the *Noar Zioni*. The author has been unable to identify the particular Zionist group which published it. See *Chaverim News* (July 1941), No. 4, p. 2.

80. Kraemer, *Zionismus*. Cf. also *Unser Leben* (October 30, 1942), p. 1 (English Supplement); Paul Parnes, *Die Kulturellen Aufgaben der Zionistischen Organisation* (unidentified news clipping, dated November 14, 1943), YIVO No. 29; various tickets to Zionist cultural evenings.

81. Kraemer, *Zionismus*. For the views of the Japanese "Zionists", see the confidential cable sent from London to the Joint (New York), ca. September or October 1942. (Context indicates this approximate period.) [Joint Cable, Repatriation, September 1942], p. 3 (JDCCA). See also Captain Inuzuka, *Japan's Stellung zur Judenfrage, S.J. Chronicle* (November 24, 1970), p. 7 [Inuzuka, *Judenfrage*]. See also above, Chap. 7 for the concept of Zionism in the *Weltanschauung* of this "Japanese antisemite".

82. Kraemer, *Zionismus*.

83. *Ibid*.

84. *Ibid*. Cf. also "Brith Trumpeldor in Hongkew" [*Almanac*, "Betar"], *Shanghai Almanac*, p. 59. This article gives the date as the beginning of 1939. This date probably refers to the establishment of the Betar youth group, as distinct from the Revisionist older element.

85. *Almanac,* "Betar".

86. Kraemer, *Zionismus.* Also F. Kaufmann Interview. For the Russian Betar helping their German counterpart, see "Shanghai, Betar", p. 87.

87. Kraemer, *Zionismus.*

88. *Ibid.*

89. Dobekirer Interview. Kraemer, *Zionismus,* cites the lower figure, while Margulies agreed that 100 was quite accurate. Interview.

90. Kraemer, *Zionismus.*

91. *Ibid.* These certificates were distributed by the Palestina Amt.

92. Kraemer, *Zionismus.*

93. See above, Chapter 12.

94. Such as an equitable distribution of the money sent from outside Shanghai, or the "Repatriation" schemes, for which the Zionists pushed hard, to gain as many representatives as possible. Another problem involved the struggle by the Zionists and the orthodox elements against the Polish assimilationists for Kashruth in the "Polish Kitchen No. 1", Margolies Interview.

SECULAR EDUCATION

*Happy laughter resounded again in a world that had
forgotten how to smile.*

(*Visitor to the "Kadoorie" School.*
L. Hartwich. *"Erziehung"*)

The education of the young was one aspect of their
life that shone brightly amid the generally dreary memories of
their stay in Shanghai. The refugee community, as we have seen,
strove fervently to brighten their own cultural life in spite of
the gloomy conditions in Shanghai. Even more so did they bend
their every effort to see that their children should not be educa-
tionally deprived. All the many differing factions among them,
as well as among the old-time Shanghailanders, gave a high
priority to education, and this accounts in a large measure for
the success of the schools. Perhaps even more did their good
fortune depend on the personal and very active interest of Horace
Kadoorie, a member of a prominent Sephardi family already
known for establishing educational centers in the Far East and
the Holy Land.[1]

One large school—free for those who could not afford
the tuition—and a smaller private school provided the three

389

R's for the majority of the refugee children throughout their stay in Shanghai. These two schools were going concerns, whose course ran relatively smoothly in spite of many difficulties. The problem of finding a suitable location, the forced evacuation and the search for a new home, the Japanese occupation, and finally the establishment of the ghetto and the ensuing financial crisis were among the hardships they faced and triumphed over.

About 120 refugee children, who arrived during the last months of 1938 and in the beginning of 1939, attended the old-established Shanghai Jewish School. Their tuition, when necessary, was paid for by the Shanghai Jewish Youth Association (SJYA) which was under Kadoorie's leadership, and a bus service was instituted to bring the refugee children in from distant Hongkew and elsewhere. Some of these children remained in the Shanghai Jewish School even after the refugee schools had opened.[2] Elementary school classes were also held in the Chaoufoong Road Heim under the supervision of the CFA.[3]

Since the Shanghai Jewish School was already overcrowded, it was obvious that a separate school would be necessary for the newly arriving refugee children. Furthermore, the old school's location in the Settlement, away from the *Heime* and the majority of the refugees, made transportation from Hongkew a major problem. Quarters were finally secured, by June 1939, in the recently acquired Kinchow Road *Heim*, which was turned into a lovely school, called the SJYA School, by November 1, 1939, almost exactly a year after the mass immigration had begun.[4]

The Kinchow Road building was originally a Chinese college, leased from the Shanghai Municipal Council, prior to the Chinese evacuation of the area during the 1937 hostilities. Through the influences of the Kadoories, the Council leased it to the refugees in mid-1939. The return in 1941 of some of the

Chinese who had fled Hongkew during the fighting of 1937, precipitated pressure on the Jews to return the building and the SJYA School had to find a new location for its now 600 students. Again, Kadoorie came to the rescue and helped raise funds required for a new building from the local Jewish community. New, and even more attractive quarters were secured at 627 East Yuhang Road, which were officially opened on January 2, 1942 (after the Japanese occupation), and this facility was often referred to as the Kadoorie School. It was justifiably regarded as the pride of the refugee community.[5]

An experienced staff of 17 teachers under the guidance of Lucie Hartwich, the headmistress, maintained high standards despite the war. In the opinion of one student, most of the teachers were excellent, despite the strict discipline they maintained. A few were considered below standard. In fact, in 1946, the seniors competed successfully in the official Senior Cambridge Examinations toward which the curriculum was geared, and those that came to the United States entered the university on this basis.[6]

The SJYA School was essentially secular in orientation, the language of instruction being English. Religious youth services were held on the premises on Friday evenings, and subjects such as Hebrew, the Bible and Biblical history were taught in an integrated fashion with math, art and history, etc.[7] The languages taught included Chinese, English and French. German was not included. Kadoorie, a British patriot, objected to any inclusion of the German language, despite its being the mother tongue of the overwhelming majority of refugees. Only after the transfer of the school's control to the *Juedische Gemeinde* after Pearl Harbor, when Kadoorie was no longer in authority, were German and Japanese introduced.[8] The language of instruction remained English, which increased the speed with which the youth learned this "foreign" tongue.

The school consisted of two kindergartens and nine grades, and a student body of about 600. Extension courses for those over 14 were also offered. The school's schedule was patterned after the European standard, which began at 8 a.m. and finished at 1 p.m., Monday through Friday. Many children, however, stayed on the school grounds during the afternoons to participate in sports, games or private instruction.[9]

Everything was done to help the children by maintaining a happy and healthful environment, which included the provision of special food, and games in spacious, airy rooms. They also had their own sports field and a flower garden from which they decorated their rooms. In the words of a visitor, "Happy laughter resounds again in a world that had forgotten how to smile."

A very strong beneficial influence on the youth was exercised by Leo Meyer, a well-known soccer player and sports figure in Shanghai's recreation circles. He was a great teacher, who encouraged sports activities among the young, for whom he also provided moral guidance. He helped many of them to avoid unsavory company in the nearby Alcock *Heim,* where those having contracted venereal diseases were maintained. The students under Meyer's tutelage who were "out of line" had to "play"—tossing the medicine ball with him—an experience they did not relish for a second time.[10]

SPORTS

Sports in general played a very important role in the lives of the refugee children as well as the adults; probably more so than it would have under other circumstances. For the adults, especially the many unemployed in the *Heime* and the even larger number idle during the difficult times of the ghetto, sports achieved the status of an obsession rather than as a mere pastime. People would spend their last penny for the inexpensive tickets, say, to a soccer match, and come in droves, with as many as 1,600 spectators, to cheer for their team or a particular idol on the playing field of Chaufoong Road *Heim*. It became the chief topic of conversation for many to create some excitement for an otherwise dull existence.[11]

The youngsters, too, found sports and gymnastics a very healthy outlet for their energies. Although their meager diet left much to be desired, in spite of the free milk and lunch at school, and they tended to be on the thin side, these youngsters eagerly participated in all sports activities. This included a daily period of gym with Leo Meyer, as well as games of all sorts during the afternoons and weekends.[12]

JEWISH RECREATION CLUB

The highlight of the adult sports scene were the exhibitions provided by the Jewish Recreation Club or the JRC whose top team in soccer, for example, competed with the best Shanghai could offer. The JRC began as a recreational and social club back in 1912, with both Sephardi and Ashkenazi finding a rare common ground in friendly competition.[13] With the arrival in Shanghai of many really talented sports figures such as Olympic boxers and professional soccer players, the JRC continued to provide this friendly atmosphere, where talent encountered no barriers. It was not long before the refugees began to dominate many of the sports, with, for example, eight out of 11 places on the soccer team filled by refugees. In boxing and ping pong, the refugee domination was even more complete. Thus, the sports scene was completely revitalized with the infusion of refugee talent.[14]

On the Jewish sports scene there were two major levels. The top teams, headed by the professional JRC team, played the best competition Shanghai had to offer. The Jewish League sponsored a variety of sports, eight teams in soccer alone.

Among these were such names as the *Barcelona* and the *Shang-hai Jewish Chronicle,* named after their sponsors, the popular cafe and the newspaper, respectively. In addition to soccer and boxing, there were teams and meets for handball, hockey, mini-soccer, gymnastics and chess.[15]

For the youngsters, there was a parallel setup called the Junior League where teams regularly compefed in all these sports. One of the major refugee sports events was the *Yom-Hamaccabi* (Day of the Maccabbi) sponsored by the JRC. From a program journal of the May 1940 event, we can get some idea of the scope of the sports and the names of the competitors. All ages participated in numerous track and field events. For the adults there was the added interest created by the guest teams such as "The Shanghai Municipal Police," "The U.S. Fourth Marines," "The Foreign YMCA," and "The British Military Forces," which competed against the "Jewish Team." Such meets, among others, brought the Jewish refugee athletes into contact with their peers among the diverse elements residing in prewar Shanghai.[16]

GHETTO PERIOD

The ghetto period did not pose a major threat to sports. Only at one point during the 1944-45 season was there a several-month suspension of all official sports activities which of course did not involve the school children at all. With the help of Mr. Toochinsky, the president of the JRC, who had good relations with the Japanese authorities, all the sports activities other than boxing were resumed.[17]

A clinic provided care for the children's health, while a Junior Club organized by Prof. William Deman, took care of their leisure time needs. The older youths, who had already left school, established a club of their own, known as the "SJYA ex-scholars club" on the premises of the Kadoorie School. There they participated in discussions, lectures, amateur performances of plays, dances and parties. During the ghetto period, these youths were provided with "group passes" to enable them to get to the school outside the "Restricted Area."[18] Many social functions were held in the school's beautiful facilities. Adding to the building's usefulness were the classes in English for over 1,000 adults, sponsored by the SJY Association.[19]

The smaller private Freysinger's Elementary and Middle School was founded in April 1941, by Ismar Freysinger, a German pedagogue. His school, with a staff of four teachers, provided a more Jewish-oriented curriculum than the SJYA school, as well as a good secular education, to about 100 to 150 students.[20] It struggled along on a small tuition charge until 1944, when the establishment of the ghetto and its ensuing economic crisis drove it, as well as the SJYA School, to apply for subsidies from the Shanghai Joint. The Joint continued to bear the major share of the financial burden of both schools throughout the remaining years of their existence.[21]

In addition to these two schools, several kindergartens were established, one of which was run by the I.C. Among the private kindergartens, the most notable was that run by Mrs. Alexander.[22]

Mention has been made of some extension courses offered to youngsters between 14 and 21 at the SJYA School. These youths were in the difficult situation of having completed only elementary school and were either unskilled or too young for a job.[23] Although some training had been previously offered at the Pingliang and other *Heime,* it had not been too successful. ORT, an international Jewish organization specializing in training Jewish youth in various trades, attempted to fill this need. When Ch. Rozenbes, a representative of this organization, came to Shanghai in early 1941 with the East European refugees, he immediately got together a group of the Russian

Jews, as well as a few individuals from the German refugee and Sephardi elements interested in establishing a trade school.[24] Opposition, on the part of the old-timers, who were skeptical about the possibilities of competing with the Chinese in any area of physical labor, had to be overcome before community support could be expected. Still, it was not long before some Chinese establishments, who hired such skilled refugee craftsmen, made it a point to advertise the "European skills" available at their shops.[25] The fact that the school did open and successfully maintain itself until the dissolution of the community in the 1950's, is indicative that a real need among the refugees was being ably filled through the work of a few dedicated individuals. It also demonstrated the possibility of cooperation between the East European and the German refugees, a rare occurrence in Shanghai.[26]

Beginning in September 1941, with a few courses such as locksmithing, carpentry and electro-fitting [sic], ORT gradually added 21 classes, including bookbinding, fashion designing, and gardening.[27] The student body averaged about 150 to 200, ranging from a low of 50 during the difficult period of 1942, to over 500 in 1944, when the Joint relief money again became available.[28]

One of ORT's most impressive achievements was a Complementary School for Apprentices, in cooperation with the Guild of Craftsmen, in 1943, which supplied the theoretical knowledge to the apprentices serving with the Guild's Masters.[29]

Adults were not neglected in the field of education. Several agencies, at various periods during the years in Shanghai, attempted to provide the refugees with a most important economic tool, command of the English language. Among them were the SJY Association which held its classes in its School; the Komor Committee (IC) which opened its School for Basic English in February 1941; and the *Juedische Gemeinde* whose

Juedisch Wissenschaftlichen Lehrhaus [sic.] taught English among its many courses, during the war years.[30]

English was also taught in the *Heime,* especially at the one on Chaufoong Road, which started out with a class of 30, but soon dwindled to eight. The truth was that the ordinary middle-aged refugee lacked the patience required to absorb a new language. They preferred to spend time directly on their economic pursuits, and for that reason the English classes which started out with a high attendance were inclined to peter out. This view was not too well appreciated or understood by many of the young men and women, who found it easier to pick up a foreign tongue and who had neither the responsibility of earning a livelihood nor the same difficulty in adjusting to a strange milieu.[31]

The most complete school for adults was the previously mentioned Asia Seminar. This institution, with a faculty of 60, including doctors, journalists, and other intellectuals, taught an amazing number of secular as well as Jewish subjects. These comprised many of the sciences, the humanities, and 16 languages, among them Indian, Hebrew, Chinese and Japanese, Sanscrit and Urdu, all taught on a very high level. One series of lectures centered around Classic Japanese, Chinese, Indian and Hebrew texts, the latter including Maimonides.[32] Though attendance at lectures ran at times as high as 70, the usual number was closer to a dozen.[33]

In order to provide a Jewish education for those youths who had already graduated from the SJYA, or had never had an opportunity to study Jewish subjects, the *Lehrhaus* offered many courses in Jewish history and allied subjects. The latter group included the 60 to 80 students who were enrolled in the Public Schools (i.e., private schools). The *Juedische Gemeinde* also established Extension Courses in commercial subjects such as math, advertising, etc., on the premises of the SJYA School.[34]

The picture of secular education for the refugees is not complete without mention of the Dancing School directed by the former dancer and ballet master, Justus-Keil-Pasqual, and the Gregg Business College founded by Professor William Deman, who promoted many other educational projects and whose facilities were used by the above-mentioned Professor Tonn to set up his Asia Seminar.[35]

The refugees' search for knowledge and intellectual stimulus was not limited to institutional channels. A number of book dealers, professionals in their homeland, opened up shops with both rare and contemporary collections, which catered to the refugees as well as the international clientele of Shanghai. Their relatively expensive imported books had to compete with the much cheaper and inferior, pirated versions produced locally. One of the refugee establishments, the Lion Book Shop, maintained a pay lending library. This library had the distinction of serving at the same time as a mecca for refugee teenagers, who had many lively debates and listened to numerous interesting lectures under the guidance of the staff. Other lending libraries soon opened, to satisfy the refugee demand for reading material on a variety of subjects. One enterprising gentleman opened a bookmobile, which eventually settled on the grounds of the Ward Road *Heim* and served over 1,000 customers. One book dealer specialized in Judaica and sold ceremonial objects among his wares. He even published a Jewish calendar for his customers.[36]

YOUTH PERSPECTIVE

After recounting some of the numerous ways in which the schools and other agencies tried to provide for the training and recreation of the children and youth of the refugee community, it will not come as a surprise to the observer to learn that the retrospective view of these former Shanghailanders is quite different from that of their parents. While most of the former refugees, at least among those interviewed, seem to recall the many difficult if not bitter moments of their experience in Shanghai, particularly during the ghetto period, this is not so for those who spent their early or adolescent years in that haven of refuge. As these youngsters, at the time, saw it, their Shanghai years were ones of "excitement," "a lark," or of "fascinating experiences." It would be useful to examine the experiences of these refugee youngsters to more fully appreciate this total variance in perspective with those of their elders.[37]

We have already touched upon the extra energies that were poured into the creation of viable educational institutions for the young on the part of the old-timers or newly arrived. This includes the Kadoorie and Freysinger Schools, the after-school clubs and the technical courses, both formal and informal, and on all levels. Nor must one forget the cultural and educational fare and plain good fun provided by such youth groups that ranged from boy and girl scouts, closely associated with their English (Sephardi) counterparts. One little song book, for example, published in 1940, by the 13th Group, "United Rovers" of the Shanghai branch of the Boy Scouts Association, contains 30 pages of melodies, in German, that raised the spirits of the youngsters at their frequent get-togethers and outings.[38]

Another cultural outlet was the heated discussions on the future of Palestine, the Jews and the methods of achieving a Jewish State, that were current fare at the meetings of Betar, Brith Noar Zioni or other Zionist youth groups. And here too, one notices the much greater contact among the diverse youth elements such as the above two groups which would frequently have their common gatherings and occasional field trips.[39] One of the latter events is recalled by one former boy scout member, in which several groups were taken on an outing to the suburbs of Shanghai.[40]

A concerted effort to work for the Youth Fund resulted in a number of charity affairs and concerts which were helped with money, time and talent by the refugees as well as the old-time residents, Sephardim and Russian Jews alike.[41] As we have seen, a youth home, modest by contemporary American standards, was finally built and named in honor of Rabbi Willy Teichner, one of the truly dedicated individuals working on behalf of the youth. The fact that a number of individuals such as Kadoorie, Teichner and others such as Professor Deman, Dr. Herbst, Major N. S. Jacobs and Leo Meyer, were involved with the youth, assured the success of such activities and enriched the memories of their youthful participants.

Not burdened by the economic cares, the linguistic deficiencies or the psychological traumas of their parents—even in the ghetto the children were treated well by the Japanese soldiers and civilians—it was a lot easier for the youth to view Shanghai as an exciting, rather than as a dreary place.[42] For them, it was not the daily routine in the *Heime,* of "what kind of beans are we having today," or "what victory have the Axis accomplished lately."[43] With a bit of curiosity, and the turn of a lane or two, one could enter the totally different world of a Chinese village, seemingly transplanted in the midst of a metropolis. There, one could savor some really exotic food and atmosphere that was a far cry from the bourgeois milieu of Vienna or Berlin or the depressing atmosphere of the *Heime.*[44] There were other varieties of free or inexpensive forms of entertainment. For example, as one refugee recalled, one could watch in fascination a Chinese funeral, with the hired wailing women, loud and strange cries, people dressed in white, and the burning of the deceased's household goods. Or armed with youthful curiosity, enjoy a Taoist procession in which penitents carried huge banners, had needles pinned into their arms, or balanced things on their foreheads, and occasionally even have some fun in a Chinese amusement park outside the city.[45]

What was perhaps of more lasting consequence for these youngsters growing up under circumstances where there were few toys, bicycles or frequent excursions to the movies, was the cultivation of intense and long-lasting friendships during the many club hours, sports, and organizational activities. As one interviewee wrote about this period,

> . . . it was this reliance on one another that was the basis for those beautiful friendships among the children, the kind that I have rarely seen in this country. Of course deprivation was present, but since everybody had more or less the same I doubt that we as children were very conscious of it.[46]

Perhaps the best commentary on the entire educational scene and the esprit de corps developed by these students and former students of the Shanghai milieu may be the future educational course they pursued in this country. If one small sampling, a graduating class of nine, may be used as an example, then the results are quite impressive. Out of these nine, including a few that interrupted their education at 14 for a few years to help supplement the family's income, seven completed their college education in the United States. These include two Ph.D.'s in chemistry, two M.A.'s in mathematics, one B.S. in chemistry, one in biology and one rabbi.[47]

NOTES : THE THREE R's

1. See Margolies to Pilpel, August 11, 1941, p. 4; July 2, 1941, p. 1. Cf. also Josef Zeitin, "The Shanghai Jewish Communal Association" [Zeitin, "SJCA"], *Almanac*, pp. 50-51; Ginsbourg, *Refugees*, p. 21; Friedrichs, *Geschichte*, p. 116.

For the institutions Kadoorie built in the Far East and Palestine, see the revised and enlarged version of Zeitin's article, titled "The Sephardic Community of Shanghai" in the *American Sephardi*, Vol. II (1968), pp. 73-76, especially p. 76, n. 2. For H. Kadoorie's work with the SJYA, both prior to and during the refugee period, see Barbash Files (YIVO No. 60).

Although Kadoorie was a member of the CFA and Chairman of its Educational Committee, he kept the educational project under his strict control, including all finances and fund raising. CFA Minutes, February 6, 1940, pp. 4-5. Kadoorie was also the only one who, in Margolies' words, "Ellis Hayim was uable to dictate [to]." Margolies to Pilpel, August 11, 1941, p. 4.

Though Margolies criticizes Kadoorie for wishing to have the school named for him, it is nevertheless true that his prestige and interest facilitated the raising of money for the upkeep of the school. For the "bus service" and students in the Sephardi-run institution, see Eisfelder, *Exile*, pp. 12, 24.

2. See CFA Minutes, April 23, 1939, p. 3. Also Speelman, *Report*, June 21, 1939, p. 4; Kann, *EE*, pp. 16, 32. For Kadoorie's leadership of the SJYA, see above, n. 1.

3. CFA Minutes, April 23, 1939, p. 3.

4. For the June date of the partial transformation of the Kinchow Road Heim into a school, see CFA Minutes, December 14, 1939, p. 5. See also Letterhead of the SJYA School dated June 25, 1941, with the address of 100 Kinchow Road (YIVO No. 44). Although most sources give the date for the opening as November 1, 1939, this date most likely refers to the complete takeover of the former *Heim* as a school. Cf. Lucie Hartwich, *Die Erziehung der Juedischen Jugend* [Hartwich, "Erziehung"], *S.J. Chronicle* (S.I.), p. 14. Lucie Hartwich was the school's headmistress throughout most of its existence in Shanghai. Cf. also "The SJYA School" ["SJYA School"], *Almanac*, p. 62. The article reads as if it were written by Lucie Hartwich. Ganther, "Seven Years", p. 4.

5. Margolies to Pilpel, July 2, 1941, p. 1. Although Margolies claims that prior to accepting the responsibility for financing the school, Kadoorie attempted to secure the money from the JDC, he did assume the responsibility after she made it clear to him that the local Jews could afford this expense by themselves. See also "SJYA School"; Ganther, "Seven Years", p. 4; Friedlander, *Sieben*, p. 43.

6. "SJYA School". Cf. also Ganther, "Seven Years", p. 4. The original curriculum of the SJYA School was based upon the plans submitted by the Superintendent of the Shanghai Municipal Council. Ganther, "Seven Years", p. 4. For the American experience concerning the entrance to the universities, the author is indebted to Mrs. V. Pardo. Pardo-Kranzler correspondence, August 5, 1975.

7. For a complete list of subjects taught, see report cards for the years 1942, 1943, 1946 (in the author's possession, courtesy Joseph Shallamacher). See also Hartwich, "Erziehung". For the Sabbath evening services held on the premises, see letter sent by Lucie Hartwich to the *Juedischen Kantoren Verband*, June 25, 1941 (YIVO No. 44).

The curriculum was very similar to that of the *Juedisches Volkschule* in Wuerzburg, Germany, attended by the author.

For the "personal" view see Kurt Fuchs, Interview, January 8, 1974. Mr. Fuchs, presently a psychologist, attended the SJYA School for several years.

8. Taped interview with Fritz Kaufmann, August 12, 1968. Kaufmann, who was active in the Juedische Gemeinde, particularly after Pearl Harbor, had many arguments with Kadoorie on this score. Interview. For the conditions after Pearl Harbor, especially for the "enemy nationals" including the British, see below, Chapter 16. Also Fuchs, Interview. For the Japanese, see Leo Meyer, taped interview, September 9, 1974 [Meyer, Interview]. Mr. Meyer taught gymnastics at the school.

9. Hartwich, "Erziehung". For the schedule and afternoon activities, see Meyer, interview.

10. *Ibid.* For the contrasting mood at the *Heime*, see above, chapter 5.

11. Meyer Interview. Cf. also Gerechter Interview. Many of the details of the refugee sports activities are found in the survey article titled the "Jewish Recreation Club" ["JRC"], *Almanac*, pp. 70-76. The short-lived *Sport* magazine, published during 1939, lists many of the events, big and small.

Most of the refugee newspapers also carried news of the major sports events. Ossie Lewin, editor of the *Shanghai Jewish Chronicle*, was a sports enthusiast himself. He sponsored the soccer team named after his newspaper, and he was active on it as a player as well. Meyer, interview. Additional information on Leo Meyer is found in an undated article titled "Die Kommende Fussball-Saison" from the *Chronicle* sometime in Spring 1940. Courtesy L. Meyer.

12. *Ibid.* Cf. also Fuchs Interview. For the Milk Fund, see above, Chapter III.

13. "JRC", p. 70. Cf. also Meyer Interview; Fuchs, Interview.

14. "JRC", pp. 70-71, 75. Meyer Interview; Fuchs Interview. Mr. Louis Greenberg from the Ashkenazi community was very active in promoting sports and in encouraging the participation of the refugees. *Ibid.* Also Greenberg, interview.

15. "JRC", pp. 70-75. Cf. also Meyer, interview. The second and third division teams were the Maccabia and Judea, respectively. *Ibid.*

16. Meyer, interview. Cf. also "JRC", *ibid.*

17. A xerox copy of the Macabbi journal is in the author's possession, courtesy of Mr. Meyer. *Ibid.*, pp. 70-71, 74. Also Meyer, interview.

18. For the scarlet fever epidemic of 1939, see above, Chapter 10. Also Hartwich, "Erziehung". For the "Junior Club", see CFA Minutes, February 6, 1940, p. 3. Cf. also Ginsbourg, Refugees, pp. 21-22.
The school clinic was run by Dr. Solomon and his wife. "SJYA School". For the "club", see Deman-Kranzler correspondence, October 22, 1974; Eisfelder, *Exile*, p. 53.

19. Speelman to Troper, December 14, 1939, p. 5. For some of the other "functions", see for example the Program for the *Feierliche Eroeffnung fuer die Jugend. Fortbildungs-kurse der Juedischen Gemeinde*, July 25, 1943 (YIVO No. 51); the Opening of the Fall Term of the Asia Seminar, August 25, 1945 (YIVO No. 51); "SJYA School".

20. Eventually over 500 students were educated in this school. See "A Short History of the School", a two-page history of the Freysinger School, on school stationery, October 1947, YIVO No. 51 [Freysinger, "History"]. Also "Freysinger's Jewish Elementary and Middle School" [*Almanac,* Freysinger], Almanac, p. 63; Friedrichs, *Geschichte*, p. 116.

21. See Ganther, "Seven Years", p. 4. Cf. also "Freysinger".

22. Ganther, "Seven Years", p. 4. Cf. also Rosenfeld, *History*, III, p. 62. The author believes that the kindergarten run by the IC was included among the two mentioned by Hartwich, "Erziehung".

23. For the cognizance of this problem on the part of the CFA, see CFA Minutes, April 23, 1939, p. 4.

24. See the ORT Minutes (YIVO No. 33), especially those of June 16, 1941; June 24, 1941. R. D. Abraham represented the Sephardic element. He was probably the Sephardi most involved in affairs involving both the refugees and the Russian Jews. Joseph Bitker, Oppenheim (also of the EASTJEWCOM), Kopelevich and Covit, and others, represented the Russian Jews, while Drs. Lesser and Rosenberg were from the German community.
Rabbi Ashkenazi greeted the newly founded organization, and as always, requested that the religious regulations not be disregarded. ORT, Minutes, June 16, 1941, p. 2. Most likely he referred to the observance of the Sabbath.

25. See above, Chapter 9. For the pride in the possession of "European" craftsmen, see Eisefelder, *Exile*, p. 52.

26. See *Unser Leben* (May 9, 1941), p. 1 (Yiddish Sect.). See also the plea for unity in the work of ORT. Minutes, June 16, 1941, p. 3.

This was one of the first concrete examples of Russian-Jewish support for the German refugees on a collective basis. See also *Unser Leben* (March 13, 1942), p. 1 (Yiddish Sect.).

27. See Chart I, p. 8 of *ORT in China 1941-1947* (YIVO No. 38).

28. *Ibid.,* p. 21. For the fluctuating number of refugees, see *ibid.,* p. 11.

29. *Ibid.,* p. 7. Also see *Guild of Craftsmen, Shanghai 1943-1947* [*Craftsmen*], pp. 7, 17 (JDCCA).

30. For the courses offered by the SJYA, see Speelman to Troper, December 14, 1939, p. 5. Also Kann, *EE,* p. 16. For the IC School for Basic English, see the ad in an unidentified news clipping, probably the *Shanghai Jewish Chronicle* (YIVO No. 51).
For the *Wissenschaftlichen Lehrhaus,* see correspondence and program dated February 18, 1942 (YIVO No. 51). English was taught in the language section of the opening of the *Elementar-Kurse* of the *Erziehungsdezernat der Juedischen Gemeinde Shanghai,* March 11, 1945 (YIVO No. 51).

31. Rosenfeld, *History,* III, p. 42. See also Friedlander, *Sieben,* p. 17; Eisfelder, *Exile,* p. 18.

32. See "Modern Adult Education at the Asia Seminar", *Shanghai Almanac 1946-47,* p. 63. Cf. also the program of the Asia Seminar *Volkhochschule* for the Fall Semester 1945 (YIVO No. 51). This links the texts used in that series of Chinese, Indian, Japanese and Hebrew literature series. Ganther, "Seven Years", p. 4; *Unser Leben* (October 9, 1942), p. 1 (English Supplement); Friedrichs, *Geschichte,* pp. 116-17.

33. Friedlander, *Sieben,* p. 43.

34. See the *Program der Fortbildungskurse der Juedische Gemeinde* for the period of November-December 1943 (YIVO No. 51) and the announcement for its opening July 25, 1943. See also the *Juedisches Nachrichtenblatt,* January 12, 1945, p. 2. (Copies of entire set of this newspaper made with the kind permission of Mrs. P. Kohn.) Eisfelder, *Exile,* pp. 53-54.

35. For the dancing school, see "Dancing School Pasqual", in *Almanac,* p. 60. Also Ganther, "Seven Years", p. 4. For the Gregg School, see Ganther, "Seven Years", p. 4. Cf. also YIVO *Catalog,* p. 18; ad in the *Almanac,* p. 63; Deman-Kranzler correspondence, September 12, 1974. For another dancing school, see Eisfelder, *Exile,* p. 39.

36. Ganther, "Drei Jahre", pp. 129-30. Also Ganther, "Seven Years", p. 18, as well as the ads in the *Shanghai Jewish Chronicle,* especially the Special Edition, *Ein Jahr Aufbau;* Friedlander, *Sieben,* p. 45. Four lending libraries are listed in the ADEB Classified Directory [*ADEB Direct*], Col. 104 (YIVO). Cf. also Eisfelder, *Exile,* p. 40; *Branchen-Register 1943,* p. 42 (copy reproduced by author, courtesy of Mrs. P. Kohn).

37. See, for example, the brief unpublished memoirs of Mrs. Karin Pardo, 1939-1947 [Pardo, *Memoirs*] of July 12, 1975, a copy of which was sent to the author. Cf. also Eisfelder-Kranzler correspondence, July 14, 1975; the taped oral memoirs of Mr. Ernst G. Hepner [Hepner, *Memoirs*], June 15, 1975, kindly sent to the author; Fuchs, interview.

38. Xerox copy in author's possession, courtesy of Mr. Hepner. Cf. also Hepner, *Memoirs*.

39. *Ibid.*

40. *Ibid.* Also Pardo, *Memoirs*. The British (Sephardi) Boy Scouts usually met at the SJYA School grounds. Abe Jacob, telephone, interview, June 30, 1975. An AZA chapter was formed sometime in 1940 or 1941 in which boys from all three groups participated. Mrs. Rose Horowitz-Kranzler correspondence, July 7, 1975.

41. The Youth Fund Committee was composed principally of Sephardi and Russian Jewish supporters. See, for example, the two small journals published by "The Youth Fund for the Grand Charity Concert for June 10 [1940?] and the Charity Ball scheduled for April 26, 1941, respectively. Copies in author's possession courtesy of H. Hepner. The ads give some indication of some of the supporters of these drives for the youth. In these, as in many other such drives, one always finds the names on full-page ads of such staunch friends, as the Ellis Hayim and D. E. J. and R. D. Abraham families, as well as smaller ads by numerous other Sephardi and Russian-Jewish supporteers. Rev. Mendel Brown, Ezra Shahmoon, Edward Ezra, Edmond S. Sassoon, Arthur and Theodore Sopher, among the former, and H. Kammerling, M. Birman, B. Chaikin, Klebanoff, Major N. S. Jacobs among the latter. An interesting footnote to Major Jacobs, the head of the Jewish Volunteer Corps, is the fact that he was a convert to Judaism. Abraham interview.

42. For the decent treatment of children by the Japanese, see Hepner, *Memoirs*. Cf. also Pardo, *Memoirs*. They also were quite liberal in granting permission for students from the ghetto to attend St. John's University outside the ghetto throughout the War in the Pacific. Eisfelder-Kranzler correspondence, July 14, 1975. Even Ghoya was nice to children. See below, Chapter 17.

43. Salter, interview.

44. *Ibid.* Cf. also Eisfelder, *Exile*, pp. 25-26.

45. Salter, interview.

46. Pardo, *Memoirs*.

47. *Ibid.*

15 | A *GEMEINDE* FOR SHANGHAI

RELIGIOUS AND COMMUNAL LIFE OF THE REFUGEES

> . . . *how they strove, out of their Jewish conscious-*
> *ness, to establish a kehilla, a "Gemeinde," that should*
> *satisfy their religious needs, help them to identify*
> *themselves with Judaism and restore some dignity by*
> *having duly elected representatives taking care of*
> *their interests.*
>
> (Dr. Kurt Redlich *to author. June 6, 1973*)

We have seen how divided the refugees often were, and how the very circumstances that might have united them (flight into common exile, fear of a common enemy) served often to tear them more apart. Yet one important common denominator was to help draw a sufficient number of them together to eventually form the single largest refugee organization in Shanghai, the Jewish Community of Central European Jews or, as it was better known, the *Juedische Gemeinde*.[1] Many of the refugees hailed from the large Jewish centers of Europe: Berlin, Munich and Vienna, where it was the norm to belong to *Einheitsgemeinde,* or unified Jewish communities, which covered the full spectrum of religious commitment from Orthodox to Liberal to Reform, and were even able to include nonbelievers. Unlike the American congregation, or synagogue, with very limited functions, the scope of the European *Gemeinde* (or Kehilla in Hebrew) covered a much broader range of religious and communal services and activities, including Jewish education, ritual slaughter, welfare, Jewish hospitals, the ceremonies, and the keeping of all statistics involving marriage, divorce, death, etc. Such *Gemeinde* were legally incorporated bodies supported by government enforced taxation from which were paid the salaries of the religious functionaries.[2]

THE SEARCH FOR A COMMUNITY

The *Juedische Gemeinde* in Shanghai did not, however, blossom into its all-encompassing structure and size overnight. Its start was rather inauspicious, and, even when on the road to some measure of success, it had to contend with numerous internal and external obstacles. Among the former were, of course, the lack of unity among the mass of newly arrived refugees, who came from diverse localities. Indifference was common, with many too preoccupied with their search for a livelihood to be concerned about reestablishing a community. A similar attitude of apathy, though for other reasons, prevailed among many of the "successful" refugees who resided in the Concessions. They tended to adopt an attitude of superiority toward their poor coreligionists who huddled in the crowded and dismal quarters of Hongkew.[3] Moreover, the numerous non-Jews (converted, or children of converts) and totally assimilated Jews resented being brought into a specifically "Jewish" organization.[4] Nor can one ignore the real difficulties posed by personality clashes and, worse, intra-group strife, that brought the *Gemeinde* close to disaster more than once, especially during the ghetto period.[5]

These internal problems were interrelated with and compounded by extraneous factors, which affected the refugees in general and the *Gemeinde* in particular. Foremost among these, as one astute participant observer noted, was the "schizophrenic concept" which governed the checkered relationship of the *Gemeinde* and the Japanese authorities, from its inception in 1939 until the end of the War in the Pacific. As viewed by the refugees at the time, this meant that while, on the one hand, they could only feel gratitude toward the Japanese for permitting them to enter Shanghai, thereby saving their lives, on the other hand, they could not help being sympathetic to the Allies, Japan's enemies, whose cause they espoused openly in numerous ways.[6] Nor were the refugees, at the time, able to comprehend the various attempts of the Japanese to utilize them for their own ends. Pearl Harbor, the establishment of the ghetto with its attendant change in the Japanese policy toward the refugees, and the use made of the Russian Jews to supervise the relocation to the ghetto, as will be noted, all these later developments were to have repercussions to a greater or lesser degree on the largest of the refugee organizations.

In addition, the *Gemeinde* had to consider at every step the views of the CFA, which looked askance at any "independent" groups, and of the Orthodox leadership of the older-Jews, including such individuals as Rabbi Ashkenazi and the members of the devout Abraham family, and even the large majority of the non-observant laiety who viewed the religious scene with a totally different *Weltanschauung*. To them, what was traditional was "religious," and any change in form or current, whether or not it had the sanction of decades of practice by German and Austrian Jews, was considered a deviation and damaging to the community. Rabbi Ashkenazi also looked with suspicion at what he considered "assimilationist" tendencies by many of the refugees.[7] These in turn thought that such suspicion simply reflected the rabbi's negative attitude toward the German refugees in general, but in this they were wrong. One has only to contrast the "splendid isolation" of Laura Margolies of the JDC, in her sumptuous suite at the Cathay Hotel, with the cordial hospitality extended to all refugees, by Rabbi Ashkenazi, the chief rabbi in Shanghai, in his humble apartment of four small rooms. And into this small apartment he took a total stranger, a poor refugee girl of assimilated background, to stay with his two daughters of the same age. This girl has testified that she was always treated as one of the family.[8]

It was simply a clash of different religious and cultural values. It created a situation where, as Dr. Zeitin has said, they simply talked on "different wavelengths."[9]

At first, as we know, while few in number, the refugees performed their religious practices within the existing institutions of both their predecessors, the Sephardim and the Russian Jews. In this they were following the example of the latter, who upon arrival in Shanghai had made use of the religious facilities of the still earlier-settled Sephardim.[10] During the winter of 1938 to 1939, the German refugees at first joined the services at the Sephardi Beth Aharon and Ohel Rachel, and the Ashkenazi Oihel Moishe synagogue.[11] As their number increased steadily, they requested permission to conduct their own services, within these synagogues, in their own familiar German rite. Such permission was granted by the leaders of the Sephardi and Ashkenazi communities under the general leadership of Rabbi Ashkenazi, whose only condition was that the services be conducted according to the Orthodox tradition.[12] As will be noted, this condition was to affect the relationship between the "establishment" and the future refugee communal organization.[13]

In cooperation with the CFA, and the Abraham family, Rabbi Ashkenazi was able to establish religious services and kosher kitchen facilities in the *Heime*.[14] In addition, he set up a *Beth-Din* (Rabbinic Court), which dealt with religious and rabbinic functions such as marriage and divorce.[15] In these activities, he involved representatives of the refugee body, for example, Dr. Josef Zeitin, who was ordained by Rabbi Ashkenazi and served as his liaison with the refugees on religious matters, The *Beth-Din* also was responsible for some general religious problems. It helped the refugees by making available kosher provisions such as salami and margarine, and had stands set up in the Chinese and Japanese food markets which the refugees frequented, where kosher meat and poultry could be bought.[16]

THE FIGHT FOR INDEPENDENCE

However commendable these efforts were on the part of Rabbi Ashkenazi and his Sephardi and Russian supporters, they were not satisfactory solutions to the religious needs of the majority of the refugees, whose "liberal" (equivalent to the left-wing American "Conservative" practice) upbringing did not allow them to feel comfortable in the Orthodox setting. The refugees, therefore, in their early attempts to establish their own religious institutions, ran headlong into the opposition of the early settlers. As a result, the refugees, with initial success, tried to walk the tightrope between independence in worship and avoiding any break with Rabbi Ashkenazi.[17]

Nevertheless, the groundwork for independent refugee services was laid, some time in March 1939, when individuals experienced in Jewish communal and social work, such as Leopold Steinhardt, Gerhard Gottschalk and Dr. Bernard Rosenberg, met for this purpose. They arranged for the first completely refugee services to be held on the *Shevuot* Holy Days, and these were held at the Broadway Theater with great success.[18] to maintain its ties with the CFA, the fledgling refugee religious organization was first formed as a separate Department of Public Worship of the Committee (*Abteilung Kultusgemeinde des Committee* for the Assistance of European Refugees) with Dr. Kurt Marx as liaison with the CFA.[19]

The next step to independence was taken in July 1939,

when the *Juedische Kultusgemeinde* was established under Dr. Georg Glass, and preparations were soon made for the coming High Holy Day services, which were held in the Broadway Theater and the Shanghai Jewish School.[20]

Though a typical Shanghai typhoon and flood greeted the refugees on their first High Holy Day (Rosh Hashanah) Services, this neither dampened their spirits nor diminished their gratitude for finding a haven from their oppressors.[21] The great success of these "German" services undoubtedly added to the refugees' desire for a fully independent *Gemeinde*.[22] But as neither Rabbi Ashkenazi nor the Committee looked with favor on such separatist ideas, friction soon arose between the temporary *Vorstand* (Board of Directors), headed by Dr. Glass, and the CFA. Nonetheless, sometime in November 1939, on Leopold Steinhardt's initiative, the die was cast and a clean break made with the CFA. Steinhardt was appointed chairman of the newly created *Juedische Gemeinde*.[23]

They had little financial backing and of course no prospects of support from their former patrons (the CFA), but the *Gemeinde* struggled to recognize itself, to seek a wider membership, and to embark on an ambitious program of religious and communal offerings.[24]

INDEPENDENCE AT LAST

Located in its own quarters on East Seward Road, the *Juedische Gemeinde* soon opened a Department of Welfare, which was to grow in scope, particularly during the war years. Eventually, other departments were established to handle specific problems such as youth activities, religious as well as secular education, cemeteries, etc.[25]

A shortage of rabbis made the task of providing all the religious services and rabbinical functions difficult. Its first rabbi, Dr. J. Winter, left Shanghai for the United States shortly after conducting his first services in October 1939.[26] He was replaced by Dr. Josef Zeitin. The other rabbis who served the refugees included Rabbi Karl H. Sober (he and Zeitin were the Orthodox rabbis), "Liberal" Rabbis "Willy" Teichner and Dr. Georg Kanterowski, and Dr. E. Silberstein, who was considered a member of the radical Reform wing, with extreme anti-Zionist views, He went as far as to preach the substitution of Sunday for Saturday as the Jewish day of rest. Rabbi Teichner was a dynamic preacher, who could deeply move an assembly by the eloquence of his sermons, especially in his appeals for the poor refugees in the *Heime*. He was greatly in demand as a speaker.[27]

Despite all the obstacles, the two years prior to Pearl Harbor was a time of progress for the *Gemeinde* toward its goal of establishing an *Einheitsgemeinde* to serve all factions of the community equally well. Many individuals rose to meet the challenge for their newly independent *Gemeinde*. Rabbi Teichner endeared himself especially to the youth, by his constant preoccupation with their problems. His untimely demise in 1942 was deeply mourned, and the new youth hostel was named The Willy Teichner *Heim*.[28] Others we shall come across again in different contexts; still others appeared for a brief time to make their contribution to the communal life in Shanghai. Among the latter, three who were probably the architects of the *Gemeinde*, and who shouldered its burdens through the difficult years until the end of the War in the Pacific should be singled out: Dr. Fritz Lesser pulled the *Gemeinde* through its initial difficulties until he fell into disfavor with the Japanese authorities after Pearl Harbor; Dr. Felix Kardegg succeeded him and held the *Gemeinde* together in the face of conflicting forces from within and without; and, finally, Lutz Wachsner, later with the Shanghai JDC, who as head of the important religious department, led the *Gemeinde* along its difficult path of independence, yet retained the respect and trust of Rabbi Ashkenazi and the Abraham family.[29]

Others involved in the *Gemeinde* in different aspects should also be mentioned: Dr. Otto Koritschiner, who later became prominent in the Zionist activities in Shanghai; Dr. Kurt Redlich, who worked for the *Gemeinde's* legal department and became one of the key figures on the Arbitration Board; Sigmund Fischel, who helped create an active *Chevrah Kadsicha* and assumed the presidency of the *Gemeinde* during the postwar period.[30]

LIBERAL CONGREGATION

Although the services at the Broadway Theater were conducted for the refugees by their own rabbi in their own rite, there were still many, brought up in the liberal tradition, who felt ill at ease in what they considered too Orthodox a service. These refugees wanted to form a Liberal Congregation, with organ and mixed choir.

Lutz Wachsner, in charge of the religious (*Kultus*) department, had early recognized the need for such a service within the *Gemeinde*. He hesitated, however, to introduce one for fear of a rift with Rabbi Ashkenazi. Now, this splinter group, headed by Hugo Alexander, insisted on creating a true liberal service, and they held their first service on Passover of 1940 at the Eastern Theater. Its overflow crowd was a clear indication of the need for such a congregation. Another such liberal service was held during the High Holy Days of that year, and for the Sukkot holiday, the newly formed *Juedisch-liberale Gemeinde,* headed by Hugo Alexander, engaged Dr. Silberstein as its rabbi.[31]

The very success of the liberal services engendered even more opposition on the part of the more conservative elements, both among the refugees and the older settlers, since this constituted a serious threat to the unity of the *Gemeinde*. When Lutz Wachsner discovered, however, that Rabbi Ashkenazi did not actively oppose the newly formed liberal service, he decided to find room for such services *within* the *Juedische Gemeinde,* under the dynamic leadership of Rabbi Teichner, in competition to the splinter group officiated by Dr. Silberstein. He succeeded in enticing back many of the new congregation even before its official demise following Pearl Harbor.[32]

ELECTIONS

On June 29, 1941, the *Juedische Gemeinde* held its first broad-based elections in which every faction was represented and in which over 1,000 men and women voted. This was probably one of the first truly democratic elections held in the Far East. It proved also to be the last important independent political act by the refugees as a whole until the end of the war, since events were to move quickly in other directions.[33]

The first organizational meeting was held at the estate of R. D. Abraham, the honorary president, with Rabbi Ashkenazi, Laura Margolies and the *Gemeinde* rabbis present. At that meeting, the 21 elected representatives (or board) chose the seven-male *Vorstand* (board of directors), which included Dr. Lesser as president and Dr. Felix Kardegg as vice-president. Dr. Kurt Redlich was selected as chairman of the board.[34]

The representatives were a cross-section of the refugees, who, in the words of one participant, . . . gathered in [its] leadership the strongly Jewish oriented: the religious men, the Zionists, the men experienced in politics and especially Jewish politics, the intellectuals. Though many of them were independent and many even well-off, some successful businessmen and professionals, in general it was a cross-section of the refugee population. The goal of these men was to create a Jewish representative body in the democratic tradition of the European Jewish communities, subject to the scrutiny of the members.[35]

PEARL HARBOR AND THE GEMEINDE

Pearl Harbor and the advent of the War in the Pacific on December 8, 1941, wrought many changes both in the internal and the external forces affecting the refugees. The dual allegiance which had compelled them to consider every action in terms of its effect on the relief organizations controlled by the old-time Shanghailanders, and in terms also of the Japanese authorities, now shifted strongly in favor of the latter. The fortunes of war had made many of the old-timers "enemy nationals," a term now applied to citizens of the Allied powers. And the Japanese were no longer as hampered by their policy of utilizing the so-called "Jewish power" to placate the British and the Americans. These were now their declared enemies, and the Japanese moved at once to acquire stronger control of the *Juedische Gemeinde,* and to eliminate the "undersirable"—or anti-Japanese—elements in its leadership. The *Gemeinde* was a natural choice for this purpose, since the authorities preferred to deal with a single, all-encompassing refugee body rather than the many existing relief and service organizations. From its former position as a voluntary, elected, representative body, with emphasis on relig- ious and communal affairs, it now became a political entity and the sole representative of the refugees in their relations with the authorities. Such a change in status was to have a number of negative as well as positive effects.[36]

Among the positive results was the broadening of its scope: it took over completely the religious services of the *Heime;* it finally eliminated the splinter group, the *liberal-Juedi- sche Kultusgemeinde,* thereby creating a genuinely unified and expanded *Einheitsgemeinde.* The financial resources and con- sequently the power of the CFA and the IC quickly dwindled after Pearl Harbor, and the *Gemeinde* created the *Patenschaft* concept to alleviate the distress among the poorest in the *Heime.* This method of raising funds was soon adopted by the first IC, and continued later by the Kitchen Fund.[37] Further, Dr. Kardegg tried, although unsuccessfully, to secure some kind of international status for the stateless refugees and to get them Nansen passports.* Moreover, as a result of outside pressures and isolation, following Pearl Harbor and later the establishment of the ghetto, the *Gemeinde* membership increased markedly.[38]

The negative aspects of its new political status, however, far outweighted the positive. The *Gemeinde* was now the organization which had to deal with the Japanese policies concerning the refugees, and this intensified the dilemma of those refugees who had openly expressed dislike of Nazi Germany, Japan's ally, and of Fascism in general, and who had now to find a *modus vivendi* with the Japanese without becoming collaborators. A dramatic event brought things to a head when Dr. Fritz Lesser, the *Gemeinde's* popular president, and Julius Weinberger of the *Vorstand*, were called in by Captain Inuzuka and asked to resign. Dr. Felix Kardegg, the vice-president, was asked to reorganize the *Vorstand*. The Japanese were evidently settling old scores, in which Lesser and Weinberger were considered *persona non grata* Dr. Lesser had displeased the authorities during the crucial SMC elections of April 1940. He had equivocated when Inuzuka had tried to make use of the Jewish refugees by persuading the *Gemeinde* to have its members vote for the Japanese. Weinberger was undoubtedly disliked as a member of the CFA with its British—or anti-Japanese—leadership, such as D. E. J. Abraham and Ellis Hayim.[39]

Although the *Gemeinde* complied with the Japanese orders, they did not let the incident pass without a gesture of defiance. Dr. Lesser was made the first honorary life member of the *Gemeinde*, and his appointment was reported in its newspaper, the *Juedisches Nachrichtenblatt*, on April 17, 1942. He was retained on the board, so that his experience was not lost to the *Gemeinde*. More serious interference into its affairs, and further acts of defiance by its leadership were to occur a year later after the proclamation of the ghetto.[40]

ARBITRATION BOARD

It is necessary to go back a little in time, to consider the legal status of the refugees in the International Settlement. They had been profoundly grateful, of course, after their recent traumatic experiences in Germany and Austria, to find themselves in a place where the authorities were the protectors of individual safety. But the rapid increase in the refugee community and their intra-group relations, made it imperative to have recourse to an indigenous legal-aid organization. This was especially evident in cases involving disputes between tenant and landlord, in the necessity of observing legal forms, and in the documentation of important acts or events. The unusual legal circumstances of international Shanghai aggravated this need.[41] The refugees had been German subjects (*Staatsangehoerige*) until November 29, 1941, and were now completely stateless.[42] They were, therefore, subject to Chinese law, even in cases of domestic relations. In this, they were unlike the subjects of countries with "extrality rights"—as the term was used locally— such as Britain, the United States, and Japan, These countries administered their own laws, including criminal, in their consular courts.[43]

It followed, of course, that for the refugees it was feasible to bring to court only very serious disputes. All briefs had to be submitted and all hearings were conducted in the Chinese language, and the cost of hiring a Chinese lawyer was prohibitive.[44] Not that the Chinese courts were necessarily unfair or unsympathetic by any means. For example, in one case the litigation involved a refugee en route to Shanghai. The firm, in accordance with the usual shipping contracts, requested that the case be tried in its home territory, that is Hamburg, Germany.

This was obviously impossible for a refugee from that country, and after his lawyer (a fellow refugee) explained this to a sympathetic Chinese court, the judge ruled that the case must be tried in Shanghai. Incidentally, the refugee won the dispute.[45] Moreover, it was not uncommon for bribery or "squeeze" to determine the outcome of a case; a fact of life in Shanghai which affected almost all aspects of business, dealing with the police and even the fire department.[46]

Thus, it became increasingly clear, at an early stage, that a refugee body of over 15,000 would have to be able to air and settle amicably the hundreds of petty, as well as important disputes that arose. The resulting machinery became so much part and parcel of the very woof and warp of the refugee community that it is difficult to envisage the relatively normal life in Hongkew without it. It therefore behooves us to give some detail to the development and functions of the Arbitration Board, To serve such needs, both the CFA and the IC had established the machinery to deal with grievances: the former created *das Schiedesgericht fuer Europaeische Emigranten* (the Arbitration Board for European Emigrants) in the summer of 1939, and the IC soon after formed a Conciliation Board, geared primarily to the needs of non-Jewish refugees. The latter concerned itself only with the first steps in settling disputes, by compromise; the *Schiedesgericht* included the process of arbitration as well.[47]

Both undoubtedly served a useful function in providing legal remedies for the harried refugees. That they were not more successful can be in part ascribed to the pressure imposed from above by the committees, run by well-intentioned local individuals who had little understanding of the refugee's problems or appreciation of his *Weltanschauung*. They never gained the complete trust and respect of the refugee body, and the outbreak of War in the Pacific, in December 1941, merely terminated already moribund institutions.[48] As we have seen, at this point the *Juedische Gemeinde*, the largest refugee organization, because it represented all the refugees, became in effect a political entity.[49] Its president, Dr. Felix Kardegg, formed and headed a committee of six refugee lawyers, in conjunction with the Association of Central European Attorneys, who proposed the establishment of an arbitration board, to set up the machinery for settling civil disputes among the refugees. They chose men who were respected authorities in their fields, and who also had greater empathy with the plight of the refugees.[50]

This organization, founded in early 1942, was called *das Schiedesgericht bei der Juedische Gemeinde*, the Arbitration Board in conjunction with the *Juedische Gemeinde*. The term *"bei"* (in conjunction with), instead of *"der"* (belonging to), was used deliberately to indicate the independent nature of the organization. This made it easy for both Jewish and non-Jewish refugees to make use of it. And further, it made it possible for key people on the former IC Conciliation Board to serve on the new panel.[51]

What kinds of disputes were most common among the thousands processed during its six years of existence? There were, of course, litigations between landlord and tenant, storekeeper and customer, small claims, and problems of inheritance (however meager the possessions might be). There were also cases of domestic harmony and strife, in other words, marriage (civil) and divorce. The marriage certificate was drawn up by one of the lawyers (in English) as part of a civil ceremony, before or after the religious ceremony, in order to meet the formal requirements of Chinese Law.[52]

Among the numerous scraps and disputes that occurred in the *Heime*, only the more serious were handled by the Arbitration Board, the minor ones being settled by the manager (*Heimleiter*). There were even instances where the residents sued the Kitchen Fund, a relief agency overseeing the *Heime,* set up after Pearl Harbor. These, of course, came up before the Board.[53]

Three steps were involved in the serious cases: first, a hearing before an arbitrator usually settled amicably by compromise. The results were formalized in writing and became a contractual agreement recognized by the Chinese courts. The next step, if a compromise was not reached, was for the litigants to agree in writing to place their case before an arbitration panel and to accept its decision. The panel consisted of a new lawyer arbitrator, who chaired the rather formal session, and two lay assessors, chosen from a list of prominent and respected communal figures such as Max Brandt, head of the Craftsman's Guild, or Sigmund Fischel, later president of the *Juedische Gemeinde.* The last step, if a compromise was still not arrived at, as was often the case, was to submit a written decision.[54]

At a later stage, a fourth procedure was added: an arbitration appeals court (*Ober-Schiedesgericht*), composed of a panel of five, and presided over by a former German District Judge, Dr. Alfred Laskowitz.[55] The law applied was Chinese Civil Code, not as strange to refugee lawyers as might be expected. Chinese law, as codified in the 1930 English version, had been based on the 19th century German code, with some later Swiss, Turkish and Italian modifications. And the English version of the code was also considered official. Even a German version was available, since a translation had been made years earlier by a similar arbitration board for the old German colony.[56] The fee for the lawyers' services was low, and on a sliding scale appropriate to the sums involved. Free legal service was provided when necessary, through the Association of Central-European Attorneys-at-Law.[57]

There were very few cases of other nationals suing refugees before the Arbitration Board, and these seem to have been settled amicably by compromise. These few were landlord-tenant disputes, involving Chinese, White Russians and Russian Jews. No cases are on record between refugees and Sephardim, or members of the old German colony. One episode involved a Japanese who sued a refugee, and who at first behaved in a threatening manner. However, as the Arbitration Board proceedings developed, he seems to have been impressed with the polite and dignified manner of the arbitrator, Dr. Schaefer, and after the amiable settlement, he departed with a deep bow of respect to the judge.[58]

The incident reflects the success of the Arbitration Board, in contrast to the attempts of the earlier versions provided by the committees. The people selected by the community itself were rated high in intelligence, integrity and especially in empathy for the refugee needs. As in the case of the development of other Jewish organizations in Shanghai, such as the *Juedische Gemeinde,* the early fumbling of the relief committees had to give way to indigenous talent among the refugees. The resulting institutions were then, in effect, recreated and maintained by an emerging Jewish community.[59]

The refugee physicians had had to adapt themselves to radical differences in sanitary and health conditions in Shanghai, and the attorneys also found the need for accommodation to their new environment.[60] The language barrier alone presented grave difficulties, and only one lawyer, Dr. Robert Michaelis, to the present author's knowledge, mastered Chinese sufficiently to be able to handle cases in the Chinese courts.[61] However, no examinations were required for the practice of law in Shanghai, and a number of refugee attorneys were able to represent their compatriots in the regular and consular courts, often teaming up with a Chinese lawyer to surmount the language barrier. Several of the refugees built up a sufficient reputation to be able to represent clients of other nationalities.[62]

The less distinguished eked out a living from the low fees paid for arbitration cases. Dr. Michaelis had organized the Association of Central-European Attorneys (*Vereinigung zentraleauropaeischer Rechtsanwaelte in Shanghai*), and about 100 refugee lawyers were members. Among the aims of this organization was the provision, by rotation, of legal services for poor refugees at the Arbitration Board, and it was here that many of the lawyers were able to serve.[63]

The success of this venture, actually the legal backbone of the refugee community, is evident in the statistics. In less than a decade, the Arbitration Board achieved a level of settlements in 85 to 95 per cent of their cases (depending on different estimates), all without recourse to the Japanese, who not only desired to impose their authority in these internal matters, but frequently demanded to do so. It is a true testimony to the remarkable self-restraint displayed by the Board and the refugees that they refused to assert their authority, even where desirable, at the cost of interference from the Japanese.[64]

THE CASE OF THE ROLLMOPS

One interesting case involved both the Medical Board and the *Schiedesgericht*.[65] Some refugees had started a business making a popular North German dish called rollmops. These consist of rolled herring filets marinated in spice with onion rings and whole black peppercorns. No herring were available in Shanghai, so they used small fish, some kind of whitefish, caught in the Wangpoo River. Their business was a hit; the fish was cheap and the German refugees had found a form of food with which they were familiar and could afford.

All of a sudden a new disease appeared in the refugee community. In this case, the liver seemed to be affected, and, in exchanging experiences and discussing case histories, the doctors soon found that only refugees from Germany seemed to be contracting the disease. They narrowed the field further, and found that everyone that had the symptoms had eaten rollmops.

The Medical Board took up the case and consulted with physicians who had been practicing medicine in Shanghai for a long time. An old Russian doctor came up with the answer: the fish were carriers of a parasite which invades the human liver. The refugees quickly named it the *Leber wurm*.

An official warning was issued against the consumption of such fish and the business of the producers and retailers of the delicacy was ruined. They brought suit for damages to the Arbitration Court, claiming that there was no clear proof that the rollmops were accountable for the liver worm. However, the Court dismissed the case after hearing expert testimony. It concluded that uncooked fish from the contaminated water of the Wangpoo were a health hazard anyway, and the Medical Board was only discharging its duty in warning the refugee population.[66]

LADIES' AUXILIARY

A very active and beneficial role in the Jewish refugee community was taken by the *Frauenbund,* a ladies' auxiliary, of the *Juedische Gemeinde,* under the leadership of Gertrude Wolff. From the time of its inception in 1940, to the dissolution of the refugee community, this group of dedicated women, whose membership at one point reached 1,000, dispensed services that brought cheer and comfort to many. Such services included visiting the sick, especially those older refugees who lacked both friends and family, supplying the poor with medicine and preparing special Sabbath and holiday meals. For a while, the women also ran a special kitchen for the needy at the *Gemeinde* headquarters.[67]

Until Pearl Harbor, much of the financial burden of this organization was taken care of by Mrs. Reuben D. Abraham, who, as we have seen, extended her philanthropic efforts to many areas of refugee life.[68]

CHEWRA KADISHA [sic.]

Among the most important functions of any Jewish community is the care and burial of the deceased, a task usually assigned to the *Chewra Kadisha*. The *Chewra Kadisha*, however, did not limit its assistance to the dead, but also extended a welcoming hand to the living, particularly the sick, the indigent and the old. In view of the importance of such a society in the Jewish community, and the fact that so many other organizations were formed even during the first months after the arrival in Shanghai, it is rather surprising that it took over a year and a half before such a *Chewra* was established in Shanghai.[69] The answer to this, according to one of the *Chewra's* former officers, was that the refugees depended on the Russian Ashkenazi community in this respect. Unable to afford their own cemetery, the German Jews were forced to pay the SAJCA for each plot in the existing Ashkenazi, Baikal Road Cemetery. Their own members also had to work under the supervision of the Ashkenazi *Chewra* when performing the burial rites on the refugee dead. Only with the organization of their own *Chewra Kadisha* by Friedrich Gluckstern of the *Juedische Gemeinde,* in August of 1940, and the purchase of their first cemetery on Columbia Road the following month, did the refugee community really become independent.[70]

A continuing rise in the death rate among the refugees necessitated the purchase of a second cemetery, on Point Road, which was inaugurated with great ceremony on November 16, 1941 by the CFA. It too filled up very quickly.[71]

The work of the *Chewra* was particularly noteworthy during two brief, but tragic periods of refugee life. The first occurred during the terrible heat wave of August 1942, when 31 refugees succumbed; the second was the air raid of July 17, 1945, when the wounded were rendered first aid and the dead buried.[72] Even at the cemetery, in the terrible heat, attendants from the ambulance corps (who carried the bodies on bicycle carts during the wartime gas shortage) were on the lookout for potential heat victims. One young man died in this manner at a funeral.[73]

As noted, the *Chewra* did not limit its activities to the dead, but performed many worthwhile services for the living. Though there was a women's division of the *Chewra,* in many ways its activities paralleled those of the Ladies' Auxiliary of the *Gemeinde,* with whom they cooperated in visiting the sick and caring for the poor. The popularity of the *Chewra* can be gauged from the membership rolls which rose to over 1,800 under Sigmund Fischel's guidance.[74]

ASSOCIATION OF JEWISH PRECENTORS (CANTORS)

Among the various religious and cultural functionaries in Shanghai after 1938, were about 20 cantors who served the Jewish community in different capacities. We have already noted the role played by Max Warschauer in the musical life of the refugees. He was also the chief cantor for the *Gemeinde,* conducting the liberal services held at the Kadoorie School of the McGregor Synagogue.. Some cantors performed the services in the *Heime,* while others found jobs in both the Ashkenazi and Sephardi synagogues, adding a more traditional flavor to the services of the old-time Shanghailanders.[75]

Since most of these cantorial jobs did not pay more than subsistence wages, the cantors were forced to secure second jobs. The majority found positions teaching English, Hebrew and/or music at either the SAJYA School or the *Talmud Torah.*[76]

To further their interests and security, the cantors,

like many other groups in Shanghai with common interests, formed the *Gemeinschaft Juedischer Kantoren Shanghai (Chew-rath-Chasonim-Association)* of Jewish Precentor [sic] in 1939, with 20 members.[77]

TALMUD TORAH

The approximately 500 to 600 Orthodox refugees in Shanghai were dissatisfied with the smattering of Jewish education offered by the otherwise excellent curriculum of the SJYA School. With the help of Rabbi Ashkenazi and a committee of his Russian and Sephardi supporters, originally called *Machazike Laumde Thauro* [sic], they attempted to rectify this situation by establishing a Talmud Torah. Essentially an afternoon religious school, the Talmud Torah provided a more solid Jewish education.[78] It opened in December 1939 with a student body of 35, and by 1941, it had increased to 120 students and a faculty of six. Eventually, by 1944-45, it reached a maximum of close to 300 students with branches in both Hongkew and the Concession.[79] The latter location was opened on October 18, 1942, with the view of reaching the children of the Russian Jews, as well as those of the refugees.[80] That some Russian children eventually did attend the Talmud Torah which their own community could not have established on their own, is still another indication of the strong cultural influence wielded by the Polish refugees on the Russians.[81]

The extremely varied background of the students compelled the curriculum of the Talmud Torah to provide for both the very elementary *Aleph-Bet* classes and more advanced classes for Talmud.[82] The Talmud Torah also provided special classes and group activities for youngsters on Sabbaths and Sundays.[83] Moreover, since the majority of the students came from indigent homes, the Machzikei Talmud Torah, the supporting agency, provided daily snacks, as well as periodic distributions of clothing and food on a wider scale.[84]

The Talmud Torah venture proved so successful, particularly after the arrival of the East European refugees, that it became necessary and feasible to provide still more advanced Jewish studies for its graduates. This matter was resolved with the establishment of an all-day Yeshiva, which specialized in higher Talmudic studies and was known as the Yeshiva Ketanah or the Far East Rabbinical College. This school grew within a relatively short time to about 30 or 40 students and a staff of four. The latter, headed by Rabbi Hershel Millner, the son-in-law of Rabbi Ashkenazi, were students of the large Mirrer Yeshiva in Shanghai.[85] The better graduates of the Yeshiva Ketanah entered the ranks of the higher yeshivoth in Shanghai, such as Mir, Lubavitch, or Lublin.[86]

Special effforts were made by students of these higher yeshivot to enlist the Sephardi children into the Talmud Torah and Yeshiva. This posed a language problem for a while, since the language of instruction at these two schools was either German or Yiddish, both foreign to the English-speaking youth. This hurdle was soon overcome by the zeal of these Talmudic scholars, who taught themselves English quickly in order to reach the Sephardim. After a period of intensive tutoring, about 15 to 20 Sephardi boys were able to enter both the Talmud Torah and eventually the Yeshiva.[87]

Such efforts found favor in the eyes of the Sephardi parents, and changed the formerly cool and condescending attitude on their part into one of friendliness and appreciation.[88]

BETH JACOB

If great efforts were required on the part of Rabbi Ashkenazi, his supporters, and the refugee scholars to overcome the initial opposition to the establishment of a Talmud Torah and Yeshiva Ketanah on the part of many fairly assimilated Jewish Shanghailanders, it proved even more difficult to establish a Beth Jacob, or girls' parochial school.[89] Opposition to the idea is understandable because such schools for girls were unknown even among the Orthodox Russian and Sephardi Jews. The Beth Jacob School movement had only originated and developed in Poland, in the two decades prior to the Second World War.[90] It took the concerted and dedicated efforts of a few feminine idealists from among the Polish refugees, such as Bessie Shaffran, and the help of Rebbetzin Ashkenazi, to change the negative views of the Jewish community into one favorable to such a novel institution.[91]

Two branches of the Beth Jacob school were eventually established, one in the Hongkew section, the other in the Concession, with a combined student body of over 100 girls. The school was fortunate in securing teachers from among the former students of Sarah Shenirer, the founder of the Beth Jacob Movement.[92]

AGUDATH ISRAEL

One of the catalysts in the growth of most of Shanghai's religious institutions, and a mainstay of its Orthodox elements, was the relatively small group of about 50 to 70 members of Agudath Israel, or *Agudah* for short. Part of a worldwide organization of Orthodox Jews dedicated to the "Observance of the Torah" ((Jewish Law and Traditions), the Shanghai branch began an active life in 1941, after an earlier abortive attempt on the part of a few German Agudists in 1939. Their success in 1941 can be attributed to the number of active Agudists who came to Shanghai among the Polish refugees, both lay members and students of the Yeshivot.[93]

Under the guidance of active leaders such as Rabbis Mordecai Schwab, Joseph Fabian, Naphtaly Horowitz, and

Prediger Cohn, the Shanghai Agudah played an important role within certain areas of the religious life, particularly education and Sabbath observance.[94] For example, the Agudah was an important factor in the establishment of the Beth Jacob school, It also played a primary role in the establishment of the adult evening lectures on Judaism founded by Rabbi Fabian (*Juedisches Wissenschaftliches Lehrhaus*).[95]

With the assistance of Rabbis Meier Ashkenazi and Shimon Kalish, (Hassidic Rebbe of Amshenov), the Committee *Machzikei Hadas,* the Agudah initiated a very successful campaign for the Sabbath observance. Through synagogue lectures, leaflets, newspaper articles and personal contact, they were able to convince a large portion of the community, both the store owners and their patrons, to observe the Sabbath. By the end of the war, over 50 per cent of the stores were closed on that day among a population containing only a small per centage of Orthodox Jews. This was accomplished in spite of general economic privation suffered by the refugees, and against their seemingly normal economic interests.[96] To encourage the public to patronize Sabbath-observing firms, the names of such firms were listed by the Gemeinde in its *Juedisches Nachrichtenblatt.*[97]

The campaign was, of course, not always successful, and the useful friction arose between the Orthodox, East-European Jews and some of the liberal German refugees. An elderly, bearded gentleman [Rabbi Kalish?] was observed approaching a German refugee and asking him to please refrain from smoking on the Sabbath. The refugee not only refused the request, but added that he had a private agreement with G-d whereby he was permitted to smoke on the Sabbath, so that he need not sin during the rest of the week.[98]

The Agudah also helped bring the Sabbath atmosphere to many refugees in the *Heime,* again with the help of Rabbi Ashkenazi, by providing them with supplementary Sabbath meals every Friday evening and Saturday noon at the Wayside Road *Heim,* within a religious setting. Funds for this purpose were raised by benefit concerts and the sale of "Sabbath-Host" tickets to supporters of this cause.[99]

MIRRER YESHIVA

The largest group among the East European refugees, and one whose presence probably had the greatest impact on the old-time Jewish residents, was the Mirrer Yeshiva. We have already seen some aspects of its incredible saga of escape from Russian-occupied Lithuania to Shanghai, via Siberia and Japan. Almost the entire Yeshia arrived in Shanghai from Kobe in August 1941, on the eve of the High Holy Days.[100]

Prior to their arrival in Shanghai, arrangements had been made with the recently formed EASTJEWCOM and Rabbi Ashkenazi to aid in settling the Mirrer Yeshiva.[101] The major refugee relief agency, the CFA, had done nothing to prepare for their arrival, and had even complicated relations with the Japanese authorities by failing to secure permission for the refugees to reside in Hongkew.[102]

A delegation of Russian Jews, headed by Rabbi Ashkenazi, greeted the Yeshiva and led them to the beautiful Beth Aharon Synagogue on Museum Road, where room was found for study as well as for meals.[103] Sleeping accommodations, however, presented a problem, which was not satisfactorily resolved until several months later, when the students were able to rent private quarters through aid from the Joint, JEC and the Vaad Hatzalah. In the meantime, the students slept on mattresses on the floors in the halls of the synagogues.[104] Since the seating capacity of the synagogue was exactly the same as the number of students, and the building had been used relatively infrequently in recent years, the students felt that the synagogue was now fulfilling its true destiny.[105]

The Yeshiva students, like many other refugees, experienced great difficulties in adjusting to Shanghai's radically different atmosphere. At one point about 70 students were stricken with what seemed to be an epidemic. After a doctor had carefully analyzed this epidemic, he allayed their fears by informing them that they were merely suffering from a lack of vintamin B, which could be supplied with larger rations of yeast.[106] One of the causes for the outbreak of this, and other illnesses which struck the Yeshiva students, was the extreme scrupulousness they exercised in their observance of Kashruth,* even under the most adverse conditions.[107]

While the financial burden was carried by a combination of subsidies from the Joint (via EJC), the Russian Jewish community (via EJC), and Rabbi Kalmanowitz, the Yeshiva quietly continued its uninterrupted schedule of study, 14 to 20 hours a day.[108] In the face of, or perhaps to some extent because of, discomfort and sickness and an alien environment, they delved all the more deeply into the "Sea of the Talmud" and its commentaries, which became a substitute for their lost families and homes. Study of the Torah also became their sole source of hope for the future. Even during the terribly hot and humid Shanghai summers, particularly following Pearl Harbor when air-raid security required all windows to be covered tightly during the period following the alarms, the students would study, with one towel tied around their heads and another in their hand to absorb the steady downpour of perspiration.[109]

Life in Hongkew for the Yeshiva involved the added dimension of a *Torah Weltanschauung* towards seemingly mundane and routine matters. For example, when, during the ghetto period, the Yeshiva was permitted for a while to leave the ghetto en masse for study in the *Beit Midrash* in the Beth Aahron Synagogue on Museum Road, there arose the *halachic* problem

---

* Rules for the *kosher* preparation of food.

of carrying the "exit passes" on the Sabbath, and pinning the lapel buttons on their coats. These were solved, for example, with the help of a non-Jew who carried the passes, and a ruling permitting the wearing of the lapel pin.[110]

In other circumstances, when the students felt uneasy, as did many of the refugees, about using the human-drawn rickshaws, they were enjoined by their spiritual counselor, the Dean of the Yeshiva, to use this means of transportation all the more. He reasoned that such abstention merely deprived the rickshaw driver of his chance to earn a livelihood. Rather, he advised, that they give, if possible, a large tip, and act as decently as possible towards him.[111]

Their unflagging spirit and enthusiasm became a source of awe and wonder to all who saw the Yeshiva at study. Their faith in eventual redemption was perhaps best illustrated by the words of a *Niggun* (melody), sung hours on end during one *Simhat Torah* (festival). While dancing with the Torah scrolls in their hands, they sang in Yiddish:

Fun danen treibt men uns arois
Und dorten losst men nit arein
Sog shoin Tatenyu,
Vee lang vet dos zein?
(Here we are driven out,
And there we may not enter,
Tell us, dear Father [in Heaven]
How long can this go on?)[112]

One of the problems facing the Yeshiva was the dearth of the Talmudic and other texts required for their study. While still in Kobe, they had received a shipment of 200 copies of the Tractate *Kiddushin* from the United States, through the efforts of Rabbi Kalmanowitz in New York.[113] After Pearl Harbor, when such shipments were no longer possible, they resorted to

other means. Original copies of needed texts were found in the
possession of the refugees, and copies were lithographed by
Chinese printers. Copies were also secured from the libraries of
the synagogues, and a few scholarly Russian Jews. Rabbi Ashkenazi headed a committee of Russian Jews who financed the
early part of the long reprint project.[114]

The first offset volume was the Tractate *Gittin*, a run of
250 copies being made during May 1942. The completion of
this first Tractate, marking a milestone in the history of Jewish
printing in the Far East, became a cause of public celebration in
the Russian-Jewish Club, which was attended by dignitaries of
the Ashkenazi community. Such an event would hardly have
been dreamed of even a year before.[115] One Polish non-observant
journalist who witnessed this scene, remarked that:

> One who did not witness the Amshenover Rebbe and
> Yeshiva students dance at receiving this marvelous gift, has
> never seen true Jewish joy and felt the secret of the Jew's
> eternity.[116]

This project, which eventually reached close to 100 titles, made
the Yeshiva students inadvertent pioneers in the reprint publishing trade.[117]

The first Tractate was soon followed by the entire
Talmud except for one title, the Bible and commentaries, Maimonides and other classics of philosophic, ethical and/or
religious nature. Even a few original works by Yeshiva students,
including two journals devoted to *Torah Novella*, were published.[118]

The small group of Yiddish writers and journalists also
participated in the printing venture, and many Yiddish classics,
such as Peretz and Sholom Aleichem, were reprinted. The group
also published original works of fiction, poetry and literary
criticism.[119]

The student body of the Mirrer Yeshiva was forced to relocate in the Hongkew area, following the establishment of the ghetto. Through the intercession of Dr. A. Cohn, the Yeshiva received permission, for about a year, to leave the ghetto every morning to study in the Beth Aaron Synagogue in the Settlement. While outside the ghetto, the Yeshiva students were able to use the *Bund* Garden, situated near the Beth Aaron Synagogue, and to enjoy a bit of nature not found in the ghetto, although a ticket had to be purchased for this. In fact, Kubota, in charge of the Bureau of Stateless Refugees, personally distributed the individual passes to the Yeshiva students. Since they had to be back in the ghetto by 11 p.m. to meet the curfew, the Yeshiva rented several rooms in Hongkew to use for the late evening study sessions, which often lasted until 3 or 4 a.m.[120]

For some unknown reason, this permission for the Yeshiva to leave the ghetto was restricted after about one year, so they temporarily rented an old, dilapidated structure, until a better location at a former hotel on Wayside Road was purchased.[121]. Many of the yeshiva students, with their unusual garb, beards and earlocks, made as profound an impression on the Chinese residents of Hongkew as they had earlier made on the Japanese in Kobe. The Chinese, however, due to their familiarity with the tall, turbaned, bearded and highly respected Sikh (Indian) police, assumed their smaller European counterparts to be related and referred to them as "little Indians."[122]

NON-JEWISH REFUGEE BODIES

On the opposite, extreme end of the religious spectrum of the refugee community in Shanghai were the 1,500 or so non-Aryan Christians, of Jewish or part Jewish descent, as determined by the Nuremberg Laws.[123] These refugees were cared for by the IC and the CFA without regard to their religious affiliation.[124] At the same time, some of the local Protestant missions offered aid to all the refugees in the form of rent-free use of their various properties, part of which were utilized for the *Heime,* as well as other forms of assistance.[125] The Catholics, however, were not as generous with their assistance. Their help consisted merely in the offer of housing to a small number of their coreligionists.[126]

Among the contributors to the various relief drives sponsored by the IC and the CFA were a number of non-Jews. The latter were also included among the original directors of the IC.[127] The CFA, through the Joint, made contacts with various American Christian relief agencies such as the American Committee for Christian German Refugees, which donated some money for the Shanghai refugees.[128]

Feelings, however, between the Jewish and non-Jewish refugees were not always very tolerant, particularly on the part of the more nationalistic East Europeans, who considered converts as traitors to their people.[129]

For their mutual benefit, the non-Jewish refugees organized themselves into the following four separate bodies:

1. The Shanghai Hebrew Mission;
2. The Quakers (Friends Center);
3. The Committee for Catholic Refugees and
4. United Mid-European Protestants.[130]

The Shanghai Hebrew Mission maintained an elaborate system of seeking converts among the Jewish refugees. For example, the fruit parcels sent to patients at the Jewish refugee hospitals were wrapped in the Gospel and other Christian doctrinal works. The Orthodox Jews were especially annoyed by the boxes of candy and toys offered to the poor refugee children during the Christmas season.[131] The mission also boasted of having enticed those refugees who were cut off from relief previously provided by the

CFA, which probably refers to the time, after Pearl Harbor, when the *Heime* no longer served free food to those outside the *Heime*.[132]

The mission also maintained a small *Heim* and conducted an elementary school called the Paul School, which taught English language courses to the refugees.[133]

The Committee for Catholic Refugees was under the direct patronage of the Bishop of Shanghai. They also maintained a *Heim* which sponsored many social and religious functions.[134]

The United Mid-European Protesetants was first organized during the summer of 1942, with Dr. L. Behrendt, a dentist, as their representative. Their aim was to incorporate all stateless Evangelic refugees in Shanghai who had come from Central Europe since 1933, and to preserve and propagate Protestantism. They, too, conducted much charitable and social work, including the operation of a free kitchen.[135]

Intermarriage was not a burning issue, since, according to the ERU Census, only seven families were required to remain in the ghetto because of the marriage of one of the partners to a stateless refugee. These involved three Chinese, one Portugese and three Englishwomen, married to refugees. We are not certain whether these refugees belonged to the Jewish or non-Jewish refugee element.[136]

CONCLUSION

Undoubtedly the refugees' spiritual heritage, whether of the "liberal" variety of the majority or the Orthodoxy of the minority, whether they were of German, Austrian or Polish descent, whether Zionists or anti-Zionists, secularists or Yeshiva students, provided the single most effective means of forging a relatively heterogenous, amorphous mass of refugees into a fairly close-knit community. Combined with the fact of living in a voluntary ghetto even before the "Proclamation," in the words of one participant:

> . . . many refugees experienced for the first time living in a closed Jewish society and that most of them liked it . . . [it] created a closeness in personal relationship and an intense Jewish life . . . being Jewish became more meaningful and Jewish consciousness was intensified.[137]

NOTES: A GEMEINDE IN SHANGHAI

1. The most detailed analysis and reconstruction of many aspects of the *Gemeinde* in Shanghai is found in the very comprehensive correspondence of Kurt Redlich to the author [Redlich correspondence]. Dr. Redlich, a lawyer from Vienna, was very active in numerous communal and civic affairs in the refugee community in Shanghai almost from the moment he stepped ashore in May 1939, until his departure for the United States in April 1948.

He was connected with the *Gemeinde* for his entire stay in Shanghai as director, elected representative, legal counsel and chairman of the arbitration board. He was responsible, among other things, for drafting the *Gemeinde's* by-laws together with Dr. Zeitin. He was also involved with the Craftsman's Guild, the Zionist organization "Theodor Herzl" and after the war, with the JDC as legal counsel. (See among his correspondence, especially November 12, 1975).

The author is greatly indebted to Dr. Redlich for his numerous suggestions, documents, criticism and general information, which have been instrumental in the author's revisions of this chapter. Still, the author accepts full responsibility for any statement or error.

2. For the geographic background of the refugees, see Redlich correspondence, August 25, 1973, pp. 1-2. The size of the *Gemeinde's* membership is found in *ibid.*, June 6, 1973, p. 6. Cf. also Heinz Ganther, "Das Religioese Leben" [Ganther, "Relig. Leben"], Herald (S.E.), pp. 3-4; "Unsere Juedische Gemeinde" [*Gemeinde*"], *SJ Chronicle (SI)*, pp. 18-19.

For the *Gemeinde* in Central Europe, see Kurt Wilhelm, "The Jewish Community in the Post-Emancipation Period," *Leo Baeck Yearbook II* (London: Leo Baeck Institute, 1957), pp. 47-75. Cf. also Arthur Ruppin, *The Jews in the Modern World* (London: *Macmillan*, 1934), pp. 343-47. See also Redlich correspondence, February 13, 1975, pp. 1-2.

3. For the superiority complex, see Redlich correspondence, December 11, 1973, p. 1; August 25, 1973, p. 3.

4. *Ibid.*, July 13, 1973, pp. 3, 5; December 11, 1973, p. 1.

5. See below, Chapter 18, Cf. also Redlich correspondence, February 27, 1974, pp. 6-9.

6. For the "schizophrenic concept" see Redlich correspondence, August 10, 1973, pp. 4-5.

7. Taped interview with Dr. Josef Zeitin, August 5, 1968 [Zeitin Interview]. Cf. also Ganther, "Relig. Leben"; Silberstein-Mars Interview; Redlich correspondence, Margolies to Pilpel, August 11, 1941, p. 4. Margolies character-

440   JAPANESE, NAZIS & JEWS

izes the Abrahams as "the only people who look at the refugees as human
beings instead of as the derelicts of the world . . . very charitable; but
absolutely blind on the subject of their orthodoxy . . ."

One may also add to these characterizations, Miss Margolies' anti-religious
feelings which are evident throughout her correspondence.

8. The "young girl" is presently Mrs. Malvens (nee Langberg) Rosengarten.
Phone interview January 22, 1975 [Langberg Interview]. Mrs. Rosengarten
noted that Rabbi Ashkenazi, noted for his strict orthodoxy, nevertheless
took into his household a girl from a then totally assimilated German-
Jewish family. Ibid.

For a comparison of Margolies and Ashkenazi, see Zilberpfenig, "Shagrire."
See also Margolies to Pilpel, May 28, 1941, p. 1.

9. Zeitin Interview.

10. Although, as Dr. Redlich pointed out, there was little help offered by
the Shanghailanders in actually starting the refugee organizations, nevertheless, many communal and religious groups began their activities as part
of the existing institutions. These include the various Zionist groups, and
religious functions of all sorts. See Redlich correspondence, August 30,
1974.

11In one instance, there was a permanent relationship between German
refugees and the Russian Jews. This involved the almost complete takeover
of the Oihel Moishe Synagogue at 62 Ward Road by the orthodox elements
among the refugees. This was so because very few Russian Jews remained
in Hongkew at this time. Even prior to the erection of the large "New
Synagogue" in Frenchtown there was a branch of Oihel Moishe there, due
to the earlier-mentioned shift of population. See above Chapter II.

Most of the refugee congregants of the 62 Ward Road Synagogue were
Orthodox German Jews of East European origin, who felt at home in this
setting and were welcomed there. Later, some of the Polish Jews who came
from Kobe joined this congregation. Rabbi Ashkenazi retained his overall
supervision of activities in the synagogue, though he only came there once
in a while. The refugee, Josef Shallamach, served as the cantor, while
classes in Talmud and other subjects were given by various refugee scholars.
Oral interview with Rabbi Boruch Borchardt, October 10, 1969, and subsequent dates. [Borchardt Interview]. Cf. also Zeitin Interview; Rabbi
Ashkenazi, "Ein Jahr Religioese Aufbauarbeit" [Ashkenazi, "Aufbau"], S.J.
Chronicle (S.I), p. 17; the special Hanukah services conducted at this time
in the same synagogue, in which the prayers and sermans were conducted by
refugee rabbis. S.J. Chronicle (December 9, 1939), p. 1. Courtesy Dr.
Zeitin; Redlich correspondence, August 25, 1973, p. 1; December 11, 1973,
p. 4. Cf. also Chapter 14 re JRC.

12. Zeitin Interview. Also Ashkenazi, "Aufbau"; Borchardt Interview.

13. See especially below, in this chapter, re the establishment of the "liberal" congregation.

14. Margolies to Pilpel, August 11, 1941, p. 4. Cf. also Ashkenazi, "Aufbau"; Weinberger, *Report* 1939, pp. 7-8, 13-14.

15. *"Beth-Din,* the Shanghai Jewish Spiritual Body" [*"Beth-Din"*], *Almanac,* p. 57. During this early period it was not technically a *Bet-Din* (Court of Jewish jurisprudence), since most of its members were not trained rabbis or scholars of Jewish law. The activities of the *Beth-Din* were restricted primarily to such "religious" activities as the arrangements for *Kashruth* (kosher or ritually-prepared or supervised food) in different institutions and business establishments. They also helped in the setting up of the Talmud Torah, etc., as noted below.

With the arrival of the East European refugee Torah scholars, the *Beth-Din* took on its more formal rabbinic functions. Borchard Interview. The following were the later representatives of the various groups: Rabbi Meyer Ashkenazi (SAJCA), Reverend Mendel Brown (SJCA), Rev. Dr. Josef Zeitin (German Refugees), Rabbis Joseph Mannes and Hersh Millner (East European Refugees). *"Beth-Din."*

The original *Beth-Din* included such laymen as Reuben D. Abraham, I. A. Toeg, Cantor Rotenberg and Mr. Plessner. *"Aufbau."* All marriages and divorces were under the jurisdiction of the Beth-Din, even after the *Juedische Gemeinde* and the "Liberal" *Gemeinde* were set up. No other authority in religious matters was recognized. *S.J. Chronicle* (November 20, 1940),an unpaginated article found in the YIVO No. 67. Also Borchard Interview.

16. Ashkenazi, "Aufbau." Cf. also Josef Zeitin, "The Shanghai Jewish Community [Zeitin, "Shanghai"], *Jewish Life,* Vol. XLI, October 1973, p. 58. Redlich correspondence, August 25, 1973, p. 3.

17. Redlich correspondence, *ibid.,* pp. 2-3, 5.

18. "Unsere Gemeinde" ["Gemeinde"], *S.J. Chronicle (S.I.),* p. 18. See especially Redlich correspondence, August 25, 1973, pp. 1-5.

Ganther, "Relig. Leben." Also an earlier version of Ganther's article published in his *Drei Jahre Immigration,* pp. 47-54 [Ganther, Rel. L-3].

19. Redlich correspondence, August 25, 1973, pp. 1-2. Cf. also Ashkenazi, "Aufbau"; Ganther, "Rel. L-3," pp. 48-49; "Gemeinde."

20. Ganther, Relig. "Leben." Cf. also "Gemeinde"; Redlich correspondence, August 25, 1973, p. 2.

21. For the typhoon, see Eisfelder, *Exile,* p. 22. The success is detailed in Redlich correspondence, *ibid.* Cf. also Ganther, "Rel. Leben"; "Gemeinde."

22. Redlich correspondence, *ibid.* Cf. also Ganther, "Rel. L-3," p. 49; "Gemeinde"; Ganther, "Rel. Leben."

23. Redlich correspondence, ibid., Cf. also Ganther, "Relig. Leben."

24. Redlich correspondence, ibid.

25. Ibid. Cf. also "Gemeinde"; Ganther, "Rel. Leben." Some aspects of the courses offered by the Gemeinde are discussed in the previous chapter.

26. "Gemeinde." Cf. also Ganther, "Relig. Leben"; YIVO Catalog, p. 13.

27. Zeitin Inter. Cf. also Ganther, "Relig. Leben"; "Gemeinde"; Zeitin, "Shanghai," p. 57. For Silberstein's views and Teichner's personality, see Redlich correspondence, ibid., pp. 3, 5; December 11, 1973, p. 7.

28. Ibid. Cf. also Ganther, "Relig. Leben."

29. Redlich correspondence, August 25, 1973, pp. 5; February 27, 1974, pp. 12;
See below in this chapter re some of the problems involved. See also Chapter 18.
Cf. also Ganther, "Relig. Leben" "Gemeinde, for the early days. Re Abraham, see Redlich correspondence, December 11, 1973, pp. 4, 5.

30. For Koritschiner and Fischel, see Redlich correspondence, August 25, 1973, p. 4;
For Fischel see also below re the Chewrah Kadischa; Ruth Fischel Interview. All the names are found in Ganther, "Relig. Leben"; "Rel. L-3";
Some aspects of Redlich's activities other than for the Gemeinde can be gleaned from some of the following correspondence. Leopold Steinhardt to Redlich, October 25, 1939; Rudolph Glaser to Redlich, April 10, 1940; Albert Trum to Redlich, May 1, 1940; Trum to Redlich, January 13, 1941; Bruno Prager for the Juedische Gemeinde, November 15, 1945; Karl Redisch to Redlich, May 28, 1947. All of these letters were by officers of the Juedische Gemeinde. Copies in author's possession, courtesy Dr. Redlich.

31. For the hiring of Rabbi Silberstein, see Silberstein-Mars Interview. Cf. also Redlich, August 25, 1973, p. 5. See ibid., for the development of the liberal congregation. Cf. also Ganther, "Relig. Leben"; Ganther, "Rel. L-3," p. 49; Zeitin, "Shanghai," p. 58. Zeitin calls it a Reform congregation, which is incorrect. Other than having an organ, this congregation maintained separate seating and their congregants covered their heads. Redlich Interview. There were choirs in all services, including the Orthodox ones, an old tradition in Germany, familiar to the author from his childhood days. See also Redlich correspondence, May 6, 1974.

32. Redlich correspondence, August 25, 1973, p. 5; December 11, 1973, pp. 6, 10.

33. Ganther, "Relig. Leben." Cf. also Redlich correspondence, December 11, 1973, pp. 4-7, for a detailed account.

34. Ibid. See also Juedisches Nachrichtenblatt, May 20, 1941; June 13; July

11; July 25, 1941. Copies of this newspaper reproduced courtesy of Dr. Redlich. The constitution of the *Gemeinde*, according to Dr. Redlich, was a "One-Chamber System," as in Switzerland, unlike the American Two-Chamber Systems. See esp. correspondence, February 13, 1975, p. 2.

35. Redlich correspondence, February 27, 1974, p. 3.

36. Ganther, "Relig. Leben." Cf. also Redlich correspondence, December 11, 1973, pp. 7-10.

37. Ibid. For *Patenschaft*, see p. 7. Cf. also September 6, 1973, p. 6. See circular re the origin of this means of fund-raising, distributed by the *Gemeinde*, dated January 11, 1942. Copy reproduced courtesy Dr. Redlich. For the later use of the *Patenschaft* by the Kitchen Fund, see below, Chapter 16.

38. For the Nansen Pass, see Redlich correspondence, February 27, 1974, p. 4.

39. *Ibid.*, December 11, 1973, p. 9. The identification of the Japanese officer as Inuzuka was given by the author. See Margolies, *Report*, pp. 2, 9 and *JRC*, p. 287.

40. Redlich correspondence, December 11, 1973, pp. 9-10. For additional acts of defiance, see below, Chapter 18. A copy of the article was sent to the author by Dr. Redlich.

41. The author's basic source for the history and work of the Arbitration Board as in the case of the *Gemeinde*, is the thoroughly detailed and analytic correspondence of Dr. Redlich. Dr. Redlich, as a founding member, who helped to write the rules and procedures for the Board, plus his experience as a lawyer-arbitrator, in charge of administration from 1942 until 1947, make him uniquely qualified as an authority on this subject. In addition to his experience, Dr. Redlich, where possible, backed up his contentions with documentation, of which copies were supplied to the author. These are all part of the author's Redlich Papers (RP).

For general background and history of the Board, see especially Redlich correspondence, June 19, 20, 1973; July 13, 1974; January 14, 1975; February 7, 1975. Among the other sources utilized by the author are: Hans Norbert Freundlich, "Das Schiedsgericht fuer Europaeische Emigranten in Shanghai" [Freundlich, "Schiedsgericht"], *S.J. Chronicle (S.I.)*, March 1940, p. 16; Victor Sternberg, "Die Rechtsverhaeltnisse der Emigranten" [Sternberg, "Recht"], *Almanac*, pp. 98-99; Victor Sternberg oral interview [Sternberg Interview]; Ganter, *3 Jahre*, p. 103 [*Ganther, 3 Jahre*].

For the legal background and problems for the refugees, see Redlich correspondence, June 6, 1973, p. 4; June 20, 1973, pp. 1-2; February 7, 1975, pp. 2-3. For some of the legal problems of the Settlements in Shanghai, see above, Chapter 2.

42. See below, Chap. 18. According to the "Table of Anti-Jewish Legislation in Germany 1933-1943" in the *Black Book* (insert p. 106), the date for the deprivation of citizenship of Jews residing abroad is given as November 25. RGBL, I, pp. 772 ff. The 29th was the date when it became publicized in those countries, as announced for example in a document from the *Schiedesgericht* (A Board) titled "Ausbuergerung," quoting the *S.J. Chronicle* of November 29, 1941. Copy in author's possession, courtesy Dr. Redlich (RP).

43. See above, Chap. 2. Cf. also Redlich correspondence, June 20, 1973, pp. 2-4.

44. Sternberg, "Recht." Cf. also Redlich correspondence, November 5, 1974, p. 2.

45. Sternberg, "Recht."

46. Eisfelder, Exile, pp. 19, esp. 22-23 (re judges), 20, 48-49. Redlich notes that Eisfelder's examples probably refer to criminal cases, whereas to his knowledge the little contact and the lack of bribery refer to civil cases. Correspondence, November 5, 1974, pp. 1-2.

47. Sternberg, "Recht." Cf. also Redlich correspondence, June 20, 1973, pp. 2-3; June 20, 1973, p. 2; Freundlich, "Schiedesgericht." Freundlich cites the exact title. The author has been unable to find the German title for the IC organization, and the "IC Kammer" came at a later date, in 1942; Ganther, *3 Jahre;* Margolies to Pilpel, September 26, 1941 (JDCCA).

48. Sternberg, "Recht." Cf. also Redlich correspondence, July 13, 1973| pp. 1-3.

49. See above, n. 36.

50. Redlich correspondence, July 13, 1973, pp. 1-2.

51. Redlich correspondence, June 20, 1973, pp. 2-3 Cf. also Sternberg, "Recht"; Ganther, *3 Jahre.* The setup and technique of the Board were modeled after the similar arbitration board procedures established for labor disputes in the Ruhr territory under the Weimar Republic in the 1920's. Redlich correspondence, June 20, 1973, pp. 2-3.

52. For the types of cases, see Freundlich, "Schiedesgericht." Cf. also Ganther, *3 Jahre;* Sternberg, "Recht." Redlich correspondence, July 15, 1973, p. 6. A copy of such a marriage contract in author's possession, courtesy Dr. Redlich.

53. Redlich correspondence, July 13, 1973, p. 3.

54. Redlich correspondence, June 20, 1973, pp. 2-3.

55. *Ibid.,* p. 3.

56. *Ibid.,* p. 4; January 14, 1975, p. 1. Dr. Redlich has also brought to the

attention of the author (and a xerox copy) the introduction to the English translation of the Chinese Civil Code. The two volumes, containing Books I-V, are titled *The Civil Code of the Republic of China*, translated into English by Ching-Lin Hsia, *et al.* (Shanghai: Kelly and Walsh Ltd., 1930, 1931).

57. Redlich correspondence, June 20, 1973, p. 3; June 19, 1974, p. 1. Cf. also Sternberg, "Recht."; Margolies to Pilpel, September 26, 1941.

58. Redlich correspondence, July 13, 1973, pp. 2-3.

59. *Ibid.*, pp. 1-2. Cf. also Sternberg, "Recht."

60. See above, Chapter X.

61. Sternberg, "Recht." Cf. also Redlich correspondence, July 13, 1973, p. 1; Michaelis, *Testimony.*

62. Redlich correspondence, July 13, 1973, p. 3. Cf. also Sternberg, "Recht."; Margolies to Pilpel, September 26, 1941.

63. See Redlich correspondence, June 20, 1973, pp. 4-5. Cf. also Sternberg, "Recht."; *Bericht* (Report) *der Juedischen Gemeinde an den World Jewish Congress,* June 24, 1946 (Shanghai). This valuable summary of statistical and other data concerning various aspects of the *Gemeinde's* work includes a brief half-page review of the Arbitration Board's accomplishments. Copy reproduced by the author, courtesy of Dr. Redlich (RP).

64. Redlich correspondence, June 20, 1973, p. 4; February 4, 1975, p. 4.

65. Redlich correspondence, November 5, 1974.

66. *Ibid.* As Redlich pointed out, this case points to the fact that the Board was involved with not only petty cases, but major ones, in which even the Medical Board accepted its decisions. Correspondence, February 20, 1975, p. 1.

67. *Der Frauenbund der Juedischen Gemeinde [Frauenbund]* (a two-page unidentified manuscript of a history of the Ladies' Auxiliary, dated February 12, 1947), YIVO No. 45. Cf. also Ganther, "Relig." Leben."

68. *Frauenbund,* p. 1.

69. Ganther, "Relig. Leben," p. 4. Cf. also "Chewra Kadischa for Immigrants" ["Chewra"], *Shanghai Almanac,* p. 58.

70. Interview with Leo Meyerheim, April 14, 1971. Cf. also "Chewra." Dr. Josef Schaefer became its President in 1941 and was succeeded two years later by Siegmund Fischel. *Ibid.*

71. See the Appendix for the mortality statistics. For the program for the Inauguration on November 16, 1941, see YIVO No. 28. Cf. also "Eine

446   JAPANESE, NAZIS & JEWS

Staette der Ruhe und des Trostes. Die Einweihung des neuen Juedischen Friedhofes," *Shanghai Jewish Chronicle* (November 18, 1941), p. 8 (courtesy of Dr. Zeitin); Friedrichs, *Geschichte*, pp. 163-64.

72. "Chewra." Cf. also Ganther, "Relig. Leben," p. 4. See below, Chapter XIX, re the July 7, 1945 air raid.

73. For the heat, and the deaths caused by this heat, see Friedrich, *Geschichte*, p. 164.

74. Ganther, "Relig. Leben." Cf. also "Chewra"; *Almanac*, "Chewra."

75. For Warschauer's contribution to the refugees' cultural life, see above, Chapter XIII. Other examples are Josef Shallamach who was the cantor at the Oiheil Moishe Synagogue on Ward Road, and Cantor Podrabenek who served the large, 1,000 seat capacity, Ashkenazi Russian "New Synagogue" at Rue Tenant de la Tour (Concession). Cf. also "Association of Jewish Precentors, Shanghai" ["Precentors"], *Almanac*, p. 58; "The Shanghai Jews Re-inspire Loyalty to Torah Yiddishkeit," *Orthodox Tribune*, Vol. V (December 1946), p. 15 [Yiddishkeit"].

For the services of the cantors in the *Heime*, see for example Lesser to Kantorenverband, March 1, 1942 (YIVO No. 26) and the many other documents in the YIVO Folder No. 32.

76. "Precentors."

77. See the letterhead, dated July 11, 1941 (YIVO No. 32). See also, for example, the correspondence of the *Gemeinschaft* to the IC, March 7, 1941 (YIVO No. 32).

Among the documents in the YIVO folder No. 32 are scattered sections from the minutes of this organization.

78. Ashkenazi, "Aufbau." The committee's English title later to be known as Committee of the Talmud Tora [sic], was originally called the Machasike Laumde Thauro [sic]. [Joseph] Zeitin, "The Talmud Thora and Beth Jacob in Shanghai," *Almanac*, for the older form of the title, p. 56 [Zeitin, "Tal. Thora"]; Birman, *Report*, January 16, 1940, p. 2; correspondence Chaim Drucker to S. Barbash, April 5, 1942. The letterhead gives a slightly different spelling for the title of the committee as Mahazike Talmud Torah (YIVO No. 60).

79. Zeitin, "Tal. Thora." Cf. also Ganther, "Relig. Leben," p. 4. For the 1941 figures, see the *Jewish Calendar 5702, 1941-1942* [*Calendar*] ([Shanghai:] Elenberg [1941], p. 2 (YIVO No. 50). Cf. also Chunah Hertzman, *Mirrer Yeshiva in Golus* (Yiddish) [Hertzman, *Golus*]. The Talmud Torah conducted classes at the Ward Road Synagogue, the Chaoufoong Road Heim and the Shelter House. *Ibid*. For the figure of 300, see below, n. 92.

80. *Unser Leben* (October 23, 1942) (English Supplement), p. 1.

81. See above, Chapter XII. It was the Polish refugees who provided the impetus for the Talmud Torah to expand far beyond its original scope. Borchardt Interview.

82. Zeitin, "Tal. Thorah."

83. Borchardt Interview.

84. Zeitin, "Tal. Thora." Also *Calendar*, p. 2; Drucker to Barbash, April 5, 1942.

85. Zeitin, "Tal. Thora." Cf. also Receipt (n.d.) of the "Far East Rabbinical College" (YIVO No. 60); *Calendar*, p. 3. The latter gives a pupil enrollment of about 20.
Rabbi Borchardt said that this figure of 20 must have referred to the earlier period of its existence. He claims that 30-40 is more accurate. Interview.

86. See Zeitin, "Tal. Thora." Also Schechter Interview. Borchardt Interview. Also interview with Rabbi David Schechter, October 10, 1969 [Schechter Interview]. Rabbi Schechter was involved in the establishment of this Talmud Torah and was especially close to the Sephardi youth.

87. Schechter Interview. Confirmed by interviews with Rabbis Borchardt and Walden. At least a half-dozen of these Separdic boys were graduated from similar institutions of higher learning in the United States and became principals of Day Schools, rabbis, and Talmudic scholars. For the example of the influence of the Mirrer Yeshiva on the Sephardic boys, see "New School Brings Oriental Background to Dade," *Miami Herald* (August 8, 1968), p. 17 (courtesy Pearl Kardon). Attempts to reach the Russian children were less successful. Schechter Interview.

88. Schechter Interview. Also Borchardt Interview.

89. For such opposition, see *Unser Leben* (March 6, 1942; also February 27, 1942, p. 1 (Yiddish Sect.)). Also Schaffran Interview. (Bessie Schaffran was the first organizer of the Beth Jacob in Shanghai. Walden Interview). For Beth Jacob School, see also Zeitin, "Tal. Thora"; Ganther, "Agudas Jisroel"; "Marat Zissel Eisenberg" (Hebrew), *Beth Jacob*, Vol. 8, No. 1 (2 Adar I, 1957), p. 7.

90. See Zvi E. Kurzweil, *Modern Trends in Jewish Education* (New York: Thomas Yoseloff, 1964), pp. 266-74. See also Isaac Lewin, "Religious Judaism in Independent Poland," *Israel of Tomorrow*, Leo Jung, ed. (New York: Herald Square Press, Inc., 1946), p. 393; Miriam Eisenstein, *Jewish Schools in Poland*, 1919-1939 (New York: Columbia University, 1950), Chapter 6.

91. See above n. 89. Interview with Bessie Schaffran, October 11, 1969. Shaffran, who arrived in Shanghai with a few other Polish refugees from

Japan a few months prior to the large Yeshiva groups, noted that she encountered less opposition after their arrival.

92. Walden Interview. Shaffran Interview. Borchardt Interview. Cf. also *Unser Leben* (March 6, 1942 (Yiddish Sect.)), p. 1, which places the number of students at 100. Based upon this figure, which the author deduced from the 400 given for the combined enrollment of the Talmud Torah and Beth Jacob, he arrived at the number 300 for the Talmud Torah. Hertzman, *Golus*, p. 25. See also Lewin, *Churban*, pp. 220, 224.

93. Ganther, "Relig. Leben," p. 4. Also Borchardt Interview. Here is still another example of the prevasive influence of the East European refugees on the Jewish communal life in Shanghai.

94. Borchardt Interview. "Prediger" is not a first name; it is the German title for preacher or the equivalent of the American "Reverend." The owner of such a title lacks rabbinic ordination. The author was unable to ascertain Cohn's first name.

95. Zeitin, "Thal. Thora." Cf. also Ganther, "Relig. Leben," p. 4; Borchardt Interview.

96. For the "Sabbath Observance" campaigns, see the following: *Juedisches Nachrichtenblatt* (February 16, 1945), pp. 1, 4 (YIVO No. 25); *The Word (Dos Vort) A Jewish Weekly for the Religious Revival in the Far East* (November 21, 1941), p. 3 (a sporadically appearing Yiddish weekly published by the Agudah in Shanghai) (YIVO No. 54); Leaflet circulated by the "Machzike Hadass" urging the women not to buy on the Sabbath, and a sticker identifying a store as "closed on Saturday" (YIVO No. 25). Invitation to a mass meeting at the Ward Road *Heim* Synagogue, November 19, 1941 (YIVO No. 27). For Rabbi Kalish's efforts in this campaign, particularly in the Concession, see Flakser, "Poilishe Yidn." See also Lewin, *Churban*, pp. 220, 224.

For the effectiveness of the "Sabbath Observance" campaign, see "Yiddishkeit," pp. 15-16; Naphtaly Horowitz, "Reiligiese Renaissance in Vayten Mizrakh" (Yiddish), *Orthodox Tribune*, Vol. V (December 1946), pp. 44-42. Borchardt, however, maintains that the 80 per cent mentioned in the former article is an exaggeration and that "over 50 per cent" is more accurate. Interview.

97. Numerous issues, such as the one noted above, carried these names. For an additional example, see the issue of February 2, 1945, p. 2. The *Gemeinde* as the publisher of this newspaper was of course an active partner in the Sabbath Observance campaign. See Redlich correspondence, December 23, 1975, p. 2.

98. Friedrichs, *Geschichte*, pp. 195-96.

99. See YIVO No. 27 for sample tickets. Cf. also *Unser Leben* (No-

vember 21, 1941) for an advertisement inviting fellow Jews to attend the *"Oneg Shabbat"* in the French Concession.

100. See above, Chapter XI

101. See, for example, the letter to Rabbi Ashkenazi from Kobe, 2 Sivan 5701 (May 1941) signed by the representatives of all the yeshivot and rabbinical groups. Cf. also Shoshana, *In Faier,* pp. 278-79. Birman to HICEM (Lisbon), March 21, 1941, p. 1 (HH XV C-10); Rottenberg, *Shanghai,* pp. 324-27. Or, the correspondence of Zorach Wahrhaftig to Rabbi Ashkenazi, from Yokohama, Passover Eve (April 11, 1941). Mr. Wahrhaftig, who was very active in promoting the evacuation of the yeshivot and other groups from Lithuania to the Far East, and the reemigration to Palestine *(Palestina Amt),* was later to become Israel's Minister of Religion. The two letters are part of the correspondence loaned to the author by Rabbi Joseph D. Epstein. Epstein Papers (EP).

102. See above, Chapter XII. For the "complications" see Margolies to Pilpel, October 26, 1941, pp. 1-3. Cf. also Inuzuka to Herzberg, September 17, 1941, pp. 7-8.

103. See for example the cable of Rabbis Ashkenazi and Schmuelowicz to Rabbi [Eliezer] Silver, August 27, 1941 (EP).

104. *Ibid.* Cf. also Epstein, "Mir," p. 127.
Prior to the arrival of the Yeshiva, this synagogue had been used as a refugee center almost two years earlier. See above, chapter 3. For the use of this synagogue by the Mirrer Yeshiva, see Epstein, "Mir," pp. 127-28. Cf. also Margolies to Pilpel, October 26, 1941, pp. 2-4; Hertzman, *Golus,* p. 22; EASTJEWCOM to SAJCA, September 9, 1941 (JDCCA).
For the arrangements of the EJC and the CFA with the U.S. Joint for granting aid to the East European refugees in general, including the Yeshiva groups, see above, Chap. 12. Cf. also Margolies to Pilpel, October 26, 1941, pp. 1-6, especially pp. 2-3, in reference to the difficulties encountered by Rabbi Ashkenazi in getting support for the Yeshiva.
A number of refugees supported themselves by renting rooms and/or feeding Yeshiva students. Fischel Interview. Gerechter Interview. Kunstliger Interview. Charles Kungstliger's parents provided such a private restaurant for Yeshiva students.
The remnants of a few other well-known European Talmudic centers of learning, such as the Yeshivot of Telse, Kletsk, Lublin and Lubovitch, were given lodging at the old Jewish "Club" at 35 Mulmain Road. Margolies to Pilpel, October 26, 1941, p. 4. There was also a group of about
—8 pt. TIMES Roman on 10 pt .BODY ——— — ....
70-80 rabbis from Poland to Lithuania among the East European refugees. YIVO *Catalog,* p. 14. The married among the Yeshiva students or rabbis were provided with private quarters in Hongkew or the Concession. Walden Interview.

105. Zackheim Interview. Cf. also Epstein, "Mir," pp. 127-28; Hertzman, *Golus*, p. 22. The latter source quotes an apocryphal story to the effect that the assimilated Sephardi magnate, Silas Hardoon, had built the synagogue as a result of a dream in which he was requested to do something for his own people. Furthermore, according to Epstein, it was hardly ever used prior to the arrival of the Mirrer Yeshiva.

Joseph Abraham, grandson of D. E. J. Abraham, claims that it was the latter who persuaded Hardoon to build this beautiful edifice, to replace the old Shearith Israel. Moreover, he maintained that the synagogue was used quite frequently for prayers until the 1937 hostilities. As a result of the fighting, a major shift of population ensued, and many Sephardi and Russian Jews moved from that part of the Settlement, near Hongkew, where the synagogue was located, to the Concession, a move which automatically limited its use. Interview. Cf. also above Chapter II.

106. Epstein, "Mir," p. 128. Dr. Abraham Seligson, a follower of the Lubovitch Hassidic Movement, was the unofficial "guardian" of the Yeshiva students' health. Epstein Interview.

107. See, for example, Margolies to Pilpel, September 10, 1941, p. 3. Cf. also Shoshana, *In Faier*, p. 298.

108. For the subsidies supplied by the Joint and the EJC both prior to and for six months following Pearl Harbor, see Margolies to Pilpel, November 9, 1941, pp. 1-2. Cf. also Margolies, *Memo*, November 5, 1941 (JDCCA); Margolies, *Report*, 1941-44, pp. 10-11. For the role of Rabbi Kalmanowitz and Vaad Hatzalah, see below, Chapter XIX. Cf. also Epstein, "Mir," p. 129; Lewin, *Churban*, pp. 229-30; Epstein Papers; the cables from the Yeshiva group (and individuals) to and from Rabbi David Bender. The author is grateful to the family of the late Rabbi Bender z"l, for giving him this collection. Bender Papers (BP).

109. Hertzman, *Golus*, pp. 25-26.

110. "Yeshivat Mir Begolat Shanchai" [Shapiro, "Mir"] (Heb.), *Beth Jacob* (March-April 1974), p. 4.

111. *Ibid.* For another refugee's qualms about the rickshaw ride, see Eisfelder, *Exile*, p. 25. The ghetto passes and buttons are discussed below in Chapter XVII.

112. Hertzman, *Golus*, p. 27.

113. Epstein, "Mir," p. 129.

114. Interview with Mrs. Meyer Ashkenazi. Cf. also Epstein, "Mir," p. 129; Interview with Rabbi Joseph Malinowski, October 15, 1969 (Rabbi Malinowski was involved in this reprint project).

See the margins of various volumes, e.g., the tractate Erubin, for Chinese printers' instructions. The financing of most of the later volumes was carried out by the students who collectively subscribed to the printing of a particular volume. In addition, many volumes were later printed by individuals as private enterprises. Malinowski Interview.

115. Epstein, "Mir," pp. 129-30. Cf. also *Unser Leben* (May 15, 1942) (Yiddish Sect.), p. 1; Lewin, *Churban*, pp. 226, 229.

116. Flakser, "Poilishe Yidn" (free translation from the Yiddish).

117. YIVO *Catalog*, pp. 23-25. Cf. also Epstein, "Mir," p. 130; Appendix.

For the "pioneering" aspects of the reprint field, see Samuel Gross, "Judaica Reprinting: Past, Present and Future," *Proceedings of the Fourth Annual Convention of the Association of Jewish Libraries, June 17-20, 1969,* pp. 22-27, especially p. 24.

118. YIVO *Catalog*, pp. 23-25. Cf. also Epstein, "Mir," p. 130.

119. YIVO *Catalog*, p. 25. Cf. also *Unser Leben* (May 29, 1942) (Yiddish Sect.), p. 1; (September 4, 1942), p. 1 (English Suppl.); Yaakov Fishman, *Farvogelte Yidn* (Yiddish) (Shanghai: Committee, 1948). Copy in author's possession, courtesy of Rabbi Shmuel Walkin.

120. Interview with Rabbi Abraham Krupnik, June 30, 1974. Included among the original documents presented to the author by Rabbi Krupnik is such a season's ticket, dated March 1, 1944—December 31, 1944.

For the group passes and the rental of rooms in the ghetto, see Epstein, "Mir," p. 131.

121. Epstein, "Mir," p. 132. Cf. also Gerechter Interview. Perhaps there is a correlation with the general suspension of "three-month passes" after the first year in the ghetto. See below, chapter. 18. The old building collapsed right after their evacuation. Epstein, "Mir," p. 132. Gerechter was the agent in the sale of this former hotel. Interview. Also Drucker Interview. (DP).

122. Eisfelder, *Exile*, pp. 21-22.

123. For the statistics of these non-Jewish refugees, see the Confidential Joint Report of October 28, 1945 [Joint, Report, October 28, 1945], which gives a breakdown of the immediate postwar statistics for the refugees according to the following religious groupings: Jews, 13,927; Catholics, 420; Protestants, 603; Others, 50; Total 15,000. These figures, though based on a census taken several months after the war, indicate about 1,000 to be the more accurate figure. However, an UNRRA list of statistics of refugees registering as of March 1946 gives a total of 15,511 out of which Jews amounted to 87 per cent and others 13 per cent, which would bring the figure closer to 2,000. This figure is substantiated by Ganther in his article, "Die Anderen Religioesen Gemeinschaften" [Ganther, "Anderen"], *Shanghai Herald* (Special Ed.), p. 4. However, the UNRRA figures also include 639

Italians, who were definitely not part of the refugee group we are dealing with.

The author, therefore, feels that 1,500 as a rough figure is probably correct. See also FOS 9460-3-1687 No. 159, January 19, 1940 for a lower estimate (DP).

124. See, for example, Speelman Report, June 21, 1939, p. 3; Katzki Memo, June 6, 1939, p. 2; Hilfsfond Report, p. 3; Joint (N.Y.) to Speelman, December 26, 1940; Kann, "European Refugees," p. 1; list of original directors of the IC, *Bylaws of the International Committee for Granting Relief to European Refugees* [IC Bylaws] (a six-page copy of the original charter), YIVO, No. 38, p. 1; Paul Komer Phone Interview, September 26, 1969.

125. See above, Chapter V.

126. Speelman, *Report*, June 21, 1939, p. 3.

127. See, for example, Speelman to Troper, December 14, 1939, p. 4. Cf. also Speelman, *Report*, June 21, 1939, p. 3; IC Bylaws, p. 1.

128. Speelman, *Report*, June 21, 1939, p. 3.

129. For example, see *Unser Leben* (October 9, 1942), p. 1 (Yiddish Sect.). Cf. also Shoshana, *In Faier*, p. 258; Lewin, *Churban*, pp. 224-25. Siegel, *Report*, November 4, 1945, p. 9 (JDCCA).

130. Ganther, "Anderen."

131. For such activities, see especially the publication of the Mission called *The Quarterly Mission*, of which the April 1941 issue is located in the YIVO No. 64 [Mission, April 1941], p. 57.

132. *Ibid.*, p. 56.

133. *Ibid.*, pp. 54-55.

135. *Ibid.*

136. *Unser Leben* (November 3, 1944), p. 1.

137. Redlich correspondence, August 30, 1974, p. 1; June 6, 1973, p. 6. Cf. also Didner Interview.

> *Due to the outbreak of the Greater East Asia War*
> *it has become necessary that our Jewish measures be*
> *subjected to reconsideration.*
>
> (*Japanese* Foreign Minister Togo to Shigemitsu,
> Ambassador to China, *January 17, 1942* FO
> S-9460-3-2516, DP)

On December 8, 1941, a few hours after their attack on Pearl Harbor, the Japanese fired on a British gunboat, HMS *Petrel,* moored in the Yangtze near Shanghai, the then lone symbol of former British naval power in China.[1] This action was followed by the complete and rapid occupation of Shanghai by the Japanese, with minimal resistance. For the first time, the "foreigners" were directly involved in the undeclared war in China.[2]

The "old China Hands" who had refused to leave, despite early warnings by the British and American embassies, on the grounds that "this too will pass away," suddenly found their whole world order collapsed. This order, in which the "foreigners" (or White Men) were superior to Orientals, would, in fact, never return.[3] The Japanese occupation of Sassoon's splendid Cathey Hotel, and of opulent foreign clubs, symbols of the foreigners' former reign in Shanghai, served not only to

453

accommodate the new conquerors, but also to convey to the Chinese open defiance of the rule of the White Man.[4]

A new chapter was to open also for the Jewish refugee community in Shanghai. The United States, their chief source of relief funds, was now at war with Japan. The wealthy Sephardim had become "enemy nationals." And the Japanese authorities themselves were changing their policy toward the Jews. This change was to reach its climax in the proclamation of the ghetto, but that was still almost two years off.

The speed and thoroughness with which the Japanese occupied every part of Shanghai is evidence of careful preparation.[5] Thus, already on the morning after Pearl Harbor, the Japanese forces displayed their might by marching long columns of troops and light tanks throughout Shanghai. Moreover,

> Proclamations, made to look handwritten, but printed, with only the date inserted by hand and obviously prepared well in advance, informed the population that Japan was at war with the USA and Britain. It promised that law and order would be maintained and that everyone was to carry on as before the occupation.

Enemy nationals, such as Americans, British and Dutch, were allowed relative freedom for the time being, but were warned that internment was not far off.[6] Red armbands were distributed to them and all foreign businesses were now supervised by Japanese managers.[7] Bank accounts were frozen, except for small withdrawals for living expenses, and all short-wave radios were confiscated, unless the short-wave attachment was removed. Most newspapers, especially those with a record of anti-Japanese views, ceased publication. A few journalists known for such opinions were whisked out of Shanghai to Australia, by an English ship, one step ahead of the Japanese occupation. Among these was a refugee journalist and writer named Mark Siegelberg.

Gasoline quickly disappeared and the few substitutes that were tried were not very successful. Buses ceased operation and most goods were carried in heavy, two-wheel cars, which were pulled by as many of the readily-available coolies as necessary. The bicycle became a socially-acceptable means of transportation, used even by the well-to-do foreigners.[8]

Notices were soon posted to the effect that all British and Americans had to register with the Japanese *gendarmerie* no later than December 13, 1942, which made them, within the year, liable to internment in special camps.[9]

How did this Japanese occupation affect the Jewish refugees and residents? About one-third of the Sephardi Jews, as we know, had chosen British protection or citizenship; the rest held either Iraqi papers or were stateless.[10] The former group included most of the wealthier elements, who were in communal leadership and in the refugee committee.[11] They had long been at odds with the Shanghai Japanese authorities because of their open pro-British stand, and their policy of ignoring Japanese regulations concerning the illegal movement of refugees into Hongkew.[12]

As they were *personæ non gratæ* with the Japanese, and were, in any case, preoccupied with the effort of salvaging the remains of their enterprises, now under Japanese overseers, the Sephardi leaders withdrew almost completely from relief affairs.[13] Members of the Ashkenazi and refugee communities had to take over. Ironically, the "stateless" newcomers enjoyed a more privileged status than the enemy nationals.[14]

The outbreak of the war in Europe, in September 1939, had had no appreciable effect either on refugee immigration or on their life in Shanghai. Nor was communication cut off, and some of the products and services provided by the refugees were greatly sought after when they were no longer available from Europe. For instance, one product in great demand and whose price soon skyrocketed, was caffeine. This derivative from tea was marketed in crystallized one-pound blocks. As the demand increased, buyers no longer insisted on these blocks, but accepted and even requested the smaller, compressed tiles which were easily transportable and even more easily smuggled. Their manufacture now proved to be a challenge to some of the resourceful refugees with chemistry background. This was so because, although tea was plentiful, the process of extraction required the use of chloroform or carbontetrachloride, which were in short supply. Several successful methods were devised by ingenious refugees which provided a lucrative source of income throughout the War in the Pacific. There was also a marked increase in the scope of refugee press and radio, when news from other sources was limited.

However, the outbreak of the War in the Pacific had a directly detrimental effect on the refugees in Shanghai. The Japanese takeover of American and British firms precipitated unemployment among the refugee workers. This condition, of course, aggravated the already overwhelming relief problem.[15]

The break in communication between Shanghai and the United States was catastrophic for many refugees. It closed the former two-way traffic of export by refugees to the United States, and import of relief aid from friends, relatives and organizations in the States. Still, commerce was not completely halted. Some limited shipping trade continued mainly with other Chinese ports, Japan and Japanese-occupied territories such as Formosa, Indo-China, Korea and Manchuria. However, most of the business that was maintained during the next several years was primarily internal.

Soon, the former relatively slow-moving inflation grew rapidly worse by mid-1942, as the confidence in the new CRB currency, printed by the Japanese puppet government in Nanking, grew less and less. Statistically this meant that while the official rates of exchange of the Chinese dollar for an American in 1939 was approximately six to one, it increased to a ratio of almost fifty to one in 1942, and reached ridiculous rates during the worst period of 1944-1945. Thus, it jumped from 599 to one in December 1944, to 3,000 to one a half year later. Even these figures do not give the full picture, since the "official" rates were usually far below the going "black" rates, as the common parlance had it.

As one refugee recounted these years of rising prices, when he arrived in Shanghai at the end of 1938, one could buy a pound of meat for (Sh) 18c. to 30c., depending on the cut and variety. Sugar, a higher-priced commodity, sold for 20c. a pound white margarine went for 32c. per pound. By early 1943, sugar had risen to (Sh) $9 ($25 on the "black") and margarine to (Sh) $32 ($50-$60 on the "black"). A can of American cigarettes, air-sealed for freshness, went from $100 to $300, a pound of candy, such as lollies, sold for (Sh) $20 to $100, while rice, the staple Chinese food, rose from (Sh) $11 a sack of a bit over 100 lbs. to over $1,700.

At the same time, this same refugee, in his teens at the time, was earning a "meager" salary of (Sh) $600 a month in April 1943, which enabled him to purchase perhaps two cans of cigarettes or a few pounds of candy. Even a coolie earning twice this salary could not manage with such a meager sum.

As a hedge against such inflation, companies began a mad scramble of buying and selling. The following illustration recalled by the same individual, but corroborated by others, goes like this:

> One would bring, for instance, a case containing a few dozen tins of sardines, not with any intention of ever eating any one of them, but solely as a hedge against inflation, to be sold again to someone else who in turn would sell it and so on. Of course, some fool, would one day, open the case

and find all the tins rusted, leaking and their contents spoiled, but that was his fault. After all, he was not meant to consume the contents of the box, but simply and only to use it as a substitute for cash.

Actually, one of the best of such substitutes were

. . . flints, yes, simple flints as used in gas or cigarette lighters, perhaps because they would not perish and they became so much sought after, that weight for weight, they obtained a higher price than even gold.[16]

The economic repercussions of the new war on the refugees were bad enough; the psychological impact was even more severe. It eliminated the last shred of hope of leaving Shanghai. The view of Shanghai as a transit station had not been helpful to long-range relief planning by the committees, but it served as a safety valve against frustration.[17] This source of hope was now gone.

RELIEF 1942-1943

Laura Margolies and her recently arrived JDC colleague, Manuel Siegel, were just beginning to make headway in reorganizing the previously amateurish and cumbersome refugee machinery, when the Japanese took over.[18] By this time, the monthly allotment of the Joint to the CFA and EJC relief efforts totaled (US) $30,000 a month, which went toward the feeding of about 8,000 refugees and the housing of close to 2,500.[19]

Since, right after Pearl Harbor, no money seemed to be forthcoming from the United States, Captain Herzberg, at the time the paid executive of the CFA, reduced the two meals a day to one, and cut down the individual bread allowance from 16 to 12 ounces, as a stopgap, money-saving device,[20]

Fortunately, a cable arrived on December 13, 1941, from the Joint in New York, extending Margolies' two-month "Joint Guarantee" loan for local borrowing of funds up to six months and (US) $180,000.[21]

The Japanese permitted the borrowing of this sum. Three members of the CFA Executive, Speelman, Hayim and Abraham, went therefore to see Captain Inuzuka, head of the Bureau of Jewish Affairs. Inuzuka listened patiently to their story—and then practically threw them out of his office. Presumably, he still remembered their prewar anti-Japanese stand.[22]

In contrast, Inuzuka dealt with both Joint representatives in a most courteous and cooperative manner. He permitted the loan, but restricted its sources to neutrals and required the submission of the donors' names. Inuzuka also released 5,000 sacks of cracked wheat donated by the International Red Cross.[23]

Margolies was less successful in her attempts to interest the Russian Jews in the plight of the refugees. Their avoidance of involvement in general was now aggravated by the fear that the Japanese would discover that they had available "ready cash."[24] There thus appeared to be little alternative but to close down all relief operations, and face possible food riots, which would have been put down in characteristic, ruthless manner by the gendarmerie.[25] At great personal risk, the Joint representatives resorted to publicity, giving all the heartbreaking details to the newspapers and on the air. This was successful, though it was only the intercession of someone "in" with the gendarmerie that prevented the arrest of both Margolies and Siegel by the angry authorities. The Japanese did not want any adverse publicity to disturb their "peaceful" takeover of Shanghai.[26]

The first breakthrough in the quest for loans resulted from this publicity. It came from Fritz Kaufmann, an old-time

German-Jewish resident of Shanghai, who had recently come
into a lot of cash by "selling" stocks of essential goods to the
Japanese military.[27] He gave the equivalent of (US) $10,000
towards the Joint Guarantee Loan, which sufficed to keep the
relief operations going for over one month.[28] With the help of
two members of the Ashkenazi community, Joseph Bitker and
David Rabinovich, the editor of *Unser Leben,* the Joint was
able to raise the entire (US) $180,000 loan by the end of
April 1942.[29]

In order to stretch the relief money, Laura Margolies
cut the number of refugees receiving food from the CFA from
8,000 to 4,000, leaving only the poorest in the *Heime,* the aged,
the children and the sick who were housed elsewhere, and she
put even these on reduced rations. The rest had to fend for
themselves. This often meant selling their last bit of goods or
clothing.[30]

The staff of the *Heime,* numbering over 500, was told
of the financial situation, given a month's salary and notified
of the impending drastic cuts in personnel. However, almost the
entire staff showed up the next morning to work.[31]

Laura Margolies also indicated her desire to introduce
more democratic methods in the administration of the *Heime.*
She was helped by the Shanghai Society of Friends to expand
representative government. Margolies was amazed at the new
spirit among the people, despite hunger and physical exhaustion.[32]

Self-help did not stop with self-government: gardens
were planted on the grounds surrounding the *Heime*; laundry
and mending services were organized; benefit performances and
evenings of entertainment became the scne of friendly competition. The residents of one of the *Heime* even built and rented
out for profit an outdoor skating rink.[33] Once again, one
wonders how much more could have been accomplished, had

experienced, professional social workers been sent to Shanghai, one, or better, two years earlier, as requested by the harried, local, amateur relief committee.[34]

In her campaign for economy, Margolies was able to eliminate a prime source of waste, the cumbersome kitchen. A. Levenspiel, a Polish refugee engineer, figured out that in the old kitchen only 10c out of the average cost of a meal of (Sh) 60c ("Fapi" currency, backed by the Chinese Nationalist Government) per person was used for food, with 50c spent on coal. A simple, efficient steam kitchen of his design, he calculated, would feed as many as 10,000 refugees a day at only (Sh) 2c per meal for fuel. Needed were two steam boilers, then unobtainable in Shanghai. Laura Margolies "borrowed" two from a lot belonging to a former Sassoon plant, then under Japanese supervision, and gave the protesting British director an IOU for future repayment.[35]

The new kitchen was dedicated in November 1942, at a ceremony graced by many Japanese and Jewish dignitaries. Because of insufficient funds, however, it served only around 5,000 per sons.[36]

The ultimate setback suffered by Laura Margolies was communicated on May 21, 1942 in the last cable from the Joint representative in Paraguay, Moses Beckelman. It instructed her to discontinue all communications.[37] Since January 10, 1942, Margolies had persistently requested an extension of the Joint commitment for local loans beyond the six months. Despite exhaustive efforts, the JDC in New York was unable to convince the State and the Treasury Departments to grant authorization for such communications.[38] The Joint, as a "super patriotic" American organization, felt duty-bound fully to honor the restrictions imposed upon even telegraphic communications by the Anglo-American Trading with the Enemy Act. This act prohibited both the sending of money and the communicating by any means with the enemy countries.[39] The JDC's policy, however, was postulated upon the premise that "we as an American organization cannot be involved in anything that has the remotest color of trading with the enemy."[40]

The JDC would not even take a "hint" offered by the Treasury Department to send an "unauthorized" cable. On May 13, 1942, M. L. Hoffman of the Foreign Funds Control Office of the Treasury noted that all communication, whether direct or indirect, as a matter of policy, is prohibited between Americans and persons in enemy-occupied countries.

He [Hoffman] said, "of course, that if we [JDC] wanted to send such a cable we would be at liberty to do so, but the Treasury could not authorize the sending of such a cable" [italics mine].

Margolies was not alone in her feeling of shock and dismay at the JDC's refusal to continue help for the refugees. The Japanese (for instance, Inuzuka), who had given their permission for US money to enter via the Red Cross, were dumbfounded when they heard of the denial. Inuzuka had also given permission to the Gemeinde to send its own appeal for funds to the JDC and the State Department.[41]

So, unlike HICEM and the Vaad Hatzalah, whose representatives in neutral European countries maintained an unbroken line of communication with the Jews in Shanghai, the Joint broke off contact with its representatives and the refugees in Shanghai until December 1943.[42]

With the financial situation becoming increasingly hopeless, Margolies initiated several measures to at least partially alleviate the relief situation. First, she planned for the greater participation of the Ashkenazim, who, though stateless, were not enemy nationals and thus not subject to the restrictions that inhibited their Sephardi coreligionists. She was able to convince some of the Russian Jews, who had hitherto limited their aid to the Polish refugees, to support at least 600 to 700 destitute German refugee children. These Russian Jews formed a new organization called CENTROJEWCOM (Central European Refugee Committee), an obvious counterpart to the earlier Russian-Jewish organization, the EASTJEWCOM.[43]

Feelings ran very high among the Russian Jews, so high that in some cases brothers were no longer on speaking terms, on the vexing question of aid to the German refugees. The schism was exacerbated because EASTJEWCOM and CENTROJEWCOM both derived their income essentially from the same people.[44]

The IC, which after Komor's brief arrest in February 1942, was run by Robert Peritz, a German refugee, adopted the idea of *Patenschaft* (sponsorship) as a means of raising money among the wealthier refugees. This idea, as we know, had originated and been used successfully by the *Juedische Gemeinde*.[45]

Margolies also cut down on expenses by closing the three units of the refugee hospital in June 1942. She had always felt that the hospital was an unnecessary financial drain, both in its physical plants and large staff.[46] Dr. Friedrichs, who was present when the decision to close part of the hospital was made, agreed that, under the circumstances, there was no alternative.[47] The elimination of this medical staff helped Margolies to reduce the number of personnel from 500 to about 100.[48] This reduction was made at a time when the hospital was overcrowded, especially with victims of typhus, which was then rampant in Shanghai, and heat prostration.[49] For example, during one summer day in 1942, 16 refugees died of heat prostration and physical exhaustion.[50] Margolies shifted the more seriously ill patients from the refugee hospital to about twenty beds in the Shanghai General Hospital. The outpatient clinics were still maintained at the *Heime*, while the rest of the patients had to be treated at home.[51]

464   JAPANESE, NAZIS & JEWS

She also completely overhauled the system of keeping books and statistics at the *Heime,* and applied new methods of investigating both their present and potential residents. The latter procedure was long overdue, since many of those in the *Heime* were bettter off than those trying to live independently.[52]

By the middle of 1942, both Margolies and Siegel became increasingly aware that their days of free movement as enemy nationals were limited and that they would soon be either repatriated or interned. This awareness was reinforced by the increasingly prevalent antiforeign climate of opinion in Shanghai. Margolies felt this to be particularly true in her dealings with the new Japanese officials arriving in Shanghai. Captain Inuzuka, with whom she had established good working relations, had been replaced at this time by Captain Saneyoshi, who was indifferent to the problems of the Jews and the refugees.[53] Margolies and Siegel, therefore, pressed for the transfer of responsibility for the relief problem to the refugees themselves, as well as to the Ashkenazi community. Thus, at the time CENTROJEWCOM was being organized, Margolies was training three responsible refugees, Lutz Wachsner, Glueckman and Dr. Lang, to help administer the relief program as members of both the Shanghai JDC and the Kitchen Fund. Through both these organizations, they attempted to broaden the base of the smaller contributions from the better-off refugees, as well as from the Russian Jews.[54] With the hope that at least some semblance of order in the relief picture had been set up, Margolies and Siegel resigned on July 15, 1942.[55]

An extraneous event, whose full significance was only realized about a half-year later, greatly altered the plans of Laura Margolies: the arrest by the *gendarmerie* in August 1942 of an *ad hoc* committee representing the leaders of the three Jewish communities in Shanghai. They had met in Speelman's house to seek ways to prevent an alleged Japanese scheme to liquidate the refugees by placing them on a ship and sinking it out at sea.[56]

Though the Jewish leaders were released from their detention in the Bridge House jail after several weeks, all those remaining from the reorganized CFA resigned, including Speelman.[57] Margolies felt that something should be done to reestablish the relief apparatus, and she attempted to enlist some of the Ashkenazi and refugee leaders to this cause. Joseph Bitker, who had been among those arrested in August, pledged his participation in her efforts. He placed his wide business experience at the service of the newly established Shanghai JDC, which sought to raise local money for the American JDC conditional loan.

Unlike the first loan of (US) $180,000 which was backed by a written (cable) JDC guarantee, the second loan, was arranged by Margolies without the JDC's authorization and guarantee due to the above-mentioned break in communications with the United States. Its only guarantee was a moral one, whereby Margolies, who knew of the American Joint's desire to help, affirmed that the "Joint had the money to help and would do so after hostilities cease."[58]

Obviously, a contract backed only by a moral obligation, however sincere, could not carry the same authority as the earlier guaranteed loan. The second loan was more difficult to raise and the rate of exchange for Swiss francs was drastically lowered.[59] Ironically, Margolies also limited the amount she permitted the Shanghai JDC to borrow on these conditional loans to (US) $210,000 (or 900,000 Sw. fr.), a six-month budget. This loan was raised by Bitker from neutral firms such as French and Swiss.[60] Money was also raised among the Ashkenazim and even the Chinese, some loans being as low as (US) $15-25.[61]

The three refugees previously referred to, Wachsner,

Glueckman and Lang, who had been trained by Margolies, were appointed by her to work for the Shanghai JDC, together with Bitker and the chairman, Brahn. According to Margolies, the latter's primary qualification was his close connections with the Japanese *gendarmerie*.[62]

In August 1942, several refugees formed a Kitchen Fund Committee (Kitchen *Fond Kuratorium*), later shortened to Kitchen Fund, or KF, in order to raise funds from the more prosperous refugees, to feed at least the most indigent. This committee adopted the aforementioned *Patenschaft* (sponsorship) system of relief.[63] With the completion of Levenspiel's steam kitchen in November 1942, the Kitchen Fund was able to serve over 5,000 hot meals daily.[64] According to an agreement worked out by Margolies and Siegel, the Kitchen Fund and the Shanghai JDC were to share responsibility for refugee relief. The former organization was to be responsible for the raising of funds, primarily through the conditional loans, while the latter was to care for the feeding and housing of the poorest refugees. As economic conditions in the ghetto deteriorated, especially during the latter part of 1943 and the early part of 1944, the relief activities of the Kitchen Fund increased tremendously.[65] This broadened scope included the reopening of the Refugee Hospital by the spring of 1943, though on a smaller scale.[66]

The KF refugee leaders, strong-willed, independent and successful businessmen, clashed with the Margolies appointees, which resulted in the resignation of the latter and restricted their activities to the Shanghai JDC.[67] One of the bitter ironies of refugee life in Shanghai, according to Margolies and Siegel, was that greater harm was inflicted on their cause by internal and intergroup dissension than by Japanese regulations.[68]

On January 31, 1943, Manuel Siegel was interned by the Japanese, along with other enemy nationals, in the Pootung

Camp. His coworker Margolies suffered a similar fate about three weeks later.[69] Their confinement, however, did not deter either of these resourceful relief workers from keeping in contact with the refugee situation, since both were able to leave the camps for brief periods and maintain an underground system of communications.[70] Margolies feigned illness in order to consult with Bitker from the Shanghai General Hospital, despite close supervision by Japanese guards.[71]

It was during her last meeting with Bitker, when she was looking for ways to send money from the United States to Shanghai after her awaited repatriation, that they improvised a coded signal to indicate the approval of the United States Government for renewed communication. This signal was to be a cable from Margolies, via a neutral country, congratulating Bitker upon his daughter's birthday. One can readily imagine the joy spread by the arrival of such a telegram in the spring of 1944, when conditions were at their lowest ebb.[72]

A brief table summarizing the sources of funds received by the Kitchen Fund during the period from August 1942-June 1943 indicates how the relief program was primarily supported during this period.[73]

Source	Per cent
1. Kitchen Fund (*Patenschaften* and one-time contributions)	17
2. Income—from refugees (some paid minimal amount for food tickets) ..	14 3/4
3. Shanghai JDC	59 1/2
4. Central Jewcom [sic]	8 3/4

Two other sources of financial aid must be included to round out the 1942 to mid-1943 relief picture. The first is the steady subsidy sent to Mir and other yeshivot and rabbinical groups by Rabbi Kalmanowitz and the *Vaad Hatzalah,* via neutral Switzerland, Portugal, Sweden, Argentina and Uruguay, despite many obstacles.[74]

The second was the vital, dual role played by HICEM in Shanghai. It too continued its network of communications with friends, relatives and organizations throughout the world, though on a reduced scale, despite the entry of the United States into World War II. These contacts, through the above-mentioned neutral nations, enabled both small amounts of money, and some news about relatives in parts of Nazi-occupied Europe, to reach Shanghai. Appeals by hundreds of refugees in Shanghai for aid from their friends and relatives in Europe were broadcast by means of "collective cables" sent by HICEM, whereby many names were attached, for a relatively small fee, to an otherwise prohibitively expensive cable.[75]

The funds received by HICEM from abroad enabled it to grant many small loans to both needy individuals and organizations.[76]

These events, from December 8, 1941, through December 1942, illustrate the complexities and hardships faced by the refugees and their relief organizations amidst the turmoil of a Japanese-occupied Shanghai.

NOTES : PEARL HARBOR

1. For a description of this opening incident of the War in the Pacific, see *Yellow Creek*, pp. 171-73. Also Carey, *War Years*, pp. 27-28.

2. Cf. the detailed divisions given by Fritz Friedlander in *"Einkresung."* Cf. also Gruenberger, "Refugees," p. 337; Rosenfeld, *History*, III, p. 3.

3. See Dave Rudan, "China Youngson Knew," *The Independent Forester*, Vol. 87 (Don Mills, Ontario, December 1967), p. 9. Courtesy Gerechter.

4. See, for example, Carey, *War Years*, pp. 72-73, 164. Also Fitzgerald, *Communist*, pp. 201-203.

4. Carey, *War Years*, pp. 33-34, 58-59, 74. See especially chapter 8 in which the author beautifully delineates the world and *Weltanschauung* of the "Old China Hands." Another such view can be seen in Spunt, *Place in Time;* Hauser, *Shanghai*, p. 315.

5. See Hinzelmann, *O China*, pp. 59, 73. Also Carey, *War Years*, p. 25; *Yellow Creek*, p. 174; Siegelberg, *Pearl Harbour*, p. XII; Eisfelder, *Exile*, pp. 34-35.

6. Margolies, "Race," p. 12. Cf. also *Yellow Creek*, p. 176; Carey, *War Years*, pp. 81-88. For the quote, see Eisfelder, *Exile, Ibid.*

7. The Americans had a large *A* on their armbands, while the British carried a *B* and the Dutch an *H* (for Holland). Carey, *War Years*, pp. 87, 89, 135-36. Cr. also *Yellow Creek*, p. 176.

The sight of all the Jews registering on order of the Japanese authorities, whether Sephardic, German, Russian or Czech, at the old Jewish Club at 35 Mulmain Road, prompted one Jewish journalist to note that "necessity, by uniting all these Jews, had done what they themselves had been unable to accomplish." (Translated from the Yiddish) *Unser Leben*, January 2, 1942 (Yiddish Sect.), p. 1.

8. Carey, *War Years*, p. 38. Also Kaufmann, "Experiences," p. 6. For the short-wave radio removal, see Friedrichs-Kranzler Corres. July 29, 1973. Cf. also Eisfelder, *Exile*, p. 35. For the journalists, see the introduction to Siegelberg, *Face.*

9. *Yellow Creek*, p. 176. Also Carey, *War Years*, p. 34; Margolies, *Report*, p. 1.

10. Abraham Interview.

11. *Ibid.*

12. See especially Inuzuka to Hertzberg, September 17, 1941; Margolies, *Report*, pp. 2, 9.

13. Abraham Interview. Actually the total withdrawal by all of these Sephardi leaders did not take place until July 1942, following their arrest after the special meeting of all the Jewish communal leaders.

14. See *Unser Leben* (April 17, 1942) (Yiddish Sect.), p. 1.

15. Gruenberger, *Refugees*, p. 337. See also Friedrichs, Geschichte, p. 155. For the caffeine production, see Eisfelder, *Exile*, pp. 33, 37-39, 47.

16. According to one estimate (prior to Pearl Harbor), over 70 per cent of the refugees were receiving private aid from the United States (Peckel Corres.). Cf. also Friedlander, "Einkreisung"; Ganther, "Seven Years," p. 2; Birman to HICEM (Lisbon), November 12, 1942, p. 1 (HH XV C-7). Birman to ISRAV, January 19, 1943, p. 2 (HH XV C08); Eisfelder, *Exile*, p. 37.
Some ingenious refugees attempted unsuccessfully to move to the nearby neutral Portuguese island of Macao, in order to continue to receive funds from the United States. *Unser Leben* (February 6, 1942; February 27, 1942), p. 1. (Yiddish Sect.). For the inflation statistics, see Young, *Inflation*, chapters 17-18, and especially the chart on p. 265. For the story and other examples of inflation and the refugees, see Eisfelder, *Exile*, pp. 35-36.

17. See, for example, Farb Corres., p. 2; Peckel Corres., p. 3. For the "transitional" attitude on the part of both the refugees as well as the relief committees, see Margolies, "Race," p. 12. Cf. also Rosenfeld *History*, III, pp. 2, 6; Shoshana, *In Faier*, p. 289; Raymist, "Sh. Myth," p. 17; Burkhard, *Tanz*, p. 152. For the panic created among the refugees by the outbreak of the War in the Pacific, see *Unser Leben* (December 12, 19, 1941), p. 1 (Yiddish Sect.).

18. Margolies, *Report*, p. 2. See also Birman to HICEM (Lisbon), January 21, 1942, pp. 2-3; Gruenberger, Refugees, p. 337.

19. Margolies, *Report*, p. 5.

20. *Ibid.*, p. 2. Herzberg was the only one able to move about freely during the first two weeks following Pearl Harbor since he was the only "nonenemy national" on the CFA staff.

21. See Cable No. 3227 dated December 13, 1941 (JDCCA). For the confirmation of this cable sent to the Joint representative in Paraguay, Moses Beckelman, on December 15 (a copy of which was sent to Margolies), see Cable No. 3229 (JDCCA). Cf. also Margolies, *Report*, p. 2.
This procedure by the Joint of "local borrowing" upon guarantee of re-imbursement had already been established practice during World War I. See Buchanan to Isaac Seligson, January 5, 1942 (JDCCA). When the author asked Dr. Joseph Schwarz (the then Acting Director of the European

JDC) why the Joint imposed a six-month limit on its guarantee, he replied that the six months already far exceeded its "normal" two months' budgetary commitment. Taped Interview, July 28, 1969.

22. Margolies, *Report*, p. 2.

23. *Ibid.*, pp. 2-3, 14. Cf. also Margolies, "Race," p. 12.

24. See Margolies, *Report*, p. 5. Cf. also Kaufmann Interview, Fritz Kaufmann, an old-time German businessman, had come to Shanghai in 1931 and became more deeply involved in refugee affairs during this period, though he had already worked earlier with the *Hilfsfond*. See also Kaufmann, "Experiences," p. 1.

25. Margolies, *Report*, p. 5.

26. *Ibid.*, pp. 5-6. The "influential" Japanese was Mrs. Nagomi, a good friend of Mr. Brahn, an old-time German-Jewish Shanghai resident, who was soon to become involved in refugee affairs. Cf. also Kaufmann, "Experiences," p. 9.

27. Kaufmann, "Experiences," pp. 6-7. Such essential goods belonging to enemy nationals were simply confiscated, *Ibid.*, p. 6. See also Howard Ling to L. Margolies, Joint (N.Y.), April 3, 1944 (JDCCA).

28. Margolies, *Report*, p. 6. Also Kaufmann, "Experiences," pp. 6-7.

29. Most of it, (US) $138,000, came from the first loan by J. Shriro (Margolies, *Report*, pp. 6-7).

30. Margolies, *Report*, pp. 5, 7. Cf. also Rosenfeld, *History*, III, p. 6.

31. Margolies, *Report*, p. 8. Cf. also Gruenberger, "Refugees," p. 337.

32. Margolies, *Report*, pp. 11-12. Cf. also Margolies, "Race," pp. 14-15; Gruenberger, "Refugees," p. 337.

33. Margolies, "Race," p. 15.

34. Cf. Margolies, *Report*, p. 12.

35. Margolies, "Race," p. 14. Cf. also Margolies, *Report*, p. 8. For the IOU, see Margolies-Kranzler Corres., September 15, 1968.
The "Fapi" money was that issued by Chiang Kai-shek's Chungking government. See Margolies, *Report*, p. 7. Also Young, *Finance*, pp. 5, 164-74.

36. *Unser Leben* (November 20, 1942) (English Suppl), p. 2. See Birman to HICEM (Lisbon), November 12, 1942, p. 1; Margolies, *Report*, 1941-43, p. 18. See also Margolies, "Race," p. 14.
According to Margolies, in both her *Report* (p. 18) and "Race" (p. 14),, December was the date. Since Margolies wrote both of these from memory over a year later, I assume that the discrepancy of a few days is due to a lapse in her recall.

By December 30, 1943, the number of meals served reached 6,000 Birman to Lisbon, December 30, 1943 (HH XV C-8). Though according to one source, poor financial conditions cut down the number of meals, during July 1943, to about 3,500. Shanghai JDC, data regarding relief work, July 20, 1943 (HH XV C-8).

37. Margolies, *Report,* p. 12. Cf. also Birman to HIAS (N.Y.), August 28, 1946, p. 2 (HH XV C-11); Bitker, *Memo* (date unclear, ca. 1943) (JDCCA); Leavitt, *Memo* re U.S. Treasury, May 8, 1942 (JDCCA); Kwapiscewski to Leavitt (Cable), June 5, 1942 (JDCCA).

38. Such efforts can be seen from the many trips to Washington and meetings with representatives of these two departments of the United States Government. See, for example, Hyman to Leavitt, January 9, 1942; Hyman to J. Hollzer, January 19, 1943; Leavitt to J. W. Pehle, January 22, 1942; Leavitt to Kwapiszewski, June 7, 1942; Leavitt, Memo to U.S. Treasury, May 8, 1942; Evelyn M. Morrisey, Memo, May 20, 1942; Hyman to Morgenthau, August 24, 1942 (JDCCA). Cf also related documents in the files of State Department, Decimal File No. 840.48 (Refugees), Nos. /3132-3140.

39. For "Trading with the Enemy Act," see Feingold, *Politics,* p. 239. Cf. also Blum, Morgenthau, pp. 215-19.

40. Buchman to Seligson, January 5, 1942 (JDCCA). Although the letter refers specifically to monetary transfers, this policy represented the Joint's views even in regard to formal communications with the enemy. For example, see the letter by Joseph Hyman (JDC) to J. Hollzer, January 19, 1942, p. 2. Hyman stated, "We have no right to request a person in the Argentine to communicate with anyone in territory at present occupied by the enemy" (JDCCA).

Under such a policy, the Joint would not even honor the request made by the Polish Embassy in Washington for the JDC to raise (US) $5,000-$10,000 which they would get to the Polish refugees. (See Kwapiscewski to Leavitt, June 9, 1942) (JDCCA).

For this interpretation of the "Trading with the Enemy Act" on the part of the State and Treasury Departments, see Excerpts from Memo re Visit to JCH [Hyman] and MAL [Leavitt] to Washington, D.C., July 22, 1942 (JDCCA). Cf. also Evelyn Morrissey, Memorandum for Leavitt, September 3, 1942 (quoting John Pehle of the Treasury Department) that, "the Treasury cannot approve any communication to Shanghai." For the "hint," see also Memo.

Excerpts from Memo.

Rabbi Kalmanowitz, on the other hand, continued his communications and transfer of money via neutral countries, or deposits of money in American accounts for its equivalent release in Shanghai. This, despite several warnings by the FBI of impending arrest. Joshua Ashkenazi taped Interview. January 10, 1970. Mr. Ashkenazi was involved in such transfer of money.

41. Inuzuka, "Faith," p. 8. For his permission to the Gemeinde to send a cable to the U.S., see Redlich-Kranzler corres., December 11, 1973, p. 7.

42. The Joint did have some idea of the general refugee picture in Shanghai by virtue of the few reports sent to its New York office by the International Red Cross. See for example, Cable sent by the IRC to JDC, June 27, 1942; IRC Report, June 15, 1943 (JDCCA); HIAS-HICEM, which sent dispatches to New York via neutral countries (see HH XV C-2); also James Bernstein (HICEM, Lisbon) to JDC (N.Y.), January 22, 1943; Reports from some of the refugees repatriated in 1942 (see for example confidential memo, JDC), September 1942 (JDCCA). See also "29 Jahre HIAS," p. 19.

43. Margolies, Report, pp. 13-14. Margolies spells it Central Jewcom. The author follows the more frequently used spelling, especially as used by Meyer Birman. See also Birman to HICEM (Lisbon), October 15, 1942, p. 2; November 12, 1942 (HH XV C-7); Unser Leben (September 18, 1942; September 25, 1942) (English Suppl), p. 1; CCB, Minutes, May 23, 1945, pp. 1-2.

44. Margolies, Report, p. 13. For the agreement by the EASTJEWCOM to turn over its collected funds to the CFA, in return for one-fifth of the total relief, see ibid., pp. 10-11; David Rabinovich Interview, July 25, 1971. Rabinovich, editor of Unser Leben, was one of the founders of CENTRO-JEWCOM.

45. See leaflet published on January 11, 1942 by the Juedische Gemeinde, which called for such type of sponsorship. According to Dr. Redlich, the idea originated with Dr. Jacob Wachtel, a physician and member of the board of directors of the Gemeinde (xerox copy in author's possession). (Redlich Papers).

For Komor's arrest, see Margolies, Report, pp. 3, 12. Cf. also Robert Peritz, "Eidesstattliche Versicherung" [Peritz, "Affidavit"], for the United Restitution Office [URO], p. 1; Erich Faerber, "Affidavit" [Faerber, "Affidavit"] for the URO. These and other affidavits by former refugees from Shanghai were made available for reproduction to the author by Dr. Ganther Kamm of URO.

Paul Komor, in a telephone interview with the author, claimed that several refugees were responsible for instigating his arrest by Captain Inuzuka. Interview. An important factor in his arrest must also have been Komor's close association with Sir Victor Sasson, who was an old foe of both Inuzuka and the Japanese policies in China, had funded the IC.

46. Margolies, Report, p. 13.

47. Friedrichs Interview. For an opposing view, see Kunfi, "Medizinische," p. 9.

48. Margolies, "Race," p. 15. Cf. also Margolies, Report, p. 13; Unser Leben (July 10, 1942; July 24, 1942) (English Suppl.), p. 1.

49. Margolies, *Report*, p. 11. Cf. also unidentified article (ca. 1942) from the *California Jewish Voice* (JDCCA); Almanac, "Chewra," p. 58.

50. Gruenberger, "Refugees," p. 338. Also *Almanac*, "Chewra," p. 58.

51. Margolies, *Report*, p. 13. Cf. also Kunfi. *"Medizinische,"* p. 10; Friedrichs, *Geschichte*, p. 162.

52. Margolies, *Report*, p. 11. Cf. also Rosenfeld, *History*, III, p. 44; Margolies to Pilpel, August 11, 1941, p. 6. Similar attempts at such a "house cleaning" in 1944 prove that this problem was never really solved.

53. Margolies, *Report*, p. 14.

54. *Ibid.*, pp. 13-14, 16.

55. Margolies, *Report*, p. 14. Cf. also *Unser Leben* (July 24, 1942), p. 2 (English Suppl.), for their resignation.

56. Kaufman, "Experiences," p. 8. Also Bitker, *Memo,* p. 2; Peritz, "Affidavit," p. 2; Inuzuka, "Secret" p. 6.

57. Margolies, *Report*, p. 15.

58. Margolies, *Report*, pp. 16-17. For the complete text of this "conditional contract," see Margolies, "Affidavit," September 17, 1942 (JDCCA). See also the detailed correspondence of the lawyers for J. Shriro and the JDC (N.Y.) concerning the repayment of his share of the loan of (US) $138,000 (JDCCA).

59. Margolies, *Report*, pp. 17-18, 22. Margolies noted that while the market price of the Swiss franc into which the dollar had to be converted, according to new Japanese currency regulations, was at the rate of 10-12 CRB to one Swiss franc, she was only able to get 3 CRB per Swiss franc for one loan. Margolies, *Report*, p. 17. The CRB or Chinese Central Reserve Bank notes of Nanking was the currency issued by the pro-Japanese Nanking regime in June 1942, at which time the Chungking Government's Fapi currency was taken off the market at a rate of 2 CRB to one Fapi dollar. Margolies, *Report*, p. 7. See also Bitker, *Memo,* p. 4; Young, *Finance*, pp. 172-73.
The value of the Swiss franc in dollars during the mid-1942 period was at a ratio of approximately 4½ Swiss franc to one U.S. dollar. *Ibid.*, p. 22.

60. Bitker, *Memo,* p. 4. The French, Vichy Government, then already out of the war, was considered neutral. Meskill, *Hitler,* pp. 106-107.

61. Anderson, *Memo,* American Reb Cross, August 28, 1942, p. 1 (JDCCA). Mr. Shriro, for example, who had a major share in both the original "Guaranteed" loan, as well as the "Conditional" one, was a member of the Ashkenazi community.
Margolies did not inform any of the Jewish leaders of the "Shriro" loan except for Bitker and Shiffrin, who helped raise it, since she was afraid of

dulling that initiative for local fund-raising started by the Kitchen Fund. This money was quietly invested by Bitker, who had it "donated" piecemeal in anonymous form, toward various relief projects. In this manner the local JDC-sponsored money accomplished a great deal of relief work during 1943-44, unbeknown to almost anyone in Shanghai. Cf. Birman to HIAS (N.Y.), August 28, 1943, p. 2. A complete list of such anonymous relief projects can be found in the "List of Payments Made Out of the Money Received from G. Shiffrin during 1944-1943" [sic] signed by J.B. [Joseph Bitker]. The loan is attributed to Shiffrin, due to the wartime circumstances. See Margolies, *Report*, pp. 17-18.

On her own initiative, Margolies was also able to raise one million Swiss francs from Jewish communities in neutral Switzerland, Portugal and Sweden. Margolies, *Report*, p. 13. See also Shanghai JDC to Lisbon, June 5, 1944, p. 1 (JDCCA).

62. Margolies, *Report*, p. 15. Cf. also Siegel, *Report*, August 26, 1945, p. 5 (JDCCA). Kaufmann, "Experiences," pp. 17-18.

63. For the Kitchen Fund and the "Patenschaft," see Margolies, *Report*, pp. 15-16. Also Birman to HICEM (Lisbon), November 12, 1942 (HH XV C-7); Birman to ISRAV, January 19, 1943, p. 3 (HH XV C-8); Siegel, *Report*, August 26, 1945, p. 4; *Unser Leben* (July 24, 1942) (English Suppl.), p. 1, which gives the original name of Kitchen Committee, formed as early as July 20, 1942.

64. See Unser Leben (November 20, 1942) (English Suppl.), p. 2. Cf. also Eisfelder, *Exile*, p. 34.

65. Margolies, *Report*, p. 16. Margolies, *Report*, pp. 16-17. See also Birman to Comm. Israelita, December 30, 1943.

65. See Siegel, *Report*, August 26, 1945, p. 6.

66. Gruenberger, "Refugees," p. 338. Cf. also Kunfi, *"Medizinische,"* p. 9. By June 1944 the hospital was enlarged from a 40- to 125-bed unit. Shanghai JDC to Lisbon, June 5, 1944, p. 3 (JDCCA).

67. Margolies, *Report*, p. 17.

68. *Ibid.*, pp. 1, 16-17, 20. Also Siegel, *Report*, August 26, 1945, pp. 1-5; International Red Cross Cables, March 2, 1944 (JDCCA;)); ICR to Joint, Report, June 15, 1943 (JDCCA). The latter source draws unfavorable comparison between the disunity among the Jewish refugees and the unity displayed by the White Russian emigres. See also Redlich-Kranzler corres., corres., February 27, 1947, pp. 1-9.

69. Margolies, *Report*, p. 18. Also Margolies, "Race," p. 15; Siegel, *Report*, August 26, 1945, p. 1.

For the internment of enemy nationals in general and life in such internment camps, see Carey, *War Years*, especially pp. 89, 91-93, 165-213. Also

Langdon Gilkey, *Shantung Compound*: *The Story of Men and Women Under Pressure* (New York: Harper and Row, 1966).

For a brief but incisive comparison between the *Heime* and the internment camps, see Margolies, "Race," pp. 15-16.

70. Letter by Laura Margolies-Jarblum to Joseph Bitker, February 12, 1951 (Bitker-Dicker Corres.). Cf. also Siegel-Bitker Corres., February 13, 1951, p. 1 (Bitker-Dicker Corres).

71. Agar, *Remnant*, p. 17. Though this work is far from scholarly, and contains numerous errors even within the brief space allotted to Shanghai, this incident is substantiated by Margolies in her correspondence with this writer. Margolies-Jarblum-Kranzler Corres., September 25, 1968. See also Bitker, *Memo*, p. 4.

72. See Bitker, *Memo*, pp. 4-5. Cited by Dicker, *Wanderers*, p. 132.

73. Margolies, *Report*, p. 21.

74. Epstein, "Mir," p. 129. Cf. also Birman to ISRAV, November 19, 1943, p. 2. (HH XV C-8). Also interview with Pincus Schoen, formerly of the *Vaad Hatzalah*.

75. See Birman, *Report*, February 10, 1944 (HH XV C-9). Cf. also Birman to Jewish Community (Lisbon), February 14, 1944; February 24, 1944; March 10, 1944 (HH XV C-9). For communications with Nazi-occupied Europe, see Birman to Commissao Portuguesa de Assistencia aos Judens Refugiados, July 8, 1943 (HH XV C-8).

76. See "Thirty Years in the Far East," *Shanghai Jewish Almanac* 1946-47, p. 43. Also "29 Jahre" "HIAS" (HICEM) in "Fernen Osten," *Shanghai Herald* (Spec. Edit.), p. 19.

At first, HICEM used the money that remained from the (US) $10,000 grant that was to have been employed for refugee emigration from Shanghai prior to Pearl Harbor. Speelman to Troper, December 14, 1939, p. 6.

Funds were received by HICEM in Shanghai from HICEM in Lisbon and other Jewish relief organizations in Switzerland and Sweden. See Birman to HICEM (Lisbon), January 21, 1942, p. 1 (HH XV C-10). Cf. also Birman to ISRAV, January 19, 1943, p. 1; Birman to Masaiska Foersamlingen (Sweden), January 4, 1943, pp. 1-2; March 5, 1944 (HH XV C-9). Birman to Jew. Comm. Lisbon, March 2, 1944 (HH XV C-9). For information concerning the transfer of money from Jewish Communities in North China and Manchuria to Shanghai, see Birman to ISRAV, January 19, 1943, p. 3; SACRA Minutes, July 5, 1943, p. 1. The minutes for the meetings of the Executive Committee of HIAS (N.Y.) on January 11, 1944 showed an allocation of (US) $6,000 for the Far East in 1943, and one for $3,000 in 1944. It is not clear why the budget was halved. HIAS Minutes, Executive Committee (YIVO). The author went through the microfilms of the minutes of the HIAS (N.Y.) for the period of 1938-45, and found only the above-mentioned references to Shanghai.

17 | "THE LONG ARM OF THE GESTAPO,"

A GHETTO FOR SHANGHAI

*Don't be under any illusions, our reach is quite long.
Even to China!*

(Gestapo agent to Jewish prisoner leaving Dachau
to Shanghai. Burkhard. *Tanz Mal Jude*)

The policy of the Japanese had been so unexpectedly favorable to the refugees that it had, in a sense, dulled their suspicions. After Pearl Harbor, restrictions such as police surveillance of public meetings were imposed. But these were applied with equal severity to other groups, especially "enemy nationals."[1] So astute an observer as Laura Margolies, in fact, observed that relations with the Japanese authorities during the first half of 1942 were more cordial than might have been expected, considering the circumstances.[2]

However, the refugees were unaware that as a result of America's entry into World War II, the steady Nazi pressure on their Japanese allies to conform to the German model of antisemitism had borne fruit. This was to become all too evident to the refugees by February 18, 1943, in the form of a proclamation establishing the Hongkew ghetto for the victims of Hitler in Shanghai. Thus, in one fell swoop, the refugees' fears of the

477

"long arm of the Gestapo," which had inhabited their sub-
conscious for so long, was now brought to reality.[3]

The first overt indication of change was a flurry of
antisemitic newspaper articles in the middle of June 1942.
There was a strong Jewish reaction to this, especially to one
article which blamed all the Jews for the black marketeering
of a few.[4] An emergency meeting was called, at Michael
Speelman's residence, of a recently formed committee representing all Jewish factions in Shanghai, to hear a confidential
report by Shibata, the Japanese Vice-Consul.[5] Shibata, as part
of his duties, had been attending all the meetings of the new
Jewish Affairs Bureau, which a day earlier had made a crucial
decision on the refugees' fate.[6]

The following alarming story, as recalled by one of
the participants, was given at the meeting:

> He [Shibata] informed us that under heavy pressure
> from the German Consulate (particularly its commercial
> attaché, a Baron Putkammer) to isolate the Jews, par-
> ticularly refugees, from freedom of the city in Shanghai,
> the Japanese authorities were giving this matter con-
> sideration. The Germans pointed out that most of the
> refugees were Jews and hence enemies of Hitler (Ger-
> many) and desired nothing but defeat for Germany and
> accordingly should be viewed as a likely source for acts
> of sabotage. It appears that at this point during the war,
> German influence was considerable and various ideas
> were being considered, including the sending of all
> refugees to one of the islands at the mouth of the Yangtze
> River near Shanghai. Also suggested was to confine them
> to the Hongkew area in the northern part of the city
> where many of them were already residing. Mr. Shi-
> bata implied that in his opinion the Jewish community in

Shanghai might well organize all available resources to soften the severity of the conditions which might be imposed in the near future.[7]

And again,

According to Japanese military customs, being accredited members of this Bureau, they [the Japanese military authorities in Shanghai] had full authority to act without obtaining the approval of higher authorities.[8]

Shibata suggested that the Jewish leaders get in touch with these higher Japanese echelons in China and Japan. One of these, General Matsui, and another unnamed, but apparently important official in the foreign office in Tokyo, had been on good terms with the Russian Jews in Harbin, Manchuria, during the early 1930's.[9] Fritz Kaufman's task was to contact an old acquaintance, Herr Brahn, who had connections with the Japanese *gendarmerie,* reputed to be "the nastiest and most difficult of the lot."[10]

These plans did not go too smoothly since Brahn had finally divulged the source of his confidence to the *gendarmerie.* The publicity given the Japanese plans made the authorities order the arrest of all those present at the meeting.[11] After a few weeks of incarceration in the Bridge House Jail, all the Jewish leaders were released, with the "assurance" that "the possibilities that stirred up all the commotion were not realistic because the Japanese authorities are always fair and just to everyone." Among those arrested had been the Vice-Consul Shibata, who after a long imprisonment was dismissed from the consular service and sent back to Japan, according to Fritz Kaufmann. Kaufmann also relates that, after the war, a number of Jewish residents of Shanghai gathered some money for Shibata in gratitude for his services.[12]

It was most difficult to keep the disclosures of the meeting confined to the participants, and within twenty-four hours, the entire Jewish community was subjected to various rumors and speculations concerning their impending fate at the hands of the allegedly Nazi-inspired Japanese authorities. These rumors tended to unnerve the already disheartened and downtrodden. Nevertheless, the refugees attempted to suppress their gnawing fears in the hope that somehow such events would not come to pass.[13]

On the surface, at least, things did quiet down for a few months, though it is now known through top-secret Japanese Foreign Office documents, that some form of "strict surveillance" of the refugees had already been approved by the Japanese Foreign Ministry on January 17, 1942. A more concrete form of the ghetto was approved by November 15, 1942. These acts, as the documents clearly indicate, were the manifestation of a major shift in the previously favorable Japanese policy toward the Jews. This is spelled out in a message sent by Foreign Minister [Shigenori] Togo to [Mamoru] Shigemitsu, the Ambassador to China, and to others, on the subject of "Emergency Measure for Jewish People," which reads in part as follows:

> Due to the outbreak of the Greater East Asia War it has become necessary that *our Jewish measures be subjected to reconsideration.* Apart from possible changes in the decisions reached at the five Ministers' meeting [of December 6, 1938], the following items have been established as an emergency measure by the officers concerned of the Ministries of Army, Navy and Foreign Affairs. As it has been decided on the part of the military and Naval Authorities that this measure be cabled to their respective outstations to be put in practice immediately, *your office*

is hereby requested to take action as stipulated in the following. [italics mine].

Still under the spell of the alleged "Jewish Power" in the United States, the message continued:

You should be careful that the measure should be carried out in no unnecessarily provocative manner that our position might be precipitated in the interest of the enemy counter-propaganda.

These are the measures to be taken by the Japanese authorities in China, and Manchoukuo [sic.]:

1. Since Germany has deprived the Jewish people overseas of their nationality (effective as of January 1), German Jews will hereafter be treated as denationalized Jews:

2. Out of the *denationalized Jews,* and *Jews with a nationality of any neutral nation other than our allies,* those who are or will be made use of on our part . . . will be treated in a friendly way. *The rest of them will be placed under strict surveillance* so that any hostile activity may be eliminated or supressed . . .[14] [italics mine].

Most likely the reference in number two to the "denationalized Jews" refers to the stateless Russian Jews, and "Jews with a nationality of any neutral nation" might mean the Jews with Iraqi (Sephardi) citizenship, since the Japanese probably intended to still "make use" of them. The "rest of them" refers to the German and Austrian refugees, who were now to be kept under careful watch.

By November 18, "strict surveillance" gave way to more concrete measures, as noted in the top secret dispatch from the Japanese Consul-General [Seiki] Yano, in Shanghai, to [Kazuo] Aoki, the Minister of Greater East Asia, concerning "Measures Pertaining to Jewish People," which read as follows:

> Relative to measures pertaining to the Jewish People in Shanghai area, the *plan established by the Japanese Navy of that area,* having *been approved by the Central Government,* will shortly be carried into force. However, in view of the desire of the Navy, it has been decided that the Ministry of Greater East Asia will handle the *enforcement of the concrete measures,* with the Army and Navy giving the necessary cooperation.
>
> The general substance of the above plan is as follows:
> 1. To set up a Jewish district in the Yo Ju Ho [Japanese pronunciation of Hongkew] area and get the Jewish people scattered within the city to collect and live there.

This is followed by the techniques used to bring the refugees into the ghetto, as noted in number two.

> 2. The guidance? to and receiving into the above district [copyists note: "?" appears in the original text] will be accomplished with German Jews numbering [sic] approximately 20,000 as the object, and following this, the disposition of White Russian and other Jewish people will be made.

The third item poses the problem of the method to be utilized for the administration of the ghetto.

> 3. The surveillance, control and guidance after accommodation will be Military Affairs? function ["?" appears in the original text].

The last item presents the means of implementing these measures:

> 4. For the purpose of putting the above plan into effect, a committee, with the Consul-General as its chairman and officials concerned from the Military of Greater East Asia, Army, Navy, Ministry Police, Engineering Bureau, and Special City Government as committee members, will be established.[15]

Evidently, still uncertain as to the political implications of an anti-Jewish move in Shanghai, no agency was interested in taking the sole responsibility for the establishment of the ghetto. This view was even more clearly spelled out when, on February 9, 1943, the final details of the impending ghetto were sent back to Tokyo for confirmation by Consul-General Yano. In this dispatch Yano noted that:

> . . . as nearly a year has already passed since the General Headquarters *Liaison Conference, which is the* direct *basis for subject matter,* was held and, furthermore, because *this affair has delicate signs of international relationship,* the Army and the Ministry of Greater East Asia *will issue the proclamation after each one has obtained the consent of the Central Government.* (The Navy has already contacted the Central Government). It is therefore requested that a consolidated opinion of the Central Government be obtained and instructions be sent to us . . .[16] [italics mine].

Thus, we have come full cycle in respect to the Japanese policy toward the Jews. In a little over three years we find two Liaison Conferences of all the major departments of the Central Government involved in the decisions that affected the fate of the 17,000 Jewish refugees in Shanghai. The first conference in December 1938, agreed to establish a favorable policy, in effect granting them freedom, while the second conference in February 1942, decided to place these refugees into confinement.

All this, of course, was known only to a few individuals among the higher echelons in Tokyo. As far as the refugees were concerned, they were still to have a half-year reprieve, however, until the February 18, 1943 proclamation of the ghetto.

Meanwhile, in order to present a more unified front to the Japanese authorities, and to provide for greater mutual understanding, a roof organization, the Shanghai United Jewish Committee on Communal Representatives was formed in September 1942, representing the three major Jewish communities. As its title implies, it was composed of representatives of the Ashkenazi, Sephardi, and German Communal Associations. Its expressed aims, according to a memo by Dr. A. J. Cohn, whom we shall encounter again, were:

1. To act as an authorized representative body of the entire local Jewish population for furthering and facilitating closer cooperation among the various public bodies and with the local Nipponese and Chinese Authorities.

2. To lead and advise the local Jewish Communal Association in their works but without interfering with their inner life where such undertakings do not have any influence on the whole population.

3. To create and develop a feeling of mutual confidence and cooperation among the various language groups of the local Jewish population and to further closer friendships between Jewish and non-Jewish groups of Shanghai.

To endeavor to clarify and to educate the Jewish population, especially the newcomers, to a better understanding of the customs and peoples of Nippon and China as well as introduce the true status of Jewry to the Nipponese and Chinese, thus automatically better understanding will produce better relationship.[17]

Judging by the lack of reference to it in any other source, this attempt at a united front for all the Jews of Shanghai met with little success. Only a common danger could unite the splintered Shanghai Jewish Community—as was to happen later during the postwar period.[18]

NAZI INFLUENCE IN JAPAN

In Japan, too, the earlier failure of the German Embassy's efforts to promote the Nazi line against Jews and Judaism now achieved a large measure of success. The more favorable Japanese policy toward the Jews was able to predominate with Tokyo as long as the influential "experts" were able to envision various deals with Jews from which Japan's Greater East Asia plans would derive some concrete benefits. Once this notion of the use of the alleged Jewish wealth and power began to fade as a result of America's entry into the war, the experts, such as Inuzuka and his Bureau of Jewish Affairs in Shanghai, no longer served a useful function, and the Captain was returned to active duty with the Navy.

The now stronger Nazi pressures which were to have wide repercussions for Jews all over the Japanese-occupied Pacific, found expression in Japan in the increase in the volume of Japanese-language antisemitic publications subsidized by the German Embassy in Tokyo. Attempts to hold antisemitic lectures and exhibits were no longer curbed, as is evident from the success of two huge exhibits held in 1942 and 1943 in Osaka and Tokyo, respectively, that catered to a combined audience of over one million.

These exhibits were sponsored, in part, by a department store, a major newspaper, and the all-powerful Japanese Bureau of Information. At the second, larger fair in Tokyo, over 32,000 antisemitic brochures were distributed and 3,000 copies of a book by Kommoss, titled *Juden Hinter Stalin*, were sold. All this was aided by the German Embassy and duly reported to the Berlin office. Moreover, Ambassador Stahmer requested additional funds for a project to translate and publish a special small library of Nazi material on Jews.

GENERAL SHIODEN

Among the speakers at the well-attended lectures given at the Tokyo fair was the infamous General Shioden, whose ideology concerning Jews suited closely that of his Nazi friends. In April 1942, Shioden won a seat in the Japanese Diet running on an antisemitic platform.

In his platform, Shioden prided himself for attending the Conference on Jewish Problems in Germany (in 1938). He reiterated the aforementioned Japanese version of the anti-semitic line by blaming the Jews for the start of the war with China as well as the two World Wars. All this was done by the Jews to achieve their goal of world-wide Bolshevik domination. Although seemingly against this movement, the United States and Britain, who were controlled by the "stubborn secret society, Jewish power," contrived to aid and abet this cause.

Shioden pledged, among other things, to resist these powers working in Japan under the guise of "liberalism and individualism." He also vowed to:

> . . . shut out the operation of International Secret Power
> . . . [and] to find out the movement of the secret powers,
> as I studied and experienced over twenty years in the
> field . . . [18a]

ANTISEMITIC ARTICLES

Of interest is the fact that the second exhibit concluded eleven days prior to the proclamation of a Shanghai "Designated Area" on February 18, 1943, made amidst a flurry of antisemitic articles appearing simultaneously in the press in Shanghai, Peking, Tokyo and the Japanese-occupied territories in the Pacific.

As an example, one may cite the article titled "News in Regard with the Jew's Character," published in the *Sin Wan Pao* (a Chinese-language daily) on February 15, 1943.

This article summarizes a virulently antisemitic speech by Wang Ching-wei, President of Japan's puppet regime in Nanking. Wang typically identifies Jews with Bolsheviks, who dislike nationalist feelings in other nations since they lack their own homeland. That is why they are disloyal to every country that offers them a haven. The Jews, he noted, made fortunes in China and Japan at the expense of their hosts: no wonder Germany got rid of them.

An elaboration of these canards with a few new ones thrown in for good measure, is found in another article, a few days after the Proclamation. This piece reported in the *Peking Chronicle* of February 25, was titled "Heyday of Jewish Imperialism in China Has Been Swept Away," and subtitled "Shanghai Authorities Now Study Urgent Problem to Keep Financial Activities Decent."[18b]

Moreover, the tone of these Nazi-inspired articles suddenly became much harsher, especially in the propaganda barrage from Batavia aimed at the Australian audience. Among this avalanche of antisemitic rubbish is another vitriolic speech by General Shioden. The harassment of Jews in the Philippines, the closing of the Jewish newspaper in Harbin, and the mass indoctrination of Japanese school children in Manchuria with antisemitic notions about a people they did not even know existed, were all symptomatic of a breakthrough in Nazi influence on the Japanese government.

WIEDEMANN'S TESTIMONY

This nefarious Nazi influence on the radically revised Japanese policy vis-a-vis the Jewish refugees can best be summed up in the words of the former Chief German Consul of Tientsin, Fritz Wiedemann, who testified on January 22, 1951, that:

> This is to state that I (whose signature is attached below) have been Consul General for Germany in Tientsin from 1941 to 1945.
>
> I hereby declare that I was thoroughly acquainted with the situation in the part of China then occupied by Japan, and that I followed the directives of the German government in all my activities there.
>
> I therefore confirm that the internment of Central-European emigrants as a rule primarily Jews who had emigrated from Germany and Austria to China, had taken place upon the instigation of the German government then in power. The Japanese themselves were not anti-semitic, and we were under orders to instruct the Japanese authorities about the racial policies of Germany and to suggest appropriate measures. There is no doubt in my mind that the internment of Jews in the Shanghai ghetto had been instigated by German authorities,
>
> From my work with Hitler I know that in the matter of policy pressure was exerted upon friendly governments in that direction.
>
> I am also prepared to make these statements under oath before court.[18c]

PROCLAMATION OF GHETTO

Thus, nine days after Tokyo's final decision, the seemingly inevitable finale came on February 18, 1943, when the Japanese proclaimed officially, over the radio and on the newspaper front pages the establishment of a ghetto. The terms seemed almost innocuous, but they made real at last the refugees' worst fears.

PROCLAMATION CONCERNING RESTRICTION OF RESIDENCE AND BUSINESS OF STATELESS REFUGEES

I.   Due to military necessity, places of residence and business of the stateless refugees in the Shanghai area shall hereafter be restricted to the undermentioned area in the International Settlement. East of the line connecting Chaoufoong Road, Muirhead Road and Dent Road; West of Yangtzepoo Creek; North of the line connecting East Seward Road and Wayside Road; and South of the boundary of the International Settlement.

II. The stateless refugees at present residing and/or carrying on business in the district other than the above area shall remove their places of residence and/or business into the area designated above by May 18, 1943.

Permission must be obtained from the Japanese authorities for the transfer, sale, purchase or lease of rooms, houses, shops or any other establishments, which are situated outside the designated area and now being [sic] occupied or used by the stateless refugees.

III. Persons other than the stateless refugees shall not remove into the area mentioned in Article I without permission of the Japanese authorities.

IV. Persons who will have violated this *Proclamation* or obstructed its reenforcement shall be liable to severe punishment.

> Commander-in-Chief of the Imperial Japanese Army in the Shanghai Area.
> Commander-in-Chief of the Imperial Japanese Navy in the Shanghai Area.
> February 18, 1943.

The refugees were given a three-month deadline, that is until May 18, to relocate to their new home.[19]

The terms "Jew" or "ghetto" were not used. The sensitivity of the Japanese on this score prompted them to substitute "stateless refugee" and "designated area" in referring to the Hongkew sector. Even in private conversation only these euphemisms were permitted.[20]

A newspaper article which appeared at the same time as the proclamation was more explicit in its details. In line with the above-mentioned Japanese sensitivity, the article went to great lengths to anticipate all possible objections and fears on the part of the refugees by stating:

> This measure is motivated by military necessity, and is, therefore, *not an arbitrary action intended to oppress* their legitimate occupation. It is even contemplated to safeguard so far as possible their place of residence as well as their livelihood in the designated area . . . the public at large is also reguested to comprehend its significance.[21] [italics mine].

The key term "stateless refugees" is defined as those refugees who

. . . arrived in Shanghai *since* 1937 from Germany (including former Austria, Czecho-Slovakia), Hungary, *former Poland,* Latvia, Lithuania and Estonia, etc. and who have no nationality at present.[22] [italics mine].

The emphasis is on the date, since this excluded all the Russian and Polish Jews who, although stateless, belonged to the earlier-settled Ashkenazi community.[23]

Any woman married to one eligible for the "designated area" was considered in the same category as her husband. The same was true of business partnerships.[24] In an additional regulation, the phrase "It is hoped" at the start, "requested" the present (Chinese) residents to move to other areas, and offered the assistance of the Japanese authorities. This was in sharp contrast to the mandatory tone of the rest, and was an obvious appeal to the good will of the Chinese at the expense of the white man.[25]

Of utmost importance for the refugees' future in the ghetto was the rule that gave temporary permission for those refugees with jobs outside the "designated area" to leave it during working hours.[26] On the other hand, "enemy nationals" who lived outside the ghetto had to obtain a pass to enter it.

Thus, about half of the approximately 16,000 refugees, who had overcome great obstacles and had found a means of livelihood and residence outside the "designated area" were forced to leave their homes and businesses for a second time and to relocate into a crowded, squalid area of less than one square mile, with its own population of an estimated 100,000 Chinese and 8,000 refugees.[27]

In dry statistics, this meant that 811 apartments, consisting of 2,766 rooms, outside the restricted area had to be exchanged by the refugees for new quarters, and 307 concerns were forced to close down while their proprietors attempted to relocate inside the ghetto. Numbers, however, cannot convey the anguish of losing an apartment, built up literally from scratch, for a much inferior one, and usually smaller. Nor do bare numbers tell of the difficulties encountered by those refugees whose initiative and drive had helped them create a going concern, kept them off relief, and who now had to try once again, under even more trying conditions, to reestablish their businesses. Needless to say, many were unsuccessful.

The Japanese, and even observers from the Shanghai International Red Cross, did not view such a relocation as unrealistic, since they assumed that an equal number of Chinese would readily move out of the "designated area" and make an exchange of apartments greatly to their advantage. Things however did not turn out quite as anticipated. True, the more affluent refugees had little difficulty in arranging for a relatively good apartment in exchange for their well-fixed-up old ones. They could afford to absorb the loss and any additional costs. Yet, the majority could ill afford the loss of their major investment, the key money for their former apartments and places of business, and accept as substitute a dirty old apartment, often in need of disinfecting.[28]

The reluctance of the Chinese to leave their homes proved to be a blessing in disguise to the refugees: it was some comfort to know they were not totally isolated in their ghetto.[29]

Although the refugees were permitted to take furniture, goods and personal belongings with them, because of the May 18th deadline, they often obtained very low prices for their apartments. The refugees would report the availability of their premises to an agent, usually White Russian, who sold them mainly to Japanese clients, at a very low price. One refugee doctor had built an office-apartment consisting of five rooms with telephone, bath fixtures and toilet. He was forced to exchange it with a Japanese for a small, dirty apartment. The doctor was lucky in that the Japanese was not interested in such amenities as bathroom fixtures or telephone, and he was permitted to take them with him. But, in most cases, the refugee had to sell most of his personal items in order to effect the exchange.

Most of the refugees lost their former telephones, and any transfer to the ghetto had to be okayed by Kubota's Bureau for Refugee Affairs.[30]

GHETTO RESTRICTIONS

The boundaries of the "designated area" were given in the proclamation and clarified as follows in an article accompanying the proclamation:

The designated area is bordered on the west by the line connecting Chaoufoong, Muirhead and Dent Roads; on the east by Yangtzepoo Creek; on the south by the line connecting East Seward, Muirhead and Wayside Roads, and on the north by the boundary of the International Settlement.[31]

Consisting of approximately forty square blocks of drab lane housing, the ghetto was unrelieved by the green of even a small park.[32] In fact, the closest thing to greenery in the ghetto was said to be a green-painted bench.[32]

Most of the exits from the ghetto were guarded either by armed Japanese sentries or Jewish members of the auxiliary police, called the Foreign Pao Chia[33] The Pao Chia had been organized in September 1942, as part of the city-wide plan for self-policing and collective responsibility imposed by the Japanese on the city.[34] It was composed of all men between twenty and forty-five. They had to serve several hours a week on a rotating basis. The Jewish Pao Chia, consisting of about 3,500 men, was headed by Dr. Felix Kardegg under the general supervision of the Japanese Chief Inspector Yasuda (of the Wayside police station) and a White Russian assistant named Kraemer.[35]

With the establishment of the ghetto, the *Pao Chia* took on the more onerous task of guarding the exits and making certain that the refugees did not leave the ghetto without a properly stamped pass.[36] Those who did sneak out without one risked an encounter with the *Pao Chia* upon return. The refugees hated some of the *Pao Chia* for taking their job too seriously. If bearers of passes returned even one minute late, the guards might tear up the precious pass or they might threaten to report the refugees to the Japanese authorities. One such nasty episode involved two yeshiva students who crossed the ghetto boundary on the eve of the holiday of *Shevuot* to make a purchase. Upon returning across the street into the ghetto, they were stopped by a *Pao Chia* who checked their double-pass and discovered that one of the students did not fit the identity. The *Pao Chia* slapped the guilty party and had both students arrested by the authorities, who detained them in the typhus-ridden cell of the Wayside Police station. It took a great deal of "bribery and the proper connections" to bail out the two on the second day of the holiday. In all fairness it must be pointed out that these actions were perpetrated by only a few of the *Pao Chia* guards. Others helped the refugees wherever possible, especially when they were not observed by the supervising, bicycle-riding Japanese or White Russian officers. One refugee officer in the *Pao Chia,* with several stripes to denote his authority, and who proudly possessed a hard-to-come-by bicycle, attempted to assert this authority with the Japanese soldier driver of a truck which had bumped into his valuable machine. Neither the refugee nor his bicycle were ever heard of again.[37]

Occasionally, for emergencies such as a Japanese search for violators or saboteurs, the *Pao Chia* would cordon off a section of the ghetto with rope or barbed wire. However, a few exits might be left unguarded or uncordoned, and some of the refugees would make use of these open lanes to attempt trips out of the ghetto. They managed to evade the periodic checkups of identification cards outside the "designated area" as well as the *Pao Chia* guards upon their return.[38] All the exits had signs posted which read, "Stateless Refugees Prohibited Without Permission," but many of the young people especially in their desire to get out of the confinement of the ghetto and find a little green patch, would sneak out and go to a park outside the restricted area.[39]

Already by mid-1942 the German refugees had to return their most recently acquired I.D. cards known as Bridge Passes for new ones, called "resident certificates." These were issued by the Juedische Gemeinde on behalf of the Japanese authorities. This regulation similarly applied to other refugees who had secured Chinese, English or French I.D. cards prior to the Japanese occupation. The new "resident certificates" had an easily identifiable yellow stripe printed across the top and the words "German Refugee" printed in both English and Japanese. This act of being singled out again, by a familiar yellow designation, sent shudders of fear down the backs of many refugees. Their premonition of this act as a prelude to some kind of isolation was probably correct, since, as we have seen, the Japanese, at that time, had already prepared for some major change of policy concerning the Jewish refugees.[40] All other non-Chinese residents of Shanghai received similar I.D. cards, but but with a green stripe to distinguish them from the Jewish refugees. These enabled them to travel anywhere in the city.[41]

The "Aryan" wives of Jewish refugees, who had divorced their husbands, not only received green-striped I.D.'s, but were granted financial support by the German Embassy.[42]

It is to the credit of most of these divorced wives that they used their financial aid to provide extra food for their families, whom they visited every evening. The number of such Nazi-inspired divorces was estimated to be approximately 150.[43]

The refugees who received passes to leave the ghetto for employment on the outside were known to the rest of the population by virtue of red or blue metal badges worn on the lapel, on which was printed in Chinese characters "May Pass," and which only the refugees were required to wear.[44]

BUREAU FOR STATELESS REFUGEES

The Japanese military authorities gave the responsibility for carrying out all items of the proclamation to a newly created department called the Bureau for Stateless Refugees Affairs. Its headquarters was located at 70 Muirhead Road, in the "designated area."[45] This bureau was headed by Tsutomu Kubota, a former naval officer, who was, in effect, to reign supreme over the approximately 15,000-16,000 refugees residing in the ghetto until the end of the War in the Pacific.[46] Although he was far from popular among the refugees, he had relatively little direct contact with them, dealing chiefly with the representatives of various Jewish organizations and preferring to let the dirty work be done by his two subordinates, Ghoya and Okura.[47] These two men were to become objects of intense hatred and fear among the refugees who had to deal with them directly.[48]

PASS SYSTEM—GHOYA AND OKURA

The infamous Ghoya was in charge of issuing both the three-month "seasonal passes" and the monthly passes.[49] The seasonal passes were granted by the Japanese authorities to refugees with "justified occupation," i.e., permanent jobs. The temporary passes, for one month or less, were given to those with immediate needs outside the ghetto. These were dispensed quite liberally during the first year of the ghetto, when over 1,600 three-month and 2,500 briefer passes were issued.[50] According to Morris Feder, Ghoya's Jewish secretary, the distinction between seasonal and briefer passes was less dependent upon the nature of the refugee's employment than on Ghoya's whim. Depending on his mood, whether the refugee had a permanent job or no job at all outside the ghetto, Ghoya was liable or not to issue a pass.[51] Actually, it was a general policy of the Japanese authorities to pressure those refugees with permanent jobs outside the ghetto to find a livelihood within the "designated area." This was the real reason why the three-month passes were severely curtailed after the first year, leaving Ghoya in charge primarily of the one-month passes.[52]

In contrast to his colleague, and to most Japanese, Okura was tall and powerfully built. He was in charge of issuing the short-term passes, ranging from a few hours to one month.[53] It was he who was also generally the one to mete out punishment to any hapless refugee caught violating the ghetto regulations.[54]

Anyone desiring a pass to leave the "designated area" because of an outside job, had to produce a document certifying employment at a legitimate firm. This firm became fully responsible to the Japanese authorities for its "employee." Since many refugees were either self-employed or performed all sorts of odd jobs in order to earn a few dollars, they would never have been able to produce a bona fide certificate of employment without the active sympathy of many businessmen outside the "designated area." These employers were either Russian Jews, who were permitted to live outside the ghetto, or non-Jewish employers of Swiss, French, White Russian and even German (gentile) nationality.[55]

They provided hundreds of such certificates vouching

for non-existent jobs, at great risk to themselves since they faced severe punishment if caught by the Japanese authorities. The refugee would generally show up at his job once a month for a renewal of his certificate, and, in the meantime, seek ways of supporting his family.[56] He would often deal in the black market (especially that of currency exchange), as the middleman, trusted by the Occidental to carry out his mission. Or, he would peddle some wares such as saccharine or insulin, bought outside the ghetto and sold for a profit to other refugees.[57]

Every day, hundreds of fearful refugees would line up for hours in front of Ghoya and Okura's offices in the Bureau, and plead for a pass that would enable them to get a medical examination, attend a funeral, or earn a few sorely needed dollars.[58] For many this wait ended in a traumatic experience, especially if they were victims of one of Ghoya's foul moods. He was best characterized in the words of one eyewitness, a psychiatrist, as

> . . . a psychopathic personality full of pathological ambition. He called himself "King of the Jews" and loved to be photographed in front of lines of people waiting for passes. He displayed all the attitudes of a tyrant. He wanted to be feared and at the same time, to be popular. He would play with children on the one hand, and at the same time tyrannize the group with conflicting orders, passing moods and personal whims.[59]

While playing with children he would ask them if they knew who was "King of the Jews," and when they answered (being familiar with his tactics) that Ghoya was king, he would reward them with candy.

Similarly, when Ghoya would visit the Kadoorie School periodically, he loved to preside over their athletic meets, he always treated the children and their teachers very courteously. In fact, the teachers had no problems getting their passes to get to the school outside the ghetto. The children, with their school identification, were not even required to get such passes.

It was this erratic behavior more than anything else that left such deeply hostile impressions. Ghoya would vehemently denounce the man in line as a liar and gangster, and in a split-second about-face, hand the still-bewildered refugee a pass for a wider area even than requested. He always "knew" or "did" things better than the refugees, as is manifested in the episode of the musicians. Since Ghoya, among other things, was an amateur violinist, he often invited refugee musicians to accompany him. Once, when he had a clash of harmony with Professor Alfred Wittenberg, a well-known violinist, Ghoya angrily remarked, "You play as I direct, or I kill you." His ungainliness and short stature were probably the basis for much of Ghoya's psychotic behavior. This became particularly evident in his usually picking a tall refugee for attack, jumping on his desk and slapping his victim across the face.[60]

In another incident related by Feder, a refugee who evidently understood Ghoya's character, arrived wearing a fancy cylinder hat. Ghoya started to shout at him, "Are you making fun of me?" The man answered that he always wore this hat when meeting with men of high caliber. Ever since, Feder noted, the man was always granted a pass without difficulty.

Yet, despite his erratic behavior and frequent slapping (a common behavior among Japanese occupation soldiers who often endured similar treatment at the hands of their superiors), Ghoya never shot anyone, or ordered anyone to be shot, or even doomed a refugee to the typhus-ridden jail. Moreover, when Ghoya was in a good mood, he would dispense passes quite liberally.[61]

Such behavior was not to be expected of Ghoya's colleague, Okura, who, one gathers, was a great deal more sadistic, and inflicted more serious damage on the refugees. This is illustrated by accounts of his frequent beatings. Okura's powerful slaps were far more devastating than Ghoya's. He also forced the refugees to wait hours in the broiling Shanghai sun before even listening to their requests. And violators of the rules were sent to the bunker of the Ward Road jail, a sure condemnation to typhus, if not to death.[62]

One can therefore understand readily some of the proclamation's psychological impact upon the unfortunate refugees. Under increasing pressures, many panicked, although the majority were able to swallow even this bitter pill with stoicism. As Margolies saw it, the

> . . . proclamation came as a bombshell to Shanghai Jews, who were taken by complete surprise. There were not more than three or four of us who knew this was in the air. To the refugees this seemed like almost the last thing that could happen to them after what they had previously been through. It is interesting that the refugee group itself took this proclamation with considerably more calm than the local Russian Jews and the old resident German Jews, who, although the proclamation said "stateless," realized that this was the first threat to themselves, even though they were not at that moment directly affected by it. Some of the refugees were quite hysterical about it. The majority who had taken one blow after the other, took this as just another blow and their whole attitude toward the situation was that the United Nations [sic] were close to winning the war and that they simply had to tighten their belts, and see this thing through until the day of victory. I must express my admiration for the way in which the majority of these people took a proclamation which really meant the end of their livelihood.[63]

EXEMPTIONS TO THE PROCLAMATION

As noted above, the key word in the proclamation was "stateless," which included only refugees without nationality, such as those from Germany, Nazi-occupied Austria, Czecho-Slovakia, Hungary, former [sic] Poland, Latvia, Lithuania and Estonia.[64] Included among those forced into the ghetto were three persons of Chinese nationality (including two children), one Portuguese and three British, since the proclamation gave the wives of "eligible" refugees the same status as their husbands.[65]

The largest bloc of "stateless" residents to be exempt from the ghetto, as they had arrived prior to 1937, was that of the White Russians and Russian Jews.[66] There was much speculation and recrimination concerning the exemption of the Russian Jews. Although, at the time, the refugees felt quite bitter against the Russian Jews, for what they regarded as a sellout, in retrospect, even their severest critic, Moshe Elbaum, had to agree that it would have helped no one to have the Russian Jews included in the proclamation. On the contrary, by having the freedom of movement, the Russians could conduct their business and help the refugees in more ways than one.[67] In the author's opinion, it was Japan's tenuous and delicate relations with the Soviet Union during World War II that determined the fate of the Russian Jews. Japan desired at all costs to avoid any unnecessary friction even when it only involved stateless Russians, including Jews.[68] This is substantiated by the top-secret Japanese Foreign Office document on February 9, 1943, which spelled out the proclamation quite explicitly, nine days prior to its public announcement. It specifically excluded the White Russians and Russian Jews on the interesting ground "that there is no danger of causing international complications," implying relations with Germany and Russia, as Dicker has already pointed out.[69] Additional examination of the relevant Japanese documents also reveals, that until March 1944, the Japanese always used the term "Jewish people," rather than the euphemism "stateless refugees."[70] As late as May 1944, the term "Stateless *Jewish* Refugees in Shanghai" was used in a document.[71]

There were other, smaller groups that were exempt from the ghetto for one reason or another. For example, 15 to 20 refugees, hailing originally from Poland, who had arrived in Shanghai via Belgium after a brief residence there, were exempted. Unsuccessful requests were also made to SACRA for exemptions on behalf of several Yiddish writers, by the editor of *Unser Leben*. He wrote to Dr. Cohn that as steady contributors their presence was necessary for the proper functioning of the paper.[72] A few persons who resided in the French Concession and who had lived previously in a French territory were given the protection of the French (Vichy) Consul General who claimed jurisdiction over them, while others, obviously affluent, were able to remain outside by purchasing a Portuguese passport.[73]

EXTENSIONS

During the first year following the proclamation, hundreds of refugees were able to obtain extensions for residence outside the ghetto, usually for a three-month period. Although many of them practiced certain favored professions such as medicine, nursing, and related occupations, others received extensions for reasons of health, employment in fields of public interest (such as relief), or because of age—for those living with families who were not affected by the proclamation. For example, an aged mother, supported by children with Portuguese passports was permitted to remain outside the ghetto.[74]

The explanatory newspaper article attached to the

proclamation gave notice that it was possible for shops or businesses "that serve the public" such as clinics, to apply for extension permits, but leeway was also granted most commercial enterprises during the first year.[75] Prior to such approval, their financial status was carefully scrutinized and a "voluntary contribution" was "solicited" towards the upkeep of SACRA, the Russian-Jewish agency in charge of the relocation to the ghetto.[76] In addition, refugees whose rooms or apartments were not ready for occupation by the May 18, 1943 deadline were granted extensions.[77]

By May 18, 1943, the end of the three-month deadline, about 14,000 refugees, including the more than 2,800 in the *Heime*, either already resided in, or had relocated to the "designated area." According to figures supplied to the Japanese Ministry of Greater East Asia by the Consul General of Shanghai, 1,172 eligible refugees still remained outside because of one kind of extension or another. Ten months later, this number had decreased to 207.[78] In all, probably not more than about 50 refugees managed to reside permanently outside the "designated area."[79]

When Dr. Abraham Kaufman in Harbin heard via cable of the establishment of the Shanghai ghetto, he immediately protested to the authorities at Dairen and Tientsin, and telegraphed likewise to Tokyo. They replied with the same message printed in the official proclamation, i.e., it is not a discriminatory act, only one of military necessity. They further informed him that within the designated area, the Jews are free to conduct their affairs unmolested. As proof of their lack of antisemitism, the Japanese authorities pointed to the fact that confinement referred to only some of the Jews, that is, the German stateless refugees. Unconvinced, Kaufman could do little to effect any change. Still, the Japanese responded apologetically, as they did similarly in a private explanation to

a prominent Jewish businessman in Tokyo, using Colonel
Yasue as the messenger.[80]

Thus, deprived by the Nazi regimé of even the last
vestige of German nationality by November 29, 1941, the
refugees were completely helpless in face of the new Japanese
policy to follow their Axis partner's ideology toward the Jews.[81]

NOTES : "THE LONG ARM OF THE GESTAPO"

1. Cf. Gruenberger, "Refugees," p. 339. Cf. also Carey, *War Years*, p. 85, for some of the general restrictions applied to Shanghai.

2. Margolies, *Report*, pp. 1, 14. See also Kaufmann, "Experiences," pp. 5-6; Peritz, "Affidavit," p. 1.

3. For the earlier Japanese policy re the refugees, see above, chapter 8.

4. Kaufmann, "Experiences," pp. 6, 10. Also Friedlander, "Einkreisung," p. 12. *Unser Leben* (July 31, 1942), p. 1 (English Suppl.) The latter source discusses the black marketeering. For the Gestapo, see Burkhard, *Tanz*, p. 139.

5. Peritz, "Affidavit," p. 2. There exist four fairly detailed accounts of this meeting and its aftermath, three of which were written by participants: Bitker, *Memo*, pp. 2-3 (DP); Kaufman, "Experiences," pp. 8-16; Peritz, "Affidavit," pp. 1-3; Margolies, *Report*, pp. 14-15. (Although Margolies was not present at the meeting, she was informed of its details, and Peritz gave her a full account of the alleged Japanese plans).
Other references to this meeting will be noted below.
This was probably an ad hoc committee which had no direct connections with a later one formed in September, 1942, called the *Shanghai United Jewish Committee of Communal Representatives*.
This meeting was attended by Michel Speelman and Ellis Hayim. The latter represented the Sephardic Jews; Boris Topaz and Joseph Bitker, the Russian Jews; Dr. Felix Kardegg, Fritz Kaufmann and Robert Peritz, the German refugees. See Kaufmann, "Experiences," p. 8. Kaufmann could not recall Bitker's name. See Bitker, *Memo*, p. 2, where Bitker also leaves out a few names. Peritz (Affidavit," p. 2) erroneously placed Brahn among the participants, although Brahn was not even involved with any aspect of the refugees until after this meeting. Kaufmann Interview.

6. Kaufmann, "Experiences," p. 8. Kaufmann's is the only report on this meeting to give the name of the *Jewish Affairs Bureau*, [i.e. The Bureau of Jewish Affairs], which he noted was re-formed, following the departure of Captain Inuzuka whom he considered "a very considerate man and rather sympathetic to the Jews." *Ibid.*, pp. 7-8.
The Bureau of Jewish Affairs was composed of the representatives of the Japanese Army, Navy, Air Force, Consulate and the Japanese representative to the Shanghai Municipal Council, See Bitker, *Memo*, p. 2.

7. Bitker, *Memo*, p. 2. Also cited by Dicker, *Wanderers*, pp. 116-17. Baron Putkammer mentioned above was not a commercial attache but the head of

the *German Information Bureau* whose task it was to spread Nazi propaganda.

8. Kaufmann, "Experiences," p. 8.

9. Kaufmann, "Experiences," pp. 8-9. According to Fritz Kaufmann, Dr. Abraham Kaufman of Harbin was to contact the "high official" at Tokyo, who might be Premier Matsuoka. The writer attempted to correspond with Dr. Abraham Kaufman in Israel, to learn of this "contact," but received no reply. See Kranzler-Kaufman Corres., August 16, 1969.

Margolies and Siegel were suspicious of Shibata's motives (she erroneously calls him Katawa). See Margolies, *Report*, p. 14. She vetoed Shibata's idea of cabling the United States for help in this matter, although, as she admitted, she had heard from other "reliable" sources that "something was brewing among the Japanese authorities with regard to segregation plans for the refugees." *Ibid.* Margolies and Siegel maintained a "hand-off" policy and refused to have any connections with attempts to mitigate the impending harsh decrees. See *ibid.*

Fritz Kaufmann suggested that it was possible that Shibata was being paid by Ellis Hayim in order to keep tabs on Japanese plans concerning the Jews, though he still believed Shibata's story. Kaufmann Interview.

The writer (April 16, 1971) received a taped interview between Rabbi Marvin Tokayer (of the *Jewish Community Center* in Tokyo) and Dr. A. J. Cohen, former head of SACRA. See chapter 18. [Cohn Interview] in which Dr. Cohn described his role in alerting the Jewish community to the Japanese intentions, and the Nazi influence on the Japanese policy. Since there are too many things unsaid, and others, particularly names, are not too clear, further research is required to make full use of these tapes. Only brief items will be utilized. The writer gratefully acknowledges the receipt of these tapes and other information from Rabbi Tokayer. (TP).

10. Kaufmann, "Experiences," p. 9. Also Margolies, *Report*, p. 15. For Brahn's connections with the gendarmerie, see above, chapter 16.

11. Kaufmann, "Experiences," pp. 10-11. His account is the most detailed one of the treatment of prisoners in the Bridge House.

Other accounts include Ossie Lewin, "Bridge House Memories, Reunited at Social Gathering" [Lewin, "Bridge House"], *Almanac*, pp. 21-23; Burkhard, *Tanz*, pp. 152-53; *Yellow Creek*, pp. 177-78. Cf. also Bitker, *Memo*, pp. 2-3; Margolies, *Report*, p. 15; Peritz, "Affidavit," p. 2; Bitker, *Memo*, p. 3.

12. Kaufmann Interview. Cf. Bitker, *Memo*, p. 3. Kaufmann, Topaz and Shibata were detained longer than the rest for other reasons. Kaufmann, "Experiences," pp. 12-13. Dr. Cohn believes that Topaz was arrested for attempting to bribe a Japanese officer. Dr. Cohn had previously suggested an alternate method of dealing with the Japanese authorities. Interview.

13. Bitker, Memo, p. 3. For these "rumors" see also Shoshana, *In Faier*,

p. 294; Faerber, "Affidavit," pp. 1-2; Kaufmann, "Experiences," p. 10; Gruenberger, "Refugees," p. 341; Friedlander, "Einkreisung," p. 12.

For an early warning to Jews about a possible ghetto, see *Unser Leben* (February 13, 1942) (Yiddish section), p. 1.

14. FO S9460-3-2516, January 17, 1942. See also a similar, undated (Foreign Secret) [ca January 1942] summary of "Jewish Measures in view of the 1942 situation. (Plan adopted at the Liaison Conference).

As Dicker already noted, in his manuscript (p. 133), the date of this document can be inferred from the February 9, 1942 FO document quoted just below note 16, (No. 51464), in which it is stated that as nearly a year has passed since the General Headquarters Liaison Conference which is the direct basis for the subject matter, was held.

The German refugees lost their citizenship on November 29, 1941. See below.

15. FO 30320, 30321 (cable) No. 69. Top Secret Nov. 18 [1942].

See also "T1111 (R-118-F31243) Jikyoku ni tomonau Yudayajin no toriatsukai; Military Affairs Section, Army Ministry; January 19, 1942; *Riku A Mitsu Dai Nikki*, vol. 10, no. 98; NA 16315. Treatment of the Jews in View of Current Situation," which seems to be a copy of FO Secret (ca. January 1942) and possibly FO S9460-3-2516, January 17, 1942. This is found in Young's "Checklist of Microfilm Reproductions of Selected Archives of the Japanese Army, Navy and other Government Agencies, 1868-1945," courtesy of Andrew Y. Kuroda, Head of the Japanese Division of the Library of Congress). (DP).

16. Yano to Aoki, February 9, [1943] Dispatch No. 51464. Telegram No. 130. (DP).

17. Dr. A. J. Cohn, *Memo, September* 9, 1942 (YIVO No. 19). Cited by Kranzler, *M.A.,* pp. 86-87.

18. This organization was suggested to the rather reluctant Jewish leaders by Dr. Cohn, who had already become aware of some of the Japanese plans to set up a ghetto. Dr. Cohn seems to concur about the impossibility of getting all the Jews of Shanghai to present a unified front. Interview.

18a. For Inuzuka's return to active duty, see Dicker's interview of Inuzuka, January 28, 1958 (DP). The story of the Nazi-influenced Japanese policy in the occupied territories and the German influence in the creation of the ghetto is not yet complete. The author is presently at work on this subject, which is expected to appear in the near future.

The two antisemitic exhibits are mentioned in several sources. For the larger, Tokyo exhibit, held from January 15 to February 7, 1943, see a summary of the article in the *Yudaya Kenkyu* titled "An Exhibition Concerning Freemasonry," *JCM,* p. 59. A translation of the complete article was made for the author by Professor Kotsuji. The texts of several articles from the *Yudaya Kenkyu* were supplied to the author courtesy of the Japanese division of the Library of Congress. This exhibit was sponsored by the press ("Mainichi Shimbum") and had the support of Information Bureau. (Kotsuji terms it the "Intelligence Bureau".) It was held in the Matsuya Department Store in Tokyo. The title of the exhibit was "International Secret Power and Free Masonry" (see article). Support also came from the leadership of the *Kokusai Seikei Gakkai* (*ibid.*).

Here, as in numerous other instances, Jews are at best secondary to the major villain, "Freemasonry," which is often but not necessarily identified with the Jews.

The first evening of the exhibit (January 14) was reserved for those with invitations, while the masses were permitted attendance from the 15th on.

See also Inland II A/B April 23, 1943, in a cable by Stahmer to Berlin. Stahmer reported an attendance for both exhibits at one and a half million visitors. He is also the source for the sale of the book by Kommass, and the brochures, as well as support by the German Embassy. Cf. also Kaufman, *Manchuria*, pp. 30-33 for the first exhibit at Fukuoka, which was stopped through Jewish intervention. Another exhibit is reported to have been held in September 1941. (See *Tokyo Record*. It was attended by 1,000 people. (TP))

For Stahmer's request for money to publish antisemitic books, see Inland II, April 23, 1943, notes at bottom of telegram.

The Osaka exhibit is also reported on in the *Yudaya Kenkyu* (September 1943), pp. 85-68, 98. *JCM*, p. 262. This article was similarly translated for the author by Kotsuji, who added his personal observations at the end. The slogan for this smaller exhibit was "To Expose *Yudaya* [the Jews] that Manipulate America and Britain." This was directed by Shioden and Masao Masuda (the Executive Director of the *KSG*). Both lectured there as well. Kotsuji called Masuda the Japanese "Streicher." Cf. also Inland II, July 6, 1942.

Another antisemitic lecture, one by the editor of the same Mainichi, Hichiro ("Soho") Takutomi, was given on October 22, 1943 (*Peking Chronicle*, October 24, 1943) (LP).

For Shioden's election campaign, see KP, April 30, 1942, which is a detailed copy of the platform and a biographical sketch. (DP)

The Jews living in Japan at the time were aware of these exhibits. See, for example, M. Moiseff to Tokayer, July 6, 1973. (TP)

18b. An English translation of the *Sin Wan Pao* article is found in YIVO No. 11; the second article is part of the Loewenthal Papers.

18c. For the closing of the Harbin Jewish newspaper *Yevreskaya Zhizn*, at the end of 1943, see Kaufman, *"Itonot,"* p. 86. Cf. also Kaufman, *Manchuria*, p. 40.

For the Nazi propaganda in Manchuria see *ibid.*, pp 17, 22, 30-35. I am indebted to a colleague, Professor P. for information concerning the indoctrination of Japanese school children with Nazi propaganda. Conversation with the author, June 26, 1975. Professor P. related his experiences. He said that at the time he had no idea what Jews were.

An earlier, brief attempt, had been made by the author to ascertain the Nazi influence on the Japanese policy toward the Jews, especially concerning the establishment of the ghetto. See Kranzler M.A. Chap. 7. The quotation from Wiedemann is cited there on p. 112, based on Michaelis, *Testimony*, p. 27. Dicker, *Wanderers*, p. 115, uses this quotation (the author's free translation) from Kranzler, M.A.

Much additional research is still required before one can make a more definitive statement on this theme. As noted, the author is in the process of completing such research.

19. *Shanghai Herald* (February 18, 1943), p. 1 [*Herald*, "February 2, 1943"] (YIVO No. 67). See Appendix.

The complete wording of this proclamation, with the Japanese enunciation of the street boundaries, and lacking a specific date, had already been issued by the combined authority of the Japanese Army, Navy and Ministry of Greater East Asia on February 9, 1943. This can be found in the (Top Secret) FO message No. 51464, February 9, 1943, sent by Yano, the Japanese Consul General of Shanghai to Aoki, Minister of Greater East Asia [FO No. 51464, February 9, 1943]. Cited by Dicker, *Wanderers*, etc., p. 118.

For the element of surprise in this proclamation, see the Introduction to the Shanghai Consular Police Secret Correspondence No. 302, sent by Yano to Aoki, May 18, 1943, p. 1, titled "Re: Activities of Jewish Refugees in Shanghai For the Past Three Years." (Actually, the body of the report is but a summary of Heinz Ganther's special edition of the *Shanghai Herald* (1943) titled "Drei Jahre Immigration in Shanghai," which was later published in Shanghai as a separate book. Copy in writer's possession, courtesy R. Loewenthal). Cf. also *Unser Leben* (July 31, 1942) English Suppl.), p. 1, for the Jewish reaction to the general accusation of black-marketeering on the part of the Jews. See also Friedrichs, *Geschichte*, p. 166.

20. M[oshe] Elbaum, "18 February 1943: Die Geschichte des Hongkewer Ghettos," *Herald* (*S.E.*), pp. 24-25 [Elbaum, "18 Februar"]. Cf. also editorial in the *Juedisches Nachrichtenblatt* (May 28, 1943), p. 2 (in which the author, echoing the Japanese view, exclaims "dass der Distrikt weder ein 'Ghetto,' noch ein 'Gefaengnis' darstellt"). Copy, in writer's possession, courtesy G. Gerechter. Margolies, *Report*, p. 6; Shoshana, *In Faier*, p. 298; Burkhard, *Tanz*, p. 153; Epstein, "Mir," p. 130. Cf. also speech by Kubota, quoted in the *Shanghai Jewish Chronicle* (May 9, 1943), p. 1; (June 4, 1943), p. 3.

21. *Herald* (February 18, 1943), p. 1. Cf. also above, no. 20.

22. *Herald* (February 18, 1943), p. 1.

23. For the resentment that this "exclusion from the ghetto" aroused among the refugees towards the Russian Jews, see below, at end of chapter.

24. *Herald* (February 18, 1943).

25. Elbaum, "18 Februar," p. 24. Elbaum also reported that the Chinese newspapers contained similar appeals.
For the Japanese attempts to humiliate the white man for the benefit of the Chinese, see above, chapter 16.

26. See below. For the prohibition to "enter" the ghetto, see Greta Didner Interview September 22, 1973. Mrs. Didner was of Turkish descent and lived outside the ghetto across the street. She managed to sneak in occasionally.

27. For the population statistics of the ghetto, see Appendix.
Also see the "Amendment to the Statistical Data as to the Nationality and Residence of the Stateless Refugees" published in SACRA Bulletin No. 3 (Supplement to *Our Life* [*Unser Leben*], No. 103, n.d., ca. February-May 1943) (YIVO No. 12) [SACRA Bulletin No. 3], for the most complete statistics of refugees residing both in as well as out of the ghetto area prior to the proclamation. It is also a basic source for accurate statistics in general of the refugees.
The total number of refugees is given in this source as 15,342, although admittedly it is not complete, since the registration returns upon which it was based had not been 100 per cent tabulated at the time of its issuance.
See also FO Yano to Aoki, May 4, 1944, p. 1, where another, similar count etotalled 15,257; List of Refugees Registered by May 17, 1943 (YIVO No. 12). Cf. International Red Cross, "Notes" [IRC, "Notes"], June 24, 1943, p. 1 (JDCCA). Also Gruenberger, "Refugees," p. 342. The author adds several hundred refugees to these statistics since none included those refugees who got extensions for up to a year. Nor were even the best of the several counts 100 per cent accurate.
Margolies estimated the size of the ghetto to be less than three-quarters of a square mile. *Report*, p. 19.

28. See *Herald* (February 18, 1943), article II. For the views of the Red Cross, see IRC, "Notes," June 24, 1943, p. 1. See also *Shanghai Jewish Chronicle* (May 9, 1943), p. 1. Key money involved a sort of bonus given to the landlord, usually amounting to about 2-4 months' rent, for the Lane House apartments (i.e., single rooms). Where one rented a whole house (i.e., several rooms, to be sublet), the key money amounted to thousands of Shanghai dollars. Gerechter Interview. In one case, the key money for a house ran to (U.S. $200.00). Friedlander, *Sieben*, p. 22.

29. Elbaum, "18 Februar," p. 24.

30. Gerechter Interview. Cf. also Siegel, *Report*, August 26, 1945, p. 2; Gruenberger, "Refugees," p. 342; Elbaum, "18 Februar," p. 24. See, however, Kaufmann, "Experiences," p. 24.
Both Gruenberger and Gerechter felt that the Japanese authorities were in on the deals, and made fortunes on these sales, especially since they knew

who had to sell and were thus in a position to make a deal with the proper Japanese buyer. Gerechter Interview. Feder, on the other hand, maintains that the only problem was the loss due to the short deadline, not any deals. Feder Interview. Neither was able to bear out his contention with additional evidence. For the example, see Friedrichs, *Geschichte* pp. 167-168.

31. *Herald* (February 18, 1943).

32. See SACRA Bulletin, No. 5, May 21, 1943 (YIVO No. 12). See also SACRA Minutes, July 21, 1943, pp. 1-2; Fuchs, Interview, Eisfelder, *Exile*, p. 41.

Robert Michaelis, *Bericht und Gutachten Ueber den Sonderbezirk fuer Staatenlose Fluechtlinge in Shanghai (China) (Shanghai-Ghetto* 1943-1945) [Michaelis, *Testimony*] August 18, 1961, Buero-Hannover, a 30-page transcript of Dr. Robert Michaelis' testimony concerning conditions in the Shanghai Ghetto for the restitution cases. Dr. Michaelis practised law in both foreign settlements in Shanghai. He was also head of the *Vereinigung Mitteleuropaeischer Rechtsanwaelt* in *Shanghai* (1941-45); on the Executive Board of the *Vereinigung Mitteleuropaeischer Protestanten* in Shanghai (1942-48). After the war, until his retirement in 1969, he served as Landsgerichtsdirector, Mainz, West Germany.

Gerechter got a carbon copy of this valuable document for the author from the late Ludwig Lazerus (Germany).

33. Feder taped Interview, August 9, 1968, and subsequent dates. Mr. Morris Feder first served on the Shanghai Municipal Police Force, and during the ghetto period, he acted as an interpreter and assistant to Ghoya on behalf of the refugees. Also Gerechter Interview; Dr. Gunther Kamm, "Affidavit," April 1954, p. 3 (URO); Martin Bernstein, "Affidavit," June 14, 1954, p. 4 (URO); Dicker, *Wanderers*, pp. 126-27; Gruenberger, "Refugees," pp. 342-43; FO Yano to Aoki, May 4, 1944, p. 2; FO Yano to Aoki, July 21, 1943, p. 3; Kaufmann, "Experiences," p. 14.

34. See "Statement of the Foreign Pao Chia," August 29, 1945 (YIVO No. 21) [Statement, "Pao Chia"]. Also *Unser Leben* (October 9, 1942) (English Suppl.), p. 2.

For the general organization of Pao Chia units in Shanghai, see Carey, *War Years*, pp. 137, 147. "Pao Chia" literally means "Protect the Armor," i.e., the "Home." Each ten households were one Pao under the direction of a Pao Chang or head man. *Ibid.*, p. 136. The Pao Chia wore armlets which (in Chinese characters) said "International Settlement Foreign Pao Chia Vigilance Corps [Statement, "Pao Chia"].

35. *Shanghai Jewish Chronicle* (September 29, 1943), p. 10. Cf. also Statement "Pao Chia"; Michaelis, *Testimony*, p. 9; Feder Interview. Feder felt that Inspector Yasuda was a friend of the refugees.

36. See the Notice (Bekanntmachung) distributed by the Pao Chia on

November 11, 1943, detailing the regulations the refugees were expected to
follow (YIVO No. 21) [Notice, "Pao Chia"].

37. For the most critical view of the Pao Chia, see Elbaum, "18 Februar,"
p. 25. For more balanced opinions, see Shoshana, *In Faier*, pp. 315, 328, 330,
332, 335; Siegel, *Report*, August 26, 1945, p. 3; Burkhard, *Tanz*, p. 164. For
the incident involving the Pao Chia and the Japanese soldiers, see Fuchs,
Interview. This seems to be well known and was related to the author by
various individuals.

The episode involving the arrest of the two students, was related to the
author by one of the participants. Levi Fleishaker, Interview, June 23, 1975.

38. Feder noted that some of the exits were unguarded. Interview. For
the periodic checkup by the Japanese of the refugees' ID cards outside the
ghetto, see Shoshana, *In Faier*, p. 317. Cf. also Carey, *War Years*, p. 146.
Mrs. Sommer, in her testimony concerning the Shanghai ghetto, claimed
that the exits were barred by barbed wire, ropes and signs, although Feder,
Gerechter and Bitker maintain that barbed wire was not used to close the
ghetto. *Sommer vs. Hessen*, Germany, March 23, 1955. Restitution claims
court cases 8 U 2/53-Wike; 563 LG. Wiesbaden. Copy given to writer,
courtesy Dr. Gunther Kamm of the URO. Also cited in Kranzler, *M.A.*, pp.
106, 138. Dicker follows this citation. Feder explained that it was used only
occasionally by the Japanese as a temporary means of enclosing or preventing access to a house or a whole block, both inside and outside the
ghetto, for a specific purpose such as a search after an assassination of a
Japanese. See Bitker-Dicker, Corres., August 31, 1959; Gerechter, *M.A.*, p.
106. Feder Interview. Dicker, *Wanderers*, p. 126; Kaufmann, "Experiences,"
p. 14; Bernstein, "Affidavit," pp. 3-4 for views supporting Mrs. Sommer's
contention; Eisfelder, *Exile*, pp. 46-47.

39. See photo of such a sign (YIVO No. 11). Cf. also Bloch, "Unser
Graphiker," for a collage of various restrictive signs used in the ghetto,
including one which reads, "Stateless Refugees are Prohibited to Pass Here
Without Special Pass." Cf. also Margolies, *Report*, p. 21; FO Shanghai
Consular Police Corres., No. 663, Yano to Aoki, July 21, 1943, p. 6 [Yano
to Aoki, July 21, 1943]. For the sneaking out of the ghetto, see Fuchs,
Interview.

40. For an original yellow-striped ID card, the author is grateful to Ruth
Fischel. See also photos of such in YIVO No. 11, 62. Dr. Shick-Hong, the
author's colleague at QCC, kindly translated the Japanese identification
terms.

For the assignment of the exchange of ID's to the Gemeinde, see the
Juedisches Nachrichtenblatt (June 4, 1943), p. 1. The fear posed by the
yellow-stripes is related by Redlich, along with the entire problem of the
various identification cards. As his correspondence with the author indicates,
this problem is still not solved satisfactorily. Cf. Redlich-Kranzler Corres..

May 7, 1975, and especially Deman-Kranzler Corres., February 2, 1975. Ms. Deman raised some valid points which the author has been unable to solve.

41. Siegel, *Report,* August 26, 1945, p. 3. Also Bernstein, "Affidavit," p. 4; Gertrude Schellenberger, "Affidavit," January 15, 1954, pp. 1-2 (URO) [Schellenberger, "Affidavit"]. Julius Wolff, "Affidavit," July 2, 1954, p. 1 [Wolff, "Affidavit"] (URO); Michaelis, *Testimony,* p. 3; *Juedisches Nachrichtenblatt,* June 4, 1943, p. 1.

42. Schellenberger, "Affidavit," p. 1. Also Wolff, "Affidavit," p. 1; Michaelis, *Testimony,* p. 3; Kamm, "Affidavit," p. 1.
One interesting case came to light whereby the daughter of a mixed marriage, who possessed a five-year German passport (without a *J*), received a green-striped ID and resided outside, whereas both her parents had to live in the ghetto, with their yellow-striped resident certificates. The daughter frequented the ghetto with impunity, despite various attempts by the German Embassy to get back her passport. Wolff, "Affidavit," pp. 1-2.

43. Gerechter Interview. Also Burkhard, *Tanz.* p. 167. For the number of divorces, see Michaelis, *Testimony,* p. 8.

44. The red badges were given to those with passes for one month or less, while the blue were worn by those with three-month passes. Feder Interview; See also Siegel, Report, August 26, 1945, p. 3. A photo of such a badge is found in YIVO No. 11; Gerechter Interview; Michaelis, *Testimony,* p. 3; Bernstein, "Affidavit," p. 4; Burkhard, *Tanz,* p. 165; SACRA Minutes, July 5, 1943, p. 1.
All this evidence is contrary to Bitker's emphatic statement that "no Jews [sic] in Shanghai were wearing at any time red badge marked in Chinese [sic] characters, "May Pass." (Bitker-Dicker Corres., August 31, 1959, p. 2). Not only does the author have such a badge, (courtesy of Rabbi Joseph D. Epstein) but Bitker himself was present at the SACRA meeting on July 5, 1943, at which time the badges, their use and the charge paid by the refugees, was discussed. SACRA Minutes, July 5, 1943, p. 1. His name is among those marked present. Perhaps his usually sound judgment was clouded by some feelings of guilt concerning the refugees who had to remain in the phetto.
See Appendix, for picture of such a badge.

45. *Herald* (February 18, 1943). Also *Shanghai Jewish Chronicle* (May 9, 1943), p. 1 (YIVO No. 11). Also *Unser Leben* (February 26, 1943) (English Suppl.), p. 1 (YIVO No. 68). This article also contains the official map of the "designated area."

46. His first name is rarely given. He usually signed *T. Kubota.* The only source the author found citing his first name was the *Shanghai Jewish Chronicle* (June 9, 1943), p. 1.
He had already made his public acquaintance with the refugee com-

munity by attending the inauguration of the new kitchen erected in November 1942, at which time Dr. Cohn translated his remarks into English. *Unser Leben* (English Suppl.) (November 20, 1942, p. 2). The author has no solid evidence to identify T. Kubota with Michiatsu Kubota who wrote antisemitic articles in the *Yudaya Kenkyu,* e.g., "The (Jekyll and) Hyde-like Character of the Freemasons—Criticism of the Masonic Society of Japan," "*Yudaya Kenkyu* (Tokyo), 2:1 (January 1942), pp. 10-28. Cf. also *JCM* p. 107. Cf. Elbaum, February 18, 1943, p. 25.

Dr. A. J. Cohn, also thought that the Kubota of the antisemitic articles was identical with the head of the Bureau. Interview. From the name on the article, it would seem to refer to another Kubota. Still, the question is an open one. Prof. M. Kobayashi is inclined to view them as two individuals. Interview.

47. Feder Interview. He generally dealt with SACRA and other Jewish organizations.

48. See below, in this chapter for details.

49. Feder Interview. Cf. also Burkhard, *Tanz,* p. 164.

50. See especially FO S-9460-3-2868-2871 (Jososohi No. 255), Yano to Aoki, June 24, 1944, pp. 1-3 [Yano to Aoki, June 24, 1944]. See also SACRA Minutes, July 5, 1943, p. 1.

51. Feder Interview. For Feder's role as Ghoya's assistant, see Burkhard, *Tanz,* p. 157. Also Shoshana, *In Faier,* p. 323.

52. See Yano to Aoki, June 4, 1944, p. 2, concerning the Japanese policy. For Ghoya's one-month passes, see Shoshana, *In Faier,* pp. 311-24. Cf. also Feder Interview.

53. For the Pass System in general, see the following sources in addition to the previously mentioned ones: Burkhard, *Tanz,* pp. 156-67, especially p. 164; Bernstein, "Affidavit," p. 4; *Juedisches Nachrichtenblatt* (May 29, 1943, p. 2; June 4, 1943, p. 1; Gruenberger, "Refugees," pp. 342-43; Bitker, *Memo,* p. 5; Siegel, *Report,* August 26, 1945, p. 3; SACRA Minutes, April 6, 1943, p. 2; Kaufmann, "Experiences," pp. 14-15. For copies of several such passes, see YIVO No. 11.

54. Burkhard, *Tanz Jude,* p. 167.

55. Kaufmann, "Experiences," pp. 14-15. See copy of one such job certificate, made out by the "Star" Transportation to the Shanghai Stateless Refugee Affairs Bureau, July 26, 1944 (YIVO No. 32) [Star, "Employment"]. Cf. also Shoshana, *In Faier,* p. 330; Burkhard, *Tanz,* p. 157; Fuchs, Interview.

For the fact that some German (Gentile) old-time firms in Shanghai provided such certificates of employment *see* Levin, Interview. Levin said that some of these German residents would pay storekeepers to send packages of food to poor refugee families anonymously, *Ibid.*

56. Kaufmann, "Experiences," pp. 14-15. Cf. also Gruenberger, "Refugees," p. 343.

57. Kaufmann Interview. The Japanese were well aware of the dealings in black market and currency speculation, by both refugees and others outside the ghetto. In fact, they too made money on such deals, occasionally even on a grand scale. Kaufmann Interview; also Margolies Interview. As mentioned, Kaufmann gave as an example bank certificate manipulations, whereby the Japanese defied their own regulations, to turn a neat profit.

They probably permitted such dealings, with an occasional arrest for public show, since they did not want to cut off completely the source for the refugees' livelihood and thereby place a greater burden upon the Japanese authorities. Moreover, such a move would simultaneously eliminate a lucrative source of gain for themselves. Interview with Professor Georges Ginsbourg, June 7, 1969. Also Siegel, *Report,* August 26, 1945, pp. 3-4; Carey, *War Years,* pp. 55, 69.

For an example of an arrest for black market activities, see Shoshana, *In Faier,* p. 308. (Szechuan Road was known as the center for black market in currency dealings.) Margulies Interview. Cf. also Carey, *War Years,* p. 146; *Yellow Creek,* pp. 176-77; Zikman-Dicker Corres., June 20, 1959, p. 2.

For sale of saccharine and insulin, see Gerechter Interview. See also Burkhard, *Tanz,* p. 168. For peddling chocolates and other goods outside the ghetto, see Shoshana, *In Faier,* pp. 327, 329-30. For speculation in "sugar tickets," see SACRA Minutes, October 8, 1943, p. 2.

58. For examples of medical examinations taken outside of the ghetto, particularly those requiring X-rays, (lacking in the ghetto), see CCB Minutes (SACRA Central Control Board), January 4, 1945, p. 1. Also Feder Interview. See Shoshana, *In Faier,* pp. 314, 317, for permission to leave for a funeral and the 17-hour wait in the heat for a pass. In some some cases, whole groups were permitted to leave the ghetto as units, as on the two occasions when an audience was permitted outside the ghetto to listen to a concert, or the daily exodus of the Yeshiva students to their *Bet Hamidrash* outside the ghetto.

59. Gruenberger, "Refugees," p. 342. Cited by Dicker, *Wanderers,* p. 126.

60. Feder Interview. Feder also attested to the fact that at home, Ghoya could be as charming as anyone. *Ibid.* Similar testimoney is given by Margulies. Interviews. Cf. also Eisfelder, *Exile,* p. 43; Gruenberger, *ibid.*

For the incident concerning the hat, see Protokoll Fritz Fabisch, p. 6 (Yad Washem). Concerning Ghoya and the musicians, see Friedrichs, *Geschichte,* pp. 185-190. Dr. Friedrichs also noted that most of the newly transferred doctors joined the *Hongkewer Aerzte Verein,* since Ghoya would only give passes to physicians belonging to this association and who could present its membership card. True to his whimsical character, Ghoya favored doctors with very large diplomas, (which be could not read in any case). Doctors with smaller certificates, or who possessed only duplicates, or none at all often fared badly. As president of the association, Dr. Friedrichs often had to deal with Ghoya to substantiate claims of identification of MDs. *Ibid.*

For Ghoya's attitude toward children and teachers, see Meyer Interview. See also above, chapter 14.

61. Burkhard, *Tanz,* p. 167. Cf. also Feder Interview; Eisfelder, *Exile,* p. 43; Shoshana, *In Faier,* p. 310. For the conditioning of the Japanese soldier, see Hanami Tasoki, *Long the Imperial Way* (Boston: Houghton-Mifflin, 1950). For some of these slapping incidents see Shoshana, *In Faier,* pp. 311-12, 323-24; Fabisch, p. 6.

The best portrait of Ghoya, in pictures and words, is found in the nine-page, fold-out booklet of caricatures drawn by Fritz Melchior, a refugee artist (YIVO No. 23). See also Melchior's illustrated article, "The Hongkew Ghetto," *Jewish Horizon,* Vol. 15 (October 1952), pp. 12-14.

Another caricature, in verse, by Herbert Zernik, "Ein Affe Wurde Mensch!" is quoted by Burkhard, *Tanz,* pp. 161-63, 156-61. He is also well characterized by the Yiddish writer, Fishman, in a short story called "Ghoya's Concert," *Farvogelte Yidn* (Yiddish), pp. 34-38. Margolies believes that Ghoya sincerely felt himself to be, in a benign, patronizing manner, a protector or "king of the Jews."

62. For examples of Okura's beatings, see Shoshana, *In Faier,* pp. 310-11. See also Bernstein, "Affidavit," p. 4. When Dr. Laudau offered Polish prisoners soap to prevent their contracting typhus, Okura refused this request. Laudau Interview.

Ghoya seems to have intrigued the refugees much more, as evidenced by the numerous and varied descriptions of him, in contrast to the few accounts of Okura. This, in the writer's opinion, was due to two factors. The first is the comic character and erratic behavior of Ghoya, which easily made him a laughingstock and very caricaturable. The second is the volume of requests for one-month passes which far surpassed the number of short-term ones. Moreover this situation was reinforced by the fact that the refugees preferred to take their chances with the erratic Ghoya rather than risk encounter with the sadistic Okura.

This opinion was subsequently substantiated by Feder, who knew both Ghoya and Okura quite well. Interview.

63. Margolies, *Report,* p. 19. For the panic caused by the proclamation, see Shoshana, *In Faier,* p. 294. Cf. also Gruenberger, "Refugees," p. 342; Siegel, *Report,* August 26, 1945, p. 1; Friedrichs, *Geschichte,* p. 166. See also the various attempts by Kubota to allay the fears of the refugees, in

Shanghai Jewish Chronicle (June 4, 1943), p. 3; *Juedisches Nachrichtenblatt* (May 28, 1943), pp. 1-2; (June 18, 1943); SACRA Minutes, March 2, 1943, pp. 1-2.

64. See above, p. 320. See also Dicker, *Wanderers*, p. 118; IRC, "Notes," June 24, 1943, p. 1; Birman to HICEM (Lisbon), April 25, 1943, p. 1.

65. See ERU (Emigrants Residents Union), undated census (ca. mid-1944) (YIVO No. 12) [ERU Census].

Other odd cases included in the ghetto proclamation were 74 former Russians, 38 Rumanians, 20 from Danzig, 22 Hungarians, 4 Turks, 1 Yugoslavian, 1 Latvian, 1 Spaniard. *Ibid.*

66. For a list of close to 900 names of Jews who arrived prior to 1937 and were thus exempt from the proclamation, see "List of Persons Not Subject to the Proclamation; Official Confirmations Handed Through SACRA," June 19, 1943 (YIVO No. 17) [SACRA, Official Exemptions]. Those desiring exemptions on any grounds had to complete a special form, where the reasons and documentation were listed. *Ibid.*

67. For the view of the refugees on this point, see Margolies Interview; Elbaum Interview; Zvi Zackheim Interview.

Others were angry at the older-settled, well-to-do Polish residents who were also excluded from the effects of the proclamation. Margolies Interview. Shoshana also refers acrimoniously to the rich who were exempt, though they had come after 1937. *In Faier,* p. 299. For Elbaum's critical view, see [Moshe Elbaum], "Die Herren von der SACRA Eindrucke Eines Opfers," *Unser Velt* (Spec. Ed., 1945) (YIVO No. 12) [Herren von SACRA]. For the retrospective view, see taped interview by the author, June 6, 1966 [Elbaum Interview]. Margolies and Redlich concurred.

68. For the tenuous relationship between Japan and the Soviet Union, see, for example, George Alexander Lensen, *The Strange Neutrality: Soviet-Japanese Relations During the Second World War* 1941-1945 (Tallahassee, Fla.: The Diplomatic Press, 1972. Jones, *Far East,* especially pp. 103-26; Meskill, *Hitler,* pp. 17, 21-24; cf. also Moses Beckelman, "The Jewish Community of Tientsin" [Beckelman, "Tientsin"], *The Jewish Center,* Vol. XXIV (June 1946), p. 13. Beckelman maintained that part of the reason no ghetto was established in Tientsin was due to the attitude of the Soviet consular representative, who viewed those who merely took out an application for Soviet citizenship as "being under their protection." Also Carey, *War Years,* p. 87.

69. FO Yano to Aoki, February 9, 1943, p. 2. Cf. also Dicker, *Wanderes,* pp. 118-19. Actually, neither were the Russian Jews Soviet citizens, but since they had applied for Soviet citizenship, the Soviet Union considered them under their protection, and the Japanese were reluctant to intern them at this time. See also above, n. 68.

One interviewee, a long-time friend and neighbor of Dr. A. J. Cohn of SACRA, still from his residence in Hankow (he moved to Shanghai in 1939), added another partial solution to the problem of why the Russian Jews were exempt from the ghetto. She related that Dr. Cohn rushed home one day (near the date of the proclamation) in an almost frenzied state, and told her that he had only been able to buy off the Russian Jews, but the Japanese were unyielding concerning the refugees. Mrs. Kling Interview.

Dr. Cohn seems to have alluded to such a view during his opening remarks at a meeting of SACRA, in which he said, "Originally the proclamation was intended to have a wider scope, but fortunately many residents were not affected by it. It was then the absolute duty of all these people to do their utmost and help their brethren." SACRA Minutes, June 7, 1944, p. 1. Dr. Cohn, in his recent taped interview, substantiated this contention. If this view is correct, then the writer feels that the Japanese merely took advantage of a situation to make some additional money, since their policy concerning the stateless Russians, we believe to have already been a foregone conclusion.

70. For example, see FO S-9460-3-2516, January 17, 1492. Cf. also FO. S-9460-3-2554, November 18, 1942; FO Yano to Aoki, February 9, 1943; FO Yano to Aoki, May 18, 1943; FO Yano to Aoki, July 21, 1943; FO Yano to Aoki, November 22, 1943. The first document to use the term "Stateless Refugees" is FO "Refugees Postponement List," March 31, 1944.

71. FO Yano to Aoki, May 4, 1944. A later account, in FO Yano to Aoki, July 7, 1944, again uses the term "Jewish People."
Moreover, the author feels that the ERU census of March 1944 probably used the term "Stateless Refugee" only because the census taken was in the ghetto where the term "stateless" was mandatory.

72. Interview with Arthur Gottesman, September 15, 1968. A student at the time at the Aurora University in Shanghai was permitted to continue his studies outside the ghetto throughout the rest of the war.
For the appeal for the writers see carbon of this letter addressed to Dr. Cohn by David Rabinovich, the editor, dated April 16, 1943. Copy in author's possession, courtesy of Rabinovich.

73. Margolies Interview. For the forms filled out by those claiming exemption from the "designated area," see YIVO No. 17. For example, one Polish resident, claiming arrival prior to 1937, attached a certificate from the Polish Residents Association, verifying his contention. See application dated May 17, 1943, *ibid*. See also SACRA Minutes, March 30, 1943, p. 3.
For the Portuguese passport, see Eisfelder, *Exile*, pp. 41, 44-45.

74. FO Yano to Aoki, May 4, 1944. Also FO S-9460-3-2872-2882, "Refugee Postponement List," March 31, 1944.

75. See *Herald* (February 18, 1943), article No. 3. An example of the

former would be the Polish Kitchen No. 1 which twice received a three-month extension without claiming any undue hardship. Margolies Interview. Isaac Margolies was the manager of this refugee restaurant.

76. SACRA Minutes, March 30, 1943, p. 2. For SACRA's role, see below, Chapter XVIII. See also Kubota's statement re the proclamation in the *Shanghai Jewish Chronicle* (May 9, 1943), p. 1 (YIVO No. 1); Dicker, *Wanderers*, p. 123.

77. For example, SACRA Bulletin No. 5, Notice No. 21. (Supplement to *Our Life—Unser Leben*, May 7, 1943, and Notice No. 24, *ibid.*), May 21, 1943 (YIVO) No. 12). Also SACRA Minutes, April 28, 1943, pp. 1-2.

78. FO, "Refugee Postponement List," March 31, 1944. There is a large discrepancy in the number of refugees still residing outside the ghetto by May 28, 1943, as cited in this document, which totalled 529, whereas Yano to Aoki, June 4, 1944, cited in the previous note, gives a number of 1,172. These could not have decreased by over 600 during the ten days between May 18-28.

If no error is found in the sources for the documents, one can perhaps conjecture that the larger figure included all the Polish refugees that had not even registered for relocation during the first few months following the proclamation.

79. Siegel, *Report,* August 26, 1945, p. 3.

80. For Kaufman's intervention, see his *Manchuria*, pp. 25-27. Mr. Z. conversation with Yasue is found in Z-Dicker correspondence, May 20, 1959, pp. 7-8.

81. Even the stateless Russians, Jews and non-Jews alike, had some measure of protection, as we have seen, which prevented their being incarcerated in the ghetto. For the November 1941 date, see Arbitration Board Information Sheet, November 29, 1941 (RP). See also above, chapter 15.

Although additional research is still required to pinpoint the Nazi influence on the Japanese, the author is presently working on this project, it is clear that the Japanese would never have created a ghetto had the Jews any semblance of national protection. See also below, Chapter 19.

18 | RELOCATION AND RESISTANCE:

SACRA AND THE MOVE TO THE GHETTO

> *. . . why do you compeled [sic] us to be stateless?*
> *everyone knows that we are not stateless . . . we are*
> *not and we will not be stateless! . . . The whole*
> *world will know that you had compelled us !!! [sic]*
> *We informed from this to the Swith [sic] [i.e. Swiss]*
> *consulate and to the international red cross! Better*
> *for you and for us give us a red belt [i.e., red arm-*
> *band worn by "enemy nationals"] and take us to the*
> *[internment] camp . . . The war is not finish and you*
> *can not know! We are and remain Polish citizens till*
> *our die! . . .*

> (Anonymous letter by Polish group to the Japanese
> authorities opposing relocation to ghetto.
> Landau Papers).

SACRA

Although the Ashkenazi community, did not have to move to the "designated area," its members were, however, to become the unwilling tools of the Japanese authorities in carrying out the unpleasant task of relocating the refugees into the ghetto.[1] This task was outlined for the Russian Jews, and a delegation of the refugees, at a general meeting held in the Club, a few days after the proclamation of February 18, 1943. Tsutomu Kubota, the principal speaker

who had recently been designated as the Director General of
the Japanese Bureau of Stateless Refugees Affairs, began his
talk with the explanation that the proclamation had nothing
to do with antisemitism. Rather, he stressed, it was due to the
critical problem of housing and feeding the refugees in Hongkew.

As noted above, this explanation convinced no one;
it was the latter half of his talk that was of great significance.
Here Kubota offered a "gentle" ultimatum to the Russian Jews
to cooperate in the job of relocating the refugees, or the
Japanese would "take matters into their own hands and do it
their own way."[2]

That evening the representative body of the Shanghai
Ashkenazi Communal Association elected a committee of 18
members to carry out this task. At its first meeting, on February 28, 1943, this new committee, named the Shanghai Ashkenazi Collaborating Relief Association, better known as
SACRA, inaugurated its activities under the chairmanship of
Dr. A. J. Cohn.[3]

DR. COHN

Dr. Cohn, a physician of Rumanian-Jewish ancestry,
raised and educated in Japan and fluent in its language, was
chosen by the Russian Jews to be their spokesman to the
Japanese authorities.[4] However, his close relations with the
Japanese and his relative obscurity in the Jewish community
made him suspect even among members of SACRA itself.[5]

The very nature of the opprobrious task delegated to
SACRA by the Japanese authorities made it intensely disliked
by the refugees. They had always been conscious of the Russian
Jews' indifference to their plight and now considered them
traitors at best. What was even worse was the thought, common at the time, that the Russian Jews had "sold" them out.

Yet, the objective outsider must consider the other side of the coin, as seen by the members of SACRA. Membership on this committee was neither to their liking nor one of choice. In the words of Joseph Bitker, one of their active members:

Our community very reluctantly submitted to the suggestion of the authorities, but in confidential deliberations among ourselves, we decided to assist the refugees but to delay as long as possible their removal from the International Settlement and French Concession, using every form of sabotage that was possible . . . The work of this new committee was thankless, unpopular and misunderstood by many refugees, as it was not feasible to explain to thousands what we were trying to do. We hoped that by stalling the implementation of the relocation as long as possible, we might hope for a turn in the fortunes of war.[6]

SACRA'S FUNCTIONS

To more efficiently manage the move, six subcommittees were created to deal with specific aspects of the relocation. These included a subcommittee on Finance, whose job it was to raise the required funds—primarily from the Ashkenazi community—and to finance the relocation; Housing; Application, to take care of applications for extensions; Economic; Bylaws; Judicial; and Press; whose task it was to send in news concerning SACRA activities to the two Jewish newspapers, as well as to make certain that only the "right" news was printed.[7]

Membership on the Executive Board, as well as on any of the six subcommittees, derived almost exclusively from the Ashkenazi community. The refugees themselves however, did most of the actual work. They were represented by the creation of five additional subcommittees with similar scope, and these in turn were headed by a Joint Administrative Committee, otherwise known as JAC. JAC would report periodically to either the specific subcommittee involved or to the main SACRA body.[8] Since many of the refugees working for JAC were also on the board of the Kitchen Fund, these two organizations were often in close association.[9]

The two most pressing immediate problems facing SACRA were finding sufficient housing in the ghetto, and financing the purchase and/or renovation of such housing into tolerable living quarters. As we have seen, the more well-to-do among the refugees seemed to experience little difficulty in finding such suitable quarters in the "designated area," since they were able to exchange their previous residences for less satisfactory quarters among the primarily Japanese element living in the poorer quarters of Hongkew.[10]

HOUSING PROBLEM

Most of the refugees, however, who were required to move within the deadline, could ill afford the high prices asked for rooms in the ghetto.[11] The Japanese authorities promised to make available several housing units, including a former Chinese school, a Salvation Army compound and 48 houses, still occupied by Chinese tenants. SACRA had also hoped to negotiate with the tenants for about 200 houses in the "designated area" owned by members of the Ashkenazi community.[12] But most of these plans did not materialize, certainly not in time for the May 18 deadline. To begin with, not all the premises that were promised to SACRA became available.[13] Only two, the Chinese school and the Salvation Army compound, were actually given to SACRA, and these required extensive renovation before the refugees could move in.[14]

Thus, by April 26, about three weeks before the deadline, there was room in the ghetto for only about 2,000 relocated refugees, while at least another 5,000 remained without accommodations.[15]

PROCRASTINATION

In order to head off criticism by the Japanese authorities for the delay in meeting the deadline, SACRA called a meeting with Kubota for April 28, to "explain" the situation.[16] Kubota, however, was perfectly aware of the conditions, having forearmed himself with data supplied by the local *gendarmerie*.[17]

The picture he presented was not as pessimistic as that portrayed by SACRA, although he admitted that only about 2,500 persons had completed their arrangements for apartments. He expected very shortly that an additional 1,500 refugees would follow making a total of 4,000 settled before May 18. SACRA promised to have accommodations for about 2,700, as soon as repairs were completed at the various locations. These 2,700 would be granted extensions until they received notice of the availability of their apartments—or better, rooms. An additional 500 professionals, mostly doctors, nurses and teachers, would be granted extensions, while the rest of the refugees had to fend for themselves.[18]

The second major problem was the financing of the relocation of the several thousand refugees unable to afford their own rooms.[19] Most of the immediate expenses would be required for the repair and alteration of the former Chinese school and the Salvation Army compound. For this purpose, SACRA envisioned a fund of $1,500,000 (Sh. CRB) as a "loan" from the Ashkenazi community. That the term "loan" was a euphemism for "tax" was obvious to all—despite Dr. Cohn's assertion to the contrary.[20] This can be discerned even from the carefully edited form of the SACRA minutes, particularly so from the use by SACRA's Financial Committee of the phrase "to request—if necessary—that Kubota and Kano address the Russian Jewish Community and place his [Kano's] signature on the notification for obligatory contributions."[21]

OTHER PLANS

In addition to the immediate financial plans, SACRA envisioned a long-range, 15-to-20-year loan amounting to 5 million yen, to be obtained from Kubota—toward the building of houses in the "designated area." Another related project involved the setting up of a private SACRA corporation with a capital of (Sh.) $20,000,000, one quarter of which, they hoped, would be subscribed to immediately.[22]

Still other plans, of smaller scope, included the setting up of a market in which food would be made available at reasonable prices; a relief lottery within the ghetto for raising additional funds for the poorest refugees, a tax on all food bills in restaurants, cafés and bars, to collect for the indigent sick; a pawn shop to enable the poor refugees to borrow money at low interest rates, instead of having to sell their last bit of clothing and household goods, (which would have ended up in Chinese hands).[23] The latter was a stopgap measure, since a Japanese Police Report noted that 400 such stalls for selling their winter clothes had already been set up by the refugees.[24] A bakery, with an allotment of 10,000 pounds of flour a day was also supposed to be set up, although no record of its existence has been found.[25]

Among the financial burdens shouldered by SACRA in its task of relocating the refugess, one must consider the upkeep of Kubota's Bureau of Stateless Refugees Affairs, which included, the furnishing of Kubota's and Kano's new apartments at a cost of (Sh. CRB) $18,000, Kano's salary of 1,000 yen, and that of a Japanese secretary at 400 yen per month.[26]

SACRA "TAXES"

These funds were to be raised by SACRA, through an assessment on the wealthier members of the Ashkenazi community by a financial subcommittee. The "donors" were divided into 13 categories, the total numbering 317 members by May 1944. These categories ranged from the top, *A* Class, assessed at (Sh. CRB) $18,000 per month, t othe lowest group, whose members had to pay only (Sh. CRB) $100 per month.[27] The total assessment for one month equalled close to (Sh. CRB) $600,000 which, however, as noted above, was never fully collected.[28]

At a time (May 1944) when the total SACRA budget reached (Sh. CRB) $600,000 per month, this still amounted to only 10 per cent of the total relief budget, towards which the Shanghai JDC contributed the remaining 90 per cent, or (Sh. CRB) $5,400,000.[29]

POLISH RESISTANCE

SACRA found itself encumbered not only by the pressure to meet a deadline on the one hand, and the manifold problems of finance and relocation on the other, but in addition, of even graver consequences—resistance on the part of the Polish refugees. This resistance manifested itself in various forms, but appeared first during the organization of some of the subcommittees formed by SACRA to work under JAC. The Polish groups refused to submit the names of their representatives.[30]

This initial refusal to partake in SACRA activities was part of the concerted Polish effort to remain out of the "designated area." Their stand was predicated upon the view that, since Poland maintained its government-in-exile in London, and had never repudiated their citizenship, they could not be

considered stateless, and, consequently, should not be required
to live in the ghetto.[31] Moreover, they claimed that they awaited
repatriation, and 43 of the Polish refugees had already been
evacuated from Shanghai in August of 1942. They coupled
their gratitude towards the Japanese for the latter's earlier
hospitality—particularly during their stay in Kobe—with a
plea to permit them to remain at their present domiciles outside the "designated area." Their views were submitted to the
Japanese authorities by their two representatives, Dr. Ernest
Landau and Aleksander Fejgenbaum, in conjunction with the
larger Polish Residents Association in China, headed by the
old-time Polish residents in Shanghai.[32]

The Japanese, of course, rejected the Polish claims,
with the argument that since Poland no longer existed, there
could not exist any Polish citizens.[33] Although a number of
the Polish refugees accepted the Japanese decision and consequently registered with the other refugees for relocation to
the "designated area," others were not ready to give up their
struggle. This group accused its own elected representatives of
selling out to the Japanese, and sent a petition to the Swiss
Consulate for delivery to the International Red Cross, as well
as a letter reiterating their demands in even stronger tones—
to be recognized by the Japanese as "enemy nationals." They
asked:

> , . . why do you compelled [sic] us to be stateless? every-
> one knows that we are not stateless . . . we are not and
> we will not be stateless! . . . The whole world will know
> that you had compelled us !!! [sic]. We informed from
> this to the Swith [sic] consulate and to the international
> red cross! Better for you and for us give us a red belt [i.e.,
> red armband worn by "enemy nationals"] and take us to
> the [internment] camp . . . The war is not finish and you
> can not know! We are and remain Polish citizens till our
> die![34]

Many of this splinter group did not register until months later, hoping against hope that somehow they could remain outside the ghetto.[35] Their defiance earned them the hostility of the Japanese authorities, the antipathy of SACRA, and of course, the anger of some of the German refugees.[36] Many of the latter, however, openly admired and/or envied the solidarity and spirit manifested by *"die Arroganz der Polnischen Fluchtlinge."*[37]

To counter such a challenge on the part of the refugees, the Japanese authorities promulgated regulations whereby anyone moving to the "designated area" later than their allotted schedule would be given due punishment, i.e., sent to Okura, who usually meted out one day in the detention cell of the Wayside Road Police Station for every day overdue.[38]

PENALTIES

Six of the "defiant" Polish refugees who were sent to jail on this account paid the ultimate penalty of death as a result of contracting typhus in the cell while others suffered serious illnesses.[39]

SACRA applied its own pressure on any refugees who challenged its authority, by letters to various members of the Polish group, threatening that "if they do not obey and fail to register within the time specified, the SACRA Committee will not be responsible for the consequences."[40]

In applying these pressures, they closed down the Polish Kitchen No. 1, which was supported by the EAST-JEWCOM, whose heads were also part of SACRA.[41]

STUDENT REBELLION

Another unlikely challenge to SACRA came from a small group of Yeshiva students, or rather, postgraduate students of higher Talmudic studies. When SACRA assigned the entire Mirrer Yeshiva to lodge in the Salvation Army compound, the yeshiva students refused to relocate. They told SACRA that they represented a yeshiva, that is the cultural elite of the Jewish People, and therefore would not reside in a place still partially occupied by the dregs of Shanghai's society —former prison inmates, drunks, etc. Neither were they ready to give up their long-standing tradition of privacy and residence in private quarters. Moreover, their greatest fear, ever since their narrow escape from the Germans after the invasion of Poland, was a roundup of the entire Yeshiva, which would have been greatly facilitated by their all being concentrated in one place.[42]

These yeshiva students revolted by smashing all the furniture in the SACRA office and throwing it out the window. The *gendarmerie* quickly arrested 33 of them and only quick intervention on the part of Rabbi Ashkenazi and his supporters prevented long prison terms for the "revolutionaries." Shoshana claims that SACRA paid a tidy sum to the Japanese to hush up the affair. However, the students won their demand to rent private quarters at their own expense, and they became the heroes of the day.[43] Little did the students know, at the time of their revolt, that their victory in getting other places of domicile probably saved their lives. The compound was later hit directly during an air raid.

OTHER FORMS OF RESISTANCE

Although the resistance of the Polish-Jewish refugees to the Japanese was well publicized in Shanghai at the time, there were other forms of defiance to the authorities which required the same courage and audacity. This is true whether it involved the unpublicized acts of German refugee and Russian Jewish cooperation with the allied underground or the simple opposition to and obstruction of Japanese-dictated policies in internal matters of the Gemeinde.

For example, the Allied efforts to oppose the Japanese occupation forces, which involved indigenous Chinese guerillas or those led by OSS or SACO-trained men, were by their very nature secretive, and most of these heroic chapters of World War II have yet to be written.[44]

One group composed primarily of German refugees— which after the war became the nucleus of the *Gemeinschaft der Demokratischen Deutschen in Shanghai*— maintained an underground organization throughout the period of the War in the Pacific. Led by such men as Dr. Ernst Aschner, Gerhard Gerechter and Professor Richard Paulik, this group was able to be of assistance to the refugees in various ways.[45] For example, they were able to establish contact with certain sympathetic German officials in the Shanghai Embassy and even with the Nazi Intelligence in Shanghai. These contacts were achieved chiefly by Dr. Paulik, a non-Jewish political refugee from Nazi Germany since early 1933. He was able to maintain steady communication with a Captain Louis Siefkin, a German Naval Intelligence Officer stationed in Shanghai, and Captain Fritz Wiedemann, Consul General of Tientsin, who frequently visited Shanghai. Both of them belonged to the anti-Hitler "Canaris" group.[46]

Clandestine meetings of the refugees and these sympathetic Germans usually took place at such public locations as the Race Course or in certain cafes. In this manner, the refugees were often given advance notice of Japanese moves. For example, prior to the Japanese order for all short-wave receivers or radios to be confiscated, the refugee underground was made aware of it and was able to hide many of their sets.[47] These radios, together with TASS News Agency, were the basic source used by the refugees to keep informed of much of the war news, especially in the European theater. In this manner, at least some of the refugees found out about the atrocities committed by the Nazis in Europe.[48]

Such a contact with the sympathetic Germans forewarned the refugees not to turn in their "Bridge Passes" to the *Juedische Gemeinde* (upon order of the Japanese authorities) after the establishment of the "designated area" in 1943.[49] Of greater significance for the refugees, however, was the information passed on by Captain Siefkin about the existence of a few traitors in the employ of the Nazis in Shanghai, among the Jewish refugees themselves.[50]

The underground often kept the refugee body informed of important developments by fact sheets, which were distributed clandestinely or posted at night in key locations. They were able to cooperate with the Sikh police of the Municipal Police Force, some of whom worked for the Allied cause. Thus, they helped the Sikhs carry out the escape of several downed American pilots from their cells in the Ward Road Jail to behind the Chinese lines. [51] Another group of German refugees worked directly with the Chinese Underground in their sabotage work on Japanese installations.[52]

RESISTANCE BY THE GEMEINDE

It was a well-known policy of the Japanese to plant "spies" among differing, competing and rival groups (and they were extraordinarily astute in finding where such rivalries existed), in order to keep abreast of their activities. It was a deliberate policy of Inuzuka's, based, he claimed, on the British colonial strategy of "divide and rule." The *Juedische Gemeinde,* though, by no means always submitted to Japanese demands, as we have seen in the case of Dr. Lesser's removal as president of the *Gemeinde.* A great deal of self-discipline and restraint was also manifested by the Arbitration Board in its steadfast refusal to make use of dreaded *gendarmerie* to enforce its decisions.

Another episode gives evidence of that quiet but determined defiance of the Japanese when they attempted to impose their will on the *Gemeinde*. Soon after the proclamation of the ghetto, Kubota's office instructed the *Gemeinde* to provide certain statistics and to complete some registration related to the relocation. The data was not provided on time, nor was it correctly done, and the authorities accused the *Gemeinde* of sabotage. Such pressure was successful in producing the correct statistics, but the Japanese were still not satisfied. An "urgent" meeting was called by Dr. Cohn of SACRA and attended by Wachsner, Redlich and Wachtel for the *Gemeinde,* Silberstein and Pulvermacher for the Kitchen Fund, and a few others.

Dr. Cohn informed them that the authorities were dissatisfied with them on several counts (which included in-fighting among various "ambitious" persons, friction between the *Gemeinde* and the Kitchen Fund, and the refusal of the Arbitration Board to take advantage of the "enforcement powers"), and intended to dissolve the *Gemeinde*. He had, however, been able to mollify them and suggest that it would be sufficient punishment to replace the top executives by five commissioners who would be under the direct supervision of SACRA, which they controlled completely.

The *Gemeinde* leadership succeeded in convincing Dr. Cohn to retain five of the former *Vorstand*, including Kardegg, alongside the commissioners. These five commissioners were younger, less experienced men, hand-picked from the Kitchen Fund, the longtime antagonists of the *Gemeinde* leadership in Shanghai's "Jewish politics," who were thus imposed on an unwilling refugee organization. However, it did not take long for these "puppets" to become aware of the lack of confidence they inspired. They tried in vain to bolster their image by appointing some respected individuals such as Max Brandt and Paul Parnes, a leading Zionist figure. Soon they either resigned or were removed by Kubota.[53]

These events may seem petty, but what emerges is that the *Gemeinde* defied the authorities in their own quiet way.

RUSSIAN-JEWISH RESISTANCE

Among the Russian Jews there were also a few who at great personal risk worked for the Allied cause. According to one of the leaders of the American OSS Underground in Shanghai, such Jews were of primary importance in the carrying out of their objectives. These included the destruction of barges containing synthetic fuel produced and stored in Shanghai. They also directed American bombers to their targets during the 1944-45 air raids.[54]

INDIVIDUAL RESISTANCE

A few instances of individual resistance to the enemy, and aid to the Allies, are worth recounting. One prominent Jewish Zionist and figure in the sports world was allegedly arrested and tortured for helping to secure the escape of downed American pilots. A refugee kept in contact with both the Japanese internment camps and the Swiss Consulate through the help of a Chinese messenger. In this way she was able to help spirit out Judge Cornell S. Franklin, the chairman of the Shanghai Municipal Council, and to keep the Red Cross aware of the Japanese cruelty to internees. On a lighter note, a group of 15-year-old students at the Kadoorie School resisted the authorities when they ordered that Japanese be taught as a mandatory subject. They simply refused to return to school.[55]

CONCLUSION

Among the distasteful by-products of the Nazi-inspired ghetto was the use of indigenous manpower to put into effect the more onerous tasks. Among these, we have seen the use of the "free" Russian Jews to carry out the relocation to the ghetto, while the refugees were ordered to provide their own police: the Pao Chia.

On the one hand, this situation fomented internal strife; brought to light some of the more unfortunate qualities among a number of individuals; exacerbated the already existing cool relations between the Russian and German Jews and created an intense dislike for some of the more overbearing among the Pao Chia. On the other hand, the establishment of the ghetto helped to fuse even more the bond of brotherhood among most of the refugees and removed the former ambiguity in the refugee attitude toward Japan. Resistance to Japan, now considered a full-fledge Axis partner in the eyes of the refugees, found expression in a variety of guises and among all elements of Shanghai's Jews.

Still, the refugees most heroic and tragic hour came to pass toward the end of the period of the ghetto, and forms part of the final chapter.

NOTES : RELOCATION AND RESISTANCE

1. See Bitker, *Memo*, p. 4. Also Bitker-Dicker Correspondence (August 31, 1959), p. 2. Cited by Dicker, *Wanderers*, p. 120.

2. Margolies, *Report*, p. 19. Margolies gives the date for this meeting as February 23, 1943, which is doubtful, particularly in view of her obvious error in placing the proclamation on February 8th instead of the correct date of February 18th. A Sacra Memo (March 15, 1944), p. 1 (YIVO No. 12) states that *"simultaneously* with the issuance of the proclamation of February 18, the Shanghai Ashkenazi Communal Association elected and appointed a committee of 18" [italics mine], which is most likely the correct date.

See also above, n. 1. Bitker uses the term "emphatically advised the resident Jews . . . to form their own committee to aid the Jews in the resettlement." Bitker, *Memo*, p. 3.

3. SACRA Minutes [SACRA Min.], February 28, 1943, p. 1. Also SACRA, Memo, March 15, 1944, p. 1; Birman to HICEM (Lisbon) (April 25, 1943), p. 1; Shoshana, *In Faier*, p. 299; Siegel, *Report*, August 26, 1945, p. 2.

For the problem of early identity of SACRA to foreign sources, see IRC to Joint (N.Y.), October 4, 1943; IRC Cable, October 2, 1943; IRC Cable to JDC (N.Y.), October 24, 1943; IRC to JDC (N.Y.), October 25, 1943. JDCCA.

4. Bitker, *Memo*, p. 3. Cited by Dicker, *Wanderers*, p. 120. For Dr. Cohn's ancestry, see Cohn Interv., also Kranzler, *M.A.*, p. 83, cited by Dicker, *Wanderers*, p. 120.

Already in November of 1942, when a delegation of Japanese dignitaries attended the opening of the new steam kitchen, Dr. Cohn translated Kubota's Japanese talk into English. *Unser Leben*, November 20, 1942 (English Suppl.), p. 2.

Dr. Cohn's first wife, who bore him three children, was Japanese. He had lived in Hangkow until 1939, when he moved to Shanghai. Kling Interview.

5. Dicker noted that the members of SACRA would cease their private conversation the moment Dr. Cohn walked in. *Ms.*, p.136, n. 36. Based upon an interview with a former member of SACRA.

For Ghoya's opinion of Cohn and a more favorable view see Shoshana, *In Faier*, p. 324.

6. Bitker, *Memo*, p. 4. Quoted by Dicker, *Wanderers*, p. 120. For the most devastating attack by the refugees on SACRA, see "Die Herren von SACRA," by [Moshe Elbaum]. See also Shoshana, *In Faier*, pp 9, 301-302.

7. SACRA Minutes, February 28, 1943, pp. 1-2. For the censorship of the

news in the Jewish newspapers the *Shanghai Jewish Chronicle* for the refugees and *Unser Leben* for the Ashkenazi community, see SACRA Minutes, March 2, 1943, pp. 1-2. Other subcommittees were created as the need arose.

8. SACRA Minutes, February 28, 1943, pp. 1-2.

9. For example, Wachsner, Pulvermacher and Silberstein. See Margolies, *Report*, p. 15, re their membership in the Kitchen Fund, and SACRA Minutes, February 28, 1943, p. 3; March 2, 1943, p. 1, for membership in JAC. See also Birman to HICEM (Lisbon), April 25, 1943, p. 1.

JAC is not to be confused with the Shanghai Joint Distribution Committee (*Shanghai JDC* for short). See above, pp. 300-301, although Wachsner was involved in the Shanghai JDC as well. See Margolies, *Report*, pp. 16-17.

10. See SACRA Minutes, March 30, 1943, p. 2. About 3,000 Japanese residents in 476 houses or apartments, registered for such an exchange. *Ibid.*

11. See Kubota's speech, *Shanghai Jewish Chronicle*, (May 9, 1943).

12. SACRA Minutes, March 16, 1943, pp. 1-2; March 23, 1943, p. 1.

13. SACRA Minutes, April 26, 1943, p. 1.

14. *Ibid.*

15. *Ibid.* Dicker gives the April 28th date, at which meeting the figures given by Kubota were quite different. *Wanderers*, p. 124.

16. SACRA Minutes, April 26, 1943, p. 1.

17. *Ibid.* Cited by Dicker, *Wanderers*, pp. 124-25.

18. *Ibid.*, pp. 1-2. For publicity of the availability of rooms to the potential residents, see *SACRA Bulletin*, Nos. 4, 5 (YIVO No. 12).

19. See above, chap. 17.

20. SACRA Minutes, March 9, 1943, pp. 1-2. Mrs. Kling and Mrs. Lew in an interview also remarked that the Russian Jews considered this SACRA "loan" a tax, and they resented it, accusing Dr. Cohn [wrongfully, in their opinion] of making a fortune out of these "taxes." See also Margolies, *Report*, p. 23.

The fact that the very committee assigned to assess the other members and to collect these "contributions" were themselves delinquent in their payments, gives an idea of how popular these "taxes" were. For example, see SACRA Minutes, October 26, 1943, p. 2; June 27, 1944; August 1, 1944; August 5, 1944; August 22, 1944; August 28, 1944; Cf. also Dicker, *Wanderers*, pp. 130-31.

21. Cf. Kano's salary of 1,000 yen per month from SACRA's treasury (cited by Dicker, *Wanderers*, p. 123) or the 400 yen a month to be paid for a Japanese secretary.

For this plan see SACRA Minutes, March 16, 1943, p. 2. An indication of the cost relation can be seen from the estimate of $500,000 (Sh. CRB) required for the renovating of only the former school building, or the (Sh.) $1 million cost of the proposed bakery. SACRA Minutes, July 27, 1943, p. 1.

22. SACRA Minutes, June 7, 1943, p. 2.

23. For the *Market*, see SACRA Minutes, May 31, 1943, p. 1; June 28, 1943; p. 2. For the *Relief Lottery*, see SACRA Minutes, June 18, 1943, p. 1; October 26, 1943, p. 1. For the *Tax*, see SACRA Minutes, December 8, 1943, p. 2. For the *Pawn Shop*, see Police Report to the Japanese Consul and General Yano, November 16, 1943. Yokeikohi No. 4303, pp. 1-2 [*Police Report Yano*, November 16, 1943] (cited by Dicker, *Wanderers*, pp. 127-28).

24. SACRA Minutes, November 24, 1943, p. 1. Also *Police Report Yano*, November 16, 1943.

25. See SACRA Minutes, May 31, 1943, p. 1; July 27, 1943, pp. 1-2. Cited by Dicker, *Wanderers*, p. 128.

26. SACRA Minute, March 15, 1943, p. 2. See also above, n. 21.

27. SACRA Minutes, Finance and Tax Committee [Fin. and Tax Com.], May 19, 1944.

28. SACRA Minutes, Fin. and Tax Com., May 23, 1944, p. 3. Changes in fortune and complaints of too high evaluation made the Financial Committee re-evaluate the categories periodically and change the standing of some members to lower categories, while occasionally the reverse was done. See SACRA Minutes, Fin. and Tax Com., May 14, 1944, pp. 1-4; June 6, 1944, p. 1; August 5, 1944, pp. 1-2.

29. SACRA Minutes, Fin. and Tax Com., May 14, 1944, p. 1. The exchange rate of the CRB during May 1944 was approximately CRB 80 to Swiss Franc 1 (Shanghai JDC to Lisbon, June 5, 1944) (JDCCA) and the Swiss franc at about 4 to (US) 1. Cf. Margolies, *Report*, p. 22, and Hyman to Jackson Martindell, March 28, 1944, p. 2. In the latter, Hyman of the JDC indicated its monthly remittance of (US) $25,000 to Shanghai at the exchange of Swiss franc 100,000. By the time of the reorganization of SACRA (March 1944), all pretense of using the term "loans" abandoned for the more realistic form "taxation." SACRA Minutes, March 22, 1944, p. 1.

30. See SACRA Minutes, February 28, 1943, pp. 1-2. For criticism by the Polish refugees of SACRA's handling of the "Relocation to the Ghetto," see SACRA Minutes, July 30, 1943, p. 2.

31. See the correspondence between the Polish groups and Dr. Cohn, and the former with the Japanese authorities. YIVO No. 11 and No. 40. See

also the undated letter sent by a Polish splinter group to the Japanese authorities [Anon. Polish citizens] (copy in author's possession, courtesy of Dr. E. Landau, who was one of the chief delegates of the Polish refugee group in Shanghai and who dealt with the Japanese on this problem). Also Landau Interview.

32. Letter on behalf of Polish citizens, April 23, 1943 (YIVO No. 40). Landau Interview. Cf. also letter to Dr. Cohn. For first repatriation, see above, p. 207. For the appeal by the Polish Residents Association, see the letter of April 9, 1943, on behalf of the Polish refugees by Dr. Stan. [sic] Tomaszeweki and Marian Krzyzanowski, Chairman and Secretary, respectively, of the organization. Attached to this letter was a list certifying that the names included were valid Polish citizens under the protection of the Association. YIVO No. 40.

33. Landau Interview. See also above, chapter 17 re the use of the term "former Poland," in the article accompanying the announcement of the proclamation.

34. Anonymous. Polish Citizens, pp. 1-2. For the Polish refugees' fairly common preference for interment to the ghetto, see Shoshana, *In Faier*, p. 300. For the red armbands worn by the "enemy nationals," see Carey, *War Years*, p. 25.

Both Margolies and J. Epstein have testified to the accuracy of Landau's and Fejgenbaum's contention that they had attempted to secure rights for the Polish refugees from the Japanese authorities. Cf. Margolies Interview; see also *Polish War Refugees*, p. 80. It seems that the anonymous letter was sent by a group organized by someone named Apfelbaum.

35. Margolies Interview. Also Shoshana, *In Faier*, pp. 308-309.

36. See esp. *Shanghai Jewish Chronicle* (May 7, 1944). Cf. also "Die Herren der SACRA"; Shoshana, *In Faier*, p. 310; "18 Februar," p. 25; SACRA Minutes, April 6, 1943, p. 1; Yano to Aoki, July 21, 1943, p. 5.

37. Shoshana, *In Faier*, p. 310. Cf. also Gruenberger, "Refugees," p. 343; Burkhard, *Tanz*, p. 167.

38. See "Herren der SACRA." Cf. also Shoshana, *In Faier*, pp. 310-11; Feder Interview.

39. Shoshana, *In Faier*, pp. 311-15. Elbaum, in "18 Februar," lists the names of the five Polish victims. *Siegel Report*, August 26, 1945, p. 3, states that there were six victims. "Die Herren der SACRA" cites seven, although the "List of Detained Persons" (YIVO No. 65), which notes the dates, names and former nationality of all refugees detained in the Wayside Road Jail for various infractions, including the "late removal" to the "designated area," lists seven names of prisoners who died as a result of imprisonment. At least one, if not two, are not Polish refugees.

Polish War Refugees, p. 80, gives the names of eight Polish refugees who died due to imprisonment on account of resistance. At least one, H. Rapaport, was imprisoned for a completely different reason. See Shoshana, *In Faier,* p. 306.

The period of detainment, according to this "List," ran from March 3 (1944, since the deadline was first set for May 18, 1943) to May 25 (1944). Generally, for the first few months, i.e., March and part of April 1944, the major number of detentions consisted of 1-2 day periods, whereas from April 20, 1944 on, most of these periods of detention lasted from 1-2 weeks, sometimes for as long as 30 days. *Ibid.*

40. SACRA Minutes, April 6, 1943, p. 1.

41. Shoshana, *In Faier,* p. 300. For example, Oppenheim and Tuchachin-sky of EASTJEWCOM were both on SACRA. Cf. SACRA Minutes, February 28, 1943; March 9, 1943, p. 1.

42. This incident is related in Epstein, "Mir," p. 131, and *In Faier,* pp. 301-320. Also Epstein Interview; Gerechter Interview.

The last reason, the fear of a round-up, was related to me by Rabbi Epstein (Interview). He stated that ever since they fled Poland, the Yeshiva did not stay in any one place (even in Vilna) as a unit. See also Weisfogel, "Mir," pp.

43. Shoshana, *In Faier,* p. 302. Also Epstein Interview.

44. One book by Vice-Admiral Milton E. Miles has been published about the role played by SACO (Sino-American Cooperative Organization) in establishing a network of Naval stations along the China Coast including Shanghai for relaying information to the United States Navy in the Pacific and for training and organizing guerrilla units vs. the Japanese forces. Milton E. Miles, *A Different Kind of War* [Miles, *War*] (New York, Doubleday and Co., 1967).

For the role of OSS (Office of Strategic Services) in Shanghai and its underground activities, and especially in the relation to the assistance of the Russian Jews, I am indebted for a taped interview of one of its leaders, Willie Soong, of Korean extraction, August 26, 1968.

For the information concerning the clandestine activities on the part of German refugees against the Japanese occupation, the author is grateful to Mr. Gerhard Gerechter for several interviews as well as documents loaned for reproduction. For general notices of Chinese guerrilla and underground activities in Shanghai, see Carey, *War Years,* pp. 189, 199.

45. Gerechter Interview. See also *Aufbau,* January 11, 1946, p. 26. Other names included Ludwig Lazarus, Hans Kempner and Bruno Heinsius. Cf. also the *Shanghai Jewish Chronicle* (January 19, 1945), p. 10.

For the relation of these names to the *Gemeinschaft der Demokratischen Deutschen in Shanghai* (Association of Democratic Germans in Shanghai) during the postwar period, see "Association of Refugees from Germany, *Almanac*, p. 81.

46. Gerechter Interview. For the activities of the Nazis in Shanghai, including the role played by Captain Siefkin, see Proceedings Before a Military Commission by order of the Commanding General, Nanking Headquarters Command, at Shanghai, China. *U.S. of America vs. Lothar Eisentraeger alias Ludwig Ehrhardt*, August 26, 1946— January 17, 1947. National Archives [*Bureau Ehrhardt*]. Cf. also Kranzler, M.A. chapter VII, especially p. 112, upon which Dicker (*Wanderers*, p. 115) based his remarks. Also Dicker, Ms., p. 134, n. 18; Carey, *War Years*, pp. 36-37, 64-65. See also below, n. 7.

47. Gerechter Interview. For the confiscation of shortwave radios, see Carey, *War Years*, p. 31.

48. Gerechter Interview. Cf. also Elbaum Interview; Carey, *War Years*, pp. 84-85, 87; Eisfelder, *Exile*, p. 54.

49. Gerechter Interview. These refugees who were forewarned claimed to have lost them and were given their ID anyhow. *Ibid.*

50. The entire problem of the Nazi activities in Shanghai and their relations to the Jewish refugees was intentionally left out of the "Bureau Ehrhardt" trial and its 3,000 pages of testimony. The reason for such a glaring omission is *not* the lack of Nazi activities and antisemitic propaganda vs. the Jews. Rather, it was due, as Captain F. T. Farrell (USMC), the chief prosecutor at the trial, noted in a separate two-page testimony of February 20, 1947: "However, out of consideration for the predicament of the entire refugee community in Hongkew, the prosecutors in the recent Nazi trials *eliminated all mention of Jewish refugee participation in this despicable business.* The prosecutors felt that to set forth any such evidence it had acquired would prejudice the position of the entire Jewish refugee community . . ." [italics mine]. Form a sworn statement by Captain F. T. Farrell and verified by an additional statement of Lt.-Col. Jeremiah J. O'Connor (JAGD War Crimes Officer AAG U.S. Army, March 15, 1947). Copy in author's possession, courtesy of G. Gerechter.

This material was also utilized and verified by the F.B.I. as evidence from such correspondence from the F.B.I. to Gerechter, August 11, 1950 (copy in author's possession, courtesy Gerechter). See copies in Appendix of dissertation pp. 516-20.

For the justification of the fears of the Jewish refugees about the condemnation of all the refugees—due to a few collaborators—see Siegel, *Report*, October 22, 1945, pp. 6-7 (JDCCA).

51. Gerechter Interview.

52. Hinzelmann, *O China*, pp. 83-100.

53. The Gemeinde episode is detailed by Redlich, a participant in the events. See Redlich-Kranzler corres. June 6, 1973, p. 3; especially February 27, 1974, pp. 6-13; October 10, 1973, p. 3; December 11, 1973, pp. 2-10. Cf. also Dicker, *Wanderers,* pp. 123-124; Ganther, "Religioese," p. 3.
For Inuzuka's policy of "divide and rule," see Inuzuka "Secret," p. 4 (tr.) (TP). The internal strife is described above, chapter 16.

54. Soong Interview. For additional information concerning OSS activities in Shanghai, see Miles, *War,* Index, pp. 622-23.

55. For the arrest of the sports figure, Herman Natowic, see the "Natowic Story," a two-page manuscript by Redlich. Redlich-Kranzler corres. June 19, 1974. Cf. also Didner Interview; Fuchs Interview. The incident involving Judge Franklin was told to the author by Ruth Linn, a participant. Linn Interview. Kurt Fuchs related the episode of the "Youth defiance." Fuchs Interview.

19 | TRAGEDY AND TRIUMPH, TWILIGHT OF THE GHETTO

> *by September 3, 1945 [the ghetto opened and] the refugees once more took to the street dancing, this time without restraint and with real hope for a brighter future.*

The move to the ghetto imposed tremendous economic, physical and, above all, psychological burdens on the refugee community. While the entire exodus from Europe and the adjustment to life in Shanghai had been traumatic for many, the ghettoization proved for some less damaging than might have been expected.

Given the recent Nazi reversals at Stalingrad (as the refugees heard over the TASS news broadcasts), they now perceived that time was on their side and sooner or later they anticipated the defeat of the Axis Powers and the crumbling of the ghetto walls. But before this optimism was to become a reality they would yet undergo many moments of severe anguish as well as of triumph. These experiences would finally mold the earlier amorphous and heterogeneous group of refugees into a genuine community. Living in close proximity in a real Jewish atmosphere (even many non-observant refugees closed their shops for the Sabbath and Jewish holidays), and

543

forged by adversity, the ghetto created for many, warm and
lasting friendships that continued well into the postwar years.[1]

RELIEF 1944-1945

The latter part of 1943 and the beginning of 1944
were in some ways the most difficult for the refugees. During
this period, the results of the economic dislocations, and the
full psychological impact of their removal to the "designated
area" began to have a marked effect. The three-month passes,
which at first enabled many refugees to maintain their jobs
outside the ghetto, were becoming increasingly difficult to
renew, and the short-term ones were dispensed as liberally
as before. Moreover, Ghoya and Okura's manner of distribution had a telling effect on the nerves of those who risked asking for passes[2]

The shrinking economic opportunities increased unemployment further, which in turn aggravated the relief problem.
At the time, the refugees were largely unaware of how close
to total bankruptcy the relief program was. The basic source
of funds, the Shanghai JDC, found it increasingly difficult
to raise money on the American Joint's "conditional" guarantee, and would not have been able to continue financing the
Kitchen Fund much longer.[3]

POVERTY

During this period in the ghetto, the living conditions
deteriorated drastically, as evidenced by the large number of
refugees driven to bare subsistence level. A few of the more
desperate ones resorted to begging, a practice previously rare
among the non-Chinese elements in Shanghai. Others, especially
inmates of the *Heim* for recalcitrant youthful offenders, went
around in sack clothes, after having sold the very shirts on
their backs. Some of these youths were so desperate for a few

pennies to buy a piece of cheese or salami, they were willing
to provide the human energy required to grind the millstones
in a Chinese peanut butter establishment. The proprietor,
fully aware that the spectacle of a white man doing coolie-type
labor would arouse the interest of bystanders, maintained such
an advertising ploy to sell his products.[4] Also, seven refugee
women were registered prostitutes, and several lived with men
in order to improve their financial situation. In some cases,
the arrangement was made with the full knowledge of the
husband, who shared the advantages. As many as 20 mothers
are said to have sold their newborn babies, to raise their low
standard of living. Children of refugee families were sent to
gather leftovers around the market, where they competed with
Chinese children for a little half-rotten fruit.

But despite the desperate measures resorted to for the
sake of survival, there was apparently little psychological disturbance among the refugees, according to the report of a
practicing psychiatrist who lived through this period in Shanghai.[5]

AFFLUENCE AMIDST POVERTY

The harsh winter of 1943 caught many unprepared
and without proper clothing. Some had already sold most of
their clothes for food and relocation expenses.[6] At this very
same time, there was a small group of refugees who enjoyed
financial independence, even some measure of wealth. The
owners of a bakery were reputed to be among the wealthiest
families in the ghetto. Others made money selling commodities
of value in the ghetto such as caffeine, or dealt in the profitable
black market. These residents of the ghetto were able to
patronize expensive restaurants and cafes, such as the Roofgarden and the Cafe Louis, along with members of the affluent
international class. At the Roofgarden, hundreds could eat at

leisure while listening to a fine four-piece band. Cafe Louis specialized in delivering exotic and costly cakes and ice cream outside the ghetto, using a refugee who, as the son of a mixed marriage, possessed a valid German passport and could leave and reenter the Restricted Area at will.[7]

DETERIORATING CONDITIONS

The physical health of the ghetto residents deteriorated fast, despite precautions taken by the authorities during the relocation, such as mandatory mass inoculations to prevent any outbreak of epidemics.[8] A conference of the *Hongkewer Aertzteverein* on December 20, 1943, commented that malnutrition in one form or another was rampant among the inhabitants of the ghetto. It resulted in the death of 102 residents of the Heime during the months of January to November 1943—"double the norm." In November of that year 12 out of 15 patients afflicted with sprue (a sickness caused by malnutrition) died.[9] This brought the total mortality for 1943 to 311.[10]

Approximately 5,000 to 6,000 refugees were dependent upon relief from the Kitchen Fund by the beginning of 1944. In terms of food this relief meant one hot meal a day with nine ounces of bread, a total of about 1,350 calories—not starvation but not sufficient to build up any resistance even under the best conditions. About 1,000 children and the sick and aged received a supplementary meal in the evening.

The harshness of the winter was aggravated by a shortage of coal caused by the Allied blockade. The price of coal also rose steeply after electricity was rationed, and this rationing, two kilowatt a month, was stringently enforced. This amount was sufficient to operate a 15-watt bulb for about two hours. An alternative was to use an acetylene lamp, which gave a bright light but emitted an obnoxious odor.

Problems soon arose from the rationing of electricity on a per-house basis, the most serious of course being the sharing of light and cost among tenants and subtenants. Even when submeters were installed, the matter of the cost of installation became a bone of contention. The services of the Arbitration Board were in constant demand to settle such minor problems in time to prevent the electricity from being cut off for non-payment.

Food was cooked on small Japanese charcoal stoves which looked like flowerpots with a hole on one side. Fuel consisted of briquettes made from a mixture of coal dust, cinders, ashes, straw and sand, in about equal proportions. This "porridge" was mixed with water and shaped in small iron moulds, then left to dry in the sun. It is easy to imagine the difficulty an inexperienced housewife would have, first in starting the fire, then in keeping it going. The wet-straw content, which produced a lot of smoke, made it necessary to use the stoves outdoors only, either in a courtyard or even the street.[11]

SACRA REORGANIZES

Among the most detrimental aspects of the ghetto experience was the use of "free" Russian Jews who formed the SACRA committee, making them an object of hatred among the refugees. But SACRA was not popular with the Russian Jews either. It had to tax them in order to support the *Heime* and the indigent refugees, and the refugees themselves did not trust the members of SACRA. In turn, Dr. Cohn, Chairman of SACRA, was not trusted by members of his committee. According to one former SACRA member, all private conversation among this group would stop the moment Dr. Cohn came near.[12]

Yet SACRA was the only relief organization that represented them before the Japanese authorities and, as we know, Kubota liked to deal with a single organization.

As a prelude to such reorganization, one may look at the results of a very important SACRA meeting, reported on in detail in the *Chronicle* of April 27, 1944. This meeting was chaired by Kubota and Kano, the secretary of SACRA. This bulletin speaks of Jews, per se, not only stateless refugees, etc., "but simply of all Shanghai Jews," although the word "Jew," had been studiously avoided in all previous public notices.

At this meeting the Japanese proclaimed their authority and established the following regulations:

1. All stateless Jewish inhabitants of Shanghai, not subject to the proclamation of February 18, 1943 are considered regular members of SACRA and are required to register as such.

2. All non-stateless Jewish inhabitants of Shanghai are considered supporting members of SACRA and their voluntary support is asked for the charity work of SACRA in favor of the refugees.

3. SACRA has to control and supervise, to support and administer all Jewish organizations in Shanghai, if and when necessary.

So by the end of 1944, when the relocation and the housing problems it had created had become minor matters, SACRA was forced to reexamine its place and function in the refugee community. Its minutes during this period, though carefully edited, reveal a dissatisfied membership, aware that they had become a superfluous, cumbersome bureaucracy, whose few remaining functions could be better handled by other existing relief organizations. Many of these members were, in fact, involved in the other organizations, such as EAST-

JEWCOM, CENTROJEWCOM and the Shanghai JDC. They resented what they considered to be SACRA's duplication of services.[13]

Dr. Cohn wanted to respond to the Jewish community's needs and realized that radical changes would have to be made, and Kubota agreed.[14] As the first move toward this goal, SACRA turned over the administration of the Jewish Hospital, the Shanghai Jewish School and other Jewish institutions to the Ashkenazi Jewish Community.[15] Then, to reflect the shift in policy, it announced the creation of five new departments.[16] These were to be headed by experienced paid workers rather than by volunteers.[17] In order to finance its new activities, the euphemistic loans were to be replaced by a more efficient system of taxation and collection.[18]

KUBOTA, HONORARY CHAIRMAN

To give the reorganized SACRA greater authority, Kubota took the title of Honorary Chairman, and Kano acted as an advisor. Dr. Cohn, the previous chairman, would serve as president and head of the Administration Department. This shift in titles made little difference in practice, though, as Kubota retained the ultimate authority.[19]

Even as reorganization was going on, complaints began to circulate that the new system accomplished little beyond a more effective means of collecting taxes.[20] Something more drastic was required to revitalize SACRA, and a Central Control Board (CCB) was established, to act as an umbrella agency covering the various refugee relief organizations. Dr. Cohn would serve as chairman, but SACRA would only be one unit, and the new CCB would be composed of representatives from the Kitchen Fund and the Shanghai JDC.[21]

This system allowed Kubota to keep a vigilant watch on all the relief organizations and their expenditures, without departing from the Japanese practice of employing a minimum of their own manpower in an occupied area, in this case himself and his three assistants, Kano, Okura and Ghoya.[22]

While the slow process of reorganization was going on, the CCB tried to correct a few of the more disagreeable aspects of the relief. Foremost among these was the amount of red tape involved in every detail of relief work, which by 1944 had become almost unmanageable. The Kitchen Fund had rapidly expanded, and now supported 11,000 refugees almost totally, where it had only fed about 4,000 in the beginning of 1942. It had grown with a "maximum of inefficiency and minimum of direction."[23]

PIC

To alleviate this situation, the CCB set up the Permanent Investigation Committee (PIC), to investigate both old recipients of relief and all new applicants. It was composed of delegates from the *Juedische Gemeinde,* the Refugee Hospital, *Pao Chia,* the Chamber of Commerce ERU and the Kitchen Fund, as well as EASTJEWCOM and a Czech group for cases affecting the Polish or Czech refugees.[24]

The leaders of the Kitchen Fund feared that their shortcomings would be exposed. They need not have worried, as the PIC, far from eliminating the bureaucratic bungling, merely exacerbated it.[25] Shortly after its establishment, a haggard refugee applied for a pair of shoes and socks. He found that his application for socks had to be investigated by the *Juedische Gemeinde,* which made the decisions for minor items, while his request for shoes, a major item, must await approval, for up to four weeks, while the PIC investigated the case.[26]

Such bureaucratic behavior on the part of PIC made many refugees prefer to sell their few belongings rather than submit to a humiliating investigation.[27] Other independent souls asked for loans to enable them to keep off the relief rolls. Many of these refugees, especially those on salaries, had to live on far less money than those on relief, who by mid-1945 were receiving an inflationary (Sh) $350,000 a week for a family of three,[28] After much debate, and a number of meetings, it was decided, in June 1945, that a refugee applying for relief would receive aid immediately, and PIC's investigation of his case would take place afterwards.[29]

In addition to the red tape, friction and rivalry among the various relief organizations had begun to create problems. Between members of the Kitchen Fund and the Shanghai JDC it went beyond mere personal recriminations, and involved both organizations in the already existing feud between the Japanese *gendarmerie* and Kubota's Bureau.[30] This kind of friction would reach the point where food purchased by the JDC was rejected as inedible by the Kitchen Fund Purchasing Department, and had to be forcibly imposed on them by the JDC.[31] This kind of discussion particularly disgusted the International Red Cross who, as a result refused to let the JDC distribute the funds from the United States when they arrived in the spring of 1944.[32]

As the CCB gained greater control over the activities of the Kitchen Fund, the former eliminated some of the inter-organizational friction and streamlined its cumbersome administrative machinery. Some of the volunteers were replaced by skilled paid workers.[33] After the department was reorganized, there remained three clearly defined activities: Purchase, Delivery and Storing; Feeding, Payment and Social; Housing and Works.[34]

The last recorded minutes of the CCB, dated July 16, 1945, indicate Kubota's approval of this plan, which would have greatly benefited the refugees if it had been put into effect a year, or a year and a half earlier. As it happened, the events

of the following day, July 17, 1945, created a far greater
crisis for the refugees than the petty bureaucratic annoyances.
In fact, it served to unite them in a way previously unimagin-
able, in what turned out to be their most tragic as well as
heroic hour.

AIR RAID

      On July 17, 1945, the refugee community experienced
a brief but devastating air raid, and when it was over, 31 of
them were among the 250 dead in Shanghai. Over 500
were wounded, of whom about half were refugees, many in
serious condition. About 700 refugees were left homeless.[35]
Shanghai had become a secondary target for the air strikes of
United States military aircraft ever since the summer of 1944.
These raids, covering the Nanking-Shanghai strip, were greatly
intensified during the months that followed January 1945. They
had as their primary objective the blockading of China by
destroying Japanese shipping lanes, and the neutralization of
such military establishments as docks, airdromes, supply depots,
oil tanks and arms plants.[36] Although the United States pilots
were given strict orders not to bomb strictly civilian areas,
there was always the danger of stray bombs hitting nearby
non-military targets. A few refugees, foreseeing a possible
Allied landing and heavy fighting, prepared for all eventuali-
ties, including flight into the interior. They began to study
Chinese seriously and exchanged their best valuables into
"illegal" Chinese silver dollars, carefully hiding them in a
money belt on their person.[37] The Japanese, of course, ordered
blackouts, and curfews in restaurants, which had to close at
nightfall. The disruption of normal electricity and water supplies became commonplace for all Shanghai residents. Emergency first-aid centers also had to be set up and air raid drills
organized.

      Few of the refugees took these drills seriously. They
believed that the United States would not bomb their sector of

Shanghai. That the Japanese, in line with their "Jewish Power" theory, shared this belief, is clear from the fact that they stored ammunition in many parts of the ghetto.[38] In fact, many refugees, especially among the young, used to enjoy the sight, and take pride in, the awesome power of the American Air Force in action. Little did they realize that they, too, might become its victims.[39]

DEATH AND DESTRUCTION

All the more was it a shock when, at exactly 12:13 p.m. on July 17, 1945, a hot summer day, death rained from the skies, as Okinawa-based United States bombers carried out an attack on the Japanese radio station located in Hong-kew, which had been directing the Japanese shipping lines.[40] Within a few minutes, the appalling destruction became apparent. Hundreds of both Chinese and refugee victims lay buried in the rubble. The fragile houses collapsed under the shock waves, and the SACRA compound at Tongshan and Kungpin Roads, which housed hundreds of refugees, received a direct hit which killed 12 and wounded 40. A nearby nursery caring for 35 young children narrowly escaped destruction.[41]

EFFECTIVE REACTION

Never before had the moral, physical and mental resources of the refugee community been marshalled so quickly and effectively as in this moment of tragedy. The reaction is best described in the words of an eyewitness:

The air raid services organization proved, as expected, to be completely useless. But the spirit of the group was beyond description. There were no signs of panic, The refugees rushed from where they happened to be to the medical offices and to other emergency stations created

JAPANESE, NAZIS & JEWS

on the spot. Chinese casualties received aid together with the refugee victims. The supplies of bandage and dressing available were used up in a few minutes. The camp inmates brought their shirts and bed linens and turned them over to be used for bandages. People who had previously been frightened at the sight of blood rushed to the emergency stations to offer their help. Women, otherwise nervous and fussy and given to tears easily, worked conscientiously and carried out the instructions of the doctors. The women of the old-age room made tea and coffee for the wounded and gave up their pillows and blankets. A guard service was hastily organized to prevent looting. The spontaneous action of the refugees in meeting the catastrophe called forth the admiration as well as the appreciation of the native population. They brought food to the bombed out refugees and offered money to the camps. When this was refused, with thanks, they brought Chinese cakes to show their gratitude. The refugees felt they had passed this test with credit.[42]

When the raid was over, as we have seen, the refugee dead numbered 31 and the wounded 250.[43]

The massive Ward Road jail was opened to the public for shelter, since it was the only really solid building in this area. The courtyard was turned into a first aid station for hundreds of wounded. Though the jail had its own well-equipped hospital, with the finest German instruments, and was manned by clinical doctors, neither the refugees nor the Chinese would be treated until the families of the wounded came and paid for the medical care. This was because of the family-centered structure of Chinese society which limited concern and responsibility for the welfare of individuals to members of one's extended family. The Jewish refugee doctors, both private and those employed by the Refugee Hospital, teamed up to aid all the victims of the raid, Jews and Chinese alike.

The Chinese also appreciated the fact that the refugees did not flee, but stayed in the lanes and guarded all homes from looting. This gratitude not only reflected the events of the day, but was indicative of a basic change in the former neutral, even occasional hostile attitude of some of the Chinese inhabitants of Hongkew toward the refugees.[44]

The Japanese naturally attempted to capitalize on the feelings of the refugees by encouraging them to cable a protest to the United States. Joseph Bitker of the Shanghai JDC told the Japanese authorities that, as a recipient of United States relief aid, he could not take issue on a "political matter." He did, however, consent to send a cable to the United States authorities, giving the factual information about the number of casualties and the damage suffered.[45]

Following the air raid, representatives of all the organizations within the Ashkenazi Jewish community, headed by Rabbi Ashkenazi, appealed to Kubota to open up the ghetto and permit freedom of movement to the refugees. No answer is recorded, but the response was obviously negative. However, the ghetto was not to remain a restricted area much longer.[46]

This heroic, tragic chapter of refugee life has two, somewhat sad, footnotes. The first was the detention of three unidentified refugees who had attempted to rob victims of the raid, and who were severely punished by the Corrections Department of the *Heime*.[47] The second had to do with a misunderstanding that served to widen further the gulf between the German refugees and the Russian Jews. This concerned Rabbi Ashkenazi's refusal, in accord with Jewish Law, to perform the preburial ritual of *Taharah* (which involved the cleansing of the dead) on the mutilated victims of the air raid.[48] The German refugees regarded this as another rebuff on the part of the resident Russian Jews.[49]

LABOR SERVICE

A shortage of Chinese labor and a rise in its cost, as well as difficulties in managing the Chinese, made the Japanese seek means of utilizing unemployed refugees, especially from the *Heime,* to work in their industries.[50] The first of several such attempts was initiated by Kano in April 1943 at a SACRA meeting, and was followed by a plan proposed by the five board members of the *Juedische Gemeinde* who had recently been placed in charge by the Japanese. This plan envisioned a Labor Service *(Arbeitsdienst)* of all the refugees, with the exception of the aged, the sick and the children cared for by the charity organization.[51]

Evidently, this plan did not materialize, for in May 1944, a report by the Japanese Consul General of Shanghai, S. Yano, reiterates a similar proposal for recruiting the unemployed residents of the *Heime* "to serve as collective labor."[52]

YESHIVA RESCUE PLAN

Confined in their ghetto, the refugees were totally unaware of several dramatic efforts to extricate them. One of these focused on the small yeshiva group, while the other included the entire refugee body.

Although they were able to decipher Kalmanowitz's cryptic messages from the United States with their great talmudic knowledge and logic, not even the heads of the Mirrer Yeshiva were privy to the schemes he devised to save the Yeshiva. Dissatisfied with merely dispatching life-saving funds to Shanghai through legal and extra-legal channels, he left no stone unturned in his determination to protect the students from possible harm in the war zone. Creative and restless, Kalmanowitz devised some fantastic plans to solicit aid from neutral countries vis-a-vis Japan, such as the Soviet Union, Sweden and the Vatican, to pull out all the rabbinical students from the ghetto to such destinations as Mexico or Sweden.

From one telegram by the American Legation in Stockholm, for example, we learn that rabbis Wolbe and Jacobson (the latter, Chief Rabbi of Sweden) had since 1944, actively negotiated with the Russians, the Japanese and the Swedes for the release of the entire Yeshiva and rabbinical group, consisting of almost 500 individuals. The Japanese, in keeping with their policy of concern for the alleged Jewish influence, even after Pearl Harbor, readily gave their approval to such evacuation plans with only the reservation that transportation be provided to Vladivostok. The Russians were less enthusiastic about providing transportation across Siberia, claiming that the Trans Siberian railroad was already over-crowded. The Swedes pointed out that they had no shipping in East Asian waters, and the American Government, unwilling to provide shipping, declared this plan "technically impossible," although it found the means to transport almost 150,000 POW's to the United States.[53]

NISEI REFUGEE EXCHANGE PLAN

While Rabbi Kalmanowitz tried to snatch to safety a relatively small group among the Shanghai refugees, another plan, on a much broader scale, and equally imaginative, was created by the World Jewish Congress. In line with a resolution by Congressman Dickstein and Senator Barbour to create a temporary haven in the United States for religious and racial refugees, Dr. Kubowitzki proposed in November 1943 to exchange the entire Jewish refugee body in Shanghai for an equal number of interned Japanese-Americans (Nisei).

Although over 100,000 Nisei were incarcerated at the time in a number of internment camps, Kubowitzki suggested that a particularly "troublesome" group of 15,000 at the Tule Lake (California) camp, dubbed "disloyal" because of their refusal to sign a loyalty oath, be returned to Japan in exchange for the Jewish refugees. He further noted that this would take place after prior exchange of Americans confined by the Japanese authorities.

As in the first instance, the State Department was not very receptive to this suggestion for saving Jewish lives.[54]

RESUMPTION OF COMMUNICATIONS

The brightest moment for the refugees in the generally bleak ghetto period, which obviously spelled survival for the majority of the over 15,000 refugees, was the resumption of communication between the American Joint and Shanghai in December of 1943.[55] We can imagine the joy with which the long-awaited cable from Laura Margolies (who had been repatriated in that month) to Bitker, concerning his daughter's birthday, was received. This meant, of course, the renewal of financial aid, particularly from the end of March 1944, It came via Switzerland at an ever increasing tempo throughout the war and into the postwar period. This rate of aid was maintained and even increased as economic conditions in Shanghai steadily deteriorated.

The American Joint, ever since its last cable had reached Shanghai in May 1942, had not ceased in its efforts to convince an indifferent United States government to grant official resumption of communications with enemy-occupied Shanghai.[56] Several factors influenced the change in the government's policy. One of these was Laura Margolies' report on the refugee situation following her repatriation in 1943. There was also the steadily increasing moral pressure on the American government, particularly the State and Treasury departments, following the early disclosures of Nazi atrocities. Above all, there was the relentless efforts of Rabbi Abraham Kalmanowitz and several of his rabbinical colleagues from Vaad Hatzalah.

This moral pressure proved decisive. Henry Morgenthau, Jr., then Secretary of the Treasury, was able to use it to reverse the government's formerly inflexible stand on the Trading with the Enemy Act. Permission was granted for the resumption of communication with enemy-occupied territory in China and Europe, by December 1943. By the beginning of 1944, it became possible to transfer money legally via Switzerland.[57] It is interesting to note that while the United States granted this request at this late date on humanitarian grounds only, the Japanese did nothing throughout the War to prevent money from coming in. They even permitted the entry of relief money from Tokyo and Harbin. For instance, in 1943, a Jewish businessman from Manchuria, residing in Tokyo, successfully sent 5,000 yen to the Shanghai refugees, a transaction requiring approval by the finance ministry as well as by the military authorities. Similarly, the Jewish Far Eastern Council in Harbin sent several relatively large sums to the refugees in Shanghai.[58]

By December 29, 1943, the American Joint's first cable to Shanghai's JDC, via the International Red Cross in Switzerland, sent authorization to borrow up to (US) $25,000 in Swiss francs (which was the only currency permitted to be imported by the Japanese) per month for up to one year. By January 1944, Rabbi Kalmanowitz had received authorization to send (US) $100,000 also in Swiss francs to his yeshiva in Shanghai.[59]

Although the resumption of communications with the United States (and especially the guarantee from the American Joint for loans) came as welcome news to the harried refugee committees in Shanghai, apparently conditions had reached the point where it became difficult to raise the necessary funds locally, even with the "Joint's Guarantee."[60] By the end of March 1944, the American Joint was able to transfer the equivalent of (US) $25,000 in Swiss francs through its emissary, Saly Meyer, in St. Gallen, Switzerland, which pulled the Shanghai JDC out of a precarious position.[61]

Due to steadily rising inflation in Shanghai, during 1944, which went completely out of control by mid-1945, the rate of relief sent by the Joint soon increased. Starting with (US) $35,000 per month, it reached a sum of (US) $100,000 (400,000 Swiss franc) by January 1945.[62] This rate continued until the end of the war, when the Joint opened an entirely new chapter of relief work in Shanghai. Even these large sums would hardly have sufficed were it not for the fact that the Shanghai JDC was able to make withdrawals from the banks in Shanghai dollars equal to ten times the official rate. This was done "on the black," with the obvious complicity of the Japanese authorities, who upon humanitarian grounds chose to ignore it.[63]

NEW FUNDS—NEW LIFE

These steady Joint remittances were the primary factors mitigating the effects of the worsening economic conditions for the refugees during 1944-1945. These conditions are manifest in the number of refugees requiring assistance, which rose from approximately 6,000 by the end of 1943 to 7,300 by April 1944 and 11,000 by June 1945.[64]

Such funds from the American Joint, supplemented by the smaller amounts sent by other Jewish organizations, especially Vaad Hatzalah, were not only responsible for the improved level of food at the *Heime,* but they also enabled the

Kitchen Fund to substitute cash subsidies for food—since the summer of 1944—to those who desired it. This money also infused new life and vitality into various educational and cultural institutions and organizations which could now continue and even expand their activities at a time when the economic situation was at its lowest ebb.[65]

Among such organizations receiving aid were the *Juedische Gemeinde* and the various schools, such as the SJYA, the Freysinger school, the Craftsmen's Guild, the ORT Trade School, as well as the various yeshivot. In addition, the Refugee Hospital's facilities were expanded with 125 beds, a pharmacy and a dental clinic.[66] The rate of malnutrition and its concomitant diseases was already lowered by the summer of 1944, and declined even more so the following winter. This decrease is reflected in the decline of the mortality rate from a high of at least 311 in 1943 to 260 in 1944. Still, according to the evidence of one refugee, six infants froze to death during one bitter cold evening in the winter of 1944-1945.[67]

Moreover, the lack of proper equipment, even with the improved situation, made decent diagnoses and treatment difficult. The Ward Road laboratory, for example, possessed only two microscopes to cope with the needs of a hundred patients daily requiring the inspection of the stool. Since such inspection took ten minutes each and the stool was no longer suitable for this purpose beyond four hours, it was impossible to do justice to more than a fraction of the patients.

The arrival of JDC money in Shanghai at this period of acute economic difficulty provoked a slightly comic situation. The banks and even some of the commercial enterprises had resorted to issuing notes, referred to as *"bons,"* to substitute for cash, which lack of confidence in the current paper money had left in short supply. There was, of course, a slight discount on these *bons,* but so high was the JDC credit that when its Shanghai branch began to issue JDC *bons,* signs immediately appeared in store windows, "JDC-Bons Pari"— that is to say, they were as good as ready money.[68]

PEACE FEELER

Before the conclusion of the War in the Pacific, the notion of "Jewish Power" was to appear once again as a factor in the Japanese policy. This involved the use of Jews in China as intermediaries in at least one and possibly three attempts in quest for peace with the United States, One instance for which details are available is based on two taped interviews by Rabbi Marvin Tokayer of two of the Jewish participants in the event. Both knew Japanese and one of these served as the interpreter. Although there are a few discrepancies between the two versions they agree on the essential story which goes as follows:[69]

On a Saturday during the early part of 1945, the Jewish Community in Tientsin received a cable from the Peking Military Mission (which had jurisdiction of Tientsin), requesting the Jewish leaders to meet a delegation of Japanese officers at the train station the following day. The meeting took place and the Jews took the Japanese to the Jewish Club *(Kunst)* for lunch.

Colonel Tomiaki Hidaka, who headed this delegation of about ten officers, claimed to speak on behalf of the Tokyo authorities. Considering the size of the group and the public forum at the Club with an equal number of Jews present, it is highly unlikely for the Colonel merely to have voiced his private opinion.

Hidaka began by noting how long the War had been going on and how many Americans, Jews and Japanese had been killed. He stated that it was high time to put an end to this slaughter. As the Jews listened in amazement and in fear, Hidaka went on to tell them their role. Hidaka explained that everyone knew that Roosevelt, Morgenthau and Morgan (the banker) were Jews, as were all the powerful and rich men in America. As residents in the Far East, the Jewish delegates must be fully aware of how well Japan treated the Jews who sought sanctuary in Shanghai and Kobe, and how they had never been persecuted.

On behalf of the Tokyo Government, Hidaka ordered the Jews with their "international connections and power," to go with him to Peking and to broadcast an appeal to their brothers in the United States to use their influence on the American Government to stop the conflict. The Jews realized that they had to do something quickly and could not put off answering the Colonel. Groping for time to at least discuss the matter, the Jewish delegation launched into a series of toasts: anything to keep Hidaka drinking. Though red in the face and full of alcohol, he got up and demanded an immediate response.

Speaking on behalf of the Jewish community, one of the delegates replied that they would glady make the broadcast. But, as Jews, and knowing their correligionists better than did the Japanese, the delegates were certain that such a broadcast would leave the wrong impression. The American Jews would automatically assume that a call for peace after more than three years could only mean that Japan was too weak to carry on, and the United States would surely double its efforts to knock out Japan militarily. Hidaka acknowledged the wisdom of these remarks and said that he would bring this message to the authorities and report back. To their relief, the Jews of Tientsin never heard from him again.

Although it would be idle to speculate about the significance of such an appeal in view of the negative response to numerous other unofficial peace feelers in Stockholm, Zurich and Moscow, it is doubtful, to say the least, that this one would have fared any better.[70]

REMOVAL OF GHOYA

The news of D-Day in June 1944, which was the beginning of the end of the war in Europe, inspired a jubilant mood among the Jews of Shanghai. However, the first real sign of the approaching demise of the ghetto did not appear until the close of that year when, at the request of some members of SACRA, Ghoya was removed from his post.[71] He was replaced by Harada, a more rational administrator, who ushered in a period of greater leniency in the press system. For instance, he returned all the passes confiscated by Ghoya.[72] He even permitted his assistant, Morris Feder (who held the same position under Ghoya) to renew any pass issued originally by Ghoya. Ghoya disappeared after losing his post, but reappeared in the ghetto shortly before the conclusion of the war. He was thrown out of his apartment by an irate Jewish landlord. Later, the astonished "king of the Jews" was beaten in the street by a group of refugees, who recognized him as the former erratic ghetto administrator. To the end the deposed Ghoya had really thought himself to be benign ruler of his loyal Jewish subjects.[73]

NEWS OF NAZI ATROCITIES

After Germany's surrender on May 8, 1945, reports about Nazi atrocities began to circulate, reports too horrible for the mind to grasp. While many of the refugees were still unable to accept their truth, Russian newsreels on the concentration camps began to be shown, and forced the reality on them all too graphically. One man had the awesome experience of witnessing, on film, his own brother, a survivor of such atrocities acting as guide to the Russian liberators of the camp. On the other hand, the conclusion to the War in Europe naturally encouraged the hope of seeing the end of Japanese occupation.[74]

Serious proposals were presented at a CCB meeting—with Kubota's apparent approval—advocating an entirely new kind of pass, more in the nature of a passport, which would eliminate some of the red tape.[75]

PEACE RUMORS

With the greater intensity of American air strikes in China during July, came the first solid rumors of the impending end of the War in the Pacific. When at one point, early in July 1945, it was rumored in the ghetto that traffic was henceforth unrestricted to and from the "restricted area," the refugees eagerly seized their first chance of freedom in over two years. To their dismay, they found that restrictions, if anything, were tighter, as the authorities were making a special attempt to clamp down on the flourishing black market.[76]

The expectations and the spirits of the refugees soared once more as news of the two atomic bombs dropped on Japan, and of Russia's late entry into the Pacific theater of war, spread throughout the ghetto, via secret underground radios and clandestine newsletters, as well as through the still openly functioning Tass radio network.[77] With Russia's declaration of war on Japan on August 9, it became the turn of Russians in China and Manchuria, including the Russian Jews, to fear the retribution of the Japanese authorities. And indeed the Japanese were soon checking who was a "White" Russian, and who had applied for Soviet passports. Luckily there were little time left for any real damage to be done before the war ended.[78]

For the next two weeks, all of Shanghai lived under uncertain, paradoxical conditions, with conflicting rumors and orders following one another in rapid succession, as the War in the Pacific came to a close. For example, on August 10, the Allied flags were raised on various public buildings, and within 24 hours peace rumors burst upon the ghetto. Pent-up feelings overflowed and everyone danced in the streets. Russians,

Chinese and refugees kissed each other in a rare display of solidarity—and took the opportunity to beat up a few Japanese. Both these forms of celebration were however premature, as the flags were hauled off by Japanese sentries and the jubilant crowds subdued by ever-increasing patrols.[79] One final exhibition of authority was attempted by the Japanese when they rounded up the refugees and made them stand bareheaded in the broiling sun. This was quickly stopped when the *Juedische Gemeinde* got in touch with the Japanese commander-in-chief. The Japanese remained in control until August 22, when the last of the notices was posted, announcing the end of the pass system, though the "designated area" remained in effect for a few days longer.[80] During these last days, when the Japanese authorities practically disappeared and the city was not yet under Chinese control, the *Pao Chia* protected Jewish property from potential vandals.[81]

THE GHETTO WALLS FALL

The delay in the liberation by the Allied forces resulted from logistic difficulties as well as politics. The Chinese Army was still far up in the north, but the Americans were following Chiang Kai-shek's request that his army should be the one to liberate Shanghai.[82]

The failure to open up the ghetto, "the shame of Shanghai," was denounced both by the refugees and by the Russsian-language newspaper *Novosti Danya,* which pointed out that when the Allied Commission entered Shanghai the ghetto was still in existence.[83] Not until September 3, 1945, can it be said to have been officially closed. On that day the American Rescue and Goodwill Mission toured the designated area and the *Heime* with Manuel Siegel, the Americant Joint representative, himself recently freed from an internment camp. The refugees once more took to the streets, dancing, this time without restraint and with real hope for a brighter future.[84]

NOTES : TRAGEDY AND TRIUMPH

1. See esp. Redlich-Kranzler correspondence August 30, 1974; December 23, 1975; Redlich-Tischler correspondence April 9, 1974.

2. See above Chapter XVII.

3. Bitker, *Memo*, p. 5.

4. Fuchs Interview. Cf. also Rosenfeld, *History*, III, pp. 6, 10. *Ibid.*, p. 18; CCB, May 23, 1945, p. 3.

5. Gruenberger, "Refugees," pp. 340-41. For the picking of the fruit, see Fuchs Interview.

6. See FO *Police Report to Yano*, November 16, 1943, p. 1 (DP).

7. Eisfelder, *Exile*, pp. 37-39, 44-45.

8. See SACRA Supplement to *Unser Leben* (April 30, 1943), n.p. YIVO No. 12. The Medical Committee of SACRA carried out the inoculation program for the entire refugee ghetto population.

9. "Hongkewer Aertzteverein," pp. 1-2.

10. Kranzler M.A., p. 140. See also Appendix for statistics.

11. For the number of refugees dependent on relief, see Shanghai JDC to Switzerland, June 6, 1944. Enclosure No. 2 (JDCCA). See also Kunfi, "Medizinische," pp. 9-10.
For examples of the inflation, see Eisfelder, *Exile*, p. 55. The amount of electricity used is also cited by *ibid.*, p. 51. For the Arbitration Board and the electric meters, see Redlich-Kranzler correspondence, April 18, 1975, p. 4.

12. See Redlich-Kranzler correspondence, February 27, 1974, p. 5, re dislike of SACRA by refugees and distrust of Dr. Cohn. See also above, Chapter XVII. For the distrust of Dr. Cohn by SACRA, see Dicker, *Ms.*, p. 136, n. 36, based on an interview of a former member of SACRA. For Kubota's pressure on SACRA, see Margolies, *Report*, p. 19.

13. See, for example, SACRA Minutes, January 13, 1944, pp. 1-2; January 26, 1944, pp. 1-2; March 14, 1944, pp. 1-2; February 1, 1944, p. 1; June 16, 1944. Cf. also Bitker, *Memo*, p. 4. For the SACRA meeting and the regulations by Kubota, and Redlich's remarks, see Redlich-Kranzler correspondence, February 27, 1974, p. 11. Dr. Redlich sent the author a copy of the *Chronicle* article, Redlich also observed about this article that:

In Kubota's speech there is a very interesting point: He declares himself in favor of self-government of the Jewish colony and points as an example to the Japanese Residents' Association. The SACRA (stateless Jewish inhabitants, not subject to the proclamation) are subject to taxation, while all supporting members (non-stateless Jewish inhabitants) are requested to make donations.

I wish to stress Kubota's remarks, that the Jewish organisation, though under supervision, should be permitted to organize and govern themselves.

In the same bulletin it is said, that a general meeting of all Jewish inhabitants will be held. I don't remember such a meeting and doubt that it ever took place.

14. SACRA Minutes, February 1, 1944, p. 1; March 14, 1944, p. 1.

15. SACRA Minutes, March 14, 1944, p. 1.

16. *Ibid.* The number of personnel appointed to each of the new departments indicated the degree of the importance of each. *Ibid.*, March 16, 1944, pp. 1-2. For example, the Housing Department which used to be the most important and fully staffed section, was now reduced to the three members, while on the other hand, the Social Welfare Department increased its scope of activities, and now included seven members. *Ibid.*

17. *Ibid.*, March 14, 1944, p. 1.

18. *Ibid.*, March 22, 1944, pp. 1-2.

19. *Ibid.*, March 16, 1944, p. 1. The post of Honorary Chairman is crossed out and President is written above it. Cf. Dicker, *Wanderers,* p. 131. The new title, however, was never accorded any status, since all later Minutes carry the heading of Dr. Cohn as Honorary Chairman. The author doubts whether the new title was meant for anything more than for carrying the authority of Kubota's name to collect the taxes.

20. SACRA Minutes, March 14, 1944, p. 2.

21. *Ibid.*, CCB, June 6, 1944, pp. 1-2. In fact, by May 1945, SACRA was dropped completely. See also CCB, May 2, 1945, p. 1; June 6, 1944, p. 1.
Within the year the CCB would also include representatives of the *Juedische Gemeinde* and the Permanent Investigation Committee (PIC). See CCB, May 2, 1945; May 23, 1945. Cf. Dicker, *Wanderers,* p. 132. For the PIC, see below, in this chapter.

22. Similarly in Kobe, Japan, during 1941, a period of heavy Jewish refugee influx into Japan, the Japanese dealt only with the local Jewish organization JEWCOM, which they held responsible for the entire Jewish

population. See Moiseff, "Kobe," pp. 2-3. Also Gerechter Interview. Tarshansky Interview.

23. The quote is from Siegel, *Report*, August 26, 1945, p. 6. For the statistics of the Kitchen Fund aid, see below, this chapter; also CCB, June 6, 1945, p. 4. The 4,000 figure for early 1942 is found above, chapter 16.

24. *Ibid.* January 11, 1945, pp. 1-2; February 9, 1945, pp. 1-2.

25. For the fears of the Kitchen Fund, see *ibid.*, February 9, 1945, p. 2.

26. *Ibid.*, May 2, 1945, p. 3, and June 15, 1945, p. 2. Cited by Kranzler, *M.A.*, p. 88, and Dicker, *Wanderers*, p. 133.

27. CCB, June 15, 1945, pp. 1-4.

28. *Ibid.*, June 6, 1945, pp. 3-4; Cf. also June 15, 1945, pp. 1-4. At this point (Sh) $30,000-40,000 bought only enough food for a few days. *Ibid.*, June 6, 1945, p. 3.

29. *Ibid.*, June 19, 1945, p. 2.

30. See Margolies, *Report*, p. 20; Siegel, Report, August 26, 1945, pp. 1-3; July 12, 1945, p. 2. A detailed discussion of the problem of internal strike is found in Redlich-Kranzler correspondence, February 27, 1974, pp. 2-5, 8-9.

31. *Ibid.*, July 14, 1945, p. 5.

32. ICR Cable, March 2, 1944. Also Peter to Leavitt, March 3, 1944; CCB, July 3, 1944, p. 2; June 6, 1945, p. 2; July 4, 1945, pp. 1-3. For the newly-arriving funds, see below, in this chapter.

33. CCB, July 16, 1945, p. 1; July 12, 1945, p. 1.
The individual within the Shanghai JDC presenting the greatest personality problem was finally asked to resign on August 8, 1945, a bit late to be of much benefit. Siegel, *Report*, August 26, 1945, p. 5.

34. CCB July 12, 1945, p. 6; July 16, 1945, p. 1. The Housing Department of the now almost defunct SACRA had already been integrated into its counterpart in the Kitchen Fund by May 1945, leaving SACRA primarily with the task of raising "taxes" from the Russian Jewish community. *Ibid.*, May 23, 1945, p. 2.

35. For detailed reports of this raid, see Ernst Pollak, "Das Heldenlied vom 17 Juli," *Herald (S.E.)*, p. 26. [Pollak "17 Juli"]; "Der Herr hat Gegeben, der Herr hat Genomen" ("The L-rd Gave and the L-rd Took Back"), *Juedisches Nachrichtenblatt* (July 27, 1945), pp. 1-2 [*Nachrichtenblatt*, July 27, 1945] (YIVO No. 13); "Erinnerung an die Toten des 7 Av 5705," *The Jewish Voice of the Far East* (August 2, 1946) ["7 Av 7505"],

p. 2. Copy in writer's possession, courtesy of Gerechter). This issue contains the names of 25 of the 31 refugee victims; Shoshana, *In Faier,* pp. 337-42; Gruenberger, "Refugees," pp. 344-45; Burkhard, *Tanz,* pp. 170-72.

36. Wesley F. Craven and James L. Cate, *The Army Air Forces in World War II; The Pacific: Matterhorn to Nagasaki June 1944 to August 1945* [Craven, *USAF*] (Chicago: University of Chicago Press, 1953), Vol. V. See the following pages: 141, 135, 159, 215, 258, 264, 346, 491, 496, 497, 499-500, 697, especially pp. 111, 695. See also *Yellow Creek,* pp. 184-85; Carey, *War Years,* pp. 190, 204-205, 208, 210; Hinzelmann, O China, p. 150; Shoshana, *In Faier,* pp. 340-41.

37. Craven, *USAF,* pp. 111, 695. Also Carey, *War Years,* pp. 207-208. For the "money belts," see Eisfelder, *Exile,* p. 55.

38. Redlich-Kranzler correspondence, February 27, 1974, p. 13. Cf. also Eisfelder, *Exile,* p. 55.

39. Eisfelder, *Exile,* p. 55.

40. Pollak, "17 Juli." Also Burkhard, *Tanz,* p. 170; p. 170; Shoshana, *In Faier,* p. 337.

41. Pollak, "17 Juli." Also Burkhard, *Tanz,* pp. 170-71; Shoshana, *In Faier,* pp. 337-38; Gruenberger, "Refugees," p. 344; Friedrichs, *Geschichte,* pp. 199-205.

42. Gruenberger, "Refugees," pp. 344-45.

43 The statistics for the number of dead presents a problem since the sources differ in the number of refugees killed. Pollak, "17 Juli," gives the number as 32, with 27 of German-Austrian and five of Polish origin. This figure of 32 is also given by Burkhard, *Tanz,* p. 171. The "JISKOR" (Memorial) Services announcement in *The Jewish Voice* (August 2, 1946), p. 1, lists the names of 25 victims belonging to the *Juedische Gemeinde.* Since five of the victims were of Polish nationality, the remaining two might possibly have been unaffiliated. In this same issue, however (p. 2), the total figure is given as 31. The writer has been unable to establish the correct total.

44. For the use of the Ward Road Jail see Levin Interview and Didner Interview. The latter, a medical doctor, also related the matter of the treatment of the wounded. Also Fuchs Interview. Pollak, "17 Juli." The clinics at the *Heime* also handled close to 600 wounded Chinese and refugee victims, while the Refugee Hospital cared for 200-300. *Ibid.* Also Gruenberger, "Refugees," p. 345.

The American Joint sent a special allotment of (US) $35,000 to cover some of the expenses resulting from the raid. Joint, News Release, August 31, 1945, p. 2.

Some of the neutral, if not hostile, attitude towards the refugees can be attributed to several causes. The most important is probably the fact that some of the "White Man's Superiority Complex" had rubbed off on some of the refugees. Fuchs Interview. There is also a good likelihood of the influence of Nazi antisemitic propaganda having some effect on the Chinese; this is especially evident in the immediate postwar period. The author hopes to complete research on this aspect in the near future.

45. Bitker, *Memo*, p. 5. For the views of some of the refugees towards the United States in relation to this raid, see Shoshana, *In Faier*, p. 339.

46. See the letter signed by representatives of 18 Jewish organizations to Kubota, July 23 [1945]. The original carbon given to the author by David Rabinovich, one of the signatories.

47. Shoshana, *In Faier*, pp. 341-42.

48. For the Jewish laws concerning these circumstances, see *Shakh, Shulhan Arukh, Yore Deah* 3, 64:4; 11.

49. The German view was related in Gerechter Interview.

50. FO Yano to Aoki, July 21, 1943, p. 3. For the problem of Chinese labor, see FO Yano to Aoki, May 5, 1944, p. 2. See also Dicker *Wanderers*, p. 192.
Gruenberger mentions a "voluntary labor service" sponsored by the relief committee [K.F.?] which granted special food rations. He claims that it was discontinued due to the numerous offers of volunteers. "Refugees," p. 341. Since he gives no particulars, I am not certain which period or occasion he refers to.

51. For Kano's original suggestion, see SACRA Minutes, April 1, 1943, p. 2. At this meeting it was "suggested" that the present leaders of the *Juedische Gemeinde* be replaced by more cooperative members. *Ibid.*, p. 1.
For the plan submitted by the *Juedische Gemeinde*, see "Juedische Gemeinde to T. Kubota, May 4, [19]43" and the attached three pages, "Report Concerning the Foundation of a 'Labour Service'." YIVO No. 42.

52. FO Yano to Aoki, May 4, 1944, p. 2 (DP). Perhaps there is a correlation between this plan and the "employment Agency" noted in the CCB Minutes, June 6, 1944, p. 2. The refugees interpreted the questionnaire as a prelude to a "concentration camp." See Burkhard, *Tanz*, p. 169.

53. The full story of Rabbi Kalmanowitz's rescue work, with that of *Vaad Hatzalah* and Rabbi Eliezer Silver, has yet to be told.
Some of the fascinating diplomatic maneuvers involving the various neutral countries, including Spain, Sweden, the Vatican, etc., can be gleaned from the following documents in the Kalmanowitz Files, courtesy of the Rabbis Shraga Moshe Kalmanowitz (the son of Rabbi Abraham) Shmuel Birenbaum and Mrs. Kalmanowitz, who kindly put the files at the author's disposal, (except for the cables with coded messages,) permitting the repro-

572 JAPANESE, NAZIS & JEWS

duction of important documents. See, for example, Michael Hoffman, Director of the Foreign Funds Control under the Treasury Department, to Rabbi Abraham Kalmanowitz, July 11, 1945; Kalmanowitz Memo to Joseph Grew, Under Secretary of State, July 17, 1945; Warren G. Magnuson to President Harry S. Truman, July 21, 1945, and Grew's reply July 26, 1945; Florence Hodel, Acting Executive Director for the War Refugee Board, to Rabbi A. Kalmanowitz (strictly confidential), February 3, 1945; cf. also Epstein, "Mir," p. 32. Corresponding and related documents are located in the NA/SDDF No. 840.48 collection. For example, one letter from the Polish Ambassador, J. Ciechanowski, to the Union of Orthodox Rabbis, February 16, 1943. He cites the Polish Government's willingness to include 500 students (Polish) for evacuation to Mexico (840.48/3800). Cf. also *Vaad Hatzalah,* pp. 227-45.

Copy of Paraphrase of Telegram from the American Legation of Stockholm, the Special War Problems Division of the State Department, April 12, 1945; substance of a report dated April 9, 1945, from American Legation, Stockholm. (Kalmanowitz Files). Cf. also memo to the Hon. Joseph C. Grew, Washington, D.C., July 17, 1945. In reference to America's unwillingness to use shipping for rescue work see especially Saul S. Friedman, *No Haven for the Oppressed: United States Policy Toward the Jewish Refugees, 1938-1945* [Friedman, *No Haven*] (Detroit: Wayne University Press, 1973), pp. 194-202.

54. See the exchange of memos between Dr. Kubowitzki, Dr. Wise [Stephen S.?], and Dr. N. Goldman concerning this project during 1943. The World Jewish Congress had also been involved in assisting Rabbi Kalmanowitz in his quest to get the Yeshiva out of Shanghai. See A[rye] Tartakower to Nahum Goldman, March 30, 1942. (World Jewish Congress Archives). The author is grateful to Rabbi Arthur Hertzberg and Rabbi M. Tokayer for making these documents available.

Dr. Kubowitzki noted in a memo to Dr. Wise (December 2, 1943) that Secretary of State Hull had begun negotiations with Japan for the further exchange of interned civilian nationals. (See *New York Times,* November 24, 1943). In his talk with Hull, Kubowitzki countered Hull's desire to repatriate only 15,000 Japanese with the fact that over 135,000 Japanese reside in the Continental United States. He also pointed out to the unsympathetic Hull that

> The country now suffers from a shortage of manpower [sic] and that the press recently discussed with seriousness the advisability of bringing to the United States 1 million Italians for a temporary stay as an effort to remedy this shortage.

Ibid. For some of the literature on the internment of Japanese-Americans, see Dillon S. Myer, *Uprooted Americans: the Japanese-Americans and the War. Relocation Authority During World War II* (Tucson, Arizona: University of Arizona Press, 1971); Paul Bailey, *City in the Sun: The Japanese*

Concentration Camp at Poston, Arizona (Los Angeles: Westernlore Press, 1971); Audrie Girdner and Anne Loftis, *The Great Betrayal: The Evacuation of Japanese-Americans During World War II* (New York: Macmillan Company, 1969): Morton Grodzins, *Americans Betrayed: Politics and the Japanese Evacuation* (Chicago: University of Chicago Press, 1949).

55. See below, note 59.

56. For the "birthday message," see Bitker, *Memo*, p. 5. Cf. also Margolies-Jarblum correspondence, February 12, 1951 (for JDC and sent to Bitker) (DP).

57. For Margolies' repatriation, see Margolies-Bitker Correspondence, February 12, 1951, p. 2 (DF).

For the part played by Henry Morgenthau, Jr., in the reopening of communications and the transfer of money to enemy-occupied territory in Europe via Switzerland, see Blum, *Morgenthau*, Chapter IV, Section 6, especially pp. 219, 223. Blum does not mention Shanghai, although part of the money sent through St. Gallen, Switzerland (via Saly Meyer) for rescue work went towards the relief of the Shanghai refugees. Morse, too, in discussing the role of the War Refugee Board, writes about the money sent by the JDC since the beginning of 1944. *Six Million*, Chapter XVII, especially pp. 329-30.

For the role played by Rabbi Kalmanowitz in influencing the State Department, especially through the good offices of Henry Morgenthau, Jr., see writer's taped interview with Dr. Joseph Schwarz, head of the European JDC. When the writer asked Dr. Schwarz what finally enabled the Joint to send the badly needed funds to Shanghai, he replied that "there was a rabbi [Kalmanowitz] with a long white beard, who, when he cried, even the State Department listened." See also interviews with Pincus Schoen and Rabbi Alex Weisfogel, both of whom worked for Rabbi Kalmanowitz during the wartime in his relief projects for the Mirrer Yeshiva and Vaad Hatzalah. Rabbi Weisfogel, who was Rabbi Kalmanowitz's assistant and translator, was directly involved in the discussions with Henry Morgenthau, Jr. See for example, the photo of Rabbis Kalmanowitz and Weisfogel with a few of the rescued students of the Mirrer Yeshiva after the war, thanking Henry Morgenthau, Jr., for his efforts in the rescue work. *Letters and Documents* (in memory of Rabbi Abraham Kalmanowitz) (New York: published by the Mirrer Yeshiva, n.d. [1967], p. 128.

See also the correspondence between Rabbi Kalmanowitz and the State Department found in the National Archives File Series No. 840.48 (Refugees [NA 840.48], especially Nos. /5061, /5528 and/5138. The last is a letter of thanks sent by Rabbi Kalmanowitz to the State Department in January 1944, for authorizing the transfer of (US) $100,000 to be sent via Switzerland.

58. For the relief money sent from Harbin, see Kaufman, *Manchuria*, p.

28. Mr. Z. sent the 5,000 yen from Tokyo, Z.-Dicker correspondence, May 20, 1959, p. 8.

59. For Kalmanowitz authorization see above, note 57, NA 840.48/5138. For the JDC, see Marc Peter to Moses Leavitt, February 1, 1944. Also Joseph Hyman to Jackson Martindell, March 29, 1944; Robert Pilpel to JDC (N.Y., November 13, 1944). See also the cable of Moses Leavitt to the IRC, Geneva, Switzerland, sent on December 24, 1943, with the government authorized Federal Reserve Bank License No. N.Y. 595343-R; Moses Leavitt to John Pehle, December 10, 1943. (JDCCA).

60. See Shanghai JDC to Switzerland, June 5, 1944, p. 1. See also Bitker, *Memo*, p. 5.

61. According to Shanghai JDC to Switzerland, June 5, 1944, Enclosure p. 1, the budget for January-March 1944 derived almost solely from loans. See also C. Brahn per Howard Ling to Laura Margolies, April 3, 1944, at which time Brahn mentions the receipt of 100,000 Swiss francs, and the improvement in the relief this money made possible. JDCCA. Although Siegel in his *Report* noted that the Joint funds were received regularly from abroad starting May 1, 1944, it does not negate the funds sent at the end of March and in April, for which there is concrete evidence. *Report*, August 26, 1945.

For the role of Saly Meyer in the Joint relief work in Switzerland, see Agar, *Remnant*, pp. 174-51, 156-58. See also the many documents, including cables and general correspondence between Saly Meyer, as well as about his activities, in the JDCCA (1942-1945). For example, the cable No. 122 from the War Refugee Board to the American Legation (Lisbon), December 19, 1944 (JDCCA).

62. For the increase of the remittances from (US) $25,000 to (US) $35,000 per month, see Cable War Refugee Board to Lisbon, No. 119 (JDCCA). For the (US) $100,000 per month, see John Pehle to Moses Leavitt, December 26, 1944. Also Moses Leavitt to War Refugee Board, December 29, 1944; Joint Memo, June 26, 1945 (JDCCA).

For the steady inflation in Shanghai, especially during 1944 and the sudden jump by mid-1945, see Young, Finance, especially charts on pp. 181, 265; and Shun-Hsin Chou, *The Chinese Inflation 1937-1939* [Chou, *Inflation*] (New York: Columbia University Press, 1963). For Shanghai, particularly during the war years, Young's book is more useful. Young also gives the value and comparison of the Japanese occupation yen (see, e.g., pp. 182-86).

Some of the Jewish sources from Shanghai also give evidence of the inflation for the various periods. For the years of 1938-1941, see Margolies to Pilpel, October 26, 1941, p. 6 (JDCCA).

For 1943, see Margolies, Report, pp. 9, 22. For 1944, see C. Brahn per Howard Ling to Laura Margolies, April 3, 1944; Carey, *War Years*, pp. 129, 148.

For the runaway inflation of May, June 1945, see especially CCB Minutes, May 23, 1945, p. 3; June 6, 1945, p. 2; June 19, 1945, p. 1; Shoshana, *In Faier*, pp. 307, 330, 333-34.

63. The total figure for the relief funds sent by the American Joint to Shanghai for the period of December 1938—August 31, 1945 amounts to close to (US) $2,200,000. This includes the close to (US) $500,000 which was borrowed through the two Joint loans (the "Guaranteed" and the "Conditional"). Joint News Release, August 31, 1945 (JDCCA).

For the black market exchanges, see Luftig Interview.

64. For the 6,000 and 7,300 figures, see Shanghai JDC to Switzerland, June 5, 1944, Enclosure No. 2. For the 15,000 figure, see Florence Hodell to Moses Leavitt, June 8, 1945. Also CCB Minutes, July 12, 1945, p. 4 (JDCCA).

The figures of 11,000 for April and 12,000 for June 1945 reported by Siegel, *Report*, August 26, 1945, p. 5, appear to be exaggerations, unless perhaps one stretches the number of refugees assisted to include the indirect help extended via the various organizations, institutions and their activities, partly subsidized by JDC money.

65. The cash subsidies were first granted in June 1944 when, due to the heat the Kitchen Fund found it difficult to cook for the large number (over 7,000). This type of subsidy was maintained throughout the rest of the war period. See, for example, CCB Minutes, June 6, 1944, pp. 1-2; CCB Minutes, December 15, 1944, p. 1.

66. Shanghai JDC to Switzerland, June 5, 1944, p. 3. Cf. also "List of Payments" by J. B. [Joseph Bitker] (ca. Fall 1944) (JDCCA). Cf. also Shanghai JDC to St. Gallen, Switzerland, June 5, 1944, pp. 2-4.

67. For the rate of malnutrition, see Kunfi, "Medizinische," p. 10. The infant deaths were reported by Linn Interview. For the statistics, see YIVO *Catalog*, p. 9. Cited by Kranzler, *M.A.*, p. 140. The figure of 350 for 1942 is based on those given in the Shanghai JDC Report. The figures of 320 from the YIVO catalog are based on the statistics provided by the *Juedische Gemeinde*, which was in charge of all birth and death records. The author took the latter figures since they are most complete, although he is not certain if they are more accurate. Dr. Friedrichs related the problem concerning the lack of proper equipment.

68. See "List of Payments" by J. B. [Joseph Bitker] (ca. Fall 1944) (JDCCA). Cf. also Shanghai JDC to St. Gallen, Switzerland, June 5, 1944, pp. 2-4. For the humorous incident concerning JDC funds, see Eisfelder, *Exile*, p. 50.

69. The author is grateful to Rabbi Tokayer for copies of these two tapes. One of the accounts, by Mr. K., is dated November 17, 1975, and the other, by Mr. B., took place several weeks earlier. See also Tokayer-

Kranzler correspondence, May 20, 1975 (TP). Most of the detail comes from B's longer account, although he places the date as far back as mid-1944. Still he is uncertain of this. Mr. K. is more definite for his 1945 date, though both agree on the day of the week. Mr. B. also alludes to another, earlier peace feeler.

The author has grounds to believe that Ishiwara and Yasue were involved in an earlier attempt to seek peace by using Jews as intermediaries. (See the brief biographical sketch of Colonel Yasue by his son Hiroo).

According to a report of a recent interview of Ayukawa's son by Tokayer, this industrialist, who wanted to settle 50,000 Jews in Manchuria, also attempted to start negotiations for peace by contacting a former administrator of his company, a Jew, who remained in Japan during the War. Tokayer to Kranzler, January 7, 1975. Toland seems to be hinting at such a peace feeler, when he brings an unpublished photo, in his book, *Rising,* of a group of Japanese, including Ayukawa. Many of these, Toland noted, "were later involved in efforts to seek an early peace."

New research being conducted by Tokayer should shed light concerning this attempt as well.

In addition, the author is aware of still another peace attempt via the Jews, as early as 1942, but the individual involved will elaborate on his story as part of a forthcoming autobiography.

70. For some of the numerous peace feelers, see Toland, *Rising Sun,* Chapter 31; Lester Brooks, *Behind Japan's Surrender: The Secret Struggle that Ended an Empire* (New York. McGraw-Hill, 1968); Kase, Journey; Butow, *Surrender.* Cf. also Professor Ernest N. Paolino to New York Times, August 17, 1975.

71. For the jubilant mood following the report of the invasion of France, see Shoshana, *In Faier,* p. 316. Also the FO Report No. 347 sent by Seiki Yano to the Japanese Foreign Minister Mamoru Shigemitsu, July 7, 1944 [FO Yano to Shigemitsu, July 7, 1944], p. 2.

For the removal of Ghoya, see Shoshana, *In Faier,* p. 328. Also Bitker, *Memo,* p. 5 (cited by Dicker, *Wanderers,* p. 154); Feder Interview; Burkhard, *Tanz,* p. 166.

72. Shoshana, *In Faier,* p. 328. Also Feder Interview.

73. Feder Interview. Feder stated that Harada left the renewal stamp with him. See also Burkhard, *Tanz,* p. 177.

74. Shoshana, *In Faier,* pp. 333-34. Also Gruenberger, *Refugees,* p. 344. For the newsreel incident, see Eisfelder, *Exile,* p. 56.

75. CCB Minutes, May 2, 1945, p. 2.

76. Shoshana, *In Faier,* p. 336.

77. Gerechter Interview; also Elbaum Interview. The Tass radio station

and the Russian newspaper were closed only upon entry of Russia into the war. Cf. Carey, *War Years*, pp. 87, 187, 202; Shoshana, *In Faier*, p. 343.

78. Shoshana, *In Faier*, p. 344. See also *Yellow Creek*, p. 185. In Hailar, Manchuria, the White Russians massacred the Soviet citizens, including 20 Jewish families. William Pratt, "Exodus from China" [Pratt, "Exodus from China"], *Hadassah Magazine*, Vol. 51 (February 1970), p. 24; Friedrichs, *Geschichte*, pp. 205-207.

79. For the "flag" incident, see Carey, *War Years*, p. 211. For the street demonstrations in the ghetto see Shoshana, *In Faier*, pp. 346-47. Also Burkhard, *Tanz*, p. 177.

The increased street patrols are noted by Shoshana, *In Faier*, pp. 346-47; and Hinzelmann, *O China*, p. 158; Levin, "Kriegesende," p. 3. For the beating up of the Japanese soldiers and the incident of the sun treatment, see Redlich-Kranzler correspondence, February 27, 1974, p. 14.

80. *Ibid.* Cf. also Shoshana, *In Faier*, pp. 347-51. The Japanese "Notices" gave contradictory orders from day to day, for the dates of August 15, 17, 18, 22. These may be found in YIVO No. 11; Fabisch, p. 10.

81. Gerechter Interview. He claimed that the Pao Chia prevented Chinese rioters from looting the Jewish section.

82. Carey, *War Years*, pp. 217, 219. For the United States agreement with Chiang Kai-shek, see Samuel Eliot Morison, *Victory in the Pacific 1945* [Morison, *Victory*], History of U.S. Naval Operations in World War II, Vol. XIV (Boston: Little, Brown and Company, 1968), pp. 354-56. Actually a small contingent of the U.S. Fleet was the first to enter Shanghai. Craven, *USAF*, Vol. 7, p. 149. Also Carey, *War Years*, pp. 217-18; Finch, *Shanghaii and Beyond*, p. 328. Miles, *War*, pp. 528-31.

83. Shoshana, *In Faier*, p. 350.

84. *Ibid.*, p. 351. Also Feder Interview. See Siegel, *Report*, August 26, 1945, p. 1, for his release from internment, and *Report*, September 25, 1945, p. 1, for the dancing of the refugees and the welcoming of the Commission.

נלאתנו את העיר

עם סגירת החוברת הנוכחית, מסתיימת גם תקופה מיוחדה בחיי
קהל תופשי התורה אשר בשנגהאי . . . הלא המה עיטויידם
הרפתקאותיהם דעדו עלייהו ולא התלאה אשר מלאתם, יען כל
אלה זקוק לספר מיוחד, בו יסופר חסדי ה' ונפלאותיו אשר הראנו
כל העת.

כנאתנו את העיר נפרוש כפינו אל ד' בתודה על העבר, על אשר
הצילנו מתוך החורבן הגורא וזכינו לעסוק בתורה בימי הזעם
האיום. כן נעמוד בתפלה על העתיד, שקולות לעקת עמנו יחדלון,
ומצול הרשעה לא יתך עוד. ויצליח ד' דרכנו לבוא ולקומס הריסות
עמינו הרלון — ברוח ובחומר, ונזכה לראות בשוב ד' עמו בב"א.

(מאור תורה ח' ב' שנגהאי, תש"ו.   בהכרת טוב
למוה"ר הלל דוד שליט"א)

EPILOGUE

The end of the War in the Pacific found the three
Jewish Communities in Shanghai under differing circumstances
and with independent approaches toward their future in
China.

The fortunes of the formerly successful Sephardim had
declined drastically during the War, since their most prominent
members, as British subjects, were interned with other "enemy
nationals." This situation left the rest of the Sephardim, who
were primarily lower-middle class, and who were either stateless or possessed Iraqi citizenship, to fend their way through
the difficult War years. The return of the "internees" after the

579

War signalled a temporary return to "normalcy," that is, to some of their preeminent status in Shanghai's social and economic sphere and their role of leadership in the Jewish community. Still, the revitalized nationalist fervor fed by the wartime Japanese campaign of "Asia for Asians," and other imperialistic slogans, prevented any real perpetuation of the pre-War era of the White Man's supremacy.

With the fall of the Kuomintang regimé in 1949, the fate of the Sephardim was no longer independent of that of their coreligionists from Russia and Germany. They migrated to the newly established State of Israel, though a few, like the Kadoories, reestablished themselves in Hongkong. Others, especially the Abraham family, maintained their long-time concern for the rest of the Jewish community and exerted their leadership over the dwindling flock almost until the very end.

The Russian Jews were in the best position, having suffered no wartime disabilities. Except for a brief period of fear accompanying Russia's entry into the War in the Pacific, they carried on business as usual. In fact, since most of the Sephardi communal leaders were interned, the Russian Jews now administered the Sephardi-run institutions, such as the synagogues, the school and the hospital, a sign of communal maturity not previously displayed. With the War at an end, all intentions were to continue their communal lives in China.

Events, however, were not to bear out their hopes and the advent of the Maoist Communist Army forced the majority of these Russian Jews to take one of two courses. As stateless citizens, though Russian-born, they could have secured status as displaced persons, since they were not permitted to remain in China without Soviet papers. Or, as did a small percentage, they could have chosen to return to Russia, a move which proved fatal to more than a few of them. The majority of these sought asylum as "Displaced Persons," along with the rest of the Jewish community of Shanghai, in the Western hemisphere or in Israel during the 1940's and the early 1950's.

For the German-Jewish refugees, however, the Allied victory could not even reprieve for them a brief return to their homeland, since the full details of the Nazi slaughter of their families made this impossible. Nor could they even envision a future in China, as their Russian and Sephardi coreligionists did. For them, emigration was the only solution, and those able to were the first to make their way to the United States or to Latin America. The bulk of the refugees, however, discovered the doors of the world's nations not much more ajar than before the War. Moreover, as the Maoist armies pressed on toward Shanghai, it became evident that the remaining 10,000 Jews desired to leave more than ever.

Nineteen forty-eight, however, was not 1938, and the newly-established State of Israel was the one place that offered a refuge to all homeless Jews. The new State quickly dispatched its consul to Shanghai, and visas began to be issued. Within six years, 9,700 of the 10,000 left for Israel with the cooperation of the Maoist regimé. By 1957, only about 100 remained in Shanghai. To the author's knowledge, there are presently about a dozen or so old Jews left in Shanghai, the remnant of an uprooted community in a turbulent time.

Sadly enough, it was only during the period of the Maoist regimé that the first communal cooperation existed among the three factions, when the Baghdadi, Russian and German Jews pitched in together to maintain the rapidly dwindling but now unified Jewish community.

Although the thousands of refugees from Shanghai were dispersed among numerous countries, especially in the

Western Hemisphere and Israel, the strong ties forged in adversity and kinship have been maintained to the present. This is manifest in both the voluminous ongoing correspondence between the refugees and the active associations of former refugees from Shanghai in the United States, Israel and Australia.

Despite its fascinating saga and importance to the understanding of the Holocaust and Far East History, the future of Shanghai as a Jewish enclave is rapidly approaching the same fate as that of the ancient Jewish community of Kaifeng. Like the *Kikayon* plant in the Book of Jonah that grew and blossomed for only one day, the twentieth century settlement of Jews among the one billion Chinese will have been only an ephemeral phenomenon in the Diaspora history of the Jewish People.

BIBLIOGRAPHY

BOOKS

Adler, Cyrus. *Jacob H. Schiff*: *His Life and Letters*. 2 vols. New York: Doubleday, 1928.

Adler, H. G. *The Jews in Germany*: *From the Enlightenment to National Socialism*. Notre Dame, Ind.: University of Notre Dame Press, 1969.

Agar, Herbert. *The Saving Remnant*: *An Account of Jewish Survival*. New York: The Viking Press, 1960.

Barnett, Robert W. *Economic Shanghai*: *Hostage to Politics 1937-1941*. New York: Institute of Pacific Relations, 1941.

Bauer, Yehuda. *From Diplomacy to Resistance*: *A History of Jewish Palestine, 1939-1945*. Philadelphia: Jewish Publication Society, 1970.

Bentwich, Norman. *They Found Refuge*: *An Account of British Jewry's Work for Victims of Nazi Oppression*. London: Cresset Press, 1956.

Betar in China 1929-1949. n.p. [Israel]: n.p. [Betar], n.d. This commemorative volume contains numerous articles in Russian, Hebrew and English concerning Betar's activities in various Jewish communities in China and Manchuria. Copy in author's possession courtesy of M. Tokayer. (TP)

The Black Book: *The Nazi Crime Against the Jewish People*. n.p.: The Jewish Black Book Committee,1946.

Blum, John Morton. *From the Morgenthau Diaries*: *Years of War 1941-1945*. Boston: Houghton Mifflin Company, 1967.

Bondy, Louis. *Racketeers of Hatred*: *Julius Streicher and the Jew-Baiters' International*. London: Newman Wolsey.

Brown, Delmer. *Nationalism in Japan*. Berkeley: University of California Press, 1955.

Burkhard, Hugo. *Tanz Mal Jude*: *Von Dachau bis Shanghai*. Nurnberg: Richard Reichenbach AG, 1967.

Butow, Robert J. C. *Tojo: and the Coming of the War*. Princeton: Princeton University Press, 1961.

Carey, Arch. *The War Years at Shanghai 1941-45-48*. New York: Vantage Press, 1967.

Chou, Shun-hsin. *The Chinese Inflation 1937-1949*. New York: Columbia University Press, 1963.

Compton, James V. *The Swastika and the Eagle*. Boston: Houghton Mifflin Company, 1967.

Cohn, Norman. *Warrant for Genocide*. New York: Harper & Row, 1967.

Crowley, James B. *Japan's Quest for Autonomy*: *National Security and Foreign Policy, 1930-1938*. Princeton, N.J.: Princeton University Press, 1966.

Davidson-Houston, J. V. *Yellow Creek*: *The Story of Shanghai*. London: Putnam, 1962.

Davidowicz, Lucy S. *The War Against the Jews, 1938-1945*. New York: Holt, Rinehart and Winston, 1975.

Dickinson, John J. *German and Jew*: *The Life and Death of Siegmund Stein*. Chicago: Quadrangle Books, 1967.

Ducker, Abraham G., ed. *Europe Between the Two World Wars*: *1919-1939*. Jewish Post-War Problems; a study Course, Unit IV. New York: American Jewish Committee, 1942.

Eisenstein, Miriam. *Jewish Schools in Poland, 1919-1939*. New York: Columbia University, 1950.

Feingold, Henry L. *The Politics of Rescue:The Roosevelt Administration and the Holocaust, 1938-1945*. New Brunswick: Rutgers University Press, 1970.

Feis, Herbert. *The Road to Pearl Harbor*. New York: Atheneum, 1966.

Finch, Percy. *Shanghai and Beyond*. New York: Scribners, 1953.

Fishman, Yaakov H. *Farvogelte Yidn*. (Yiddish) Shanghai: Gezelschaftlichen Komiete, 1948.

Fitzgerald, C. P. *The Birth of Communist China*. Baltimore: Penguin Books, 1964.

Frankel, Josef, ed. *The Jews of Austria*: *Essays on Their Life, History and Destruction*. London: Vallentine, Mitchell and Co., Ltd., 1967.

Friedman, Elisha. *Inquiry of the United Jewish Appeal*: *Report for Refugees and Overseas Needs 1940*. New York: United Jewish Appeal, 1941.

Friedman, Saul S. *No Haven for the Oppressed*: *United States Policy Toward Jewish Refugees 1938-1945*. Detroit: Wayne University Press, 1973.

Ganther, Heinz. *Drei Jahre Immigration in Shanghai*. Shanghai: Modern Times, 1942.

Ginsbourg, Anna. *Jewish Refugees in Shanghai*. Shanghai: The China Weekly Review, 1940.

Habe, Hans. *The Mission*: *A Novel*. New York: Coward-McCann, 1966.

Hall, Robert King. *Kokutai No Nongi*: *Cardinal Principles of the National Entity of Japan*. Cambridge: Harvard University Press, 1949.

Hamburger, Ernst. *Juden in Offentlichen Leben Deutschlands*: *Regierungemitglieder, Beamte und Parlamentarier in der Monarchischen Zeit 1848-1918*. Tuebingen: J. C. B. Mohr, 1968.

Hansen, Marcus Lee. *The Atlantic Migration, 1607-1860*: *A History of the Continuing Settlement of the U.S.* New York: Harper Torchbooks, 1961.

Hauser, Ernst O. *Shanghai*: *City for Sale*. New York: Harcourt, Brace and Co., 1940.

Hausner, Gideon. *Justice in Jerusalem*. New York: Harper and Row, 1966.

Havens, Thomas R. H. *Farm and Nation in Modern Japan*: *Agrarian Nationalism, 1870-1940*. Princeton, N.J.: Princeton University Press 1974.

Hertzman, Chunah. *Mirrer Yeshive in Golus*. (Yiddish) New York: C. Hertzman, 1950.

Higham, John. *Send These to Me: Jews and Other Immigrants in Urban America*. New York: Atheneum, 1975.

Hilberg, Raul. *The Destruction of the European Jews*. Chicago: Quadrangle Books, 1961.

Hilsenrad, Helen. *Brown Was the Danube: A Memoir of Hitler's Vienna*. New York: Thomas Yoseloff, 1966.

Hinder, Eleanor M. *Life and Labour in Shanghai*. New York: Institute of Pacific Relations, 1944.

Hinzelmann, Hans H. *O China: Land Auf Alten Wegen*. Braunschweig: IM Schlosser Verlag, 1948.

Hirschler, Eric E. *Jews from Germany*. New York: Farrar, Strauss and Sudahy, 1955.

Hofstadter, Richard. *The Age of Reform*. New York: Random House, 1955.

Hsia, Ching-lin. *The Status of Shanghai: A Historical Review of the International Settlement*. Shanghai: Kelly and Walsh, 1929.

Ike, Nobutaka. *Japan's Decision for War: Records of the 1941 Policy Conferences*. Stanford: Stanford University Press, 1967.

————"War and Modernization," *Political Development in Modern Japan*. Robert E. Ward, ed. Princeton, N.J.: Princeton, University Press, 1968.

Institute of Jewish Affairs. *Jews in Nazi Europe, February, 1933-November, 1941: A Study Prepared by the Institute of Jewish Affairs*. Baltimore: Inter-American Jewish Conference, November 23-25, 1941.

Jackson, Stanley. *The Sassoons*. New York: E. P. Dutton & Co., Inc., 1968.

Jakobovitz, Immanuel. *Jewish Law Faces Modern Problems*. Studies in Torah Judaism. Series No. 8, edited by Leon D. Stitskin. New York: Yeshiva University, 1965.

Johnstone, William C., Jr. *The Shanghai Problem*. Stanford: Stanford University Press, 1937.

Jones, Francis C. *Japan's New Order in East Asia: Its Rise and Fall*. London: Oxford University Press, 1954.

Kaufman, Abraham. *Rofeh Hamachanah* (Hebrew) (Doctor in the [Bolshevik Labor] Camp). Tel Aviv: Am Oved Publishers, Ltd., 1971.

Kaznelson, Sigmund. *Juden in Deutschen Kultureich*. Berlin: Juedischer Verlag, 1960.

Kober, Adolph. *Cologne*. Trans. by Solomon Grayzel. *Jewish Communities Series*. Philadelphia: Jewish Publication Society, 1940.

Kochan, Lionel. *Pogrom: 10 November 1938*. London: Andre Deutsch, 1957.

Kogon, Eugene. *The Theory and Practice of Hell: The German Concentration Camps and the System Behind Them*. New York: Berkley Publishing Corporation, 1950.

Kotsuji, Abraham. *From Tokyo to Jerusalem*. New York: Bernard Geis Associates, 1964.

Kublin, Hyman (ed.). *Jews in Old China: Some Western Views and Studies of the Chinese Jews: Selections from Journals East and West*. New York: Paragon Books Reprint Corp., 1971.

Kurzman, Dan. *Kishi and Japan: The Search for the Sun*. New York: Ivan Obolensky, 1960.

Lensen, George Alexander. *The Strange Neutrality: Soviet-Japanese Relations During the Second World War 1941-1945*. Tallahassee, Fla.: The Diplomatic Press, 1972.

Leslie, Donald David. *The Survival of the Chinese Jews: The Jewish Community of Kaifeng*. Leiden: E. J. Brill, 1972.

Letters and Documents in Honor of Rabbi Abraham Kalmanowitz. New York: Mirrer Yeshiva, 1967.

Levin, Nora. *The Holocaust: The Destruction of European Jewry 1933-1945*. New York: Thomas Y. Crowell Co., 1968.

Lewin, Ossie (ed.). *Shanghai Jewish Almanac 1946-1947*. Shanghai: *Shanghai Echo*, 1947.

Lewis, Isaac. *Churban Eiropa: Gezamelte Mamorim* (Yiddish). New York: Research Institute for Post-War Problems of Religious Jewry, 1948.

Lipset, Seymour M., and Raab, Earl. *The Politics of Unreason: Right-Wing Extremism in America, 1790-1970*. New York: Harper, 1970.

Lowenthal, Marvin. *The Jews of Germany: A Story of Sixteen Centuries*. New York: The Jewish Publication Society, 1939.

Masao, Marisyama. *Thought and Behavior in Modern Japanese Politics*. Expanded edition edited by Ivan Morris. London: Oxford University Press, 1969.

Meskill, Johanna M. *Hitler and Japan: The Hollow Alliance*. New York: Atherton Press, 1966.

Miller, G. E. *Shaghai: Paradise of Adventurers*. New York: Orsay Publishing House, Inc., 1937.

Morison, Samuel Eliot. *Victory in the Pacific 1945*. History of U.S. Naval Operations in World War II. Vol. XIV. Boston: Little, Brown & Co., 1968.

Morley, James William. *The Japanese Thrust Into Siberia, 1918*. New York: Columbia University Press, 1954.

Morris, Ivan, (ed.). *Japan 1931-1945: Militarism, Fascism, Japanism?* Boston: D. C. Heath & Co., 1963.

Morris, Ivan. *Nationalism and the Right Wing in Japan: A Study of Post-War Trends*. London: Oxford University Press, 1960.

Morse, Arthur D. *While Six Million Died: A Chronicle of American Apathy*. New York: Random House, 1968.

Murphy, Rhoads. *Shanghai: Key to Modern China*. Cambridge, Mass.: Howard University Press, 1953.

Muto-Teiiti. *Angriff der Juden gegen Japan*. Tokyo: Naigari-Syobo, 1938.

Myerson, Abraham, and Goldberg, Isaac. *The German Jew: His Share in Modern Culture*. Lonodn: Hopkinson, 1933.

Norman, Herbert E. *Japan's Emergence as a Modern State*. Westport, Conn.: Greenwood Press, 1940.

Peattie, Mark R. *Ishiwara Kanji nad Japan's Confrontation with the West*. Princeton, N.J.: Princeton University Press, 1975.

Pott, F. L. Hawks. *A Short History of Shanghai*. Shanghai: Kelly and Walsh Ltd., 1937.

Prager, Moshe. *Disaster and Salvation: The History of "Vaad Hatzalah"* [sic] *in America*. (Yiddish) New York: "Vaad Hatzalah" Book Committee, 1957.

Reischauer, Edwin O. *Japan, Past and Present*. London: Duckwirth, 1947. *Japan: The Story of a Nation*. Revised edition. New York: Knopf, 1974.

Reischauer, Edwin O.; Fairbank, John K.; and Craig, Albert M. *East Asia: The Modern Transformation*. Vol. II of *A History of East Asian Civilization*. 2 vols. Boston: Houghton Mifflin Company, 1965.

Reitlinger, Gerald. *The Final Solution: The Attempt to Exterminate the Jews of Europe 1939-1945*. New York: Barnes & Noble Co., 1961.

Reports of the Council of the Jewish Community in Shanghai 1952-1957. Shanghai: Council of the Jewish Community in Shanghai, 1952-53, 1954-55, 1955-56, 1956-57. (DP).

Report of the International Red Cross on its Activities during the Second World War, September 1, 1939-June 30, 1947. Geneva, 1948.

Rollin, Henri. *L'Apocalypse de Notre Temps*. Paris: Gallimard, 1939.

Rosen, Ber I. *Geklibene Shriften*. (Yiddish) Melbourne: Ber Rosen Committee, 1957.

Roth, Cecil. *The Sassoon Dynasty*. London: Robert Hale Ltd., 1941.

Rottenberg, Joseph. *Fun Varshe Biz Shanchai*. (Yiddish) Mexico City: Gezelshaft Fun Kultur un Hilf, 1948.

Ruppin, Arthur. *The Jewish Fate and Future*. London: Macmillan, 1940. .*The Jews in the Modern World*. London: Macmillan, 1934.

Salvetti, T. *Juden in Ostasien*. Berlin: Nordland-Verlag, 1941.

Sassoon, David Solomon. *A History of the Jews in Baghdad*. Letchwirth: S. D. Sassoon, 1949.

Schwab, Hermann. *A World in Ruins: History, Life and Work of German Jewry*. London: Edward Goldston, 1946.

Shigemitsu, Mamoru. *Japan and Her Destiny: My Struggle for Peace*. London: Hutchinson, 1958.

Shillony, Ben-Ami. *Revolt in Japan: The Young Officers and the February 26, 1936 Incident*. Princeton, N.J.: Princeton University Press, 1973.

Shirer, William L. *The Rise and Fall of the Third Reich: A History of Nazi Germany*. New York: Simon and Schuster, 1960.

Siegelberg, Mark. *The Face of Pearl Harbor: A Play*. Melbourne: View Publishing Co.

Simpson, Sir John Hope. *Refugees: Preliminary Report of a Survey*. London: The Royal Institute of International Affairs, 1938.
. *The Refugee Problem: Report of a Survey*. London: Oxford University Press, 1939.

Singer, Kurt. *Mirror, Sword and Jewel: A Study of Japanese Characteristics*. New York: George Braziller, 1973.

Sopher, Arthur and Theodore. *The Profitable Path of Shanghai Realty*. Shanghai: *Shanghai Times*, 1939.

Spunt, Georges. *A Place in Time: Shanghai Between the Two World Wars*. New York: Putnam's, 1968.

Storry, Richard. *A History of Modern Japan*. Baltimore: Penguin Books, 1960.

Strack, Hermann. *The Jew and Human Sacrifice: Human Blood and Jewish Ritual*. London: Cope and Fenwick, 1909.

Szajkowski, Zosa. *YIVO Catalog of the Exhibition: Jewish Life in Shanghai*. New York: YIVO, 1948.

Takehiko, Yoshikashi. *Conspiracy at Mukden: The Rise of the Japanese Military*. New Haven: Yale University Press, 1963.

Tartakower, Arieh, and Grossman, Kurt R. *The Jewish Refugee*. New York: Institute of Jewish Affairs of the World Jewish Congress, 1944.

Tasoki, Hanami. *Long the Imperial Way*. Boston: Houghton Mifflin Company, 1950.

Thelmann, Rita, and Finerman, Emanuel. *Crystal Night: 9-10 November 1938*. New York: Coward-McCann, 1974.

Tikozinsky, Jechiel M. *Sefer Hayomam Bekadur Haarets*. (Hebrew) Jerusalem, 1943.

Toland, John. *The Rising Sun*. New York: Random House, 1970.

Ward, Robert E., and Rustow, Dankwait A., (eds.). *Political Modernization in Japan and Turkey*. Princeton, N.J.: Princeton University Press, 1964.

White, William Charles. *The Chinese Jews: Compilations of Matters Relating to the Jews of Kaifeng Fu*. 3 vols. Toronto, 1942, 2nd ed., 3 vols. in 1, with an introduction by Cecil Roth. New York:

Weinryb, Bernard D. *Jewish Emancipation Under Attack*. Pamphlet Series Jews and the Post-War World No. 2, edited by Abraham G. Duker. New York: American Jewish Committee, 1942.

Wilson, George M. *Radical Nationalist in Japan: Kita Ikki, 1833-1937*. Cambridge: Harvard University Press, 1969.

Wischnitzer, Mark. *To Dwell in Safety: The Story of Jewish Migration Since 1800*. Philadelphia: Jewish Publication Society, 1948.
. *Visas to Freedom: The History of HIAS*. New York: World Publishing Co., 1956.

World Jewish Congress. *Unity in Dispersion: A History of the World Jewish Congress*. New York: World Jewish Congress, 1948.

Wyman, David S. *Paper Walls: America and the Refugee Crisis 1938-1941*

Young, Arthur. *China's Wartime Finance and Inflation, 1937-1945.* Cambridge, Mass.: Harvard University Press, 1965.
Zimmels, H. J. *Ashkenazim and Sephardim.* London: Oxford University Press, 1958.
Zimmerman, Aaron Chaim. *Agan Hasaar.* (Hebrew) New York: Balshon Press, 1956.
———. *Kviat Kav Hataarikh.* (Hebrew) New York: Hakerem, 1954.
Zweig, Arnold. *Bilanz der deutschen Judenheit 1933.* Amsterdam: Querido Verlag, 1934.

ARTICLES

Adler-Rudel, S. "The Evian Conference on the Refugee Question." *Yearbook of the Leo Baeck Institute.* Vol. 13. London: East and West Library, 1968, pp. 235-73.
Ahlers, John. "Economic Threat Caused by Jewish Refugees." *Shanghai Evening Post and Mercury,* p. 8.
Akira, Iriye. "Japan's Policies Toward the United States," in James William Morley (ed.), *Japan's Foreign Policy, 1868-1941:A Research Guide.* New York: Columbia University Press, 1974, pp. 407-58.
Aronsfeld, C. C. "Jewish Bankers and the Tsar." *Jewish Social Studies.* Vol. 35 (April 1973), pp. 87-104.
Ashkenazi, Rabbi Meyer Z. "Ein Jahr Religiese Aufbauarbeit." *SJ Chronicle* (SI), p. 17.
"Ashkenazim." *Encyclopaedia Judaica.* Vol. 3, pp. 319-22.
"Association of Jewish Precentors, Shanghai." Ossie Lewin (ed.). Shanghai Jewish *Almanac,* [Almanac] Shanghai: *Shanghai Echo,* 1947, p. 58.
Ball-Kaduri, K. J. "Die Vorplanung der Kristallnacht." *Zeitschrift Fur Die Geschichte der Juden.* Tel Aviv: Olamenu, 1966. pp. 211-16.
Barnett, Robert W. "Shanghai's Refugees Face Uncertainties." *Far Eastern Survey.* Vol. VIII (October 25, 1939), pp. 251-53.
Beckelman, Moses. "The Jewish Community of Tientsin." *The Jewish Center.* Vol. 24 (June 1946), pp. 10-14.
Benz, David. "Refugees in Shanghai." *Congress Weekly.* Vol. 8 (May 9, 1941), pp. 11-12.
Berlin, Meir. *"Mitziyon Tetsey Torah." Hatzofeh* (Hebrew) (October 2, 1942), p. 2.
Bernard, William S. "American Immigration Policy: A Reappraisal." *Immigration as a Factor in American History.* Oscar Handlin, (ed.). New York: Prentice-Hall, Inc., 1959, pp. 192-99.
"Beth-Din, The Shanghai Jewish Spiritual Body." *Almanac,* p. 57.
Black, Abraham, "Jews in Japan." *Review Jewish Community Center 1957-1958* [Tokyo]: n.p., n.d., pp. 27-37.

Blau, Bruno. "The Jewish Population of Germany, 1939-1945." *JSS*, 12: 161-172, 1950.

Borg, Dorothy and Shumpei Okamoto (eds.). *Pearl Harbor as History: Japanese-American Relations, 1931-1941.* New York: Columbia University Press, 1973.

Brieger, Lothar. "Emigration und Kuenstlerische Produktivitaet." *Herald* (SE), p. 18.

Brisk, Simcha Selig. "A Letter on Sabbath in Japan." *Talpioth* (Hebrew). Vol. 2 (June 1945), pp. 177-78.

"Brith Trumpeldor in Hongkew." *Almanac*, p. 59.

Brown, Mendel. "The Jews of Modern China." *The Jewish Monthly.* 3:159 (June 1949).

"Chewra Kalischa for Immigrants." *Almanac*, p. 58.

Cho, Yukio. "An Inquiry Into the Problem of Importing American Capital into Manchuria: A Note on Japanese-American Relations, 1931-1941," in Dorothy Borg and Shumpei Okamoto (eds.), *Pearl Harbor as History: Japanese-American Relations, 1931-1941* [*P. Harbor*]. New York: Columbia University Press, 1973, pp. 377-410.

Contemporary Jewish Record 1939-1942. Edited by Abraham G. Druker.

Crowley, James B. "Japanese Army Factionalism in the Early 1937's." *Journal of Asian Studies.* Vol. 21 (May 1962), pp. 309-26.

————— . "Japan's Military Foreign Policies," in James W. Morley (ed.), *Japan's Foreign Policy, 1868-1941.* New York: Columbia University Press, 1974. Pp. 3-30.

"Cultural Life and Emigration." *Almanac*, p. 64.

"Dancing School Pasqual." *Almanac*, p. 60.

"Der Wirkungskreis der HICEM in Shanghai." *SJ Chronicle SI*, p. 23.

Diamond, Sander A. "Kristallnacht and the Reaction in America." *YAJSS*. Vol. 14. New York: YIVO Institute for Jewish Research, 1969, pp. 196-208.

"Die Zentralheimleitung erstattet ihren Taetigkeitsbericht." *SJ Chronicle* (*SI*), p. 9.

"Die Jewish Company des Shanghai Volunteer Corps." *Shanghai Jewish Chronicle* (SE), March 1940, p. 20.

Dreifuss, Adolf. "Unser Theater." *Herald* (SE), pp. 13-14.

Eck, Nathan. "The Rescue of Jews with the Aid of Passports and Citizenship Papers of Latin American States." *Yad Vashem Studies, I: On the European Jewish Catastrophe and Resistance:* Edited by Ben Zion Dinur and Saul Esh. Jerusalem: Yad Washem, 1957, pp. 125-52.

"Ein Jahr Internationales Komitee." *SJ Chronicle* (*SI*), pp. 15-16.

Elbaum, Moshe. "18 Februar 1943: Die Geschichte des Hongkewer Ghettos." *Herald* (SE), pp. 24-25.

————— . "Die Herren von der S.A.C.R.A. Eindrucke Eines Opfers." *Unser Velt* (unpagin.). Special Edition, 1945 (YIVO No. 12).

Elberg, Simcha. "Golus Shanchai" (Yiddish). *Dos Yiddishe Vort.* Vol. 13 (December 1966), pp. 14-18.
———. "Shanchai und ir Rov" (Yiddish). *Dos Yiddishe Vort.* Vol. 13 (January 1967), pp. 14-16.

Elberg, Dr. Simcha. "Yiddish in Shanchai." *Unser Leben* (Yiddish Sect.). May 8, 1942, p. 2.

Epstein, Joseph D. "Yeshiva of Mir." *Jewish Institutions of Higher Learning in Europe: Their Development and Destruction.* (Hebrew). Edited by Samuel K. Mirsky. New York: Histadruth Ivrith of America, 1956, pp. 87-132.

Felber, Irwin. "Prominent Artists and Musical Teachers at Local Conservatory." *Almanac,* pp. 65-67.

Fishman, Yaakov H. "Shiffn." *Farvogelte Yidn* (Yiddish). Shanghai: Communal Committee, 1944, pp. 7-18.

Flakser, Menachem. "Toizend Poilishe Yidn in Shanghai." *Jewish Daily Forward.* December 31, 1962, p. 5.

"Freysinger's Jewish Elementary School and Middle School." *Almanac,* p. 63.

Friedlander, Fritz. "Die Einkreisung der Emigration." *The Shanghai Herald.* German Language Supplement (SE), April 1946, p. 12.

Friedlander, Henry. "The Holocaust: Anti-Semitism and the Jewish Catastrophe." *The Study of Judaism: Bibliographic Essays.* New York: Ktav, 1972, pp. 207-29.

Friedman, Dr. S. "Ein Jahr Ambulanzdienst." *SJ Chronicle (SI),* p. 13.

Friedrichs, Dr. Theodor. "The Refugees as a 'Folks Unit,' Their Acclimatization and Their Causes of Death." *Journal of the Association of Central European Doctors.* Vol. 3 (July-August 1942), pp. 99-100, 123-24, 140.

Fujiwara, Akira. "The Role of the Japanese Army," in *P. Harbor,* pp. 189-95.

Ganther, Heinz. "Aus Dem Wirtschaftsieben." *Herald (SE),* p. 1.
——— . "Das Religoese Leben." *Herald (SE),* pp. 3-4.
——— . "Sieben Jahre Immigration." *Herald (SE),* pp. 2-3.

"The General Zionist Organization of Shanghai." *Almanac,* p. 59.

Gross, Samuel. "Judaica Reprinting: Past, Present and Future." *Proceednigs of the Fourth Annual Convention of the Association of Jewish Libraries,* June 17-20, 1969, pp. 22-27.

Gruenberger, Felix. "The Jewish Refugees in Shanghai." *JSS.* Vol. 12 (1950), pp. 329-48.

Guggenheim, Ludwig. "Sport." *Herald (SE),* pp. 22-23.

"Hadiyun Besheelat Yom Hakipurim Bejapan." (Hebrew) *Hatzofeh,* September 30, 1941, p. 1.

Hartwich, Lucie. "Die Erziehung der juedischen Jugend." *SJ Chronicle (SI),* p. 14.

Ike, Nobutaka. "War and Modernization," in Robert E. Ward (ed.), *Political Development in Modern Japan.* Princeton, N.J.: Princeton University Press, 1968, pp. 189-212.

Ikle, Frank W. "Japan's Policies Toward Germany," in James William Morley (ed.), *Japan's Foreign Policy, 1868-1941*: *A Research Guide.* New York: Columbia University Press, 1974. Pp. 265-339.

Imai, Seiichi. "Cabinet, Emperor, and Senior Statesmen," in *Pearl Harbor.* Pp. 53-80.

Inuzuka, Koreshige "The Imperial Navy Protected the Jews: Historical Testimony Now Clarified by the Secretary of the Department of Intelligence during the Period of Jewish Refugee Influx in Shanghai." *Jiuy Magazine.* Vol.   (English translation), (February 1, 1973), pp. 236-45.

Inuzuka, Koreshige. "Japan's Stellung zur Judenfrage." *Shanghai Jewish Chrnoicle,* November 24, 1940, p. 7.

Inuzuka, Koreshige. "The Secret History of Japanese Jewish Policy: The Japanese Auschwitz was a Paradise, My Great Effort against Pressure Exerted Upon Jews to Set Up a Unique Japanese Policy Concerning Jewish People." *Jiyu Magazine. Vol.* .. (English translation), Febru- (February 1, 1973), pp. 228-35.

Isgour, A. "Shanghai—Jewish Center in Eastern Asia." *Unser Leben,* August 21, 28, September 4, 1942 (English Sect.), p. 2.

Ito, Takashi. "The Role of Right-Wing Organizations in Japan," in *Pearl Harbor.* Pp. 487-510.

Ivri, Samuel. "Drei Kehillos—Drei Zeitungen." *Unser Leben,* May 5, 1942 (Yiddish Sect.), p. 2.

Jansen, Marius B. "Changing Japanese Attitudes Toward Modernization," in Marius B. Jansen (ed.), *Changing Japanese Attitudes Toward Modernization.* Princeton, N.J.: Princeton University Press, 1965. Pp. 54-61.

Jansen, Marius B. "Modernization and Foreign Policy in Meiji Japan," in Robert E. Ward (ed.), *Political Development in Modern Japan.* Princeton, N.J.: Princeton University Press, 1968. Pp. 149-88.

Jewish Calendar 5702 (1941/1942). M. Elenberg, 1941. (YIVO No. 50).

"Jewish Community of Central European Jews." *Almanac,* p. 55.

"Jews in the Far East." *Jewish Affairs.* Vol. 1 (January 1942), pp. 2-7.

Jovishoff, Albert. "A City of Refugees." *The Menorah Journal.* Vol. 27 (Spring 1939), pp. 209-16.

Kahn, Alfred. "Das Musikleben in Shanghai." *SJ Chronicle (SI),* p. 24.

Kann, Eduard. "Europaeische Emigration nach China." *SJ Chronicle (SE),* April 1940, p. 7.

————"The Problem of the European Refugees in Shanghai." (Section of an unidentified Shanghai periodical), August 24, 1939, pp. 15-16, 32, 38-39. (JDCCA).

Karelitz, Abraham Yeshayahu. *"Kuntrus Yud-Heth Shaoth"* (Shabbat, Section 64). (Hebrew), Hazan Ish. Bnei Brak: Shmuel Greineman, 1957, pp. 185-92.

Kase, Hideaki. "Jews in Japan." *Chuo-Koron*. Vol. 86 (May, 1971), pp. 234-47.

Kasher, Menachem M. "The Sabbath of Genesis and the Sabbath of Sinai." (Hebrew) *Talpioth*. Vol. 1 (April-September 1944), pp. 604-50.

————The Sabbatt [sic] and the East of the World." (Hebrew) *Hapardes*. Vol. 26 (January, 1954), pp. 1-31.

Kiseleff, Moshe A. *Sefer Imre Shefer* (Hebrew). Tel Aviv: Published privately by Rebetzin Fayge Kiseleff [1952]. TP.

Kiseleff, Moshe A. *Sefer Mishbere Yam* (Hebrew). Harbin: Published privately, 1926.

Kobayashi, Masayuki. "Kametaro Mitsukawa's War against Antisemitism in Japan: Sidelight on the early years of antisemitic propaganda (1919-1932)." *Kaigai Jijo*. Vol. 21 (English Translation), November 1973), pp. 1-9.

————. "Kametaro Mitsukawa's War against Antisemitism: Sidelight on the early years of antisemitic propaganda in Japan." *Kaigai Jijo*. Vol. 22 (English translation), (February 1974), pp. 61-72.

Komor, Paul. "Meine Arbeit fuer die Immigration." *SJ Chronicle (SI)*, p. 15.

————. "Twelve Golden Health Rules." *SJ Chronicle* (August 3, 1941) (YIVO No. 67).

Koritschoner, Otto. "Allgemeine Zionistische Organisation Theodore Herzl." *SJ Chronicle (SI)*, p. 19.

Kraemer, Alphons. "Der Zionismus in der Immigration." *Herald (SE)*, p. 5.

Kranzler, David. "How 18,000 Jews Survived the Holocaust While Europe Burned." *Jewish Life,* (September, 1975), pp. 29-40.

Kranzler, David. "Restrictions Against German-Jewish Refugee Immigration to Shanghai in 1939." *Jewish Social Studies*. Vol. 36, No. 1 (January 1974), pp. 40-60.

Kranzler, David. "The Two-Day Yom Kippur in Japan." *Yom Kippur Anthology*, edited by Philip Goodman. Philadelphia: Jewish Publication Society, 1971, pp. 201-203.

Kublin, Hyman. "Star of David and Rising Sun." *Jewish Frontier*. Vol. 25 (April, 1958), pp. 15-22.

Kunfi, Dr. Tibor. "Der Existenzkampf der Refugee Aerzte." *SJ Chronicle (SI)*, p. 26.

————"Die Medizinische Betreung der Immigranten." *Herald (SE)* pp. 9-11.

LaFrance, Alfred Alphonse Kramer. "Die Presse der Emigration." *Herald (SE)*, p. 11.

Leonof, George. "Jewish Refugees Here Facing Lean Future." *China Press,* April 14, 1939, pp. 1, 3.

Levin, Horst. "Rundfunk fuer die Refugees." *SJ Chronicle (SI)*, p. 26.

Levitan, Dagobert. "The Jewish Recreation Club." *Almanac*, p. 7.

Lewin, Ossie. "Bridge House Memories. Reunited at Social Gathering." *Almanac*, pp. 21-23.

Loewenthal, Rudolph. "Harbin." *Encyclopaedia Judaica*. Vol. 7, p. 1331.

Levithan, Dagobert. "The Jewish Recreation Club." *Almanac*, pp. 70-76.

Lury, Robert M. "Jews in Japan." *Review Jewish Community Center 1956-1957*. n.p: n.p., n.d.

Margolies, Laura. "Race Against Time." *Survey Graphic*. Vol. 33 (March 1944), pp. 11-16.

Margolinski, Henry. "Musical Characters in Shanghai Commissions." *Almanac*, p. 68.

Mars, Alvin. "A Note on the Jewish Refugees in Shanghai." *JSS*. Vol. 31 (October 1969), pp. 286-91.

Melchior, Fred. "The Hongkew Ghetto." *Jewish Horizon*. Vol. 15 (October 1952), pp. 12-14.

Mitteilungen der Vereiningung der Emigranten Aerzte. Vols. 1-2 (January-October 1940). Dr. Theodore Frierichs, editor.

"Modern Adult Education at the Asia Seminar." *Almanac*, pp. 63.

Nissim, Lucie. "My War Years in Japan." *India and Israel* (April 1952), pp. 18-19.

North-China Herald (Shanghai), September 14, 1938-November 5, 1941.

Hausdorff, Martin. "Das Musikleben der Immigranten." *Herald (SE)*, pp. 16-17.

————. "Gefuchlsgehalt der Musik." *Herald (SE)*, p. 21.

Henkin, Joseph E. "On the International Date Line." (Hebrew) *Talpioth*. Vol. 2 (June 1945), pp. 179-83.

Hilfsfond Fuer Deutsche Juden. Shanghai Report 1934-1938. YIVO No. 38.

Hirsch, W. "The Sephardi Jewish Community of Shanghai." *South African Jewish Observer, September* 1957, p. 7.

Horowitz, Naphtaly. "Religieze Renaissance in Vayten Mizrakh." (Yiddish) *Orthodox Tribune*. Vol. 5 (December 1946), pp. 42-44.

Hosoya, Chihiro. "Japan's Policy Toward Russia," in James William Morley (ed.), *Japan's Foreign Policy, 1868-1941: A Research Guide*. New York: Columbia University Press, 1974, pp. 340-406.

————. "The Role of Japan's Foreign Ministry and its Embassy in Washington, 1940-1941," in *Pearl Harbor*, pp. 149-64.

Hubner, Samuel. "Anashim Hanosim Lejapan Keytsad Yinhagu." *HaDarom* (Hebrew). Vol. 15 (April 1962), pp. 78-91.

"135 Schiffe Brachten 12,000 Emigranten." *SJ Chronicle* (SS), p. 23.

Parnes, Paul. "Die Kulturellen Aufgaben der Zionistischen Organisation." (Unidentified news clipping of November 14, 1943, probably from the *Shanghai Jewish Chronicle*) (YIVO No. 29).

Parry, Albert. "The Jews in East Asia." *Asia*. Vol. 39 (September 1939), pp. 513-16.

————"The Jews in East Asia." *Asia.* Vol. 39 (September 1939) pp. 513-16.

"Polish War Refugees in Shanghai." *Almanac,* p. 80.

Pollak, Ernst. "Menschen die uns Helfen." *SJ Chronicle* (SI), p. 6.

Pratt, William. "Exodus from China." *Hadassah Magazine.* Vol. 51 (January 1970), pp. 10-11, 28-30; (February 1970), pp. 14-15, 24; (March 1970), pp. 12-13.

Prinz, Arthur. "The Role of the Gestapo in Obstructing and Promoting Jewish Immigation." *Yad Vashem Studies, II*: *On the European Jewish Catastrophe and Resistance.* Edited by Saul Esh. Jerusalem: Yad Washem, 1958, pp. 205-18.

Rabinovich, David. "Yidn in China" (Yiddish). *Goldene Keyt,* 7:218, 1951.

Rabinovitch, Shmuel. "Hayishuv Hahehudi Besin, Shigeshugo Vehurbano" (Hebrew). *Gesher.* Vol. 3 (July 1957), pp. 108-21.

Rapoport, O. "A Voice in the Winderness." *Unser Leben,* September 25, 1942 (English Sect.), p. 3.

Raymist, Malkah. "The Shanghai Myth." *The American Hebrew.* Vol. 145 (September 29, 1939).

Reiss, Dr. Frederick. "Die Aerzliche Fuersorge der Emigration." *SJ Chronicle (SI),* pp. 11-13.

Reiss, Dr. Frederick. *Report of the Medical Board (CFA) 1939-1940.* (YIVO).

————*Report of the Medical Board (CFA) 1940-1941.* (YIVO).

Ronall, Joachim O. "Jews in Japan." *Jewish Spectator.* Vol. 16 (February 1958), pp. 19-21.

Rosenberg, Ing M. "Die Embankment—Kueche." *SJ Chronicle (SI),* p. 11.

Rosenstock, Werner. "Exodus 1933-1939: A Survey of Jewish Emigration from Germany." *Yearbook of the Leo Baeck Institute.* Vol. 1. London: East and West Library, 1956, pp. 373-90.

Rosenthal, Eric. "Trends of the Jewish Population in Germany, 1910-1939." *JSS.* Vol. 6, pp. 233-74, 1944.

Roth, Cecil. "Past, Present and Future of Sephardim." *Le Judaisme Sephardi,* New Series, No. 13. Pp. 570-75, January 1957.

Rudan, David. "China Youngson Knew." *Independent Forester.* Vol. 87 (December 1967). Don Mills, Ontario. Pp. 8-11, 29.

Sadao, Asada. "The Japanese Navy and the United States," in *Pearl Harbor.* Pp. 225-60.

Salvotti, T. "China, Japan und die Judenfrage." *Mitteilungen Uber die Judenfrage* (October 17, 1939), p. 5. (Unidentified sheet in Wiener Library).

Scapalino, Robert A. "Elections and Political Modernization in Prewar Japan," in Robert E. Ward (ed.), *Political Development in Modern Japan.* Princetton, N.J.: Princeton University Press, 1968.

Schechtman, Joseph B. "Failure of the Dominican Scheme." *Congress Weekly.* Vol. 10 (January 15, 1943), pp. 8-9.

"Sephardim." *Encyclopaedia Judaica.* Vol. 14, pp. 1164-1177.

Shanghai Herald (German Language Supplement). "3 Jahre Proklamation, 7 Jahre Aufbau" (Special Edition). Edited by Heinz Ganther (YIVO No. 68).

Shanghai Jewish Chronicle. "Ein Jahr Aufbau" (Special Issue). March 1940. Edited by Ossie Lewin. (Courtesy Mr. Joseph Abraham).

"The Shanghai Jews Re-inspire Loyalty to Torah Yiddishkeit." *Orthodox Tribune.* Vol. 5 (December 1946, pp. 15-16.

Silbert, Layle. "Report from Overseas: Shanghai." *Congress Weekly.* Vol. 15 (January 16, 1948), pp. 14-15.

Sissons, D. C. S. "Early Australian Contacts with Japan." *Hemisphere* (April 1972), 13-15. (TP).

"The S.J.Y.A. School." *Almanac,* p. 62.

Soref, Harold, "Jewish Life in Japan Today." *London Jewish Chronicle,* October 4, 1957, pp. 27-28.

"Spotlite on a Party." (Shanghai) *Spotlite.* Vol 1 (January 1939), pp. 9-15. (LF).

Steiner, J. Arthur. "American-Japanese Tensions in Shanghai," *Annals of the American Academy of Political and Social Science* (May 1944), pp. 215 : 140-146.

Steiner, Sebastian. "Als Erste Emigrantenfamilies in Hongkew." *Shanghai Jewish Chronicle (SI),* March 1940, p. 27.

Swartz, Mary I. "Jews in Japan" *Hadassah Magazine.* Vol. 57 (October 1975), 10-11, 50-53.

Szajkowski, Zosa. "Paul Nathan, Lucien Wolf, Jacob H. Schiff and the Jewish Revolutionary Movement in Eastern Europe 1903-1917." *Jewish Social Studies.* Vol. 29 (Fall 1967), pp. 75-91.

Tenenbaum, Joseph. "The Crucial Year 1938." *Yad Washem Studies II: On the European Jewish Catastrophe and Resistance.* Edited by Saul Esh. Jerusalem:YadWashem, 1958, pp. 49-78.

"Thirty Years in the Far East." *Almanac,* p. 43.

Tiedemann, Arthur E. "Big Business and Politics in Prewar Japan," in James William Morley (ed.), *Dilemmas of Growth in Prewar Japan.* Princeton, N.J.: Princeton University Press, 1971. Pp. 267-318.

Tikozinsky, Jechiel. "On the International Date Line." *Talpioth.* Vol. 1 (April-September 1944), pp. 579-89.

"Twenty-Nine Jahre "HIAS" (HICEM) in Fernen Osten." *Herald (SE),* April 1964, p. 19.

"Unsere Juedische Gemeinde." *Shanghai Jewish Chronicle (SI),* pp. 18-19.

"Unsere Theater." *Almanac,* p. 13.

Usui, Katsumi. "The Role of the Foreign Ministry" in *Pearl Harbor,* 1973. Pp. 127-149.

Weinberger, Julius. *Annual Report of the Central Management of the I.C.R. Homes 1939.* (YIVO No. 3).

Weltsch, Robert. "Introduction." *Yearbook of the Leo Baeck Institute.* Vol. 1. London: East and West Library, 1956. Pp. xix-xxi.

Wischnitzer, Mark. "The Historical Background of the Settlement of Jewish Refugees in Santo Domingo." *Jewish Social Studies.* Vol. 4 (January 1942), pp. 45-58.

Wood, Stanley. "The International Press of China." *Almanac,* pp. 17-19.

Yamamura, Katsuro. "The Role of the Finance Ministry," in *Pearl Harbor.* Pp. 287-302.

Zeitin, Josef. "The Sephardic Community of Shanghai." *American Sephardi.* Vol. 2 (1968), pp. 73-76.

————"The Shanghai Jewish Communal Association." *Almanac,* pp.

————"The Shanghai Jewish Community." *Jewish Life,* Vol. 41, pp. 54-68, October 1973.

————"The Talmud Thora and Beth Jacob School in Shanghai." *Almanac,* p. 56.

Zilberpfenig, Zacharia. "Shagrire Yisrael Bemizrakh Harachok." (Hebrew) *Hadoar.* Vol. 12 (May 1, 1942), pp. 371-73.

INTERVIEWS

Abraham, Joseph Hayim, (taped) January 16, 1969 (and subsequent dates).

Altman, Dr. Avraham, (oral) May 27, 1970.

Ashkenazi, Joshua, (taped), January 10, 1970.

Ashkenazi, Rebetzin (Mrs.) Taube (taped), February 4, 1968.

Benda, Professor Harry (taped), June 29, 1970.

Borchard, Rabbi Boruch. (phone), October 10, 1969 (and sebsequent dates).

Dobekirer, Jechiel, (oral), June 23, 1968.

Didner, Dr. Samuel and Mrs. Greta, (taped), September 22, 1973.

Epstein, Rabbi Joseph D. (taped), October 15, 1968 (and subsequent dates).

Feder, Morris (taped), June 20, 1968 (and subsequent dates).

Flakser, Menachem (oral), June 16, 1968.

Fischel, Mrs. Ruth (taped) December 6, 1965 (and subsequent dates).

Friedrichs, Dr. Theodore (oral) (various dates).

Fuchs, Curt (taped) January 8, 1974.

Fleischaker, Rabbi Levi (phone), June 23, 1975.

Gerechter, Mr. and Mrs. Gerhard (taped), April 16, 1968 (and subsequent dates).

Gottschalk, Gerhard (taped), November 24, 1973.

Heuman, Israel (oral), August 15, 1968.

Kamm, Dr. Gunther (oarl), June 27, 1968.

Kaufmann, Fritz (taped), November 13, 1969.

Kling, Mrs. (taped), September 15, 1968.

Kohn, Mrs. Kattie. (oral), June 18, 1975.

Komor, Paul (phone), October 20, 1969.
Kotsuji, Professor Abraham (taped), December 6, 1967 (and subsequent dates).
Kranzler, Dr. George (oral), November 25, 1969.
Kaufman, Theodore (oral), August 15, 1971.
Kuenstler, Charles (oral), August 17, 1970.
Landau, Dr. Ernst (taped), June 20, 1968.
Levinson, Rabbi and Mrs. Joseph (oral), September 21, 1970.
Levitas, Dr. Irving (taped), July 28, 1968 (and subsequent dates).
Lew, Mrs. David (taped), September 15, 1968.
Levin, Horst (taped), August 6, 1974 (and subsequent dates).
Luftig, Ernst (taped), September 25, 1975.
Malinowski, Rabbi Joseph (phone), October 15, 1969.
Margulies, Isaac (taped and oral), August 4, 1968.
Meyer, Leo (taped), September 9, 1974.
Meyerheim, Leo (phone), April 14, 1971.
Millner, Rabbi Hersh (taped), February 4, 1968.
Perutinsky, Rabbi Israel (oral), September 7, 1968.
Rabinovich, David (taped), August 1971.
Rosenberg, Mrs. Malvena (nee Langberg) (phone), January 22, 1975.
Salter, Les (taped), June 1975.
Schechter, Rabbi David (phone), October 10, 1969.
Schoen, Pincus (taped), January 5, 1970.
Shaffran, Mrs. Bessie (phone), October 10, 1969.
Shkop, Rabbi Abraham (oral), July 1, 1968.
Soong, Willie (taped), August 26, 1968.
Sopher, Arthur and Theodore (taped), October 17, 1969.
Steinman, Dr. Max (taped), July 5, 1975.
Stenby, Dr. Victor (Steinberg) (phone), December 30, 1974.
Tarshansky, Rabbi Solomon (taped), June 11, 1968.
Tobias, Herman (oral), August 20, 1967.
Tuchachinsky, Saul (oral), February 7, 1967.
Walden, Rabbi Moshe (oral), October 10, 1969.
Wahrhaftig, Zorach (taped), August, 1971, (also transcript of interview at Institutee of Contemporary History, Hebrew University).
Weisfogel, Rabbi Alex (oral), June 23, 1968 (and subsequent dates).
Zackheim, Rabbi Zvi (oral), February 18, 1968.
Zeitin, Rabbi Josef (taped and oral), August 5, 1968.
Zupnik, Rabbi Moshe (oral and taped), June 23, 1968.

INTERVIEWS BY DR. HERMAN DICKER (notes on) (DP)

Albans, Dr. Jan
Citrin, W.
Drucker, H.
Elkan, Bertha
Ionis, Shriro
Inuzuka, Capt. Koreshige
Krasno, Mrs.
Matterman
Piastunovich
Shannon

INTERVIEWS OR BRIEF MEMOIRS. (Transcripts)
YAD WASHEM (Jerusalem)

Allgemeines zur Geschichte der Refugees in Shanghai, No. 01/91.
Berglass, Dr. Emanuel, No. 03/2880.
Das *ASIA SEMINAR* in Shanghai, No. 01/89.
Fabisch, Fritz, No. 03/2763.
Brand, Jechiel, No. 03/2942.
Liss, Rabbi Joseph, No. 03/2276.
Rosenstock, Josef, No. 01/90.

INTERVIEWS (transcripts) IN WIENER LIBRARY (London)

Cohn, Georg
Hoenigsberg, Hugo

INTERVIEW BY ALVIN MARS (MP)

Silberstein, Walter, (taped), April 27, 1964.

INTERVIEWS (taped) BY RABBI MARVIN TOKAYER (Tokyo) (TP).

Cohn, Dr. A. (with DK).
Mr. K.
Kobayashi, Professor Masayuki (with DK).
Mr. B.

CORRESPONDENTS

Bliss, Charles

Deman, Professor William

Deman, Ms. Joan

Eisfelder, H. Peter

Gutwirth, Nathan

Heppner, Ernest

Horowitz, Mrs. Rose

Kinderman, Dr. Karl

Kobayashi, Professor Masayuki

Kotsuji, Professor Abraham

Murphy, Professor Rhoads

Pardo, Mrs. Karin

Redlich, Dr. Kurt

Salter, Les

Tokayer, Rabbi Marvin

MANUSCRIPTS AND MANUSCRIPT COLLECTIONS

Bender Papers (BP). Dozens of original cables to and from Rabbi David Bender and the Yeshiva group in Kobe (as well as Lithuania and Shanghai) during 1940-1941. Courtesy of the Bender Family.

Bye-Laws of the International Committee For Granting Relief ot European Refugees. Six page copy of the Original Bye-Laws includes all the signatories. (YIVO No. 38).

China Archives at the JDC. (JDCCA). This extensive collection of documents, reports and correspondence for the period of 1937-1960 is arranged in chronological order. American Jewish Joint Distribution Committee.

Committee For Assistance of European Refugees. *Annual Report.* 1940 (DF).

Der Frauenbund der Juedischen Gemeinde. A two-page, unidentified manuscript history of the Ladies Auxiliary, dated February 12, 1947, (YIVO No. 45).

Dicker, Herman. *Wanderers and Settlers in the Far East.* This manuscript version of the printed book has all sources omitted in published edition. (Courtesy of author).

Deman Files. Copies of news clippings and other documents relating primarily to educational and cultural aspects of the refugee life. Many involved activities originated or conducted by Professor William Deman. Reproduced courtesy of Professor Deman and his daughter, Ms. Joan Deman.

Eisfelder, H. Peter. *Chinese Exile: My years in Shanghai and Nanking 1938-1947.* A 78 page typed, unpublished manuscript, 1972. Reproduced courtesy of Mr. Eisfelder.

Entwicklung des Musiklebens in der Emigration 1939 bis zur Beendigung des Pazifikkriegs. Three page typewritten, unidentified manuscript. (YIVO No. 32).

Epstein Files. A collection of correspondence and other documents relating primarily to activities of the Yeshiva group in Shanghai, and Rabbi Epstein's correspondence with Professor Kotsuji. The first group reproduced and the last items received the originals, courtesy of Rabbi Joseph D. Epstein.

Flakser, Menachem. *Yapan und China: Zeier Baziung zu Yidn in der Tzveiter Milchome.* A 13 page manuscript in Yiddish. (In writer's possession).

Friedlander, Irma. *Sieben Jahre Shanghai 1939-1946.* A 56 page unpublished, handwritten manuscript in the Leo Baeck Institute. Utilizes courtesy of Mrs. Friedlander and the Leo Baeck Institute.

Friedrichs, Theodore. *Geschichte Unser Auswanderung aus Deutschland:* 1963. A 321 page unpublished manuscript of the author's memoirs, including the Shanghai period. (Leo Baeck Institute) (Writer's copy reproduced from author's manuscript).

German Records Microfilmed at Alexandria, Va. No. 15. Records of Former German and Japanese Embassies and Consulates 1890-1945. Roll T-176 Serial 67. Also Inland II A/B Roll 120 Microcopy No. 4667, Juedisch-Japanische Beziehungen.

Guild of Craftsmen, Shanghai 1943-1947 (JDCCA).

HIAS-HICEM Collection at the YIVO. It is cataloged by File numbers. The Far East section (HH-XV) contains the Birman Papers for HICEM in the Far East.

HIAS Minutes. Minutes of the Office of HIAS (N.Y.) on microfilm at the YIVO, in chronological order. The writer went through the years 1938-1945.

Hongkewer-Aerzte-Verein (Association of Central European Physicians) *Report* (YIVO).

Jewish Consulate. The author, used several pages of this unpublished memoir of Mr. S. as well as the S.-Tokayer correspondence. (TP). The author also corresponded with Mr. S., a long-time resident of Japan who was active in helping the Jewish refugees.

Kahan, Lazar. *Togbukh.* (Diary). Kobe, (Japan), March-July 1941. A 102 page handwritten manuscript in Yiddish, by one of the Polish journalists who recorded his experience in Japan. His wife is Rose Shoshana, the actress, whose own published diary (In *Faier und Flamen*) was used more heavily by the author.

Kalmanowitz Files. The private collection of documents of the late Rabbi Abraham Kalmanowitz. Many documents reproduced courtesy of the Kalmanowitz Family.

Kaufman, Abraham. *Testimony Concerning Jewish Life in Manchuria.* An 85 page, typed interview, originally in Yiddish, and translated into Hebrew, May 1967. (Yad Washem No. 03/3168).

Kaufman, Fritz. *The Experience of the Shanghai Jewish Community under the Japanese in World War II.* (From a 16 page manuscript of a speech by Fritz Kaufman on February 12, 1963, before the Shanghai Tiffin Club, New York) (AJC Library).

KOGAN and FOREIGN OFFICE PAPERS. A collection of top secret Japanese documents from the Foreign Office and other departments relating to the Jews in the Far East. The translations of an important segment of this valuable collection were used by Dr. Dicker, who made them available to the author. The author used the translations as is although some were not very smooth. Dr. Dicker received them from Mr. Micha Kogan who in turn got them from a Peter Berstein (Burton) at the end of the war in the Pacific. (DP).

The author received a xerox of complete Japanese version from Mr. Hideaki Kase, in an exchange of documents. Some of these documents are also found in Arthur Young's *Checklist of Japanese Army and Navy Archives 1968-1945* (L.C.)

Kohn Newspapers. Reproductions of several Shanghai Jewish newspapers from the private collection of Mrs. Kattie Kohn, wife of the journalist and editor, Philip Kohn. These include: *8 Uhr Abendblatt* (September-December 1940), *Juedisches Nachrichtenblatt* (August 1940-1946), which became *The Jewish Voice of the Far East* (January-August 1946).

Kranzler, David. *The Jewish Community of Shanghai 1937-1957* Unpublished Master's thesis at Brooklyn College. 1958.

Lankin, Eliyahu. *Interview.* A 300 page memoir of Jewish life in Manchuria and China. Reproduced from a copy in the Oral History Division of the Institute of Contemporary Jewry, Hebrew University. No. 850.

Levin Files. A collection of newsclippings, documents, photos and especially the text for a series of radio programs conducted by Mr. Horst Levin on station XMHA in Shanghai. Reproduced courtesy of Mr. Levin. (LF).

Library of Congress. Newspaper Collection. Contains the full run of a number of English language Shanghai newspapers utilized by the author.

Loewenthal Papers. The private collection of newspaper clippings (especially the *Peking Chronicle*), booklets German, Chinese and Japanese material relating to the Jews, collected by Dr. Rudolph Loewenthal, while at the Yenching University in Peking, 1937-1947. These papers include the various bibliographies of the Jewish Press in the Far East, published by Dr. Loewenthal. Entire collection reproduced courtesy of Dr. Loewenthal. (LP).

Loewenthal, Rudolph. *Japanese and Chinese Materials Pertaining to the Jewish Catastrophe 1939-1945.* (A 292 page manuscript with summaries of important, primarily Japanese, antisemetic material). Prepared for the YIVO. 1955 (LP).

Mars, Alvin. *A Community by Necessity: The Story of the German Jewish Flight to Shanghai.* Unpublished History Seminar Paper at Temple University, May 1964. (Copy in writer's possession courtesy of Mr. Mars).

Michaelis, Dr. Robert. *Bericht und Gutachten Ueber den Sonderbezirk fuer Staatenlose Fluechtlinge in Shanghai (China) (Shanghai Ghetto 19431945).* Buero-Hannover, August 18, 1961. 30 pages (Author's collection). A carbon copy of this valuable document was given to the author by Ludwig Lazarus (Germany) through the influence of Gerhard Gerechter.

National Archives, State Department Decimal File. Especially Nos. 893.55 J; 840.48 Refugees. (NA/SDDF).

National Refugee Service Archives (NRS) (YIVO).

Newman, Frank. *Kobe Diary.* A brief, handwritten 35 page entry in a 1941 diary by a representative of Agudath Israel and Vaad Hatzalah sent to Kobe, Japan, to help the Yeshiva group. Copy reproduced courtesy of Mr. Newman. Some aspects explained or clarified in a related taped interview.

Pardo, Karin. *Shanghai, 1939-1947.* July 14, 1975. A five page, handwritten manuscript in which Mrs. Pardo recounted her experiences in Shanghai as a teenager, sent to the author.

Redlich Papers. A collection of documents relating primarily to activities of the *Juedische Gemeinde,* as well as a 130 page correspondence by Dr. Kurt Redlich with the author. The latter is especially valuable as a primary source for the history of the Gemeinde and Arbitration Board as well as other aspects of refugee life. (RP).

Report of the Activity of the Committee for Assistance to Refugees The' Jewish Community of Kobe. (JEWCOM) (Ashkenazim) July 1940-November 1941-1942. A 33 page unpublished, typed manuscript recounting the activities of the JEWCOM of Kobe for the Jewish refugees. Reproduced courtesy of Dr. Dicker. (DP).

Rosenfeld, Manfred. Untitled, incomplete, three part manuscript of a history of the Jewish Community of Shanghai. Part I is concerned primarily with the refugees. Part II is a partial revised English translation of Part I, titled *History of the Jews of Shanghai.* Part III is titled *Brief Information Concerning the Ashkenazi Jewish Community in Shanghai.* (YIVO No. 1).

SACRA Minutes. A 200 page manuscript containing the minutes of SACRA (Shanghai Ashkenazi Collaborating Relief Association) 1943-1945. (YIVO No. 12-16).

"A Short History of the School," (A two page history of the Freysinger School, typed on school stationery) (YIVO No. 51).

Shanghai Collection at the YIVO. It is catalogued and arranged by folders. (YIVO No. 1-68).

Shanghai Hebrew Relief Society and the Shanghai Jewish Women's Benevolent Society. Financial Statement for the period of 1933-1943. (YIVO No. 35).

Shanghai Jewish Youth Association Founded February 1937: Its Foundation and Short History of its Activities, 1940. A 12 page unpublished, mimeographed report of the SJYA activities which included the refugee children after 1938. Probably written by Lawrence Kadoorie. Copy sent to the author courtesy of Rabbi Tokayer. (TP).

Sinclair, Michael L. *The French Settlement of Shanghai on the Eve of the Revolution of 1911.* Unpublished dissertation, Stamford University, 1973. Made aware of its existance by Mr. Frank Shulman.

Sugihara, Senpo. July 15, 1968. A four page memoirs (translated into Hebrew) and related correspondence. By the Japanese consul in Riga concerning the episode of the Japanese transit visas. (Yad Washem) (TP).

United States State Department Papers concerning refugees. Decimal File Numbers 840.40 and 893.55/36 (National Archives).

United States of America vs. Lothar Eisentraeger alias Ludwig Ehrhardt, August 26, 1946-January 17, 1947. Bureau Ehrhardt. Proceedings Before a Military Commission by Command, at Shanghai, China. (NA).

World Jewish Congress. Institute of Jewish Affairs. Information Series. Includes the following: *Jews in Shanghai,* February 1949; *Jewish Communities of China in Dissolution* by Nehemiah Robinson; *400 Jews Left Amoung* 600,000,000 *Chinese!* September 25, 1957.

YIVO Shanghai Files. The major Shanghai collection at the YIVO Institute for Jewish Research (N.Y.) arranged by file numbers 1-68.

STATISTICS OF JEWS IN SHANGHAI

VITAL STATISTICS OF REFUGEES

Source: YIVO Catalog, pp. 9-10.

YEAR	BIRTHS	MARRIAGE	DIVORCE	MORTALITY
1939	2	14	--	131
1940	67	51	13	130
1941	64	34	12	167
1942	36	30	12	320
1943	37	28	11	311
1944	48	31	18	260
1945	50	52	38	262
1946	114	126	--	145
TOTAL	408	366	104	1,726

On March 25, 1934, the number of Jews in Shanghai was 1,671; 881 males (including 260 children) and 790 females (including 240 children). Of these, 14 arrived prior to 1900, 21 in 1900-1904, 51 in 1905-1913, 116 in 1914-1919.

Statistics of Jewish commercial and industrial establishments outside the Ghetto of Shanghai, according to zones. On February 18, 1943, these establishments were ordered removed to the Ghetto or closed. The order involved a total of 307 such establishments. Of these, 68 were clothing stores, 50 cafes and restaurants, 26 secondhand stores, 24 grocery stores, 19 tailor shops, 14 bookstores, 12 crockery stores, 9 chemists and apothecary laboratories, 9 radio and electrical appliance shops, 8 leather goods stores, 7 jewelry stores, 6 booteries, 5 photographic studios,

4 stamp and rubber good factories, 2 fur shops, and 44 miscellaneous shops.

Statistics of apartments and rooms occupied by refugees outside the Ghetto. Most of these had to be exchanged for living quarters in the Ghetto. The total of apartments was 811 (2,766 rooms).

The number of Jews in the Ghetto, according to statistics of the Emigrant Residents Union—ERU—November, 1944. The Ghetto then housed 14,245 refugees (8,283 men, 5,863 women) of whom 1,171 were under 15 years. Of these, 8,114 were from Germany, 3,942 from Austria, 1,248 from Poland, 236 from Czechoslovakia, three Chinese women who were married to refugees, and others.

Marriage and divorce: In 1939 there were 14 marriages; in 1940, 51 marriages, 13 divorces; in 1941 34 marriages, 12 divorces; in 1942, 30 marriages, 12 divorces; in 1943, 28 marriages, 11 divorces; in 1944, 31 marriages, 18 divorces; in 1945, 52 marriages, 38 divorces, in 1946, 126 marriages.

Births: in 1939, 2; 1940, 67; 1941, 64; 1942, 36; 1943, 27; 1944, 48; 1945, 50; 1946, 114.

Mortality: In 1939, 131; 1940, 130; 1941, 167; 1942, 320; 1943, 311; 1944, 260; 1945, 262; 1946, 145. Mortality according to age groups in 1942: Below 20 years, 9; 21-30, 10; 31-40, 17; 41-50, 53; 51-60, 76; 61-70, 104; over 70, 44; age unknown, 7.

Mortality in the months and years of 1939-1946. (The date of Nos. 76-78 are based on the statistics of Juedische Gemeinde in Shanghai and include only refugees from Central Europe and some from Poland).

European refugees in Shanghai, statistics of the UNRRA, after the liberation. Of 15,511 European refugees in Shanghai, 13,496 or 87 per cent were Jewish.

In 1946, 2,175 and in 1947, 5,555 refugees re-emigrated. Toward the end of 1947 there were still 7,270 refugees in Shanghai, of whom 516 were below 15 years. According to a report of the JDC, there were in Shanghai, together with the earlier Jewish settlers, 11,270 Jews.

A list of 1,497 refugees who died in Shanghai from January 1, 1939 to April 1, 1945, including the causese of death (among them 36 suicides). The list was compiled by the HIAS. (Other lists compiled by HIAS indicate that 123 refugees died from September 1, 1945 to April 1, 1946, and 118 in the year 1947).

A list of 36 refugees from Vilna, deported toward the end of 1941 from Japan to Shanghai, who died during the period 1941-45 and were buried in the cemetery on Baikal Road in Shanghai. The list was compiled by the HIAS.

APPENDIX—B

[FO]   13 October, 1938
S9460-3-750

FROM: Prince KONOYE, Fumimaro
          Minister of Foreign Affairs.

SUBJECT: Forwarding the Transcribed Text of Col. YASUE's
         Lecture on the Jewish Problem Delivered to the Jewish
         Problem Research Council.
         On September 19, Col. Yasue, Chief, Army Special Service,
Dairen, delivered a lecture on the Jewish Problem at this Ministry
in the presence of persons concerned from the Ministries of Army,
Navy and Foreign Affairs.
         Admitting that the contents of the lecture may contain
some points which are still questionable, and that even in the
Army, the said colonel's view cannot always pass without causing
controversy, I am forwarding its transcribed text, inclosed herewith,
for your information.

Distribution: Ambassador in Manchoukuo
               Consul-General, in Mukden, Harbin, Nanking,
               Shanghai, Chingtao, Peking and Tientsin.
               [The first of a nine-page rceport]

Appendix—C
[KP No. 5 (DP)]

Summary of the May 25, [1939] *interview between the members of the Jewish Investigation Committee and Victor Sassoon and Haim.*

Remark: Haim is political advisor to Sassoon and Director-General of the Jewish Relief Committee.

Members of the Jewish Investigation Committee.

Consul Ishiguro

Col. Yasue

Capt. Inuzuka.

1. *The Jewish Relief Committee's Course of Action on Jewish Refugees:*

The Relief Committee has been hard pressed with its daily relief activities, in which great difficulty has been felt due to the shortage of funds, that it does not know how it could manage to continue its activities.

The ultimate cause of this question is the fact that Germany has been releasing her Jewish nationals without restraint, and the stoppage of this action will be the best solution of the question. The Committee has already lodged a petition through various foreign consuls to Germany for the release of Jews to be discouraged. Now that this has turned out ineffective, we believe it more effective if the matter be negotiated by Japan.

*   *   *

4. *Copy of Telegram to Foreign Minister from Consul-General in Shanghai:*

On the meeting with Sassoon concerning the Jewish Problem, Col. Yasue, Capt. Inuzuka and Consul Ishiguro (the Committee on the spot) had an interview with Mr. Victor Sassoon, President of Jewish Community and Mr. Haim, the Chief Director of Jewish Community on 25th, so as to hear the opinion of the leaders of Jewish Community concerning the disposition of Jewish refugees. They appreciated our thoughtful consideration for this matter and it seemed that the result of the meeting was good. The measures are now under consideration. We will send the details by mail. Please report the above as a telegram from the Committee to Army, Navy Authorities.

APPENDIX—D

[FO S9460-3-1722]

[January 1940]
[by Yoshiuori Inuzuka]

CONTENTS

1. Explanation for Doubt "Without confirming the details of the other party's conditions and in view of the several reply telegrams from the other party, it is difficult to determine that we are hopeful as stated by Murata."
2. Explanation for Doubt "The sincerity of the other party is doubtful and in view of the intrinsic nature of the Jews, carrying out of the conditions is not readily believable. Even if it is admitted, the financial and material aid to Japan is difficult, at least from out common sense, in the present situation of the U.S. Government."
3. Explanation for Doubt "Because of this, the Jews in Shanghai and those in America are at odds with each other and it can not be said that there is no possibility of a result reverse to what was intended being brought about."
5. Explanation for Doubt "It seems utterly hopeless as it is opposed positively by the Army in Manchuria and ignored by the Army in China."
6. Conclusion.

Explanation For Doubts In Operations On Jews In America

Yoshinori Inuzuka
Resident Naval Officer
Shanghai

1. Doubt "Without confirming the details of the other party's conditions and in view of the several reply telegrams from the other party, it is difficult to determine that we are hopeful as stated by Murata."

This view is an argument of one who is not familiar with the present circumstances of the Jews. In other words,

(a) The Jews are clever at bargaining by habit of 2,000 years' standing and do not employ such a foolish policy as to show their real intentions on their face. The stronger their desire is, the cooler attitude they pretend to take, showing a firm mouth attitude. This fact will be admitted by any person who has an experience of association with the Jews. If this is viewed as diplomatic policy of a nation, the real situation will be immediately understood.

(b) If you change the positions by putting our country in their difficult position, it will be natural tactics to hide our weak points, and to show a firm attitude purposely, taking advantage of the other party's weak points.

(c) Further, it is considered too careless and hasty to presume their attitude through their simple telegrams.

(d) In addition, Marata met and conferred with "Blandes" and other responsible and powerful Jews in America. As Murata inferred their earnest desire from his 20 years' experience of association with the Jews, he took part in this difficult negotiation chivalrously. In view of this fact, it is not proper to stick to the simple reply telegrams alone.

(e) Something or other may be said about a change of the situation only after considerable time is wasted since Murata started negotiations with powerful Jews in America. As the war in Europe develops, to obtain a place of refuge for Jews there, is a pressing necessity and their desire to obtain a place of safety at any cost obviously becomes more and more earnest. The leader in this district has revealed to me that as they are too many in number, there is no adequate place of accommodation at this critical moment of the race and that it is a matter of great concern for them. The heads of the Jews in every country have the same worry as well. It is to be noted that the Jews in America have the same earnest desire as 80 per cent of them are of German origin and have the strong same blood consciousness.

(f) Therefore, it serves two ends for Japan to satisfy their desperate eager desire and to make them realize by means of fact our great spirit of the universe-is-one principle and the racial equality which we advocate all the times but the Westerners can not understand, thereby advertizing our great spirit with their advertizing skill and at the same time, making them cooperate for our construction of the Continent. We should say the European War is the time of all times for this purpose.

(g) But as they were not fully aware of the circumstances because of the lapse of considerable time and the proposal was not by a responsible official such as outstation authorities, it is not unreasonable that they have had a sort of fear and have not expressed their full sincerity. It is considered that such a doubt as this on both parties will be dispelled when a representative comes to Japan. I can make this statement positively, judging from the result of my contacts with the leaders in this area since this spring.

2. Doubt "The sincerity of the other party is doubtful and in view of the intrinsic nature of the Jews, carrying out of the conditions is not readily believable. Even if it is admitted, the financial and material aid to Japan is difficult, at least from our common sense, in the present situation of the US Government.

As to the question of the other party's sincerity, it is desired that the matter be judged by unbiased proper reasoning as stated above.

One who says "carrying out of the conditions is not readily believable" is open to the criticism that he rather lacks the understanding of the nature of the Jews and the distressed circumstances of the Jews in Europe. In other words,

(a) To be full of wiles and a pretty keen hand at bargaining is the natural self-defense of the Jews who do not have a motherland and arms since 2,000 years ago. If they encounter with a life-or-death issue of the race, they get together to remedy the situation with disinterested religeous homo-racial consciousness unlike other nations. This is the reason why they, as a vagrant and ruined people, have continued the deep-rooted prosperity for twenty centuries.

(b) Their reality, namely the immeasurable golden power of control over the financial, political and industrial worlds and their characteristic that they do not have a country for peaceful living and military force, are absolutely favorable to our country. There is a strong probability of success.

(c) Next, the view that "in the present situation of the US Government . . ." is an opinion of a person who only knows about the existing state of affairs.

Once Murata's plan is put into operation, they will start changing suddenly. In other words, the current anti-Japanese policy

A. LITTLE VIENNA

Top: Hongkew ruins prior to refugee arrival. (*Courtesy H. Eisfelder*) Middle: Ruins rebuilt by refugees. (*Courtesy H. Eisfelder*) Bottom: Refugee relaxing in midst of rebuilding a bombed-out shell in Hongkew. From the *Spotlight*, July 1939. (*Courtesy R. Loewenthal*)

Life in the "lanes" of Hongkew. (*Courtesy K. Redlich*)

Top: Lane "599 Tongshan Road." (*Courtesy H. Eisfelder*)   Middle: The Tongshan Restaurant and Provision store. The son of the owner (Glogauer) is in the doorway. The inscription on the window advertises the "house specialty": EISKALTES WASSER (ice-cold water) and underneath: TRINKWASSER' WASSER M. SAFT, (drinking water, water with cordial). (*Courtesy H. Eisfelder*)   Bottom: Chusan Road Market. (*Courtesy H. Eisfelder*)

DISTRIBUTION OF MEALS IN "HOMES"
FEB – DEC 1939

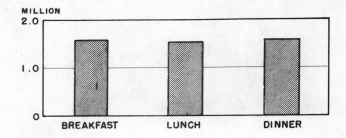

SOURCE : ANNUAL REPORT OF THE CENTRAL
MANAGEMENT OF THE I.C.R. HOMES

CAMPS AND NUMBER OF RESIDENTS

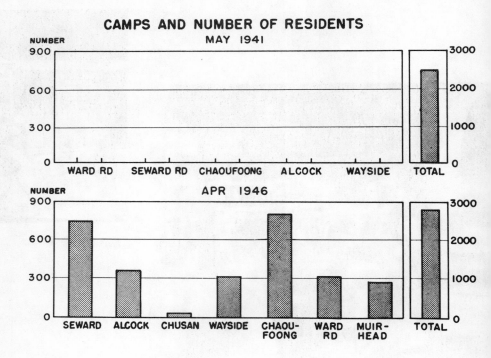

SOURCE : AMERICAN JOINT DISTRIBUTION COMMITTEE

CHART   A

B. HEIME

Top: Refugees arrive at distribution center (probably the Embankment Building). (*Courtesy M. Tokayer*)   Middle: Refugees loaded on trucks, driven by volunteers to one of the Heime. (*Courtesy M. Tokayer*)   Bottom: Luggage of new arrivals on grounds of Chaoufoong Road Heim. (*Courtesy H. Dicker*)

Top: Refugees lined up for meal at the Ward Road Heim kitchen. Notice gardens being tended. (*Courtesy M. Tokayer*) Middle: Dormitory room in one of the Heime. (*Courtesy M. Tokayer*) Bottom: Kitchen-duty in one of the Heime (probably Ward Rd.). (*Courtesy M. Tokayer*)

PERSONS ASSISTED BY
AMERICAN JOINT DISTRIBUTION COMMITTEE

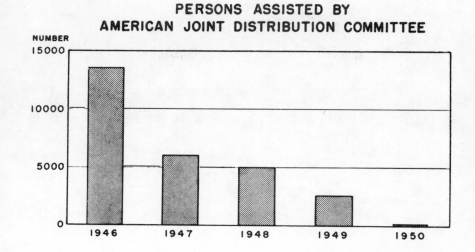

NUMBER

15000

10000

5000

0

1946   1947   1948   1949   1950

AGE DISTRIBUTION
1946

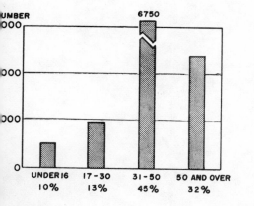

NUMBER
000

000

000

0

UNDER 16   17-30   31-50   50 AND OVER
10%   13%   45%   32%

6750

RELIGION

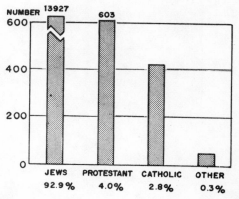

NUMBER   13927   603
600

400

200

0

JEWS   PROTESTANT   CATHOLIC   OTHER
92.9%   4.0%   2.8%   0.3%

URCE : AMERICAN JOINT DISTRIBUTION COMMITTEE

CHART B

THE SCHOOL BUILDING

C. YOUTH

Top: Shanghai Jewish School (Sephardi) attended at first by many refugee children. Bottom: Part of the Shanghai Jewish Youth Association (Kadoorie) School on Tongshan Road, about 1944 (a U-shaped building). (*Courtesy H. Eisfelder*)

op: Outing with the Boy Scouts. Among the more "carefree" days of the youth. *Courtesy E. Heppner*) Middle: Refugees in the Boy Scouts. (*Courtesy E. eppner*) Bottom: Soccer match. Refugee soccer team (right side, white shorts) s. the White Russian team in Frenchtown. (*Courtesy L. Meyer*)

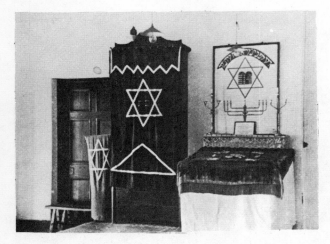

D. RELIGIOUS AND COMMUNAL LIFE

Top: Sephardi "Beth Aharon" Synagogue. (*Courtesy Mrs. Rose Horowitz*) Middle: Inside of "Beth Aharon" Synagogue, when used as refugee reception cente[r]
(1939), showing clothes and mattress. (*Courtesy J. Abraham*) Bottom: Front o[f]
refugee synagogue (Ward Rd. Heim?). (*Courtesy M. Tokayer*)

Lewensztejn, Prof. of Ethics and Educator;   Rabbi Ch. L. Szmuelowicz, Acting Dean;   Rabbi J. D. Epstein, Secretary.
(First from left)   (Second from right)   (First from right)

Top: Beth Aharon Synagogue used as Beit Midrash (Study Hall) by Mirrer Yeshiva. (*Courtesy Rabbi S. M. Kalmanowitz*) **Bottom: Rabbi Meir Ashkenazi, Spiritual Leader of Russian (Ashkenazi) Jewish Community of Shanghai from 1925-1947. Died in New York City, 1956.** (*Courtesy H. Dicker*)

Top: Members of the Arbitration Board (Schiedesgericht). (l. to r.) Erna Weiss (sec'y), Dr. Otto Koritschoner, Dr. Kurt Redlich, Dr. Josef Schaefer, Bernard Cohn. (Standing) Mr. Goldmann, (messenger). (*Courtesy K. Redlich*) Bottom: Craftsman's Guild graduation ceremony for apprentices, with issuance of journeyman's certificates. Speaker, Max Brandt. (*Courtesy Mrs. Max Brandt, Dr. K. Redlich*)

Top: Juedische Gemeinde Staff. Front: (l. to r. seated) R.A. Cohn, Dr. K. Redlich, Rabbi Dr. Kantorowsky, Mrs. Kessler (sec'y), Dr. Schaefer, Mrs. Weiss (sec'y), Fritz Tuch (Manager). (*Courtesy K. Redlich*) Bottom: Zionist Gathering. Speaker Max Brandt, on head table, (center), Rabbi Ashkenazi, Siegmund Fischel (with hat). (*Courtesy K. Redlich*)

Top: Yeshiva students "in conference" at corner of lane, 599 Tongshan Road, Hongkew. (*Courtesy H. Eisfelder*)   Bottom: Rabbi Abraham Kalmanowitz thanking Henry Morgenthau, Jr. for assistance in rescue work. On left is Rabbi Alex Weisfogel, assistant to Rabbi Kalmanowitz.

E. JAPANESE AND JEWS

Top: Captain K. Inuzuka and his staff at the Bureau of Jewish Affairs, (according to Mrs. Inuzuka, the third one on the left, standing, is Ghoya). (*Courtesy M. Tokayer*) Middle: (l. to r.) Sir Elly Kadoorie, Capt. and Mrs. Inuzuka, Horace Kadoorie, Ota (builder). Probably had conference re working on one of Inuzuka's plans for joint realty company with Jews in Shanghai. In Sir Victor Sassoon's suite on 10th fl. of Cathay Hotel. (*Courtesy M. Tokayer, J. Abraham*) Bottom: (l. to r.) Masaki (interpreter), Mrs. (Shimei) Inuzuka, Capt. Koreshige Inuzuka, Frank Newman, Reuben D. Abraham, Jack Ezekiel. (*Courtesy M. Tokayer*)

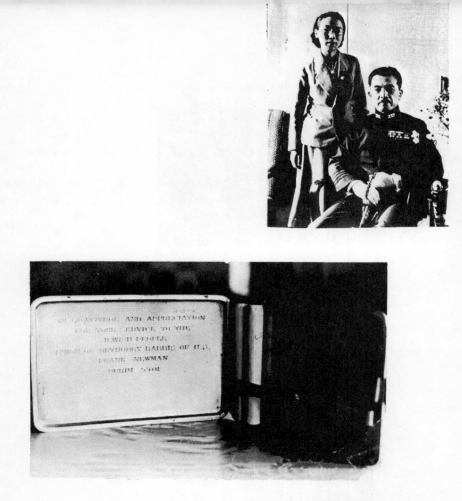

Top: Mrs. Shimei and Captain Koreshige Inuzuka. She was the brains behind his plans. Rabbi Tokayer received most of these photos and many documents from Mrs. Inuzuka. (*Courtesy M. Tokayer*)　Middle: Silver cigarette case presented to Capt. Inuzuka by Frank Newman on Purim 5701 (March 1941) on behalf of Union of Orthodox Rabbis of the U.S. (Agudas Harabanim) for providing 300 Shanghai Permits for Yeshive students. (*Courtesy M. Tokayer*)　Bottom: Kadoorie's Marble Hall. (*Courtesy M. Tokayer*)

Top: D.E.J. Abraham residence. (l. to r., top.) Julius Weinberger, Mrs. R. D. Abraham, Ezekiel Abraham, (Mrs. Mowlem), D.E.J. Abraham, Jack Ezekiel. (3rd row) Mrs. J. Weinberger, Capt. Inuzuka, Mrs. D.E.J. Abraham, Shimei (Mrs.) Inuzuka, (?). (*Courtesy M. Tokayer, J. Abraham*)   Middle: Letter of introduction for Frank Newman by Rabbi L. Seltzer, head of Union of Orthodox Rabbis of the U.S. (Agudas Harabanim). (*Courtesy M. Tokayer*)   Bottom: Letter by Dr. Stephen S. Wise, president of the American Jewish Congress, to Dr. Karl Kindermann concerning Japanese plan to settle German refugees in Manchuria [*not* Japan proper as noted in letter]. (*Courtesy M. Tokayer*)

Top: Dr. Abraham Kaufman (center) speaking at (third?) Far Eastern Conference of Jewish Communities, in Harbin, Manchuria, flanked by Japanese military notables. Behind him are Betar (Zionist) guards, and the Japanese, Jewish and Manchurian flags (left to right) Gov. I Kan Sho, Gen. ? Deputy Gov. of Yuhinko Province, Maj. Irimura repres. of Harbin Secret Military Agency, Dr. Kaufman, Col. Yasue chief of Dairen Secret Military Agency, Major Sato Chief Military Police of Harbin. (see FO S-9460-3-1640-1654 Jan. 11, 1940 re 3rd Convention) (Courtesy M. Tokayer) Middle: Sir Victor Sassoon and Captain Inuzuka (4th and 5th l. to r.). (Courtesy M. Tokayer)

F. KOBE

Top: Left to Right: Rabbi Shapiro, Prof. Abraham Kotsuji, Rabbi Shimon Kalish (Amshenover Rebbe), Rabbi Shatskes, (Lomsher Rov), Capt. Fukamachi, Leo Hanin. This group met with Japanese Shinto priests and generals in a discussion of Judaism, sometime in the first half of 1941. When asked by the Japanese [according to one version] why the Germans persecuted the Jews, Rabbi Kalish replied, "Because we too are Asians." (*Courtesy M. Tokayer*) Middle: Japanese distributing gifts of apples to the refugees in Kobe. Man on right is A. Triguboff of JEWCOM. (*Courtesy M. Tokayer*) Bottom: Polish refugees arriving in Kobe, ca. early 1941. (*Courtesy M. Tokayer & H. Dicker*)

Top: Members of JEWCOM, the Jewish Community of Kobe. The Committee for Assistance to Refugees. (*Courtesy M. Tokayer*)   Middle: Refugee group in Kobe, mostly from the Yeshiva group. Included are a few members of JEWCOM. Leo Hanin is in the second row, second from left. (*Courtesy M. Tokayer*)   Bottom: Refugees in front of JEWCOM in Kobe. (*Courtesy M. Tokayer*)

A WARNING

To all Chinese, Japanese and Gentiles Alike

THE "CHOSEN PEOPLE"
HAVE INVADED SHANGHAI!

Be Prepared to Resist

An Economic Invasion and

Be Prepared for

An Era of Crime, Sin and Intrigue

G. ANTISEMITISM

Top: Title page of antisemitic booklet greeting arriving refugees. (Probably by Nazi-German elements and/or White Russians in Shanghai), 1939. (*Courtesy R. Loewenthal*)   Bottom: Illustration from the above booklet, manifesting all the basic antisemitic notions from the *Protocols of the Elders of Zion.* (*Courtesy R. Loewenthal*)

一圖は、漫畫といふには、餘りに陰慘な彼等の意圖を象徴して描かれたの、鷄頭の似顔に注目せられたし

(G.Szajkowski)

illus. originally taken from popular Jewish picture postcards

A Japanese antisemitic cartoon showing a Jew (schlogging kapores) with the Czar of Russia.

Illustration from the Japanese antisemitic journal *Yudaya Kenkyu* showing a Jew (*Schlogging Kapores*) or "twisting the tail of," the Russian Czar (probably Nicholas II) the caption reads: "This picture, purported by be a caricature, symbolizes their (Jews') extremely sinister plot with special attention to the resemblance to the chicken head." (*transl. Courtesy S. Hong*) (*Courtesy H. Kublin*)

H. GHETTO

Top: One of the numerous signs indicating boundary of the "Restricted Area." (*Courtesy H. Eisfelder*) Middle: Button worn on lapel of those leaving ghetto, Chinese characters state, "May Pass." (*Courtesy H. Eisfelder*) Bottom: Line of refugees waiting for Pass to leave ghetto. Note Pao Chia guard with white armband in middle and at right. (*Courtesy H. Eisfelder*)

Top: Front of Pass to leave ghetto, Notice time. On bottom right corner is oval stamp with signature of Ghoya (?). Stamp more authentic for Japanese than written signature. (*Courtesy H. Eisfelder*) Bottom: Jewish Pao Chia checking pass of fellow refugee desiring to leave ghetto. (*Courtesy H. Eisfelder*)

Top: Refugee I.D. (yellow strip across top right. (Front) (*Courtesy R. Fischel*)

ttom: Pao Chia Meeting in the courtyard of the Wayside Road Heim. (Seated l. to r.): Owner of coffeehouse, Josef Cohn, butcher, District Commander, Wilhelm Stricks, Commander air warden corps, Capt. Wernberger (?) former Austrian army officer, inspector, Paul Leichter, Deputy Commander, Japanese police inspector in charge of Foreign Pao Chia, Dr. Felix Kardegg, Commanding officer, White Russian Police Inspector, Kovacs, refugee police officer, Otto Weinberger, District Commander, Max Rechenberg, engineer, Director of ORT Training Center, Fritz Sello, youth leader, unknown. (Among standing in back) (first on left) Zadeck, Mgr. of Wayside Heim, (last on right) Alfred Heller, Mgr. Alcock Rd. Heim, (2nd row behind Rechenberger) Eyck, Mgr. Ward Rd. Heim (last row center, in front of tree) Gerhard Gottschalk. (*Courtesy K. Redlich*)

Top: Refugees selling clothing on street for a little money to buy food during ghetto period. (*Courtesy H. Eisfelder*) Bottom: The relatively "affluent" of the ghetto (1944 or 1945). Afternoon tea on the "Roy Roofgarden Restaurant," overlooking the ghetto. Some of the larger buildings of the Ward Road Prison can be seen at the top right. (*Courtesy H. Eisfelder*)

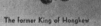

I. GHOYA "KING OF THE JEWS"

Top: The "King" surveys the boundary of his kingdom (ghetto). (*Courtesy H. Eisfelder*) Middle: Refugee receiving "Pass" from Ghoya to leave ghetto. (*Courtesy H. Eisfelder*) The "King" dethroned. Ghoya beaten up by refugees after War. (*Courtesy E. Heppner*) Bottom: Caricatures of Ghoya by Fritz Melchior. (*Courtesy M. Bloch*)

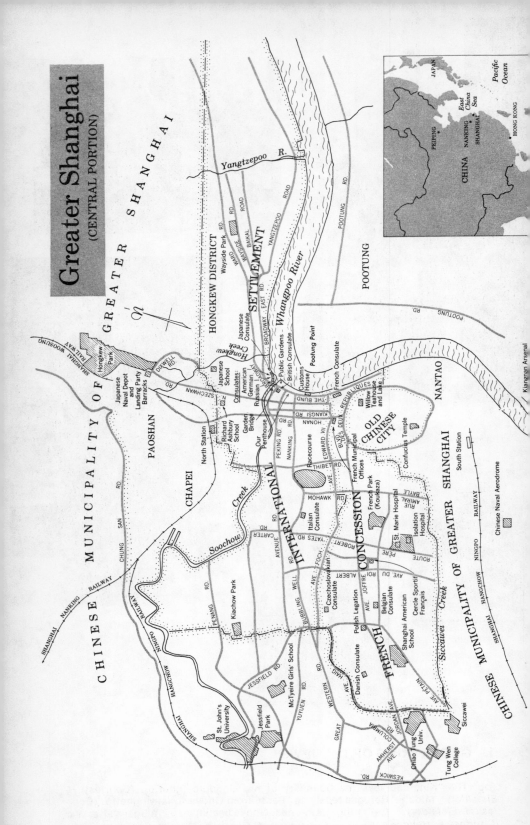

Greater Shanghai
(CENTRAL PORTION)

GREATER SHANGHAI

JAPAN

East China Sea

Pacific Ocean

PEIPING

NANKING

SHANGHAI

CHINA

HONG KONG

Yangtzepoo R.

HONGKEW DISTRICT

Wayside Park
WAYSIDE RD.
BAIKAL RD.
YANGTZEPOO ROAD

SETTLEMENT

Whangpoo River

Japanese Consulate

BROADWAY EAST

Honkew Creek

Public Gardens
British Consulate
Customs House
French Consulate

POOTUNG

POOTUNG RD.

POOTUNG RD.

Pootung Point

Kiangnan Arsenal

Hongkew Park

Japanese Naval Depot and Landing Party Barracks
DIXWELL RD.
Japanese School
SZECHWAN RD.

Consulates:
American
German
Russian

THE BUND

KIANGSI RD.
HONAN RD.

NANTAO

PAOSHAN

SHANGHAI WOOSUNG RAILWAY

North Station
Richard Ashbury School
Garden Bridge
Our Penthouse

PEKING RD.
NANKING RD.
Racecourse
EDWARD VII
THIBET RD.
AVE.

BD. DES DEUX REPUBLIQUES

Willow Teahouse and Lake

OLD CHINESE CITY

Confucius Temple

OLD CHINESE CITY

GREATER SHANGHAI

South Station

Chinese Naval Aerodrome

CHAPEI

Soochow Creek

Creek

MOHAWK RD.

French Municipal Offices

French Park (Koukaza)

RUE AMIRAL BAYLE

St. Marie Hospital
Isolation Hospital

RAILWAY

CHUNG SAN RD.

Italian Consulate
CARTER RD.
AVENUE RD.
YATES RD.
FOCH AVE.
ROBERT RD.

INTERNATIONAL CONCESSION

PÈRE ROBERT
ROUTE

St. Marie Hospital

SHANGHAI NANKING RAILWAY

NINGPO RAILWAY

Kiachow Park

PENANG RD.

BUBBLING WELL RD.

AVE. DU ROI ALBERT
AVE. JOFFRE

Czechoslovakian Consulate

Polish Legation

Belgian Consulate
Shanghai American School
Cercle Sportif Français

FRENCH CONCESSION

AVE. PETAIN

Siccawei Creek

HANGCHOW RAILWAY

CHINESE MUNICIPALITY OF GREATER SHANGHAI

NINGPO

HANGCHOW

St. John's University

Jessfield Park

JESSFIELD RD.
McTyeire Girls' School

Danish Consulate

YUYUEN RD.
WESTERN RD.
HAIG AVE.
JORDAN AVE.
GREAT WESTERN RD.
AMHERST AVE.
COLUMBIA RD.
KESWICK RD.

Chiao Tung Univ.

Tung Wen College

Siccawei

SHANGHAI HANGCHOW RAILWAY

CHINESE MUNICIPALITY OF GREATER SHANGHAI

of the U.S. Government is rather based on the ideological reasons and backed up by the public opinion. The American public is, needless to say, made up by the press and advertizing agencies and Congressmen. If the Jewish leaders in America who control these agencies should be inclined to become pro-Japanese, the American public opinion would obviously change in one night and attack the anti-Japanese policy. At a conference attended by the Jewish leaders living here in Shanghai, I was advised that they were sure they could contribute to a change of the public opinion toward Japan if the Murata's plan was put into operation.

(d) No one can deny the fact that there is a possibility of the financial and material aid to Japan being facilitated by the above-mentioned power of the public opinion and the political influence although it is difficult to smooth the aid in the present position of the US Government. Implementation of the subject plan has a purpose, among others, to make the public opinion toward Japan change for the better. Therefore, we should say this argument fails to properly evaluate importance.

(e) Even if the plan should fail to make a change in the public opinion and contributions to the withdrawal of the moral embargo law and to a revision of the commercial treaty because of failure to move the US Government, a way for supply of materials could be worked out and carried out by the well-known ability of the Jewish financial groups and trademen dealing in munitions, construction and materials when once improvement is made of their feelings toward Japan. There was many a instance during the World War I where the materials were obtained from the hostile country by using the international connections and smuggle organizations of the Jews. In view of those instances, I assume it is an easy job for them to furnish supplies to Japan which holds a neutral position. Especially, we have an advantage of using Shanghai strongly tinged with neutrality. In addition, if you realize that the pro-Japanese key figures among the Jews in the Far East are wishing for the great expansion of Japan in the Continent and are expecting Japan to be their final resort, you will see that there is high probability that the acceleration of the Jews' pro-Japanese sentiment in America will result therefrom.

(f) To cope with the complicated and inscrutable international political situation, prompt construction of the Contient and completion of armaments are urgent needs for our Empire which has declared new order in the Estern Aisa [sic]. These national requirements, we can not neglect for a moment. It is needless to say that this unparalleled most difficult time can be overcome by the unequal spiritual strength of the Japanese and by having enough time. But in the present pressing situation, it is a great mission charged to the agencies dealing with the Jews to strive for sufficiency of the national strength by obtaining sufficient supplies and completing the armaments at the earliest date even if it costs considerably. Yet if we do not consider the "speed" element, we will be foolish enough not to adapt ourselves to a new situation after the European War.

(g) For this reason, there can be no gainsaying that to make most use of whatever is available, is the best policy. There are too many cases to mention in the history where the root of calamity in future was left uneradicated due to use of the Jews without knowing their instrinsic nature. But we have sufficient study of and counter-measure against the precedents. We are confindent [sic] that it is God's will allowed only to Japan to settle the Jewish Problem, a scourage in the world and to find a key to the world peace through the characteristic of our country that the supreme national spirit of the "Emperor First" principle really exists since Jummu era.

(h) Further, to accommodate 30,000 Jews under our influence in this national emergency, has a sort of "hostage" sense and, in utilizing their financial power, brings an effect of holding their weapon before the breast. Such an utilization is seen in Imperial Russia, i.e.,

(1) The history tells us that although Imperial Russia took a barbarous and inhuman anti-Jewish policy such as the well-known "Jew-hunting (hogrom) [sic], the Jews could not oppose to it openly as they feared that such open opposition against Russia would bring an immediate bad effect on them.

(2) In the recent history, we can point out the very timid attitude of the Jews toward Nichist Germany. Because of their

having assassinated a diplomatic secretary, they had to pay a tax amounting to a billion leich mark and met with a misery of deportation with no penny. Though they always had a grudge against such a cruel and heartless anti-Jewish policy, they could not take direct and effective measures in fear of suffering another misfortune. In short, they keenly felt a weak point that the hostage was taken.

(3) At the time Col. Yasue, Consul Ishiguro and I attended a conference held at Sassune, they made a frank statement that "To Japan which holds tens of thousands of the Jews in the Far East under her influence, how can we possibly have a will to oppose?" This implies their weak point.

(4) In our history, there is no precedent for such unreasonable oppression of a weak minority as is seen in the precedents of the other countries. As the character of the nation does not allow us to do such a thing, they will not plot like in the precedents in Russia and Germany.

(i) Is a Jewish problem fearful as alleged by the anti-Jewists? No; there is nothing to be afraid of unless we oppress, persecute and discriminate them without reason. "Wherever the Jews go, there is a Jewish problem." stated by Helltel holds true only in society of Western individualism where a strong religious prejudice exists but such assimilative power as in Japan does not exist. In Japan where we treat the Jews without any racial or religeous prejudice, the probability for a calamity by them is very lessened. Proof is better than argument. You can see the point if you examine the actual proof that the Jews presently living in Manchuria are praising the realm of peace and prosperity and deepening their gratitude to Japan that gave them a place for peaceful living.

(j) In short, the accommodation of 30,000 persons in question is of much benefit to the increase of the national strength at a small cost to us.

(3) Doubt "As a practical problem, it is difficult to accommodate 30,000 persons in China or Manchuria (mainly in view of future operations on Wang [Ching-Wei]." [sic]

This is a groundless argument. Removal of no more than 30,000 Jews to the vast area of China is merely a drop of water into a large river. It is said that 2 million people were drowned owing to the overflow of the Yellow Riber [sic] but that the decrease in the population was not particularly noticebale [sic]. It can not be accepted, therefore, that an inflow of tens of thousands of persons into China will cause a big problem in future. Expecially, as the immigrant refugeess are those people who are highly cultivated and well educated dwellers in Europe, consideration should be given to the fact that their technique can be utilized as good cooperators for the construction of the Continent. Further, we have the advantage of having authority to select and limit the immigrants and particularly, we have the way to ask for the agricultural immigrants. Therefore, what should be done as a first thing, is a negotiation with the representatives of the Jews in America.

(4) Doubt "Because of this, the Jews in Shanghai and those in America are at odds with each other and it can not be said that there is no possibility of a result reverse to what was intended being brought about." [sic]

This is also unnecessary care with no knowledge of the actual state of affairs. That is;

(a) As a result of the conference with the Jewish leaders in Shanghai and the officers of the Refugee Relief Committee, a *telegram was sent* to the representatives of the *Jews in America, requesting their visit* to Japan in order to expedite the subject matter, as stated in the attached paper. It has been expressed that the Jews in Shanghai also have a strong desire for the settlement of the refugee problem by Japan.

(b) Many of the Jews in Shanghai have kinship with the Jews in America and the greater part of the expenses for the equipment of the refugee reception center established in our naval guarding area are covered by the grants-in-aid from America. They are already in close contact with each other.

(c) Among the refugees in the reception center, those who have blood relationship particularly with the Jews in America number as high as 30%. As is clear from this fact and as the majority (80%) of the Jews in America are originally of German-Austrian descent, the present concern of the Jews in America is about their people suffering oppression by Nichist Germany.

(d) As a result of our operations during the past one year,

the leading class of the Jews in Shanghai has become very pro-Japanese and it is now an evident fact that their attitude toward Japan has been improved. On this occasion, if our great spirit of the universe-is-one principle is proved by means of actually carrying out the accommodation of the refugees, it is considered that their atmosphere of reliance on Japan will be furhter [sic] facilitated and that they will make every effort for furtherance of Japan-US tie-up.

(e) Accordingly, a fear for reversion of the result is really a groundless worry and I can state definitely with confidence that the result will be increased by a few times.

(5) Doubt "It seems untterly [sic] hopeless as it is opposed positively by the Army in Manchuria and ignored by the Army in China."

As to the objection by the Army, they may change their mind, depending on the conditions of the other party. Especially, as to the Army in Manchuria, as it is assumed that Col. Yasue has the same opinion as stated above, it is recognized that there is room for negotiation, depending on the conditions of the other party.

Or if we take such a method as having them move in a small group partially to the south, partially to the middle and partially to the north of China, the friction with all quarters will be reduced and it is not definitely considered as a desperately difficult problem. In short, as there is much possibility of moving the Army, depending on the conditions proposed by the Jews in America, it is desired that further assistance be offered.

CONCLUSION

In the nutshell, these doubts originate in a lack of understanding of the present circumstances of the Jews. Again I urge that if you look at the actual situation that their places for peaceful living are being narrowed every hour in an atmosphere of the aggravated world-wide anti-Jewism, you can necessarily see through their wishes. Recently, our Empire declared to the world our great resolution of the release of the Yangtze River. However, you can not expect this measure alone to improve the atmosphere of third powers' anti-Japanism. That is:

(a) As is seen in the reaction to our frequent diplomatic gesture, it is being considered to be a release for the form's sake and as the power of control of the Yangtze River must, in fact, be secured by our Empire, indirect restraining operations are required for a third power which expects a restoration of the old order of the river.

(b) It is feared that if these restraining operations are ignored, we will come to be compelled to make a concession of this kind more frequently than ever in the future if the world-wide anti-Japanese sentiment in the past few years is to be improved.

(c) In short, the perfect settlement of this Incident requires concurrent operations for the betterment of the international feelings toward Japan, i.e., operations for the international ideological war. Without these operations hundreds of release statements of the Yangtze River may be meaningless. In this case, from the viewpoint of the research work on the Jewish problem, utilization of the Jews who maintain the international press and advertizing agencies for the purpose of shifting the anti-Japanese atmosphere, is the best and most effective way.

(d) Even if the operations should fail to obtain the desired result of securing prompt supply of materials, the effect of guiding the international feelings toward Japan to our advantage will be very great. Particularly, at least a few years from now are the most important time for the development of our country's destiny. During this short period of time, we must make rapid strides by avoiding international friction as much as possible and making use of and adopting everything available. By so doing, we can live up to the accomplishment of the purpose of the Holy War.

Being faced with such a situation as this, I, as a person who has devoted himself to the study of the Jewish problems for many years, would like to emphasize the effective use of the study for the sake of the Empire. It is earnestly desired that such a wish be taken into consideration as an uncontrollable expression of true feeling. Unless carried out with the relations of third powers taken into consideration, even the operations on Wang will no doubt become a matter for regret as the finishing touch is forgotton. [sic] The establishment of new order is not merely a management of the internal affairs of China. A far-reaching policy for the peace of the Orient can not be established unless the complicated foreign rights and interests in China are adjusted.

As these complicaled [sic] and strong foreign powers were out-wardly considered to be third powers of various nationalities such as England, America and France, we have heretofore negotiated separately with each country. But as far as the Orient is concerned, the leading center of the third powers is the Jewish plutocracy in China and it is clear from the past instances that no matter what cooperation or agreement is made with the home government, no effect will come out if those people on the spot are ignored.

In other words, if a complete pro-Japanese view is estab-lished among the Jews who fix their permanent homes and keep their family graves in China, a great advantage of having the Orient policy at home changed by their peculiar power, is also thinkable. If we make an enemy of them, they will plan for an expulsion of the Japanese influence from the Continent in such a big scale as in that revision of monetary system. It is not too much to say that the calamity of the present incident has its root in blindness to the powers of the Jews in China. They pitched a splendid camp in the strategical war against Japan by moving England and the League of Nations. We should know that immeasurable profit will be obtained by making a reverse use to our advantage of such secret power they have.

We will lose little and gain much if the subject plan is carried out. The subject operations should be carried out con-currently with the operations on Wang; nay, they should be carried out as a great national policy surpassing the operations on Wang. In other words, the operations on Wang are mainly related to the internal affairs of China, but the subject operations cover every phase of the international political situation. It is keenly felt that the operations may be called a basis for the development of the future of the Empire which will be the center of the world peace in time to come.

We should say that their having extended a hand of earnest desire to us is really a Heaven's dispensation. Should this good chance be missed, it is considered that the great ideal of the 2600th year of existence of the Empire and the Imperial will that the universe is one, will not be complied with.

[FO PAPERS (DP)] (FOREIGN SECRET) (SUMMARY) APPENDIX—E

[ca. February 1942]

Jewish Measures in view of the 1942 Situation
(Plan Adopted at the *Liaison Conference*)

Measures pertaining to the Jewish people due to the outbreak of the Greater East Asia War will be enforced based on the
following policy plan.

POLICY PLAN

(1) With the exception of those having special reasons, the
entrance of Jewish people into Japan, Manchuria, China and our
other occupied territories will be prohibited.

(2) As a general rule, the Jewish people who are already
residing in the various areas mentioned above will be handled
according to nationality, but in view of their racial characteristic,
strict surveillance of their dwelling and business operation will be
made and, furthermore, hostile activiites will be eliminated and
suppressed.

(3) Jewish people who can be used by Japan (includes
those among the ones who can be used by the Axis powers and who
are not opposed to Japan's policy) will be given good treatment,
but Jewish racial movement will not be given support.

Remark: The policy plan for Jewish measures adopted by
the 5-Minister Conference on 6 December, 1938
will be abolished.

EXPLANATION

Heretofore, Japan's policy concerning Jewish people was
based on the Jewish policy plan which was adopted at a 5-Minister
Conference on 6 December, 1938. The purport of this policy plan
was to treat the Jewish people well, and thereby promote introduction of foreign capital and avert aggravation of relationship with
England and the United States. However, due to the outbreak of
war, this necessity has been eliminated and, furthermore, even look-

ing at the Jewish policy trend of our allies, Germany and Italy, it has become unnecessary for Japan, in her policy pertaining to the Jewish people, to give consideration to relationship with a third power. On the other hand, with the expansion of our occupied territories, the number of Jewish people coming under our power has continued to increase and, in view of their racial characteristic, unless appropriate security measures are taken immediately, there is danger of incurring unforeseen adversities. However, an over-all rejection of the Jewish people will not only be contrary to our national policy of world unification but will also be bound to be utilized as counter-propaganda by England and the United States. Therefore, as a general rule, the Jewish people who formerly held German nationality will be considered stateless and will be accorded the same treatment as White Russians (—because, since, January this year, Germany has taken away the nationality of the Jewish people of German nationality who reside in foreign countries), and it is deemed appropriate that only so much surveillance as is necessary be made of them.

[FO PAPERS (DP)] (TOP SECRET)   (SUMMARY)   APPENDIX—F
           Office in Charge: Consulate-General in China
1942 30320   Code   Dispatched from Sphanghai: P.M., 18
                           November [1942]
       30321   Received at This office: At Night, 18
                           November

TO: Minister of Greater East Asia AOKI

FROM: Consul-General YANO

NO: 69 TOP SECRET

Re: Measures Pertaining to Jewish People

Relative to measures pertaining to the Jewish people in Shanghai area, the plan established by the Japanese Navy of that area, having been approved by the Central Government, will shortly be carried into force. However, in view of the desire of the Navy, it has been decided that the Ministry of Greater East Asia will handle the enforcement of the concrete measures, with the Army and the Navy giving necessary cooperation.

The general substance of the above plan is as follows:

(1) To set up a Jewish district in the YO JU HO (Japanese pronunciation) area and get the Jewish people scattered within the city to collect and live there.

(2) The guidance? to and receiving into the above district (copyist's note: "?" appears in the original text) will be accomplished with German Jews numbering approximately 20,000 as the object, and following this, the disposition of White Russian and other Jewish people will be made.

(3) The surveillance, control and guidance after accommodation will be Military Affairs? function. ("?" appears in the original text).

(4) For the purpose of putting the above plan into effect, a committee, with the Consul-General as its Chairman and officials concerned from the Ministry of Greater East Asia, Army, Navy, Military Police, Engineering Bureau, and Special City Government as committee members, will be established.

APPENDIX—G

(TOP SECRET)   (SUMMARY)   [February 9, 1943]
Office in Charge: Consulate-General in China (General Affairs
               Section of the Consulate).

1943   51464   Code   Dispatched From Shanghai: A.M., 9
                        February

                        Received At This Office: A.M., 9th
TO: Minister of Greater East Asia AOKI

FROM: Consul-General YANO

No. 130

         Matter Concerning Movement of Jewish People
         In re telegram No. 69 dispatched last year:
    (1) Subsequently, as a result of studying the concrete
method of effecting the movement of the Jewish people, the Com-
manders of the Army and Navy will shortly issue a proclamation
prescribing the following:
    (i) Because of military necessity, the residential and busi-
ness areas of stateless refugees in the Shanghai Area will be restricted to an area within the International Settlement east of the
line connecting CHOHORO, MOKAIRO, and TODATSURO
(TH: all Japanese pronunciations), west of YOJUHO Creek,
north of the line connecting TOSHIKOBAIRO, MOKAIRO, and
KAISANRO (TN: Japanese pronunciations), and south of the
boundary line of the International Settlement.
    (ii) Stateless refugees presently residing and/or operating
business outside the area mentioned in the preceding paragraph
shall move their residence and/or places of business inside the
above-prescribed area by   (month)   (day) from the
date of this proclamation. Those desiring to buy and sell or rent
houses, stores, and other installations located outside the above
area which are homes and/or business places of stateless refugees
shall obtain prior approval of the authorities concerned.
    (iii) Those other than stateless refugees may not move
into the area designated in paragraph 1 without permission.

(iv) Any person who violates this proclamation or interferes with its enforcement shall be punished.

Furthermore, it has been arranged that by a statement of Army and Naval authorities dated the same date, it will be indicated that the "stateless refugees" mentioned in this proclamation refers to refugees from Germany (includes former Austria and Czechoslovakia), Hungary, former Poland, Latvia, Lithuania, Estonia, etc. who arrived in Shanghai after 1937 up to the present time and who are actually stateless.

(2) However, as nearly a year has already passed since the General Headquarters Liaison Conference, which is the direct basis for subject matter, was held and, furthermore, because this affair has delicate signs of international relations, the Army and the Ministry of Greater East Asia will issue the proclamation after each has obtained the consent of the Central Government. (The Navy has already contacted the Central Government). It is therefore requested that a consolidated opinion of the Central Government be obtained and instructions be sent to us. Furthermore, not only the Jewish people of Soviet nationality, but also the Whites, are excepted from being subject to this proclamation. It is considered that there is no particular danger of causing international complications.

It is also the desire and intention to put into effect an armband system and to issue permits for going out of the area after the move is effected.

APPENDIX—H

Paraphrase of telegram from
American Legation at Stockholm

SPECIAL WAR PROBLEMS
DIVISION

APRIL 12, 1945

DEPARTMENT OF STATE

Rabbis Wolbe and Jacobson have been very active for several months in discussing with Japanese, Russians and Swedes the possible release of the Rabbinical Group at Shanghai.

The question was taken up with the highest levels of the Swedish Government. Even the Crown Prince took a personal interest in the matter. The Rabbis obtained a promise which still is valid that the Swedish Government would give the group a collective visa, would receive them in Sweden and that it would support them in that country.

From the beginning the Japanese indicated consistently that they would permit the release of the Rabbinical group. They never indicated that they would ask for anything in return. In fact they stated that it would be an advantage to them to let the Rabbinical group go, since the congested situation at Shanghai has lead to unmanageable living conditions in that city. However, the Japanese Legation pointed out that they could not handle the question of transportation of the group from Shanghai since they have no ships to go to Vladivostok and since all facilities on the railroad to the Russian border, a week away, is reserved for military purposes.

The Rabbis state that the Russians have consistently been sympathetic to their proposals but have maintained throughout that they cannot provide means of transportation. They have pointed out that it would be foolish to promise transportation facilities, since the Siberian railway is overloaded and no Russian vessels run between Shanghai and Vladivostok.

The Swedish Government has pointed out that it has no shipping in East Asian waters.

It appears that the problem of moving the Rabbinical group out of Shanghai has been thoroughly explored from every possible angle and that the way things are going to be, it is technically impossible to solve such a problem. Any further efforts which might be taken could only go over the same ground that has previously been covered and existing developments in relations between Russia and Japan have only served to introduce new difficulties.

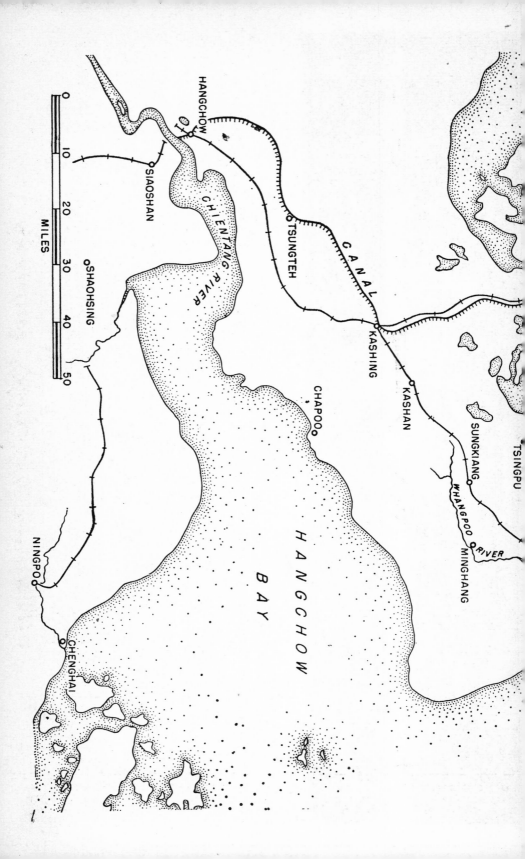